A History of Western Education

Volume Three
THE MODERN WEST
EUROPE AND THE NEW WORLD

James Bower

A History of

Vestern Education

Volume Three

THE MODERN WEST
EUROPE AND THE NEW WORLD

METHUEN & CO LTD

11 NEW FETTER LANE · LONDON EC4P 4EE

First published in 1981
by Methuen & Co. Ltd
11 New Fetter Lane, London EC4P 4EE
© 1981 James Bowen and M. J. Bowen
Printed in the United States of America

British Library Cataloguing in Publication Data

Bowen, James
A history of Western education.
Vol. 3: The modern West: Europe and the New
World
1. Education – History
1. Title
370'.918'2   LA91
ISBN 0-416-16130-8

For our three sons

CHRISTOPHER
TORQUIL
ANEURIN

Contents

List of Illustrations

Title page: A French schoolroom of 1700.

The author and publishers wish to thank the following for permission to reproduce the illustrations that appear in this book:

Associated Press Limited for no. 17
British Museum for no. 9
Cheshire Libraries and Museums, Warrington, for no. 7
Greater London Council for no. 11
Guildhall Library, London, for no. 4
Incorporated Froebel Educational Institute, London, for no. 13
Jacob A. Riis Collection, Museum of the City of New York, for no. 14
Janine Wiedel for no. 18
Mansell Collection for the title page
Musée Bonnat, Bayonne, for no. 1
National Portrait Gallery, London, for no. 3
Novosti Press Agency for no. 16
President and Fellows of Sion College, London, for no. 6
Radio Times Hulton Picture Library for nos 12 and 15
University Library, Prague, for no. 5

Every effort has been made to trace the locations of plates 2, 8 and 10, but their whereabouts remain unknown to us.

Preface

'Terre, terre' – 'Land in sight' – wrote Denis Diderot in 1765 when he completed the famous *Encyclopédie* after more than fifteen years' labour. This present work has some parallels: the three volumes have also taken some fifteen years, and, by coincidence, I began writing at the same age as Diderot when he commenced his editorial task. The past fifteen years, however, have seen even more momentous changes than those of the mid-eighteenth century when Europe was entering its age of revolutions, and this has created some profound difficulties. While, like Diderot, I looked forward to a safe landfall, the 1980s are emerging as the most troubled years in mankind's historical experience. Throughout Western history, in every epoch, there has been a rush of ideas that threatened the stability of the existing social order, and, as these volumes have recounted, our heritage is one of continued challenge and, generally, resolution. At present, however, it does seem that events may overwhelm us before conceptual clarity can be achieved and appropriate responses determined, and that situation should be of central concern to the educational historian. Originally, in the early 1960s, while teaching in the United States and then Canada, reacting to this trend of events, I had conceived a revisionist history on what, as I look back, was a modest scale; as the 1960s wore on, the theme of popular affluence and progress increasingly became counterpointed by a troubled bass, especially as, in the course of essential fieldwork, I visited not only the established historical locations but also a number of those places where modern educational history was being made, beginning with Paris, Rome, Athens in 1968, San Francisco in 1969, and during the 1970s not only throughout the developed world of Europe, North America and Japan but also the socialist world of the Soviet Union, eastern Europe and the People's Republic of China.

My original aim, expressed in the Preface to both Volumes 1 and 2, has not changed, and it remains true, as I wrote there, that the entry of the state into education has accelerated the controversies and conflicts on the nature, purpose and practices of education; and that, moreover, the only really acceptable generalization we can make about the modern period is the popular aspiration that education must be extended as widely as possible. I added that there is, however, no great clarity in the public mind as to why or how this extension should and can be made. The events of the late 1970s served to show that such an observation was both accurate and prescient, chiefly because the educational crisis we shall experience in the 1980s was generated then, when contest for the control of education assumed its current polarized form. The conflict between conservation and creativity on which this work was originally based has remained a central theme, heightened by the fact that the conflict, in recent times, has become ever more highly politicized.

Until recently, educational historiography has not served us well; as several contemporary revisionist historians have argued, most educational histories have concentrated excessively on the development of schools and schooling, and have generally been written from a comfortable Eurocentric viewpoint, recording the inevitable rise of a deserving middle-class, male meritocracy, and promising continued progress to some kind of well-structured democracy in which education would serve to locate each person in his and her proper place. Along with a number of my colleagues, I can no longer accept that earlier twentieth-century Whig conception of educational history, and this work is a contribution to the construction of a new past. In order better to understand the thrust of the entire work, it may be helpful to know that the original working title was *Western Culture and the Process of Education*, and I proposed to examine the interplay between the history of ideas and their institutionalization in the process of education. Even though the title was changed, that concern has remained, and the achievement might profitably be assessed against that original intention. This final volume, then, covers the period of educational dissent, which became conspicuous in the early seventeenth century and reached crisis proportions in the late twentieth, when the dominant ideologies of progress and equality, generated at the beginning of the nineteenth century, were questioned for the first time on a widespread, popular scale.

Equality was the demand of the *parvenu* bourgeoisie of the age of revolutions (1776–1815); throughout the nineteenth century that *arriviste* class contended with the aristocracy, and, because it gained control over commerce and industry, the bourgeoisie triumphed. In particular, it was supported by the new technologies and methods of science – built upon either pragmatic or positivist assumptions and developed out of seventeenth- and eighteenth-century endeavours – which offered unlimited possibilities of exploitation. Yet the bourgeoisie could not reject the aristocracy: the latter necessarily had to be joined in alliance, and used as a legitimizing force; its traditions were adopted (usually in heightened and ornate forms) by the bourgeoisie as its own. The conservative tradition of education and its privileged system of the grammar school and university, therefore, were retained intact. Indeed, they were strengthened during the age of classical archaeology. The intellectual structures of established nineteenth-century bourgeois society, like its architectural structures, were clothed in the authority of the classical era: as homes, banks, churches and wealthy schools imitated the Parthenon, so education became a romantically heightened and revived imitation of *paideia*.

Throughout the twentieth century this approach continued to characterize the dominant bourgeoisie, now generally known as the middle class. To sustain its new position of dominance it refused to extend equality to the servile working class, and instead adopted an ideology of superiority which it found in the two concepts of culture and natural order. The Eurocentric notion of culture, interpreted here basically as the bourgeois lifestyle, was given heightened expression by James Mill in *On Government*, expanded by Matthew Arnold in *Culture and Anarchy*, and has since been argued by a succession of retainers. At the same time, while there was considerable opposition to Darwin's theories of evolution, paradoxically, his work, despite his intentions, provided a powerful support to middle-class claims for superiority in the concept of natural selection, first developed in *The Origin of Species* of 1859, and almost immediately applied to social hierarchies by Herbert Spencer, who vigorously and successfully promoted the idea of middle-class ascendancy under the title of 'social Darwinism'. To legitimize these concepts the doctrines of progress and equality were maintained, their effect being to defuse popular, especially working-class unrest.

With this ideology the middle class, manipulated by its élites, held control of education by means of a dual system for more than a century. Working-class cohesion, meanwhile, had grown steadily in the late nineteenth century, but it had not shown an excessive interest in changing the ideals of education or the structures of the schools; generally, it sought greater access and, in large part, accepted the notions of progress and equality. It is important to observe that determinedly progressive liberal forces, in the same period, had been successful in establishing a system of popular schools, although these offered little access to the higher levels of society, much less to power. The Bolshevik Revolution of 1917, therefore, assumed considerable significance because it was the first overt recognition of the belief that, if society is to be changed, so also must the schools – thereby running counter to the attitudes of many working-class activists who accepted the tenets of Jeffersonian equality of opportunity and believed that they could make equal attainments within the dual system. Attempts by enlightened European and American liberals to implement reforms, however, were ineffectual on any thorough-going scale: progressive educational practices were outlawed in Europe by Pius XI, Hitler, Mussolini, Franco and Stalin; in the United States these were excoriated as 'soft' and 'pink' pedagogy by conservatives holding privileged power under the élitist doctrines of social Darwinism. After 1945, this attack was recommenced in the United States in such works as *Educational Wastelands* by Arthur Bestor and extended in Britain with the *Black Papers* by Cox and Dyson.

The question arises: what was the real cause of such violent opposition to progressivism? We must look for answers in the allegedly dangerous and subversive doctrines of holism. Progressivism, in its general and broad sense, stressed the wholeness of the child as an individual and as a social being, and the interrelatedness of knowledge, even when expressed as a curriculum. The privileged élites opposed holism, both as theory and as practice, from its first appearance as *Naturphilosophie* in the work of Goethe, Humboldt and the Weimar Circle: industrial society requires the training only of 'hands'; whole persons threaten the privileged social order. Moreover, the holist view of man's place in the unity and harmony of nature was less congenial to the expansion of Western exploitative industrialism than the dualist world-view offered by positivism, with its ideal of man's progress in the mastery of material nature. So this volume is centrally concerned with an analysis of the holist movement in the educational work of Rousseau, Pestalozzi, Froebel – and, to an extent, Herbart – and traces the process by which the thought of these educators was debased, and put into schoolroom practice in the late nineteenth and early twentieth centuries in mechanized, degenerate form.

As Marx argued, however, even privilege and wealth are alienating, and class conflict increased throughout the twentieth century; the flashpoint came in the 1970s with a popular rejection of the hypocrisy of privileged morality and leadership. In the 1960s, the threat of ecological crises had begun to appear, and confidence in progress began to decline as industrial development showed up as vast corporate profits for a wealthy élite and as global pollution, poverty and loss of resources for the many. The Vietnam War symbolized public disillusion: young men refused to be slaughtered in a conflict that served the interests only of a secure, manipulative minority. The growing body of research – epitomized in W. L. Guttsman's *The British Political Elite*, Pierre Bourdieu's cultural and social reproduction studies and Richard Titmuss's work in the economics of inequality – showed that ballot-box democracy did not provide for genuine interactive participatory democracy. The people remained, in effect, largely powerless. When President Johnson attempted to mitigate the extremes of deprivation and poverty in the United States and inaugurated the Great Society programme, the commissioned Coleman Inquiry (1966) revealed how badly cancerous the body social was; Christopher Jencks in *Inequality* showed how impotent the people were, and how completely deceived they were about the ability of education to effect democratic social justice. Accompanying this was a rhetoric of dissent and even rage – Illich, Freire, Goodman, Kozol, *et al.* – which was expressed in sustained student violence and teacher-led campaigns that were to end, fortuitously for conservative governments, with the energy crisis and collapse of the world economy in the mid-seventies.

Much of the blame was projected on to the people, and especially on to the 'disruptive' influences of higher education, as the Trilateral Commission report of 1975, *The Crisis of Democracy*, illustrates; consequently, the privileged forces reacted vigorously and, given that they controlled most of the media, induced fear and stimulated a sense of insecurity by heightening the dangers from external chaos: from the overthrow of Allende in Chile to the Soviet invasion of Afghanistan. Welfare for the weak was reduced, thereby weakening them further; in education, campaigns were mounted urging 'back-to-basics' and vocational training, while tertiary enrolments were reduced in order to return universities and colleges to middle-class membership. In 1971 every European government, west and east, had at least a socialist component in the government; by 1980, among the democracies, only Norway had a socialist element in government. Reaction has held the line for privilege, and educational thought is increasingly becoming understood as a primarily political activity.

Against this background, much current educational activity can be seen as a movement – if not yet clearly articulated – towards changing the entire conception of both society and education. Throughout the world a new morality is emerging which rejects the idea of progress, meritocracy, psychology as an instrument of electronic manipulation where silicon chips rank above persons, the processes of political subordination and lack of public access to decision-making, the alleged necessity of economic inequality and the conception of education as 'investment'. Above all, there is a growing rejection of the metaphysics and epistemology of positivism. One reason for the failure of the protest movements of the 1960s and 1970s was the lack of a suitable epistemology; one is now being formulated, and changes proposed in the 1970s may, it is hoped, be effected in the 1980s. In order to understand this process, a necessary, related theme here has been the tracing through of the empiricist movement from the original scientific revolution of the seventeenth century down to the conceptual and social disasters of recent positivism and so-called 'value-free' research.

Correlatively, certain elements of the new social – and educational – morality are emerging. A central notion is what has been called the 'ecology of knowledge', which argues for a return to holism as the only moral, and practical, way ahead. This necessarily involves a renewed concern for, and recognition of, history as an integral part of the present totality; it is issuing as a new 'third force' psychology based upon transpersonal and humanistic concerns; a new sociology and politics that focuses on reciprocity; an economics that assumes that people matter. And these, I believe, are being brought together in a new conception of education, amounting in reality to a revolution, which will have to contest in the 1980s with the conservative forces to decide what must eventuate: mankind must either come together in some version of holistic amity or else remain alienated and polarized as a consequence of the continuing ravages of privileged exploitation.

Inevitably, this present volume is highly compressed, and much detail had to be eliminated; indeed, this final version is little more than half of the first draft. In particular, I would like to have written at greater length on the nineteenth and twentieth centuries, although it was necessary to remain conscious of the scale of a narrative that began in Volume 1 with Sumer and Egypt. At the same time, the fact that this study is being translated into other languages has imposed the need to write for more than an English readership; consequently, I have sought to give as wide a coverage of Western education as possible and this, necessarily, has prevented a fuller treatment of some topics. Obviously the impact of late twentieth-century dissent upon educational thought and practice demands more exhaustive treatment; much of this, in effect, has to be the subject of a more specialized monograph, now in progress.

Throughout the preparation of this present volume, I have been assisted by many persons and institutions, and it is a pleasure to acknowledge these sources. Central to all scholarly inquiries, of course, is the patient, tireless work of librarians: I am grateful for their considerable assistance in the Dixson Library at the University of New England, the Fisher Library of the University of Sydney, the Menzies Library of the Australian National University, the Australian National Library in Canberra, the Bodleian at Oxford and the libraries at the University of Toronto and the Ontario Institute for Studies in Education. Many institutions gave support, and I benefited greatly from the kind assistance of officials in many countries, particularly Dr Joncić of Matica in Belgrade, the officials of the Chinese Ministry of Education who organized my visits in 1975 and 1977, and Professor Markeshevitch, Deputy Director of the All-Union Ministry of Education in Moscow. In particular, I found the preparation of this work immensely strengthened through the good offices of the UNESCO Institute of Education in Hamburg which invited me to act as General Editor of its 1979 Silver Jubilee theory issue of the *International Review of Education*, thereby enabling me to visit a large number of educational institutions and to be in close contact with many significant international educators. In writing the section on the Soviet Union I should particularly like to acknowledge the generosity of the University of Wisconsin Press which allowed me to use material from my monograph on *Soviet Education*.

Over the years I have been assisted by many persons in my work; and I should like to make express recognition of the sustained encouragement of Richard St Clair Johnson, Professor of Classics at the Australian National University, Henry Silton Harris, Professor of Philosophy at York University in Toronto, and Emeritus Professor H. Lionel Elvin, formerly

Director of the University of London Institute of Education and now Fellow of Trinity Hall, Cambridge. As well, I should like to acknowledge the scholarly assistance in the Spanish sections given by Dr Olives Canals of Barcelona and my Spanish publisher, Editorial Herder. Further, I should like to express my appreciation for the support of the Italian publishers, Arnoldo Mondadori of Milan. Standing quite apart, and contributing in an unfailing way, have been my primary publishers, first Peter Wait and then John Naylor of Methuen who undertook the hazardous task of bringing this trilogy to completion, and my editor of all three volumes, Linden Stafford, for whose scholarship and patience I am deeply grateful.

My greatest debt, as acknowledged in the dedications to Volumes 1 and 2, remains to my wife, Margarita, from whose researches in the history of scientific ideas I have drawn freely, chiefly from her doctoral work in the holist movement of the nineteenth century and her monograph on *Empiricism and Geographical Thought*, with its concepts of 'social empiricism' and the 'ecology of knowledge'. Quite properly, this volume is dedicated to our children who must grapple with the problems that our generation has created; I hope that works like this will be some guide. None the less, I feel that a dedication might equally have read, as for the other volumes, *uxori carissimae Margaritae*.

September 1980   JAMES BOWEN

CHAPTER I

The Educational Heritage of the Modern West

Prologue: the modern tradition of educational dissent

In the later decades of the sixteenth century, Western educational thought began to change significantly. This was made evident in the first instance by the appearance of a serious literature of discontent. Quite independently, in many places, a growing number of thinkers began arguing that much was fundamentally wrong with education as it was being conducted and that reforms had to be made. The criticisms that were advanced, moreover, were not ignored; on the contrary, they were often readily accepted into the intellectual life of Europe and exerted increasingly stronger influences on educational practices, curricula and institutions. As a consequence, in the sixteenth century Western education began to acquire many of the attributes that we consider to be distinctively modern, and it is their development that is the subject of the present volume. These attributes are many and varied, and are often in conflict with one another; indeed, Western educational thought and practice throughout the modern period exhibit none of the broad patterns of unity and consistency found in either of the two great previous eras of classical antiquity and medieval Christianity.

From the beginning of the seventeenth century to the present day a major defining characteristic of Western education is that of argued dissent. Since the sixteenth century, Western education has built up a tradition, still in vigorous operation, of institutionalized dissatisfaction along with a heightened consciousness of the need to seek for solutions through deliberate innovation, often with the implicit utopian assumption that there is a better world to find or, perhaps, to create. Criticism and dissent, however, draw their strength from immediate circumstances; reaction is a form of contemporaneity and is rarely governed by a longer view. This was, in fact, the problem of the sixteenth-century critics, inasmuch as they found it difficult to determine what precisely was wrong. The burden of the educational traditions of the past weighed so heavily that critics were only too readily aware of what was irksome and so became quite articulate in denouncing particular ideas and practices that they wanted to discard; they were not, however, equally clear about what should be introduced by way of improvement. Consequently, the climate of educational thought in the initial phases of the movement to reform was basically one of critical, often hypercritical, rejection; there was little appreciation, much less acceptance, of the idea of systematic development, orderly reconciliation of competing demands and the introduction of worthwhile innovation. On the contrary, the history of Western education in the modern period exhibits a continued record of acrimonious debate, mutual hostility, lack of goodwill and agreement and an often intransigent refusal to compromise.

When educational debate became particularly acute in the sixteenth century, there were a number of contributing factors. In the first instance, Europe itself had changed markedly throughout the millennium of its historical emergence, having become a troubled and divided society, racked by more than a century of bitter religious and political conflicts, generated in large part by the continued efforts of the Holy Catholic Church to maintain its primacy. These conflicts, moreover, were not recent developments but were the continuation of a process that had been set in operation at the beginnings of Christian Europe. From the time of its emergence to power during the disintegration of classical civilization that resulted from the barbarian migrations of the fifth and sixth centuries, the church in Rome had attempted to maintain authority over Europe. To strengthen its position, it supported the Frankish kings of the eighth and ninth centuries, to whom explicit recognition was given by Pope Leo III when in AD 800 he crowned Charlemagne as 'great and pacific emperor of the Romans'. This concordat, however, created more problems than it settled, and throughout the eleventh, twelfth and thirteenth centuries the Holy Catholic Church and the Holy Roman Empire were in frequent conflict. Thereafter crises and confrontations increased rapidly and the history of the fourteenth, fifteenth and sixteenth centuries is a record of the continued erosion of Rome's authority in matters both spiritual and temporal as one upheaval after another convulsed the continent.

Much of the problem lay in the vexed issue of the relative jurisdictions of church and state. As European civilization developed, national states began to emerge on the basis of linguistic groupings, and their efforts to attain some kind of secular identity continued to bring them into conflict with the church, which itself sought actively to keep the temporal states subject. This was to prove patently impossible and, as the centuries progressed, the confrontations became increasingly serious and on a wider scale. By the fourteenth century France had become the largest single national state in Europe and was so strong that it could, and successfully did, challenge the papacy, to the extent that throughout that century the pope in Avignon was, for many purposes, a French subject. In the fifteenth century other states gained further strength and national unity, but none on a scale sufficient to match France, until the two major Iberian kingdoms of Aragon and Castile were united after the marriage of Ferdinand and Isabella. From 1480 onwards the joint monarchy produced the unified kingdom of Spain and made it a growing force in European politics.

By the end of the fifteenth century Spain had colonized much of the New World by a vigorous programme of exploration, and at home continued to expand into the Arab Maghreb following the expulsion of the Moors from the Iberian mainland, occupying all of the north-west Atlantic coast of Africa by 1511. Spain was now in command of the Atlantic; under these circumstances it was inevitable that Spain and France as the two great emerging centralized powers in Europe should come into conflict early in the sixteenth century. In contrast to France and Spain, England was still a minor power, engrossed in many internal conflicts and without a strong crown; Italy remained occupied alternately by France and Germany. In effect, at this time there was no political state of Germany: the term was used to designate the Holy Roman Empire, ruled over by an emperor but consisting in reality of about 2300 separate and virtually autonomous territories. Throughout the sixteenth century the Spanish House of Habsburg dominated the Holy Roman Empire when Charles V (r. 1519–56) inherited some of these lands and subsequently intrigued his way to election as Holy Roman Emperor. Neither of the Habsburg emperors, Charles and his son Philip II (r. 1556–96) who succeeded him, conceived of himself as a purely secular ruler. On the contrary, both were devout communicants of Rome and referred to themselves quite explicitly as *los reyes Católicos*, 'the Catholic kings'.

For more than forty years Charles used his two offices of Holy Roman Emperor and King of Spain to extend and consolidate the authority of both Spain and the Catholic Church in a bitterly divided Europe, and charged the continuation of this policy to Philip II. The advent of the Habsburgs, however, and their attempt to bring Europe back under the suzerainty of a single Holy Roman Emperor, who in turn supported the supremacy of a Holy Catholic Church after the Lutheran revolt became serious in the 1530s, came to be considered a mixed blessing in Rome, since Charles was not disposed to let the papacy hinder his pursuit of Catholic unity. Throughout the century Spain waged war against the Protestant nations, involving all of western Europe, but without success. By the beginning of the seventeenth century Spain had declined as a major power, and Europe reached a position in which the Holy Roman Empire had ceased to have effective political authority and the Holy Catholic Church had ceased to be 'Catholic' in the asserted sense of the word as 'universal'. Europe then entered its modern period in which political power becomes exercised by independent nation states, with religious allegiance shared among a large and ever-growing number of different communions.

Education as the instrument of Christian civilization

The medieval achievement

It was, then, within this context of seething conflict – and partly as a consequence of it – that Western education began to assume its modern character. In the sixteenth century it came to be appreciated as a highly important social process, especially after the stimulus given by Erasmus and Luther, who argued very persuasively that the propagation and maintenance of religious beliefs – and hence political loyalty – could be controlled to an appreciable extent through the school and the procedures of education. Both sides, Catholic and Protestant, began to give considerable attention to the problem of how education could best be used as an instrument for securing their particular religious persuasions, and this was carried forward into the seventeenth century when the intellectual justification of religious dissent and nonconformity of all kinds led to as much continued conflict in education as it did in politics and other social matters. Education was influenced, moreover, not only by these religious movements, pre-eminent as they appeared at the time; it was affected also by a second and much more diffuse concern to develop it as a wider social process than simply that of providing support for Catholic orthodoxy or Protestant schism. This latter concern began to appear throughout the sixteenth century in a number of places, first as a literature of criticism, often very negatively and even violently expressed, but subsequently moderated by quite widespread efforts to effect improvement. The early period of modern Western education, then, is dominated by the interaction of several elements: the conservative concern to make it the deliberate instrument of religious and political policy, criticism of educational practices as they currently existed, and enthusiastic, often extremely idealistic, efforts to make education the means to a better, if not the best, world. What, then, was the status of education at the end of the sixteenth century? And how genuinely deserved were the criticisms which were so keenly felt at the time?

It is important to begin by taking a longer view and to appreciate that, when seen in the perspective of its own history, Western education by the end of the sixteenth century had made remarkable progress. The mastery of symbols, whereby experience can be stored and communicated, had been achieved in early antiquity and this, through the genius of the Greeks, had in turn been developed into a set of relatively simple instrumental skills. The Greeks, however, used this achievement as a means to produce what they called the process of education – *enkyklios paideia* – conceived as a heightened and intense set of experiences that collectively provide what was believed to be the worthiest form of life open to man, and cultivated through the medium of the liberal arts. Yet this remained a generally inaccessible ideal and, although it spread throughout the Mediterranean regions and subsequently into Europe, it rarely extended beyond a relatively small, wealthy, leisured class. The subsequent collapse of classical civilization in the early Christian centuries had profound repercussions in Europe, since education again became narrowly restricted, and during the early centuries of European history – the sixth to the ninth – it barely survived as the collection of instrumental skills it had been 2000 years before. Yet men struggled to recover the classical heritage, and the accession of Charlemagne to the throne of the Holy Roman Empire in the first year of the ninth century marked the beginning of the second major period in the history of Western education: that of the medieval civilization of Christian Europe.

The development of education became a central preoccupation of Europeans as they deliberately sought to build a new civilization to replace that which had been lost. Charlemagne himself proposed the goal of a new regenerated Christian world – *imperium christianum* – and this remained an inspiration to all who recognized the value of education. In the course of the following years, from the ninth century down to the sixteenth, that civilization not only was built but was brought to a higher peak of development than man had ever achieved before, and the process of education was one of its most vital and significant features. The ideology of education retained many of the characteristics it had acquired in its classical past; yet the Graeco-Roman concept of the cultivation of the *artes liberales* was transmuted throughout the centuries into the distinctively new ideal of the *pietas litterata*, so eloquently expressed in the writings of the Christian humanists of the sixteenth century. It is important to recognize how profoundly Christianity had changed the classical ideal of education. In essence, the acceptance of a personal god, guaranteed by the incarnation, along with the belief that the way to education and a heightened vision is potentially available to all, was a radical departure. Of equal significance, although manifested more concretely in everyday life, was the institutionalization of education. The labours of the Renaissance humanists had been responsible for the recovery of much classical learning, its semantic purification into Greek and Latin, and its translation into the vernaculars; the technological advances of the craft guilds provided the printing presses and the skills of book production that allowed for the dissemination of this learning, now organized into pedagogical sequences from the simple introductory Latin grammars through to the great collected works of Plato and Aristotle. And ready to disseminate this learning was a wide range of schools (in the general sense of the word) which were now in existence throughout Europe, ranging from the simple 'petty' schools and 'pedagogies' up through the grammar schools to the academies and universities that were to be found in almost every major city. The Jesuits, in particular, had even found a spiritual mission in establishing schools throughout the continent and were eagerly seeking to become, as they were later acknowledged to be, the schoolmasters of Europe.

Education was inevitably drawn, therefore, into the sixteenth-century religious-political conflict, since, throughout the millennium of the Christian civilization of Europe, it had been the handmaiden of the church. One of the most interesting aspects of education in medieval Christian Europe is that educational autonomy and secularity (with certain qualifications for Italy) were rarely proposed. On the contrary, throughout the Holy Roman Empire, education was essentially an element of Christianity, even if minor jurisdictional disputes arose at times in various cities between the bishop and the civic authorities. This, of course, recognizes that as education became increasingly institutionalized there were demands for executive independence, but that was a different matter. It was readily accepted, moreover, that the various institutions, chiefly schools and universities, had to provide for the instrumental and vocational skills of literacy, although these were always relegated to a foundational role. The clearly understood purpose of education was to secure and promote Christian faith and, if possible, beatific vision. There was an equally firm conviction that the content of a proper education was to be derived from a grammatical and literary study of the Christian classics. And in this respect it is important to note that in the sixteenth century a large body of theoretical writing appeared, concerned centrally with the ideology of education, which attempted to explain and justify its religious role, and which in volume was significantly greater than in any previous period in Western history. Concern with the Christian aims of education is a major characteristic of sixteenth-century thought.

Sixteenth-century ideologies

While many of Europe's most learned men composed pieces presenting their views, the field was dominated by Erasmus of Rotterdam, from whose writing the essential sixteenth-century ideology of education was generated, and this received a very wide dissemination and acceptance throughout western Europe. Erasmus put forward very expressively the Neoplatonist version of Logos Christianity with its central doctrine that the Word is contained within words.[1] There were, however, some serious obstacles to developing this educational theory into a workable school programme. While Erasmus, and other similar educators of the period – Luther, Melanchthon, More, Sadoleto and Vives, for example – reformulated Platonism into a more accessible literary version, the conception of two classes of people, the vulgar majority and a pious minority, of whom only the latter were really capable of a 'true education', retained a still very narrow view which went against the ethical spirit of Logos Christianity.

Aristotle had postulated a receptive capacity in the human mind which enables it to accept and order logically, in a parallel mental structure, the phenomena of the external world. This model of the mind became increasingly incorporated into Western thinking. Its really significant impact on education began in the early sixteenth century with the appearance of printed books, for these were, *par excellence*, the medium for logical organization and presentation. Aristotle's model of the mind lent itself very readily to the classroom, since it is fundamentally a theory of the interactive process of teaching and learning. Fundamental to this approach is the necessity for such learning to involve personal experience of the external world, but this step was largely bypassed: sixteenth-century educational theorists either took experience for granted or else presented it solely in the form of verbal statements, usually drawn from earlier authorities; they concentrated their energies on seeing how to transmit these predetermined patterns of verbal statements to the learner's mind. Their major interest, in effect, was in finding the best method of achieving this transmission. This became almost an obsession in the sixteenth century, and school textbooks based on such an approach flowed from the burgeoning printing presses of Europe. Erasmus, like most scholars of his day, worked at the task, and produced a treatise on classroom procedure, *On the Right Method of Instruction (De ratione studii)*. In that influential work the argument was advanced for a graded progression of studies from an elementary grammar through a series of Latin and Greek texts to the study of selected passages of classical and Christian literature, with an emphasis on grammatical, syntactical and textual exegesis.

Concurrently with Erasmus many other scholars were also seeking to translate the ideals of Christian humanism and the attainment of *pietas litterata* into a practicable school programme, and this created the phenomenon, made possible by the printing press, of the textbook movement. The process of education was suddenly transformed, as simple, intermediate and advanced grammar texts in Latin and Greek – and a few in Hebrew – along with graded readers and anthologies, known respectively as colloquies and florilegia, issued from the printing houses of Europe. By twentieth-century standards most of these are exceptionally crude; in their own day they were revolutionary. Most of them were small and would fit easily into the hand, and so the learning of Europe was now made accessible and portable. Throughout the sixteenth century hundreds of school texts appeared and found their way into the classrooms of Europe; of these, many had a short life, but others became established, often for centuries, such as Lily's *Latin Grammar*, thereby introducing into the classroom the practice of studying a set text.

Recognition of the advantages of text grading was carried across to the school itself, where the programme of instruction was similarly organized. The process started with individual schools, of which that conducted by Joannes Sturmius for the city council of Strasbourg rapidly became the European exemplar. Sturm's approach spread throughout the Protestant regions of Europe; in the Catholic areas it was disseminated by a more systematic treatment, based on his model but carried to greater lengths, in the most celebrated and significant *ratio* ever devised, the Jesuit *Ratio studiorum* – literally, the 'correct method of studies' – which received definitive form in 1599.

A further problem was the absence of a support system of schools and other institutions and this led to the appearance of quite different forms of educational procedure throughout the continent. The sixteenth century saw the first concerted, and partially successful, movements to establish schools on something more systematic than an individual, *ad hoc* basis. Such efforts laid the grounds for much future development in Europe and, in addition, provided the models that were taken to the colonies of the New World.

The provision of education: sixteenth-century patterns

It is necessary, in this connection, however, to appreciate that, despite the intense activity in theoretical and practical aspects of education in this period, there was no widespread revolution in public literacy at this time, nor was there any dramatic increase in school populations. In the absence of accurate statistics, of course, inferences for this time must be drawn from what are highly unreliable and partially extant sources such as parish registers, court documents, and literary references and allusions, many of which, as a direct result of the wars and the consequent depredations of that century, were deliberately destroyed, the most dramatic example being the burning of Huguenot educational records, of the later sixteenth century, in the seventeenth when those French Protestants were bitterly suppressed by a resurgent and vindictive Catholicism. Europe's population was almost entirely rural, with the greatest densities in France, Germany, Italy and Spain where modern estimates suggest a total for these four regions of perhaps fifty million; the British Isles had something of the order of five million. The Scandinavian countries together had fewer than Britain, while the eastern European regions were even more sparsely settled. All of the prominent cities were relatively small: the biggest were in Italy where Naples had more than 200,000 people, Milan and Venice about 150,000. London and Paris each had populations similar to Milan and Venice; Rome, Antwerp, Lisbon and Seville are thought to have contained around 100,000.[2] Although the basis for these statistics is too insecure for confident generalizations to be made, it seems reasonably clear that the twenty largest cities of western Europe for which data exist had altogether a total population of less than two million.[3]

Despite the proliferation of printed books in the mid-fifteenth century, there was virtually no popular press, and nothing of any significance in the vernacular: only learned men could write well, and when it came to preparing works for publication they avoided the vernacular, knowing that would limit circulation. Printing was too expensive for ephemera, and the relatively few popular books had to have a wide appeal to justify production on a significantly economic scale. As a result they were mostly encyclopedic works with a universal interest such as Bartholomaeus's *All the Properties of Things* of 1495.

There was, however, no continuous stimulation of a need for public literacy. The educational ideology of Neoplatonism and the *pietas litterata* was sustained in a highly specialized and erudite literature restricted to a tiny minority; that approach had no popular impact, nor did it make any attempt to provide for the more instrumental and vocational aspects of education: the sixteenth-century school was still beyond the ambit of most people's concerns, and public life was carried on by almost exclusively oral face-to-face communication. Occupations requiring literacy were dominated by clerics, or those who had been influenced by the church and had been trained in the petty and grammar schools. It was in the sixteenth century that the word 'clerk' – which had hitherto expressly denoted men in holy, generally minor orders – began to acquire its separate meaning of a person capable of keeping records, correspondence and accounts.

When schools were established on a wider scale in the sixteenth century, they were motivated largely by religious considerations: their ideology was that of attaining 'lettered piety', their curriculum was based on a programme of literary studies, secular and sacred, while support came from rulers and governments who acted from a religious stimulus. This, of course, does not deny the influences of increasing trade and economic activity, and the steadily developing urbanization of Europe. Pressure from these sources was indeed explicitly recognized and so stated by some, but generally these were covert forces. There were two fundamental processes at work in the development of schools: a Protestant initiative which occurred separately in the German territories, England and France; and a Catholic response which was limited largely to France and the Catholic regions of southern Europe.

Protestant developments: Germany and England

The Lutheran initiative in Germany

The educational challenge to the traditional monopoly of medieval Catholicism became prominent in Germany as a result of Luther's ceaseless campaign to have schools established and maintained for the Christian education of youth, girls as well as boys.[4] Although there were already in Germany a number of well-established schools and universities, some of which had deservedly good reputations and a history of several centuries, the first great stimulus to the wider establishment of schools came in the fifteenth century when Italian humanism was imported to enthusiastic German scholars who saw in the new intellectual movement a means of civilizing their emerging nation, hitherto known for cultural barbarism. This growth can be seen most dramatically in the case of the universities. In the fourteenth century there were five: Prague, Vienna, Heidelberg, Cologne, Erfurt; in the fifteenth, eleven were founded: Leipzig, Rostock, Greifswald, Freiburg, Basle, Ingolstadt, Trier, Mainz, Tübingen, Wittenberg and Frankfurt an der Oder. Schools, administered by various authorities – church and civic – also increased, although their origins and numbers are not so well chronicled. It is known, however, that Nuremberg in 1485 had four schools, each staffed by a master and three assistants, which provided, among them, places for 245 paying scholars and an unspecified number of free places; while Augsburg, a little over a hundred kilometres to the south, had, in 1503, five schools and a total of 523 students.[5] In the same period, around the beginning of the sixteenth century, the total enrolment of all German universities, Catholic and Protestant, has been estimated to have been between 3000 and 4000 students; if the enrolments of Catholic Vienna and Prague, and those Germans studying abroad, are counted, the number is estimated at around 6000.[6] Given such evidence, the figures for school and university enrolment are minuscule in proportion to the estimated population of twelve to fifteen million in Germany at that time.[7]

The Lutheran educational programme was first set out in Melanchthon's *Articles of Visitation*[8] of 1528 and, once adopted by the Elector John of Saxony, became the model for further sets of school regulations, which, drafted by various authors, were adopted by other regions and cities in Lutheran territories: Hamburg in 1529, Schleswig-Holstein in 1542, Mecklenburg in 1552 (written by Melanchthon himself) and the Palatinate in 1556. Simultaneously, Protestant universities were founded: Marburg (1527), Königsberg (1544), Jena (1558) and Helmstedt (1576).[9] Schools did not necessarily immediately follow when regulations were adopted, particularly in rural locations. The first attempt to establish an institutional system of schools – as distinct from the individual town schools – appears to be that of the Elector Maurice of Saxony who decreed in 1543 the provision of a dual system: city schools, *Stadtsschulen* (descendants of the medieval city schools); and state schools, *Staatsschulen*, established outside the municipalities, and subdivided further into two types – *Ländesschulen*, intended to train clever boys for the state service at public expense, and *Klosterschulen*, maintained in convents and monasteries.[10] The first three *Staatsschulen* were set up straightaway in Pforta, Meissen and Grimma, each being endowed with the property of former local convents. Between them they were to accept 230 boys, 100 from the cities of Saxony, 76 from the nobility and 54 of the elector's nomination. These boys had to be already literate and after six years' study were expected to proceed to either of the universities of Leipzig or Wittenberg and, after graduation, into the service of the state. This practice was followed elsewhere, although details are not certain; nor is it clear to what extent these regulations were applied outside the major cities.[11]

Generally these schools had a more modified instructional sequence than Sturm's gymnasium, employing the three-stage progression of the *Articles of Visitation*: elementary, Latin grammar, literature. Very little is known of elementary instruction, partly because there was neither an established theory nor a practice to offer guidance, partly because the schools still catered chiefly for the middle and upper classes who had no respect for the vernacular – there being no major German literary movement in this period comparable with those of Italy, England and France – and such families were in any case able to give this instruction in the home.

We are fortunate, however, in possessing a detailed account of education in sixteenth-century Germany in the autobiography of the city school-master of Basle, Thomas Platter, written in 1572.[12] This is a very personal document, in marked contrast to the excessively formal writing of Sturm, and gives a vivid picture of educational conditions in Germany and Switzerland which adds a human scale to the existing record.

Platter attended a village school, although he recalled nothing of it except a series of brutalities by the teacher which induced him to abscond and fall in with a group of wandering scholars or bacchantes,[13] there being large numbers of these bands of vagrants travelling all over Europe at the time. He fled from the bacchantes and eventually arrived in Schlettstadt in 1521 where he enrolled in the school of Johann Sapidus which at times held up to 900 pupils. Platter recorded that 'when I entered the school I could do nothing; not even read Donatus. I was then already eighteen years old. I seated myself among the little children. I was quite like a hen among little chickens.'[14] After an unspecified period he knew his 'Donat by heart to a dot', although his knowledge of Latin was still so meagre that 'had my life depended on it, I could not have declined a noun of the first declension'.[15] He left for Zürich where he attended the grammar school of Our Lady's Cathedral where, under Father Myconius, instruction began with Terence and 'we were compelled to decline and conjugate all the words of the entire comedy'.[16] Myconius also lectured on the scriptures, many of the laity attending.[17] While in Zürich he heard of the debates between Luther and Eck, and became influenced by Zwingli.

Seeking further improvement, Platter taught himself Greek and Hebrew from textbooks, and after marrying moved to Visp where he became a ropemaker. He was accepted into their guild – a precondition in that period for civic participation – and thereupon opened a school. This in itself is an interesting commentary upon the times, for schoolmastering was frequently conducted in conjunction with some other relatively sedentary occupation, and the practice continued for several centuries, being especially favoured by tailors, dressmakers, and craftsmen such as cutlers concerned with the manufacture of small objects. Platter's first school seems to have prospered, since he records that when he 'began to prepare for rope-making and to hold school . . . [he] received thirty-one scholars; most in winter, but in summer scarcely six'.[18] In 1541 he was invited to become rector of the school in the castle at Basle. Platter accepted the offer and discharged the duties of the office for more than thirty years, in the course of which time the school built up a reputation for scholarship.

Protestant supremacy in England

Meanwhile, education in England was following a similar course, stimulated in the first instance by Henry VIII's conflict with Rome and the subsequent anglicization of the church under Henry VIII and his son Edward VI. After a short interlude of attempted return to Catholicism under Mary Tudor (r. 1553–8), the thorough Protestantization of the English church under Elizabeth I (r. 1558–1603) exercised a direct and lasting influence on English education.

Education in England had already begun to change rapidly in the fifteenth century[19] when the increasing urbanization of the country produced a demand for literate persons. With the withdrawal of the monasteries at this time from their traditional concern with schooling, their place was taken by the cathedral schools and the newly emerging town and guild schools. To supplement the meagre instruction given in the elementary schools scattered throughout the churches and cathedrals of the land, the grammar schools appeared in strength in the fifteenth century. This growth of schools, however vigorous it may appear from the surviving records – and in this respect it must be remembered that England is better documented for this period than any other European country – was not one of any great magnitude. The bulk of children, despite Henry IV's statute of 1405–6, remained tied to the land and to serfdom, and received no instruction at all; the song and grammar schools were few in number and generally tiny in enrolment.

Henry VIII's movement to anglicize the church, which took place chiefly throughout the 1530s, affected education in two respects: through the dissolution of the monasteries and chantries, and the enforcement of mandatory texts for use in the church and the schools. Schools were nearly all located in churches, and the majority were conducted by clerics; the anglicization of the church made all the clergy subordinate to the crown, and Henry used this power effectively, as did Elizabeth later in the century. Henceforth Rome was no longer able to exert any influence upon the clergy and the clerical teachers.

Enforcement of mandatory texts, however, had a more direct and positive influence. Under the Vicar-General, Thomas Cromwell, the clergy were instructed to teach in English, and the Coverdale revision of the Tyndale translation of the Bible was officially authorized for use in the kingdom. The maintenance of Henry's policies, even after his death in 1547, led to the issuing in 1548 of an English vernacular Book of Common Prayer. For the first time the bulk of English society were now able to understand the religious services. Preaching, of course, was in the vernacular, and it was by these means that the people were instructed generally. The schools, too, were influenced by mandatory texts, with the setting of a standard Latin grammar – Lily's *Grammar*. So Henry VIII structured the future of the English church and English education. These were, however, relatively minor changes, and the schools remained entirely within the broad stream of the tradition of *pietas litterata* sustained by the Latin grammar method. Indeed, only Lily's *Grammar* was prescribed; alongside it appeared a multitude of Latin texts, the *vulgariae* and colloquies which were used throughout the schools indiscriminately.

Most of the educational developments of Henry VIII's reign, however, were consequences of his religious policies, of which the chief architect was Thomas Cranmer (1489–1556), who became in 1532 Archbishop of Canterbury, a position he held until his imprisonment, some twenty years later in 1553 by Mary Tudor, when he was degraded and subsequently burned at the stake in 1556. Under Cranmer the monastic cathedrals were all reconstituted as secular cathedrals and, with the exception of Winchester, were required to maintain grammar schools. It was Cranmer who secured several of Henry's divorces and remarriages, acts that led him to be considered a mere dupe of the king. Yet that charge is by no means accurate: Cranmer was an ardent Erastian in his persuasions, following the position developed and promulgated by the Swiss theologian Thomas Erastus (1524–83) who argued for the ascendancy of the state over the church in ecclesiastical matters. Moreover, Cranmer was of a highly independent mind, anxious to see that the *ecclesia anglicana* maintained its independence. And so, after Henry's death in 1547, he provided religious guidance for the young and sickly Edward VI (1537–53), Henry's son by Jane Seymour, during that boy-king's brief reign.

The features of religious policy during Edward's reign that most affected education were the suppression of the chantries and the endowment of the grammar schools. The suppression of the chantries had been initiated by Henry VIII who, on the pretext that they were improperly conducted, sought to take over their valuable lands, chiefly to finance the war against the French. In its origins the chantry was an office of prayers for the dead, and to ensure its perpetuity wealthy persons throughout the Middle Ages provided endowments of a permanent benefice for a resident priest to sing the office, along with a fund for the constitution and maintenance of small chapels for the purpose; in the course of time it was the buildings themselves that became known as chantries. In the following years chantry priests conducted schools, and by the time of Henry's Act of 1545 which put the chantries under the 'protection' of the crown there were several thousand of these, and similar small chapels, in operation. Henry himself did not live to put the Act into effect; however, in 1547, the year of his death, by a similar Act Edward VI suppressed 2374 chantries and guild chapels, causing a considerable educational loss, since many of these, unlike the monasteries, were active centres of elementary and grammar education.

The endowment of the grammar schools appears to have been an attendant consequence: in 1552 numerous churches were given grants of land to support schools which subsequently became known as Edward VI foundations. In most cases, however, the records have not survived, and such an appellation is quite misleading, attributing as it does a policy of founding schools to the reign of the boy-king. On the contrary, these foundations were in all likelihood simply a partial restoration of church properties previously seized. There remains considerable doubt, and no little controversy, over the role of Edward VI in founding schools; it seems that the letters patent granted to schools were more often confirmatory than foundational.[20]

The Elizabethan era: education as an agent of Protestantization

The chief educational developments in sixteenth-century England occurred during the reign of Elizabeth I (1558–1603), when the schools and universities – and indeed the whole conception of education – were linked with the deliberate Protestantization of the nation. There were no significant educational developments, however, during the first decade of her reign, when she was preoccupied with maintaining her own ascendancy in a difficult period. Elizabeth devoted her governmental energies to securing as much harmony as she could in England and so evolved her compromise style of religious organization in which, by the Act of Supremacy of 1559, she became 'governor' of the Church of England and the bishops became the theological and ecclesiastical authorities. The Act of Uniformity of the same year required the clergy of England to observe

English forms of worship and to follow the revised edition of the Book of Common Prayer of 1552.

These two Acts had a considerable effect upon education. The Act of Supremacy contained an oath of allegiance to the queen which all clergy were required to swear, and this effectively prevented Catholics from graduating at Oxford and Cambridge, although, since the oath was not administered until graduation, it did not prevent them from gaining a university education.[21] By this time, however, the universities had ceased to be clerical corporations and their social structure had changed considerably, many people pursuing studies with quite secular intentions. Pressure against Nonconformists increased and in 1563 a new Act, the Oath of Supremacy, demanded that the swearer should 'utterly testify and declare in my conscience that the Queen's highness is the only supreme governor in this realm'. This oath was required not only of clerics but also of all university graduates, lawyers, members of parliament and schoolmasters, and was enforced by severe penalties for breaches: forfeiture of lands, substantial fines, imprisonment and, for repeated offences, the charge of treason. To control religious sympathies even more strictly – for by now Elizabeth recognized that education was closely involved – schoolmasters had not only to take the oath but in addition to be licensed; all books, including school texts, likewise had to be approved, and school-children had to be instructed in the English catechism.

Extreme Protestantism: English Puritanism

By the year 1570 England under Elizabeth had become largely Protestant, Catholicism had been suppressed, and the religious character of the period was marked by a new phenomenon: the virtual polarization of religious activism between Protestant Puritanism at one extreme and clandestine Catholic recusancy at the other, while in between were the majority of the population, paying little heed to either faction, and following the path of orthodox conformity. Between them, Puritans and Catholics continued the religious struggle in England for the ensuing century.

The educational influence of Puritanism was quite significant, being exerted through the universities, and through the pressure of zealous Puritan congregations upon their clergymen. Cambridge was a particularly enthusiastic supporter of such evangelical fundamentalism, especially Emmanuel College, although the movement existed at Oxford too. Puritanism was, moreover, a middle-class phenomenon, supported chiefly by the mercantile groups which had increasingly been sending their sons to the universities for a general education, especially since the introduction of humanism under the influence of Erasmus. Throughout the sixteenth century the universities in England, and in numerous places in Europe, had lost their exclusively clerical, medieval character and had become, to a considerable extent, finishing schools, in which the aristocracy, the gentry and the mercantile classes increasingly influenced policies and procedures. In addition, the universities now drew their theological students from these same classes, with the result that most of the graduating clerics held Puritan views. Throughout the 1570s, moreover, legislative pressure was exerted against Catholic schools at all levels; in 1571 came the Penal Act which proscribed Catholic schools and required all schools to teach the English Catechism and the Thirty-Nine Articles; ten years later, in 1581, Catholics were virtually excluded from the two universities by the requirement that all intending undergraduates take the Oath of Supremacy to Elizabeth and the English church, not at graduation as formerly but before the commencement of studies, upon matriculation.

Although Protestant nonconformity had not yet appeared in any seriously organized forms, throughout the 1580s Puritan forces sought the replacement of the episcopal system of church government by a presbyterian one (Greek *presbuteros*, 'elder' of the church) in which authority is vested in a representative body of clerics and laymen. Puritan attacks on episcopacy reached a climax in 1588–9 with the appearance of the pseudonymous 'Marprelate Tracts' which were scathing criticisms of the current established system of church government. By means of the church courts and the ecclesiastical commission of interrogation, the Archbishop of Canterbury, John Whitgift, moved successfully against the attempt to replace episcopacy with presbyterianism.

Catholic recusancy and clandestine schools

Catholic resurgence was attacked even more vigorously, and throughout the later decades of the sixteenth century further penal sanctions against Catholics were promulgated with increasingly severe injunctions. Unlike the Puritans, moreover, who as a morally stringent reforming faction within the English church were more difficult to deal with, Catholics were readily identifiable, and with the explicit hostility of Rome in the bull of Pius V of 1570, *Regnans in excelsis*, which excommunicated Elizabeth and bound Catholics to oppose her, they were, by the laws of the realm, potential traitors. Elizabeth had originally sought a minimum of religious conflict and hoped for compromises with Catholics. When such measures failed, she was forced to respond more vigorously, this leading to the Penal Act of 1571 which included bans on Catholic schools.

Henceforth Catholic education had to be conducted in secret, and the chief effect was the emigration of English Catholics across the Channel where they established schools in considerable numbers.[22] These existed at all levels, and there are records of at least thirty-five boys' and men's schools in various parts of Europe in the period,[23] of which several were religious seminaries concerned specifically to prepare priests who could return to England and keep Catholicism alive. There were, in addition, girls' schools, but these are more vaguely documented.[24] The first of the seminaries founded was at Douai in the Netherlands in 1568 by William Allen (1532–94) who was forced to leave Oxford in 1565 as a result of the penal laws, and who subsequently devoted his life to the preparation of English émigré priests. Others followed, all generally at convenient locations near Channel ports to facilitate movement in both directions.

The émigré schools on the continent gradually began to return educated Catholic children and evangelizing priests to England. As early as 1580 the English Jesuits, Robert Parsons or 'Persons' (1546–1610), a former fellow of Balliol College at Oxford, and Edmund Campion (1540–81), formerly of St John's, Oxford, crossed from Douai to London where they began preaching Catholic doctrines, with some success. Elizabeth ordered them to be arrested; Parsons fled back across the Channel, Campion was caught and executed the following year. They had been successful, however, not only in establishing a number of Catholic schools, and training teachers for them, but also in setting up clandestine presses which produced Catholic religious and educational texts – in contravention of the Privy Council Order of 1566 which licensed all presses and restricted them solely to London, with the exception of one each at Oxford and Cambridge.

The Jesuits continued their efforts and made the infiltration of the universities a primary concern, as was recognized by a government proclamation of 1591 which, stating that such infiltrations were believed to be 'Friers, Priests, Iesuits, or Popish schollers, and of these, many do attempt to resort into the universities and houses of Lawe',[25] required all householders to report the movement of suspicious persons. Throughout the 1590s the search for Catholic infiltrators was stepped up, and altogether, between 1590 and 1603 (when Elizabeth died), fifty-three priests and thirty-five lay persons were executed under the penal laws against Catholics.[26] By the end of Elizabeth's long reign the Church of England was established as the religion of the state and the majority of the people; Catholicism was a minority faith, driven largely underground, Catholic schools were few in number and secretly conducted. The campaign against Catholicism was sustained by Elizabeth's successors throughout the seventeenth century.

Educational developments under Elizabeth: removal of church control

Under Elizabeth, English education became entirely separated from the Catholic Church and was virtually secularized, even though many teachers were in holy orders, since clerics held their livings, and conducted schools, as benefices of the crown. With the loss of church control, a number of different kinds of authorities established schools; in addition to the crown, schools conducted by guilds, city corporations, parishes and private groups and individuals came into existence. A measure of caution must be exercised in interpreting this, however, since the secularization of schools under Elizabeth implies no great expansion in numbers. Reliable statistics are still difficult to collect, but it seems that schools were relatively few in relation to the estimated total population of between four and five million in England and Wales during the sixteenth century. It is impossible to assess the number of elementary schools since these were distributed throughout the land on a totally unorganized basis and were conducted frequently in simple quarters – usually the church building itself – without any particular identity. The grammar schools, however, are easier to find since they were fewer in number, were generally located in the larger centres and had separate buildings for which title deeds were issued. Before Elizabeth's accession in 1558, fifty-one such schools are definitely known, while during the half-century of her reign a further 230 schools come into the record; of these, 135 have no documentation prior to her accession, the balance of 95 schools may have existed, but their documents are ambiguous: it is uncertain whether their letters patent are original grants or simply confirmations of existing foundations.[27]

It is equally difficult to determine the size of these schools, but they appear to have been relatively small. Many had only a single master, although some had an assistant, known as an usher. Qualifications stressed moral character and intellectual competence, particularly in Latin and, if possible, Greek. Enrolments were correspondingly limited; the median range was 40–60 pupils; many had fewer, and some, such as Shrewsbury in 1581, had as many as 360 boys.[28] Girls did not attend grammar schools.

The numbers of schools and their estimated enrolments allow some very rough guesses to be made concerning the state of literacy; 281 schools with a median enrolment range of 40–60 suggests a total grammar school population of less than 20,000, and this set against a population of five million gives a school enrolment of one in 250. If one allows for even four generations of similarly schooled persons in the total society – and this is far too generous in terms of the record of schools earlier in the sixteenth century, prior to Elizabeth's accession – the figures still give a literacy rate of much less than one per cent. This, of course, raises the issue of the meaning of 'literacy', 'illiteracy' and 'semi-literacy', but it is clear that, regardless of whatever precision we might give these terms,[29] schooling of the formal Latin grammar kind, which alone provided for access to the higher culture, and certainly to social and vocational advancement, was limited, as in antiquity and the medieval period, to a tiny minority. This, of course, refers only to Latin literacy; the social and economic conditions of the times demanded a wider range of public literacy, of varying degrees, which was met in the vernacular, where no grammar schooling was required. Thomas More wrote in 1533 that 'farre more than fowre partes of all the whole divided into tenne coulde never reade english yet', thus implying a literacy rate of under 60 per cent in the vernacular.[30] This is obviously impressionistic; it would be realistic, in the light of our more accurate knowledge of various European countries for later centuries, to estimate less than 50 per cent literacy, in terms of the ability to read the vernacular but not to write it, for the population of England in the reign of Elizabeth. It is important, however, to remember that such informal methods of acquiring the vernacular, and literacy in the vernacular itself, were not considered educational in any significant sense. The ideology of education was still avowedly Neoplatonist, dominated by the concept of Logos Christianity, and well exemplified in the morning prayer of the grammar school at Hawkshead which called on the 'divine majesty' of god 'to illuminate our understanding' and to help the boys to 'profit in good learning and literature'.[31]

Catholic response: education under the Habsburgs

The Catholic Reformation and the Society of Jesus

In response to Lutheran and Anglican secessions, Rome became even more conservative and reactionary, dominated by the policies of the House of Habsburg. In the mid-sixteenth century the Catholic Church moved to internal reforms, in which control of the schools, colleges and universities of Europe was conceived as significant and necessary for prosecuting heresy and restoring the unity of faith. Authority over education, however, was not seen in isolation; it was recognized as part of a wider mechanism of social control which the church must initiate if Europe were to be restored to Catholic unity. As events were then understood, it was necessary for the church itself to reform the abuses that led to Luther's revolt while at the same time it was considered equally important for discipline throughout the religious ranks, as well as within the laity, to be tightened and enforced. Education was seen not as an immediate agent of reform but as a long-term development for maintaining unity once it had been regained. So the four great elements of the Catholic Reformation were assembled: the Council of Trent, the Inquisition, the *Index* and the Society of Jesus.

The Council of Trent was convened between 1545 and 1563 to examine the attacks upon doctrine and church government and to effect any necessary reforms. In the first series of sessions it reaffirmed the church's right to mediate between man and god; it asserted, that is, the necessity of church interpretation of all scriptural revelation.[32] By 1563 a great deal of doctrinal clarification and redevelopment had been achieved, although this had in large part further alienated the Protestant participants (who left the sessions even more opposed to Rome's arrogation of religious authority) and so had prepared the way for the worsening of relations and the further series of major devastating religious wars of the later sixteenth and the first half of the seventeenth century. The Council of Trent, however, strengthened and rejuvenated Catholicism, which in the face of a Protestant initiative undertook a programme of reform, beginning with the re-examination of Catholic teaching. The year after the Council closed, its vast body of documents was summarized by Pius IV in the bull *Injunctum nobis*, known as the Tridentine Profession of Faith. This religious symbol was issued to all bishops and priests in 1564, requiring them at the time of its receipt to recite publicly the profession of their faith as a show of Catholic force. The text required each priest to 'acknowledge and embrace the Apostolical and ecclesiastical traditions and other observances and constitutions of the [Catholic] Church' and to accept the exegetical authority of the church in that 'I acknowledge the sacred scripture according to that sense which Holy Mother Church has held and holds, to whom it belongs to decide upon the true sense and interpretation of the holy scriptures'.[33]

While the Council of Trent, after examining the doctrinal basis of Catholicism, in effect made no changes but instead merely strengthened and affirmed the traditional position, it at least made explicit what had become the subject of continued doubt and debate. In concert with this was the establishment of an agency of enforcement which the church already had to hand in an existing institution, a court of church inquiry founded by the Emperor Frederick II in 1232 to deal with heretics and known as the Inquisition. This court was refurbished and invested by Pope Paul III in 1542 with executive authority to impose and see to the enforcement of sentences for heresy and ecclesiastical indiscipline. On the assumption that heresy could be avoided, in the main, if people were unaware of alternatives, the Inquisition in 1557 during the pontificate of Paul IV promulgated its compilation of proscribed books, the *Index librorum prohibitorum*, which, in dual lists of authors and titles, named those writers and publications considered contrary or dangerous to Catholic faith and morals. This *Index* came to include many celebrated works; indeed it became virtually a catalogue of the influential reforming literature of the modern period, and although still in use today it is no longer so restrictive.

By this time the idea of internal reform had given rise to the Theatine Order in the 1520s, followed by a Franciscan offshoot, the Capuchins, who received approval in 1529, and the Barnabites in 1530. These were all organized as reforming movements, and Ignatius Loyola followed their example when in 1539 he constituted himself and nine other enthusiasts at Paris as the Society of Jesus which received approval by Paul III in 1540, and which was to become the main instrument of Catholic educational policy. Since its early years coincided with the sittings of the Council of Trent, the Society drew into its ranks many zealots who identified with its rigorous discipline in the pursuit of Catholic unity. This discipline is set out specifically in two major documents, the *Spiritual Exercises*, written personally by Ignatius, and the *Constitutions* which became the Rule and included an educational programme, set out in the concluding Fourth

Part.[34] Towards the end of the century, this was complemented by an exhaustive method of teaching set out in the *Ratio studiorum* which in its definitive version of 1599 was to provide a practical manual of how Jesuit educational goals were to be achieved.

The Jesuits never fulfilled their original mission of combating heresy among the Turks; they remained to fight Protestantism in Europe by educational means and their domination of education was spectacularly successful almost from the start, particularly in Spain, Portugal and Italy; later the order took firm root in France, the Germanic Habsburg domin- ions and Poland. So successful was its expansion that they won back to Catholicism much of the southern Germanic territories and even threat- ened to go beyond Poland, where they enjoyed considerable acceptance. It was, in fact, the threat of Jesuit penetration that stirred a lazy Russian Orthodox Church in the 1630s to establish a Jesuit-style college in Kiev, chiefly, as their records indicate, in order 'to preserve the truths of Eastern orthodoxy'.[35] In addition, the Jesuits were to provide the most formidable opposition to Protestantism in the Germanic regions and England. It was, however, in Spain, Portugal and Italy that they enjoyed initial educational successes, due both to the intrinsically superior quality of their organiza- tion, dedication and educational procedures and equally to the lack of any firmly established tradition to oppose them.

Jesuit domination of education in the Habsburg domains

The characteristic educational institution of the Jesuits, modelled after that of their first foundation established in Gandia on the Spanish Medi- terranean coast some eighty kilometres south of Valencia in 1546, was the college.[36] Jesuit planning included not only the organization of the college but also the principles of pedagogy which were set out in the *Ratio studiorum*. These principles were based on the continuous use of Latin in question-and-answer situations, the vernacular being avoided as much as possible. By means of the *Ratio*'s techniques of prelection, concertation, exercises and repetition, the Jesuit schools developed a pedagogical system in advance of anything offered elsewhere in Europe, which, by stressing uniformity, set high standards of achievement. And, we might note, the Jesuits established, for the first time in the history of Western education, an instrument of potentially far-ranging social control, for theirs was a fully centralized system. Their colleges were strategically situated throughout Europe and by the end of the century were producing considerable numbers of graduates who moved into positions of authority as an élite able to give further preference for official appointments to other Jesuits.

At a rapidly accelerating rate the Jesuits founded new colleges and in addition smaller, more localized schools as provided for in the *Constitutions*. So enthusiastically was this done that the Jesuits in the seventeenth century dominated all boys' education in Catholic regions and were dubbed 'the schoolmasters of Europe'. This, of course, was accomplished at a price. In Italy, for example, the independent republics were suppressed under Habsburg domination, the schools came under Jesuit control, and much Renaissance learning was extinguished, apart from the continuing activities of some of the scholarly societies. Only the Republic of Venice remained independent and its university, situated in the city of Padua, attempted to maintain a humanist tradition of learning. Elsewhere in the Habsburg territories the Jesuits dominated many of the universities and schools, and, aided by the Inquisition, which they came to dominate as well, they were able to impose their will.

Catholicism divided: education in France

Only in one Catholic country – France, which lay outside the Habsburg domains – did the Jesuits encounter serious opposition. It was, of course, France almost as much as Germany that was the area of their greatest concern, since Gallicanism was as dangerous to Catholic unity as Protestantism, and France had both. France, however, was not as educationally backward as either Spain or the kingdom of Naples where the Jesuits found their earliest acceptance, and by the mid-sixteenth century French educational provisions were equal to anywhere else in Europe, although quality and effectiveness were becoming increasingly subject to challenge. Education was caught up, very intimately, in the religious conflicts of the later decades of the sixteenth century when it seemed possible that France might become independent, on an English model, or at least would split into two major divisions, with neither possessing any territorial integrity. This possibility came from the fact that the Protestants and Catholics co-existed in equal populations in many regions, and while the Catholics were more numerous around Paris, and the Huguenots had a number of major bases elsewhere, of which the chief was the citadel and port of La Rochelle on the Atlantic coast, neither had any clearly defined regions of dominance. The overwhelming danger, from the Catholic point of view, was that the Huguenots, as was being openly said, might become 'a state within a state'. The conflict, then, was very similar in its elements to that in England, and the inevitable course of events became one in which both sides contended for supremacy, although, unlike England, the struggle was protracted over a much longer period. Both sides, Catholic and Huguenot, saw the control of the schools as crucial to the maintenance of their respective obediences.

The continuing medieval tradition of education

Although France was not as educationally backward as either Spain or much of Italy, it had begun to lag behind England, parts of Germany and the Low Countries, and the more progressive Italian republics, especially Venice and Florence. Unfortunately the lack of evidence for school foundations in the Middle Ages continues through into the fifteenth and sixteenth centuries (and even, in some respects, into the seventeenth), and quite frequently we have to be content with rather generalized information. The diocese remained the unit of educational provision and administration, all cathedrals coming to have an *écolâtre* or schoolmaster – the vernacular equivalent of the medieval Latin *scholasticus* – whose duty it was to supervise the school, appoint assistants and look after the cathedral library. Each town and village church had the moral obligation (required by previous church decrees) to establish and maintain schools, while every cathedral supported a school, a number of which grew into universities, fifteen all told by the beginning of the sixteenth century, these being distributed across the entire countryside. In addition there were numerous monastic colleges and *studia particulares* which gave a general liberal arts education, almost exclusively to interns. Dominating the entire higher educational scene was the University of Paris which had remained the stronghold of unreformed Aristotelianism in Europe, and which provided an educational model for the rest of the country.

In all the larger towns and cities the church conducted elementary schools (*petites écoles*) which accepted both boys and girls, teaching the elements of literacy in the vernacular and, perhaps for the better pupils, some Latin. There were, in addition, grammar schools (*grandes écoles*), for boys only, which continued the elementary instruction and prepared the pupils for university entrance. It seems that these were generally conducted by, or operated in close conjunction with, the cathedral schools and universities, thereby inhibiting the independent growth of grammar schools as had occurred in England and elsewhere.[37] The universities developed a college system for both residence and instruction and in many cases the colleges, especially at Paris, were themselves little more than *grandes écoles* concerned fundamentally with instruction in Latin grammar.

Throughout the sixteenth century this pattern continued and efforts were made to extend the provision of schools, particularly in the face of the growing Protestant challenge. Specific educational enactments are few, one being an *ordonnance* of the Parlement of Paris of 1560 which required parents to send both their boys and girls to school, under penalty of a fine; but this Act, like so many similar to it, lacked any means of enforcement and seems to have been largely an exhortatory gesture.

Challenges to tradition: humanist influences

The continuing medieval tradition was not, however, without its challenges, most of which had a humanist origin. Humanism had made some headway in France, having become entrenched in the city of Lyon in the Rhône valley. During the Renaissance Lyon became highly receptive to humanist influences moving up from Italy, and by the sixteenth century it had surpassed Paris as the cultural centre of France, having become known particularly for its acceptance of the revived and purified Platonism of Ficino cultivated in the Accademia Platonica. From Lyon the humanist influence radiated into the rest of France, stimulating not only an interest in the revival and imitation of classical antiquity but also the equally significant humanist concern with the vernacular.

Humanism reached Paris and, although spurned by the university, took hold in the French court largely through the efforts of both Jacques Lefevre d'Étaples (1450–1536), who issued a French New Testament in 1523 and thereby initiated the vernacular tradition, and of Guillaume Budé (1468–1540), who encouraged François I to promote humanist learning. François I (r. 1515–47) came to the Valois throne in a period of rising French nationalism; stimulated by Budé, one of the leading classical scholars of the day (in Greek as well as Latin), François founded, in 1518, a new humanist-type institution of higher learning, the Collège de France. This foundation, known also as the Collège Royale, was modelled on the Collegium Trilingue at Louvain which had been established the previous year as a school of biblical-exegetical studies concerned with Latin,

Greek and Hebrew. The Collège de France began with two chairs, Greek and Hebrew (Latin being plentifully provided for at the university), and by 1530 had become so well established that it proliferated into the additional fields of Arabic, rhetoric, civil law, philosophy, mathematics, botany, medicine and surgery. Lectures were to be given freely by the professors, no tests or charges were to be made for admission, no examinations were to be conducted or qualifications awarded, and it is interesting to note that, with the necessary changes in curriculum through the centuries, the Collège de France continues in operation following the original provisions to this day.

The Collège de France, however, was able to play only a limited role; academic power was still firmly held by the University of Paris, particularly in its faculty of theology which, dominated by the Dominicans and later by the Jesuits, was a stronghold of ultramontanism – the adherence, that is, to the central authority of Rome in the face of the growing separatist tendencies of independent French Catholicism and Protestantism. As such, the university resisted the trend to humanism and continued to promote a conservative Aristotelian scholasticism, thereby endeavouring to preserve what was considered to be a continuity with medieval Christendom. But the university's dominance and rigidity came increasingly under attack, one of the most trenchant and best received of these being that of François Rabelais (c. 1495–1553). One of the major early French humanists, Rabelais was also a champion of the vernacular, and in his writings we find a strident, far-reaching voice of educational criticism. Throughout his life Rabelais, a former Franciscan monk (and later a Benedictine), was an *enfant terrible* of the Catholic Church. In 1530 he renounced his vows, studied medicine and emerged with an even greater contempt for establishment learning.

For more than thirty years Rabelais attacked French education, religion and culture generally in four books – *Pantagruel*, *Gargantua*, *Le Tiers Livre* and *Le Quart Livre* – which were published between 1532 and 1552. In 1567, fourteen years after his death, these were brought together along with a fifth book of doubtful authenticity, *Le Cinquième Livre*, in a single posthumous publication.[38] The romance as a whole concerns the giant Gargantua and his son Pantagruel and their various exploits, all of which, although described in episodes of broad farce, were such transparently devastating attacks upon the church and French educated society that the various sections were continuously denounced as they were published: Books I and II were censured by the faculty of theology at the University of Paris, as was Book III immediately on its appearance in 1546, the first eleven chapters of Book IV in 1548 and the remainder in 1552. In addition his work was proscribed in 1548 by the Parlement of Paris, the supreme legal body of the capital and its environs. The work, however, was not banned, and Rabelais was fortunate to have the protection of many like-minded friends including the king, Henri II, who even extended royal copyright protection to the romance in 1552, the year before Rabelais's death.

Gargantua and Pantagruel had a both immediate and lasting impact upon French intellectual life and contributed to the growing criticisms as Protestantism – Lutheran, Calvinist and Huguenot – spread throughout Europe; the educational attacks, in particular, found a receptive audience. These specific criticisms are diffused throughout the entire work but are particularly concentrated in two sections: I. 14, concerning Gargantua's Latin schooling, and II. 5-8, which relates Pantagruel's education in Paris. In the first instance, the work was written in the French vernacular and is concerned chiefly to denounce the derivative nature of medieval learning, especially the excessive dependence on the memorization of glosses on standard texts.

Rabelais was not, however, totally negative; on the contrary, he proposed a positive educational approach which was to comprise the entire humanist programme. These serious suggestions occur in a letter which Pantagruel received from his father Gargantua, counselling his son on the best course of study. In effect, that short letter is a panegyric of humanism as then understood in France. It begins with an affirmation of life being directed towards the attainment of divine union which can be sought through the cultivation of moral virtue and intellectual activity, with the latter best channelled through the humanist studies. First, the classical languages should be learnt perfectly: Greek, Latin, Hebrew, Chaldaic and Arabic, with the advice to 'model your Greek style on Plato, your Latin on Cicero'. Along with these should go the daily study of the scriptures, the New Testament from the Greek, the Old from Hebrew. Then should follow history, cosmography, geometry, arithmetic, music and astronomy; astrology and divination should be dismissed as merely 'vanity and imposture'. Civil law is necessary, with a knowledge of 'the texts of the Code [*Corpus juris civilis*] by heart', and these then compared with philosophy. In addition,

a knowledge of nature is indispensable [to which you should] devote yourself
. . . with unflagging curiosity. Let there be no sea, river or fountain but you

know the fish that dwell in it. Be familiar with all the shrubs, bushes and trees in forest or orchard, all the plants, herbs and flowers that grow on the ground, all the birds of the air, all the metals in the bowels of the earth, all the precious stones in the orient and the south. In a word, be well informed in everything that concerns the physical world we live in.[39]

In addition, the letter recommends a study of medicine and practice in human, not animal dissection, for acquiring a knowledge of man. The inclusion of the study of nature, the physical world and man, however, marks a distinct departure from the usual humanist programme which up to the fourteenth and fifteenth centuries had been entirely literary. In this context Rabelais reveals a sensitivity to changing conceptions of scholarship and learning, and his inclusion of the proto-sciences puts him in the vanguard of the new approach to education, although the implementation of this was still more than a century away.

Perhaps the most interesting feature of the letter is its address: 'From Utopia, the seventeenth day of September'. For, indeed, Rabelais took his inspiration directly from More's classic work of 1518, and much of the content of Gargantua's letter is drawn from the prescriptions of the original programme of *Utopia*; Rabelais, moreover, knew that he was tilting at windmills and that his new educational studies would not be easily and willingly carried out. But he did put forward an affirmation of life and promoted zest and honesty where he perceived *ennui* and deceit; he attacked the greed and concupiscence of the church, the pretensions of scholars and the shallowness of so much learning. Rabelais's work helped to create a climate of criticism in mid-sixteenth-century French intellectual life.

The attack by Ramus

Contemporaneously with Rabelais the attack upon French scholarship, particularly as it was centred in the University of Paris, was being conducted more directly by an equally redoubtable protagonist, Pierre de la Ramée (1515–72), known by the latinized form of his name, Petrus Ramus. An adept, even precocious scholar, who had entered the University of Paris at twelve years of age, at twenty-one Ramus was ready to incept for his degree of Master of Arts. Already he was rebelling against the excessive scholasticism of the university which had reaffirmed its Aristotelian stance in 1534 when the Faculty of Arts enacted that 'the works of Aristotle are given as the standard and basis of all philosophic enquiring'.[40] Two years later he showed considerable temerity in choosing as his master's examination theme: 'Whatever has been said by Aristotle is false'. In the custom of the times, the candidate was required to defend the thesis in public debate but had the privilege that his own thesis could not be used as argument against him; were his examiners to quote Aristotle in contradiction they would be committing the logical fallacy of begging the question, *petitio principii*.[41] Given the current practice of beginning every argument with an Aristotelian dictum or axiom, and bearing in mind the Dominican requirement to follow Aristotelian Thomism in their philosophy, Ramus reduced the examining faculty to virtual speechlessness; he received not only his degree but the enduring hostility of many of the scholars.

Ramus, however, continued his attacks on Aristotle unabashed. He had by now become a convinced humanist, arguing for French as the language of scholarship and even writing a vernacular grammar, and he became interested particularly in mathematics, the foremost Platonic study, along with literature, rhetoric and logic, becoming concerned to improve on the logic of Aristotle which he felt was the cause of so much backwardness. His attacks on Aristotelian teachings were outspoken in two major criticisms of 1543, *Aristotelicae animadversiones* and *Dialecticae institutiones*. By this time the Jesuits were a growing force in Paris and they led an investigation which resulted in a censure of Ramus, a record being placed on the *Index* of his having acted rashly, arrogantly and impudently,[42] an order for his books to be publicly burned and his being forbidden to teach philosophy.

Ramus turned to teaching mathematics and rhetoric but continued to press for university reform. He was fortunate that the support shown by François I for humanism was continued by Henri II (r. 1547–59), who was, moreover, disposed towards Protestant toleration. In 1551 Ramus moved to a chair of mathematics at the Collège de France, and in 1557 Henri appointed him a member of a royal commission of inquiry into university reform; although nothing came of the inquiry, Ramus later published his own views in 1562 in a tract addressed to the king entitled *Proemium reformandae Parisiensis academiae ad Regem*. In the meantime, Henri II had died, to be succeeded by François II, who reigned only for a year, and then Charles IX (r. 1560–74). Charles himself was a supporter of humanism and was, in fact, on his mother's side a descendant of the Florentine House of Medici. Ramus, however, was unable to gain the royal protection he needed since at the time of the Colloquy of Poissy (1561) he had openly avowed his Calvinism. The University of Paris was split, with Ramus leading the Protestant faction in his role as rector of the Collège de Presles within the university, the Jesuits opposing him in force from their Collège de Clermont. From then on, Ramus became embroiled in the bitter religious-political conflicts, having refused to abjure Calvinism by swearing the oath of fidelity to Catholicism required of all persons in the university by a decree of 1562. For the next eight years he moved around the Lutheran parts of Germany and the Calvinist areas of Switzerland until he was allowed, despite intense Jesuit objections, to return to the University of Paris, although forbidden to teach. He immediately plunged again into the now raging disputes; two years later he was murdered in his study on St Bartholomew's Day, 1572.

'Ramism', however, as his humanist position was known, remained a potent force, particularly his insistence on the priority of mathematics. In his reforming tract of 1562 he had recommended it as 'the premier liberal art without which philosophy is otherwise blind'.[43] In his will, moreover, he endowed at the University of Paris a chair of mathematics to be taught not according to someone's opinions but by the truth of logic.[44] This concern with mathematics centred on its capacity for providing deductive reasoning which Ramus considered the essential method of finding truth. Aristotelian logic, he argued, provides a misleading model of the mind, and, while he accepted the distinction made by medieval scholars between the passive and active intellect, his quarrel was with the way in which logical processes interpret the data of experience. In this, he was moving in the same direction as many other reforming scholars. What, it was being increasingly asked, is the nature of mental and logical processes? What are the links between induction and deduction? What, in effect, is the genuinely scientific model? Ramus sought answers, and his efforts, though limited, were heading in a new direction.

Huguenot education

The reforming tendencies in France – religious, educational, social – found their focus in the Huguenot movement on which Ramus was a major spokesman. At the same time there was a widespread desire for reform throughout the country, particularly among the landed nobility, many of whom became Huguenot, thereby giving Protestantism its predominantly rural character. The major stimulus came in the first instance from Calvinism in Switzerland where the Geneva Academy, founded in

1559 as an institution with a theological curriculum for the education and training of a Protestant clergy, was widely accepted as a model for further foundations particularly by the Huguenot congregations in France. The Geneva Academy itself, however, was not an educational innovator since it followed the now well-established Christian humanist pattern as earlier developed in Italy, and more latterly by Sturm.

The Colloquy of Poissy of 1561, which conciliated Protestantism to a considerable extent, stimulated the establishment of Huguenot churches. In 1559 there were seventy-two; by 1561 there were 2150;[45] and this growth in turn increased the need for pastors. So the Huguenot education movement gathered momentum, building on the Geneva Academy model. Despite the continuing political and military conflict with the Catholic forces, which held back the establishment of schools, the Huguenots maintained an optimistic spirit and with the accession of Henri de Navarre as king in 1593 they moved into an era of relatively peaceful development. To promote religious peace, in 1595 Henri IV expelled the Jesuits from France because he considered them to be 'corrupters of youth, disturbers of the public peace and enemies of king and state',[46] following this with strong moral support of the Protestant cause. The Huguenots seized their chance and in 1596 their Fourteenth National Synod urged all the sixteen provinces 'to endeavour to found a college, and all of them together to found at least two academies'.[47] In order to implement this, and to counter the influence of the University of Paris and the large number of imitative provincial scholastic universities, the Huguenots established a Geneva-type academy at Saumur, and another at Montauban the following year.

In 1598 they won recognition for their assertion as 'la religion prétendue réformée' – the religious position, that is, which claimed to have reformed the corrupted Christian faith. This was a major concession, since in the absence of an established 'Church of France' similar to the Church of England the king could grant no greater degree of recognition than that given in the Edict of Nantes in 1598 by which Henri IV gave Huguenots a wide range of freedoms: equality before the law, guarantees to practise their faith in specified places, the right to hold public offices and freedom from molestation by Catholics. As a *quid pro quo*, however, Huguenots were required to return Catholic properties seized by them. In education the consequences were significant. The Thirteenth Article forbade the education of Huguenot children outside those specified localities, the Fifteenth prohibited both persuasions, Catholic and Huguenot, from forcibly rebaptizing children in the opposite faith. The Huguenots secured the right to publish and sell books dealing with their beliefs in those certain regions, although if they sought to distribute them elsewhere the publications had first to be inspected and approved by both Catholic theologians and state officials. The Huguenots did gain a significant right in the Twenty-Second Article which asserted that 'no distinction is to be made with regard to this religion, in the reception of pupils for education in universities, colleges and schools'.[48] For their part the Huguenots recognized that they could best exercise this freedom in their own institutions and in the immediately following years they rapidly increased the foundation of schools and colleges. In the decade from their fourteenth synod in 1596 to 1606 they established six Geneva-type academies: in addition to Saumur and Montauban were Montpellier, Nîmes, Sedan and Die; while thirty-five colleges appeared on the model of Sturm's gymnasium offering boys a Latin grammar education and thereby challenging the Jesuit grip on French education whose place during their banishment (which lasted from 1595 to 1603) was taken by other, less aggressive Catholic teaching orders.

Protestantism was greatly strengthened, much to the discomfiture of the Catholic Church which still controlled Paris and the royal court, and sustained both intrigues and actions against the Huguenots. While Henri IV lived, however, they were secure and their schools became some of the finest in Europe, being in accord with the most progressive thought of the time. Elsewhere in the Protestant regions, society was changing markedly as a result of the Reformation, the voyages of exploration and the scientific and technological revolutions, and to adapt to these new conditions the Huguenot movement gave France its most modern educational institutions. Then, in 1610, Henri IV was assassinated at Ravailla; his nine-year-old son Louis XIII succeeded, with the Queen Mother Marie de' Medici as regent, and France again became unstable. The history of seventeenth-century French schools is one of conservative reaction, the forcible re-Catholicization of the country and the return of the schools to clerical control. Subsequent educational initiative was to be exercised almost entirely in the Protestant regions of Europe.

CHAPTER 2

The Scientific Revolution of the Seventeenth Century

Challenge to Aristotelianism: a new cosmology

The powerful movement of educational questioning and reform which gathered increasing momentum throughout the seventeenth century came from two major sources: a new stream of theorizing generated by a number of individual thinkers, which came to maturity in the doctrine of empiricism; and the equally important if less spectacular growth of a new system of institutions of higher learning. Throughout the West education was still dominated by the traditional procedures inherited from medieval Christendom, and indeed the great reforming activities of the medieval and Reformation periods had been in no way aimed at demolishing the basically religious conception of the world and of human knowledge as expressed in the doctrines of the Catholic Church; it is a matter of record that submission to authority was always more frequent than defiance. Throughout the sixteenth century, however, while the great doctrinal and military battles raged throughout Europe, scholars became increasingly preoccupied with questioning the framework of explanation derived from scholastic Aristotelianism.

In the forefront questions concerning cosmology – the attempt to provide an explanation of the universe and, by inference, of man's place within it – received a new stimulus with Europe's entry into an era of worldwide exploration. By then the inadequacy of medieval conceptions became increasingly apparent, and the scholastic emphasis on Aristotelian logic and cosmology proved increasingly barren in the context of the expanding intellectual and geographical horizons of the time. The structure of the universe, the relationships of the stars and planets to each other and to the earth, provided one of the most demonstrably visible and accessible aspects of the great realm of the unknown and unexplored. Further, such cosmological inquiry had always been associated with the search for answers to ultimate questions and hence with theology; it is understandable that in many societies the priests, as guardians of the temple, resisted the intrusion of any outsider in what they regarded as their legitimate area of responsibility. It was, then, within this area of cosmological inquiry that the scientific revolution of the seventeenth century had its immediate origins, and the outcome inevitably brought conflict with the established teachings of the church.[1]

The popular medieval notion of a flat earth, with Jerusalem at the centre and surrounded by the circle of water known by its Greek name of Okeanos, had been gradually displaced by the notion of a spherical earth revived from classical antiquity through the influence of Arabic and then humanist scholarship. Eratosthenes, director of the Mouseion at Alexandria in the second century BC, had calculated the circumference of the earth with a high degree of accuracy, and the circumnavigation of the earth by Magellan's expedition early in the sixteenth century provided a convincing demonstration of the spherical theory. More difficult to displace was the geocentric view of the universe, sanctioned by the church, which accounted for the celestial structure in terms of heavenly bodies moving in perfect circles around a fixed, central earth, itself the object of divine creation as scripture confirmed. To question this explanation scientifically was considered presumptuous, for it had been held by Aristotle himself and had, moreover, been elaborated in great detail in the astronomy of Ptolemy. Working in the Alexandrian school during the second century AD, Claudius Ptolemaeus produced his 'Great Collection' of astronomical observations, known in Greek as the *Megale syntaxis* and assimilated into Arabic as 'Almagest' (Ar. *al-Majisti*), which presented an extremely complex explanation of observed planetary movements in terms of a geocentric conception of the universe. Equally influential in guiding later Western concepts of the world was Ptolemy's celebrated *Geography* with its series of maps that were reprinted and gradually improved during the age of discovery: Ptolemy's estimate, for example, of the earth's circumference, smaller and less accurate than that of Eratosthenes, was shown to be in error after the voyage of Columbus. During the sixteenth century both his geography and his astronomy became increasingly subjected to scrutiny.

In 1543 the Ptolemaic cosmology was rivalled by a new system published at Nuremberg under the title *De revolutionibus orbium coelestium* by a Polish cleric, Nicolaus Copernicus (1473–1543). On the basis of his observations over many years Copernicus here proposed an alternative heliocentric theory, with circular orbits for planets, already outlined as early as 1507 in his short and poorly distributed *Commentariolus*. Curiously, Luther opposed the theory as non-biblical; the Catholic Church at first ignored it. In the following years support for the Copernican theory was provided by the Danish astronomer Tycho Brahe (1541–1601), known chiefly for his accurate catalogue of the movement of the stars, and Johannes Kepler (1571–1630) who followed Brahe as Imperial Mathematician at the Protestant court in Prague. Kepler published his explanation of planetary motion in 1609 in his *Astronomia nova* (*New Astronomy*), in which he proposed the concept of elliptical rather than circular orbits, thus breaking with the tradition of Greek astronomical theory as inherited from Plato and Aristotle.

European cosmological theory was becoming profoundly influenced by this growing corpus of work, much of it now based upon increasingly accurate observational methods, assisted by an array of newly developed precision instruments. The most dramatic developments came as a result of the application of the lens, which opened up the exciting new world of optics; by 1609 telescopes were being sold in Paris,[2] and with the later development of the microscope scientific activity changed significantly as the reach of human perception was extended. All previous instruments had simply increased the precision with which phenomena could be measured; these provided access to phenomena formerly beyond the range of physical discrimination, and the consequences were to be far-reaching.

One of the most important contributions to the growing literature of observations based on the telescope was the work of Galileo Galilei (1564–1642), Professor of Mathematics at the University of Padua. His treatise *The Starry Message* (*Siderius nuncius*) of 1610, which included the heliocentric hypothesis of Copernicus and Kepler, was not well received by the Catholic Church. Already the increasing opposition of the Catholic Inquisition to heresy had been demonstrated in 1600 when the Dominican scholar-priest Giordano Bruno was burned at the stake for his heretical views. Bruno's independent thinking included the assertion that in an infinite universe there is no point completely at rest. There was, implicitly, much more to it than that; the relatively simple physical cosmology he propounded, which challenged the comforting belief in the stability of the earth at the centre of a finite cosmos, was susceptible of social and political analogies. The whole civilization of Christian Europe was seen to be endangered, and the challenge of Bruno, by no means a centrally controversial figure, was construed as a revolt against the established authority of the church and state. The church, for its part, had reached the point where no further insurrection could be tolerated, otherwise it would lose that spiritual and moral primacy it claimed as its patrimony from early Christian times.

Galileo revived Bruno's views and was attacked, censured and counselled against further propagation of these doctrines until they could be investigated and their ramifications understood. The story is long, complex and full of intrigue: for the ensuing thirty years he remained in conflict with the church over his scientific investigations. Despite the loss of his chair at Padua, Galileo continued to develop the Platonic view, arguing that nature is mathematically constructed, and asserting furthermore that its laws can be discovered with certainty and even given mathematical expression. The book of nature, he declared in *Il Saggiatore* (*The Assayer*) of 1623, is written in the language of mathematics, and the study of geometry provides the key to its comprehension. He extended the scope of geometry to deal not only with the traditional problems of lengths, areas and volumes but also with time and motion. In 1632, despite further church warnings against heresy, Galileo published in Italian his *Dialogo sopra i due massimi sistemi del mondo Tolemaico e Copernico* (*Dialogue Concerning the Two Chief World Systems*), arguing in favour of the Copernican as against the accepted Ptolemaic theory. The issue, as Galileo realized, was the overthrow of Aristotelian physics at a time when the geocentric theory was still being adhered to by Rome. In support of his stand he advanced the empiricist position, defending conclusions drawn from observation rather than from authority. At the same time, paradoxically, he was even prepared to call on the authority of Aristotle to justify an alternative explanation of the solar system, arguing that Aristotle himself had declared 'that what sensible experience shows ought to be preferred over any argument'; therefore 'it is better Aristotelian philosophy to say "Heaven is alterable because my senses tell me so", than to say "Heaven is inalterable because Aristotle was so persuaded by reasoning" '. With the telescope, Galileo pointed out, 'we possess a better basis for reasoning about celestial things', and he argued that Aristotle would not have objected to the replacement of his own theory of the universe in this way, but indeed would have approved such an approach.[3] Dismissing also Aristotle's separation of the terrestrial from the celestial sphere, Galileo established in its place the theory of uniformity in the working of the material universe as one of his major contributions to later scientific thought. The entire universe, including the earth, he argued, operates according to mechanical relationships and is controlled by uniform laws.

The dialogue form of Galileo's *Two Systems*, in which both sides of the argument were presented, did not prevent his being brought to trial by the Inquisition of 1633 and convicted of spreading heretical doctrines. His imprisonment aroused widespread concern, and the desire to free natural science from church control encouraged an enthusiastic response to the pronounced separation of natural from moral philosophy advocated in his final publication, the *Discourses and Demonstrations Concerning Two New Sciences* of 1638, published in Protestant Holland, and which turned out to be a major contribution to modern physics and mechanics from its initial, widely successful appearance.

In Galileo's view the natural world, mechanical in its function and measurable in its effects, must be distinguished from the moral or social world; philosophy, therefore, which formerly dealt with knowledge in general, must be divided accordingly, with natural science, using the methods of mathematics, confined to a study of the mechanical world. Although the mechanistic concept was subsequently transferred to the biological sciences with the idea of the plant or animal as a mechanism, Galileo's view prevailed that it was not applicable to the social sphere. His dualist approach, with the separation of natural science from moral philosophy and his effort to distinguish between mathematical and subjective phenomena, was to be incorporated in the theory of exact and specialized science that became paramount in the following centuries. In the work of Galileo, who spent the last of his days in blindness under house arrest at Arcetri, near Florence, the modern scientific doctrine of empiricism received one of its first significant expressions.

The renovation of knowledge: Baconian empiricism

The major development of empiricism, however, in such a vigorous and persuasive form that it caught the imagination of most scholars and became the dominant theory of scientific method, occurred in the work of Francis Bacon (1561–1626). In its simplest definition empiricism – the term is derived from the Greek word for experience (*empeiria*) – is the belief that our knowledge is derived solely from experience; in the original Baconian usage, it was identified purely with first-hand sense experience. This viewpoint, revolutionary when advanced by Bacon, quickly became the intellectual fashion, particularly in England, and thereafter served as a major stimulus to scientific inquiry. In the course of the seventeenth century it was adapted by a number of persons, particularly John Locke, to educational theory and has increasingly been accepted as a guide to practice, with subsequent modifications, down to the present day.

Unlike the cosmographers who were at the centre of the great disputes of the scientific revolution, Bacon was not primarily a scientist. Born into the English gentry, Bacon followed a career – at times controversial and chequered – in the court administration, first of Elizabeth and then of James I; in 1618 he was ennobled as Baron Verulam; in 1621 he became Viscount St Albans. Despite a very busy life as a senior administrator, and a period of political intrigue and disgrace between 1621 and 1624 when he was accused of administrative malpractice and corruption and debarred from parliament, he spent all his spare time in a passionate endeavour to reform the totality of human learning. During his long fight against criminal charges he had more time to give to this interest; after he was completely exonerated in 1624 he remained out of public life and devoted himself completely to his ambitious project until his death in 1626.

Bacon's literary and intellectual endeavours were considerable; a recent bibliography of his works and subsequent 'Baconiana' to the year 1750 catalogues 256 separate editions.[4] Yet within this vast corpus the essential arguments and supporting texts are easily identified, chiefly in three books – *The Advancement of Learning*, *Novum Organum* and *New Atlantis* – each of which formed part of his scheme for the total reorganization of learning to which he gave the general working title *Instauratio magna*, literally, as it was translated in his own day, 'The Great Instauration', although the term instauration (from the Latin *instauratio*, renewal) has since become obsolete in English. As early as 1605 Bacon published the

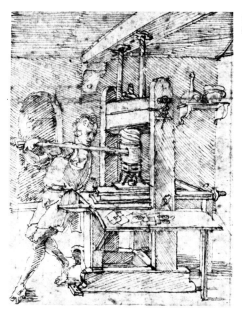

1 One of Koberger's presses, drawn by Dürer in 1511.

2 Portrait of Petrus Ramus (Pierre de la Ramée), 1515-72, by an unknown artist.

3 Portrait of Francis Bacon, *c.* 1600, by an unknown artist.

first part, *The Advancement of Learning*, as a preliminary treatise which had two purposes: to set out, with supporting argument, the evidence for the decay of learning which was causing so much disquiet among scholars; and to provide a comprehensive classification of knowledge as it then existed. Once that reordering were achieved, then the advancement of learning could be more easily pursued.

The current difficulties in Western learning, he argued, were created by obsolete medieval Aristotelian conceptions of nature, along with the ineffectual scholastic reliance on Aristotelian logic. Aristotle's four books on scientific method had been organized in antiquity, by various editors, as the *Organon* (the Greek word for 'instrument' and, by metaphorical extension, method). Bacon sought, as did many others, to find a better, more productive methodology of scientific investigation and, believing this to come from the processes of observation and logical induction, he set this out in direct opposition to the Aristotelian *Organon* as a 'new instrument' or, in the Latin in which he first wrote the text in 1620, a *Novum Organum*.[5]

In his period of legal tribulations he began to work at the full Instauration and developed a comprehensive schema for the complete renewal of knowledge which he proposed in a vast six-volume production organized under the following titles:

1 Partitiones scientiarum (Divisions of the Sciences)
2 Novum organum (The New Method)
3 Phaenomena universi (Phenomena of the Universe)
4 Scalla intellectus (Ladder of the Intellect)
5 Prodromi (Intimations [of a New Philosophy])
6 Philosophia secunda (The New Philosophy)

In 1623 he published the first two volumes, which consisted of *The Advancement of Learning*, a classification of knowledge and so easily retitled and rewritten as the *Divisions of the Sciences*, and *Novum Organum*, these two appearing under the new collective title, not as 'The Great Instauration' but as *De augmentis scientiarum* ('The Extension of Knowledge'). The remaining four volumes of the schema were never written; Bacon recognized his inability to do so in view of his personal difficulties and advancing years. But he did write one more work, in the utopian genre, *New Atlantis*, in which he set out his ideas on learning in an ideal state, with a description of an improved system of higher learning and better communication among the scholars of Europe.

What Bacon proposed, in effect, was a more efficient method for the 'interpretation of nature'; he sought to supplement the use of such technical devices as the telescope with improved intellectual methods of study, for the purpose of 'finding out new works' through vigorous sciences. To this end he condemned scholastic preoccupation with Aristotelian logic, arguing that it does not 'help us in finding out new sciences' but tends instead to fix errors:

> The syllogism consists of propositions, propositions consist of words, words are symbols of notions. Therefore if the notions themselves . . . are confused and over-heavily abstracted from the facts, there can be no firmness in the superstructure. Our only hope therefore lies in a true induction.[6]

Bacon's intention, then, was to provide leadership by discarding earlier forms of disputation and demonstration: 'In dealing with the nature of things I use induction throughout,' he claimed. 'For I consider induction to be that form of demonstration which upholds the sense, and closes with nature.' Reliance on the senses is basic to his theory of knowledge. Experience, in his view, commences with the senses, which can provide an accurate record of the 'particulars of nature'. Next, the reason generalizes from such data, and in some way that he did not specify produces (apparently from the available 'notions') the axioms or 'middle terms' that themselves lead by a gradual process to 'the most general propositions' or principles of nature. From these again, new particulars and, in the sciences, new experiments were to be derived. This process he described as a new kind of logic, inductive rather than deductive, commencing not with faulty notions but with facts of nature and leading not to idle debates but to exact and useful knowledge, and the ability 'to command nature in action'.[7]

With the use of the right method, Bacon was confident that truth could be reached by the human mind, in the same way that he assumed the drawing of an absolutely straight line to be possible with an appropriate instrument. It was one of his basic postulates that 'the truth of being and the truth of knowing are one, differing no more than the direct beam and the beam reflected'.[8] According to his plan, additional sciences were to be invented and organized to provide further help to the intellect, and this was one of his most valuable contributions. Those sciences, however, when they emerged, were to inherit both his urge to reach absolutes – 'the perfect circle', 'the facts of nature' – and his suspicion of intellect. A separation of senses from intellect is one of the major characteristics and inconsistencies of his theory, and in this he was clearly following the faculty theory of the mind, originally advanced by Aristotle, and rein-forced in the Thomistic synthesis of Aquinas (1225–74). Like them, furthermore, he assumed a passive role for the intellect in sense percep-tion. Taking his own metaphor from optics, Bacon described the intellect acting as a mirror to reflect 'the genuine light of nature' directed to it by the aided senses. 'All depends', he claimed, 'on keeping the eye steadily fixed upon the facts of nature and so receiving their images simply as they are.'[9] There would be no problem at all, in his view, 'if the human intellect were even, and like a fair sheet of paper with no writing on it'.[10]

Bacon's project was gigantic in its scope, and the method of inquiry that he outlined, later termed sense-empiricism, with its assurance of a reliable, even mechanical formula for the orderly progress of knowledge towards eventual control over nature, provided the basis, almost without exception, for the empirical sciences and, to a lesser extent, for formal in-struction, during the next three centuries.

Solomon's House: a college for experiment

At the same time that he was working on the text of his 'Great Instaura-tion', Bacon was also attempting to devise a new kind of institution that would further the purposes of the advancement of learning. Instead of making any direct proposals he put his ideas in the form of a fable entitled the *New Atlantis* which, unfortunately, was never completed. It was probably written around 1623–4 and then put aside as an unfinished manuscript; after Bacon's death in 1626 it was published in English, a year later, by his amanuensis, Dr William Rawley, who set out in a short preface the nature of the piece:

> This *Fable* my *Lord* devised, to the end that He might exhibit Therein, a *Modell* or *Description* of a *Colledge*, instituted for the *Interpreting* of *Nature*, and the Producing of *Great* and *Marveilous Works* for the *Benefit* of *Men*; Under the Name of *Salomon's House*, or the *Colledge of the Sixe Dayes Works*.[11]

The title itself was taken from Plato's myth of the city of Atlantis, de-scribed in *Timaeus* and *Critias*; the literary form was the utopian genre which had been increasing in popularity around that time. The influence of Plato's *Republic* and Thomas More's *Utopia* can be discerned, rather remotely; more particularly, it seems that Bacon was stimulated by the 1623 utopian social-reformation treatise by Campanella entitled *Civitas solis* (*City of the Sun*). The content of *New Atlantis*, however, was original to Bacon and, as Rawley's prefatory note indicates, the book was concerned with advancing the idea of a new kind of institution: Solomon's House. Its function was to extend well beyond the conservation of wisdom; its purpose was to seek new knowledge by means of deliberate experiment, this being expressly indicated in a declaration of purpose: '*The* End *of our* Foundation *is the Knowledge of* Causes, *and Secrett Motions of Things; And the Enlarging of the bounds of* Humane Empire, *to the Effecting of all Things possible.*'[12] No greater departure from the medieval scholastic tradition could be expressed; in this statement Bacon set out the experimental manifesto.

Solomon's House was to be equipped with a large number of 'houses', 'preparations' and 'instruments' which, in effect, were to operate as laboratories, field stations and instrumentation. Since the aim was to find knowledge in every domain that affects people, the scope is wide and the catalogue includes caves, hills, towers, lakes, wells, fountains, 'houses' (i.e. laboratories), orchards, gardens, parks, enclosures, kitchens, dispensaries and manufactories. In all of these locations experiments were conducted, most being of a technical or technological nature. The scholastic studies, in fact, are completely ignored except for mathematics, which must serve practical ends: '*We have also a* Mathematicall House, *wher are represented all* Instruments, *as well of* Geometry, *as* Astronomy, *exquisitely made.*'[13] But virtually all the experiments are in the realm of biological, social and psychological knowledge. To illustrate Bacon's conception of these operations, and how knowledge would be gained inductively from observation, the following passage is quite typical:

> *We have great* Lakes, *both* Salt, *and* Fresh; *whereof we have use for the* Fish *and* Fowle. *We use them also for* Burialls *of some* Naturall Bodies: *for we finde a Difference in Things buried in* Earth, *or in Aire below the* Earth; *and things buried in* Water. *We have also* Pooles, *of which some doe straine* Fresh Water *out of* Salt; *And others by Art do turn* Fresh Water *into* Salt. . . . *We have likewise* Violent Streames *and* Cataracts, *which serve us for many* Motions; *and likewise* Engines *for* Multiplying *and* Enforcing *of* Windes, *to set also on going diverse* Motions.[14]

In this short passage we can see the rudiments of biology, chemistry, hydrology and mechanics. Bacon's imaginative discourse in this treatise, however, anticipated many later developments as varied as submarines ('Shipps *and* Boates *for* Going under Water')[15] and organ transplants ('*As* Continuing Life *in them, through diverse* Parts, *which you account* Vitall, *be perished, and taken forth;* Resuscitating *of some that seeme* Dead *in* Appearance; *And the like*').[16]

The staff of Solomon's House is also unconventional in that each one is actively employed travelling, collecting books and information from other places, experimenting, compiling, organizing meetings and discussions; effecting, in short, all of the usual range of pursuits nowadays normal in research institutes and universities. In Bacon's day, when the universities were still engaged, regardless of faculty, in scholastic book learning dominated by the accumulated glosses on Aristotelian and classical texts, and when research institutes were almost nonexistent, his description of Solomon's House was a radical departure. It was not ignored; on the contrary, it stimulated emulation and activity, for Bacon was writing at a time when all these activities were being undertaken, randomly and piecemeal, in a number of locations. His own particular genius was to attempt a coordination of scientific and technological effort.

In considering all of his work, especially in view of the experiments and observations of the cosmologists and scientists who preceded him, it is doubtful that Bacon was as much the solitary pioneer in this as he liked to see himself. No one else, however, seems to have approached the rashness of his proposition for founding a scientific method on the myth of the fresh start. What must be done, he believed, in order to create a pure natural philosophy, was 'to sweep away all theories and common notions, and to apply the understanding, thus made fair and even, to a fresh examination of particulars'. Given the prevalence of error and confusion in the thought of his own day, the degree of Bacon's impatience with the past can of course be appreciated when he added, 'human knowledge, as we have it, is a mere medley and ill-digested mass, made up of much credulity and much accident'.[17] The important point is Bacon's evident conviction that scientific invention could be advanced by first eliminating ideas and theories altogether. This theory of knowledge was to have a lasting impact on science and education over the next three centuries. Determined to free himself from prejudice and superstition, he did not hesitate to advocate the most extreme objectivism, although it must surely be assumed there was at least some element of exaggeration in his assertion that the ideal researcher, in order to 'apply himself anew to experience and particulars', should be a person of 'unimpaired senses, and *well-purged mind*'.[18] It seems, in fact, that his belief in particulars or facts as the starting-point of observation led him to the objectivist view that the scientific method can really begin at some point with a blank mind. This, of course, is a serious deficiency in that it underestimates the active role of the mind in experience, including sense perception. This limitation, however, was not recognized, and early in the scientific revolution of the seventeenth century Baconian empiricism came to exert a significant influence.

New institutions of learning: academies and scientific societies

Italian origins and developments

Bacon's proposal for Solomon's House was not isolated from the developments of his day; although it was conceived as a state foundation and was therefore only strictly comparable with the universities which held legal charters, its aims and organization held much in common with a growing number of scientific and learned societies being formed in this period. By the early seventeenth century a new network of alternative institutions of higher learning had appeared throughout Europe, all of which shared certain common characteristics: they were composed largely of amateurs; they were voluntary associations usually commencing, and often continuing, without formal constitutions or state charters; they were devoted solely to research and the advancement of learning; and they offered neither courses nor degrees. In addition, and of greater significance, they had few of the inhibiting traditions of medieval scholastic organization and methodology.

The impetus came from Italy where the first of these alternative institutions appeared in the meetings of the Accademia Platonica under the patronage of the Medici. Throughout the fourteenth century there are records of the existence of a number of informal gatherings of scholars which seem to have contributed to the establishment of a more regular society concerned with the advancement of learning. In the Italian Quattrocento the great concern was the accurate recovery of the classical past, and the Florentine court in particular patronized this, beginning with the efforts of Cosimo de' Medici (r. 1434–64) and sustained by his grandson Lorenzo (r. 1469–92).[19] This society, the Platonic Academy, was concerned solely with recovering the corpus of Greek knowledge and using it to promote humanist learning, particularly with respect to the arts, and it continued to inspire literary and philosophical inquiry throughout the succeeding centuries. Apart from its influence on France, where Baïf's Académie de Poésie et de Musique is the major descendant, it stimulated other societies in Italy.

In understanding how humanist societies also provided the stimulus to scientific interest and research, which in turn created the revolution of the seventeenth century, it is necessary to consider the conceptions and purposes of sixteenth-century learning. All knowledge, it was believed, is interconnected, and this was supported by both the Platonic and the Aristotelian approaches which in effect have many more similarities than differences. In the Christian interpretation of both philosophies, the sensible world is the ground of a natural theology: understanding the world is coming to know god, and this explains why the cosmological quest was so important in the intellectual and educational history of the period; it further explains the distress arising from the fractures between philosophy and religion. The initial stimulus to the establishment of the Platonic Academy was the desire to effect a reconciliation between philosophy and religion[20] and this, it was believed, was largely a problem of communication. The early societies, then, directed their energies in linguistic directions. A great deal of philosophy was concerned with analytic classification, while the extension of interest from classical Greek and Latin to modern languages led to explosive debates throughout the sixteenth and seventeenth centuries on whether the vernaculars were capable of expressing and communicating serious ideas. Meanwhile the position of scientific inquiry became increasingly contentious as the Catholic Church in particular sought to retain science as an aspect of natural theology. The struggle for autonomy in scientific explanation and the emergence of separate subjects or disciplines were significant factors in the scientific revolution.

Throughout the Cinquecento in Italy societies appeared whose exact origins are hard to determine in so far as they often began very informally. In the same period as the Platonic Academy of Florence another group of philhellenic humanists began to meet at Venice under the patronage of the great printer Aldus Manutius (r. 1450–1515), styling themselves, appropriately, the Accademia dei Filleleni.[21] Other literary groups formed in the sixteenth century, with the same interests, addressing themselves particularly to the vernacular question, the first being the Orti Oricellari in Florence early in the sixteenth century; around 1540 this developed into the Accademia Fiorentina, while in the same period the Accademia della Crusca also appeared in Florence, along with the Accademia degli

Infiammati in Padua; by 1560 the Accademia degli Affidati was operating in Pavia. All these societies centred their activities on extensions of humanist themes, particularly matters of rhetoric, literary style and the value of the vernacular. The Orti Oricellari (so named because they met in the Oricellari Gardens) chose to conduct their meetings in Italian, thereby strengthening support for the *volgare*, as did the Infiammati ('the burning, passionate ones') in Padua. But these are only the prominent groups among a host of others of lesser importance.[22]

As the century progressed and societies appeared and disappeared, a bifurcation developed between those inclined towards literary-humanist studies and those more interested in experimental science. At the same time, it is important to point out that, while these humanist and scientific studies were pursued chiefly in amateur societies, this was not exclusively so in the case of Italy, in so far as they were taken up in some of the universities, especially Florence and Padua – although even here they were not studied by virtue of the specific mandate of the university but rather were followed as private interests of the professors. We might conceive in certain cases of societies and academies coexisting within universities, and, moreover, this was to continue as a pattern of development in the future; in England, for example, a great deal of university reform, innovation and development was to occur from within as a consequence of professors' divergent interests. It was in this way that Padua had become the leading medical and scientific school in Europe, since, as the university city of the Venetian Empire, it was able to attract some of the most independent minds of the time, including Vesalius, Fabricius and Falloppius – three of the greatest names in the history of medicine – and, later, Galileo and the great logician Zabarella. It was at Padua that the Englishman William Harvey gained his medical doctorate in 1602 and was exposed to the new forms of scientific reasoning that enabled him to make his great discovery of the circulation of the blood, which he published in 1628.

Notwithstanding the fact that science began to develop almost entirely outside the universities, it is important to make a significant exception for Padua, since it was not entirely cast in the traditional mould of the scholastic *studium*. Indeed, Padua was the location of some of the most important intellectual activities of the century which were concerned to overthrow the dominance of outmoded thinking, such as the inquiries of Jacopo Zabarella into the logic of scientific explanation. Using the revived purified Aristotelianism of Pomponazzi, Zabarella (1533–84) recognized that the logic of Aristotle's *Posterior Analytics* is fundamentally one of propositional proof rather than of discovery.[23] Zabarella investigated the problem much more closely, seeking to analyse the nature of experience and to find the ways in which this was observed as physical effects. The approach clearly anticipated the inductive method of Bacon, and Zabarella was able to speak of a two-way method of demonstrative proof: that of 'resolution', the study of effects back to causes; and 'composition', the study from causes to effects.[24] It was the interplay between the *metodo risolutivo* and the *metodo compositivo* that constituted the scientific contribution of the school of Padua which Galileo followed.[25] From its position as a leading European university, when Italian influences were at their height, Padua was able to extend this style of thinking widely, particularly into Protestant regions. The Studio Patavino was a student university composed of nations, one of the constituents being the 'English' nation in which Harvey was enrolled and which was a major source for conveying Paduan ideas back to the England of Bacon's time.

Galileo was the central figure of the first really scientific society which took form and much inspiration from the example of Padua: the Accademia dei Lincei founded in Rome in 1601 by Duke Federigo Cesi out of a group that had been meeting the previous year. By choosing the title 'Academy of the Lynx-eyed', they intended to suggest the penetrating search for truth. The early members planned to set up 'scientific, non-clerical monasteries'[26] for the advancement of learning, each intended to be

> . . . a gathering which, according to certain rules and regulations and united friendly councils, directs its labours diligently and seriously to studies as yet little cultivated. Its end is not only to acquire knowledge and wisdom for living rightly and piously, but with voice and writing to reveal them unto men.[27]

Galileo was their leading member, and the society was responsible for many meetings and experiments chiefly on astronomy, physics and natural science, publishing in 1609 the world's first scientific papers, the *Gesta Lynceorum*, as well as Galileo's highly controversial work *On Sun Spots*. The Accademia dei Lincei was a popular society with the Roman *cognoscenti*, boasting even the membership of Cardinal Maffeo Barberini, a friend of Galileo who defended the new forms of scientific inquiry. Following his election as Pope Urban VIII in 1623, this Florentine patron of the arts and sciences changed character completely; apparently obsessed with personal power, he sought to restore the grandeur and authority of the

Renaissance papacy and accepted Jesuit arguments that Galileo was a dangerous threat. Schooled by the Jesuits, and both temperamentally and intellectually a humanist who really understood nothing of science, Urban VIII made no attempt to save Galileo from the inexorable pressure of the Inquisition. With the death of Duke Federigo Cesi in 1630 and the condemnation of Galileo in 1633, the academy found science too hazardous and ceased operations.

The spirit of scientific inquiry, however, did not die in Italy and, in fact, Galileo served as a continuing inspiration. This led to the most distinguished of all Italian scientific societies, the Accademia del Cimento, literally the 'Academy of Experimentation', but the name also carried a play on the word *cemento* (meaning cement or structure), suggesting the idea of inquiring into the 'linkages' of phenomena. The heraldic crest of the society illustrates this: it featured a goldsmith's furnace in which metals were assayed for purity of composition. The motto accompanying the crest is most indicative of the society's attitude: *Provando e riprovando*. It is, in the first instance, in the vernacular; second, it asserts the experimental credo in its meaning – testing and retesting, the idea of retesting being explicitly that of experimental evidence confirmed by replication.

The Accademia del Cimento had secret beginnings because of the climate of fear following the trial of Galileo, and in its earliest days it was nothing more than meetings between two of Galileo's most devoted followers, Vincenzio Viviani and Evangelista Torricelli. After Galileo's trial in 1633 and even after his death in 1642, cosmology in Italy was a hazardous venture and virtually disappeared. Indeed, at this time, the Spanish grip was firm and, while Spain governed with a minimum of interference, the country languished. Venice retained her independence but her power continued to diminish as Turkish expansion choked off her overseas trading routes and concessions. The high culture of Italy continued in the ducal courts but became increasingly withdrawn and uncontroversial; painting flourished in the precious style known as Mannerism, while science restricted itself to the seemingly inoffensive studies of mathematics, physics, chemistry and biology. It was in Florence, which maintained its reputation as a centre of urbane civilization, that the Accademia del Cimento emerged. Florence remained in the hands of the Medici, who by this time were intermarried with the French monarchy and so had independent support that made both the papacy and the Habsburg court wary of provoking any serious confrontation, especially since Spain was already heavily engaged against the Protestants in the Thirty

Years War. So, when the two Florentine ruling princes, Grand Duke Ferdinand II and Prince Leopold, formally established the Accademia del Cimento in 1657 after its less structured existence for the previous twenty years, there was no opposition.[28]

The Accademia del Cimento, with a small but highly distinguished membership, continued for the next decade and was responsible for one of the most glorious bursts of creative scientific endeavour in the century. It sponsored experiments on a wide range of topics in its designated areas of interest, particularly in physics and biology; its example spread widely into the Protestant states of Europe, through a system of corresponding members. Early interest was in measurement for which they had a number of instruments constructed – thermometers, barometers, hygrometers, inclined planes – some of these remaining today in the Museum of the History of Science in Florence. Their interests developed beyond this to natural phenomena and at the end of their first decade their second secretary Lorenzo Magalotti (1637–1712) published in 1667 their work in the first such book in the world, *Saggi di naturali esperienze fatte nell' Accademia del Cimento* (*Results of Experiments in Natural Science Conducted by the Accademia del Cimento*). These *Saggi* ('tests' or 'assays') were the first systematically constructed corpus of deliberately contrived experiments that were intended to begin, as far as possible, without speculation. These papers were in the same spirit as the *Gesta Lynceorum* but were much more comprehensive, containing well-drawn illustrative plates and an accurate accompanying text. Unfortunately, because they were written in Italian vernacular which did not have a wide readership outside the country at the time, the *Saggi* lacked the circulation they deserved. They did circulate, however, in a limited way, throughout Europe; and after Magalotti had sent a copy to the recently founded Royal Society in London the volume was translated into English in 1684.[29] It was not until they were translated into Latin in 1731 that they were able to receive their fullest distribution, whereupon they rapidly became the standard laboratory manual of the age. The academy itself did not survive its first decade; in 1667 Leopold accepted a cardinal's hat and, while an official tercentenary history of the academy, the *Celebrazione*, simply states that he was subsequently unable to find time for further scientific work,[30] a more plausible suggestion is that he was offered the cardinalcy as a political diversion and on condition that the society be terminated.[31] As a consequence the most famous of Italy's scientific societies ended its brief but highly influential career, so confirming the widely repeated ironic jest of the times that Italy could lead Europe in matters of intellect and culture while ever the Inquisition would let it.

The great age of the French academies

While the academy movement declined in Italy in the seventeenth century, it prospered in France with such brilliance that the century can quite accurately be described, with respect to the development of higher learning, as a great age. The inspiration, as for the rest of Europe, came from Italy in the sixteenth century, and, while there were many influences, the one notable historical example is the creation of the Académie de Poésie et de Musique. This academy, which had rather informal beginnings as a circle of friends, came to be conducted in the Italianate mansion of a distinguished French diplomat Lazare de Baïf who had been, at the beginning of the sixteenth century, French ambassador to Venice and to Florence. In Italy he participated in the meetings of the Accademia dei Filleleni and the Accademia Fiorentina, in part because his mission was to report back to François I all Italian activities, cultural as well as political. François I was determined to make France the leader in European intellectual and cultural life, and despite the opposition of the University of Paris his court was receptive to these influences. Back in Paris, Lazare de Baïf built himself a grand château, the Hôtel Baïf, just outside the city walls. The site was chosen deliberately: it was next to the university but separated from it by the city wall, and close to the great Abbey of St Victor. The abbey was significant, for, ever since it was made famous in the eleventh and twelfth centuries by William of Champeaux and Hugh of St Victor, it had remained the intellectual centre of French Platonism; its library held the greatest collection of Platonist works in France, and there, in the convent walls, visiting scholars received hospitality. It was in this great château (demolished in the nineteenth century) that the French Platonic tradition was maintained and brought to a high level of development as a result of Lazare de Baïf's son, Jean-Antoine.[32]

Born in Venice of a Venetian mother, Jean-Antoine de Baïf (d. 1589) was one of the great founders of the French academy movement. Exposed to Italian influences as a child, he was a fellow student of the poet Pierre de Ronsard. Ronsard himself had formed a circle of seven friends who took for themselves the allegorical name of 'La Pléiade', since the Pleiades consists of seven stars. At some point the Pléiade began meeting at the Hôtel Baïf, joining in with the circle of Jean-Antoine, and devoting their energies to a search for the ultimate harmony of the universe, especially as manifested in song and dance. In this we find the most vigorous expression of the age of literary Neoplatonism. The intention was profound: by means of the study of sounds, harmony and melody, by the processes of composing measured verses 'to which are accommodated tunes likewise measured in accordance with the metric art . . . the minds of the auditors . . . may be composed so as to become capable of higher knowledge after being purged of the remnants of barbarism'.[33] So the members sought, in an age increasingly dominated by the search for cognitively given, demonstrative knowledge, to continue their quest through affective means. The group found considerable royal support, and in 1570 Charles IX granted his protection in letters patent, with accompanying statutes, jointly to Jean-Antoine de Baïf and Joachim Thibault de Courville.

This Académie de Poésie et de Musique faced a formidable task. The protection of the king was needed to fend off the bitter opposition of the university which feared that the study of poetry and music would 'soften youth', while any positive programme was fraught with difficulty. Baïf's plans, of course, encompassed all the arts and sciences that support music, and, in a limited way, the academy flourished. It was not possible, however, for it to expand, nor for it to reach a wider audience, even though it grandly sought 'to drive barbarism from Gaul'. None the less, given the great crises through which France was passing, occasioned by the Huguenot wars, the clerical split, with Gallicanism gaining wide support, and the challenges to national sovereignty coming from Habsburg Spain, the Jesuits and the Inquisition, it is easy to appreciate how the idea of moral regeneration through a properly applied programme of study might be accepted. The death of Charles IX deprived the academy of its patron; it continued under his successor Henri III but was reorganized as the Palace Academy, thereafter losing impetus.

After the Huguenot Wars, which were settled temporarily in 1598 by the Edict of Nantes, a period of reconstruction followed and Henri IV (r. 1593–1610) attempted major institutional changes, turning his attention particularly to higher learning. In 1600, as a result of his Catholic conversion, he gave new statutes to the University of Paris (by now at its lowest ebb) which confirmed its reactionary dominance by restricting entry to Catholics only, suppressing the vernacular as the language of instruction and censoring printing. The Jesuits came into control of the university and, in addition, received royal support for their new college at La Flèche, 150 kilometres south-west of Paris. La Flèche was the new symbol of

Catholic regeneration; following the procedures of the celebrated Jesuit *Ratio*, it gathered there its finest scholars and teachers in a grand plan to re-educate a new Catholic Europe. Its greatest alumnus, René Descartes, in his seminal *Discourse on Method* left an indictment of the sterility of the Jesuit teachings.

The one progressive achievement was the revival of the stagnating Collège Royal. Founded originally in 1518 by François I, it had not prospered as well as it might, again because of the hostility of the university. Its name was changed to the Collège de France, and, in the course of time, to its original chairs in Greek and Hebrew further chairs were added in medicine, surgery, mathematics, botany, philosophy, eloquence, civil law and Arabic.[34] The University of Paris now faced a real challenge, and throughout the seventeenth century it fought the Collège and virtually every other educational innovation that appeared; none the less, it could not stem the tide of change and by the end of the century it was in total decline, eclipsed by the emergence of a new comprehensive system of institutions of which the first, and one of the greatest, was the Académie Française, founded in 1635 by Cardinal Richelieu.

In 1624 Richelieu (1585–1642) became President of the Council of Ministers and by 1629 he was *de facto* ruler of France; under him, the nation became the foremost power in Europe, and Richelieu was determined to express this in the arts, scholarship and the efflorescence of French culture in general, one of his signal acts being the creation of the Académie Française as an instrument of national policy. The academy itself was already in existence as an informal society of scholars concerned with literary matters such as those studied in Baïf's academy, and there are strong suggestions of historical continuity from the Pléiade, although unfortunately the record is not clear.[35] There were, at the time, numerous shortlived groups among which the literary issues of the previous century would have easily been transmitted, such as the private circle convened by the journalist Théophraste Renaudot (1586–1653) who organized weekly symposia on current intellectual matters and published these in proceedings entitled *Conférences du Bureau d'Adresse*, beginning in 1633.[36] These meetings, and especially the printed papers, had a wide following, and they discussed topics which became the particular province of the academy. One of these – and of the first order of importance – was the question 'whether the French tongue be sufficient for learning all the sciences'.[37] Across Europe at this time the issue of the vernaculars was growing more urgent, particularly as they had become the common languages of discourse, and Latin and Greek studies were now being seen as consuming inordinately large amounts of time which could be better devoted to mastering the ever-increasing volume of secular and scientific knowledge.

The contemporary record of Pierre Pellison in 1652[38] indicates that, upon hearing of these meetings some time in the early 1620s, Richelieu recognized the opportunity to use the informal society as a means of creating a national consciousness through the purification, enrichment and elevation of the French language. Accordingly, he offered his 'protection' which they were unable to decline, and in 1635 Renaudot's circle was officially established as the Académie Française by letters patent.[39] It met these purposes quite adequately, and in 1672 Louis XIV extended it royal patronage and moved its location to the palace of the Louvre. It was in the reign of Louis XIV (r. 1643–1715), in large part through the initiative of his Chief Minister Colbert, that a range of specialized institutions of higher learning were established.

In addition to his post as Minister of Finance, Colbert, who succeeded Cardinal Mazarin in 1661 as Chief Minister and held office until his death in 1683, acquired the additional title and office of Protector of the French Academy of the Arts and through the organization of the academy system exercised a profound influence on the development of European culture. Within the brief space of ten years, five academies, all of which remain in operation to this day, were founded: L'Académie de Danse (1661); L'Académie des Inscriptions et Belles-Lettres (1663), L'Académie des Sciences (1666), L'Académie de Musique (1669) and L'Académie d'Architecture (1671). All of these were single-purpose establishments and provided an institutional breadth to French, and European, learning that had hitherto been absent; of these, one in particular was to become deservedly famous, the Académie des Sciences.

Although formally founded in 1666, the Académie des Sciences, like most of the other academies, had a lengthy period of gestation, and the spirit of scientific inquiry can be traced back to several amateur groups operating in the early decades of the century.[40] The impetus to French scientific activities, as for humanist activities, came from Italy, in particular from Padua and Florence. The link was through Nicolas-Claude Fabri de Peiresc (1580–1637) who, after a period as a mature student in both cities, particularly in the Studio Patavino, formed a corresponding group of likeminded scholars. The most prominent were Pierre Gassendi, provost of the cathedral chapter of Digne in the southern French Alps, who spent considerable time in the capital, and two Parisian brothers, Pierre and Jacques Dupuy. The two brothers had already formed a small group, later known as the Cabinet des Frères Dupuy, which began meeting some years before Peiresc joined in 1616. An interesting fact is that the Cabinet (literally, a chamber; by extension, a group meeting privately) sought a portrait of Francis Bacon to hang in a gallery of portraits of other learned men in their meeting-place.[41] The Cabinet Dupuy flourished and coordinated the scientific interests of a large group of enthusiastic amateurs; it was still meeting regularly, but rather uncertainly, at the death of Jacques Dupuy in 1656, and had come to attract visitors from outside France – particularly England, where similar groups of amateurs were holding meetings. In 1659–60 Henry Oldenburg, accompanied by Richard Jones, attended meetings; Oldenburg was later to become a secretary of the leading English scientific group, the Royal Society.[42] Lacking any firmer institutional basis for support than the enthusiasm of its members and the provision of a meeting-place by the de Thou family in their mansion, the group was forced to break up in 1662 when the family de Thou became bankrupt and the mansion was sold.

The spirit of scientific inquiry, however, by now had been strongly kindled, and accompanying the Cabinet Dupuy were the activities of an outstanding friar, Marin Mersenne (1588–1648), whose cell in the Couvent de l'Annonciade in Paris after 1620 became a regular clearing-house for scientific papers. Mersenne had been a fellow student (and later a lifelong collaborator) of Descartes at the Collège de la Flèche; in 1611 he sought a religious vocation and joined a self-abasing order of brothers known as the Minims.[43] Père Mersenne, as he was affectionately but incorrectly addressed, was a highly competent theological and scientific scholar who sought a middle way between theological conservatism and scientific discovery; by the 1630s, when the church prosecution of Galileo was reaching its climax, Mersenne was counselling caution among scientists. In 1634, the year after Galileo's condemnation by the Inquisition, Mersenne published his *Questions théologiques, physiques, morales et mathématiques*, a rationalistic discussion of problems, which revealed the influence of Descartes. Mersenne's advice comes through very prudently in the forty-fifth of his *Questions* where, discussing the heliocentric controversy, he concludes with the statement that 'if scholars were to proceed with more discretion and prudence in the sciences, they would not be so subject to censorship, and would have no occasion to complain nor to retract.'[44] Mersenne was arguing here that science can proceed if scholars simply avoid confrontations. And, indeed, that is the course he followed himself.

From 1635 to his death in 1648, the Convent of the Annunciation in Paris was the major focus of French scientific activity, and Mersenne assumed the role of scientific coordinator, corresponding in Europe with Descartes, Huygens, Torricelli, Galileo, Pascal and many others, at the same time communicating with scientists and scholars in England, particularly Theodore Haak, Thomas Hobbes and William Petty. Of these, Haak was the most frequent respondent, his exchanges with Mersenne being concerned in large part with projects of scientific and educational reform currently being pursued in England by a number of enthusiasts of whom Samuel Hartlib and Joannes Amos Comenius were the leading protagonists. Correspondence, however, was not Mersenne's sole activity; much of his time was spent organizing conferences at which papers were read and discussed.

At Mersenne's death the initiative was maintained briefly by a number of collaborators and then, more comprehensively, by an enormously wealthy Parisian aristocrat, Henri-Louis Habert de Montmor, already a member of the Académie Française. Montmor, however, was impatient of the work of the Académie which had narrowed its activities to philological and lexicographical concerns, and this view was repeated in a letter to the Dupuys by his associate Ismael Boulliau which referred to the meetings of the Académie Française as 'this stupid rabble with its reformed dictionary'.[45] Montmor was attracted to the new method of Descartes and sought to use its seemingly fresh and productive approach in the pursuit of knowledge. Coming later than Baconian empiricism, Cartesian rationalism was in many ways more attractive to the French mind, especially since it made less violent breaks with tradition than the new empiricism.

Tradition modified: Cartesian rationalism

René Descartes (1596–1650), the son of a member of the parliament of Brittany, had been well educated, recording that 'from my childhood I have been familiar with letters'.[46] He had been sent to the Jesuit college at La Flèche, where, at the end of his studies, he wrote:

> I found myself involved in so many doubts and errors, that I was convinced I had advanced no further in all my attempts at learning, than the discovery at every turn of my own ignorance. And yet I was studying in one of the most celebrated schools in Europe.[47]

There was, he felt, something profoundly lacking. Descartes accepted the necessity of much of the formal curriculum – languages, history, mathematics, eloquence, theology. Philosophy, which completed the standard Jesuit curriculum given in the *Ratio studiorum*, he regarded as totally deplorable, especially since although 'it had been cultivated for many ages by the most distinguished men ... there is not a single matter within its sphere which is not still in dispute'.[48] This led him, so he reported in the same passage introducing his *Discourse on Method*, 'to entirely abandon the study of letters ... and to seek no other science than the knowledge of myself, or the great book of the world'.

France of the 1620s, however, was unsafe for questioning intellects and in 1628 he went to Holland, remaining outside France for much of his life. In France, some years before, he developed an overmastering passion for mathematical inquiries, owing to the famous intuition of the night of 10 November 1619 when he became aware that the universe is basically mathematical in structure.[49] Thereafter he worked at his goal of explaining the world in mathematical terms. If the world were indeed mathematically structured, then the task would be first to discover the basic principles, which must be understood ultimately by direct intuition, and then to work by deductive methods. He turned to physics and attempted a treatise, based on the Copernican system, but supported by observations and experiment. In letters written during 1630 to Mersenne he promised to have his *Treatise on the World* finished in three years. By April 1632, however, he was ready to admit the problem of bringing such a cosmology to a conclusion; and with the news in 1633 of the Inquisition's condemnation of Galileo's *Massimi sistemi del mondo* Descartes announced his intention to withhold publication of his own *Traité du monde* since this, too, 'included the doctrine of the movement of the earth'. Explaining to Mersenne his firm decision to avoid conflict with 'the authority of the Church' and 'to live in peace', he expressed the hope that 'in time my *World* may yet see the day'.[50] The *Traité du monde* was never completed, although some later sections were published posthumously in 1664.

Descartes now turned directly to problems of scientific method and in March 1636 wrote to Mersenne that he had four treatises, all in French, ready to be published anonymously under the general title: 'The Plan of a Universal Science to raise our Nature to its Highest Degree of Perfection ...'[51] The work appeared, however, the next year as the *Discourse on the Method of Rightly Conducting the Reason and Seeking for Truth in the Sciences*.

In the *Discourse* the first precept of his logic was the famous principle of doubt: 'to accept nothing as true which I did not clearly recognize to be so'. The second was to divide problems into parts, and the third to order his reflections, rising from the most simple objects 'by degrees, to knowledge of the most complex, assuming an order, even if a fictitious one', among them.[52]

Of all his conceptions, the first that he accepted as certain is the existence of the self: 'I think, therefore I am' (*Cogito ergo sum*).[53] This, he added in his *Principia philosophiae* (1644), 'furnishes us with the distinction which exists between the soul and the body, or between that which thinks and that which is corporeal', since, while we are certain of the existence of our own thoughts, 'we still doubt whether there are any other things in the world'.[54] For a justification of the existence of material things, Descartes in his *Principia* appealed, somewhat surprisingly it seems now, to the reliability of god. Arguing that the necessity of god's existence is proved by man's clear conception of such a perfect being, he declared that all ideas of corporeal objects which are clear and distinct must be produced by such external objects themselves, since god is no deceiver and would not provide man with 'the light of nature, or the faculty of knowledge', in order to produce false perceptions.[55]

In many ways, Descartes was in sympathy with the empirical tradition of Francis Bacon, and indeed made his own distinctive contribution to it. Like Bacon and Galileo he was a realist, accepting the existence of an external world as revealed in experience, and like them he was a materialist in that he conceived that world to be constructed of particles of matter. However, he was even more explicit than Bacon in making a separation between matter as divisible and having extension, on the one hand, and mind, unextended and indivisible, on the other. Thought, the chief attribute of mind, included for Descartes all operations of the soul: sensation, imagination, will and feeling, as well as reason. He defended the notion of free will in man, while making an effort to reconcile this with the Christian doctrine of divine preordination'[56]

The Cartesian dualism was an attempt to overcome the inability of the mechanical hypothesis to account for everything in the world, by claiming that the human mind is itself outside the material system. Further, it enabled him to accept the determinism implicit in the mechanistic theory as applying to the material world only, without being extended to man, so justifying the argument for free will. The opposition between mind and matter was at the same time reinforced by the church doctrine, found earlier in Aristotle, that man by his power of reason is set apart from the natural order and designed to dominate it.

Descartes went further than Bacon in exploring the operation of the intellect in perception. He therefore questioned more critically the extent to which certain knowledge of the external world is possible, asserting at the same time the reality of the mind and the importance of thought. Emphasis in his philosophy is on the effective use of reason – a subject more superficially treated by Bacon – although rationalism for Descartes did not exclude an empirical approach. Within his framework of doubt, he still accepted the reliability of most sensory perception, even if he envisaged this as arising from divine influence; experiment and mathematical analysis were essential to his method of scientific inquiry. Descartes was always interested in studying the natural world, offering, for example, a mechanical theory of the universe, of light and of human physiology.

The main question on which his theories differed from the empirical view of knowledge was his assertion that some ideas, of simple notions such as existence or certainty, and of the laws laid down by god in nature, are inborn in our minds.[57] Empiricists came to take profound exception to this, arguing that all knowledge must be derived from experience, *a posteriori*. The debate as to whether *a priori* knowledge is possible continued through the following centuries, obscuring as many issues as it clarified. In particular it tended to force empiricists into the untenable position that all reliable knowledge is derived from immediate sensory experience.

With the polarization of opinions in the dispute over *a priori* ideas, few stopped to ask the question 'prior to what?' In the religious context of the time, Descartes and his rationalist followers argued that such ideas are provided by god prior to all human experience. Rejecting this possibility, scientific empiricism moved to an extreme objectivist position, denying not only innate ideas but even the importance of *a priori* knowledge in the form of concepts or expectations already in the individual's mind prior to present experience.

The Montmor Academy and the Académie des Sciences

A keen admirer of Cartesian philosophy in this period was Henri-Louis Habert de Montmor (*c.* 1601–79), who offered Descartes the use of a rural mansion at Mesnil-Saint-Denis on the outskirts of Paris.[58] This was located near Port-Royal, the convent which had become a Jansenist stronghold at the time when Jansenism, which asserted the necessity of divine grace for living a godly life, was being attacked as heretical for its determinism. Although Descartes declined, he and Montmor remained in close contact. In fact, in a confidential dossier on Montmor forwarded to Colbert it was reported, *inter alia*, that 'he professes Cartesian doctrine; and rumour has it that he has set up an academy in his house only to establish this novelty and to destroy the doctrine of Aristotle in which he has found serious contradictions'.[59] This academy began with informal meetings, apparently in the late 1640s or early 1650s; by 1656 it was strongly established and gaining a major reputation. During its early years the academy sought official recognition through royal letters patent but these were not granted, presumably because it threatened the Académie Française. None the less the Académie Montmor established itself formally in December 1657 by adopting a constitution and rules for proceedings.

The Académie Montmor flourished and increasingly turned its attention to scientific questions; a contemporary document by a skilled observer, Ismael Boulliau, dated 5 February 1658, recorded that in the academy set up by Montmor in his house 'there is discussion only of mathematical and physical matters'. These apparently did not avoid disputation over subtleties, Boulliau observing in the same document that 'the Montmorians are sharper, and dispute with vehemency since they quarrel about the pursuit of truth; sometimes they are eager to rail at each other, and jealously deny a truth, since each one, although professing to inquire and investigate, would like to be the sole author of the truth when discovered.'[60] In December of the same year Boulliau also wrote to Christian Huygens that a debate in the academy was so acrid that the group very nearly disbanded, chiefly because M. de Roberval took 'offence at an opinion of M. des Cartes which M. de Montmor approved'.[61] Tempers cooled, the academy struggled on for a while and then, for unknown reasons, left its location *chez* Montmor in 1664.

Meanwhile in England in 1662 perhaps the most famous of these amateur seventeenth-century groups received royal letters patent from Charles II as the Royal Society. Commerce between English and French scholars, especially in London and Paris, was frequent and sustained, and the Montmor Academy, like the other French societies, was visited from time to time by Englishmen along with scholars from all over Europe, particularly the German and Baltic territories. There are records of a continuous stream of English visitors to Mersenne, the Dupuys and Montmor, the Montmor Academy receiving visits from Henry Oldenburg and

Richard Jones who were associated with an Oxford group of scientists. The significance of England in this context, however, is that the Royal Society achieved what the supplications of the Montmorians could not: the ascent of English science was a threat that stimulated the intervention of the French court in matters of science by giving official encouragement and support.

The Montmor Academy had continued the amateur scientific tradition established by Peiresc, the Dupuys and Mersenne but was the most active in pressing the case for official patronage; then, at the moment it expired in 1664, the demands were renewed by one of the members, Melchissédec Thévenot (d. 1692), a frequenter of court circles who held diplomatic posts under Mazarin and was appointed royal librarian by Colbert in 1684. Thévenot drew together a circle of amateur scientists – including some from the disbanded Montmor Academy – for the purpose of conducting experiments, in chemistry and anatomy among other sciences, and reading papers. It was Thévenot who put the case for royal support in its most direct form, as he wrote in his *Autobiography* in 1662, to the effect that

> . . . I gathered around me a company of men known to be very able. In a house joined to mine I maintained another person for experiments of chemistry, but the cost of these experiments, observations, and anatomies greatly exceeding my revenue, and having borne it during two years, I suggested to M. Colbert that it be given a more lasting form under the approval of the king.[62]

Thévenot was supported strongly by a member of his group, Adrien Auzout (1622–92), a lifelong devotee of science who, having been in the Mersenne circle, in his *Ephéméride du comète de 1664* (*Astronomical Observations of the Comet of 1664*), dedicated to Louis XIV, pointed out that the work would have been much improved were better facilities available. He could not, in fact, have been more direct:

> [We] hope that your Majesty will command some place for making all sorts of celestial observations, and cause it to be furnished with all the instruments necessary for this end. This is one of the chief purposes of the *Company for the Sciences and Arts*, which awaits only the protection of Your Majesty to work mightily for the perfection of all the sciences and all the useful arts.[63]

Despite the intense objections of the Jesuits and the University of Paris, particularly the faculty of medicine, Colbert became interested, especially since the Royal Society in England promised to prosper and eclipse French learning. In the years 1665–6 he initiated preliminary studies and conducted investigations, while the Royal Society in England lent encouragement, in the form of correspondence from Henry Oldenburg to Auzout.

In December 1666, now given royal support, such a Company for the Sciences and Arts began its meetings with a restricted membership of sixteen. Subsidies came from the king to help the various activities – anatomy, physiology, physics, chemistry, biology; laboratories were set up and papers were read.

The scope of their research was less comprehensive than that of the original plan, which, conceived within the French encyclopedic tradition, had been intended to cover not only mathematics and physics but also history, grammar, philosophy, poetry and belles-lettres, each of these meeting on alternate days, in a complex interlocking schedule, in the king's library. The project was impossible to fulfil; the historians quarrelled; the grammarians retreated to the Académie Française, the library scholars to the recently established (1663) sister institution, the Académie des Inscriptions et Belles-Lettres. The shattered society was restructured with six (perhaps seven) members, all mathematicians. Knowledge was fragmenting and single-interest societies became the rule. Although it received its royal charter in 1666, the Académie des Sciences did not prosper as a mathematical institute, and after Colbert's death in 1683 it languished. In 1699 it was totally reorganized, with an enlarged membership of fifty; and in the eighteenth century it moved into a more vigorous phase of its career when its members included that galaxy of Enlightenment talent, d'Alembert, Montesquieu, Condorcet and Voltaire, who attempted to restore the original encyclopedic intention of unifying and interrelating all knowledge.

It was the reorganization of 1699 which put vigour into the Académie des Sciences. Relocated in the Louvre, it was given a grand formal opening in April 1699. Its revised statutes indicate its new temper: Article XII denied full membership to priests or members of any religious order, although they could be nominated for honorary associateship; Article XXII required each member to be a specialist in one science but to keep his work within the wider perspective of the totality of all learning; Article XXIX looked back to the motto of the Accademia del Cimento in requiring that 'the Academy shall repeat all considerable experiments and note . . . conformity or difference between their own and other observations'; Article XXX required all books published by members, *qua* members, first to receive the imprimatur of the academy; Article XXXI provided for the patenting of members' inventions.[64] The members – *pensionnaires* – were provided with handsome residential stipends, along with laboratories and ancillary rooms, which allowed them to conduct their researches in the academy's quarters and not in their own rooms or private workshops. So the notion of institutional endeavour became more strongly developed in the seventeenth century. Meeting in session, the members planned their experiments in advance and, once these were completed, discussion and analysis followed. The early experiments, however, were not systematically scheduled on a forward-looking basis of sequential discovery; rather, they covered a very wide range of concerns and were directed at first towards correcting misconceptions, fallacies and myths. Indeed, in these attempts to correct false impressions we find the origins of the concept of 'research' itself: the word has a seventeenth-century provenance in the Italian *ricercare* and the French *rechercher*. To the infinitive 'to search' the intensifier 're-' was added, giving the modern notion of 'really finding out', of seeking to settle questions in a demonstrative way.

The academy's greatest single contribution to the advancement of science was the publication of its proceedings in a journal. Precedents existed in the *Gesta Lynceorum* and the famous volume of the Cimento's *Saggi di naturali esperienze*; the Académie des Sciences was even more ambitious in proposing a yearly issue. The intention was to create a comprehensive scientific newsletter containing lists of recently published books, obituaries of scientists, reports of scientific meetings and activities across Europe, notices of current projects and, most significantly, results of experiments conducted in the laboratories of the academy. Entitled *Le Journal des Sçavans* (literally, the 'journal of the learned'), the first issue appeared on 5 January 1665 and immediately attracted the hostility of the Jesuits who, foreseeing the possibilities it would open up, had the printing licence of its editor revoked. The editorship was transferred and the journal continued, thereby achieving what it promised: a means of creating and sustaining a world of scientific thought which quickly encompassed most of liberal Europe and stimulated the foundation of further journals. The number multiplied rapidly in the late seventeenth century and throughout the eighteenth learned journals were founded in increasing numbers for virtually all the arts and sciences.[65]

Learned societies in England: Gresham College and the Royal Society

Despite developments on the continent, it was England that became the scientific pacesetter for western Europe in the seventeenth century and which was, consequently, to provide a pattern throughout the eighteenth and nineteenth centuries in the example of the Royal Society, formally founded in 1660 and later chartered by King Charles II. Like many of those in other countries, the society was stimulated by the turgidity of the universities, and to appreciate the significance of the Royal Society in the scientific revolution and the advancement of learning it is necessary to trace the steps leading to its foundation, beginning with the continuing decline of the two universities of Oxford and Cambridge, and the lack of development of the four newer foundations (fifteenth and sixteenth centuries) in Scotland and the one in Ireland at Dublin.

Oxford and Cambridge had developed to a considerable extent under the influence of Paris and it was not until the reign of Henry VIII that the ties were seriously weakened. The Protestantization of England during the sixteenth century had a marked effect upon the universities, especially after the two Acts for the Dissolution of the Monasteries of 1536 and 1539 which, in effect, closed down many halls and ejected the majority of students and teachers who, up to this point, were of necessity in holy orders. The universities faltered, but did not fall into total desuetude since in the sixteenth century a need was developing for secular institutions of higher learning to provide for the growing class of landed gentry and urban bourgeois. In addition, the anglicization of the church in England removed the celibacy requirement, and by the late sixteenth century there were a sizeable number of priests' sons who sought to follow in educated callings. Protestantism stressed both 'self-help' and 'good works' and this too influenced the universities, particularly with respect to new foundations as wealthy philanthropists endowed colleges to replace the earlier medieval hostels and halls. In this period a quarter of all private benefaction went to education – a reflection of the Puritan ethic of moral and intellectual improvement[66] – and much of this munificence went directly into the universities. By the end of the sixteenth century they were quite different institutions: their chancellors ceased to be bishops and were now prominent statesmen; students came in significant numbers from the privileged classes (ruffs, swords, capes and silk hose were being worn); instruction was centred in the colleges with the lecture system replaced by the individual or small group tutorial, facilitated by the appearance of printed texts; while the programme reflected the needs of the times in that scholastic logic was replaced by rhetoric and the curriculum constituted by the *pietas litterata*, especially at Cambridge under the influence of Erasmus.

Despite these changes, however, it was clear that the universities were not easily meeting the needs of that rapidly changing society, and late in the sixteenth century voices of protest emerged that were to continue well into the seventeenth. Clearly, the refurbishing of the universities was an *ad hoc* arrangement, and many critics of the educational and intellectual tradition were urging more radical reconstruction of the system or, to put it more exactly, the construction of totally new institutions of which prototypes were already appearing. The Inns of Court in London – which had grown up during the Middle Ages on an informal basis to provide, first, residence and, later, centres of instruction for apprentice lawyers – had by the sixteenth century become more than law schools, offering instruction in the humanities as a general education for the well-to-do. The liberal arts instruction of the Inns had already attracted attention during the late sixteenth century and prompted one of England's Elizabethan adventurers, Sir Humphrey Gilbert (*c.* 1539–83), to propose an educational reform of the country in his short submission entitled *Queene Elizabethe's Achademy*, presented to the sovereign around the year 1570. Gilbert's proposals amounted, in essence, to a plan to lead aristocratic and wealthy youth away from idleness and profligacy to the better use of their leisure and talents and, at the same time, to provide an institution concerned with the totality of learning; not just the humanities but, in addition, mathematics, political philosophy, medicine, military studies, law and music.

The proposal came to nothing, but in the years that followed other treatises continued to urge a new type of institution to encompass the wider range of knowledge and, in particular, science, known as the 'experimentall philosophie'. So appeared Edmund Bolton's plan for a Royal Academy (1617) and Sir Francis Kynaston's proposal for an institution to teach medicine, languages, astronomy, geometry, music and fencing which was named, rather inappropriately, after the Roman goddess of handicrafts, Musaeum Minervae. Kynaston actually received a licence to operate this college in 1635 but it closed upon his death in 1642. Why it came to nothing is not clearly known, but there are suggestions that it was opposed by the universities of Oxford and Cambridge, who saw in it a potential competitor.[67] Standing alone, and unrivalled in influence, was Bacon's *New Atlantis*. Among other common features, all of these treatises were calling for the inclusion of science on a systematic basis, responding to the stimulus of Bacon in his 1605 treatise on *The Advancement of Learning* in which the method of scientific investigation on an inductive basis as a means to the furthering of human affairs caught the learned imagination.

There was already in existence, however, an institution of scientific instruction of a kind in what was called Gresham College, established by the will of the founder of the Royal Exchange, Sir Thomas Gresham. In his bequest Gresham left his London mansion as a foundation for providing public lectures in the seven areas of law, physic, rhetoric, divinity, music, geometry and astronomy. In 1598 the revenues from the Royal Exchange and the availability of the mansion allowed the college to appoint its first professors. The college operated quite successfully and followed the same pattern as the European learned and scientific societies.

In 1625 the German-born Theodore Haak settled in England and enrolled at Oxford in 1629. Haak was active in promoting science and corresponded with Mersenne in Paris and with a large number of other scholars including the English mathematician John Pell, the Moravian reformer Comenius and the indefatigable Polish intellectual entrepreneur, Samuel Hartlib. Haak seems to have been particularly active in stimulating correspondence and meetings on scientific matters in the 1630s and 1640s although, regrettably, we lack precise details. England of the 1640s was a place of considerable intellectual ferment, and plans for scientific and educational reform abounded. At this time, for example, in the correspondence of the twenty-year-old Robert Boyle we find three references to an 'invisible college' which confirm the new temper of practicality.[68] In this correspondence there are references to all kinds of reforming ideas: Milton's *Tractate of Education*, the Utopian literature of Campanella and Andreae, the social democracies of Venice and Holland, the schemes for universal world reform of Comenius. Boyle's first editor, Thomas Birch, who collected and edited his various writings in 1772 – a full century later – read into the 'invisible college' the prototypical form of the Royal Society; subsequent research now discounts the theory and various alternatives have been suggested, including the notion that it was a private club either of Haak or of Hartlib, for the latter was attempting at the time, in conjunction with John Dury, to establish an Office of Address in London on similar lines to Renaudot's Bureau d'Adresse. The second interpretation seems the more likely, for in those years around the fall of the English monarchy under Charles I there was a great sense of urgency for total reform, led by Hartlib, Dury and Comenius; the 'invisible college' does seem to have been the abortive prototype for a greater scheme of wide-ranging improvement, perhaps as set out in Comenius' grand dream of a Pansophic College.[69]

This interpretation, however, does not diminish the significance of the 'invisible college' but simply provides evidence, even though insecure and intriguing, of the intellectual excitement of the day in seeking the reconstruction of society on utopian lines, guided by scientific principles. If the 'invisible college' is not the precursor of the Royal Society, it at least formed part of the general climate of ideas within which that institution arose. It is known, too, that the Oxford 'experimental club' was in existence around 1648, although the record is not as exact as for the corresponding French developments. This club drew its stimulus from John Wilkins, Master of Wadham College, and had a reasonably large number of members of whom the most constant were Seth Ward, Robert Boyle, William Petty, Christopher Wren and his cousin Matthew, and John Wallis. The group met usually in Wilkins's lodgings but also, on occasions, in London in several places, including Gresham College – although it is clear that they used the college purely as a convenient venue and not by virtue of any scientific programme it may have had. By 1651 this Oxford club moved to regulate its activities and appointed as its first secretary Henry Oldenburg, who was responsible for sustaining contact with the Parisian societies, particularly the Montmor Academy. The club continued to prosper, stimulated by intercourse with Paris and Italy in addition to its own programmes of inquiry, and in 1660 the members sought the grant of royal letters patent in a submission to Charles II who had been restored to the English throne that year after the turbulent period of the Commonwealth, 1649–60. Charles acceded and the club became the Royal Society of London, receiving its charter in 1662. The following year it was issued a slightly amended charter and was granted its motto, *Nullius in verba* ('On the word of no one'). The Royal Society continued to meet at Gresham College until that building was burned down in the Great Fire of London of 1666; after an eight months' recess it built its own quarters. The society thereupon decided to record its progress and authorized its second secretary, Thomas Sprat, to prepare what was published in 1667 as *The History of the Royal Society of London for the Improving of Natural Knowledge* and remains our major source of information.[70] Thereafter the Royal Society continued to publish its proceedings, and branch societies spread throughout the British overseas dominions in the following centuries.

The Royal Society's motto indicates its empirical character, and, indeed, from the beginning it claimed to follow the precepts of Bacon. The opening of Sprat's *History*, which was carefully supervised by the members and is probably a trustworthy account,[71] proclaimed it to be the leading such organization which might possibly provoke others 'to attempt some greater Enterprise (if any such can be found out) for the Benefit of humane life, by the Advancement of *Real Knowledge*'. The Baconian reference would have been obvious to his readership; Sprat made it explicit further on when, in a historical survey of the progress of human knowledge, he considered the recent contribution of Aristotelian scholasticism, criticizing it chiefly as a structure of theories, often very subtle but insecure because it was not based on 'a sufficient information of the things themselves'.[72] This approach, he pointed out, leads only to the construction of a barrier of 'a thousand false images which lye like Monsters in their way'; the correct approach is to follow the method of 'one great Man, who had the true Imagination of the whole extent of this Enterprize, as it is now set on foot; and that is, Lord Bacon.'[73] The fellows of the Royal Society appreciated Bacon as a philosopher of scientific method rather than as a scientist (as some later interpretations suggested), with the result that, following the precepts of empirical deduction, their experimentation soon provided the innovative edge to scientific inquiry.

Early experiments were, as among other scientific societies, random and *ad hoc*, the criterion of utility being highly valued. However, the society was also well aware of Bacon's admonitions not to be entirely dominated by such considerations, for, although science was of obvious value in producing tangible benefits – and he termed such investigations 'fruitful' (*experimenta fructifera*) – the primary goal of science should be the ordered structuring of man's knowledge of the relationships of the external world, which Bacon termed 'enlightenment' (*experimenta lucifera*).[74] Here is the belief that the natural world has a discoverable structure, that human perception is limited to accurate observation and description, and that the mind has the 'faculty' of ordering these perceptions into a pattern of objective knowledge. The seventeenth-century Baconians of the Royal Society applied themselves to this task, imagining it to be an attainable goal within a finite period of time, the final achievement being the most desired prize of all – the complete mastery of nature, as the growing utopian literature reveals. As the society proceeded, it became apparent, as one member, Joseph Glanvill, observed in *Plus Ultra*, that such inquiry 'must proceed *slowly*, by degrees almost insensible', since it is 'so immense an Undertaking'.[75]

Such, then, was the new spirit of scientific enterprise, and it is a tribute to Bacon's method that it was able to provide a means for the rapid and systematic accumulation of knowledge, although the cost has since proved greater than was earlier imagined and the goal of objective knowledge as elusive as ever. None the less, the Royal Society introduced a new era in human endeavour and was greatly to influence man's conception of knowledge and, as a consequence, the approach to education. Parallel with the scientific revolution of the seventeenth century were closely related, often integrated, endeavours to apply the methods and results of science to the process of education – indeed, as one enthusiastic reformer noted, to effect a 'reformation of schooles'.

CHAPTER 3

'A Reformation of Schooles':
Utopia and Reality in the
Seventeenth Century

Voices of dissent: rejection of the classical humanist tradition

The word 'reformation' is the leitmotiv of the significant educational
literature of the seventeeth century; it recurred constantly in the titles and
contents of books, pamphlets and essays; it was put forward everywhere as
one of the most urgent needs of European society, and like many such
terms it embraced a wide range of connotations. Everyone responsibly
involved recognized that something had to be done; that schools, colleges
and universities left a great deal to be desired; that the curriculum was in
need of considerable attention; that the process of education itself demanded serious – even drastic – revision. For many this necessitated, in
effect, a complete reformation. This notion of the restructuring of education did not occur independently; it was, of course, part of the European
response to the rapidly changing social environment which received its
most profound general expression in the scientific revolution and Bacon's
plea for a 'Great Instauration' of Western civilization.

Bacon was well aware that the social scene was changing (although
even he clearly lacked a comprehensive understanding of the scale of
operations); his response was the most prescient of the period, and the
call for a social renewal was timely. Bacon realized that much learning was

useless, some of it positively deleterious: the narrow, Latin-based humanities curriculum was outmoded and, for most, quite inappropriate; teaching methods that responded either with increasing brutality and co-ercion or by sugar-coating the pill of compulsion with ingeniously con-trived methods and *ratios* were equally futile; the future, he recognized, was with the vernacular, the sciences and technologies although the call for relevance was not always precisely understood or expressed. His stimulus, however, activated many educational reformers of the seven-teenth century, although none of them thought with the same verve; even the best wrote with greater caution and proposed far more modest re-forms. Europe's problems were not generally perceived in terms of the profound economic, demographic and technological changes then occur-ring; they continued to be interpreted as a failure of society to adjust to the break-up of medieval civilization and the consequent rapid growth of strife and hatred that divided mankind. Many social thinkers, and par-ticularly those concerned with education, considered the proper response to be the restoration of social harmony, secured by establishing a more comprehensive and beneficent social order. So education, as a key element in achieving such restoration, was still conceived as operating within the general framework of the Christian Neoplatonist approach, but suitably modified and improved by a judicious use of those advances in science which might be appropriate.

Educational reformers, and their schemes, remained within the con-servative tradition, seeking to maintain the best of the past in optimum balance with the most appropriate of the new. Because there was so much dissatisfaction with that tradition and with the state of European society, however, there developed a flight from reality, and a great deal of reform-ing energy was channelled into devising new visions of society in a move-ment of utopian theorizing. Indeed, utopianism became an important element of the reforming efforts of the seventeenth century and once introduced remained a permanent feature of Western educational litera-ture. Within this reforming movement, and drawing together virtually all of the separate elements, two people were outstanding: Samuel Hartlib and Johann Amos Comenius. As the whole thrust of educational reform in the period from the mid-sixteenth to the mid-seventeenth century culminated in their work, they became the acknowledged leaders of the movement, Hartlib through his indefatigable organizing, Comenius through his wide-ranging, highly articulate pleading for the cause. This relationship between the two was expressed in the title of an essay written

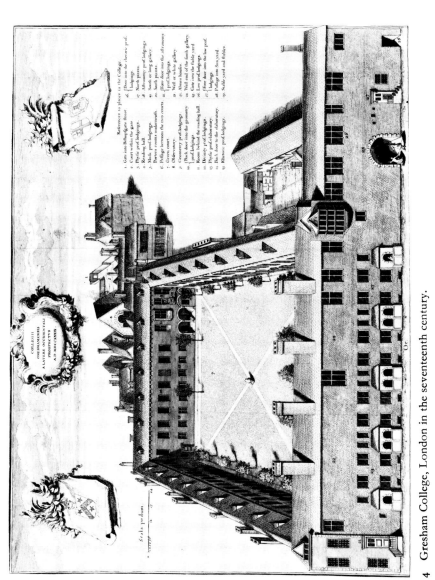

4 Gresham College, London in the seventeenth century.

5   Comenius and the *Opera didactica omnia*.

by Comenius and published in London in 1642 by Hartlib in an effort to influence the English parliament to act upon it:

> *A Reformation of Schooles,* designed in two excellent treatises. The first whereof sumarily sheweth the great necessity of a general reformation of common learning. What grounds of hope there are for such a reformation. How it may be brought to passe. The second answers certain objections ordinarily made against such undertakings and describes the several parts and titles of workes which are shortly to follow.

Neither Hartlib nor Comenius, however, much less any other reformer, really understood the complexity of the current economic and social processes. They were living in a Europe in which the population increased from 80 million in 1500 to 100 million in 1600, and which saw continued exponential demographic increases. In addition, new inventions, especially the harnessing of water power to various forms of industry, created a burgeoning technology which was changing the continent into a more closely integrated economic community, to which the American colonies had become increasingly important, both as sources of raw materials and as markets for finished products. The attention of the school reformers, however, remained focused on modifying the traditional literary curriculum. The great programme of educational 'reformation' was therefore a limited operation and, in the long term, ineffective. In assessing the importance of the efforts of Hartlib and the thought of Comenius in that period, however, it is essential to see their activities as coming at the end of an epoch rather than, like Bacon's, as the stimulus to significant change. The educational reformation had been under way for a century before they wrote and, like so many of the great movements in European civilization, it had its origins chiefly in Italy – with significant reinforcement in France – and must be interpreted in the light of the scientific, technological and economic developments of the period.

Sixteenth-century dissent in France and Italy

The first major manifesto of dissent had been published in France by François Rabelais in the mid-seventeenth century. It must be remembered, however, that Rabelais did not depart from the mainstream of Christian Neoplatonic humanism; on the contrary, his satires were written in its defence, to remind people how far they had strayed from the proper path. In *Gargantua* and *Pantagruel* Rabelais argued vigorously in defence of the vernacular, and for the introduction of a more relevant curriculum, summarizing his argument with the injunction: 'in a word, be well informed of everything that concerns the physical world we live in'.[1] And, as has already been noted, he gave his address in the *Preface* to these books as 'Utopia', indicating his own clear recognition of the difficulties of implementing his suggested reforms.

At the same time in Italy a much more powerful current of dissent and radical criticism was being generated which was to reinforce the efforts of Rabelais and to create the climate of dissatisfaction – and disenchantment – that led directly to the seventeenth-century reforming effort. This Italian movement had several aspects, all closely related to Rabelais's suggested reforms: the affirmation of the vernacular; a bitter rejection of humanist learning; and the belief – not too strongly argued – that education should be more closely related to real life. The Italian movement, however, had an added component of cynicism and despair in that its writers could see no way out of the enormous difficulties in which society was enmeshed. Several people were centrally involved: the significant proponent of vernacular education was Giambattista Gelli; the cynics constituted a group known as the *poligrafi* – Nicolò Franco, Lodovico Domenichi, Ortensio Lando, Giulio Landi and Anton Francesco Doni – who created the climate within which the utopian reforming literature was generated.

The vernacular question had long been central to education; in the sixteenth and seventeenth centuries, however, it was felt more acutely because the conflict had so many potential ramifications. Over the centuries the various European tongues had been subordinated to three major languages, Hebrew, Greek and Latin, which had provided the vehicle for the continuity of Western civilization. Europe, in particular, was largely dependent upon Latin, which throughout the medieval millennium had been a universal means of communication; the fracturing of the social structure by the Protestant Reformation and the ensuing religious wars was now in danger of being compounded, as Latin was challenged by a multitude of competing languages and dialects. The threat of barbarism was perceived as being very real.

The attack upon Latin and the arguments advanced for the vernacular by Gelli marked an important episode in the movement to educational reform, since his activities were at the centre of the major intellectual controversies of the day. Gelli was a member of the Florentine Academy and in 1546 published his controversial views in *I Capricci del bottaio* ('The Fanciful Thoughts of a Cooper'), constructed in the form of ten imaginary dialogues between a cooper, Giusto, and his soul.[2] The *Capricci* was an outstanding success; in the first five years it ran through eight editions and remained in print for a considerable time thereafter, stimulating a considerable debate in the literary academies on the role of the vernacular. In essence, Gelli was attacking the humanist position which, in the course of the previous two centuries, had become a highly conservative orthodoxy. Already the vernacular movement had its opponents, of whom a representative example was Francesco Florido (1511–47), whose *Apologia* of 1537 violently denounced the growing incursions of the *volgare*. Florido's arguments came from the mainstream of conservative thought; he affirmed the general arguments of the *quattrocentisti* that Latin and Greek have a permanent, international status, that they sustain the historical, civilized tradition, being supported by an agreed lexicon, syntax and grammar. To these he added a number of particular arguments that Latin was a 'pure' language and the vernacular only a corruption, lacking a corps of good writers, a literature, style and authority, and moreover was barbaric in origin.

Florido's attack on the vernacular of Italy as an 'infection' prompted the Accademia Fiorentino to respond by means of continued debates, discussions and articles, of which Gelli's *Capricci* is the exemplar. Clearly, Latin had to go; in its Ciceronian form – and it was that which Florido regarded as 'pure' – it is a highly contrived, complex language requiring virtually a singleminded, lifelong application to master it. If education were to be democratized and extended – and the reformers were, perhaps unconsciously, responding to the demographic-economic pressures that required this – then a simpler language would have to be devised. The Accademia Fiorentino and others, notably the Accademia degli Infiammati and the Accademia della Crusca, directed much of their attention to the question, with the result that Tuscan emerged as *la lingua madre* of Italy. In supporting the case for this particular vernacular, Gelli easily dismissed the notion of 'impurity' and 'barbarism'; the vernacular, he asserted (quite correctly), is equally capable as Latin of expressing abstract concepts, a fact illustrated in the works of the fiery reformer Savonarola whose persuasive vernacular writings involved the most complex philosophical ideas.[3]

Gelli moved aggressively to the attack. Why it is, he asked, that Latin is defended against the vernacular? His answer pointed to the vested interest of the academic establishment and the church. The former, of course, jealously guard their body of professional expertise; from grammar

masters in the elementary and grammar schools to the university professors there is a financial advantage in restricting the audience and presiding
over the mysteries of a complex subject, and one, moreover, that he regarded as 'dead' – Gelli being one of the first to advance this concept –
because it is not spoken naturally anywhere.[4] The church too has an
interest in sustaining Latin as an inaccessible language since it thereby has
a means of duping the ignorant in order to maintain its social control and
financial gain. Religion, Gelli asserted, should be based not on fear but on
love and understanding; the Bible, therefore, should be readily accessible
and hence printed in the vernacular, as should the church services. In the
period these were clearly Protestant views, and, amid quite unfounded
charges that not only Gelli but the entire Accademia Fiorentino held
Lutheran sympathies, *I Capricci del bottaio* was promptly placed upon the
Index. None the less, Gelli had made his points; he argued that the vernacular is even more suited to the cultivation of patriotism and the maintenance of the cultural tradition because it is easier and faster to teach and
therefore able to reach more people, and is superior in its concepts and
store of knowledge owing to its status as a living language. The enthusiastic response to the book, doubtless aided by the recommendation that it
was prohibited reading, kept the debate well in the foreground of public
educational concern.

Educational cynicism and the rejection of humanism

Simultaneously with Gelli, however, there was a group of far more pessi-
mistically inclined thinkers, known collectively as the *poligrafi* – so named
because they were all occasional essayists – who were totally opposed to
the humanist programme. Although Gelli's arguments in favour of the
vernacular clearly belonged to the arena of the growing debate, he had
attacked education only indirectly; the *poligrafi* attacked the *studia humanitatis* themselves, the core of liberal studies, and in the period from 1535 to
1555 a movement to reject humanist learning was created by the separate
pens of these polemicists. They sought to amuse but also to chide; behind
their efforts to stimulate there was a common theme of disenchantment
with the state of the world.

The one universal idea developed in their many popular books and
tracts was a denial of the basic humanist proposition that the *studia humanitatis* prepared people – specifically well-connected boys and youths –
for active participation in a free society; in a phrase, for the *vita civile*. In

attacking humanist education the *poligrafi* found many targets: teachers were ridiculed by Lodovico Domenichi as being ineffective in their personal lives outside the classroom, which immediately illustrated the absurdity of their claims to prepare boys for the *vita civile*;[5] Nicolò Franco in his *Pistole vulgari* (*Vernacular Letters*) attacked the foolish pretensions of scholars in that arithmeticians, he asserted, attempt to measure the height of heaven's mansions above the earth while logicians seek to prove that *si* denies and *non* affirms.[6] These attacks continued in endless variations across thousands of pages; the *poligrafi* captivated a wide and enthusiastic reading audience, and their nine basic works collectively ran to fifty-one separate Italian editions in the second half of the century (up to 1615), while there were also fifteen French editions, three in Spanish and, moreover, innumerable plagiarizations.

Despite their popularity throughout southern Europe, these criticisms, which Lando for one claimed were really only entertainment, being composed 'in jest rather than seriously',[7] had no constructive programme. They were written expressly to show that the claims of the *studia humanitatis* were incapable of being met: that *virtù* is not teachable; that history, a key study of the humanities, has only negative value since it has no predictability; that book learning prepares only for the vapid, affected life of the salon and court; that scholars themselves had no concern for scholarship but simply used teaching as a commercial activity and the *studia humanitatis* as a stock-in-trade to be peddled to the highest bidders, and for the teachers' personal gain and social advancement. And this, Anton Francesco Doni asserted, is fraud.[8] The response of the *poligrafi*, widely communicated throughout Europe, was one of cynical despair; clearly, education was a failure and they saw the only solution to be withdrawal from society, a 'psychic emigration' as it were, into the personal, interior life, something rather akin to the religious *vita contemplativa* for which Italy had already been historically famous. Their proposal was for an alternative lifestyle revolving around total disengagement: *ignoranza da bene*, the life of 'goodly ignorance'.[9]

The scepticism of Montaigne

While conservative schoolmasters attempted to solve problems by improving their methodologies, educational despair prevailed in the ideological literature and found a greater champion in the French writer Michel de Montaigne who, on account of his eminence, gave the concept of *ignoranza da bene* a much wider circulation, turning, it might be noted, to Italian examples when describing the decadence of contemporary education. Montaigne (1533–92), the son of a country nobleman, had retired from public life in an emotional reaction to the Huguenot wars. As a good Catholic he accepted the arguments for the suppression of Protestantism; as a sensitive person he was deeply distressed by the human suffering that eventuated and in 1571 withdrew to his château where he devoted himself to reflective essay writing on major social, and therefore educational, issues. Beginning this period with a stoic attitude, he moved towards complete cynicism and came to reject the rationalist assertion that man can triumph by virtue of his unaided intellect with the despairing, and famous apophthegm, which in 1576 he adopted as his motto: *Que sçay-je?* Using this question ('What do I know?') as a basis, he wrote his famous series of essays which immediately became part of the significant literature of France and, quite soon thereafter, much of Europe. Owing to his own humanist upbringing and his reading of the Italian critics of learning, Montaigne saw education as central to the human condition; he sided, however, with the *poligrafi* and was responsible for heightening the disillusionment with education as it existed. Montaigne, indeed, set loose into European consciousness some of the most devastating criticisms of schools, teachers, teaching methods and the curriculum yet made, these being threaded through all of his essays, though particularly concentrated in two: 'Du pédantisme' and 'De l'institution des enfants'. 'On Pedantry' continued the negative cynical tradition of the Italian critics, attacking the pretensions of latter-day humanist learning masquerading as erudition. The opening sentence set the tone: he remarked that he was always bothered by Italian comedies which, using a pedant as the butt of contempt, consistently chose a schoolmaster; why is it, he continued, that the word 'master' does not have a more honourable connotation?[10] The answer, obviously, is that book learning is equivalent neither to knowledge nor to wisdom, and he accepted Plutarch's dictum that the greatest scholars are not the wisest men.[11] The essay developed the expected criticisms of mannered learning, much as we find in Rabelais's attack upon the Paris clerks, with jibes at those whose conception of education is so completely obsessed with abstruse verbal accomplishment that they are nothing more than 'letter-puffed' or 'letter-struck' (*lettre férus*) pedants. We should, he observed throughout, if we really care for children, keep them away from schooling and let them devote themselves to playing games, for tennis is a much better activity for children in their years of physical agility.

'On the Education of Children' contains more positive features although it is a mixed composition, containing as it does much of the rancour that suffuses 'On Pedantry'. Brutality and meaningless learning are especially attacked; if only classrooms could be hung with festoons of flowers rather than, as they are, with blood-soaked birches.[12] The chief argument of 'On the Education of Children', however, is positive; it presents Montaigne's view that the function of education is to join learning with true knowledge to the end of cultivating judgement and moral character. For this purpose, experience of real life is the proper teacher; we should, then, provide in the first years a vigorous programme of healthy physical activities – running, wrestling, music, dancing, hunting and management of arms and horses – tied in with training in courteous demeanour and deportment. This, of course, is the best way to learn – a point he emphasized throughout one of his longest essays, 'On Experience', in which the opening paragraph declared that when reason fails we turn to experience.[13] Certainly the boy's education should contain a literary element which perforce had to be drawn from the classical and recent tradition, but overemphasis on Latin and Greek should be avoided. The vernacular is adequate for most learning and everyday life; after learning to speak good French (the language in which the *Essays* were composed) the child should learn the language of those neighbours with whom the country has most dealings.[14]

Montaigne did not propose any prescriptive, forward-looking curriculum but gave only general indications: the vernacular and modern languages, social courtesy. Basically, he was totally disenchanted with the claims of reason, and with the notion that education in any form is capable of developing ideals, judgement and morality; man still has a soul, which links him to god; ultimately, it is faith that is important. We can never really know ourselves or others, life is a quest from a position of ignorance, and it is vanity to pretend otherwise. The sad cynicism of *la ignoranza da bene* thus received further support from one of France's greatest writers.

The search for stability: early utopian visions

Given the tremendous range of prevailing conflicts – political, religious, social, economic and intellectual – that were raging throughout Europe, there is little reason to wonder at the disenchantment of many, especially since most people were directly involved with only limited aspects of the turmoil and had no easy way of achieving a wider, synoptic vision which might reconcile events into a conceptually manageable understanding. No one, not even the greatest intellects, could divine where events were leading. Yet, curiously, these tremendous conflicts did not destroy the optimism of some intellectuals, and against the background of cynicism and despair being voiced in Italy and France a rising alternative movement of hope appeared in a significant literature of utopian theorizing, which saw education as a necessary instrument for transmuting utopia into reality. And, although some was decidedly of a consolatory nature, this was definitely not the prime intention of the major seventeenth-century writers, for whom constructing synoptic visions was preparatory to action. Of these writers, three are of major significance in preparing the way for the great mid-century educational formulations of Comenius and Hartlib: these were Andreae, Campanella and Bacon.

Two Christian utopias: Andreae and Campanella

It was Johann Valentin Andreae (1586–1654) who initiated the seventeenth-century utopian movement in his highly influential *Christianopolis*, first published in 1619. Andreae had trained as a Protestant pastor at Tübingen and then Geneva; in 1614 he was ordained Deacon of Vaihingen and began his labours of writing a utopian vision, based largely upon an idealized conception of the city of Geneva. This utopia is described by means of an allegory in which the wanderer Peregrinus leaves the world in disillusionment to voyage across the seas of knowledge – *Mare academicum* – aboard the ship *Fantasy* which is wrecked in storms of academic intrigue and malicious gossip. Washed up on the shores of an island, Peregrinus reaches the city of Christianopolis and finds at the 'innermost shrine of the city what you would rightly call the centre of activity of the state . . . there, religion, justice and learning have their abode, and theirs is the control of the city'.[15] These three functions are located, respectively, in the temple, the council hall and a collection of educational institutions including a school, a library and several laboratories, under the direction of, respectively, a priest, a judge and the director of learning. The three basic institutions of education give at first reading the appearance of an acceptance of the new scientific empiricism being advanced by Bacon, but on closer inspection it becomes clear that science is conceived instead as natural theology; as we study the creator's handiwork, so we come to know god.[16] Here Andreae introduced a concept common to many seventeenth-century writers, that of the 'labyrinth of the world' through which each one of us ceaselessly wanders, seeking for understanding. For Andreae, as for all dedicated Christians, the end can only be communion in Christ, and *Christianopolis* was based, despite its ordered pattern of learning supported by enlightened institutions, not upon the discoveries of the rational inquiring mind but upon a theology of conversion, secured through the atonement of the crucifixion.[17] The utopia, then, was within the highly conservative, religious tradition. *Christianopolis* was, however, a major document in the reforming movement since it pointed the way to a better society based upon republican government, distributive justice and enlightened learning pursued in laboratories and libraries as well as in the classroom.

In the same period the theme was taken up by Giovanni Campanella (1568–1639), whose early work had influenced Andreae, in another utopia which received an even wider readership and came to exercise much greater influence: this was *Civitas solis*, first published in Frankfurt in 1623 while Campanella, a monk charged with heresy, was in a Spanish prison in Naples. Although virtually contemporaneous with *Christianopolis*, Campanella's *City of the Sun* (as it came to be translated) is a quite different utopia, for it accepted the positive role of man in influencing the human condition; it went beyond a theology of existential conversion to one bordering on a belief in perfectibility through social action, this being developed out of Campanella's philosophical position which rested firmly in the idealist tradition.

The central concern of the *City of the Sun* is to depict a society in a state of perfect justice, on the model of Plato's *Republic*, with education, therefore, being an activity of great importance. Children there learn to read quickly and competently; the emphasis is on scientific, empirical knowledge, to which the boy is introduced in his seventh year. Although this knowledge is subdivided into astrology, cosmography, arithmetic, geometry, history, poetry, logic, rhetoric, grammar, medicine, physiology, politics and morals, it is drawn together and contained in 'but one book, which they call Wisdom, and in it the sciences are written with conciseness and marvellous fluency of expression'.[18] Here Campanella gave an early indication of another hallmark of the reforming spirit of seventeenth-century utopians, namely, encyclopedism: systematic collection and organization of knowledge was believed to produce a better society because it could be learned so easily; indeed, Campanella reported that by so arranging knowledge the sciences were taught with such facility that the City of the Sun produces 'more scholars . . . in one year than [ordinary societies produce] in ten, or even fifteen'.[19] The implicit utopian assumption here is that scientifically organized, encyclopedic-scale knowledge will be not only readily learned but as easily accepted and applied to the widespread rational solution of all problems.

City of the Sun created considerable impact in the early seventeenth century and appears to have influenced Bacon's *New Atlantis*. Campanella's views, of course, were decidedly Platonic – as is indicated by the full title of his work, *City of the Sun, Based on the Ideas of Plato's Republic (Civitas solis, idea republicae Platonicae)* – with an emphasis on science, utility, first-hand learning and encyclopedism. His utopia was an advance on Andreae's in that it was based upon human rationality, the direction in which the century was moving under the great stimulus of Baconian empiricism. Campanella was, moreover, less dogmatic in his religious beliefs; his utopians worship a trinitarian god, whose three attributes are Wisdom, Power and Love; they 'do not distinguish persons by name, as in our Christian law, which has not been revealed to them'.[20]

From Andreae to Campanella to Bacon, then, there was a progressive shift of responsibility for the human condition from divine grace to man's cooperation with providence, and then to the rational control of all affairs through the application of science. Bacon's *New Atlantis* of 1627, published posthumously, and although an unfinished fragment, represented a totally new conception of society and the means of furthering human affairs by scientific methods emanating from Solomon's House; it is profoundly different in conception, spirit and operation from *Christianopolis*. Solomon's House represents the concept of reason in control, using the inductive method to harness a willing and subservient technology.

Despite the priority they accorded education, Andreae, Campanella and Bacon never really discussed details. In all their utopias there was a generalized acceptance of the necessary instrumentality of education, but there were no carefully thought-out particulars of operational effectiveness, nor, in the case of Bacon, was there any real grappling with the problem of the origins and sustaining of values – of the proper and wise choice of ends that education would serve. Bacon assumed that rationality is the same among all people and that consensus would automatically emerge as scientific induction built up a structure of absolute, demonstrable knowledge. The task of taking the utopian dreams and developing them into educational sequences was, at that moment, being undertaken by another

of the greatest visionaries of the seventeenth century – perhaps the greatest
of all time – who immediately followed Bacon: the Moravian educator,
Comenius. Indeed, the social history of utopian reform, especially in its
educational aspects, revolves around the magnificent corpus of Comenian
writings known to his contemporaries as the *Complete Educational Works*:
the *Opera didactica omnia*.

The Comenian vision: utopia through knowledge

The early years 1592–1627: faith and reason

Jan Amos Komenský (1592–1670) was born in Moravia and raised in the
minority Protestant faith of the Unitas Fratrum (Unity of the Brotherhood), an Anabaptist sect that found its inspiration in the life and martyr-
dom of the great Bohemian reformer, Jan Hus (*c*. 1369/71–1415). Komenský, known by his latinized name of Comenius, studied for a religious
vocation and in 1618 was called to be a pastor at Fulnek, in the same year
that the Thirty Years War erupted. This began a long period of persecution for the Unitas Fratrum and for Comenius personally as well. The
kingdom of Bohemia, which held sovereignty over the margravate of
Moravia lying on its eastern border, was the immediate centre of the conflict; this began as a dispute over succession to the throne of Bohemia,
which carried an electorship of the Holy Roman Empire. Bohemia had
always been marginally absorbed into the Catholic Church and, indeed,
since the days of Hus had remained factiously divided, with even the
Catholics somewhat separate in their Calixtine confession. The country
was further divided along ethnic lines, between bitterly contending
German- and Czech-speaking populations, and it was therefore of European significance when the throne became vacant. At the time, of course,
the powerful economic pressures were not seen as relevant; instead, religious schism and the great dynastic conflicts of Habsburg, Bourbon and
Stuart, along with various republican movements, were seen as the causes.

Within three years of assuming pastoral duties Comenius found himself
a member of a proscribed religion and was forced into hiding; during that
period of seclusion from 1621 to 1627 he composed in 1623, in Czech, his
first serious philosophical treatise, the *Labyrinth of the World*, and its
sequel, *Paradise of the Heart*.[21] Comenius took up the metaphor of the world

as a labyrinth through which each person in life must find a way, as suggested in Andreae's *Christianopolis*, and composed an allegory which recounted his dawning realization of the iniquities of the world and his despair at finding human society so corrupt. In his view this was caused by the abuse of learning. The *Labyrinth of the World*, with its cast of slandering scholars and its rancorous polemic, recorded his disappointment with the learning of the time and led him to compose a positive sequel which described how man can find truth, not through secular studies, but through Christian faith.

Comenius did, however, see a limited role for reason and attempted to harmonize it with faith, with the result that *Paradise of the Heart* presents his vision of the Christian way as one of educational development. In mankind, he wrote, there is

> . . . a twofold clear inward light – the light of reason and the light of faith – and both are guided by the Holy Ghost. For he who enters [upon the Christian way] must put away and renounce his reason, yet the Holy Ghost returns it to him, purified and refined. . . . Then the light of faith gleams on him so brightly that he can already see and know, not only that which is before him, but also, everything that is absent and invisible.[22]

This approach characterized all his work thereafter and provoked Andreae, years later in 1646, in a preface to *Evangelical Church Harmony*, to attack Comenius by way of a thinly veiled allusion to 'some [who], in contempt of Luther, are sowing the infelicitous tares of scholastic pansophy'.[23] Comenius was deeply hurt, recording that the attack 'stupefied him', and he curtly reminded Andreae that the faith of the Unitas Fratrum followed not the *arriviste* Luther but the first and more authoritative of the reformers, Hus.[24] The quarrel was patched up, yet it clearly marked a basic difference between the earlier fideist position of Andreae and the mid-century view that the discoveries of science had to be accommodated.

None the less, Comenius was really a conservative, defending the primacy of faith in a period of increasing rationalism. In his view the goal of education must, by the evidence of revelation, be necessarily Christian, leading us to knowledge of divine works through the ministry of Christ; secular scholarship without such divine leadership is useless, even deleterious. He saw education as resting upon a linguistic basis, which, for seventeenth-century Europe, he believed simply had to be Latin.

The Protestants fared badly in the Thirty Years War, especially in Bohemia where the first phase of campaigning occurred. The Catholic

Emperor Ferdinand suppressed Protestantism ruthlessly, and the schools of all dissenting groups throughout Austria, Bohemia and Moravia were returned to the authority of the Catholic Church which, chiefly under Jesuit leadership, began a vigorous campaign of forcible re-Catholicization. In 1627 Comenius fled to relative sanctuary in Poland, a kingdom adjoining the Holy Roman Empire. There, in a community of the Unitas Fratrum in Leszno, tolerated by the local nobility, Comenius became rector of the Latin grammar school for the ensuing fourteen years, until in 1641 he left for England to expound his new educational theories.

Towards a theory of education: the unity of all human experience

Comenius continued his theological activities at Leszno, writing religious tracts and other documents, while in his dual position of schoolmaster and pastor his educational and philosophical outlook matured and he wrote his major pedagogical treatise which was eventually to gain him universal recognition. This appeared in a Czech version between 1627 and 1632 under the title *Didaktika (Didactic)*; because of its language, at first it had only a limited circulation.[25] The universality of Latin came home to him: between 1633 and 1638 he revised and extended this treatise in Latin under the title *Didactica magna (The Great Didactic)*. However, since lack of enthusiasm by its early readers prevented him from finding a publisher, for nearly twenty years it circulated in manuscript until a collected Latin edition of his complete educational works, *Opera didactica omnia*, was published in Amsterdam in 1657, in two volumes.[26]

Central to Comenius' thinking is the idea of the underlying unity of all human experience. The reality of the perceptual world he accepted as axiomatic; its interpretation was the subject of his concern. Men, and scholars particularly, were at variance in their understanding of the nature of reality, and from those disagreements the most tragic consequences often followed. Comenius' religious beliefs provided him with the notion that a single unified world is a divine creation. His personal motto, 'Were violence absent, all things would flow spontaneously', indicated his outlook (his Latin text – *Omnia sponte fluant absit violentia rebus* – is phrased in the subjunctive, making it clear that he was yearning for a utopia). Disunity and the consequent social and political disharmony, in his view, stem from faulty understanding, and the task is therefore to seek educational solutions that direct the learner to a progressive illumination of the intrinsic order of reality.

The challenge Comenius faced was that of translating his broad theories into a specific educational programme, and for the next thirty years (1627–57) he pursued that goal. Comenius was well aware that current educational procedures were inadequate; there was no satisfactory method of teaching that took account of the developments in science, particularly the sense-empiricism of Bacon; no really usable textbooks were available; nothing in the curriculum was attractive to children. And that was his starting-point: he sought, as a simple beginning, to improve the teaching of Latin. He did not, of course, develop his pedagogy *de novo*. There was in existence a tradition of language reform, based on the sixteenth-century *ratio* and *ordine* approach which had been cultivated by a number of schoolmasters and professors. Among these, the three Englishmen Richard Mulcaster, Roger Ascham and John Brinsley were well known; equally significant were the continental reformers Wolfgang Ratke, William Bateus and Eilhard Lubinus. All these innovators experimented with improving the logical presentation of Latin. The most promising method seemed to be that of an Irish priest at the Jesuit college in Salamanca, William Bateus, who as early as 1611 had prepared a school book that taught Latin through the Spanish vernacular by placing the two texts in parallel columns. Entitled *Janua linguarum* (*Gateway of Tongues*), it enjoyed wide success and was translated into several other European languages.

First steps to reform: early educational writings of Comenius

This was the tradition on which Comenius determined to improve. His first effort was extremely modest, and as a result of the examples of Bateus, Lubinus and Ratke, after several years in the writing, he published at Leszno in 1631 the first of his pedagogical texts, *Janua linguarum reserata* (*The Gate of Tongues Unlocked*), with specific acknowledgement to the influence of Bateus' edition.[27] This was a simple encyclopedia of a wide variety of topics, ninety-eight in all, beginning with the origins of the earth, 'De ortu mundi', and ending with a section on angels, 'De angelis'. The whole work, including a short introduction and an epilogue, consisted of 100 sections, subdivided into 1000 sentences, and intended, as the introduction stated, for teaching Latin and whatever other languages were desired. The *Janua* was immediately popular and for the next fifty years was the best-known and probably the most widely used text in Europe. In the first twenty years of publication it was issued in as many editions, frequently in multi-language printings, some containing as many as four languages in parallel columns. The major languages of Europe – English, French, German and Italian – were the most popular, but Dutch, Spanish, Swedish and Flemish editions were also published. In addition there were a number of Latin–Greek editions. While London and Amsterdam were the most frequent centres for publication, copies were printed in many other cities, including Geneva, Venice, Paris, Hamburg, Danzig, Frankfurt and Prague.

The introduction of *Janua* stated as a basic principle the idea that thought and language proceed together, and its application was widely appreciated; within two years of its first publication Comenius issued a simplified version to serve as a preliminary reader. Following his metaphor of the doorway to language, the introductory text was designated a portal or vestibule, the *Vestibulum*. Also encyclopedic in content, it consisted of 427 short sentences, simple in construction if not always in content, the first three, for example, reading: 'God is eternal, the earth is but temporary. The angels are immortal, man is mortal. The body is visible, the soul is invisible.'

In the same period Comenius produced *Informatorium školy mateřské* (*School of Infancy*), written in Czech in 1630 and translated into German three years later; a Latin version did not appear until it was included in the collected works of 1657.[28] *School of Infancy* presented the methods by which the parents, particularly the mother, could begin the child's education in its first years. Basically the method consists in requiring the child to observe and then repeat the appropriate words; more abstract concepts and generalizations, such as those about the nature of spiritual forces, were not given special consideration: Comenius felt they were self-evident truths that could be grasped directly by logical intuition. Comenius was never to handle that problem adequately: his theory that knowledge is derived from sensory reality did not provide any explanation of the ways in which abstractions and spiritual truths are attained.

In *School of Infancy* the encyclopedic, logically organized approach to education of *Janua* and *Vestibulum* was applied to the child's first years. At the same time, as a result of reading Bacon, Comenius began to realize that words themselves must be derived from the objects of personal experience. He was convinced that proper knowledge of the world depends on the cultivation of the senses and on an adequate relation of language to experience, and it was as a result of writing these pedagogical texts at Leszno that he was stimulated to further religious beliefs; from these Comenius proceeded to develop an educational theory, and before long his teaching activities determined the direction of his thought and influenced his religious outlook. During the period at Leszno the writing that resulted was compounded of religious beliefs and educational activity, both of which were blended together in his major work, *Didactica magna* (*The Great Didactic*).

By the 1630s Comenius had resolved to reform all knowledge in terms of a proper ordering. In the years 1634–6 he sketched out a rationalization of his belief in the unity of the universe, claiming that the reformation of the school, and learning in general, would be instrumental in realizing the utopian vision. It was that long essay, first titled *Pansophiae prodromos* ('Intimations of a Universal Science'), which was later developed into *A Reformation of Schooles*. By this time Comenius had begun to formulate the idea that in nature there are no divisions, classification in his view being an artifice of man that does violence to the organic continuity of the real world. The world is all one; so too is knowledge. To achieve knowledge is to reach god; in attaining a completely unified view of all existence, corporeal and spiritual, man fulfils his natural end. Then, of necessity, will harmony and peace ensue. Such was Comenius' grand educational vision: simple, compelling, exciting. It caught the imagination of reformers and statesmen, for it was typical of its time, and in the mid-seventeenth century the Comenian notion of a single, universal science – of pansophism, as he termed it – was discussed in intellectual circles throughout Europe.

Pansophism for Comenius was a supremely simple concept; he had no difficulty in imagining the absolute unity of all knowledge, and believed that every element of existence is related to the totality of others. Nor did he doubt that, if those relations could be determined, then demonstration itself would carry such power of persuasion that it would overcome ignorance and evil. Already he had made a tentative elaboration of the idea in his Czech *Didaktika*, which included an outline of his projected educational scheme; the idea was developed further in the Latin *Didactica magna*, Comenius' first systematic organization of his education plans, envisaging, in effect, the reform of all civilization.

Didactica magna: *education as organic continuity*

Didactica magna was the most important educational treatise of the century: indeed, it stands as one of the greatest of all time. It was a lengthy, closely argued document of 193 folio pages in the Amsterdam edition of 1657 of the *Opera didactica omnia*, the title page itself indicating the tremendous sweep of its contents. It proclaimed a method whereby all children could be taught quickly, pleasantly and certainly the sum of all knowledge, and at the same time be imbued with such qualities of character as would be relevant for this world and the next. The method was based on a study of the growth of the child's mind and the principles by which human mentality develops. These principles should be used to replace the formal, logical structure of subject matter by a psychological patterning, thus allowing learning and teaching to proceed together naturally. In his view, both stem from the single arch-principle of organic continuity: the unity of knowledge is derived from sensory percepts which in turn are integrated into a series of concepts at levels of increasing abstraction and complexity. For each level there is a corresponding set of linguistic categories, ranging from simple substantives to complex propositions, the task of the educator being to identify and order those categories.

Comenius believed that within the child are the potentialities for development: 'everything is contained in that microcosm, man'.[29] From birth to maturity, consequently, each person should follow the laws of inner development, through a sequence marked by increasing acuity of perception, as well as by improvements in physical and motor skills and in linguistic competence. All human growth follows stages – infant, child, youth, adult – indicated by corresponding patterns of behaviour. Speech, which is his chief example, likewise has four stages: babbling (*quo modo cumque*), correctness (*proprie*), taste (*eleganter*), vigour (*nervose*).[30] Knowledge should therefore be organized to correspond to those stages: the babbling child should learn to speak simple words and phrases, the young child sentences, the youth to discourse at greater length, the adult to achieve thereby access to the world of scholarly and classical writing. For Comenius speech was not distinguished from reading but was linked in a continuous relationship. Man's earthly progress is, then, one of progressive refinement of perception and understanding, and the growth of intellect is marked by changes in degree, not in kind. From infancy throughout life the totality of knowledge is to be pursued at increasing levels of sophistication; as man grows in knowledge so he grows towards god. From that position Comenius developed a curriculum, and in doing so drew from his earlier experiences in writing *School of Infancy*, *Vestibulum* and *Janua*. From infancy to adulthood, the individual should be involved in the totality of experience; the progressive cultivation of intellect should stem from the discovery of ever-increasing meaning in experience. Knowledge becomes enriched with the finding of new and fresh relationships in existing situations.

Ideal of the graded series of pansophic texts

Comenius turned in *The Great Didactic* to the formal organization of studies. Since man needs training and cultivation to achieve his vocation, institutions must be provided. A system of graded schools and a series of graded textbooks are of the greatest significance. The four stages of linguistic development were related to a sequence of schools: the mother's lap (*gremium maternum*), the public vernacular school (*schola vernacula publica*), the Latin grammar school or gymnasium (*schola latina*), and the university followed by travel (*academia et peregrinationes*).[31] His suggestions for pre-school instruction had been expressed in *School of Infancy*; little beyond recapitulation appeared in *The Great Didactic*. Development of the same studies as outlined in *School of Infancy* continued in the vernacular school, although Comenius did not write on that institution in any detail.

The Latin grammar school was the centre of his interests and in *The Great Didactic* he discussed its reform at length. In his view, its curriculum should deal with all knowledge at increasingly abstract levels. Intended for young people between the ages of twelve and eighteen, its studies were to be based upon the six formal disciplines of grammar, dialectics, rhetoric, ethics, physics and mathematics. Latin was held to be of great importance for through it all scholarship proceeded; consequently for the grammar school Comenius planned a set of graded language textbooks employing the principles already applied in *Vestibulum* and *Janua*. Following the metaphor used by Bateus in *Gateway of Tongues*, Comenius chose titles to correspond to the features of Roman classical architecture. The increasing difficulty of the texts was symbolized by the student's movement into the 'house of learning'. By the progressive cultivation of the Latin language the young person could proceed from the vestibule, through the doorway into the courtyard, thence into the palace of knowledge, there to find in the works of the great authors mankind's earthly treasure.

In *The Great Didactic* the sequence was proposed: to *Vestibulum* and *Janua* were to be added *Atrium* (Courtyard), *Palatium* (Palace) and *Thesaurus* (Treasury). The plan, however, remained undeveloped. A beginning was made several years later with an *Atrium*, but it did not achieve any widespread application. The *Palatium* and *Thesaurus*, designed as readings from classical authors, were never written.

Comenius did not pursue the question of academic studies and wrote very little about the university.[32] It seems, however, that he intended it to be occupied with knowledge at the highest possible level and concerned particularly with the clear expression of ideas, for which responsibility in his view had to be accepted by the scholarly community. To deal with that specific problem he suggested the establishment of an institution which would form, at the same time, the apex of his system of education. This was the College of Light, or Pansophic College, about which he wrote in some detail, his ideas on the subject being recorded in a document written during his London visit of 1641 and first published in Amsterdam in 1668 as *Via lucis* (*The Way of Light*).[33] The College of Light should primarily be concerned with organizing knowledge in such a way that it could be made readily available to all people. Despite the universality of Latin in the scholarly world, Comenius considered it to be inadequate to the task of communication, and, doubtless sensitive to the many criticisms being generated, he felt that education was greatly in need of a new, truly universal language. He believed that one could be devised that would avoid the syntactical and semantic difficulties of Latin, and so be able to act as a universal antidote to confusion of thought. The ideal language should be thoroughly rational and logical, correspond completely to the objects of experience and consequently be easier and more pleasant to learn. Comenius recognized the many difficulties in the way of such a project, however, and was realistic enough to know that he would have to settle for Latin.

Utopia pursued: the Hartlib circle

In 1641 Comenius arrived in London at the invitation of Samuel Hartlib who saw in him a reformer – almost a messiah – equal to the task of advising the new society that he believed was about to eventuate. England at that moment was entering a phase of chiliastic fervour as the Puritan parliamentary faction now seemed, after several decades of struggle with the monarchy, to be gaining the upper hand and in a position to effect a new social order in England. At this moment, for the first time in history, it seemed indeed that mankind might be able to control its affairs, and that the utopian writing of the earlier decades of the century might well prove to be serious blueprints for the millennium. In understanding Comenius' role in this, two sequences of events are involved: the English political struggle between king and parliament that led to civil war; and the energetic, reforming career of Samuel Hartlib.

Political developments in England 1603–1649

James VI of Scotland, son of Mary Queen of Scots, became James I of England in 1603 after the death of Elizabeth I; peace with Spain was negotiated the following year. The nation he ruled had changed appreciably from that of the Tudors, especially as economic and demographic growth had created a new class of gentry who were becoming articulate and educated. They were now demanding an increased share in government, and throughout his reign James I had to contend with them over two particular questions: the rights of the people – meaning chiefly the emergent gentry – and the authority of the crown to raise funds through taxation, a sensitive issue since the king turned out to be extravagant and even profligate. His reign was further complicated by the Thirty Years War into which England was inevitably drawn, especially as Puritanism, with its Calvinist origins, was the dominant religious ethos of the gentry.

Under Charles I, who succeeded James in 1625, the conflict between crown and parliament intensified. Charles married a Catholic, Henrietta Maria of France, sister of Louis XIII; he also had a secret agreement with English Catholics to remove their political disabilities of Tudor provenance, and allied himself closely with Anglo-Catholics. Meanwhile, England was drawn into hostilities with Spain in the Thirty Years War; in 1627–8 the country was also at war with France, chiefly because of maritime and commercial disputes and England's support for the Huguenots. Conflict was inevitable: Charles demanded finances for the war from parliament; the Commons refused until the king satisfied their demand to be more involved in government. In 1629 Charles successfully dissolved parliament and ruled absolutely – and relatively efficiently – for the next eleven years, until he made several impolitic moves against Scotland. The first was to revoke grants of crown land made to Scottish aristocrats by his father James I; the second was to attempt to impose episcopalian government on the Presbyterian Scottish Kirk. The Scots rose in 1640, marched south, and occupied Newcastle and the northern English border territories. Charles needed funds, but parliament refused until he admitted that his autocratic actions violated the historical constitutional rights of the people. Before the issue was settled, the Irish, too, rose in rebellion in 1641. Parliament refused to put the king at the head of an army – fearing he would use it against them – and instead placed itself in command. The king, in August 1642, fled to Nottingham and raised his battle standard, parliament stood firm and in 1643 formed an alliance with the Scots. Civil war ensued and the king's cause foundered: on 14 June 1643 he was defeated and captured at the Battle of Naseby; he escaped to the Isle of Wight, from whence he attempted to lead a second campaign. This failed, and in a highly charged atmosphere the 'Rump' parliament set up a court which eventually sentenced the king to death, the execution taking place on 30 January 1649. For the next eleven years England was a republic, or Commonwealth, presided over for the first nine years by the Lord Protector, Oliver Cromwell (1599–1658).

Here, then, was the one political situation in Europe that seemed to be moving in the direction of the chiliastic cause; steadily throughout the early decades of the century the English people, in the form of the articulate, better-educated Puritan middle and gentry classes, were winning the battle to establish a new society on the basis of what seemed proper doctrines: 'natural law' and the 'social contract'. In such a climate, many intellectuals and reformers were drawn to see England as the model of the new society and the centre of intellectual freedom; it was this very situation which attracted Samuel Hartlib and convinced him that, when the millennium came, it would be in England – or at least in an English territory of the New World. Hartlib himself was the great organizer and entrepreneur of social reform through education in England, and was referred to, by John Winthrop, first governor of Connecticut, as the 'Great Intelligencer of Europe'.[34] This was in many respects an apt description of a man who assiduously cultivated, and sustained, influential contacts at high levels throughout Europe and who, through a clear recognition of his own competence, enlisted the support of others in grandly conceived cooperative enterprises. Indeed, in a later petition to Charles II he recalled that he had sought to act as 'a sollicitor for the Godly ministers and Schollers, who were driven in those days [Thirty Years War] out of the Palatinat and other Protestant Churches then laid waste.'[35]

Samuel Hartlib: the 'Great Intelligencer of Europe'

Samuel Hartlib was born some time in the first years of the seventeenth century (there are no exact records) in the Hanseatic city of Elbing, near Danzig on the Baltic coast, of a Polish merchant father and an English mother. He sought to develop his maternal links with England and was possibly there some time after 1621; certainly he was studying at Cambridge in 1625–6 at the time of Charles I's accession, when that university, at the height of its Puritan enthusiasm, was acting as a religious centre for the country. Adopting England as his permanent home, he plunged into educational reform by starting a school at Chichester in Sussex with innovating intentions; according to his own description it was designed as 'a little Academie for the education of the Gentrie of this Nation, to advance Pietie, Learning, Moralitie, and other Exercises of Industrie not usuall . . . in Common Schooles'.[36] We know very little, however, except that it failed within one year and was the last of his personal efforts at education; thenceforth he adopted an entrepreneurial role. By this time he had made the acquaintance of a future educational reformer, John Dury; he continued to enlarge and sustain his range of contacts to the point at which what virtually amounted to a Hartlib 'circle' was formed.[37]

Hartlib was a general reformer with no deeply held personal mission beyond that of seeing society improved; he was very much guided by individuals who made specific proposals, though the basis of his motivation was Bacon's *New Atlantis* which Hartlib felt a personal vocation to see realized. Early in his career, Hartlib was influenced by the language-reform movement which brought him into contact with Comenius. Indeed, as soon as *Janua linguarum reserata* was published in 1631, Hartlib initiated correspondence, obtaining from Comenius a draft of his projected plans for a total reformation of the educational system of Europe. By 1636 Comenius' *Janua* was being sold in England in an English–Latin version, and Hartlib believed that Comenius was indeed the apostle of the new era that was dawning. Further, without Comenius' knowledge, Hartlib published that draft in 1637 in London under the literal title of a 'prelude to the plans of Comenius', *Conatuum Comenianorum praeludia*, following this with a revised version in 1639 under the title of *Pansophiae prodromus* ('Intimations of a Universal Science'). Although Comenius was discomfited by Hartlib's actions, rapport was maintained.

In that period Hartlib was already dabbling in utopian ventures, having read the existing literature and visited a society in Germany that had formed some time around 1625 and lasted for some twenty years, which planned to establish a community, to be called 'Antilia' (from the Greek *antelios*, 'facing east to the sun', probably a Platonic metaphor drawn from the *Republic*, with allusions also to the Antilles, the major island chain of the Caribbean in the New World). This, and the literature, apparently stimulated Hartlib to write a utopia himself which appeared in 1641 under the title *A Description of the Famous Kingdom of Macaria*, taking the name (Greek *makarios*, happy, blissful) from the neighbours of the Utopians in More's fantasy. Indeed, in the preface Hartlib expressly indicated that he had used as his pattern both Thomas More and Francis Bacon. The utopian thinking in this case was given a practical application: *Macaria* was addressed to the new session of the Long Parliament, dated 25 October, just five days after it had assembled, and was intended to make 'this Kingdome [of England] . . . like to it [Macaria]: when you heare the manner of their government, you will deeme it to be very possible, and withall very easie.'[38] Although Hartlib claimed his treatise to be an advance on the *Republic*, *Utopia* and *New Atlantis*, its rational, pietistic formula for ordered civic life actually added little to these, although it expressed strong faith in Bacon's empiricism by claiming that the use of the inductive method, supervised by a supreme 'College of Experience', would inevitably determine proper courses of action and infallible tenets of belief.

In proposing utopian ventures Hartlib seems to have had encouragement from some parliamentarians, and he arranged for Comenius to visit England in 1641 to put directly to the Commons his educational plans for a College of Light and social reforms based upon pansophic enlightenment. The time seemed appropriate: the Puritans were in the ascendant, chiliasm was growing, and the king was on the defensive, bitterly condemning in June 1642 'that Utopia of religion and government into which they endeavour to transform this Kingdom'.[39] Political events, however, were moving too quickly for the reformers; relations between crown and Commons worsened, and civil war ensued.

Puritanism modified: Milton's Tractate of Education

Although the educational reforming cause wavered, Hartlib did not lose his enthusiasm, and while the civil war continued throughout the 1640s he sought to further his schemes, enlisting the support of the poet John Milton (1608–74), who since 1641 had become increasingly militant in the Puritan cause. In 1644 Milton published his famous *Tractate of Education* concerned, as the preface states, with 'the reforming of education' and dedicated to Hartlib since the treatise had resulted directly from the latter's 'earnest entreaties and serious conjurements'. By this time Milton had become bitterly critical of the existing regime in England and had accepted Hartlib's persuasion that utopian reform with education as a central feature was the proper solution. Milton used this treatise to attack the contemporary political world with which he so strongly disagreed.

In itself, Milton's short *Tractate of Education* did not introduce any startling new ideas; its chief value is in illustrating the degree to which the reforming doctrines were being disseminated among, and accepted by, the intellectual classes. Milton expressly disclaimed any exhaustive treatment of the topic (preferring to leave that to Comenius and others) and offered only an outline, set within the Puritan tradition and asserting that the purpose 'of Learning is to repair the ruins of our first parents by regaining to know God aright',[40] although now acknowledging the emerging empirical tradition since 'our understanding cannot in this body found itself but on sensible things'.[41] Milton accepted the reformers' argument that education had become bankrupt because of its excessive concern with language, so requiring schoolboys to 'spend seven or eight years merely in scraping together so much miserable Latin and Greek, as might be learnt otherwise easily and delightfully in one year'.[42] But his alternative approach turned out to be not the abandonment of formal learning but simply a retracing of the Comenian programme of literary studies, beginning with a 'good grammar' text and eventually progressing to reading, among others, Plutarch, Plato and Quintilian. The *Tractate of Education* was no great reforming document; basically it remained in the tradition of the *pietas litterata*, with the addition of parts of the newly emerging gentleman's training as offered in the courtly academies, along with a recognition of the claims of sense-empiricism, thereby indicating a slight departure from literary Neoplatonism.

Milton's *Tractate*, however, gave Hartlib moral encouragement, if nothing else, and as the fortunes of parliament prospered in the mid-1640s he redoubled his efforts. Inspired by the success of Renaudot's Bureau d'Adresse, operating in Paris since 1633, Hartlib proposed a similar arrangement for England consisting of two divisions: an 'Office of Accommodations', which was to be fundamentally a bureau of employment and social welfare (Hartlib was now deeply concerned about orphans, the poor, the unemployed and the disadvantaged); and an 'Office of Communications', concerned with learning generally. By 1648, with Charles I now a prisoner, parliament was actively considering this proposal and apparently had in mind some such 'office' as a preliminary to a 'College of Light' at Oxford under Hartlib's directorship. The aim was grandly philanthropic and essentially realistic: poor and underprivileged children should be given basic literacy and craft training to fit them for trade apprenticeship, while at the same time what in essence amounted to a national system of education was envisaged, with a three-level structure of 'common' schools for the ordinary people, 'mechanical' schools for pre-apprenticeship training, and 'noble' schools for training an intellectual élite.[43] Provision was made, moreover, for intelligent lower-class pupils to be admitted to the 'noble' schools, so providing some possibility of social mobility in an age when social stratification and a profound acceptance of the concept of a divinely ordained 'station in life' was general among all classes.

A radical reform: Petty's proposal for technical-scientific education

The emphasis on craft training is significant, marking as it does a recognition of changing economic and industrial conditions. Hartlib, of course, was centrally involved, and in 1648 a member of the Hartlib circle, William Petty (1623–87), produced one of the better reforming schemes entitled *The Advice of W. P. to Mr Samuel Hartlib, for the Advancement of Some Particular Parts of Learning*. This short essay advanced the scientific-technical approach of Petty which was in contrast to the literary background of most reformers. The *Advice* made almost a complete break and came out in support of practical education, recommending that book learning be postponed until the child had a sufficiently developed background of real-life experience. So the first school the child attends, he urged, should be a new institution, that of the 'craft centre', though Petty used different terms: '[Let] there be instituted *Ergastula litteraria,* Literary-workhouses, where Children may be taught as well to doe something towards their living, as to Read and Write.'[44] Although his treatise was composed in English, Petty used parallel Latin names for the various institutions he recommended. Here the terminology is revealing. In calling the primary schools *ergastula litteraria* he drew upon the classical Roman word *ergastulum* which was a debtors' workhouse and, by extension, suggested the idea of charity being extended to the lower social classes. Within these *ergastula* all children, from their seventh year on, would receive a primary education, joining in an activity curriculum organized around the belief that they should 'be taught to observe and remember all sensible Objects and Actions, whether they be Naturall or Artificial, which the Educators must on all occasions expound unto them'.[45] Petty advanced cogent reasons for such a programme, chiefly that this kind of work encourages industriousness, an appreciation of the skills of such activities and of the experimental procedures, and he listed altogether fifteen groups of activities – those concerned with carving and modelling, making mathematical instruments, watchmaking, painting, etching and engraving, lapidary arts, lens grinding, botanical arts and gardening, music, instrument making, naval ship modelling, architectural modelling, confectionery, perfuming and fabric dyeing, chemistry and metallurgy, anatomy ('making Sceletons and excarnating bowells'), marine compass and globe construction. The activities are separated into future applications, and Petty suggested that they are propaedeutic to apprenticeship for boys and housewifery for girls.

Building upon the craft centres, Petty envisaged a superstructure of practical, technical and scientific education, and in this respect his proposals closely followed Bacon; indeed, it was from him that Petty borrowed the title 'Advancement of Learning', and so he advocated the plan of Solomon's House with the setting-up of a 'Gymnasium Mechanicum or Colledge of Tradesmen' for technical education, and an advanced academy, containing the 'Fabrick of the House, Garden, Library, Chymicall Laboratorie, Anatomicall Theator, Apotheca, with all, the Instruments and Furniture belonging to each of them'; all this being part of the encyclopedic movement towards the complete classification of knowledge. Throughout the *Advice* emphasis is upon sensory learning as expounded by Bacon, reaching its highest development in the mathematical, physical and mechanical sciences. Language and literature, however, are not denigrated; they are simply put in a broader perspective as just a part of the range of human learning. Writing is recognized as an instrumental skill, as are foreign and classical languages, to be taught only to those who need them for business and professional (including academic) reasons. These, moreover, should be taught by more efficacious and pleasant means than those in current use, although Petty did not indicate how.

Reform from within the tradition: Dury's Reformed School

Petty's *Advice*, however, is a limited document; prescient it certainly was but, in its day, impractical. Reform must proceed on the basis of existing or at least realizable institutions and these were, fundamentally, elementary school, grammar school and university; Comenius' general proposals were the ones consonant with reality. Comenius, however, had left England in 1642 in despair, and in Sweden for the following six years he accepted the less interesting if more practical task of preparing improved textbooks for its schools. The Hartlib circle laboured on and in 1650 Hartlib stimulated John Dury (1598–1680) to write yet more of the great reforming documents of the period. *The Reformed School* and *The Reformed Library Keeper* both appeared in that year, and it was the former that was to be influential. First ordained in Scotland, Dury was further ordained into the Church of England in 1634, subsequently travelling around Protestant Europe in the cause of religious reconciliation, particularly between Lutherans and Calvinists. Increasingly he realized that, despite utopian dreams, little could be done with adults; change, and hence reform, could only be effected through the younger generation, and that necessarily drew him into the educational circle of Hartlib.

Although dependent upon much of the previous literature, *The Reformed School* marks a significant advance in educational thought. At first glance it is certainly less radical than Petty's *Advice* but on closer reading it reveals a major departure in that it contains a new conception of the learner's mind and therefore the sequences, and methods, of instruction. In this lies its significance; in respect of its general approach to educational aims and content it follows the general reforming tradition. Indeed, its aims are much more conservative than those advanced by Petty, whose ideas were those of a scientist; Dury showed his clerical attitudes by expressing similar views to those of Comenius and Milton in stating that, if the world is divinely created and ordered, our purpose in life is to achieve salvation. His curriculum follows that advocated by Comenius and, to an extent, Petty, beginning as it does with real-life experiences and vernacular literacy, and progressing through a sequence of practical and concrete subjects to a final stage of literary and abstract studies.

Dury's attitude to knowledge is essentially the same as that of Comenius who, in using the organic metaphor of the tree, argued that, however manifold the branches may be, they all stem from the one trunk.[46] Dury used a similar analogy – a 'circle of creatures',[47] suggesting a completely interrelated system, the task of education being to ensure that everyone comes into possession of the full range of learning. Here Dury made a departure in pressing his analogy further by arguing that 'to marshal sciences rightly [so] that they may be taught orderly and profitably, the subordination of their several ends to each other (as they jointly relate unto man to supply his defects) and the way of teaching the same (as it is suitable to the capacity of those that are to be taught) must be [properly] observed.' This can be achieved, he claimed, by ensuring that 'the encyclopedia of the sciences must answer the wheel of human faculties, and this wheel must answer the circle of the creatures whence man is to supply his defects.'[48] In this statement lies the essence of Dury's educational significance, for here he recognized the necessary correlation between the logical organization of knowledge and the psychological processes by which that knowledge is attained. In this attitude – and it existed equally in Comenius – is to be found the starting-point of most subsequent pedagogical endeavour.

Learning depends, Dury asserted, upon the proper understanding of human faculties, and in this respect he followed the Baconian view, derived from Aristotle, that the human mind has such powers. The whole notion of mental faculties is classical in origin and, although there are suggestions of this in Plato, it was Aristotle who described the soul as having separate parts or powers for which he used the Greek plural *dynameis*; in the medieval period the Greek word *dynamis* (the singular form) was translated by its Latin equivalent *facultas* (power, means); by the time of Bacon these faculties had become reified into the mental realities of sense, imagination, memory and reason. It is these four, Dury argued, that must be properly harnessed in order to make learning effective. Here, unlike many contemporary reformers, Dury did not use the inductive method so extolled by them; instead, he derived, deductively, a model of how the mind operates. So he wrote that 'as in Nature sense is the servant of imagination, imagination of memory, memory of reason, so in teaching arts and sciences we must set these faculties awork in this order towards their proper objects in everything which is to be taught.'[49] Further, it follows 'that as the faculties of man's soul naturally perfect each other by their natural subordination, so the arts which perfect those faculties should be gradually suggested, and the objects wherewith the faculties are to be conversant according to the rules of the art should be offered in that order which is answerable to their proper ends and not otherwise.' Arguing from the assumption that in children there is a natural sequence for the emergence of mental powers ordered by divine sanction, so he saw an educational programme implied: 'as children's faculties break forth in them by degrees, to be rigorous with their years and the growth of their bodies, so they are to be filled with objects whereof they are capable.'[50]

Dury distinguished four stages in the unfolding or 'breaking forth' of children's 'natural capacities', corresponding to the age groups birth to about five years, five to about nine, nine to thirteen or fourteen, then to twenty; his treatise is concerned with the latter three since these fall within the ambit of the school. The capacity of the age group five to nine is that of sense and imagination, with the beginnings of memory; the group nine to thirteen or fourteen has imagination and memory with the beginnings of reason; the group up to the age of twenty is characterized by the maturation of reasoning, judgement and prudence. Corresponding to these stages of faculty development, then, is a curriculum. For the youngest group it should be reading, writing and arithmetic in the vernacular, along with broad outline history. For the middle group it should expand to an encyclopedic coverage, in the vernacular, of the world in the categories of practical mathematics, geography, astronomy, rural husbandry, anatomy and church history. At the same time this middle group should learn the names of all familiar objects in Latin, Greek and Hebrew, and be introduced to the rudiments of grammar through Comenius' *Janua linguarum reserata*. The oldest group is now prepared to move on to 'all the useful arts and sciences which may fit them for any employment in Church and Commonwealth', specifically 'to read authors in all the sciences whereof they have gained the foundations . . . and out of them to gather to themselves an encyclopedia.'[51]

Lesson sequencing is crucial to his plan, and also marks an advance in pedagogy. For a start, 'the chief rule of the whole work is that nothing may be made tedious and grievous to the children',[52] and to this end the teacher – who needs to be a very superior person indeed – should 'prepare the particular matters of everything which shall be taught for every hour of the day throughout the whole course, and deliver the same in writing quarterly, or monthly (at least) beforehand unto the ushers, that they may be in full readiness and perfectly exercise themselves in everything which they shall deliver to their scholars.'[53] Then follows careful advice on the strict sequence for the delivery of individual lessons. First of all, the aim of the particular lesson should be made quite clear to the class, then should follow an orderly exposition in four steps: the whole, general notion involved should be given first so that it may be grasped by the imagination; second, the lesson should be broken up into its constituent parts so that reason can grasp the interrelationships; third, the whole must be represented so that it is fixed in the memory; fourth, a summary recapitulation should conclude in order to expose and correct doubts and misunderstandings. Yet another advance is suggested: lessons should be no more than half an hour each; they can be combined in two such sessions profitably 'whereof the first part shall be spent in receiving, the second in entertaining the thoughts thereof'.[54]

The Reformed School is an important document in the development of Western educational thought, bringing together many of the separate strands of the reforming movement and, in a clear way, relating the current logic of knowledge to the psychology of learning, and providing new avenues of inquiry. It was, though, in many respects ambitious and unbalanced; in particular, *The Reformed School* glossed over the question of vernacular education in the early years, the securing of adequate sensory percepts, and the easy transfer to the advanced grammar curriculum on which the essential curriculum – still basically *pietas litterata* – necessarily depended.

By this time, however, the utopian reforming movement was beginning to falter and the great expectations held for the Commonwealth, which came into existence with the execution of Charles I in 1649, were not fulfilled. Cromwell did not share any enthusiasm for educational reform; increasingly Hartlib, Milton and Dury became estranged from the government and embittered by establishment hostility towards educational change. England, in fact – on the eve of such possibilities of moving towards a national, equitable system of education – turned in the opposite direction, accepting instead a fragmented, private approach to the support of schools that was not to be seriously questioned for centuries to come.

The immediate Comenian achievement: textbook innovation

Meanwhile, Comenius continued his great labours, and around 1648, while at Elbing writing textbooks for Sweden, produced his third major educational treatise, *Linguarum methodus novissima*, which contained the mature expression of his educational thought. The tenth chapter, translated and published by later scholars under the separate title of *Didaktika analytická* (*Analytical Didactic*),[55] was his third didactic work and contains the notion that, along with the parallel use of Latin and the vernacular, occasional pictorial illustrations might well be included. In that year Comenius was elected Bishop of the Unitas Fratrum and moved back to Leszno. In 1648, too, the Thirty Years War was concluded by the Treaty of Westphalia. Disappointed greatly by the fact that the treaty gave no recognition to his church, Comenius moved yet again to the security of Sáros-Pátak in the independent Hungarian state of Transylvania. There he pursued his dream of universal peace and worked at the reform of its school system. It was there that he conceived and first drafted the book for which he was to be chiefly remembered in the following 200 years: *Orbis sensualium pictus*.

After six years in Sáros-Pátak Comenius returned in 1654 to Leszno. Within a year Poland's refusal to recognize some of Sweden's gains from the Thirty Years War led to conflict; in 1656 the Swedes overran Poland and Leszno suffered destruction. Comenius lost all his personal belongings including a precious twenty-year accumulation of unpublished manuscripts. One of the most significant of these, however, *The General Consultation on the Reform of Human Affairs*, which contains the *Pampaedia* and *Panorthosia*, long thought lost, was rediscovered in the archives of the Francke Orphanage at Halle as recently as the early 1940s.[56] At the time of the fighting Comenius fled to Amsterdam where under the patronage of the de Geer family he lived for the remaining fourteen years of his life, still writing indefatigably. It was from Amsterdam that he directed the publication of *Orbis pictus*.

During the years 1653 and 1654 Comenius outlined the general idea that was to become *Orbis pictus* in a single page, published subsequently in *Opera didactica omnia*. Since it was his belief that nothing enters the intellect except through the senses, and that all learning depends on a prior basis in adequate perceptual experiences, he asserted that a new aid to schooling was required. This was to be a small book, encyclopedic in scope, with the content organized around pictures of objects accompanied by their names and verbal descriptions. The *Janua*, already well known, was to be the basis. By 1654 at Sáros-Pátak Comenius had simplified the text of *Janua*, which, with the addition of illustrations, was to be his new Latin reader, but he noted that neither a suitable artist nor an adequate printer was to be found in Hungary, and the manuscript was sent to Nuremberg, an important centre of book production. Four years later, in Amsterdam, Comenius saw *Orbis pictus* issued in its first edition of 1658 in Latin and German.[57]

In the first edition the text was set in parallel columns, Latin on the left, German on the right. Accompanying each of the 150 chapters was a small woodcut illustration in black and white with numbers indicating objects mentioned in the text. The typography itself was arresting and included an unusual combination of four typefaces, the Latin text being set in the customary roman face with words for illustrated objects and the German text in black-letter or gothic, with specially numbered words in a bolder face. The use of such techniques of visual emphasis in a school book was a considerable innovation. *Orbis pictus* was an immediate success and the following year was published in London in a Latin–English version.

The book was so well received that it was repeated in numerous editions, at first in rapid succession, in the eighteenth century at longer intervals. Many of these were merely reprintings from existing plates; however, *Orbis pictus* appeared in numerous genuine editions in which the text was emended, occasionally updated, and reset in new type. The illustrations too were changed in various editions, in general reflecting increasing sensitivity to the demands of school-book illustration. *Orbis pictus* thereby initiated a tradition of school textbooks designed to be put in the hands of the children themselves. Throughout the eighteenth century large numbers of illustrated texts appeared, all reflecting its influence, one of the most notable being the *New England Primer*.

After the publication of the *Orbis pictus* Comenius withdrew from prominence, and the earlier promise of great educational reform faded. Hartlib and his associates also retired, disillusioned, and the immediate history of education that followed was much less spectacular than they had hoped for. In the great heyday of the reforming movement in the late 1630s the mathematician Professor Johann Adolphus Tassius of Hamburg wrote to Hartlib that 'The zeal of Pansophia and for a better didactic burns in every corner of Europe: if Comenius had furnished nothing more than the great crop of incentives which he had scattered in the minds of all men, he might be considered to have done enough.'[58] Indeed, in the ensuing century the ideals of Comenius, Hartlib and their supporters were acted upon – not always directly, and often without specific acknowledgement, but the increasing pace of educational reforming thought sustained by Locke and then Rousseau was a development of the Comenian dream. Out of the encyclopedism of the seventeenth-century utopians, indeed, was to emerge the most reforming and ambitious of such projects, the famous *Encyclopédie* itself. In its turn, the success of the utopian drive of the eighteenth-century Enlightenment depended upon the slower implementation and consolidation of these reformers' ideas, and the extension of schooling according to their theories. It is to this development that we now turn.

Reformation to Enlightenment: The Extension of Schooling I. The Catholic Conservative Tradition

Catholicism in conflict: education in France

Contemporaneously with the utopian, reforming literature of education a less conspicuous extension of schooling was proceeding throughout western Europe. Although its pace was quite uneven, a pattern can be discerned; its primary emphasis was the consolidation of religious belief through the school; its secondary motivation was to respond to economic, commercial and technological demands. Politically, the seventeenth century was characterized by the collapse of the great Spanish-Austrian Habsburg dynasty with the consequent enfeeblement of Spain, the emergence of France as the greatest nation of Europe under the absolutist rule of Louis XIV (1643–1715), and the strengthening of experiments in bourgeois democracy in England and the United Dutch Provinces. At the same time there was an increasing participation in European affairs of peripheral nations, chiefly those adjacent to England – Scotland, and to a lesser extent Ireland and Wales – along with Scandinavia, Prussia and Russia, and the newly founded European settlements in the New World. The religious crisis in France, however, remained a central issue in Europe; the action of Louis XIV in revoking the Edict of Nantes in 1685, ending a century of toleration towards Protestantism, proved completely ineffectual in stifling Protestant dissent and promoting national unity. The forces of dissent were much greater than any repressive edict could dissolve, and throughout the seventeenth century Catholicism in France was divided not only by the Huguenot confession but from within by continuing Gallicanism, along with the new movement of Jansenism. Into the conflict between these opposing religious forces the school was inevitably drawn.

The complete atrophy of French education contributed to the problem. From medieval times, the universities had retained their control over the grammar schools, Paris having thirty-six such *grandes écoles*, others proportionately less. Only in university cities was a full education available; elsewhere only elementary schooling was possible, on a desultory basis in the *petites écoles* in one-room schools run by parish churches. Nominally these were open to all, boys and girls; in practice, since neither the state nor the church provided any funds for the parish schools, which therefore had to charge fees, their clientele was limited to the merchant classes. This led to fierce competition with the writing-masters, *maîtres écrivains*, as well as teachers of arithmetic, bookkeeping and similar studies to whom the more commercially minded groups frequently sent their children, boys almost exclusively. The writing-masters claimed their rights under a monopoly granted to them in 1570 by Charles IX for the teaching of writing, spelling and accounting – which also put them under the control of the civic authorities instead of the *écolâtre* – and they frequently instigated litigation against the *petites écoles* whose role, they argued, should be solely that of teaching reading for grammatical, literary and scriptural studies.[1] Well-to-do families educated their girls at home with tutors; the working classes in the main were unable to do anything except rely upon charity, and this, in effect, was the next development in the extension of schooling in France – and much of Europe – with the appearance of a new educational phenomenon, the teaching congregations of the Catholic Church.

The teaching congregations: Ursulines, Oratorians, Piarists

Such groups had been in existence for centuries as societies of monks, priests and nuns, originally in monastic and conventual orders. These societies, as well as other groups that either developed from them or were founded independently, made contributions to education in varying degrees, especially the Dominicans and Jesuits, but none was expressly founded for educational purposes; conducting schools was only part of their mission. In the sixteenth century teaching societies came into existence and in the seventeenth century consolidated their activities widely. Within the Catholic Church there are three grades of such organization: the simplest is the loosely structured 'association'; then follows the 'congregation' whose members subscribe to a Rule with 'simple' vows which may be revoked or dispensed, according to due process of canon law; finally is the 'order' whose members must be males accepted into the priesthood with 'solemn', that is, irrevocable, vows. The word 'order' also has a wider general meaning, designating other forms of religious association.

Most of the sixteenth-century teaching congregations deliberately stayed at this intermediate level, guided by the Benedictine vow of 'stability', in order to remain steadfastly committed to their express purpose, having originally appeared as simple associations of persons providing charitable education for the underprivileged. Of these the earliest for boys were the Oratorians and Piarists, for girls the Ursulines, all originating in Italy. The Ursulines were the first of these, having been founded in the city of Brescia in Lombardy in 1535 by Angela Merici (1474–1540), of the Franciscan order, who concerned herself with the teaching of girls as well as hospital care of women. In adopting a name, Angela chose the legend of an early church martyr St Ursula who supposedly led a pilgrimage from Britain to Rome of 11,000 female virgins who on returning home were massacred by Huns near Cologne. Extension of the image to that of a celibate female teaching order was easy, and in 1535 the association began in Brescia with each member living at home under a simple promise, going out each day to teach. Papal approval was granted in 1544 by Paul III; in 1572 the association was upgraded to congregation status by Gregory XIII when a Rule and simple vows were required. The society grew rapidly, following the Rule of Augustine, with the members taking a vow of stability to devote themselves exclusively to education.

The Ursulines established a French mother house in the papal enclave of Avignon, and from there the Ursuline order, and a considerable number of others following its model, spread throughout France in the late sixteenth and early seventeenth centuries. Among these one of the most stimulating influences was that of Anne de Xainctonge (1567–1621),[2] whose early religious vocation drew her to remedy the deficiencies in the education of girls for whom she felt a Jesuit-style counterpart school should be devised, there being only three *petites écoles* for girls in the large city of Dijon where she was born. In 1595, to escape her father's prohibition on following a religious vocation, Anne fled to the city of Dôle in the nearby Spanish Habsburg territory of Franche-Comté where, under friendly Jesuit auspices, she opened a school for thirty girls, following the principles of the *Ratio studiorum* and the organizational model of the Ursulines. This religious community attracted mature women, particularly widows (a disproportionately large segment of the population, owing to the depredations of the wars), and a tighter structure developed, based upon strict enclosure and solemn vows. In June 1606 the community was approved by the *parlement* of Franche-Comté and Anne became the leader of the Ursulines' expansion from Italy to France. In 1612 all Parisian Ursuline houses were granted solemn vows and strict enclosure by Pope Paul V. The Ursuline order then grew rapidly. In Franche-Comté and adjacent Switzerland seven schools were founded on the Dôle model between 1615 and 1621; Ursuline schools, following Anne's example, spread rapidly throughout France and French Canada, and stimulated similar societies – Les Filles de la Croix, Les Filles de la Présentation, Les Filles de la Pénitence and Les Filles de Notre-Dame, among others.

Anne's school at Dôle, and the Ursulines, like most of the teaching congregations, introduced no startling innovations; nor were they influenced by the reforming, utopian literature. Their aims were simple and realistic. At Dôle the school followed a Jesuit pattern of organization into classes, beginning with learning the alphabet, and going on to simple reckoning, reading and writing, although it is significant that Anne taught in French; Latin was learned as a second language for use in reading prayers and psalms. There was, however, no French literary component to the curriculum; the aims were exclusively religious and devotional, although some practical elements were included: church singing and embroidery of ecclesiastical furnishings.

The Jesuits, having received papal approval in 1550, rapidly developed a major interest in education for boys and eleven years later established schools in France. The Jesuits provided free education and accepted poor boys if they were talented and could survive the rigorously selective programme of the *Ratio studiorum*. Popular, basic education in French for boys was supplied by others, particularly the teaching congregations of the Oratorians and the Piarists, both introduced early in the seventeenth century.

The earlier of these congregations was that of the Oratorians, which grew out of the activities of Philip Neri (1515-95) in Rome. Philip was born in Florence, the son of a notary, and after an education in the famous Dominican convent of San Marco became interested in caring for pilgrims and invalids. He took priest's orders in 1551, living in the convent of San Girolamo where he gathered a group of dedicated associates who in 1575 formed the Congregation of the Oratory, named after the chapel in which they conducted their spiritual obligations (Latin *oratio*, 'prayer' in ecclesiastical usage). Neri became a popular figure in Rome and extremely influential, being the confidant of popes and cardinals; he was, moreover, dedicated to making prayer and churchgoing attractive, and his emphasis upon liturgy and sacred music in the Oratory of San Girolamo introduced the musical form and name of the oratorio, a dramatic composition for solo and orchestra on a scriptural theme. Music, devotion, concern for pilgrims, convalescents and education were the main concerns of this congregation. It received papal approval of its Rule by Paul V in 1612.

Meanwhile, Neri's influence was spreading and in 1611 the possibilities of the Oratory were recognized by the French reforming priest Pierre de Bérulle (1575-1629), later translated to a cardinalcy in 1627, who established in France the Oratoire de Jésus-Christ which received papal approval in 1613. Basically concerned with spiritual devotions, the French Oratorians adopted a centralized administration under a Superior-General, unlike the independent Italian houses, and turned their attention to the education of boys, thereby incurring the hostility of the Jesuits. Although not originally a teaching congregation, the French Oratorians soon made this the principal focus of their work and found wide scope for their activities, beginning with a college at Dieppe given to them in 1614 and expanding to thirty-four schools by the end of the seventeenth century.[3] Like the Ursulines, the Oratorians followed the trend of teaching through the vernacular and, although Latin authors – chiefly scriptural and historical – were the staple of the advanced curriculum, Latin was approached as a second language. The emphasis in their teaching, which was given free of charge if necessary – although fees were gladly accepted – was on the *pietas litterata*; they also taught geography and French history, both through the vernacular; in addition they offered mathematics as a serious discipline, being influenced by the growing developments in the scientific revolution and the work of Descartes.

Almost simultaneously appeared the Piarists, founded in Rome in 1602 by Joseph Calasanctius (1556-1641). Born in Spain and educated at the universities of Valencia and Alcalá, José Calasanza was ordained in 1583 and went to Rome in the service of the church in 1592 when he became deeply concerned about the large number of homeless and vagabond children. He opened a free school for them in 1597 and established, five years later, an austere society of 'Poor Priests of the Mother of God' who took a vow of stability to devote themselves exclusively to educational good works, taking their popular name Piarists ('atoners' or 'supplicants') from their full title, 'Regulares pauperes Matris Dei scholarum piarum'. The school was immediately popular and by 1612, when it moved to its permanent location in the Torres Palace in Rome, it had an enrolment of more than 1000 boys, an indication of the demand for schooling in a city of some 300,000 people. By 1617 the society was given congregation status by Paul V, whereupon it expanded rapidly, like the Oratorians, as an instrument of the Catholic Reformation, houses being set up throughout Spain and its empire, France, Italy and other Catholic territories in Europe. Its political career, however, was rather chequered; Calasanctius himself quarrelled and intrigued within the order and was in danger at one time of being imprisoned; after his death in 1641 disputes increased and from 1645 to 1669 the order was degraded by the pope. After 1672, however, the Piarists were restored and in the eighteenth century became an important part of the educational system of France, although like other teaching orders, despite their universalist aims, they reached only a minority of the population, and the wealthier sector at that.

Jansenism and the Port-Royal schools

France was internally insecure in the seventeenth century and, although Richelieu guided the country through the perilous years of the Thirty Years War with consummate skill, it remained divided into three factions: Protestant Huguenots, orthodox Roman Catholics and 'puritan' Catholics known as Jansenists. A fourth group also had an existence, within the fold of orthodoxy – the Gallicans, whom Richelieu was suspected of favouring. Both the Huguenots and the Jansenists sought to implement their religious beliefs, in part, by means of education, and in both cases this led to serious division within the country. The Huguenots had reached a settlement in 1598 with the Edict of Nantes, and throughout most of the seventeenth century developed a separate educational system; Jansenism was a seventeenth-century movement which in its brief existence had a wide following and threatened to split France apart, with the obvious political consequence of collapse in the face of hostile neighbours on all borders.

Fundamentally, Jansenism was a puritan movement of reform from within which, yet again, opposed the visible wealth, luxury and worldliness of the Catholic Church. Its name came from Cornelius Otto Jansen, Bishop of Ypres after 1636, whose theological work *Augustinus*, which appeared in 1640, was taken from the teaching of Augustine of Hippo of the fourth–fifth century AD and maintained that, regardless of our acts, divine grace is necessary for salvation. The doctrine appeared to deny free will and hence man's own efforts at self-improvement as well as the intercessory and teaching mission of the church itself, and so was condemned by Innocent X as a heresy in 1653. Meanwhile, it had attracted a large following, including Oratorians, who accepted its rather Calvinist doctrine of predestination moderated by an interpretation which led them to believe that grace may be gained by leading a daily life of exemplary moral quality. The emphasis, then, was not upon weekly ceremonial churchgoing but upon a totally rigorous twenty-four-hour daily devotion to god in every act. Education, of course, assumed prime importance, for it became a principal means whereby the individual could be disciplined towards moral perfection.

Such actions were best undertaken in a community, and Jansenism was first propagated in the convent of Port-Royal in the 1630s. Although its doctrines received their full expression in the *Augustinus* of 1640, they had been circulating in more diffuse form for nearly thirty years, owing to the combined labours of Jansen and his associate Jean Duvergier de Hauranne (1581–1643), later to be known by his official title as the Abbé de Saint-Cyran (and, more simply, Saint-Cyran). Both were students at Paris between 1604 and 1610 and then at an estate owned by Duvergier de Hauranne at Bayonne to which they retreated in the years 1610–17, and where the essential theology of the *Augustinus* was developed. In 1617 Jansen went as principal of the College of St Pulcheria in Louvain in the Spanish Netherlands; Duvergier de Hauranne went to Poitiers as secretary to the bishop, moving on in 1620 to become abbot of Saint-Cyran near Poitiers. Jansen died of the plague in 1636, having barely finished the *Augustinus*; Saint-Cyran had already gone to Paris and taken up residence in the convent of Port-Royal in 1633, where as spiritual director he became the leading force in French Jansenism.

The original convent of Port-Royal, some twenty-five kilometres south-west of Paris, had become run-down and in 1608 was reformed by its abbess Jacqueline Arnauld, member of a powerful family. The new convent became so popular that in 1625 the Abbess Angélique (her religious name) moved it into the city where it was known as Port-Royal-de-Paris to distinguish it from its sister foundation of Port-Royal-des-Champs. Under Saint-Cyran the convent became the vigorous centre of the reforming movement, and he was responsible for propagating the as yet unpublished *Augustinus* of Jansen. In the same period Port-Royal became a retirement home for ageing priests or 'solitaries'[4] whom Saint-Cyran enlisted as teachers in the schools he was directing both for girl boarders and day boys. The schools slowly began to achieve distinction under his guidance, although Saint-Cyran was not to finish his work, having fallen foul of Richelieu after declining his offer of further preferment in Paris, for reasons unknown. In 1638 Saint-Cyran was arrested and imprisoned in the Donjon de Vincennes for five years, in which period he wrote his famous *Christian and Spiritual Letters* (*Lettres chrétiennes et spirituelles*). These, when published on his death in 1643, the year of his release, provided the Jansenist education movement with its necessary theoretical foundations.

Despite the opposition of Richelieu, the enmity of the Jesuits and the death of Saint-Cyran (in the same year as Richelieu), the Jansenist movement was not stopped and the schools of Port-Royal continued to offer an alternative Catholic education to that given by the orthodox teaching congregations. For the ensuing thirty years there was constant harassment of the movement. Upon the arrest of Saint-Cyran in 1638 the schools, which had been specifically designated *petites écoles* in order to avoid conflict with the Jesuits, were dispersed, but they were reassembled the following year; in 1646 they moved to larger quarters in Paris and were joined by several enthusiastic teachers. One of these, Pierre Coustel (1621–1704), was the author of their basic educational text, *Les Règles de l'éducation des enfants* of 1687; others also wrote important treatises on education, including Pierre Nicole (1625–95) and Antoine Arnauld (1612–94). In 1656 the boys' school was closed by Richelieu's successor Mazarin on the instigation of the Jesuits; the convent, moreover, was Gallican in sympathy and in 1660, having reassembled, was also shut down. The following year the girls' school was closed and, although it reopened in 1669 during a period of temporary tolerance, in 1679 it was permanently dispersed, the nuns of the convent remaining until 1709 when they too were expelled; in the period 1710–13 the buildings of Port-Royal-des-Champs were demolished and the site desecrated. Jansenism, however, was not stamped out, despite the violent antipathy of Louis XIV to schisms and the continued hostility of the papacy, dominated by Jesuits. Even after the condemnatory bull of 1705 by Clement XI and the bull *Unigenitus* of 1713 which finally condemned its theology as heretical, Jansenism continued throughout the eighteenth century, chiefly in the Netherlands and northern Italy.

In education the Jansenists made significant contributions, chiefly because their work was a distinct advance on anything else at the time. Generally, their educational ideas were drawn from Christian Neoplatonism and looked back to Augustine. The ultimate aim of education, Saint-Cyran wrote, was 'what we desire above all things for our children: their salvation', this constituting a process whereby we are able 'to lift them by degrees from their degradation'.[5] Following Bacon, however, the notion of mental faculties was incorporated in their theory, their major theorist Coustel in his important *Rules for the Education of Children* of 1687 writing that education cultivates children's 'two chief faculties, that is, the intellect and the will; the intellect by making the children study the humanities, the will by training them in virtue',[6] and to this Coustel added the third area of good manners.

Like all dedicated Christian educators of the period, the Port-Royalists remained preoccupied with the teaching of Latin, and a great deal of Coustel's writing was directed at that intransigent problem. The Jansenists were in favour of using the vernacular as the basis of instruction, recognizing that Latin by this time was the language only of the learned few and that the problem had become one of finding the best method of teaching Latin as a second language, by means of the vernacular. Coustel and his colleagues held a number of wise attitudes, urging physical punishment as a last resort, and suggesting that learning should be presented where possible in the form of pastimes and games, while sequences should be graded so that 'we should always proceed from the easy to the difficult, from the known to the unknown'.[7] Although they recognized that Latin had to be learnt, they rejected the grammar of Despauterius in the three-volume edition by Estienne, the *Commentarii grammatice* of 1536, which had been adopted in France by the Jesuits and then by other congregations as a standard text, on the grounds that Latin grammar and pronunciation are different from French, and education has to begin, and essentially remain, in the vernacular. Equally they rejected Comenius' *Janua linguarum reserata*; indeed, Nicole criticized this when he complained that the

... French, Dutch, Germans and Italians have idolized a certain book called the *Gate of Language* which comprises almost all the Latin words which are used in continuous and connected discourse; and they have imagined that by making children learn this book they would soon get to know the Latin language without the necessity of reading so many authors.[8]

Their endeavour to reform language teaching followed in the sixteenth-century tradition of seeking a rational, logical form – *ratio* or *ordine* – but, influenced by Cartesianism, they developed the belief that language has a 'natural' order which, like geometry, contains a necessary sequence through which ideas become intelligible and hence known.[9] This, of course, would be facilitated by teaching grammar first in the vernacular where the pattern of ideas could be more readily understood. So the *Grammaire de Port-Royal* of 1660, under the editorship of Arnauld, was composed in the vernacular and attempted to present language teaching by finding a 'natural' order for the presentation of ideas in French and then applying these to Latin. Although a distinct advance at the time, it inevitably led to the 'substitution' approach to language teaching whereby the known, familiar elements are presumed to correspond exactly with those in the second language.

After the boys' school had been permanently dispersed in 1660, the nuns maintained the girls' school on a much more restricted scale, concentrating on prayers, convent housekeeping, attending mass and the study of sacred literature – all this being dominated by the deliberate cultivation of a deep sense of guilt. The girls were taught 'to understand that perfection does not consist in performing a number of private acts, but in carrying out what they do in common properly, that is, with all their heart and for the love of God, with a sincere desire to please Him and to fulfil always His holy will with joy.'[10] In this admonition written by Jacqueline Pascal is the essential Jansenist position: the day-by-day, minute-by-minute search to serve god, to offer atonement, to seek grace for one's soul in the afterlife of eternity.

The puritan sombreness of Port-Royalist education, however, was normal for its period, and it should not obscure the advances contained within their practices. Their concern to make learning pleasant, sequentially graded and meaningful; to base it on the vernacular and to regard Latin as a second language; to introduce history and geography, and some mathematics; the recognition of individual differences; the stress upon positive rewards for success rather than physical pain for failure; and, in particular, their concern to seek for 'natural' order in instruction that would assist learning by following in correct sequence: these were all improvements on much prevailing thought and practice. Indeed, although their beliefs were attacked and their schools closed, the Port-Royalist influence penetrated into French educational practice in the ensuing years.

The persecution of the Port-Royalists, in fact, began after the Treaty of Westphalia which in 1648 ended the Thirty Years War. At the same time, in the late 1640s, Louis XIV was confronted with a series of civil wars known as the Fronde, which were not settled until 1653. There followed a period of relative peace in which the king sought to eliminate all further opposition. In 1667 hostilities erupted between England and the Dutch, France being bound to assist the latter by a treaty of 1662. By this time all three powers bordering the English Channel were in a commercial conflict which centred on the Channel, the North Sea and the northern European plain. Although the Anglo-Dutch war was settled within a year, instability continued for the next half-century – exacerbated by the collapse of the Habsburg House of Spain, which affected Spanish territories in Germany and the power of the Austrian house. Not until the Treaty of Utrecht in 1713 were these conflicts resolved, when the map of Europe was settled on reasonably nationalistic lines; at that time the boundaries begin to approximate their modern locations.

When Mazarin died in 1661 Louis assumed personal rule, assisted by Jean-Baptiste Colbert as his First Minister, and determined upon absolute control, seeking to sustain one faith, one law, one monarch ('une foi, une loi, un roi'). Throughout the 1670s Louis XIV was confronted by the Triple Alliance of the English, Dutch and Swedish; France, however, easily met these challenges, especially as Spain was continuing to be less of a threat from the south. During this period Louis had become influenced by François Michel Le Tellier Louvois, Minister for War, and by Madame de Maintenon, whom Louis married in 1684, in a morganatic union, upon the death of his Spanish wife Maria Teresa. Madame de Maintenon came to influence much of court life after 1683 and was particularly interested in education, persuading Louis that the Huguenot problem could be solved by a successful re-education programme. It was in such a spirit that Louis moved against that other major political and religious division within French society.

Destruction of Huguenot education

Following the Edict of Nantes of 1598 the Huguenots had seized the opportunity to establish within a decade six academies and thirty-five colleges which paralleled the Jesuit system and provided a Protestant alternative. As Europe moved into the Thirty Years War, pressure was increased on the Huguenots who in 1622 (the year Richelieu came to power) were restricted to two fortified cities, La Rochelle and Montauban. Indeed the cardinal accelerated attacks upon them and in a period of civil war the Huguenots were defeated and subdued by the final treaty of 1629, the Grâce d'Alais. They continued to be tolerated, however, and their schools remained open, providing a curriculum similar to those of the Jesuits and the teaching congregations, differing only in theology. There was no further development; indeed, a decline set in, especially after Mazarin's death in 1661 and Louis XIV began to extend the absolutism of his rule.[11] Louis gave an increasingly narrow interpretation to the Edict of Nantes and in 1670 Huguenot schools were restricted to teaching basic literacy and numeracy. Already, however, Louis's repressive policy was taking effect and Huguenots were steadily – often clandestinely – emigrating to the surrounding Protestant states of Switzerland, the Dutch Provinces, England and Prussia, and overseas to the North American colonies, thus weakening those Protestant communities remaining in France.

Pressure against the Huguenot's increased considerably in the 1670s and 1680s, as it did against the Jansenists, and in 1681 Huguenot children were given the 'right' at the age of seven to renounce their religion and convert to Catholicism.[12] The pace of physical force was stepped up from 1683 when the mounted musket-firing infantry, the Dragoons, attacked and occupied Huguenot centres in bitter offensives known as Dragonnades; by 1685 the king declared that the Huguenots had willingly abjured their Protestant beliefs and that henceforth there was no further need for the Edict of Nantes. From Fontainebleau in October of that year he issued a new edict, the so-called 'Revocation of Nantes', in which the preamble states that 'God has at last allowed our peoples to enjoy perfect quiet [and we are now able to restore Catholic unity to France] since the better and more numerous part of our subjects of the aforesaid so-called Reformed religion has embraced the Catholic religion'. It would therefore be best to efface the whole sad 'memory of the disorders' and the consequent 'confusion and evils' by 'revoking completely the Edict of Nantes and the specific articles which have been granted as a consequence of it, and everything which has been done in favour of the aforesaid religion'.[13] In a short decree of eleven articles, French Protestantism was suppressed through provisions for the destruction of Huguenot churches, banning assembly of persons for any cause, the immediate exiling of all unconverted pastors, and the closing of Huguenot schools. The latter were specifically dealt with in Article 7: 'We prohibit private schools for the instruction of children of the so-called Reformed religion and everything in general which can make any concession, whatever it may be, in favour of this religion.'

The Edict also made 'positive' provisions in that it offered to abjuring clergy pensions greater than their former stipends and concessions to enable them to graduate quickly with the degree of Doctor of Laws. Children were commanded to be rebaptized as Catholics on pain of a 500-*livres* fine; emigrants could return to France under total amnesty; those who fled the country, if caught, would have their property confiscated, the men sent to the galleys, the women imprisoned. In response, some 200,000 Huguenots fled France.[14] Like Jansenism, French Protestantism was crushed, and although it maintained a tenuous, clandestine existence it ceased to be effective and Huguenot education stopped functioning in the late seventeenth century.

More problems were created than were solved, however, since the Huguenots had made a sizeable contribution to French education and the closing of their schools merely aggravated the situation. This was in no way alleviated by the royal edict of 1698 which decreed that all children between the ages of seven and fourteen should be compulsorily enrolled in Catholic schools. There simply were not the facilities available. The decree legislated for the position of *intendant* to be appointed to each school district to supervise the collection of funds and the teaching of reading, writing and Catholic doctrine, but nothing eventuated. As it happened, many individual donations and bequests were made, usually to the parish church or cathedral, for school support. It was in such a climate of concern – heightened by the disorder caused by the suppression of Jansenists and Huguenots, which climaxed a century not only of religious and political wars but also of depression, economic stagnation and static population levels – that one of France's most illustrious teaching congregations had its beginnings, this being the Frères des Écoles Chrétiennes (Brothers of the Christian Schools).

La Salle and the Brothers of the Christian Schools

This congregation was in no way connected with the Huguenot or Jansenist problems, although even within the fold of Catholic orthodoxy it struggled for many years for recognition and acceptance. Its origins lie in the efforts of a wealthy widow, Madame de Maillefer, to found charity schools in Reims. She had, through the Franciscan, Father Barré, been able to establish several girls' schools; in seeking to complement these with boys' schools Nicolas Roland, a canon of Reims Cathedral, recommended to her the work in Rouen in the 1660s of Adrian Nyel, who had opened four schools under civic administration. Nyel offered to help and in 1679 arrived in Reims; since Roland had died the previous year, Nyel was introduced to his associate, another canon of the cathedral, Jean-Baptiste de La Salle (1651–1719). At that time La Salle had no particular interest in founding any teaching congregation; he was an intelligent, wealthy patrician of Reims who had been educated at the conservative anti-Jansenist seminary in Paris, Saint-Sulpice, and seemed destined, as befitted his social rank, to rise to high preferment within the church. He was, however, excessively pious and given to acts of considerable devotion; in his view, schooling merely made people clever; they need education – that is, Christian conversion and cultivation – if they are to fulfil their divinely appointed vocation. So he accepted an interest in Nyel's work and helped to establish schools.

The story of the early years is complex and fascinating, as La Salle attempted to draw teachers together and to develop an appropriate system.[15] There was no idea at the time of a religious congregation; the schools were to be voluntary, charitable institutions. Within three years, by 1682, three schools were operating in Reims and one in nearby Laôn; the following year, in order to devote himself fully to the schools, La Salle resigned his canonry and in 1684 gave away his fortune to the starving during a famine. Now regarded by the wealthy burghers and the church establishment as bordering on insanity, he organized the teachers (who had a rapid turnover) into a group of enthusiasts as the Institute of the Brothers of the Christian Schools, even though his headship as a priest was anomalous, and a habit was adopted for daily dress. At this stage, however, the 'institute' was not recognized; indeed it was strongly opposed, but the work grew and an organization of elementary schools developed, teaching reading, writing, singing and religion, along with a novitiate of intending brothers and a seminary for their training, particularly concerning itself with training novices for a teaching vocation. In 1686, immediately after the Edict of Fontainebleau, the Abbé Chennevières addressed a memorandum to Louis XIV urging an educational programme to restore Catholicism, pointing out the need to establish a training college for men and women teachers in each diocese.[16] This memorandum was not acted upon but in 1690 at Saint-Sulpice, where the movement had spread, such a training institute was established by La Salle, the first specifically designed teachers' college in France, and one of the first in Europe – if not the first.

Gradually La Salle was recognized as saintly rather than insane; the work was increasingly accepted, requests for foundations came in, the Brothers spread down the valley of the Rhône to Avignon, throughout the basin of the Seine, and eastwards. Sunday schools for dissolute youths were organized, technical trade training in a few basic crafts was offered; in 1705 the Institute established new headquarters at the old Château of Saint-Yon in Rouen. The sudden burgeoning of their work, however, created difficulties, for they were accused of trespassing on the rights of the Guild of Writing Masters who commenced a suit in 1706. Over the century the guild had been prepared to tolerate some overlap by the charity and congregation schools, particularly if they were under ecclesiastical control, and if the writing was of a basic kind, chiefly to assist reading; however, the craft of writing in its fullest sense – that is, calligraphy, adornment, illumination – they jealously guarded as their own preserve. After much litigation the Brothers were restrained and fined. Although this inhibited their progress, they survived and throughout the early eighteenth century developed a highly systematic method of teaching.

To guide the schools La Salle had written a manual – which circulated only in manuscript (as did their Rule), and so was continually revised – entitled *La Conduite des Écoles Chrétiennes (The Conduct of Christian Schools)*. These institutions were orthodox in educational aims and theory of learning; emphasis was upon classroom management. The chief concern of the teacher, according to *The Conduct of Christian Schools*, is to establish order among pupils and the priority of his authority. Classes of a hundred boys to a single master were the norm, so that order and authority would necessarily be paramount and should be effected by imposing silence whenever possible. Lessons in the basic curriculum, reading, writing, spelling, arithmetic and bookkeeping, should commence and conclude with prayer; lessons were given in the vernacular – thereby contrasting with the Jesuits – and emphasis was upon utility and practicality.

Discipline of the coercive kind inevitably had to follow and, although La Salle counselled against brutality, he sanctioned caning and strapping as a corrective. Thus he remained within the ascetic tradition of Christianity.

Despite the lack of innovation – or rather because of their traditionalism – the Institute of the Brothers of the Christian Schools expanded, particularly in France, and (especially as La Salle grew older) it became imperative for the congregation to be more precisely regulated. In 1717 the Brothers held a General Assembly which led to a definitive Rule in 1718, the year before La Salle's death. One provision was that all future Superiors must be brothers only and not in priestly orders. The Rule required the three regular vows of poverty, chastity and obedience, a fourth of stability which had been growing in frequency among teaching orders, and a fifth to teach the poor gratuitously. In 1724 the crown issued legal status by letters patent; in 1725 the Holy See gave papal approval to the Rule, thereby legitimizing their long struggle for recognition. In 1720 *The Conduct of Christian Schools* appeared in its first printed copy and in 1730 La Salle's *Meditations* were published. At La Salle's death there were thirty-six schools; seventy years later, at the outbreak of the Revolution, the Brothers of the Christian Schools had become a major teaching congregation in France with 121 communities and over 1000 brothers.[17] Like all the religious orders and congregations, they were roughly treated by the revolutionaries and were dispersed in 1790, but in 1803 Napoleon re-established them and in 1808 they were incorporated into the Imperial University.

Popular literacy and the education of girls

From the Edict of Fontainebleau of 1685, through into the eighteenth century under the *ancien régime*, the schools of France showed a steady expansion chiefly due to the Jesuits and the teaching congregations. The Jesuits held an almost complete monopoly of higher education, especially since the 'reformed' statutes of the University of Paris of 1600 gave them control of that institution, and with a high degree of political acumen they moved in the eighteenth century away from free schooling for the poor and underprivileged towards making their colleges the preserves of the aristocracy and the well-to-do, leaving the lower social levels to the congregations. So France developed a dual system of clerically controlled schools, although a great part of the population was still unprovided for in that basic literacy was not attained by even half of the people. Using the simple test of ability to sign the parish marriage register, the famous demographic inquiry of Louis Maggiolo, published in 1880 under the authority of Jules Ferry, Minister for Public Instruction, discovered that in the period 1686-90 some 75 per cent of the total population of France could not sign.[18] Moreover, this figure is an average; 86 per cent of women could not sign as compared to 64 per cent of men. For Catholic Europe as a whole, this is consonant with a reliable conjecture that between 70 and 80 per cent of the population was illiterate in the sense of being unable to read or write basic material, while Protestant Europe was significantly better with estimates of 55-65 per cent illiteracy.[19] These gross statistics, of course, do not reveal the internal distribution of literacy which for the urban bourgeoisie was close to universal – at least 90 per cent – compared with approximately 65 per cent for urban artisans and little more than 10 per cent for rural peasants.[20]

Even though there was considerable progress in the extension of schooling in seventeenth- and eighteenth-century France, the available demographic data, however inadequate, indicate a major imbalance: girls were considerably less well provided for, and little was to be done to redress this until the nineteenth century. Despite the success of the girls' schools in Reims patronized by Madame de Maillefer – and we read of 1000 girls being instructed there in 1670 by the congregation she supported, the Sisters of the Holy Child Jesus[21] – the provisions for girls were poorer. The Ursulines were the leading group, maintaining 320 convents in France by the year 1700,[22] while in Paris in the same period, all told, there were 167 girls' schools supported by various authorities and congregations, although most would have been small one-teacher operations. The reasons are many but, basically, they all stem from the character of social and economic life in the period. Division of labour between the sexes and status distinctions within society were very profoundly marked, and for girls there was neither the need nor the opportunity for the practical application of many of the educational skills given to boys. As a result of the congruence of the classical and the Christian traditions, the prevailing religious framework of life conceived 'true' education to consist essentially in the prior attainment of moral virtue, with intellectual achievement as a secondary desideratum: piety was the expressed goal. This, of course, was easily obtained by girls if they could read in the scriptures and be carefully counselled, by a religious director if from the upper classes, in a convent if from the lower. There were only two acceptable courses open to girls, either marriage or the convent, and these represented sanctuary in an age when the physical dangers facing women were very great. In addition, prevailing moral codes were hypocritical in the extreme and in the case of pregnancy – for married and unmarried alike – there was an appallingly high maternal death rate of around 25 per cent; for infants there was a 25 per cent mortality in the first year of life, a further 25 per cent for the first fifteen years. When half the population failed to reach puberty, when puerperal fever was endemic and often fatal, and when coition often meant pregnancy, middle- and upper-class parents took extreme care in supervising their daughters, ensuring that education took a fundamentally moral emphasis.

At the same time, moreover, women were regarded as intellectually inferior to men, and these male attitudes were brilliantly satirized in Molière's play of 1672, *Les Femmes savantes*, where male contempt for – and clearly deeper insecurity about – erudite women is given a merciless, if farcical, exposure. So Ariste abuses his sister and her interest in books by telling her to burn them all, continuing:

> ... our fathers knew what they were talking about when they said a woman is learned enough if she can tell a doublet from a pair of breeches. Their wives didn't read ... instead of books they had a thimble and needles and thread to sew their daughters' trousseaux. Women today ... want to write books and become authors. No learning is too deep for them ... and here, in my house, they know everything – except – what they need to know. .... Nobody knows how the pot is cooking.[23]

Molière, for his part, recognized the intrinsic intellectual equality of women and used his own particular skills to work towards it; so too did his contemporary, François de Salignac de la Mothe-Fénelon (1651–1715), whose *Treatise on the Education of Girls (Traité de l'éducation des filles)* of 1687, and the educational novel *Télémaque* of 1693–4, defend the intellectual education of girls but at the same time place his recommendations in a realistic setting.

Fénelon wrote his tract *On the Education of Girls* in 1681, and published it in 1687, specifically as advice for Huguenot converts in his official capacity as superior of the Paris convent of *Catholiques Nouvelles* (New Catholics), which was essentially a mission to the Huguenots. Yet it is in no way a proselytizing treatise and bears no evidence of the audience for which it was intended. 'Nothing is more neglected', he begins, 'than the education for girls. Custom and the caprice of mothers often decide the whole matter. People imagine that this sex should be given little instruction.'[24] While girls cannot aspire to most of the higher levels of authority and social life, he argued, there certainly is much more that could be opened up to them, and for this a proper education is necessary. And here Fénelon made a sustained distinction between education and instruction in that, while he followed the tradition of seeing education as basically moral and ethical, pertaining to character formation, he used the term 'instruction' in its direct sense of giving schooling in cognitive studies. But he went further and provided a treatise covering the range of the girl's life.

Basically, the lengthy essay argues that education should follow the pattern of natural development, using firm but, wherever possible, pleasant disciplined control. He recommended that children first be allowed to follow, to a degree, their inclinations: to play, learn the alphabet by games such as drawing the shapes on paper, and to move imperceptibly to books in the vernacular; certainly not in Latin which 'takes all the pleasure out of reading'.[25] When the time comes for formal lessons a definite curriculum is provided: religion, reading, writing, spelling, French (or whatever vernacular) grammar, the four rules of arithmetic and fundamentals of civil laws. For advanced studies he advised Greek and Roman history and Latin for ecclesiastical writers. Fénelon also advised certain areas for careful censorship, chiefly the salacious aspects of Greek and Roman literature (which abounded in the period); such poetry, music and art as inflames the passions; and novellas and stories in Spanish and Italian, and therefore, as well, those languages, so as to deny access to erotic literature. In addition, for high-born girls, he recommended instruction in establishing schools and other charities.

Throughout the treatise Fénelon had in mind the social realities of the day, stating quite explicitly that girls have only two vocational choices: marriage or the veil. He certainly did not envisage education as changing the system. Here he was advising well-to-do parents on preparing their daughters for marriage, and recognized that his scheme demanded a governess and individual tuition, although he argued that such constraints do not vitiate the scheme. The curriculum, quite obviously, was consonant with marriage into a bourgeois home: the basic skills provided for house and estate management, arithmetic being seen as useful for accounting procedures; the elements of law were intended for the wife to know her rights (in days when marriage contracts involved often complicated property settlements) and to help her administer the estate. Again, Fénelon was writing for the bourgeois class in which both husband and

wife shared responsibility in managing the home as part of their commercial activities. The treatise was a great success, was widely read and
inspired efforts at emulation.

Of these the most notable was a school for young orphaned girls of
bourgeois birth established in 1686 at Saint-Cyr by the king's morganatic
wife, Madame de Maintenon.[26] After an Ursuline education at Niort she
married an invalid but fashionable poet who taught her Latin, Italian and
Spanish and so prepared her for high society. Moving in salon circles, she
became governess to Louis XIV's bastards in 1669–73, receiving the title
Madame de Maintenon as a royal favour. Soon Louis's mistress, she
became the dominant influence on the king and was responsible, in part,
for urging him to revoke the Edict of Nantes and convert the Huguenots –
having herself had a Huguenot upbringing before being sent to the Ursuline convent. It was, then, in her concern for the education of girls and
particularly the peaceable conversion of Huguenots that she founded the
remarkable school of Saint-Cyr which became a European showpiece for
the application of Fénelon's theories. Indeed, Fénelon and Madame de
Maintenon were in close correspondence while he was writing *On the
Education of Girls*.

At Saint-Cyr, part of the complement of 250 girls were daughters of
Huguenots – now *Catholiques Nouvelles* – and for all of them instruction
was for marriage, not the veil. The school was divided into four groups:
the youngest, known as 'reds' after the coloured sash they wore, aged
seven to eleven, began studies in the vernacular, starting with reading,
writing, arithmetic, grammar, catechism and church history; they were
then promoted to the 'greens', eleven to fourteen, where the curriculum was
augmented by music, geography and mythology; thence to the 'yellows',
fourteen to seventeen, where they learnt French language, music, religion,
dancing and drawing; completing their schooling in the blue group,
seventeen to twenty, with further instruction in French and music, along
with morals.[27] The pedagogy and routine followed the general direction
of Fénelon's theories and, during the earlier decades of the eighteenth
century, were quite successful. This school, however, was an individual
institution that provided something of a counterpart to the courtly
private-venture academies which flourished in Paris and the larger cities
to provide a gentleman's finishing-school for the leisured classes; the
general education of girls was more a matter of growing concern than one
of widespread action.

Catholicism consolidated

Spain, Portugal and the New World

The deeply divisive religious problems of France had no counterpart in Iberia; both Spain and Portugal were profoundly Catholic. In these countries the educational development of the fifteenth and sixteenth centuries, which had seen the foundation and consolidation of ten universities of considerably uneven and conservative quality, and their related network of schools, slowed down in the seventeenth century when, as leading agent of the Catholic Reformation, Spain sought to hold the line for conservatism. The provision of education was based on the Dominican and Jesuit orders, with the latter becoming increasingly dominant, although others, such as the indigenous Mercedarians along with foreign foundations, notably Franciscans, also appeared. The bulk of Spanish and Portuguese energies in the seventeenth century were not directed into domestic development; rather, both countries were preoccupied abroad, Portugal with organizing its extensive empire stretching around Africa and across the Indian Ocean to India and the East Indies; Spain with the bitter wars in western Europe and in consolidating its hold on the New World of the Americas. The extension of education in seventeenth-century Spain, then, was largely a New World activity in which the Catholic Church played the dominant role.[28]

While the social structure in the Spanish New World was a magnified distortion of Iberian conditions, with emphasis upon a highly privileged minority exploiting the land by means of an oppressed majority, educational attitudes and practices followed a similar pattern at the higher levels, especially in colleges and universities; this was not the case at the lower levels where the simple clergy often laboured under adverse conditions for the non-privileged classes. The church was seen in the colonial periods as the natural and proper agency of all education and it was to the church that the colonies turned for educational provisions as early as the first decade of the sixteenth century as the means of proselytizing and converting the Indians – a contentious procedure, since it was by no means completely accepted that the natives had souls and needed salvation. Regardless, the cross followed the sword very rapidly, especially since the Pope had included in the Treaty of Tordesillas of 1494, which divided the New World between Spain and Portugal, a clause requiring the propagation of the gospel. By the end of the seventeenth century, however, with the collapse of the missionary movement, the attempt to provide popular schooling had failed. In contrast, education for the upper classes was quite successfully established in all of the colonies, again on the Spanish model, with university education part of the visible luxury of the leisured classes. A separate system was established by the Jesuits, who by the seventeenth century had colleges in all the major cities of Spanish America offering the full curriculum based upon the *Ratio studiorum*.

Throughout the seventeenth and early eighteenth centuries education in Spanish America remained in an academic backwater, and it was not until the new thought of the French Enlightenment entered Spain in the eighteenth century, when most of western Europe – and even far-off Russia – came under the spell of French ideas and fashions, that the New World received any stimulus to change.

Portugal was a much more limited society and its educational development even more rudimentary than Spain's. In the sixteenth century the Jesuits had begun to move into Portugal, the first three arriving in 1540, and in the course of the second half of the sixteenth century established themselves rapidly, by the year 1600 having twenty houses and 600 members dispersed throughout novitiates, schools, seminaries, hospitals and asylums. The domination of the Inquisition, moreover, reached into all areas of Portuguese life, and the ensuing seventeenth century was a period of intellectual, cultural and social stagnation in which, under the Jesuits, conservative educational practices were maintained both at home and abroad. Portugal made no serious effort to develop a vigorous system of colonial education, and so stands in considerable contrast to Spain. Throughout the early decades of the eighteenth century Portugal remained in its conservative, feudal torpor, playing a minor role in European affairs and losing control of many of its overseas possessions.[29]

It was in Portugal, however, that the Society of Jesus was successfully challenged, and their expulsion in 1759 set off a sequence of further expulsions. Despite their obvious sincerity and the enormously valuable role the society played in Catholic Europe, especially in education, at the higher levels of administration they were arousing antagonisms in other countries besides Portugal. In 1764, largely because of their involvement in the Jansenist disputes, they were expelled from France; in 1767 they were even ordered out of Spain by Charles III (r. 1759–88). Pressure against them, in fact, chiefly as a result of their excessive interference in political matters, became so intense that in 1773, by the bull *Dominus ac Redemptor*, the pope suppressed the society in France, Spain, Portugal and Italy and the Jesuits were obliged to move into an eastern exile, finding refuge in Catholic parts of Austria, Germany, Prussia and even White Russia (Byelorussia) where they managed to open a seminary in 1780. Although later allowed to reorganize in western Europe in 1814 by papal approval, and with the consent of the countries concerned, the Society of Jesus had lost its power and in those vital decades of the second half of the eighteenth century created an educational vacuum in the West which was filled by alternative institutions and procedures, many of which were influenced in varying degrees by the new pressures from the Enlightenment.

Habsburg education under the Jesuits

In the Catholic regions of the Holy Roman Empire, chiefly Habsburg Austria, Italy and the Germanic territories, the schools remained entirely conservative and under the strong control of the church, with the Jesuits maintaining an almost total monopoly of secondary education. Elementary schools followed the traditional pattern, and all progression was to a Jesuit gymnasium, of which in the German territories by 1616 there were 372 with 13,112 students.[30] Their curriculum was thoroughly conservative and lagged behind the progressive Protestant north; not until 1752 did they upgrade their syllabus in a new Order of Studies which, although Latin-dominated, included German language, some science and the acceptance of state supervision. In the second half of the eighteenth century the Jesuits were challenged by new orders, of whom the Piarists were the most successful, providing as they did, in their Order of Studies of 1775, a completely modernized curriculum which was taught in the German vernacular and offered science as part of the syllabus.

Pressures for change in the Catholic German schools did not come in strength until the latter half of the eighteenth century. In Austria the Empress Maria Theresa (r. 1740–80) ordered Abbot Felbiger to reorganize the schools on the Protestant Prussian model of the *Realschule*, which was characterized by a non-classical, contemporary curriculum; in 1774, as part of his brief, he issued the *Allgemeine Schulordnung für die deutschen Normal-, Haupt- und Trivialschulen* (*General Regulations for German Teachers' Colleges, High and Elementary Schools*). This stimulated similar regulations in Catholic Bavaria on Austria's western boundary, and a chain reaction followed north-westwards up the valleys of the Rhine and Main. The Jesuits, meanwhile – having been ejected from France, Spain, Portugal and Italy – maintained a precarious existence and, in the face of competition, clung to their colleges (*studia inferiora*) and universities (*studia superiora*) with an almost stubborn tenacity. The society was, however, now thoroughly on the defensive and although they reluctantly upgraded their Order of Studies in 1752 they retained their methodology of the *Ratio studiorum* of 1599; indeed this fossilized procedure was not revised until 1828 when their General Roothan issued new regulations. By that time, however, European society was totally changed and education in the Protestant regions had taken so many initiatives that the Jesuit approach to education, like many other educational developments of the Reformation era, had outlived its usefulness and become obsolete.

Reformation to Enlightenment: The Extension of Schooling II. The Protestant Initiative

Protestantism established in England

Grammar schools in England: the age of philanthropy

In Protestant Europe, chiefly England and the German and Scandinavian regions, the secularization of education continued from the sixteenth century into the eighteenth as a quiet process; in England it depended upon philanthropy based upon both endowments and the subscription method of funding, the latter taken by analogy from the contemporaneous innovation of joint-stock financing; on the continent it occurred through a mixture of voluntarism and state provisions.

Basic provisions for education in seventeenth-century England were made by the grammar schools and the two universities, but these catered only for a privileged minority, chiefly sons of the élite, although it was possible for working-class boys to gain an education. At the time of Elizabeth's accession in 1558 there were 51 documented institutions; by the end of her reign (1603) these had increased to at least 280 endowed schools;[1] by mid-century there were 305 endowed schools and 105 known unendowed,[2] and half a century later, around the year 1700, the endowed number had grown to 400.[3] In addition, an unknown number of unendowed and unchronicled schools existed, some of which, obviously, were Catholic clandestine institutions, others being minimal, struggling places. At the apex of the grammar-school system were the great historical foundations of Winchester (1387), Eton (1414), St Paul's (1510), Shrewsbury (1552), Westminster (1560), Merchant Taylors' (1561), Rugby (1567) and Charterhouse (1611), known subsequently as the 'great public schools' (although some of these, including Harrow (1571), gained prominence much later) to distinguish their 'public' endowments and prestige from the hundreds of lesser, often marginal schools with more localized and restricted endowments and enrolment policies, of which a growing number, especially in the late seventeenth century and throughout the eighteenth, were private-venture, profit-seeking institutions.

Clearly, the considerable increase in the number of grammar schools in England, from 51 to 400 over one and a half centuries (of the order of 800 per cent), was well in advance of population increase which was approximately only 10 per cent, from around five million to five and a half. We must, then, seek an explanation outside demographic considerations and for England it rests in religious motives. When the Archdeacon of Huntingdon, the Rev. White Kennett, preached a sermon in 1706 on the value of an education that would enable children to read the Bible and so become 'little garrisons against Popery'[4] he was repeating a Protestant conviction of the preceding 150 years that had taken root at the accession of Elizabeth. In the mid-sixteenth century Genevan Calvinism swept across England, and the Puritan ethic not only emphasized education as the way to understanding the divine plan but also made it incumbent upon those with the necessary means to help the poor and disadvantaged. So began the phenomenon of the English philanthropic movement which, allied to emerging utopianism, looked forward to a millennial world. The educational reforming movement from Thomas More to Hartlib and Comenius was no isolated, ivory-tower theorizing divorced from reality and devoid of social relevance; on the contrary, it was intimately connected with a parallel movement of founding and endowing schools on a hitherto unprecedented scale which sought to give direction and drive to the philanthropic movement.

The extent of the philanthropy was tremendous; during the 150 years of this movement there were two peak periods: an early one between 1510 and 1540 and a later, much greater one in the period 1610–50. Throughout England the emergent commercial and propertied classes, many of whom had become wealthy as a result of the Protestantization of the nation, donated huge sums for the foundation of schools. Whereas in earlier times grammar schools had been endowed by rich prelates for the benefit of boys aspiring to the cloth, the mark of sixteenth- and seventeenth-century endowments was of mercantile and commercial donors providing secular education for their own class, along with generous scholarships for the promising poor. Underlying this philanthropy was the urge to keep education, and hence English society, safely Protestant. In this connection it should be remembered that the costs of nearly all social services were borne by charities, apart from local parish rates levied for support of the poor, the latter provision being regularized in 1598 in a Poor Law and further consolidated three years later in the famous Act of 43 Elizabeth, 1601, which sought to apprentice children on such assistance schemes so as to make them self-sufficient and to ease the tax rate. Within this framework of wide-scale voluntary giving throughout the long period 1480–1660, some 27 per cent of all charitable donations were given for education and 30 per cent of these gifts were provided in the two decades from 1611 to 1630.[5] In those years when Andreae, Campanella, Bacon and Comenius were writing their major reforming tracts, the burghers, merchants and aristocracy of England were responding by pouring money into the foundation and endowment of grammar schools – although often as much for self-seeking reasons as in a spirit of generosity.

The achievement was impressive, and something closely akin to a national system of grammar-school education – certainly one that operated as a substitute for a state system for two centuries – was created in the early seventeenth century. New schools and masters' residences were built, concentrated in the more populous and wealthy locations, and in addition benefactors endowed university college libraries, chairs and lectureships, along with a total of 487 new scholarships tenable at Oxford and Cambridge.[6] By 1660 there had been an eightfold increase in schools over a century, and a twelvefold increase in the numbers since 1480 with one grammar school at the time of the Restoration now being available for each 4400 of population.[7]

The universities and the Anglican establishment

This philanthropic drive was concerned with securing educated, enlightened leadership by upgrading the quality of the clergy and by encouraging the growth of an informed middle class; hence benevolence was directed at grammar schools and university colleges, not distributed as compassionate charity for the education of the poor and underprivileged. As might be expected, these expanding grammar schools and colleges received what has been called dramatically an 'invasion by the aristocracy'.[8] Whereas in previous centuries the schools and university colleges had been largely ignored by the upper classes, throughout the sixteenth and particularly the seventeenth century they moved in, in increasing numbers; and for their sons, training in courtly and gentlemanly accomplishments, though not eliminated, was now competing with formal school and university preparation. In the late 1570s the peak of enrolments of sons of the peerage had been reached at Oxford and Cambridge; thereafter the sons of the gentry and the professional and bourgeois classes became the dominant group. Many of these, especially the peerage, did not take degrees; they were seeking a more general education in a range of studies including logic, rhetoric, philosophy, Protestant theology, modern history, Latin language and literature, geography and cosmography.[9] Responding to the economic and commercial demands of the time, these classes sought something more suitable in the way of an education. The grammar schools and university colleges were ready-made institutions with boarding facilities, and were easily expanded and duplicated by the injection of funds to provide a middle-class system of education.

Yet the lower social orders were not totally excluded; the evidence of seventeenth-century admission registers at Cambridge shows that boys of 'mean birth' at times found places. One research into two representative colleges, St John's and Caius, reveals that both in the middle and at the end of the seventeenth century more than 50 per cent of entrants came from the combined group of knights, squires, gentlemen and clergymen (with the last two in preponderance), while 15 per cent came from artisan and shopkeeper fathers. Lawyers, doctors, schoolmasters and merchants provided collectively between 12 and 30 per cent. What is most interesting is that at both periods St John's College averaged 15 per cent enrolments of sons of yeomen, farmers, husbandmen, 'plebeians' and those classified as *mediocris fortunae*.[10]

Despite such provisions, throughout the seventeenth century the universities were not completely open in their admission policies, being caught up in the wider political-religious struggles that divided the realm. Towards the end of Elizabeth's reign the universities, particularly Cambridge, had reached the zenith of their Puritan reforming enthusiasm, and it was then that the minor gentry and commercial classes – the backbone of Puritanism – sent their sons in force. Elizabeth, however, moved to control the Puritan extremists, issuing an 'Act against Puritans' in 1593 which demanded adherence to the orthodox Church of England, and the universities enforced conformity by requiring students to subscribe to a list of tenets dating from 1571 which define the Anglican faith, known as the Thirty-Nine Articles, Oxford insisting upon avowal at matriculation, Cambridge not until graduation. Cambridge, which always resisted more strongly than Oxford, thereby left a loophole which allowed Puritans, dissenters, Nonconformists and Catholics to receive an education there, although it denied them the testamur. Pressure continued to build up, however, and some faculty members emigrated – notably John Cotton and Thomas Hooker, who resigned from Emmanuel College and settled in Boston where they helped establish Harvard College on a Cambridge model.

Throughout the first half of the seventeenth century, the universities were increasingly pressed to observe complete conformity to the Church of England in the three major areas of doctrine, government and discipline (including liturgy) and, while they continued to admit persons of low social origin, they accepted them only if they were in communion with the established church. After Elizabeth, both of the early Stuart kings sustained the pressure and by 1640 the universities had been brought into line; at that point a former student of Sidney Sussex College, Cambridge, was elected as member of parliament for Cambridge – both universities having the right since 1604 to send two members each – and this began a new round of conflict: the member was Oliver Cromwell (1599–1658). During the civil war (1642–9) the universities split, Oxford under royalist occupation, Cambridge under parliament, and when Cromwell emerged victorious and became Lord Protector of the Commonwealth (1653–8) Puritanism triumphed in its various forms, with Cromwell supporting the moderate Congregationalists against the extreme Calvinist Presbyterians. The universities reflected this and again swung back to Puritanism only to be faced with yet another reaction by the Anglicans with the Restoration of 1660. Under the new regime of Charles II (1660–85) the pressure to Anglican conformity became so intense that the Puritans were finally defeated.

The defeat was caused by a series of Acts issued by Lord Chancellor Clarendon and hence known as the Clarendon Code. The Corporation Act of 1661 required everyone holding public or local government offices to swear fealty to the sovereign and the laws of the realm. The Act of

Uniformity of 1662 enforced the sole use of the Book of Common Prayer and extended to ministers and schoolmasters the provisions of the earlier Conventicle Act, also requiring them to renounce objections to the Book of Common Prayer. The Five Mile Act of 1665 went on to forbid all dissenting clergy from coming 'within five miles of any city or town corporate, or borough that sends burgesses to the Parliament within his majesty's kingdom of England, principality of Wales . . . or within five miles of any parish, town or place wherein he or they may have since the Act of Oblivion been person, vicar, curate, stipendiary, or lecturer', except while travelling along the highway, and specifically forbade them from unlawful preaching to any group.[11] The general outcome of these Acts, and the later Test Act of 1673, was to make the universities closed preserves of the established church, confirming them in their conservative policies. Henceforth the universities and their associated grammar schools – for many of the endowments at colleges were tied to specific schools – suffered a marked decline and the Anglican establishment became a closed system. Puritan benefactions ceased and the vigour of England, particularly in respect of social conscience, was channelled into other directions. In education this gave rise to the era of the so-called 'dissenting academies'.

Religious dissent and educational innovation: the dissenting academies

The Clarendon Code failed to achieve its intentions. Indeed, in 1662 the passage of the Act of Uniformity stiffened Puritan resistance and led more than 2000 clerics to resign their livings – many of them in Oxford and Cambridge – and to strike out independently. Deprived of their ecclesiastical stipends, some of these 'ejected' clergy turned to teaching and, notwithstanding provisions of the Five Mile Act, set up private schools which followed the Puritan evangelical tradition. In their earliest phase most of these were rigidly Calvinist and took their generic title from the prototype Geneva Academy. The seventeenth-century start was slow and difficult to trace because these academies were clandestine; none the less by the eighteenth century they had become a significant movement.

In the period 1662–1843 there were 73 academies of major significance,[12] of which 34 offered a theological curriculum, the remaining 39 a wider general education as well. Not all of their records have been preserved; 17 of these 73 have a foundation date but no termination recorded, while the remaining 56 had an average existence of twenty-five years. There was a wide variation in survival times: the shortest-lived were open for barely three or four years, the longest, Hoxton Academy (1701–85) and Taunton Academy (*c.* 1670–1758), for more than eighty;[13] while the majority ranged from ten to forty years. Longevity was determined by a number of factors including the personality of the master and the specific historical context in which they functioned, since the era of these dissenting academies, spanning as it did some 181 years, encompassed several phases of pressure for religious conformity. In the earliest phase (1662–89), when the first academies were founded in direct opposition to the demands of the Clarendon Code, eighteen were documented, although clearly there were many more unreported institutions.

In 1689 a new phase began with the Toleration Act which mitigated the pressures of the earlier years. The Clarendon Code was entirely a product of the reign of Charles II; under his brother James II (r. 1685–8) there was an attempted relaxation since James, while Duke of York, had become converted around 1670 to Catholicism and in 1688 issued the Declaration of Indulgence which attempted to provide freedom of public worship for all non-Anglicans. This aroused immediate organized episcopal protest, James was without support, and his son-in-law William of Orange (married to James's daughter Mary) crossed from the United Provinces, ostensibly to protect his wife's Protestant inheritance, and in a bloodless victory – the English army and navy having deserted to him – assumed the throne of England. William made concessions to Protestants and by the Act of Toleration (1689) Nonconformists, but not Catholics, were exempted from penalties if they accepted the supremacy of the sovereign as governor of the Church of England, took an oath of allegiance, including a promise not to plot rebellion, and subscribed to the tenets of the Thirty-Nine Articles.

One significant consequence was a renewed surge of foundations of dissenting academies, ten appearing by the end of the century (though several of these could have been the regularizing of earlier clandestine institutions). The peak period of these academies was from 1690 to 1735 when there were, at various times, forty-three documented institutions in operation, a number of them gaining support from various Nonconformist churches, for which many of these academies operated as seminaries. There was a distinct falling-off by mid-century; by 1843 the last had closed down.

The career of the dissenting academies was closely related to the fortunes of the universities which, in a sense, they complemented. By 1660 the grammar schools, with Anglican conservative policies, diminishing endowments and poor management, began to stagnate and this was carried through into the universities, particularly Oxford which looked to the past more fixedly than did Cambridge where in at least some colleges Bacon, Locke and Newton were taught. The latter decades of the seventeenth century saw the continued decline of the universities, which became even more marked in the eighteenth, with the cessation of both lectures and examinations and an increasing ritualization of degree awards. Intellectual vigour and standards deteriorated, a celebrated account being given by Bishop Peter Gunning (1614–84) of his Cambridge professor, Parkinson, whose preoccupation with hunting led him to rush hastily to give the perfunctory lecture still 'equipped in boots and spurs, which his gown but ill concealed'.[14] Within the universities, too, criticism was engendered: in 1717 Joseph Butler (1692–1752), later Bishop of Durham, wrote while a student of Oriel College, Oxford, that 'we are obliged to misspend so much time here in attending frivolous lectures and unintelligible disputations, that I am quite tired out with such a disagreeable way of trifling'.[15] Four years later Nicholas Amhurst of St John's College, Oxford, complained in *Terrae filius* that the universities were 'nurseries of pedantry instead of sound learning, of bigotry instead of sound religion', with 'perverted statutes', 'wretchedly neglected discipline' and 'publick exercises confined to nonsensical jargon and the mere burlesque of true knowledge'.[16] In 1744 John Wesley (1703–94), a former fellow of Lincoln College, Oxford, preached a sermon in that university vigorously denouncing its ethos and practices, and noting later in his diary that 'I see not, why a man of tolerable understanding may not learn in six months' time more of solid philosophy than is commonly learned at Oxford in four (perhaps seven) years.'[17]

Against this background the dissenting academies contributed to higher learning in England, providing both employment for ejected university teachers and an education for the sons of dissenters. Generally the first academies were quite small and were usually conducted in the master's home. Enrolments varied but were, as a rule, counted in tens or twenties, though several reached up to eighty students; in the simplest, one room served as a classroom, another as a dormitory and refectory (since most students were boarders), while larger academies were able to have several specialized rooms. With the Act of Toleration of 1689 the academies became larger, with several teachers and often with better buildings, but generally these remained single structures with few grounds. They came to attract a wide clientele, often taking the sons of devout Anglican families since, while Oxford and Cambridge became degenerate in curriculum and dissolute in social life, the academies maintained a high moral tone, with rigorous intellectual standards and modernized curricula. Some academies became, in fact, the pacesetters of educational reform in England since they deliberately sought to implement the educational theories of Hartlib, Comenius, Petty and Dury. Indeed, many attempted a comprehensive programme of contemporary encyclopedic knowledge, including the works of Descartes, Newton, Grotius, Locke and other writers in the vanguard of scientific, legal, social and political theory. Even their courses in theology tended to be in the advanced stream of biblical philology and speculation, although many Calvinist academies were as rigidly sectarian as their Catholic antagonists. While not all dissenting academies were progressive, many of them holding to the doctrine of science in the service of faith[18] (*propagatio fidei per scientia*), nevertheless this movement created the necessary conditions for innovation.

Governed by the need to prepare competent parish clergy, as well as offering a wide general education, the academies taught oratory, rhetoric, preaching, philosophy of language and grammar, logic, moral and political philosophy, history and historiography, belles-lettres, biography and even shorthand. A great deal of their textual material had to be circulated in manuscript, especially during the early proscribed period; however, enough of this survives from the seventeenth century and a larger amount from the eighteenth, when it was supplemented by printed texts, to indicate the range and vigour of the curricula.[19] Divinity, in addition to the traditional studies, included such newer courses as 'pneumatology' (from the Greek *pneuma*, spirit), an early form of psychology that attempted to analyse more closely the concept of the soul and its attributes, existence, essence and immateriality, and was concerned with mental processes, faculties, ideas, the will, habits and the passions. This led to the study of related sciences: logic, music, ethics and politics.

Beyond preparation for the ministry, the dissenting academies, particularly throughout the eighteenth century, ventured into new fields by offering courses in the sciences as these were being developed, including arithmetic, algebra, trigonometry, logarithms, astronomy, the globe and its projections, geodesy, meteorology, hydrography, geology, mineralogy, botany, zoology, chemistry and anatomy. Even more forward-looking was 'electricity', one prospectus of 1767 offering 'some observations on Electricity tending to give a general idea of the discoveries which have been made about it', while another of around 1781 claimed to supplement

Priestley's initial 1767 publication of his history of electricity with data on newer discoveries of 'animal electricity' and magnetism.[20] In their mature period towards the end of the eighteenth century the dissenting academies were teaching government and British constitution; John Horsey's lectures given at Northampton Academy in the 1790s on this subject attempted to relate such theory to emerging radical and Whig political ideas using the works of Locke, Grotius, Pudendorf, Paley, Lyttelton, Sidney, Temple, Montaigne and Priestley.[21]

Education as a commercial venture: private schools and academies

Grammar schools, universities and dissenting academies, despite sectarian divisions, followed in the tradition of Christian Neoplatonism; even the dissenting academies were founded upon the belief that science could assist in propagating faith. In the eighteenth century, however, English schooling was extended by other institutions including private grammar schools and private academies, thereby following continental examples, particularly in Italy and France.

The accession of William and Mary in 1689 marked the end of Anglican absolute authority in England, and although the established church fought hard to maintain its privileges the eighteenth century saw the increasing secularization of society and education. The clerical domination of grammar schools was challenged by private schoolmasters who, often loyal to the Anglican faith, sought to conduct schools as independent ventures, occasionally out of commercial motives but also from reforming intentions to make grammar schools better institutions. In many cases these schools were conducted in the vicarage by the local vicar to supplement a generally meagre stipend. Throughout the seventeenth century private classical schools began to appear, the term 'private' referring to the fact that they were unendowed and entirely dependent upon fees or occasional benefactions for their continuation, in contrast to the so-called 'public' schools which were based upon great endowments of public funds from previous centuries, even though these were later subverted to the use of privileged minorities. The private grammar schools were often small, local institutions and, being both closer to their students' homes and less expensive, became attractive to the lower middle class. Although the 'great public' schools continued to dominate the matriculation registers of Oxford and Cambridge, averaging 60 per cent of university enrolments throughout the eighteenth century, private grammar schools contributed some 20 per cent of enrolments, the remaining 20 per cent coming from other sources, chiefly home tutoring.[22] The numbers of these private schools in the seventeenth century are unknown but many continued their activity into the eighteenth century when hundreds are documented.

Even though financially independent, such private grammar schools remained in the mainstream of the religious tradition, offering a classical literary curriculum. Completely outside that tradition were other private ventures which gave themselves the designation of academies, a title not to be confused with the dissenting academies. The private academies, looking forward to the current wave of scientific and cultural academies, modelled themselves on what they considered to be the progressive institutions of this title already operating in Italy and France which gave a range of training in commercial practices for the merchant classes and in courtly accomplishments for the wealthy stratum of society. Among the latter type was the famous early seventeenth-century courtly academy in Paris of M. de Pluvenel which concentrated upon military equitation, with additional instruction in weapons, 'courtesy', and a gloss of such leisured accomplishments as playing the lute, singing, dancing and a minimum of French language and mathematics. Similar academies flourished in France – at Saumur, Blois, Orléans and elsewhere – and they attracted many Englishmen who sought that kind of training, and its related activity of the continental grand tour, as an essential part of their 'education'.

Efforts were made to introduce such 'accomplishment' education into England in the seventeenth century but without much success. In the eighteenth century more sober versions of the vocational academy appeared, of which the first seems to have been established in London's Soho Square in the 1680s by a Mr Meure. Thereafter the number grew to eleven verified institutions in the early decades of the eighteenth century and by the 1780s these had increased to more than 200.[23] The Soho Academy expanded to become a multi-lateral institution offering instruction in five areas: grammar, commerce, technical, naval and fine arts.[24] Most of these academies were quite commercial in their approach, offering tuition in the services that the public required as the industrial revolution and overseas expansion developed in the eighteenth century. By the middle of the century well-defined programmes had become established in literary studies, mathematics-science, vocational-technical and accomplishments (with physical training).[25] Literary studies provided a general education in either the classics or vernacular literature; mathematics-science had both a liberal and an applied character; vocational-technical studies covered a wide range including commercial principles and practices, accountancy, military and naval training, navigation and surveying; accomplishments comprised the area so highly developed in France, with instruction in dancing, drawing, music, fencing and sports.

Springing up throughout London and many of the principal cities of England, and extending vigorously into the American colonies in the second half of the eighteenth century, the private academies offered as many programmes of study as they could attract students. Most were multilateral with four or five programmes; some were single-purpose institutions, generally concerned with specific vocations: military and naval studies, navigation and surveying. In an age when commissions were purchased, and before the state established its own training establishments, officer training – by no means necessary – was offered by such institutions as the military academy at Little Chelsea, its curriculum being based upon sciences, language, drawing, arithmetic, algebra, geometry, mechanics, fortification, artillery, chronology, geography, civil law, history, dancing, fencing, riding and manual exercises. The naval academies at Chelsea and Gosport were similarly organized, preparing boys for both the navy and the merchant marine. In the eighteenth century the 'enclosure' of the English countryside and the settlement and expansion in the American colonies created a need for trained surveyors as the great process of establishing and registering land titles was inaugurated, and again the private academies met this need, as did some of the mathematical academies. As new occupations emerged, so private-venture schools offering vocational preparation appeared.

Popular education and the charity-school movement

Despite the vast philanthropic endowments for education in the sixteenth and seventeenth centuries, such benevolence should not obscure the fact that England still made no widespread provisions for the schooling of the poor, the underprivileged and the broad masses of the labouring classes: grammar schools, academies (both dissenting and private) and universities reached only a tiny percentage of the population. Further, the prevalent middle-class attitude was that education should not be generally extended since it would upset the social order and increase expectations beyond acceptable levels.

The utopian educational reformers of the early seventeenth century apparently based their plans, in part, on continuous projection of the current increase in basic schooling which was creating a relatively literate reading public, as attested by the growth of the book trade. By the late sixteenth century vernacular books were coming off English presses in considerable numbers, and this apparently created a demand that led the Stationers' Company of 1587 to limit copies of books to 1500 per typesetting. The school text trade, however, was more liberally treated, being allowed between 2500 and 3000 copies per setting of grammars, accidences, primers and catechisms, with a maximum of four impressions allowed annually; that is, up to 12,000 copies of a text.[26] Despite the fact that the standard *Lily's Grammar* expanded to 20,000 copies per annum by the mid-seventeenth century, it is clear that the book trade also sought profits by publishing what has always been second only to school books in popularity: sensational as well as erotic literature. In the ominous days of 1640 when great Puritan marches were held in London demanding 'No popery, no bishops, no popish lords!' a petition was presented in December to the king demanding that the episcopal system, with all its 'roots and branches', be abolished; this Root and Branch Petition – later embodied in a Bill – attacked also 'lascivious, idle and unprofitable books, pamphlets, play-books and ballads'.[27] The inference is that a sizeable reading public had come into existence, and it seems that by the beginning of the seventeenth century the utopian optimism had some justification in fact.

The political and civil disorders of the mid-seventeenth century checked this growth, literacy being considered a factor in the potential loss of control over the lower classes, and the second half of that century became (as for much of Europe) a period of widespread economic depression which affected education. The pace of endowments slackened enormously and elementary schools independent of grammar schools diminished, with the result that literacy percentages, however defined, decreased. This continued throughout the eighteenth century, and one comprehensive modern investigation concluded that the movement towards public literacy made no headway at all in that century, on a percentage basis, chiefly because massive population increases in England, from a reasonably reliable estimate of 5.5 million in 1700 to an official 8,893,000 in 1801 (the first national census), nullified any gains.[28] Literacy rates in England seem to have been comparable to those of France, an equally developed society, with the same generalizations applying: males were more literate than females, urban populations more than rural. For the period up to the mid-eighteenth century we have only impressionistic figures, the issue being vexed by the definition of 'literacy' which varies from the simple criterion of the ability to sign one's name through to the ability to read a book. Lord Hardwicke's Marriage Act of 1753 required reading of banns and signing (or marking) of the register for civil validity, and one study of marriage registers immediately after the Act revealed that in the period 1754–62 only 51 per cent of persons could sign their names.[29] Writing, however, demands recognition, recall and, to an extent, dexterity, so it could have been that many more people were able to read than had the ability to sign their names.

The lack of educational provision for the masses, moreover, must be assessed against the background of changes in England's economic structure as it moved faster than any other Western nation into the early industrial era, thereby creating an increasing source of social discontent and friction: the problem of poverty. In Tudor times poverty had been seen as part of a natural order and it was this viewpoint that stimulated the philanthropic movement; solutions were attempted by the crown in a number of 'Poor Laws' which obliged parishes to levy rates for the support of the poor. As the poor grew in number these laws began to fail and although the Poor Law of 1598 attempted to solve the problem constructively by providing for the apprenticeship of pauper children this in practice effectively put them out to menial service in local workshops; a century later the problem worsened as the gap between poor and rich widened. In the first demographic survey of its kind, published in 1688 and entitled *Natural and Political Observations and Conclusions upon the State and Condition of England*, Gregory King produced a table[30] which divided English society into two groups. The first included the aristocracy, gentlemen, merchants, traders, shopkeepers, lawyers, clergy, freeholders, farmers, artisans and officers in the army and navy, collectively designated as 'increasing the wealth of the kingdom'; the second was composed of seamen, labourers, cottagers, paupers, soldiers and vagrants, all designated as 'decreasing the wealth of the kingdom' and outnumbering the former by a ratio of more than three to two. King's celebrated survey illustrates the style of economic thinking in the period during which the Poor Law approach broke down as increasing numbers of people were thrown on to the parish for relief.

Already the cities were beginning to grow larger and with a series of Enclosure Acts the people's common lands were 'enclosed' – physically by fencing, walling, hedging and ditching; legally by giving certificates of title to the wealthy landowners. After 1750 this process was greatly accelerated and increasingly forced the landless rural poor off their traditionally free domains into the growing cities, as yet untouched by urban hygiene or planning. The insanitary conditions of the cities, particularly London, can be gauged by mortality rates. In 1662 John Graunt calculated that only 10 per cent of children survived to their fifth year of age; of that remainder the average life expectancy was a little over seventeen years.[31] These figures remained constant, and in the next half-century the wretched poor turned to the new drugs of tobacco and gin which showed startling increases in consumption, the latter threefold between 1710 and 1740.[32] Following Gregory King the masses of the working classes were seen not as productive members of society but as consumers who decreased the wealth of the kingdom, wealth being considered only as possession of property or money. It was not until 1776 that Adam Smith (1723–90), in retirement from his professorship of moral philosophy at the University of Glasgow, published *An Inquiry into the Nature and Causes of the Wealth of Nations* which put forward the novel thesis that the wealth of a country consists in the cycle of production and consumption on a free-market model of specialization of labour and initiative. Given the economic theories of the early eighteenth century, it is no wonder that the Poor Laws broke down and the lower classes became afflicted with the vices and squalor of uncontrolled urbanization.

It was against this background that one of the great social movements in England in the modern period was initiated, the charity-school movement. This had its origins in the 1699 foundation of the Society for Promoting Christian Knowledge (SPCK) by the Rev. Dr Thomas Bray and four lay philanthropists. Very quickly this society created from its membership a second association which had the same aims for overseas colonies and received a royal charter in 1701 as the Society for Propagating the Gospel in Foreign Parts (SPG).[33] In founding these societies the members were confronted by the dilemma of resolving two conflicting positions: on the one hand, not interfering with the pattern of divine providence which ordained the natural estate of ignorance among the labouring classes while, on the other, seeking to give them sufficient literacy to assist in reading the scriptures for salvation. In the competitive, divided society of the eighteenth century many middle-class people – probably the majority – would have subscribed to the views of Soame Jenyns who wrote in 1757 that ignorance is necessary for 'all born to poverty and the drudgeries of life . . . [since it is] the only opiate capable of . . . [enabling] them to endure the miseries of one and the fatigues of the other . . . a cordial, administered by the gracious hand of providence, of which they ought never to be deprived by an ill-judged and improper education.'[34] To this, Dr Samuel Johnson (1709–84) replied that to follow this path would 'be indulging the lust of dominion, and that malevolence which delights in seeing others depressed'.[35] To their credit, the SPCK and SPG had already been opposing the Jenyns position for more than half a century.

The charity-school movement had one specialized aim – namely, providing sufficient instruction to enable the poorer classes to read the Bible. The impetus to establish charity schools came from individuals and groups scattered all over England. From its beginning the SPCK played a stimulating and coordinating role, urging the well-to-do classes to adopt the voluntary philanthropic role that had been so effective in earlier times. Throughout the sixteenth and seventeenth centuries Europe's financial system had been revolutionized through the use of paper money and various credit instruments, and this in turn led to one of the early procedures of capitalism, joint-stock organization, which had spread from Italy to England in the 1550s. The SPCK followed procedures suggested by this method and urged the well-to-do to take out 'subscriptions' to local groups for which their return on such 'ventures' would be in spiritual terms – the satisfaction of having helped unfortunate souls merit salvation.

The SPCK began its activities in London where it enjoyed considerable success and schools multiplied quickly. In turn they spread to the rural areas where their reception was more mixed, in large part because the SPCK was supported by John Wesley and his followers (known after 1733 as 'Methodists', a term of uncertain origin and meaning) and so aroused the antagonism of those parishes where the vicar and congregation were conservative Anglicans; by the same token, the SPCK flourished in areas of evangelical and Puritan enthusiasm. Statistical returns of the society in England are unreliable; because the SPCK was merely an encouraging, stimulating organization with no control over the individual schools, it had no authority to compel returns. By the year 1724 there were 1329 schools with a total enrolment of 23,421; thereafter the returns become abbreviated and after 1736 they cease to be meaningful.[36] This does not mean, however, that activities declined; on the contrary, throughout the century the SPCK was active and, indeed, the SPG was even more so in the New World, being responsible for a considerable advancement of literacy and basic schooling. In Scotland, Wales and Ireland the returns are more accurate and indicate considerable achievement.

Various venues were used as schoolhouses; mostly they were minimal one-room operations, using whatever teachers were available, although efforts were made to draft specific requirements including Anglican communion, good character and sobriety, 'genius for teaching', good family life and sufficient attainment in religion, writing and arithmetic for the local vicar to be able to certify him or her.[37] The curriculum was almost entirely Neoplatonist in character, consisting of the rote learning of the Anglican catechism and sections of the Book of Common Prayer, the Psalms and selected passages from the New Testament. Once reading was mastered, writing was introduced, and then church singing.[38] These subjects in themselves curiously engendered controversy, meeting opposition from employers who saw the 'natural order' of an ignorant labouring class being subverted because preoccupation with books did not inure them to labour, their necessary role in life. As a result, some SPCK schools attempted to include a labour component, assisted by the General Act of Relief of the Poor of 1723 which expanded the public workhouse system whereby the poor and indigent could be employed productively in various forms of simple manufacturing.[39] The result thereafter was often a combination of SPCK school and workhouse. Too often, however, the teachers were mediocre. If they were competent, after the fashion of Wesley's contemporary, Mary Fletcher, who conducted a Methodist boarding school for destitute children, the day was grim; she recorded specifically that for such children 'we never use the term play [since] our design is to fit them for good servants, we endeavour as early as possible to inure them to labour, early rising and cleanliness'.[40] The only relief from continuous lessons was an occasional evening fifteen-minute run in the garden, the children being strictly admonished not to enjoy themselves but to consider it exercise necessary for their health.

None the less, the schools of the SPCK, and many others on similar lines – for the SPCK school movement was copied by Nonconformists, Methodists, Quakers, Jews and Huguenots – played a significant role in extending schooling among the poor in a time of rapidly increasing population. Given the statistics of the Marriage Act of 1753 which show 51 per cent of people able to sign their names, and the rapidly increasing population, these schools played an important part in initiating the education of the underprivileged of England. The SPCK itself became less influential as the eighteenth century progressed but the idea of voluntary assistance remained and in that period, for various reasons, a considerable reading public came into existence. In particular, John Wesley promoted reading as being fundamental to true devotion. By this time, too, the publishing trade had become established, and newspapers appeared along with all sorts of printed ephemera produced solely for profit such as chap-books and single-sheet ballads, which led to the steady expansion of a literate public, although in the eighteenth century this was still largely a middle-class phenomenon.

Education in Scotland

Developments up to the Reformation

Meanwhile quite different educational developments were occurring in Scotland where a dynastic succession brought its king, James VI, to the throne of England in 1603. James, adopting the title James I, King of Great Britain, brought together in even more acute conflict the two nations that had been in opposition politically and religiously throughout their history. In Scotland from the fourth century AD a separate Celtic Catholic Church had developed in direct obedience to Rome and organized on a monastic model, authority being vested not in bishops but in 'presbyter-abbots' who were elected by the monks of the abbey and consecrated by other abbots. Herein lies an essential difference from the English ecclesiastical pattern which had developed along diocesan lines; even when dioceses were established, the Scots preferred government by elders (Greek *presbuteros*, elder) and so laid the foundations for a presbyterian structure. Throughout the medieval millennium the church in Scotland steadfastly adhered to its independent organization and refused to accept subservience to either York or Canterbury. The political system followed a similar pattern, with an independent aristocracy at times barely acknowledging the king in Edinburgh, much less one in distant London. England, however, was the common enemy of church and state and so catalysed both into alliance. In the sixteenth century the Scottish church or kirk, under the great reformer John Knox (c. 1513–72), became Calvinist and adopted a presbyterian, democratic form of government.

Scottish educational history up to the Reformation is sparsely documented. The first schools, which followed a standard monastic pattern, are mentioned in twelfth-century chronicles; when dioceses were organized (eleven by the twelfth century), cathedral schools came into being.

Their concern was, of course, latinity, but by the sixteenth century it seems that many of them were giving elementary instruction in the vernacular, Gaelic,[41] which isolated Scottish learning from the wider Western context. Legislative efforts were made to extend education, with no more effect than similar attempts elsewhere in Europe. In 1496, for example, in the reign of James IV the aristocracy and gentry were required to send their eldest sons to school until they had acquired complete latinity followed by three years at a school of 'Art and Law'.[42] The nature of such schools remains unclear – perhaps they were monastic institutions of charter and manuscript writing – and the Act seems to have been largely unenforceable.

In the fifteenth century Scotland gained three of its four universities: St Andrews, Glasgow and Aberdeen. Previously, Scots attended European universities, particularly Orléans and Paris; in the latter there was a Scots colony where students were assisted by a fund established by the Bishop of Moray, in Inverness. In 1410 the Scots left Paris, and established their own *studium* in Scotland at St Andrews. Two more *studia* followed, Glasgow in 1451 and Aberdeen in 1494. Edinburgh, the fourth of the historic foundations, did not appear until 1593 when it was set up as a college teaching towards degrees at Aberdeen. In organization these early *studia* followed the continental pattern with a rector, faculties and student 'nations', but the college system did not develop strongly and the faculty organization became the determining feature, assisted by the fact that the Scottish universities, apart from St Andrews, were established in large towns, unlike Cambridge and Oxford.

The Presbyterian initiative towards a national system

Despite these foundations, Scottish education did not prosper until Knox made a serious effort to create a rigorous system. The problem was largely financial, and it was to remedy this that Knox developed a plan for a national system which appeared in Part 5 of *The First Book of Discipline*. This *Book* was composed in 1560 by a committee of six, headed by Knox, in response to a government request for a new plan for the national kirk following the Reformation. They concerned themselves with doctrine and support; Part 5 of the *Book*, headed 'Provision for the Ministers', devoted five sections to education, seeing it as necessary to the maintenance of the kirk. The chief need was for a trained ministry and the plan was for 'every several church [to] have a Schoolmaster appointed, such a one as is able, at least, to teach Grammar and the Latin tongue, if the town be of any reputation'.[43] In addition the plan included colleges of arts (logic, rhetoric and languages, at least) 'in every notable town' leading up to the apex of the system in the three universities. An egalitarian feature was that 'the rich and potent may not be permitted to suffer their children to spend their youth in vain idleness, as heretofore they have done', and indeed 'the children of the poor must be supported and sustained on the charge of the church' until their ready aptitude for learning be ascertained, and 'if they be found apt to letters and learning then they [both rich and poor] must be charged to continue their study, so that the Commonwealth may have some comfort by them'.[44] After urging the organization of an adequate inspection and examination system, the education section set out in detail the curriculum, the customary Christian humanist/Neoplatonist version, leading up to the study of Greek and Hebrew.

The attempt of the Knox committee to secure permanent endowments for a national education system was opposed by the nobility who refused to relinquish the monastic lands which they had recently added to their estates. Under Knox, however, the kirk continued to assert its rights over education and in 1565 required church control over all appointments, this being ratified by parliament two years later. Throughout the seventeenth century, education still languished through inadequate financial provisions, and the kirk attempted to secure by direct legislative means the support it argued for in *The First Book of Discipline*.[45] So followed a series of parliamentary Acts – 1616, 1633, 1646 – which sought to establish schools through local property taxes, but without effect, and not until 1696 in the Act for Settling Schools was it legislated that 'there be a school settled and established, and a schoolmaster appointed, in every parish not already provided by the advice of the heritors [freeholders] and ministers of the parish'.[46] By this time the enactment was beginning to have some effect and the parishes tried to meet the injunctions of Knox and the requirements of the 1696 Act, although such activity generally remained limited to the towns. Scotland had a completely undeveloped road system, and, since most communication was by sea, the major ports became the centres of what culture there was and schools were maintained there by the local government boroughs. But the Calvinism of Knox had penetrated deeply into the countryside, and schools, where they existed, were rigidly conservative, notoriously harsh in discipline and restricted to a minority although, owing to the egalitarian feelings of the nation, a considerable number of this minority came from the working classes.

To extend literacy among the poor, the charity-school movement appeared in the early eighteenth century in schools conducted by the SPCK under direction from London until an Edinburgh society was formed to assume control for all of Scotland. Beginning in 1711 with 5 schools, these grew to 25 in 1715, to 150 by mid-century and to a peak of 176 in 1758. Thereafter the society's fortunes fluctuated, with only 146 schools in 1760, but had increased to 189 by 1809 with a total enrolment of 13,000.[47] Clearly these were significant achievements, even if charity schools reached only a tiny percentage of the population considering that in 1700 Scotland had a total of 1.2 million and by 1800 1.6 million. To reach the remote rural areas of isolated hamlets serving herders and crofters, travelling schools were organized whereby teachers moved from place to place giving short periods of instruction. The SPCK, however, made few local concessions and in particular saw Gaelic as a language to be stamped out, teaching English only, as the language of civilization.

The Scottish Enlightenment

Despite the backwardness of most of Scotland and the gloom of Calvinist Presbyterianism, in the mid-eighteenth century Scotland became second only to Paris as a centre of the European Enlightenment; and its universities of Edinburgh and Glasgow emerged as institutions of international renown and attraction. The reasons for the 'Scottish Enlightenment'[48] are complex, but revolve around the eagerness of Scotland, after the exiling of James II, to re-enter the mainstream of European life after its long isolation from England and the continent caused by wars and the insularity of the dominating kirk. By the Act of Union in 1707 Scotland became part of a new United Kingdom, and anglophile Scots referred to their country as North Britain and anglicized their native accents. Now the emphasis was on urbanity, cultivation and modernity. Not that the anglophiles went unchallenged; Scotland was still rent with social and political discord, and Episcopalians and Jacobites (supporters of the exiled Catholic James II who died in France in 1701) challenged the dominant Presbyterians, this contributing, as events happened, to a stimulating ferment of ideas.

Paris by this time was closed to Scots; the advent of William of Orange, later William III, brought the United Kingdom close to Holland, now a leading centre of liberal ideas of all kinds; as principal adviser for Scotland the king used William Carstares (1649–1715), a divine who had received part of his theological training at Utrecht which was at the time a prominent European university. In 1703 Carstares was appointed Principal of the University of Edinburgh and set to reforming both it and Glasgow on the continental models of Utrecht and Leiden. The latter had already become the leading centre of the new scientific-empirical approach and its medical school the best in existence, largely through the efforts of Francis de la Boe (1614–72), known as Sylvius, who emphasized its empirical character by having constructed the first medical laboratory in a university. Carstares had his brother-in-law William Dunlop appointed Principal of the University of Glasgow and together they looked to Holland and other major European centres for professors and ideas, with the result that both Edinburgh and Glasgow became distinguished for their faculties of medicine and law, eventually attracting students from England, away from Oxford and Cambridge.

In philosophy the country shone equally brightly, owing to the work of Francis Hutcheson (1694–1746) who, after graduating at Glasgow, directed a dissenting Presbyterian academy in Dublin before receiving the chair of moral philosophy at Glasgow in 1730. He introduced the ideas of Bacon, Newton and Locke, arguing that morality is not divinely implanted, and that it must, on the basis of the sense-empiricist argument, come from experience. Morality was seen as arising from perceptions and subsequent reflections in the mind. Hutcheson took a great Copernican step in the realm of philosophy by introducing the notion that virtue, so beloved of moral philosophers, is equivalent to that which pleases. He influenced subsequent generations of students and, despite the obvious contradictions built into his theory (are all pleasurable experiences virtuous?), created a stream of speculation which, developing from Baconian sense-empiricism, led to the florescence of the great century of Scottish philosophy epitomized by his pupil Adam Smith. Hutcheson, who first used the phrase 'the greatest happiness of the greatest number',[49] opened the way to the school of utilitarian philosophy advanced by David Hume (1711–76) and further developed in the later thought of Jeremy Bentham (1748–1832), James Mill (1773–1836) and his son, John Stuart Mill (1806–73). Although that stream of speculation was itself a complex and controversial area of eighteenth- and nineteenth-century philosophy, its educational consequences were enormous in that philosophical bases were being established for an entirely new understanding of society and ideology of education. In arguing that sense experience is the basis of humanity, that morals are dependent upon interpretation of experience, that virtue is that which pleases, and that socially responsible pleasure issues from the greatest good of the greatest number, Hutcheson was undermining the whole of seventeenth-century educational thought and practice.

Following Hutcheson in the period 1739–58, David Hume (who was refused chairs of philosophy at both Edinburgh and Glasgow because of his scepticism) released a stream of philosophical writings which stressed the role of sensation and experience as the sole source of ideas and hence of the construction of mind: *Treatise of Human Nature* (1739), *An Enquiry Concerning Human Understanding* (1748; reissued in 1758) and the *Principles of Morals* (1751). Given the stress on the role of perception and sense experience, Hume turned philosophical thought away from deductive speculation towards psychological observations which attempted to follow the Baconian precepts of inductive reasoning. Even further, especially since the New World was producing widespread evidence of vastly differing societies, Hume led the way towards investigating society itself as the agent of human variation and, therefore, the cause of social conditions. The emphasis moved to social history, sociology and politics as explanations for the human condition.[50] The consequences for all European thought and action were profound: if it could be established that social conditions create mankind, the way was open to change the course of what had been seen as inevitable natural events. Education entered the realm of the socially controllable. This was the contribution of the Scottish Enlightenment which, stemming from the universities of Edinburgh and Glasgow, was to dominate so much of future Western thought.

England's occupied territories: Wales

The contrast between the educational experiences of Scotland and the two areas of occupation, Wales and Ireland, illustrates how English policy was varied in the face of prevailing circumstances. In the case of Wales[51] there was virtually never any effort to treat the region as a separate nation and when the kings of England after the Norman Conquest of the eleventh century expanded their kingdom the Welsh tribes were seen as little more than a nuisance. Wales had been evangelized from Rome in the fourth century, and monastic settlement followed among the sparse population scattered across the hilly terrain. In the course of the medieval centuries the Welsh were not able to sustain an independent Celtic church and in 1203 they submitted to Canterbury. By 1282 their last independent king Gwynnedd had been conquered by Edward I and the region organized as a principality in the north-west, while the 'marcher' border lands were held under feudal ties to the English crown, controlled by a series of castles. In the course of the fourteenth and fifteenth centuries these castles fell into decay as the emergent Welsh gentry came into alliance with England, this alliance being strengthened when a Welshman, Henry Tudor, became King Henry VII of England in 1485. Under his son Henry VIII the policy of integrating Wales into England was completed; by 1500 most of the Welsh marches had become possessions of the English crown and in 1536 'An Act for laws and justice to be ministered in Wales in like form as it is in this realm', known as the Act of Union, provided for Wales to be incorporated into England, the marcher lordships to be abolished as political units, English law to apply, Welsh representatives to be sent to the Westminster parliament, and English to be the official language of administration, with no person holding office under the crown being permitted to speak Welsh; the whole Act was carefully designed by Thomas Cromwell to centralize authority in London.

Imposition of Anglicanism and Welsh reactions

Clearly the educated section of Welsh society, the gentry, had no alternative and although they maintained the country manor house, the *plasdy*, as a centre of independent Welsh culture they spoke English and sent their sons to grammar schools, either in Wales or in England, where the languages were primarily Latin and secondarily English. No university or college existed in the principality and all Welsh higher education was provided by Oxford, Cambridge and the Inns of Court in London. By the time of the Restoration of 1660 the Welsh gentry had become thoroughly anglicized, many as absentee landlords living in London. In Wales very little schooling was available. Medieval schools had been established in monasteries and cathedrals around 1404–5; an independent Latin grammar school was founded at Oswestry, in the English border county of Shropshire, apparently with the intention of strengthening English learning among the Welsh border people. By 1600 there were only fourteen good grammar schools and an unknown number of church schools, elementary and secondary.

In the face of these developments the common people were increasingly disadvantaged. There were no vernacular provisions at all, so far as we know, and the enforcement of the English-language Book of Common Prayer only further isolated the people. Against this there was a brief period of Welsh humanism from the mid-sixteenth to the mid-seventeenth century when a nationalistic literary movement sprang up which encouraged a fervent pride in their language, Cymric, and on the model of Italian humanism some Welsh patriots attempted to revive the history of their own culture and language. A great deal of philological and literary activity was undertaken but, owing to the indifference of the majority of the anglicized gentry, the movement failed; the chief effect was the assembling of a considerable body of material for scholarly research in later centuries. The Welsh language, then, became spoken chiefly in rural areas and among working-class people while the anglicized well-to-do looked to England for the education of their children. Indeed there was no higher education in Wales until the late nineteenth century when a rudimentary university college was built around the nucleus of the 1822 theological college foundation of St David's.

The story of popular schooling, however, is different and illustrates the tenacity of the common people in asserting the dignity and intrinsic worth of their language and culture. This particular story, in fact, begins in the Commonwealth period under Oliver Cromwell with the 1650 Act for the Better Propagation of the Gospel in Wales, the administration of which was charged to Colonel Thomas Harrison and seventy commissioners. The purpose of the Act was to strengthen Puritanism in Wales after the civil war when the country had strongly supported the royalist cause. The Welsh clergy in the Reformation century had been quite malleable, only a handful – fifteen at most – having refused to take the Henrician oath of supremacy, and for the century up to the civil war they were content to follow the Anglican path. Under Harrison 300 Anglican clergy were ejected from their livings for their intransigence and a programme was initiated for appointing schoolmasters and establishing schools to strengthen Puritanism. Altogether sixty schools, most of them near the English border, were set up; they were open to all classes and some even admitted girls.[52] Scarcely had these schools been established when in 1660, at the Restoration, they were closed down, Anglicanism was restored and even Catholicism quietly encouraged.

In 1690 the dissenting-academy movement also spread into Wales, continuing in the eighteenth century, but as in England it reached only the privileged. The schooling of the common people was still unprovided until the visit of Thomas Gouge, a dissenting minister ejected from St Sepulchre's, Southwark, in London, who gained firsthand acquaintance in 1671-2 with the need for scriptures in Cymric. Returning to London he set up, with support from a number of both Anglican and dissenting clerics, the Welsh Trust in 1674 which established schools, chiefly for adults, of which twenty were located in the north and more than seventy in the southern counties; the sparsely populated central counties had fewer than ten. These schools, however, did not survive; the need was for more systematic provisions, particularly for children. The Welsh Trust did make one major, lasting contribution: the translation and distribution, gratis, to the poor of a Welsh Bible which did much to fix and disseminate the vernacular. In addition, the Trust provided a good foundation for the extension of popular schools by creating an eagerness for learning which enabled the SPCK to become accepted, under the stimulus of Sir John Philipps (d. 1737) of Pembrokeshire who was able to enlist the enthusiasm and support of the clergy and squirearchy. These schools at first spread quickly in the south, as did the Trust schools, ninety-five appearing between 1699 and 1737;[53] moreover, similar foundations followed and in the same period twenty-nine other schools were endowed privately; thereafter the rate declined although there are records of a further thirty-four being established in the ensuing years of the eighteenth century.

The charity-school movement in Wales: the SPCK and the circulating schools

There were, of course, conditions that the SPCK had not anticipated. Extreme poverty and sparse population – perhaps never more than half a million in the period – made child labour necessary for production, thereby preventing their release into schools. Moreover, the Welsh were more interested in scriptural literacy than vocational programmes. For the poor and working classes, Cymric was their language and English a foreign tongue, and so their demand was for a vernacular religious schooling. The SPCK attempted to meet the needs of this intensely religious people and by 1717 had issued 10,000 copies of the Welsh Bible, with another impression ten years later,[54] while those too poor to pay for their Bibles, psalters, prayer books, catechisms and similar devotional literature frequently received them as gifts from Sir John Philipps. This, however, was checked with his death in 1737 and it was the loss of his leadership which slowed the impetus of the SPCK; yet, just as that society replaced the faltering Welsh Trust, so, as it declined, yet another movement came to take its place – that of the circulating schools.

The leading figure in this was Philipps's brother-in-law Griffith Jones (1683–1761) who taught at an SPCK school at Laugharne in 1708 and was appointed rector of Llandowror in 1716. Stimulated by Philipps, who gave him every assistance, Jones devised a more suitable alternative to the SPCK schools by taking account of the Welsh need for child labour. These were the circulating schools which comprised chiefly a teacher with the necessary books who moved into a village or township in the slack season, offering instruction in reading Welsh. The 'school' then moved on to another area with a slack season, in each place seeking support from the local clergy who were asked to allow the use of church halls and to assist in the instruction. So the voluntarily subscribed funds were put to the best possible use, chiefly teachers' salaries and the purchase of books. The teachers themselves were enthusiasts and gained barely two or three weeks' training at Llandowror from Jones himself through the catechetical method; no inspectors were employed, the task being to race time for the salvation of souls.[55] In a few large centres permanent schools were established which provided instruction in writing and reckoning, but the intention remained basically to provide reading skills.

Results were spectacular: in the first report issued in 1738, 37 'school sessions' were listed and in 1761, the year of Jones's death, 210 sessions had been conducted with an enrolment of 8000, while in the entire period of twenty-three years a grand total of 3498 'schools' had been held, and altogether 15,800 scholars instructed. The task was continued by Jones's long-time wealthy patron Bridget Bevan, wife of the member of parliament for Carmarthen. Under this great woman the circulating schools flourished – the year 1773 being the apogee of the movement with 243 'schools' and 13,205 pupils[56] – until at her death in 1779 they abruptly stopped when her will bequeathing £10,000 for their continuation was contested and put into chancery (the court of disputes presided over by the Lord Chancellor) for the next thirty-one years. The achievement was still there and in the eighteenth century the long-neglected Welsh common people began their movement towards educational provisions. So impressive was Jones's work that even in Russia it was reported to the Empress Catharine II who requested a memorandum on the method.

England's occupied territories: Ireland

The Irish fared even worse under English military occupation and their education at all levels had a most unhappy history resulting from the turbulence of the Reformation years. Although converted to Christianity at the same time as the rest of the British Isles some time in the fifth century, throughout the medieval period the church fluctuated in devotion and strength and became quite a weak influence after the Norman invasions of that same century. Left alone by the Romans the island of Hibernia was later intermittently settled in the seventh and eighth centuries by Vikings who became absorbed into the population. The Normans, however, were different: they invaded from England and set up fortified castles, then unknown to the Gaelic inhabitants, which in the course of time evolved into the larger cities of the nation, and from then on the English were an occupying power, the Irish a restive occupied people; both sides remained in an uneasy relationship which kept erupting in violent military clashes. The English held hegemony by concentrating their forces in Dublin and pacifying a surrounding region of varying area known as the Pale (Old French *pal*, a boundary) beginning in the early fourteenth century; in 1488-94 they attempted physical definition by digging a ditch along the demarcation line but later abandoned the task. As an administrative device, however, it was retained; and most English activity was restricted within the Pale, the rest of the nation in effect going its own agrarian way.

Henry VIII carried the Reformation into Ireland by declaring himself in 1536 supreme head of the Church of Ireland and organizing the church on an Anglican episcopalian model. Under Elizabeth, a determined effort was made to anglicize the country by means of a series of military expeditions; by 1603, the year of her death, the last Gaelic chieftain Hugh O'Neill surrendered; the people, however, remained obdurate and in 1642, with the heightened political crises in London, further rebellion broke out, the Catholic religion serving as an integrating factor. At this time faith and nationality came together and the Irish as Catholics saw themselves in opposition to the English as Protestants. In the following decade, particularly when Oliver Cromwell led a military force across, the land was devastated; with the Restoration of 1660 the Irish hoped for better treatment, which indeed eventuated, only to be lost when James II was forced to flee his throne in the face of the popular English defection to William of Orange. After escaping to Europe James went to Ireland

and raised a force to confront William who had meantime crossed the Irish Sea and landed at Carrickfergus in 1690. The two armies met at the Battle of the Boyne, named after the river crossing midway between Carrickfergus and Dublin, and the Catholics were defeated, this encounter becoming engraved in Irish consciousness as the most divisive of all conflicts within the country. Throughout the eighteenth century the Irish were demoralized; there was widespread emigration to Europe and the New World, and a triumphant Anglican establishment attempted yet again to change the character of the people.

Anglican domination and Irish responses

Throughout this unhappy history, education was vitally affected. Ireland, in common with the rest of Christendom, had developed along the usual medieval pattern of song, collegiate and cathedral schools, although it had no universities, probably because of its small population (always under a million), its students going instead to Oxford, Cambridge and Europe. The country felt the force of Henrician policies as early as 1537 when the king enacted that English Church parish schools were to be maintained within the Pale, with fines for defaulters. The Act was impossible to effect, if for no other reason than that there were only 600 impoverished clergy for 2300 parishes in the area;[57] the effort was ineffectually repeated by Elizabeth in 1570 and William in 1695. Higher education for English communicants was provided; originally it was proposed to establish a university college in the disendowed church buildings of St Patrick in Dublin, but nothing came of this and instead in 1591 the abandoned monastery of All Hallows was chosen; it began with a charter, three fellows and ten scholars in 1597. It was exclusively established church and the Jesuits wrote to the pope that it was a place where 'Irish youth shall be taught heresy by English teachers'.[58]

These educational enactments were accompanied by other equally futile efforts to 'eliminate popery'; the most ambitious scheme came in the reign of William of Orange with the Act of 1697 which required Catholic priests to take an oath of allegiance to the crown and prohibited ordination of any future priests.[59] It seems that, while up to a thousand priests took the oath of allegiance, the majority simply ignored it and continued to discharge their offices clandestinely, with the support of the people, and even the repetition of this Act in 1709 under Anne failed to eliminate the priesthood. Irish Catholicism was strengthened in that, denied free exercise of practice, including education at home, the clergy established émigré facilities abroad. Throughout the seventeenth century Irish students and clergy founded and maintained Catholic schools and colleges, generally seminaries, in Europe, chiefly France where there were fourteen, while Spain, Italy and the Austrian Netherlands (modern Belgium) each had five, Portugal had two and one was situated in Prague, making a total of thirty-two.[60] These, of course, overlapped with the émigré colleges established and used by English Catholics in the same period. The Act of 1709 in Ireland forbade instruction by Catholic schoolmasters but was generally unsuccessful and in 1731 there were estimated to be approximately 549 illegal Catholic schools, mostly in country areas.[61]

Eliminating popery: the charity-school movement

Meanwhile these negative enactments were accompanied by a positive effort, born of an earnest sense of Protestant enlightenment, to rescue the Irish from a religion seen as a mixture of idolatry and superstition. In this spirit the Society for Promoting Christian Knowledge began operating in Ireland and in the period 1704–17 established fifteen schools; in 1717 an Anglican vicar from Cork, Dr Henry Maule, formed the Dublin branch of the SPCK and the movement grew steadily. From 1717 to 1719 schools increased to 130, and in 1725 they numbered 163 with a total enrolment of 3000 children; by 1730 there were 172 schools operating, the maximum number reached. By this time the effort to help the Irish overcome their Catholicism was being stepped up with plans for a new, local version of the SPCK, the Incorporated Society,[62] which was projected as a result of alarm at the continued existence of secret Catholic schools, generally known as 'hedge schools' since they were conducted in clearings within the great hedges marking off the fields, but also in barns, farm buildings and stables. These hedge schools, although obscure because of their clandestine nature, continued to grow throughout the eighteenth century and into the nineteenth as a basic institution of Irish Catholic elementary education.[63]

The Incorporated Society project began in 1730 when the Anglican Primate of Ireland and most of the Anglican 'establishment' – the Lord Chancellor, the Archbishop of Dublin, six earls, five viscounts, twelve bishops, six barons, and more than 100 gentry and Anglican clergy – petitioned the crown (Walpole's government in Westminster) for approval to organize a countervailing force, in the form of a society with letters patent.[64] There can be no doubting the conviction of the petitioners, whose document indicated that the 'popish natives' because of their domination by a Catholic clergy lack loyalty to the English crown and are kept in 'gross ignorance' so that there 'seems little prospect but that superstition, idolatry, and disaffection will, from generation to generation, be propagated among them'. The Incorporated Society therefore offered to conduct a system of Protestant schools 'wherein the children of the Irish natives might be instructed in the English tongue, and the fundamental principles of true religion, to both of which they are generally great strangers'.[65] In 1733 letters patent were granted and the Incorporated Society was greeted with widespread enthusiasm by Anglicans. Gifts of money, land and buildings were made and the society prospered; from its first school in 1734 it had erected thirty-eight by 1754, all of these teaching Anglican religion through the English language, and existing in addition to the earlier network of SPCK schools organized in Dublin as a branch of the London society. In 1747 the society was given a grant from the Dublin parliament and continued to receive annual, increasingly larger grants for the remaining seventy-seven years of its life (it did not cease operations until 1824), thereby becoming the first educational support system in the United Kingdom to receive parliamentary funding.[66]

Yet the Incorporated Society attracted criticism from a number of sources. There was very little enthusiasm for an educated working class among employers or even the philanthropically minded; book learning was seen as particularly dangerous, and a contemporary letter in *The Grub-Street Journal*, referring to the dangerous spread of schooling among the lower classes, asserted that 'nineteen in twenty of the species were designed by nature for trade and manufacture [and] to take them off to read books was the way to do them harm, to make them not wiser or better, but impertinent, troublesome and factious'.[67] By the mid-eighteenth century this attitude was spreading rapidly throughout the charity-school movement as the perplexing problem was confronted of what to do with children kept in school all day; if indeed they were born to the working class, a liberal education as given in the grammar school – however illiberal it may be in its effects – would be deleterious, and so grew the notion of practical instruction combining scriptural literacy with work programmes. If the charity schools could operate on the model of workhouses, then the children, many of whom were paupers, orphans or even those forcibly taken from destitute Catholic parents, could make the schools self-supporting. This approach spread throughout England,

Scotland and Ireland to the extent that in the late eighteenth century the charity schools had entirely subverted their own purposes and had become so grim, even vicious, that they attracted the attention of John Howard himself. Indeed, Howard interrupted his tour of Irish prisons in 1779–82 to investigate the scandalously conducted charity schools, reports of which had already disturbed John Wesley. Howard (*c.* 1726–90) was a devout Calvinist who had dedicated his life to the horrible abuses of the prisons; the conditions of the Irish charity schools he considered worse than the prisons of the day. Children within them were more badly used than many in factories, being starved, unwashed and clothed in rags; girls' bodies were wasted and distorted by the twelve- to sixteen-hour days spent in spinning flax, making brooms, weaving cambric from the flax and making it up into shifts and shirts; the boys were equally exhausted and physically broken by spending long hours from early childhood in farm labouring of the most menial kind, particularly at hedging, including growing and transplanting seedlings, ditching and pruning.

Howard exposed these schools; Wesley took up the cause and examined the educational consequences, reporting that, so far as he could tell, the children learnt 'just nothing'.[68] The teachers, moreover, were themselves marginally competent and saw their roles as custodial rather than educative, being criticized as 'brutal and incompassionate' and 'the refuse of other callings' in contemporary reports.[69] But then from the general Anglican viewpoint these children were only Irish, and papists at that; they were, moreover, necessary to the growing industrial factory system. Only slowly were the worst abuses corrected, the schools now being very similar to the increasing number of factories with their forbidding prison-like structures that were being erected in many regions of Britain. Criticisms by Howard, Wesley and a number of other prominent people led the Dublin parliament to appoint an inquiry, after hearing Howard present evidence in 1788; Howard died two years later, and a year after that, in 1791, the commissioners presented an innocuous and evasive report. Another virulent critic, Robert Steven, wrote in his *Demand for an Inquiry into the Abuses of the Chartered Schools in Ireland* (1818) that he could 'find no trace of any steps having been taken by the Irish Parliament in consequence of the report'.[70] A further report in 1825 of the Commission of the Board of Education in Ireland observed that little had been done to correct the abuses disclosed by Howard and Wesley. By the early nineteenth century this was not exclusively an Irish problem; it was an affliction of all of the industrializing regions of the West. Meanwhile the bulk of the Irish people – who were told that their vernacular Erse was a barbarous tongue – were forced to transmit their common culture in secret in their hedge schools, or abroad, or to emigrate, in the face of a vast denial of their rights that in the future had to be accounted for.

Education in Europe: the Protestant north

Reformation provisions: efforts at extending the schools

The Protestant north of Europe in the seventeenth century remained a political mosaic of hundreds of separate states within the Holy Roman Empire. Its efforts to form cohesive national units were seriously frustrated by the devastations of the Thirty Years War since most of the military campaigns occurred in its territories. The enthusiasm for educational reform, however, which had prompted Tassius to write to Comenius from Hamburg in the late 1630s that 'the zeal of Pansophia and for a better didactic burns in every corner of Europe' was quite widely shared and was reflected in a continuing effort to extend educational provisions.

At the elementary level the Protestant regions had taken the lead under the stimulus of Luther and Melanchthon to provide schools, the *Articles of Visitation* being adopted widely as a model plan. The first compulsory school-attendance requirements were in Saxony where the city of Weimar passed laws in 1619 requiring all children between six and twelve years of age to be in attendance the full year except for the harvest month when they were to work in the fields,[71] and this precedent was followed at nearby Gotha in 1642 which prescribed fines for noncompliance. Similar regulations spread throughout Protestant Germany, the Scandinavian kingdoms of Denmark and Sweden and the United Netherlands Provinces, although they were widely ignored and in fact were almost impossible to honour, given the lack of any clear conception of an elementary school, or any adequate support system in the form of proper buildings, trained teachers and adequate funding. In Prussia similar regulations were issued in 1716 and 1717 by Frederick William I (r. 1713–40), and reissued in more comprehensive form in 1763 by his son Frederick II, the Great (r. 1840–86). These were the famous *General-Land-Schul-Reglement* which required all children between the ages of five and thirteen to attend school daily between the hours of 8–11 a.m. and 1–4 p.m., Sundays excluded and

Wednesday and Saturday afternoons free, until they had reached prescribed levels of proficiency in religion, reading, writing and elementary arithmetic. Provisions were made for fines for non-attendance and inspection by, originally, the local clergyman, later, a school superintendent.[72] Even more than a century after the Gotha regulations, however, it seems that little advance was made in providing schoolhouses and trained teachers; indeed, there is a considerable literature on the poor quality of teachers, including the common requirement that pensioned soldiers and other public servants be given charge of schools in order to save teachers' salaries, and schoolmasters given the tailoring monopoly to supplement their stipends, while in consequence of the 1763 regulations there was widespread parental evasion and underpaid inspectors tried, often unsuccessfully, to collect the 16-groschen fine that was prescribed.[73] The improvement and extension of elementary schooling was a more elusive process than enthusiastic regulation enactment supposed, and in Protestant Europe, as everywhere else, it proceeded slowly.

Advances in Prussia: Francke's schools at Halle

The significant lead was taken by the newly emerged state of Prussia, when to strengthen the independence of his new kingdom Frederick I founded his Friedrich University in 1694, locating it not in the capital Berlin but in Halle to the south-west. Frederick sought leading scholars for this new institution, planning it to follow the most progressive teaching of the period, and, among others, attracted two of Germany's great educational reformers, Christian Thomasius (1655–1728) and August Hermann Francke (1664–1727). Thomasius was, in effect, the founder of the new university which he upgraded from a courtly academy or *Ritterakademie* after moving to Halle from nearby Leipzig where he lectured in law. In educational matters, Thomasius was a modernizer and in a series of pedagogical texts, beginning with *Introductio ad philosophiam aulicam* of 1688 ('An Introduction to Philosophy for the Courtier'), he showed his concern to blend the best of the training in the *Ritterakademie* with progressive legal theory. Thomasius, lecturing in vernacular German, also attacked arid scholastic Aristotelianism and was responsible for displacing it from most of the Protestant German universities.

Complementing Thomasius, in a curious opposition, was Christian Wolff (1679–1754) who taught mathematics at Halle in the period 1707–23 from a modified Aristotelian standpoint. Wolff's career was stormy; in

1711 he was elected to membership of the recently founded (1700) Berlin Society of Sciences, of which the guiding spirit had been the great German scholar Gottfried Wilhelm Leibniz (1646–1716). This institution, modelled on the scientific academies of Europe, and the Royal Society of England in particular, and later renamed the Prussian Royal Academy, offered membership to the most distinguished German scholars, but this did not prevent Wolff's being exiled by the king under pressure from the then ascendant Pietists. He went to the Protestant university at Marburg and later returned to Halle when the new king Frederick II acceded in 1740. From then on he was showered with official recognition and honours; Wolff's teachings, based upon the precept of 'nothing without sufficient reason' – a mathematical concept – spread throughout German universities, Catholic as well as Protestant, in the eighteenth century and led to widespread reforms. During the Thirty Years War German universities had seriously declined when theology overshadowed everything else and universities had been severely disrupted by rampaging armies. As companions to theological bigotry went idleness and debauchery – not as unrelated as might be naïvely supposed – and in the age of reforming utopian writing it was seriously being questioned whether universities were suitable places for training youth.[74]

It is against this background that the work of Thomasius and Wolff must be understood. By the end of the eighteenth century the universities were successfully rehabilitated: their spirit was dominated by concern with rational philosophy and experimental science, and the medieval *lectio* method was replaced by the new techniques of the lecture and seminar, the latter term being an attempt to describe literally the process of mental fertilization that takes place during discussions. In addition, academic freedom became more widespread, lectures were given in German (except for the obvious exceptions of Latin and theology), while classical Latin courses moved away from formal stylistic studies towards historically oriented content.[75] By far the most significant were Halle and Göttingen; in the latter, founded in 1737, under the influence of Christian Heyne (1729–1812), Latin studies flourished and led a neo-humanist revival – so laying the groundwork for the great nineteenth-century movement – and his philological seminar was so distinguished and its graduates subsequently so influential that it was described as 'almost a training college which supplied the whole of northern Germany with higher teachers'.[76] And this tendency marked a European innovation: for research to be conducted in universities instead of within academies and societies.

The link between elementary schooling and the university in Germany still remained the Latin grammar school, and this, too, during the seventeenth century had become excessively conservative, under rigid Jesuit domination in the Catholic German lands, under equally inflexible Protestant churches in the Lutheran north. One of the achievements of Comenius and the other reforming theorists was to expound the concept of graded sequences of learning instruction. Such ideas were not yet widely known and their successful dissemination was the achievement of Thomasius' colleague at Halle, August Francke (1663–1727). Born at Lübeck on the Baltic coast, after a theological and philosophical training Francke became a lecturer at Leipzig in Saxony; in 1687 he met Philipp Jakob Spener (1635–1705) at the Saxon capital of Dresden. In his *Pia desideria* of 1675 Spener urged a more active faith in place of the official lifeless formalism of Lutheranism, and his movement of Pietism bears a relationship to Lutheranism similar to that of Methodism *vis-à-vis* the Church of England. Francke was converted to Pietism and at Leipzig demanded that lectures in theology be conducted as devotional sessions. Since Francke also gave his lectures in German, he aroused considerable hostility and in 1692 was ejected, finding an academic position at the new Friedrich University at Halle and a beneficed living as pastor of suburban Glauchau.

It was in Halle that Francke carried out the educational work that laid the foundations for German secondary education.[77] In addition to lecturing duties he saw his pastoral role as including concern for the poor, and since clergy were commonly charged with school tasks he became involved in educational matters. In 1694 Francke organized a school for poor and destitute children from his church which was so successful that he had to find larger quarters; this led him to open the following year on behalf of the city a separate school for well-to-do children (boys and girls) who paid fees, known as the *Bürgerschule* – that is, 'town school' – thereby providing the basis for a systematic elementary schooling for Halle, teaching basically reading and writing in German. Gifts and endowments came in liberally and enabled Francke to buy the previously rented buildings as a permanent site. Meanwhile he had also opened a Latin grammar school as a continuation of the *Bürgerschule*, for the sons of the prosperous, which was named the *Pädagogium*, its latinized Greek title suggesting a place where boys were 'led to learning'. The intention was to revitalize the lifeless formalism of the traditional grammar schools along Comenian reforming lines, and over the next few years the Lutheran, or more strictly the Evangelical Church, doctrine was the core of studies, with lessons taught in Latin – following the *Bürgerschule* vernacular grounding – supplemented by Greek and Hebrew.

Beyond this, however, there were the innovations that made the *Pädagogium* the most advanced school of its kind at the time. It taught German language, but, since there was still less vernacular literature than France or England possessed, Francke concentrated upon religious writings and German philology, and in addition, in both Latin and the vernacular, the study of history and geography; French and arithmetic were offered as well. What made a considerable departure from tradition, however, were the practical activities so earnestly recommended by the reformers. In the *Pädagogium* Francke introduced *Rekreationsübungen* ('pleasant exercises'), both indoors and out. The former consisted of workshop activities including carpentry, model making, drawing and lens grinding, this last being a fascinating craft when the exploration of nature through microscopes and telescopes was one of the most challenging new areas of study; the outdoor activities extended the study of nature through the lens by means of field trips, while manual activities were reinforced through visits to various craft studios in the city. Francke's *Pädagogium* initiated the study of reality, after nearly a century of exhortation in the reforming literature. Further realistic activities were introduced: in 1698 a school dispensary, in 1701 a printing office and bookshop, and beginnings were made on a library and museum of art and natural history.[78]

Francke's schools flourished from the start and in 1697, just two years after opening the *Pädagogium*, he established a parallel free school for poor but talented boys known as the Latin school which provided a pathway to the university; in 1709 he established a fee-paying girls' school to parallel the *Pädagogium*. In the year of his death, despite criticism from conservative sectarian quarters, his schools – conducted in addition to his university and pastoral duties – were well established, employing 167 masters, eight mistresses and an additional number of inspectors to educate 1725 children in the poor school, the orphanage and the *Bürgerschule*. As well there were eighty-two in the *Pädagogium* and 400 in the Latin school.[79] Francke's achievements in the charity field were highly significant, as these figures illustrate, and it was he who gave considerable support in the early years to the London SPCK which followed many of the ideas and practices of his poor school and orphanage. In addition to these achievements, Francke also achieved further advances in the concept of a professional preparation for teachers and as early as 1696 he was conducting daily two-hour discussion sessions for his elementary school teachers, often under-graduates at the Friedrich University, in what he termed the *Seminarium praeceptorum* (teachers' seminars), extending this in 1707 to teachers in the *Pädagogium* and Latin school. Today the Francke schools remain in opera-tion in Halle, still known as the Francke Foundations: *Franckesche Stift-ungen*.

Under Francke's influence Prussia took the educational lead in Europe early in the eighteenth century and in the concept of the professional preparation of teachers gained an initiative that was long sustained. The school system of Halle, in particular, became the model for Prussia and, by example, for other German states. As the Enlightenment progressed, the Pietist curriculum and its heavy religious emphasis proved to be un-fashionable and so declined, but the schools themselves continued through into the nineteenth century. German education, however, never shook itself entirely free of the religious element that the Pietistic schools propagated so assiduously.

Emergence of the Realschule *and the modern curriculum*

Francke provided a second avenue of development which German educa-tion fostered and thereby produced a universal model which was trans-mitted throughout the world: the notion of a curriculum based upon the study of the objects of the external world, termed *realia* in the common Latin word of the day, a concept that traces its genealogy from Bacon through Ratke and Comenius up to Francke's *Pädagogium*. In the plan of studies for the *Pädagogium* the notion of *Rekreationsübungen* provided the stimulus, although Francke, following the intellectual climate of his day, saw reality as evidence of divine handiwork; neither he nor many other educators of the period, given the religious context of the times, en-visaged *realia* to be otherwise.

Yet these were the beginnings of new developments, which Francke stimulated, albeit negatively, in Halle where a professor of philosophy Christoph Semler (1669–1740), as one of the inspectors of the schools, was concerned with the pedagogical procedures and in 1705 published a tract on 'Practical Suggestions for Establishing a Mathematical-Handwork School', following this up in 1708 by opening a *mathematische und mechan-ische Real-Schule*.[80] Conceived as a technical school, which offered part-time instruction for apprentices and craftsmen, and although forced to close three years later through lack of students, it none the less pointed the way, and some decades later Johann Julius Hecker (1707–68) opened in Berlin an *ökonomisch-mathematische Realschule* in 1747. The title is not easily translatable into English, but the underlying concept is that of a school of real studies based upon readily grasped mathematical foundations, this being illustrated by the prospectus, which listed its studies as religion, German, French, Latin, history, geography, geometry, mechanics, architecture and drawing, the emphasis clearly being on the latter part of the list.[81] In his school Hecker stressed the notion of studying the world as a structure of external objects – not transcendent ideas – by means of perception and mental reflection, and in so doing he pioneered the German *Realschule* which before long dropped Latin altogether and developed into an independent, non-classical type of secondary school. Moreover, the whole notion of studying *realia* as entities, and as evidence of an external world dependent upon the activities of the learner, was part of a wider European process of educational change of the greatest significance. This was the movement to discount immanent, revelatory knowledge and to accept the evidence of the senses as reliable. That, of course, was part of the Thomistic synthesis of the thirteenth century; in the eighteenth century the effort was made to take the step that the Catholic Church had long feared: to accept sensation and reflection as the only means of knowing, and the objects of such knowledge as the only reality.

CHAPTER 6

Education and the Enlightenment: The Conceptual Revolution

Changing conceptions of education: the influence of science and empiricism

From the scientific revolution to the Enlightenment

Despite its many achievements, the extension of schooling throughout the seventeenth and eighteenth centuries remained a limited operation characterized by the absence of any widespread appreciation of overall purpose, hampered by the primitive and undeveloped state of educational theory. It was a diffuse movement scattered across Europe, conducted by voluntaristic groups with a variety of unusually limited aims, and it is not surprising that in the second part of the eighteenth century many of the philanthropic efforts became exhausted and declined. Inadequately funded, conceptually shortsighted and often administratively inept, and universally based upon the prevailing class structures, they failed to develop because, among other reasons, the circumstances of the times were making different demands; the West, in all of its aspects – intellectual, economic, social and political – was changing at an accelerating pace.

In the second half of the eighteenth century the West entered an age of revolutions – industrial, social, political – which, among other things, introduced major changes in education, of which two features were highly significant: the increasing participation of governments in educational provision – in distinction to merely passing decrees as they had done, ineffectually, for centuries – and the emergence of new conceptions of man and society that were to provide controversial, challenging and, for many, exciting alternatives to the conventional assumptions, with stimulating possibilities for future development. Both these features, of course, were interdependent; neither could be realized without the other; both, in addition, had been in process of gestation throughout the seventeenth and eighteenth centuries. Moreover, the conservative mainstream tradition of grammar schooling was equally constrained by the absence of an acceptable theory. Despite the efforts of the utopian reforming movement of the seventeenth century, there remained no adequate body of educational theory to guide the processes of instruction: no understanding of the nature of infancy and childhood, no awareness of the psychology of learning, of the role of play, fantasy or imagination, of the appropriateness of age grading or stages of growth and interest; everything was concerned with the external logic of the ordering of subject matter, attitudes to human existence remained dominated by preoccupation with sin and the need for salvation. At the same time that these various efforts to extend schooling were being undertaken, however, a new approach to educational theorizing was also in process of development, as part of the general phenomenon of the Enlightenment; it depended essentially upon the thought of John Locke and Jean-Jacques Rousseau and slowly came to affect educational practice in the later decades of the eighteenth century and to be much more influential in the nineteenth.

The notion of the Enlightenment itself is an eighteenth-century idea and, although the movement had grown steadily out of the initial stimulus of Baconian and Cartesian thought and the subsequent scientific revolution, in the eighteenth century it gathered momentum and a heightened self-consciousness as the self-styled *philosophes* sought to overthrow the intellectual and cultural fashions of previous centuries on the grounds that they were obscurantist, and to adopt a questioning posture drawn from a faith in the efficacy of the scientific method based upon sense-empiricism and inductive reasoning. These *philosophes* – the term is French and means not philosophers in the technical sense so much as sophisticated, 'advanced' thinkers – formed a conspicuous vanguard of French intellectual society, of whom Montesquieu, Voltaire, Diderot and Rousseau are the best known, although there were many more, particularly as the movement spread rapidly outwards from Paris in all directions across Europe, and they came in fact to consider themselves as those who cast light on the prevailing darkness. The century itself came to be known in France, at that very time, as *le siècle des lumières*, literally 'the century of enlightening thinkers'; in the same period the new movement was adopted in the Prussian court of Frederick the Great as *die Aufklärung*; it was this German term that was directly translated into English early in the nineteenth century as 'Enlightenment'. With their customary dedication the Prussians pursued Enlightenment to a fault: in October of 1788 the first issue of the *Berlinisches Journal für Aufklärung* appeared and the question of exact definition was discussed, the concept of Enlightenment being expressed as that 'effort of the human spirit fully to illuminate, in accordance with the principles of pure reason and with a view to the advancement of the useful, every object in the world of ideas, every human opinion and its consequences, everything which has any effect upon man.'[1] The German enthusiasm, which took on the character of a national movement, followed the French initiation of Enlightenment thinking safely after the event; this enthusiastic credo, moreover, is nearly two centuries later than Bacon and contains essentially the programme he had advocated. The French *siècle des lumières*, the German *Aufklärung*, the English Enlightenment, the Spanish *las luces* and the comparable movements in the rest of Europe were essentially a phenomenon of the mature period of the later eighteenth century, drawing their inspiration chiefly from Voltaire and Rousseau; before them, laying the groundwork and providing the initial stimulus to all Enlightenment thinking – and especially with respect to education – was John Locke.

Descartes and Newton: towards a new science

In order to understand the essential ideas of the Enlightenment and its impact upon Western civilization it is necessary to consider briefly the development of the scientific revolution after Bacon, in the thought of Descartes and Newton, as a prelude to appreciating the contribution of Locke. It will be recalled that Descartes had considerable sympathy with the Baconian theory, but he affirmed the independence of the mind more explicitly than Bacon: indeed, *cogito ergo sum* contains the assumption of mind existing prior to, and independently of, matter. For Descartes, mind includes all the operations of sensation, imagination, will and feeling and is able, by its own operations, to achieve knowledge, of which he considered mathematics to be the highest form. Moreover, since such knowledge is attained by deductive reasoning from the mind's own resources, independently of sensory experience, he assumed the existence of innate ideas. Yet he also accepted the Baconian view that there is extensible matter which constitutes the external world and which is therefore the basis for sensory knowledge; so Descartes sought to bridge the gulf between the traditional Platonist concept of all knowledge being of pre-existing, *a priori* forms, and the Aristotelian position of knowledge being derived solely through the senses from experience, *a posteriori*. Throughout the later decades of the seventeenth century this Cartesian view reigned supreme, offering a reconciliation between two extreme positions, and by positing the independence of mind and *a priori* knowledge it thereby allowed for the existence of god.

The effective challenge to Cartesian theory came in the work of Isaac Newton (1642–1727) who, because of his pre-eminence in European scientific thought, was elected President of the Royal Society in 1703, a position he retained for twenty-four years until his death. While at Cambridge he published in 1687 the *Philosophiae naturalis principia mathematica* (known by its short title of the *Principia*), which was immediately acclaimed, because of its exposition of the universal law of gravitation, as a triumphant justification for the mechanistic view of the universe. Newton had, of course, to be careful of the religious sensibilities of the times so, quite wisely, following the established Aristotelian tradition, he accepted a first cause of the universe which is certainly not mechanical; however, like Robert Boyle and other members of the Royal Society, he asserted that the concern of science is not with causes but with observed effects, its aim being to calculate and give mathematical expression to mechanical laws. To some extent, then, he agreed with Descartes in using mathematical analysis to proceed from the known to the unknown. At the same time he diverged strongly from the Cartesian view that scientific proof can be deduced purely from ideas provided by the intuition. Following Bacon instead, Newton attempted to base his assumptions on experiments and observations of phenomena. Where direct experiment was impossible in astronomical calculations, he favoured the method of analogy, using, for example, that of a projectile such as a stone in calculating the orbits of planets.

Like Bacon before him, Newton did not inquire too closely into the relation between phenomena and ideas, nor into the way in which particulars themselves might give rise to knowledge. Nevertheless, to the satisfaction of his many followers, Newton brought together the two competing strands of seventeenth-century thought, Baconian empiricism and Cartesian rationalism. From this point forward, Descartes was in turn eclipsed and Newtonian thought became dominant; Newton's synthesis gave rise to a new form of scientific empiricism and provided a basis for the physical science of the eighteenth century. He offered a mechanical view of nature acceptable even to religious authorities by stressing it to be the divine will that the material universe should operate as an autonomous and ordered mechanism – the clock implies the clockmaker – and, although in the twentieth century Newton's absolutes of space, time and motion have been superseded by the theory of relativism, his ideas for a long time remained dominant. By the end of the seventeenth century Newton's theories were already widely accepted among English scientists, and during the first half of the eighteenth century they gained wide acceptance on the continent, especially through the interpretation of Voltaire.

John Locke: empiricism and knowledge

With the thought of Newton the scientific impetus to the Enlightenment commenced; the extension of such a scientific view not only to man and society but also to education was the achievement of John Locke (1632–1704). Locke was born near Bristol to a Puritan family and in 1652 went to Oxford, where he remained for some thirty years as student, lecturer and fellow. While at Oxford he became attracted to the thought of Bacon and Descartes, and this set him in the direction of a scientific career, which in his case was medicine. He was elected to the Royal Society in 1668 and received his medical licence in 1674. Being of republican background, Locke found it expedient in 1683, after the Restoration, to move to Holland, whereupon Oxford deprived him of his Christ Church fellowship. He remained there until 1688 when he returned on the same ship as William and Mary of Orange. The next years were the most productive; in 1689 he met Newton whose *Principia mathematica* had appeared two years previously, and then followed Locke's period of significant publishing; in 1690 came the controversial *Essay Concerning Human Understanding* which made great headway in sales once Oxford banned it from undergraduates in 1703; also in 1690 appeared his *Two Treatises on Government* and the *Letters on Toleration*, followed in 1693 by *Some Thoughts Concerning Education*. The last-mentioned proved to be immensely popular and in the course of the eighteenth century was reprinted in two editions while the French translation saw sixteen printings; by the end of the nineteenth century it had gone through a further ten English editions, seven German, six Italian and five French. Throughout the eighteenth century Locke was increasingly quoted with approbation as an authority on education.

It was, however, in political theory that he first attracted attention with his attacks in the two *Treatises* on divine right and absolutist forms of government. The first was a refutation of divine-right rule; the second opposed the *Leviathan* of Thomas Hobbes which, published in 1651, had argued that the social contract granting sovereignty to the state is a necessity, for otherwise anarchy and self-interest would lead to a condition of war, making man's life in the natural state merely 'solitary, poor, nasty, brutish and short'.[2] Hobbes argued, however, that once granted to a sovereign the social contract is irrevocable; Locke opposed that view in his *Treatises* and argued that the contract is between free men and therefore both revocable and renegotiable. Men are subject not to sovereigns but to the 'laws of nature', which are discoverable by the proper use of the faculties of 'understanding, reason, and sense-perception'. Above all, he stated, following Bacon closely, sense perception is 'the basis of our knowledge of the law of nature'. To begin with, such knowledge 'is derived from those things which we perceive through the senses'. After this, in his view, 'reason makes use of these elements of knowledge, to amplify and refine them, but it does not in the least establish them'.[3]

The growing recognition of society as the source of morals, along with the assertion that societies themselves are created by individuals and can be changed by them, was to have far-reaching effects during the eighteenth century. The idea that man can achieve social progress through political change and programmes of education gained strength with the decline of belief in divine authority as the source of all personal enlightenment and of all organization in the world. A tendency to replace divine determinism with social or economic determinism was something, however, that Locke had no wish to encourage. He preferred to minimize the social aspects of knowledge and emphasize that the way to truth requires the individual to pay proper attention to the evidence of his own senses.

The two *Treatises of Government* set the stage for a conceptual revolution in political theory; in his *Essay Concerning Human Understanding* Locke provided a second attack on established thinking. In this *Essay*, first published in 1690, although he commenced drafts as early as 1671 and continued to make additions until 1700, Locke set out to inquire into the origin, certainty and extent of human knowledge. His intention was to apply the scientific method of his day to a study of mental operations, producing in effect what Bacon had called a natural history of the mind. Bacon himself had not explored in depth the relationship of ideas to experience; it was Locke who provided an extension of Baconian empiricism by developing what was virtually an empiricical psychology.

Locke began by rejecting again the doctrine of innate knowledge. Denying that there are 'certain innate principles, some primary notions, *koinai ennoiai*; characters, as it were, stamped upon the mind of man', he set out to show 'how men, barely by the use of their natural faculties, may attain to all the knowledge they have, . . . and may arrive at certainty, without any such original notions'.[4] He followed Aristotle and Bacon in favouring the *tabula rasa* theory of the mind: 'Let us then suppose the mind to be, as we say, white paper, void of all characters, without any ideas; how comes it to be furnished? . . . To this I answer, in one word, from experience.' Experience, for Locke, depends chiefly on the senses, although he recognized another source of knowledge in the functioning of the mind itself: 'Our observation, employed either about external sensible objects, or about the internal operations of our minds, perceived and reflected on by ourselves, is that which supplies the understanding with all the materials of thinking.' These two aspects of experience he called *sensation* and *reflection*: 'external material things, as the objects of sensation; and the operations of our own minds within, as the objects of reflection, are to me the only originals from whence all our ideas take their beginnings.'[5]

Though Locke considered the mind to be passive when receiving simple ideas, he assigned it an active role when combining these to form complex ones, such as those indicated 'by the names obligation, drunkenness, a lie, etc.'. He developed some of Hobbes's views by pointing to the importance in learning of the association of ideas, and he drew attention to the role of language in ascribing constant names to complex ideas, pointing out that these are closely related to the customs of the societies concerned, so that languages themselves change as new terms are annexed to new combinations of ideas. Locke was thus an early proponent of linguistic analysis, recognizing the function of words in enabling ideas to be 'represented to the mind'. Indeed, he stated: 'now that languages are made, and abound with words standing for such combinations, an usual way of getting these complex ideas is by the explication of those terms that stand for them.'[6] Like Bacon, however, Locke was not confident in dealing with complex ideas and the whole problem of vicarious experience, this difficulty having an important bearing on his attitude to scientific knowledge. In the manner of Newton he combined the prescriptions for scientific method of both Bacon and Descartes, retaining the Cartesian preference for proof by mathematical demonstration, while arguing as an empiricist that certainty or truth can also be attained through experience, by the reception of simple ideas that correspond directly to elements of external reality. On this account complex ideas presented something of an obstacle to his theory.

Progress in the study of the external world, then, according to Locke, depends primarily on attention to the evidence of the senses, which can provide direct contact with particulars; the view that the mind is passive in perception was to remain for a long time a basic tenet of scientific methodology[7] and to exercise a profound influence on educational theory. Yet the mind was not conceived by Locke to be totally blank; indeed he drew, rather uncritically, from the long-surviving Aristotelian doctrine of mental faculties and was responsible for putting this into renewed circulation. While he admitted quite freely that the separate simple ideas that make up complex ideas somehow become a mental unity, 'all united together in an unknown substratum',[8] he saw this substratum as having certain pre-existing powers or faculties of organization. Aristotle similarly had asserted that this feature of the soul has a 'congenital discriminative capacity',[9] so prefigured as to receive perceptions through the powers (*dynameis*) which order these into concepts and thereby yield knowledge.[10] Locke followed closely in this tradition, referring throughout the *Essay* to 'faculties' of the mind, identifying these as 'knowledge' whereby perception is accurately understood, and 'judgement' which enables decisions to be taken about matters of imperfect or ambiguous perception or of a non-demonstrative kind.[11] To these he added a super-faculty of 'reason' with two aspects – 'sagacity' and 'illation' – these being posited as necessary because 'sense and intuition reach but a very little way. The greatest part of our knowledge depends upon deductions and intermediate ideas', and to effect these steps sagacity enables us to see possible meaningful relationships between ideas; illation (a sixteenth-century word for 'inference') enables the mind to test sequences of ideas and thereby enables it 'to see either the certain agreement or disagreement of any two ideas, as in demonstration, in which it arrives at knowledge; or their probable connection, on which it gives or withholds its assent, as in opinion'.[12] Locke did little more than analyse the Aristotelian model of the mind and devise names for the various operations; in the process, furthermore, he advanced them as reified concepts. So education, like science, attempted to implement a Baconian empirical, inductive method of knowing using the unrealized, contradictory model of the prestructured, faculty-ordered mind.

John Locke: empiricism and education

After his return from Holland in 1688 Locke was given a well-paid, un-demanding job in London as Commissioner of Appeals which allowed him to live in Essex at the home of Sir Francis Masham. While there he wrote a series of letters to Edward Clarke on the education of the latter's child – a common literary genre of the day – which were printed in 1693 as *Some Thoughts Concerning Education*. Like his other works this manual for mothers was well received with numerous editions and printings and marked a major turning-point in Western philosophical and social, as well as educational, thought.[13]

The point of departure was Locke's denial of an inherently depraved nature for mankind. Following through the notion of a *tabula rasa*, he argued for the primacy of nurture, and, since the mind of the child is 'only as white paper, or wax, to be moulded and fashioned as one pleases',[14] so 'the difference to be found in the manners and abilities of men is owing more to their education than anything else',[15] and therefore 'of all the men we meet with, nine parts of ten are what they are, good or evil, useful or not, by their education'.[16] This led to his assertion that education is primarily a moral affair, since its results are shown in the producing of persons who are 'good or evil, useful or not'. Given that he was writing for a privileged stratum of society, he saw the purpose of education being 'that which every gentleman desires for his sons', namely, 'virtue, wisdom, breeding and learning',[17] and of these he wrote, 'I place virtue as the first and most necessary',[18] and, he continued, 'I put learning last, especially if I tell you I think it the least part'.[19] The intention was to emphasize the active quality of life rather than bookish preoccupations which in his day often meant pedantic, narrow and irrelevant attainment. But there was a deeper concern than a simple demand for relevancy in learning, important as that may be for most people; rather, Locke opposed the doctrine of original sin and challenged conventional religious attitudes by maintaining that virtue can be taught by a purely secular, civic programme of educational procedures.

Essential to the cultivation of virtue is a proper awareness of the

child's natural propensities and of effective methods. Here Locke reflected the limitations of his times, since there existed only a theological
theory of human nature based upon the notion of original sin, and methodology in child rearing and education consisted, respectively, in conventional practices and the graded sequences of textbook subject matter.
His *tabula rasa* theory lacks detail on the development of the child's mind,
although in a few places he did show an intuitive awareness when he
wrote of 'the natural make of the mind', 'the unalterable frame of [people's]
constitutions' and 'native propensities'.[20] There is an inevitability about
individual differences in that 'God hath stamped certain characters upon
men's minds, which, like their shapes, may perhaps be a little mended but
can hardly be totally altered and transformed into the contrary'.[21] He did,
moreover, go beyond his contemporaries in recognizing rationality in
growing children and the need to treat them as capable of reasoning, and
advised that a wise approach would be to keep within their range of experience. His observation that there are degrees of mental development
implies a primitive developmental-stage theory, and he also remarked on
the need to respect 'the child's capacity and apprehension'.[22] Unfortunately, Locke's discussion of this aspect of educational procedure went no
further and his model of the mind is almost entirely ontological rather
than developmental; further, he recommended thoroughgoing habituation as the main methodology, and in this he leant upon classical Aristotelian theory; the need is for a strong discipline which will enable man
'to deny himself his own desires, cross his own inclinations and purely
follow what reason directs as best, though appetite lean the other way'.[23]
This discipline is attained through habituation:

> What you think necessary for them to do, settle in them an indispensable
> practice as often as the occasion returns. . . . This will beget habits in them,
> which, being once established, operate of themselves easily and naturally
> without the assistance of the memory.[24]

Even though Locke proposed the cultivation of virtue and character as
the primary aim of education, he saw the need for cognitive attainment
and recommended a programme of the kind offered in the dissenting
academies: literacy, history and science; in particular, he stressed the value
of the English vernacular. He followed in the reforming sixteenth-century
tradition and like William Petty considered that the boy should have an
acquaintance with various crafts and even 'learn a trade, a manual trade,
nay two or three, but one more particularly'.[25] It is significant that Locke

advised Edward Clarke, however, to avoid schools and to choose a tutor for his child, thereby educating him in a home rather than a boarding environment, the objection to schools stemming from their poor quality and the possibility that children might be exposed to vice. Indeed Locke discounted the residential grammar school with the advice not to 'hazard your son's innocence and virtue for a little Greek and Latin'.[26]

Perhaps the greatest lack in *Some Thoughts Concerning Education*, and a rather surprising omission, is a consideration of the attainment of moral – and intellectual – autonomy, especially since these were major concerns of Plato and Aristotle and of much educational thought after them. He did not indicate how the processes of habituation and discipline would lead to moral and intellectual independence; the implicit assumptions seem that they would be attained by the exercise of habit and emerge in a social context. Such is the consequence of the *tabula rasa* theory. Locke seemed to imply, in contradistinction to classical ideas, that virtue is merely the formation of habits.[27] This, of course, puts him in opposition to the Platonic belief that there is an inborn capacity in people to rise above habituation, by intellection, to a vision of the good, this being a consequence of attaining virtue; Locke was also opposed to Aristotle's dictum that once a certain point is reached the habituated mind becomes autonomous and able to become virtuous (displayed as *eudaimonia*) through its own efforts. Locke's position contains an inbuilt contradiction: if man is created by sensation and reflection from a neutral beginning, from whence do values arise and how can morally worthwhile goals be determined and pursued? This was a problem that his followers attempted to resolve.

Empiricism pursued: ideas of the Enlightenment

Locke's ideas spread rapidly throughout English educated circles and into Scotland where they were propagated by Francis Hutcheson at the University of Glasgow; Hutcheson stimulated a following that established empiricism as a dominantly British philosophy: David Hume, Adam Ferguson, William Robertson, Adam Smith and John Miller.[28] Newton and Locke were quickly accepted by some French thinkers who were seeking an alternative doctrine to Cartesian *a priorism*, and in 1700 the Huguenot expatriate Pierre Coste translated Locke's *Essay Concerning the Human Understanding* for a receptive French readership. This had the effect of dividing French intellectual life even more strongly, the University of Paris under Jesuit control proving highly reactionary.

The philosophers: Voltaire, La Mettrie, Helvétius

Voltaire (1694–1778) was the chief agent of promoting British empiricism in France. Born François-Marie Arouet, of a wealthy bourgeois family, and educated at a Jesuit college (as were many of the anticlerical *philosophes*), he adopted in early adult life the *nom de plume* of Voltaire. He quickly plunged into controversy because of his critical and anti-conservative writings and before the age of twenty-six had been banished several times from Paris, exiled to Holland and imprisoned for nearly a year in the Bastille; in 1726–9 he was again in political exile in England where he immersed himself in a thorough study of Newton, Locke and empiricist thought, recording all this in his *Lettres philosophiques*, published in 1734. These famous letters extolled the liberalism, both political and intellectual, of England – the major section is entitled *Letters Concerning the English Nation* – and in them Voltaire expressed his intention to promote the ideas of Locke in France. This so disturbed the conservatives that Voltaire's arrest was ordered at the time the *Letters* were published and he fled into exile for the next fifteen years. After a brief return to Paris in the period 1746–9 under the protection of Madame du Châtelet, he moved to Berlin where Frederick's court became enthusiastic about the new movement, Frederick himself being determined to turn the desolate marcher swampland around Berlin into a major European capital and to force Prussia into the ranks of the great powers.[29] Voltaire's popularity lasted barely three years; he returned to France close to the Swiss border and continued his literary campaign for social justice, producing the greatest single body of French Enlightenment writing, thereby inspiring, and complementing, that of the growing number of likeminded *philosophes*.

The general course of the Enlightenment is too complex to trace here; it is significant, however, that many of its concerns were educational in both broad and specific senses, and Locke's ideas remained the central inspiration. Yet they were not fully worked out; there were areas of ambiguity which led to various interpretations, one of these being a mechanist theory based upon behaviouristic empiricism of which the leading philosophical exponent was Julien Offray de La Mettrie (1709–51). La Mettrie produced a number of treatises, of which his best-known work, *L'Homme machine* (*Man the Machine*), was the ultimate development of *tabula rasa* theory. Published in 1747, it is by no means as mechanist as its title might suggest.

Following the Leiden school of empirical medicine, *L'Homme machine* rejected any metaphysical considerations. In studying man, it argued, we must 'lean on the staff of experience, eschew the history of all the unprofitable opinions of the philosophers', and follow the empirical method: 'it is only *a posteriori* or by seeking to unravel the soul, as it were, via the organs of the body, that one can, I do not say lay bare human nature itself in a demonstrative fashion, but attain to the highest degree of probability possible on this topic.'[30] La Mettrie argued for the empirical study of physical man which was, in effect, the course taken by medicine in the nineteenth and twentieth centuries. In a sense, however, the title of this work is misleading since La Mettrie's attitude is more in the direction of 'man the organism' rather than 'the machine', and indeed it was this organic approach that the majority of educational theorists favoured.

The most extreme educational application of this view came somewhat later in the treatise *De l'homme, de ses facultés intellectuelles, et de son éducation* by Helvétius, published posthumously in 1772. Claude-Adrien Helvétius (1715–71), after an education at the Collège de Louis-le-Grand, the leading Jesuit school, obtained through influence an appointment as a tax collector, spending his subsequent wealth on philanthropic ventures. He embraced the doctrines of Locke and La Mettrie but went further, rejecting every form of theorizing about internal human processes. His belief that people are uniformly blank at birth and completely formable by external influences led him to his celebrated and controversial dictum *l'éducation peut tout*: 'education is everything'. He thereby put forward the notion of absolute reductionism – that is, the elimination of all human moral or willpower components – with the environment providing all developmental and educational possibilities. This created two insuperable problems: first, the denial of any kind of 'mind' within the person leads to an inability to determine common experience and, therefore, social agreement; the second, stemming from that, is the difficulty of determining values. The significance of this theory is that it swept away absolutism and privilege and through a belief in external, behaviouristic education prepared the way for egalitarianism. The problems created by this viewpoint are enormous and, despite the popularity of his approach, which caused his earlier, similar work of 1758, *De l'esprit* (*On the Spirit*), to be suppressed for its heretical views, Helvétius's work remained a vigorous educational offshoot of the Enlightenment but provided no real direction of growth.

The Encyclopédie

Meanwhile the Enlightenment in France in mid-century was developing the character of an intellectual crusade of the *philosophes* against the Catholic Church and the Society of Jesus. At that time, in addition to Voltaire, a number of activists became prominent, chiefly Denis Diderot (1713–84), Jean Le Rond d'Alembert (1717–83) and his cousin, Étienne Bonnot de Condillac (1715–80). The great monument of these three, and their associates, is the controversial and provocative thirty-eight-volume *Encyclopédie ou dictionnaire raisonné des sciences, des arts et des métiers*, known simply as the *Encyclopédie*. This vast undertaking was originally conceived as a modest two-volume translation of Ephraim Chambers's English-language *Cyclopedia or an Universal Dictionary of Arts and Sciences*, published in the early part of the century when encyclopedism came into vogue in many countries as a response to the rapidly increasing accumulation of knowledge. Projected in 1746 and published between 1751 and 1765 with stormy interludes of suppression, censorship and prosecution, the *Encyclopédie* reflected the new intellectual and educational spirit of the age, arising from the belief that knowledge, even though expanding exponentially, still reflects a unity: behind man's discoveries is a systematically integrated corpus of knowledge. The purpose of the *Encyclopédie* was to bring knowledge into an ordered structure of 'proper' relationships.

This conception is expressed on the title page: the encyclopedia will 'set forth as well as possible the order and connection of the parts of human knowledge' and to achieve this it will follow Bacon's schema of a 'tree of knowledge' with three major branches: memory, reason and imagination, as set out in his *Advancement of Learning*. The central organizing theme is man 'as he is placed in the universe . . . [in] the very centre'.[31] This was to provoke wide church protests, as were such statements in d'Alembert's *Preliminary Discourse to the Encyclopedia* as 'all our direct knowledge can be reduced to what we receive through our senses' and truth is 'the fruits of the first reflective ideas that our sensations occasion'.[32]

In the many articles commissioned this revaluation was carried forward vigorously, and education is a key example. In the entry on 'College' written by d'Alembert, the controversy, which provoked the instant objection of the Jesuits, can be appreciated. D'Alembert (who had been educated in a rival Jansenist school, the Collège de Mazarin) launched into an attack in the first paragraph, stating that he proposed not to make a descriptive account of their history but to take up a serious public concern, 'the type of education given to our young in these colleges'.[33] This short entry begins with a survey of the subjects taught – humanities, rhetoric, philosophy, customs, morals and religion – and then devotes the remainder of the article to attacking them, summing up the net result in the words:

> All this means is that a young man, if he has spent his time wisely, leaves the college after ten years – among the most precious years of his life – with a very imperfect knowledge of a dead language and with precepts of rhetoric and principles of philosophy which he should endeavour to forget; often with impaired health, which is the least of the effects of the corruption of morals; sometimes with principles of misunderstood worship; but more frequently with such a superficial knowledge of religion that he succumbs to the first blasphemous conversation, the first dangerous reading.[34]

In the vein of the reforming spirit of the times, d'Alembert recommended a curriculum taught in the vernacular instead of Latin, and including English and Italian (and perhaps German and Spanish), along with history, geography, fine arts (especially music) and the barest necessary minimum of rhetoric and philosophy.

Religion was given cursory treatment by d'Alembert in the same article, and similarly to Locke he objected to excessive religious observances and performative rituals. He criticized Catholic schools in which,

> Under the pretext that Jesus Christ said that one must always pray, some teachers, and especially those who are very rigid in their principles, would like to see most time destined for study spent in meditations and catechisms; as if work performed conscientiously and with precision were not the best prayer before God![35]

The anticlericalism was thinly veiled; the Jesuits knew their opponents and the conflict between conservatism and the 'enlightened' empiricists continued unabated.

Despite all the efforts of the church establishment, however, the Enlightenment gathered strength; its iconoclasm reached into most aspects of European intellectual life and became the prevailing fashion, increasing the level of dissatisfaction with the conservative tradition; cultivated taste sought change even for the sake of novelty, and literature was produced to satisfy the demand. Education, as might be expected, was seen as fundamental in fostering this new enlightened society in process of gestation, and the thought of Locke was seized upon avidly; however, it remained a limited theory.

The revolution in educational thought: impact of Rousseau

In 1762 appeared the book that was to change Western educational thought and to have increasingly significant effects upon subsequent practice: this was *Émile* by Jean-Jacques Rousseau which immediately upon publication became the most censored, banned and therefore sought-after book of the century. *Émile* made Rousseau the *enfant terrible* of the establishment and the pride of the *philosophes*; apart from its sustained, free-ranging and vivacious attacks upon most conservative institutions of the day, it proposed in exhilarating form a development of Lockeian thought, not in the ultra-behaviourist direction of Helvétius, but following the organic interpretation already touched upon by La Mettrie. Rousseau's educational theory as expressed in *Émile* and his other widely acclaimed works must be interpreted not as an isolated phenomenon but as part of the grand stream of Enlightenment thinking and as a further contribution to the continuing tradition of utopian theorizing. Unlike many *philosophes*, Jean-Jacques Rousseau (1712–78) came from a humble background; his mother died in childbed a few days after he was born, leaving him to the care of an incompetent watchmaker father. Jean-Jacques was always sickly, he had little formal schooling and was largely self-taught, assisted by his erratic father who put a selection of books in his hands, both classical and contemporary. After a number of years of illness, then travel, and a time spent in ineffectual private tutoring, he arrived in Paris where he became acquainted with the editors of the *Encyclopédie*, Diderot and d'Alembert. In this period Diderot encouraged him to enter an essay for the prize offered by the Academy of Dijon on a topical Enlightenment theme: 'Has the restoration of the arts and sciences contributed to the corruption or purification of morals?' Diderot suggested that the sensational view – the negative position – would be more likely to attract attention; Rousseau argued the case for corruption and won the prize in 1749, the essay being published under the title *Discours sur les sciences et les arts* the following year.

From then on, Rousseau began writing in a vein of increasing social criticism; in 1752 he sought the Dijon prize again with an essay on the origins of inequality, the *Discours sur l'origine de l'inégalité*, but failed; none the less the work created an impact on its publication in 1755 and his corpus of radical major works appeared within the following decade: *Julie, ou La Nouvelle Héloïse* (1761), *Du contrat social* and *Émile* (both in

1762). Given his intention to shock the public conscience, he was not disappointed, and *Émile* in particular outraged clerical opinion since Book IV
contains an attack upon the Catholic Church under the title 'Profession de
foi du vicaire savoyard' – literally, the profession of faith of a curate from
Savoy. The curate, after learning to read, went on to study the *philosophes*
who opened his eyes to a much wider world than that provided within
the framework of conventional thinking. The Savoyard confession is, in
effect, a mock-ingenious affirmation of the Enlightenment programme
which becomes increasingly anticlerical as it progresses, accusing the
church of opposing truth, natural justice and social equity by its narrow
dogma and domination of the schools. Such an education leads not to an
ennobling vision of the good but to prejudice; nothing, the curate asserts,
is more stupid than wasting much of the child's life teaching it the catechism under the delusion that such would lead to the cultivation of human
potential for virtue. The Archbishop of Paris immediately condemned all
of *Émile* and in 1765 Rousseau left for England where he was temporarily
befriended by David Hume, who was by this time famous for his empirical
treatises *Of Human Nature, Concerning Human Understanding* and *Principles of
Morals*. Quarrels between them, however, broke out, Rousseau left for
France in 1767 and settled in Paris in 1770, all the time composing his
monumental *Confessions*, on the model of the famous Augustinian revela-
tions, until his death in 1778.

Traditions of ignorance: child-rearing practices in the eighteenth century

Apart from the anticlerical section on the Savoyard curate, most of *Émile*
is an account of how education should be conducted according, not to
convention, but to the dictates of right reason in a now-enlightened age.
To appreciate the inventiveness and impact of the theory of education in
Émile it is necessary to sketch the conventional wisdom against which
Rousseau was reacting. There was, for a start, no embryological theory
at the time to explain the origins of the individual; the church taught a
literal biblical interpretation of Eve as the mother of mankind who held,
within her body, the seed of all future generations, and so because all
mankind was present, *in utero*, at the Fall everyone is tainted with original
sin. This doctrine varied somewhat and a more acceptable version in the
eighteenth century was that each generation is contained, as seed, within
the seed of its progenitors. The character of neither the ovum nor the
sperm was understood, and there was no genetic theory; it was believed

that the ovum is the whole person and that the sperm does no more than 'fertilize' it.

Once fertilized, the ovum faces a hazardous gestation in the womb. Devils abound and can easily penetrate the maternal abdominal wall and infect the child with marasmus, the wasting disease. Pre-natal development of the personality was explained according to Aristotelian theory: the soul becomes individuated into various aspects, chiefly the vegetative (or appetitive), the affective and the intellective. Related to the soul in obscurely understood ways are the 'humours' of the body, namely, black bile, red bile, blood and phlegm which by their intermixed proportions give rise to the four 'complexions', choleric, aqueous, melancholic and sanguine, referring respectively to dominating temperamental qualities of excitability, calmness, broodiness and detachment. All four are present in each person, but their various mixture produces individual differences. Throughout gestation and post-natal life, the child is susceptible to maternal influences: moods, illnesses, attitudes, even those of nearby persons, are easily absorbed by the foetus and neonate.[36]

Despite maternal inclinations, mothers were counselled against breast-feeding the new-born baby for the first three days since colostrum was considered detrimental to good digestion. The mother's milk was considered to impart personality characteristics and, moreover, to be more beneficial for boys than for girls. If the mother were dry, it was important to choose a wet-nurse with the right personality and temperament since these would be transmitted in her milk. Nursing lasted a long time and weaning – by smearing the nipples with mustard – was usually begun when the child's first teeth appeared. Associated with the nursing theory was an anxiety about the 'unnatural' reflex of sucking which was believed to be caused by the membrane holding the tongue to the floor of the mouth. If the parents could afford it they sent for a surgeon to cut the membrane in the first three days; otherwise they or the midwife would pinch it with the nails of thumb and forefinger.[37]

Great care was taken to prevent the child from regressing to the foetal position by swaddling it with long bandages to a flat board, while the head was bound with a *cercle* to produce the fashionable long-tapered skull. In Comenius' *Orbis sensualium pictus* in the late seventeenth century a baby is illustrated with the description 'Infans involvitur fasciis reponitur in Cunas': the baby is wrapped in swaddling strips and is laid in a cradle.[38] Swaddling, however, caused hygiene and health problems such as itchiness, lice and other parasites; skin eruptions, which were almost universal, were attributed to imbalances in, or excesses of, the bodily humours.[39] The arms were generally freed after the first three or four weeks of life; the whole body between nine months and a year.

Early childhood was no release. Indeed, there was only a poorly developed conception of a stage of childhood; even though Comenius recognized sequences of development in *School of Infancy*, these were seen as imperfect versions of adulthood which the parent and educator should correct as quickly as possible; in everything, adult models were forced upon the child. The constant companion of childhood was fear of the rod, and the maxim of 'spare the rod and spoil the child' was universal. Few children went to school; most laboured in the fields or in cottage industries and, as the century progressed, went into factories and mines without any schooling, living, as Hobbes so correctly stated, lives that were 'solitary, poor, nasty, brutish and short'. One-half of the French population, at the time Rousseau took up their cause in the mid-eighteenth century, did not reach their fifteenth birthday.

Émile: *the doctrine of natural education*

Rousseau objected strenuously to this traditional method of child rearing which, apart from imposing excessive constraints upon the helpless infant, demanded that the child's natural affective propensities be eliminated as far as possible so that it might quickly become susceptible to 'reason'. 'Locke's great maxim was to reason with children and that is the current vogue,' Rousseau wrote in Book II of *Émile*, 'but it doesn't seem to me to be shown in results, and, for myself, I see no more stupid children than those who have been reasoned with.'[40] All of Rousseau's works concentrated upon a single theme, the utopian desire to reconstruct society by means of a new theory of natural order – a theme he expressly acknowledged as Platonic, writing that 'The *Republic* of Plato . . . is the finest treatise on education ever written.'[41] Rousseau's proposed society must be classless or at least radically different from that of the *ancien régime* of France. The need was for a social organization in which 'the people and the sovereign would be the same person', he wrote in the 1755 *Discourse on the Origins of Inequality*.[42] After a preliminary sketch of an educational system that would foster this in *Julie, or the New Héloïse* (an epistolary novel), he produced in 1762 his two major works, designed as a set: *Émile, or On Education* and its sequel *The Social Contract*.

Central to Rousseau's thought is the belief that education not only is integral with social reform but is even a prior and necessary condition. His ideas were radically utopian; as his contemporary J.-H.-S. Formey observed, 'Rousseau had turned his gaze towards Geneva but had really seen a utopia' – adding, in another context, that Rousseau took 'Geneva as a model for political organization with the purpose of proposing it as an example for all of Europe'.[43] Rousseau's ideal society, however, was not to be achieved simply by copying the independent city of Geneva, even though it was the most democratic of existing European societies; it required the institution of a totally new social order, that in turn being secured only through a radically different form of education modelled on the order of nature. Nature – and Rousseau consistently used the cognate French term *la nature* – is a fundamental concept throughout his writing, implicit in the famous opening sentence of *Émile*, 'Everything is good as it comes from the hands of the Maker of things; everything degenerates in the hands of man.' His objection was that man, through bad institutions and practices, deforms his own nature and therefore his society; in consequence even those with power fail to lead a life of genuine fulfilment. Only a careful study of nature and its processes can bring us to achieve appropriate ends in life. Our entire formation, he wrote in *Émile*, is derived from three possible sources: nature, men and things. The proper end of man is the completion of nature's own goal which is the harmonious blending, in correct sequence, of these three formative influences.[44] Education had been ineffectual up to the Enlightenment because it stemmed only from the latter two, men and things, ignoring as a proper basis that which comes first, nature. Calling for a form of public education similar to that described in Plato's *Republic*, he made a point of rejecting the Jesuit colleges – those 'ludicrous establishments called colleges'[45] – as a possible model. The first step, he said, is to establish, to get to know, the 'natural man'.[46] And this gives us our vocation in life: the attainment of humanity, which comes only in a natural order: 'dans l'ordre naturel, les hommes étant tous égaux, leur vocation commune est l'état d'homme.'[47]

To illustrate how the 'natural order' is to be followed and a good society attained, Rousseau described, in the bulk of *Émile*, how education should be effected in correct sequence: nature, things, man. The story outlines in a simplified form the education of a boy Émile and a girl, Sophie. Of its five books the first four deal with Émile, the last with Sophie, chiefly to illustrate the necessary differences in girls' education; most of the formation of Émile would apply to girls. In its internal division, Book I deals with infancy and early childhood, II with childhood, III with early adolescence, IV with late adolescence and early adulthood, these sections corresponding to natural stages of the growth of the individual and the appropriate forms of education.

In the stage of infancy, which should be supervised mainly by the mother, with the father taking a general interest, the child should be left as unconstrained as possible, completely directed by the basic forces of pleasure and pain. In order to avoid artificiality the environment should not be excessively simplified; the child should build up sensory experience by direct encounters, while the parents and other adults remain discreetly in the background. This accords with the unfolding of the child's nature, since at birth it knows nothing and has only a 'capability for learning' and a need, from its first moments, to stretch and exercise its limbs and to explore the environment. Following Bacon and Locke, Rousseau adopted the theory of a hierarchical development of mental faculties, arguing that 'at the beginning of life, when the memory and imagination are still quiescent, the child is concerned only with that which stimulates his senses',[48] and since the last are the 'primary materials of knowledge' the natural order is followed by letting the senses experience first, and this in turn allows memory to furnish such experiences to the understanding.

Education is, then, a continuous process that begins at birth and follows the natural unfolding of the child's latent powers in the sequence sensation–memory–understanding; the treatise provided a simplified model (much misunderstood by subsequent critics who failed to read it in conjunction with the *Social Contract*) of the education of Émile who, for convenience, is described as an orphan under the care of a tutor. The overwhelming purpose of such education is to produce the new moral person and here – although he explicitly acknowledged the influence of Plato – Rousseau apparently absorbed and followed Aristotelian ideas unconsciously, for he claimed that the chief characteristic of such a reborn person is to be absolutely happy. Aware of the sophisticated literature on happiness, Rousseau extended the concept to 'true happiness' which is a product of a 'perfect equality of power and will'.[49] With this concept comes the first check upon the hitherto unbridled freedom of the infant: in childhood Émile learns the constraints of necessity. We must recognize childhood as a stage and treat the child as a child, the adult as an adult. So the growing child, having first been allowed free rein of sensory experience, moves in childhood to the second realm of educational direction, that of things. Infancy follows nature; childhood is shaped by the continuous unfolding of inner nature operating in conjunction with the objects of the environment.

Childhood, in his view, is still pre-rational and so pressures from the world of people are to be avoided: Émile's tutor, in this stage, does not enter into rationally based arguments; Émile is told on occasions what to do by fiat, chiefly because he is unable to appreciate logical arguments involving concepts of duty and obligation and is responsive instead to pressures of force, necessity and dominance. Indeed, for Rousseau, the realm of things has a necessary, inevitable domination over people. As the child climbs trees and falls, steals fruit from a peasant's orchard and is chased and perhaps beaten, as he carelessly handles coals from the fire, the concepts of environmental pressures become appreciated. Rousseau termed this 'negative education': 'la première éducation doit donc être purement négative'.[50]

Throughout childhood, right up to puberty, this is the pattern of education. The tutor may, of course, at times be vexed by the caprice of the child and even express anger, but must avoid moralizing if possible since an appeal to reason is outside the natural scope of this stage. On the other hand, an angry adult does belong to the world of things and so is an appropriate 'negative' learning experience for the child. By the same token, then, the tutor must not deliberately teach any cognitive materials; there are to be no formal lessons in childhood: no reading, writing, reckoning – indeed, no books at all. If Émile wants to draw, paint, keep pets or dig a garden those, as affective, sensory experiences, are well within the ambit of the natural stage. 'Never give your student any verbal lessons,' he warned; nothing should be given but experience.[51]

This model was based on the Bacon–Locke theory (of Aristotelian provenance) of the tripartite mind governed by faculties which themselves emerge through a developmental process, and Rousseau presented the crucial argument:

Although memory and reason are two essentially different faculties, neither, however, develops without the other. Before the age of reason the child receives not ideas but merely images; and there is a major difference between them in that images are but clear pictures of sensible objects, while ideas are concepts of them, given by their relationships. An image may exist independently in the mind but ideas presuppose the existence of other ideas. When one imagines, one is merely seeing mentally; one conceives, however, by an act of comparison. Our sensations are purely passive and different from all our perceptions or ideas which are generated by the active principle of judgement.[52]

Rousseau therefore regarded book learning for the child as premature: books consist essentially of vicarious experience in verbal, symbolic form (and given both the curriculum and methods of verbal education in his day there were good grounds for his denunciation). Languages are one of the most unprofitable of educational activities; geography a meaningless mixture of abstractions on the surface of a cardboard globe; history a narrative of 'facts', mere verbal statements devoid of causal relationships which the child's pre-rational mind can't appreciate; fables are meaningless, their subtleties beyond childhood's comprehension.[53]

At puberty comes the stage of dawning reason, and it is then that the third of the educative influences – people – can be added to the earlier two of nature and things. Dawning reason is manifested by curiosity and the child's drives to extend his physical and mental horizons, and at this stage Rousseau introduced the concept that genuine science is the discovery, through a combination of experience and reason, of the structure of events. So Émile's tutor has him attend to the phenomena of nature and, rather than teaching him science, lets him discover it for himself.[54] Now he introduced geography, which is learned in the field with a compass, and the treatise deals at length with learning by means of a geography in which sensations and ideas are developed experientially. Further, it is essential not to hurry and crowd the child's mind but rather to let concepts form naturally and permanently, so that he conceives only clear, precise ideas ('idées justes et claires').[55]

Émile: *natural education and cultural demands*

Yet the world of abstract learning, the realm of books, cannot be ignored; even though Rousseau says at this juncture: 'I hate books: they only teach us to talk about things we do not know.'[56] Again the problem can be overcome by following the principles of natural learning – make the books relevant to experience – and as a first reader Émile is given a copy of *Robinson Crusoe*, man in a world of nature learning by experience. How Émile learns to read up to this stage is not made explicit, but Rousseau is clearly depending upon the intuition that maturation and enthusiasm will enable Émile to make quick progress. From then on, reading of useful books, within the realm of experience, may be introduced. In this respect we can more easily appreciate the force of Rousseau's argument when we consider that by contrast in the Port-Royal curriculum a boy at the same age (twelve or thirteen) was being required to read the sixteenth-century Latin grammar of Lubinus, the seventeenth-century grammar of Tursellinus, the *Phaedrus* of Plato, the *History* of Flavius Josephus of the first century AD, along with selections from the Bible, French literature and history, and French grammar – by the method of the *Ratio studiorum* if in a Jesuit college, by a Comenian or similar method if in a Protestant grammar school.

As adolescence proceeds the intellect soars, as sensation and memory feed the maturing faculties of reason and judgement; Émile can read voraciously now that he has a store of prior personal experience. Manual workshop activities are highly recommended, especially carpentry, while physical exercise, a simple diet and regular hours are recommended as conducive to good health. While sex is not yet a drive to be considered, the energies of the boy (and girl, for hitherto the educational programme is common to both) should be directed towards fulfilling the growth of nature. When the child becomes a young adult, however, a new set of circumstances prevails.

We are, says Rousseau, born twice: the first time for existence, the second to live; the former as members of a species, the latter as human beings.[57] This second stage implies both the development of adult sexuality, and therefore sex roles, along with participation as responsible members of society. So Émile becomes less egocentric and more involved in social relationships; he must learn from the third educative force – people – and, given the proper development of his personality through the earlier stages, he should be well prepared. Even so, life in this stage will not be easy. So Émile, who has been reared to become a fully moral person, must acquire judgement and taste; he must be able to move freely among people. Precisely what the curriculum should be is left open, for it is wise to be reserved about the future; indeed, Rousseau remarks, presciently, 'we are approaching a state of crisis and an era of revolution,' adding as a footnote, 'it is impossible that the monarchies of Europe can last much longer, . . . even if they are shining brightly now in their moment of decline. . . . Who can tell what will eventuate?'[58]

Concerning the passions, sexual drives and the mating impulses, Rousseau is ambivalent; heightening or stimulating such interests excessively or morbidly should be avoided, but when questions of curiosity are asked they should be answered either honestly or not at all. Given the conditions of his day, especially medical and psychological knowledge, his advice is quite reasonable; certainly it accords, if conservatively, with his principles. In his opinion, however, there are weightier matters involved in the attainment of a wider morality – which doubtless would include sexual behaviour as a component.

By the age of eighteen the youth has entered early adulthood, which Rousseau considers to be the moral realm (*l'ordre moral*).[59] He defines justice and goodness not as abstract terms but as 'genuine affections of the soul, enlightened by reason',[60] but avoids further definition with the disclaimer that he does not feel constrained to write, at this point, a treatise on metaphysics or morals. Yet, clearly, some deeper grounding is necessary, since by Rousseau's time these ideas had generated a considerable literature. His statement is Neoplatonic and his verb 'enlighten' a Platonic metaphor. In this Rousseau reveals an eclecticism that was characteristic of the period, mixing Aristotelian and Platonic ideas as it suited the argument; processes of thinking drew upon the Aristotelian model of the mind with its doctrine of faculties, ideologies were derived from Platonic or Neoplatonic concepts of 'illumination' or 'enlightenment' and the vision of the good. In fact, the conjunction of the two classical positions was not new to the Enlightenment but reached back at least to the twelfth and thirteenth centuries.[61] Rousseau, however, provided a new development – one not anticipated by Locke – with the idea of latent faculties that mature in the course of time. The notion of maturation explains the way in which understanding develops; it does not, however, explain the concepts of justice and goodness which Rousseau considered in greater detail in the *Social Contract*.

It is, then, by obscure mental processes that Émile comes to an understanding of the moral realm, beginning with personal experience which is amplified by increasingly wider social experience and the now highly useful verbal literature. Once rational maturity is reached, the vicarious experience of the past makes sense; we can learn from history and the experience of others. Religion is discounted here and Book IV, which contains the confessions of the curate from Savoy, goes to some length to deny the church interpretation of religion, although Rousseau professed a belief in a supreme being and his writings give the impression of a deist standpoint. To help form taste and to provide a wider literature of human experience, Rousseau recommended in *Émile* the study of French and Latin contemporary literature with progression to Latin and Greek classical literature.

The education of girls is described in Book V which gives an account of the rearing of Émile's future spouse, Sophie. Although Rousseau postulated complete equality between males and females, he stated that males are by nature active and strong, females passive and weak; accordingly, Sophie's upbringing should be more sheltered, with the emphasis on cultivating grace and accomplishments such as needlework and tapestry, preferably in a convent where innocence can be maintained. He maintained that girls need religion more than boys but stressed the need for short prayers and the inculcation of a deistic view of god as an abstract 'divine spirit' rather than a retributive patriarch. Extensive education does not have to be given to Sophie, for she needs only as much as is necessary to 'live properly'; any deep intellectual sophistication – despite her name – can be provided, after marriage, by Émile himself as tutor. Marriage and motherhood are the destiny of girls; at the wedding ceremony, however, Rousseau counselled that the bonds of matrimony should not be too tightly drawn else the knots break. Marriage should be a relationship of mutual respect and tolerance. At that point *Émile* ends.

Social conscience and moral growth

The concepts of nature and natural law and the basis of morality (itself the end of education) are examined in the *Social Contract*, the companion volume to *Émile*, published the same year. *Émile* was intended to show how by proper sequences according to natural principles the morally autonomous person would be formed; if this practice became universal, a new uncorrupted moral world would eventuate. The questions remained, what precisely is the order of nature, and how binding is this order upon mankind? Further, if Émile is raised according to the processes of nature, how is it that he will develop a moral and hence social consciousness and appropriate behaviour? How can freedom, moral autonomy, be attained by that means? Would the outcome of following nature be a personality, not free in the sense of possessing moral autonomy, but rather the perpetual slave of natural forces? Finally, is the message of *Émile* that education for social renewal, the utopian millennium, is to be achieved by individual tutoring – the ultimate paradox?

Rousseau considered these questions in *Émile* and the *Social Contract*, and to a limited extent in *Considerations on the Government of Poland*. Although his presupposition was the Hobbes–Locke theory of contract society, as the title indicates, the nature of the contract must not be coercive, as Hobbes argued, but mutually accepted. Now the famous opening lines of the *Social Contract* are frequently quoted: 'Man is born free yet we now find him everywhere in chains'. What is usually overlooked is that in the *Social Contract* he went on to say that he does not wish to pursue the history of why that has happened; instead, given that it is a fact of social life, he seeks to know what it is that legitimizes it: 'Qu'est-ce qui peut le rendre légitime?'[62] We can easily formulate a concept of universal justice by reason alone (and Plato's *Republic* is the obvious *locus terminus* of the idea), but if justice is to be realizable it must be reciprocal among all persons.[63] In view of the variety of human personality and behaviour, sanctions are necessary, and so 'it is necessary to have conventions and laws to unite rights and duties in order to make justice obtain'.

Unlike the laws of physics, such as gravitation, which are self-fulfilling, there is on earth (setting aside the notion of ultimate divine retribution) no such automatic self-enforcement; human laws must be enforced by society itself, so reciprocal action among people must be instituted. This is the essence of the concept of justice, and hence education, developed in the *Social Contract*. There has to be, therefore, a law other than the natural one (which in essence is undefinable since it consists in each one of us independently following the dictates of nature), and this exists in the broad consensus of society, in the understanding that individual inclinations have to be subordinated to a rule of law that has a universal application. That broad consensus he termed the 'general will'. It is the making and enforcing of laws conforming to the general will that is the proper (legitimate) function of the legislative process. This, as Rousseau recognized, is a circular argument, and his answer is that the ultimate source of all justice is god;[64] it is the search for divine sources and their embodiment in statute law that makes for good legislation. Throughout the *Social Contract* there is constant discussion of bad laws and bad society; Rousseau's mission was to show how good laws, of divine provenance, may be determined and enacted.

At this point the argument returns to the theory of nature. The 'divine author of all things' is responsible for creating all natural processes and has implanted in each person a capacity for following divine principles. Although Rousseau accepted the empirical position of rejecting innate ideas, his theory postulates the notion of innate faculties as the means by which each individual is enabled to understand and appreciate or empathize with the design of divine providence.[65] The Savoyard curate makes this clear in a long disquisition on the empirical approach of knowing only by particulars and the Humean pessimism of never getting beyond immediate sensations and perceptions. There is an 'established order' which 'I call God',[66] and this I feel in my heart,[67] the curate affirms.

Rousseau postulated three latent capacities implanted by god within our nature: in addition to reason, by which we know the good, and which was the major preoccupation of Bacon and Locke, he also stressed conscience and free will, conscience being the faculty whereby we come to love the good, and free will the faculty whereby we consciously seek it.[68] Here is the route to moral autonomy, to becoming a good person. Conscience is independent of social conditioning; being an innate faculty, it provides a source of independent moral judgement which enables man to seek the good, to enact good laws and thereby produce a good society. Of course, conscience may be socially inhibited, and the whole argument of *Émile* is that, by avoiding traditional corrupt social practices, including education, each person, properly educated according to the right processes of natural development, will be enabled properly to cultivate all three faculties, reason, conscience and free will. Further, Rousseau maintained that the only worthwhile life is the morally good life. Certain deeper considerations emerge. First of all, the natural education set out in *Émile* is only the beginning of a genuinely educative process since, were we always to follow nature, life would be devoid of crucial decision making and would, like that of plants and animals, be dominated by appetition. Humanity comes from conflicts that demand choice, which in turn requires moral judgement. There are many times when our natural inclinations run counter to the dictates of conscience; we become morally good in the degree to which we are able to satisfy conscience through the exercise of free will. Moral autonomy, genuine freedom, involves discipline of the natural impulses; it requires recognition of the wider good as determined by the 'general will' and our conformity to it.

The morally good person, then, is able to override self-love (*amour de soi*) in order to act upon wider principles of the common good which, ultimately, are those of divine providence. Again, there is a circularity involved in that the common good, as expressed in the general will and enacted in good laws, requires morally good members of society to produce it; morally good persons can only emerge in a good society with good laws. Such is the dilemma of all utopian reformers. Rousseau recognized that it would be a slow, interactive process of improvement. Again, Rousseau's dependence on classical tradition is apparent; his arguments for justice are strikingly similar to those in the *Republic*, although Rousseau takes the form of justice back to divine provenance; at the same time the adoption of the Aristotelian notion of faculties – virtually a psychology of learning rather than an epistemology – shows his allegiance to Enlightenment thinking. Rousseau was simply unable to accept the unmitigated empirical argument which after Locke was taken by David Hume to its ultimate development of total scepticism about knowledge. The continued acceptance of a 'Platonized Aristotelianism' by Rousseau, though, was not unusual; in fact, the purely empirical approach continued to be opposed and, following Rousseau's lead, the problem of finding ultimate values in a world of sensation and reflection became the dominating spirit of late eighteenth- and all of nineteenth-century philosophy.

Role of the school: Considerations on the Government of Poland

What of the final dilemma: is the morally good person, the highly sociable person, best educated by individual tutorship? Too often the simplified model given in *Émile*, virtually a pedagogical paradigm, is taken literally rather than as an inspirational ideal. When it came to specific instances, Rousseau was able to make concrete proposals as he did in 1772 in *Considerations on the Government of Poland*. Poland's geographical position was politically unfortunate in that its land frontiers consisted of easily crossed rivers on the great northern European plain, and it was bounded by Russia, Prussia and Austria – all modernizing nations with territorial ambitions. The country was in a state of near-anarchy due in large part to its enserfed peasantry, an excessively large, parasitic nobility constituting some 5 per cent of the population, and a lack of central authority. Even their titular king was elected by the nobility. In 1772 Count de Wielhorski wrote to Rousseau for advice on preserving the country from impending foreign domination. As events turned out, he was too late: in the same year those neighbouring powers annexed large Polish border regions; in 1793 and 1795 they completed the total partition of Poland.

Rousseau's reply to Wielhorski, however, contains a concrete development of the principles set out in *Émile* and the *Social Contract* and needs to be read in conjunction with those two works to round out Rousseau's educational theory. Hitherto Poland had been under Jesuit educational domination which had established a *collège* system, divided along class lines into colleges proper for the richer nobility and academies for the poorer nobility; the traditional parish and cathedral school system provided for the eight million inhabitants. Rousseau recommended the immediate abolition of all existing institutions (the Jesuits had by this time been suppressed) and the establishment of a single system, completely free of charge,[69] or else, if that were not possible, with fees low enough for all to afford them. The rationale was implicit in the *Social Contract*, since 'it is education that gives to all souls a national form, so directing their opinions and tastes that they become patriots by conscious affirmation'. Then followed an ambiguous passage: education belongs only to free men (*hommes libres*) who have a common interest in the rule of law.[70] By 'free men' he seems to be referring only to the nobility and gentry, but the principle extends to all people. Perhaps Rousseau was recognizing the tactical exigencies of the excessively stratified society in Poland and that change were better begun at the top, rather than not at all.

Nothing specific is recounted of the detailed sequences on education set out in *Émile*; indeed, in the *Considerations* only the fourth chapter deals with education, even though Rousseau does call it the 'all-important article'. Yet the general advice echoes, in more realistic form, the programme of *Émile*, the whole sequence leading up to the most significant aspect of the curriculum: the appreciation of the rule of law and correlative individual moral growth. The social environment is paramount, and so every school should have a gymnasium in which all the children can play together, especially since communal physical activity has not only a beneficial bodily effect but also a moral effect in that it accustoms children from an early age to discipline, equality, fraternity, rivalry and – under the constant gaze of their fellow citizens – to the need for approbation.[71] Given a good constitution and good laws, this will lead to proper moral growth.

Response to Rousseau: action and reaction

Rousseau's thought, both political and educational, had an immediate and profound effect upon Europe and, in addition, the New World. He was writing in an age of intellectual ferment, and expounded more successfully than anyone else a theory of education that accorded with the trends of Enlightenment thought. Reaction and hostility from conservative forces was instantaneous, the opening salvoes being a condemnation in the year of *Émile*'s publication by the Jesuit-dominated Faculty of

Theology of the University of Paris. A hostile literature appeared almost overnight, the French Jesuit Giacinto Gerdil attacking Rousseau in a tract that appeared in an English translation as early as 1765 entitled *Reflections on Education, relative to both theory and practice, in which some of the principles attempted to be established by M. Rousseau in his Emilius are occasionally examined and refuted*, similar arguments appearing also in the Abbé Poncelet's *Principes généraux pour servir à l'éducation des enfants, particulièrement de la noblesse française*. Both works, and many others, argued that profound truths are beyond the reach of the juvenile mind and must, at first, be accepted on faith and, by implication, on authoritarian dogmatic assertion.[72]

Despite valiant church opposition, the trend of the times was otherwise, and the Jesuits, as the main advocates of a Catholic approach to education, were themselves under attack, being expelled from Portugal in 1759, France in 1764, Spain in 1767, and suppressed in those countries by papal order in 1773. In Paris – and the pattern was generally followed elsewhere – the Jesuit schools were handed over to other religious authorities; their forty colleges in the capital were divided up, twelve going to other orders, chiefly the Oratorians, and twenty-eight to a secular commission of seven members whose composition included a bishop.[73] Meanwhile, Rousseau's works spread quickly throughout liberal Europe in numerous editions, authorized, clandestine and pirated, and became just as eagerly read – if illegally – in Italy, Spain and Portugal. In Prussia, where the *Aufklärung* became a national movement, his ideas were taken up by Christian Salzmann whose school at Schnepfenthal was based upon an attempt to translate *Émile* in institutional practice, although the school remained small, not rising above sixty-one pupils by 1803,[74] and by the very ambitious school project of Basedow at Dessau.

Émile *in practice: Basedow and the Philanthropinum*

In its short-lived existence of several years, the experimental school at Dessau known as the Philanthropinum was the chief centre for the putting of Rousseau's educational ideas into practice, attracting Europe-wide attention. Its founder was Johann Bernhard Basedow (1724–90), a wig-maker's son from Hamburg who became interested in educational reform after reading *Émile*. He proposed to publish a manual for parents whereby Rousseauian educational ideas could be followed methodically, calling this his *Methodenbuch für Väter und Mütter der Familien und Völker (Method*

Book for Fathers and Mothers of Families and Nations). In a preliminary publication of 1768 he solicited subscriptions and was almost overwhelmed by the response, so enthusiastic were the intelligentsia of Europe to follow this latest trend. Issued in two parts, the first appearing in Leipzig in 1770, the second in Dessau in 1772, it became famous under the title *Das Elementarwerk* (*The Elementary Primer*),[75] and continued to be issued at least until 1909, although by then as a curiosity. *Das Elementarwerk* is a mixture of advice for parents and an illustrated reading primer for children, on encyclopedic lines, strongly influenced by Comenius' *Orbis sensualium pictus*, and containing ninety pages of copper-plate illustrations, four pictures to a page, all cut by Daniel Chodowiecki, one of Europe's foremost engravers.

At the same time that he commenced his book, Basedow had received an invitation from Prince Franz Leopold of Anhalt-Dessau, a small principality on the south-western border of Prussia, to establish a progressive school in Dessau. Basedow accepted but spent so much time on his book, meantime delaying the opening of the school, that Franz Leopold lost interest and withdrew patronage. Without princely support, Basedow opened it in 1774 and accepted students in two classes: sons of the well-to-do as boarders and those of working-class families who, supported by a charitable sponsor, were given their board and tuition in return for menial service, usually as servants to the boarders. Basedow was himself an accomplished and well-regarded theologian and philosopher of the period and had developed an ideology similar to that of Rousseau, although he was by no means an uncritical follower. The school, designated a 'Philanthropinum' – a place of human love – had a structured curriculum and sequential lessons; its departure came in that it followed the then developing concept of the *Realschule* already pioneered by Semler in Halle and Hecker in Berlin by building the content around vernacular German, mathematics, natural science, history and geography. Latin was taught as a second language: given its universality as the medium of most scholarship, it could not be ignored. Important, however, was the addition of Rousseauian ideas, chiefly handicrafts and outdoor activities – nature excursions, local geography learnt on field trips, and even an annual summer camp of one or two months. The school included a laboratory for natural science of a museum type, where collections were displayed, observed and discussed, such a room being illustrated in Plate XLVIII of *Das Elementarwerk* with wall charts of plants and animals, and a protractor, maps and books on a table.

Despite the ordered curriculum, the Philanthropinum introduced several startling innovations derived from *Émile*. The first was the concept of learning readiness, especially in presenting sequential cognitive activities such as language and mathematics; with respect to the study of grammar, Basedow counselled waiting until the teacher knew intuitively when the moment was ready, arguing that 'by delaying until the appropriate moment and with a suitable method the difficulty will be diminished ... one should wait until the student's mind develops a capacity for abstract generalizations'.[76] Allied to this was his conviction that all cognitive learning must be voluntarily undertaken by the child and self-directed; the teacher should assist by making the lessons as interesting, playful and varied as possible, and in this way the problems of coercion and chastisement would cease to exist. In particular Basedow's method relied upon games, competitions and student involvement. By these means, he asserted, the dreariness of memorization – the staple of most educational procedures of the time – would be mitigated if not eliminated. So successful were his methods that at the end of its second year of operation, in 1776, the Philanthropinum held an open demonstration of its methods which attracted visitors from all over the continent.

Basedow was the centre of European educational attention, Prince Franz Leopold restored patronage, and the school appeared to prosper with increased enrolments. Almost immediately Basedow quarrelled violently with his deputy Wolke and the other teachers. The school by its very nature could not withstand such conflicts; Basedow left and the Philanthropinum foundered. In 1782 Wolke left for Russia to establish a school in St Petersburg while the school struggled along, without the distinction or drive imparted by Basedow, until it ceased operations in 1793. By this time, however, several similar progressive schools had been established in Germany and Switzerland, all seeking to develop Rousseau's ideas; in fact, at that moment the Rousseauian impetus was being given early tentative expression by the German-Swiss educator Heinrich Pestalozzi whose career, although similar in many ways to that of Basedow, was to have a lasting influence.

In the same period Rousseau's ideas reached Russia, which in this period was enthusiastically attempting to modernize by importing French culture under the influence of Catherine II (r. 1762–96), formerly a German princess whose education had been based on the ideas of the French *philosophes*, and who introduced Enlightenment thinking to St Petersburg. One idealistic proposal was the reform of education and, in

6 View of the convent of Port-Royal-des-Champs, engraved by Madeleine Hortemels.

7   Warrington, a dissenting academy in eighteenth-century England.

fact, significant headway was made. Originally, the scheme included Ivan Betskoy's utopian plan to create a new humanity through Rousseauian ideas by setting up a widespread system of boarding-schools wherein children could be raised according to the principles of *Émile*. The ideas were disseminated; unfortunately, the schools were not, apart from two which had a lasting existence, the Institutes of Smolny and Novodevichi,[77] although their interpretations of Rousseau were significantly modified.

Jesuit reaction: the imitation of Émile

Rousseau's ideas spread just as rapidly throughout the Catholic world, by two means: one was the widespread illegal dissemination of his books; the other, equally significant, was a quite legal propagation of his ideas by the religious authorities. The former process had a curious beginning in that *Émile* and the *Social Contract* appeared legally in Habsburg territories; only too late were they recognized as a threat to orthodoxy. Not until 1764 were they placed upon the *Index* and ordered to be burnt. In a solemn high mass in Madrid in 1765 a volume of *Émile* was ceremonially burned, although this turned out to be a fake copy.[78] Perhaps the gesture was all that was needed; the reality was that Rousseau symbolized to liberal Spaniards the hope of reform. For, indeed, during the eighteenth century, Enlightenment ideas penetrated Spain and provoked demands, among other things, for educational improvement. However, conservative opposition was so strong that it was to be a long exercise in gradualism throughout the rest of the eighteenth and all of the nineteenth century before effective changes were instituted.

Paradoxically, the widespread acceptance of Rousseau's thought was stimulated, quite unwittingly, by the religious authorities and – supreme irony – by the Jesuits themselves. The Jesuits and Rousseau were in open enmity, Rousseau accusing them of having caused his works to be banned. Far from denying the accusation, the Jesuits sought to eradicate Rousseau's educational doctrines by what now seems an incredible approach: in exile, and with time on their hands, some wrote detailed refutations of *Émile* which necessarily entailed presenting the book's essential arguments, at times in lengthy quotations, in order, they hoped, to refute them; in several cases, they even tried to write alternative versions of *Émile* from an orthodox Catholic viewpoint. Of these, two were particularly noteworthy. A French Jesuit, Jean-Baptiste Blanchard, produced a version in 1782 entitled *L'École des mœurs* (*The School of Morals*) which appeared in Madrid in 1786 under the same title *Escuela des cos-tumbres* and, after several further editions, was published in Mexico in 1822.[79] The other important version was the best known of all, the *Eusebio* of Pedro Montengón, published in Madrid in 1786 and in a re-vised, Inquisition-amended edition in 1807–8.[80] The title immediately sets the tone (the Greek work *eusebis* means 'pious' or 'religious'); the analogy is carried through in the story of a noble-born orphan who is shipwrecked on the coast of America and rescued by benefactors who put him under the tutelage of a bachelor basket-weaver who teaches Eusebio the way of the simple, frugal life. Eventually, on returning to Europe, Eusebio marries and, in rearing his son, adopts the same principles of natural development as are given in *Émile*; *Eusebio* takes two generations to achieve the aim. It was to emphasize the religious component in Eusebio's education – too lightly treated in the first edition – that led to the second version under instructions by the Inquisition. *Eusebio* spread throughout Spain and Italy; it was not, however, read for its intrinsic merit but as an introduction to *Émile* against which it was critically compared. Montengón wrote a sequel, *Eudoxia* (the girl's name means 'glory' or 'honour'), which follows, in general, the education of Sophie in Book V of *Émile*.[81]

So the Jesuits unwittingly spread Rousseau's ideas which became a significant theoretical component of the groundswell of demands for the rights of man that were being expressed throughout western Europe and its New World colonies in the late eighteenth century. Everywhere the utopian ideal of a new moral world was being discussed and, in respect of education, *Émile* was the seminal work. No one was deceived by the individualized model; clearly it was recognized that the ideas of *Émile* needed to be given a fuller theoretical analysis before they were susceptible of institutional treatment, and to that task several of the greatest figures in the history of educational thought directed their efforts.

An Age of Revolutions 1762–1830: Theoretical Foundations of Education for the New Order

Revolutions: political, economic, industrial

The social contract and political action

In his writings Rousseau not only set the tone for much subsequent eighteenth- and nineteenth-century thought; he also sensed the spirit of the times in his observation that Europe was entering an age of revolution in which it was doubtful whether monarchy would survive. As events developed, the half-century following the publication of *Émile* and the *Social Contract* was the most turbulent of all of Europe's experiences hitherto; indeed, it entered an age not of revolution but of many revolutions, political, economic, industrial and intellectual.

Politically, ideas and actions were strongly influenced by an outpouring of radical literature on contract theory which can be traced from its source in Hobbes through Locke and Montesquieu to Rousseau's *Social Contract* of 1762. Thereafter this style of political thought burgeoned, providing an ideological rationale for popular movements of social protest in Britain and France,[1] and it received its most famous and enduring expression in *The Unanimous Declaration of the Thirteen United States of America*, popularly known as the Declaration of Independence, of 4 July 1776.

Drafted by Thomas Jefferson (1743–1826), a Virginia lawyer and later third president of the new nation (1801–9), and an enthusiast for the empirical thought of Bacon, Locke and Newton, the Declaration drew directly from Locke's *Second Treatise of Government*. Its second paragraph asserted that 'we hold these truths to be self-evident, that all men are created equal, that they are endowed by their Creator with certain inalienable Rights . . . that to secure these rights, Governments are instituted among Men, deriving their just powers from the consent of the governed';[2] in making these assertions it echoed the *Second Treatise*'s claims of 'man, being born . . . with a title to perfect freedom and uncontrolled enjoyment of all the rights and privileges of the law of nature equally with any other man or number of men of the world, [and who therefore] has by nature a power not only to preserve his property – that is, his life, liberty and estate – . . . but to judge of and punish the breaches of law in others'.[3] Equally popular in the period was Thomas Paine's manifesto *The Rights of Man*, a historical justification of equality which stated that 'every history of the creation, and every traditionary account . . . agrees in establishing . . . that men are all of *one degree*, and consequently that all men are born equal, and with equal natural rights'. Paine asserted, following contract theory, that people have come together in society for the express purpose of improving their lives; the surrender of part of one's individual freedom is not 'to have fewer rights than before, but to have those rights better secured'.[4]

A quiet revolution: economic and industrial developments

Along with social and political conflicts, economic and industrial changes were inextricably involved as the slow movement to an industrial-urban economy that had begun in the early eighteenth century continued, especially in Britain and France, the English Midland region being the pacesetter. By the 1790s France led the continent, but Britain led Europe, although not by any large margin. The pressure was greater on Britain than on France; the latter's extensive territory, great forests and rivers, larger population and milder climate, particularly in the south, gave it a range of natural resources that helped sustain a rate of productivity unmatched on the continent. Britain's population of some 9 million, as against France's 27 in the year 1801, was, however, relatively denser and put a greater strain on the small land area. By this time the forests of Britain were disappearing and timber ceased to be a plentiful source of construction materials, and of energy in the form of charcoal, as it still was in France; the more level topography of England allowed no great fast-flowing rivers that could provide mill power such as the Rhône, Seine and Loire yielded. Britain turned to the new construction material of iron and the energy source of coal, both of which were abundantly available, and a new kind of manufacturing economy was generated. One, moreover, that was self-spurring; one invention stimulated another and throughout the late eighteenth and much of the nineteenth century Britain was the source of continued industrial technological invention and application. With the development of the steam engine industrial growth in Britain surged ahead.

The Baconian 'renovation of knowledge' through a combination of the scientific revolution with the methodology of empirical induction had now begun to show its promise in the application of science to technology. In that period, empiricism was employed as a technique for isolating a problem, collecting the relevant data and constructing a hypothesis that would be demonstrated in fact; this approach of scientific empiricism was a wonder of the age that led exuberant devotees to believe it would solve all problems. We read in David Hartley's influential *Observations on Man, his Frame, his Duty and his Expectations* (published in 1749) that, given the proper application of Lockeian empiricism, inequalities in human experience, which create social imperfections because most fail to reach the highest levels of human excellence, will be overcome and all people will be made 'perfectly similar, in a finite time, by a proper adjustment of the impressions and associations'.[5]

Curiously, the Clarendon Code of the Restoration era played a part. Having enforced Anglican conformity, it stimulated the dissenting and private academies which, through their modernized curricula and their recognition of the commercial need to meet consumer demands, provided England in the late eighteenth century with more schools producing technically trained students than any other region in Europe. While this remains a largely unexplored topic,[6] England clearly led the rest of Europe in technical education, although this was beginning to develop in France, Germany and Russia with the establishment of military and naval academies of engineering and related areas. French education, predominantly in the hands of the clergy – and such clerical control was little affected by the suppression of the Jesuits – had little concern with science, technology or commerce.

In Britain, however, business activities were accorded far more prestige than in France; Adam Smith had developed a labour-oriented economic theory, and Britain followed *laissez-faire* policies more freely than any other country. Despite the loss of the American colonies, the new United States remained a major market for British manufactures and a source of raw materials far greater than France or any other European power; the British Empire was continuing to grow with the acquisition of India, Australia and New Zealand – all secure sources of trading strength now that Britannia ruled the high seas. And of major significance to British dominance in the industrial revolution was its comparative freedom from continental entanglements. Despite festering relationships with occupied Ireland, it had no border disputes, no masses of hostile troops on the frontier ready to invade. Yet British leadership in the industrial revolution must not be overemphasized; the same process was occurring in the iron–coal regions of northern Europe in the basins of the Saar and Ruhr, and the industrial revolution was a European and not an exclusively British phenomenon.

The scale of all these changes was massively disturbing to many Europeans and in the course of those years there was a movement to impose a perspective on events; especially, to find a proper moral basis for human actions in order that an appropriate discipline and a moderation might be employed, consonant with the needs of reform and enlightenment. Unbridled empiricism and *laissez-faire* morality were unacceptable to a wide sector of thoughtful society; particularly to Rousseau who introduced his notion of the 'good' and a faculty of conscience implanted in man whereby the good can be appreciated, and free will whereby it can be pursued. His political and educational theory was not libertine and opportunist, in contrast to the lack of sincerity in some alternative interpretations; it was controlled, responsible and morally sincere. In particular, Rousseau had raised questions that could not be ignored: what is the good? how do we know it? how do we pursue it? He was not alone in sensing a need for responsible morality, one free from the authoritarian caprice of either despotic rule or the other extreme of mob-democracy, from tax-farming greed or *laissez-faire* commercialism. By the time of his death a successor had already appeared to take up the task, Immanuel Kant, who brought Rousseau's ideas together in a coherent philosophical system, a synthesis that was to provide the basis – even if fiercely rejected – for all subsequent philosophical theory and its applications to science and education down to the present day. Kant saw the role of education as absolutely central and made it his task to promote public concern. In taking up this issue, Kant, although following Rousseau, was also working within a growing German philosophical tradition of idealism previously expounded by Leibniz. After Kant the idealist approach to education, with its deep sense of moral responsibility, was to remain a distinctively German movement, being developed in the work of Pestalozzi and Herbart to such an extent that it permeated most continental educational thought and practice in the nineteenth century and spread, in specialized forms, to Britain and the New World.

German idealism and the Kantian synthesis

Towards a new empiricism: Leibniz and the dynamic world-view

In understanding the German educational movement and its confrontation with the tradition of British sense-empiricism that dominated the French Enlightenment, it is necessary briefly to consider its origins in the philosophy of Leibniz. The model of Newton and Locke proved a compelling one, as their theories, and those of Hume and Berkeley, were translated and popularized by Voltaire and his followers, thereby becoming converted into the more extreme versions of sensationism and mechanical materialism that provided the basis for positivist science in France. The scientific empiricism of this time offered not only a widely accepted dualist view of man versus a mechanistic world but also some clear directives that the proper manner of studying it was through the method of sense experience. Any major modification of that empiricism involved, therefore, an alternative theory of both nature and knowledge. At the beginning of the eighteenth century only one thinker of international stature proved capable of attempting that task: the German philosopher Gottfried Wilhelm von Leibniz.

A contemporary of Newton, and a leading figure in the foundation of the Berlin Academy in 1701, Leibniz (1646-1716) was a many-sided genius whose vast volume of writings defies any brief assessment of his work. What he offered, however, in his enormous output of ideas – obscure and even contradictory as many of these proved to be – was a major challenge both to the mechanistic view of the world, with his own dynamic concept, and to the sense-empiricist's theory of knowledge. Leibniz's great hope for progress in the sciences was an improvement in the method of reasoning, and he considered probability theory to be an important factor in achieving this; in addition, he made an early contribution to the development of symbolic logic. While defending the importance of effective logic and clear ideas, he pointed out that concepts without distinct referents are merely symbolic, describing this kind of knowledge as *blind* a century before Kant made famous a similar statement with regard to concepts unsecured by experience.[7]

An important source for Kant's later work was the lengthy criticism of Locke's theory of knowledge, composed by Leibniz between 1693 and 1709 under the title *New Essays Concerning Human Understanding*, but not published until 1765, when it appeared in a collection of his philosophical works in French and Latin, at Leipzig and Amsterdam. In this work Leibniz mounted a strong attack against Locke's sense-empiricism, denying that in the acquisition of knowledge so much can be attributed to the senses. Instead he stressed the operation of the reason, the function of ideas, and the importance of logical demonstration, as well as the value of comparative and historical studies in science.

Rejecting Locke's theory that the mind is a *tabula rasa* on which the senses provide the material for all knowledge, Leibniz argued that intellectual ideas do not come from the senses. At the same time he accepted, as did Locke, the Aristotelian separation of the senses from reason. His response was to reassert with Descartes the Platonic doctrine of innate ideas, although he differed from the Cartesians to some extent by defining these as principles arising from the original constitution of the soul itself. He argued that we are born with general conceptions or necessary truths without which the evidence of the senses cannot be united with ideas and so lead (in Platonic terms) to universals. 'The senses, although necessary for all our actual knowledge,' in his view, 'never give us anything but examples, i.e. particular or individual truths.' Such examples, he pointed out, as Hume was to do later, 'do not suffice to establish the universal necessity of that same truth': it remained in his terms a contingent truth or 'truth of fact'.[8]

For an assurance of perfect universality and necessity in knowledge, Leibniz turned to the innate principles that in his view distinguish human knowledge from that of the brutes and confirm the divine plan of universal harmony. Experience, for Leibniz, implies no more than induction and examples; principles or necessary truths are innate; and he rejected the possibility that general notions (*koinai ennoiai* in the Greek) on which uniformity of opinion has been reached can be acquired in any other way.[9]

Moving from this position, Kant was later to develop a more complex notion of experience in his effort to provide a synthesis of rationalist and empiricist views.

Kant: experience, knowledge and morality

Immanuel Kant (1724–1804) was one of a number of outstanding thinkers in Germany in this period who attempted to reconcile the scientific and philosophic doctrines of the British and French Enlightenment with their own traditions. Prior to his celebrated contributions to philosophy and education, published in the period 1781 to 1803, Kant produced, in addition to twelve philosophical works, two treatises on anthropology, one on education, and at least ten on natural science, including two on the motions of the earth, one on the origin of the winds, three on earthquakes, and his *General Natural History and Theory of the Heavens*, published anonymously in 1755.

Born in the Prussian city of Königsberg, Kant was educated there in the Collegium Fridericianum and then in the city's university, where he was appointed in 1770 to the chair of logic and metaphysics, lecturing until his retirement in 1796. All his major work was produced during this period in the chair, and of this the so-called 'critical philosophy' was the most influential: *Critique of Pure Reason* (1781), *Prolegomena to any Future Metaphysics* (1783), *Critique of Practical Reason* (1788), *Critique of Judgement* (1790). He was simultaneously involved in the relationship of philosophy to education and gave four series of lectures in pedagogy in the years 1776–7 and 1786–7 which were later edited by his associate Theodor Rink in 1803 under the published title *On Education* (*Immanuel Kant, Über Pädagogik*).

Throughout his life, Kant endeavoured to effect a synthesis of the main schools of contemporary thought, working always within the common Aristotelian framework of the faculty theory of the mind. Strongly influenced by the rationalism of the Cartesian school, he joined with Leibniz, Spinoza and Wolff in asserting the power of human reason. At the same time he was to a large extent in sympathy with the tradition of British empiricism, being a close reader of the works of Hume, whose scepticism provided him with a major challenge. Writing on metaphysics in 1783, he stated that no event, 'since Locke's and Leibniz's Essays', had been 'more decisive in respect of the fate of this science than the attack which David Hume made on it'. Kant admitted that it was Hume's remarks, with his questions on cause and effect, and his challenge to reason, 'that first, many years ago, interrupted my dogmatic slumber and gave a completely different direction to my enquiries in the field of speculative philosophy'.[10]

Moreover, the Enlightenment search for a secular morality concerned him deeply, along with the problem, already considered to some extent by Locke and Hume but raised more aggressively by Rousseau, of the role of the feelings in human knowledge. Kant's theory of how man comes to know the world, although considerably modified in the course of his long career, involved at each stage some kind of dualism, and in 1781, in the *Critique of Pure Reason*, his mature position was expressed. His emphasis here on the objective aspect of human knowledge has been called objective idealism. Arguing that all phenomena are perceived in the relations of space and time, Kant stressed that all perception is interpreted in terms of mental concepts. Although he continued to recognize empirical concepts, for Kant it was primarily the categories, pure concepts or principles of understanding, inborn in the mind, that make possible the objective reference of experience. Among these he specified quantity, quality, matter and causality. Yet these concepts, he claimed, remain useless unless they can be applied in experience: 'Thoughts without content are empty, intuitions without concepts are blind.'[11] He maintained, therefore, that the categories do not enable man to arrive by pure thought at valid conclusions about objects as they are in themselves: such knowledge cannot in effect pass beyond the limits of sensibility. Accordingly, Kant proposed a new dualism: on the one hand, a natural world of phenomena or appearances in space and time, perceived by man's senses and providing the basis for empirical knowledge; and, on the other, a transcendental reality that gives rise to these phenomena – a world of noumena which affect the mind and yet are inaccessible to sensible experience. At the same time, in attempting to define the limits of rationality, Kant claimed in his theory of transcendental idealism that knowledge concerning ideas can be achieved by pure reason, independently of sense experience.

Kant's absolute moral theory

Kant's objection to empirically grounded scientific knowledge is that, since it accepts a Cartesian model of mathematics as the touchstone of absolute demonstration, science claims to be determinate and hence to direct human purposes. In fact, the whole thrust of the Enlightenment was to discover the ultimate structure of events and hence to know the world and, at the centre of this, as Hartley argued in his *Observations on Man*, to make all people 'perfectly similar . . . by a proper adjustment of the impressions and associations'. Hartley was arguing, of course, for the perfectibility of man; he did not realize that he was presenting a case for the moral annihilation of man in that empirical science would have to be at the same time method and source of both values and decision making. Kant saw the threat to civilized values, and his own work was to stimulate a major school of German philosophy furthered by Hamann, Lessing, Herder, Fichte and Hegel.

The natural world of phenomena allows us to construct a descriptive account of how things do happen; the account of how things ought to happen is the province not of empirical science but of morality which is concerned with human freedom. Now we can only act freely – that is, with free will – in an indeterminate world; to argue otherwise is to make every human action subject to external necessity; and an indeterminate world is an unknowable world. This, then, denies empirical science any authority over human values; at the same time, it poses a serious problem: how can we act towards the good if it is, by definition, unknowable since it too is part of an indeterminate world? Kant's solution was to posit the theory of two worlds: one of the determinate and knowable, that is, the phenomenal; another of the indeterminate and unknowable, the noumenal. We cannot, therefore, know morality; we can only by *a priori* reasoning arrive at the conclusion that it must exist logically as a corrective to the determinate world, as a source of values. At this point his philosophy becomes most controversial, since his moral theory is one in which we are obliged to recognize a moral law and to strive towards its imperatives even though we cannot know it.[12] Indeed, by definition, the moral law cannot be known; if it were, it would be part of the external, determinate order. The problem as Kant posed it is virtually insoluble; either the separate moral realm must be affirmed or else morality must be accepted as part of the determinate world, with the inevitable consequence that it has no absolute value.

Kant's theory of education

It was, then, within this context of philosophical controversy that Kant constructed his theory of education. He freely admitted the influence of Rousseau's thought – in his austere home he had only one picture on the wall, an engraved portrait of Rousseau – and his ideas on education were originally stimulated by *Émile*. At Königsberg all professors were required to accept a rotating allocation of lectures in pedagogy, since by this time Prussia was moving towards the serious professional preparation of teachers; Kant was rostered to do this in the academic year of 1776–7 and a decade later in 1786–7. His method was to take an existing worthwhile text and expound it with a commentary, rather in the medieval *lectio* tradition. In 1776–7 he took the currently fashionable Rousseauian popularization, Basedow's *Das Elementarwerk*, recently published in 1772–4, calling his course *Pädagogik über Basedow's Methodenbuch*,[13] and it was the content of these lectures that was rewritten by Kant, edited by Rink and published in 1803 as *Über Pädagogik*.[14]

Essentially, *On Education* is an attempt to give greater philosophical coherence to the educational ideas of *Émile* by presenting them in a logical rather than in Rousseau's psychological order, the entire work hinging on what Kant saw as 'one of the greatest problems of education, how to unite submission to the necessary restraint with the child's capability of exercising his freewill'.[15] Once this is grasped, the theme of the lectures and the title of the work, *Pägadogik*, become clear, since this word contains the notion of the controlled intervention of the teacher (*Pädagog*) in the process. German, like many other European languages, has no single word for *education*; it also uses *Bildung* when scholarship, culture and moral character are implied, and *Erziehung* for rearing and personality formation, especially in the disciplined sense when it overlaps with the term *Zucht*. Kant agreed with Rousseau's organic theory of the child's nature but sought to provide a more carefully guided path of development. His own work *On Education* echoed Rousseau's ideas on infant care and presented an extremely progressive set of prescriptions, arguing that since nature works to a purpose it is necessary to follow it. In the early years, moreover, Kant recognized a pre-moral stage in children's thinking and urged, consequently, the avoidance of any early effort at moral training.[16]

As early childhood is reached, however, Kant argued for more formal direction of growth; man, he asserted at the outset, is the only animal needing an education which comprises nurture, discipline (*Zucht*), and cultivation of cognitive and moral aspects (*Bildung*). He was directly opposed to Rousseau's theory of 'negative discipline', stating that an important reason for sending children to school is 'not so much with the object of their learning something, but rather that they may become used to sitting still and doing exactly as they are told. And this is to the end that in later life they should not wish to put actually and instantly into practice anything that strikes them.'[17] Given this stress on the disciplined ability to set aside impulse and even to defer worthwhile goals, the major thrust of *On Education* follows in a relentlessly logical exposition of the concept of the controlled development of the growing child. Having treated nurture as the stage of infancy, Kant then considered childhood, the years from five or six to puberty, as the stage requiring discipline. Consequently, his advice departed markedly from that of *Émile* in that he urged careful and continued control of the child's experiences. He remained, however, within the realm of organic thinking by accepting natural stages of unfolding, even suggesting that like the primula, which 'blooms in many colours' because 'nature has placed these manifold germs in the plant and their development is only a question of proper sowing and planting',[18] so it is with man, although, pursuing the metaphor of cultivation, he extended it to include pruning and shaping so as to influence the pattern of growth. Somewhat following Rousseau's notion of the second stage – that after nature come 'things' – Kant extended the organic analogy to argue that 'a tree which stands in a field alone grows crooked and spreads wider its branches, while a tree which stands in the middle of a forest, with the pressure of other trees around, grows tall and straight'.[19] Although his observation was directed specifically at the education of future rulers, it has a universal application.

Man's organic development must therefore be corrected of its faults, and it is the proper application of discipline (*Zucht*) that restrains our animal nature and, followed by cultivation (*Bildung*), in its aspects of providing both information and instruction, leads to the development of the traits of discretion (*Klugheit*), manifested in good social conduct, and refinement (*Civilisierung*), as demonstrated in manners, courtesy and discretion. Even more important than these, and consequent upon their attainment, is the area of moral training – the highest goal of the educative process. In this respect and with regard to the whole of the child's education, Kant rejected any notion of a morally pre-existent nature, and it is precisely for this reason that moral education is necessary.[20] Equally, Kant rejected, along with the doctrine of original sin, its correlative of paradise; arcady, he asserted, 'is tormented with ennui', adding in the growing tradition of the Protestant ethic that 'man is the only animal who is obliged to work'.[21]

It is this belief in the moral neutrality of the new-born child that prompted Kant to recommend the careful exercise of cultivation (*Bildung*).

This contrasts with the Rousseauian theory which, assuming the child's inherent goodness, claimed that the removal of constraints by a policy of negative education would see the flowering of the natural personality within. Kant did, however, accept the Aristotelian concept of latency, including a predisposition to develop towards moral goodness. Here he entered one of the most contentious areas and appeared, in effect, to beg the question, by denying inherent goodness in man but asserting that 'Providence has not placed goodness already formed in him, but merely as a tendency and without the distinction of moral law',[22] or, as he stated further on, 'in man there are only germs of good'. Kant then showed how much formation should proceed, his emphasis being on enlightenment rather than training (although he recognized that the latter, in the sense of habit formation and even coercion, has a necessary role).

Emphasis throughout the educative process should be on leading the child to see the relationships of events to themselves and to other people, and this is accomplished by a parallel process of instruction in cognitive and moral learning. In the cognitive area Kant included physical activity, not just as play, but as a constructive part of instruction, although this was arrived at more by intuition than any deeply considered process of argument. The intellect, however, must be carefully cultivated and, unlike Rousseau who avoided any explicit discussion, Kant provided a clear set of directives. Following closely the faculty theory of the mind, he argued:

> . . . with regard to the cultivation of the mental faculties, we must remember that this cultivation is going on constantly . . . the principal rule that we should follow being that no mental faculty is to be cultivated by itself, but always in relation to others; for instance, the imagination to the advantage of the understanding.[23]

In this context he mentioned, in passing, the usually accepted faculties of memory, judgement, intelligence, understanding (knowledge of the general) and reason (connections of the general with the particular).

In proceeding with the cultivation of the mental faculties – and this was the overwhelming purpose of intellectual learning – he strongly advised practical activities, 'to do ourselves all that we wish to accomplish'. So, following Rousseau's stress upon the immediacy of experience, he gave examples:

> . . . for instance, by carrying out into practice the grammatical rule which we have learnt. [Further] We understand a map best when we are able to draw it for ourselves. The best way to understand is to do. That which we learn most

thoroughly, and remember the best, is what we have in a way taught ourselves.[24]

At this time in Europe the classical revival had begun and the seminar, following Socrates' practice of psychic midwifery, was being introduced into Germany. Kant supported this on the grounds that reason is best cultivated by the Socratic method. As an accompaniment to these methods of doing and discussing Kant recommended the illustrated textbook, referring to the two in wide current use: the *Orbis sensualium pictus* of Comenius, then at the height of its second wave of popularity with multiple-language editions (many with four, some with six languages) published in Moscow (1768), Vienna (1776, 1780) and Leipzig (1784); and Basedow's *Das Elementarwerk*. So he urged that 'a well-constructed so-called *orbis pictus* will prove very useful. We might begin with botany, mineralogy, and natural history in general. In order to make sketches of these objects, drawing and modelling will have to be learned, and for this some knowledge of mathematics is necessary.' Continuing his proposals to develop an integrated activity curriculum in which science and geography are taught together, each thereby illuminating the other, he used the example that 'tales of travel, illustrated by pictures and maps, will lead on to political geography'.[25] In all cognitive learning Kant stressed that theory and practice must proceed conjointly wherever possible so that 'the rule and its application should be studied side by side'[26] in order that proper understanding will develop, though he recognized that some rules need to be abstracted and learnt separately, such as grammar.

Given his philosophy of morality, it is rather surprising that he prescribed no training in morality. Training and discipline (*Zucht*) are necessary, but only to develop predispositions towards moral growth. Kant argued that wherever possible we must avoid punishment by direct means; it should (as Rousseau argued) come as the result of 'a certain law of necessity',[27] and it is this that should compel children's obedience. Morality itself is an exercising of virtue and hence cannot be taught by discipline or punishment. In this he stood in complete opposition to Locke who saw morality as being totally inculcated through habit formation.

The ultimate aim of such education is a morally and socially regenerated world; Kant's belief in the centrality of the educational process could not be more directly expressed than in his statement that 'good education is exactly that whence springs all the good in the world'.[28] This will lead to

earthly regeneration through achieving the now-fashionable Enlightenment goal of the perfectibility of man:

> It may be that education will be constantly improved, and that each succeeding
> generation will advance one step towards the perfecting of mankind; for with
> education is involved the great secret of the perfection of human nature. It is
> only now that something may be done in this direction, since for the first time
> people have begun to judge rightly, and understand clearly, what actually
> belongs to a good education. It is delightful to realize that through education
> human nature will be continually improved, and brought to such a condition
> as is worthy of the nature of man. This opens out to us the prospect of a
> happier human race in the future.[29]

In this we are compelled to observe a new conception in educational
thought, latent in earlier writers, but brought to unambiguous expression
by Kant: the perfectibility of man through his own efforts. There is no
hint of clerical assistance; Kant showed no interest in religion in education
and, following the deistic approach of his enlightened contemporaries,
saw religion as 'the law in us insofar as it derives emphasis from a Law-
Giver and a Judge above us. It is morality applied to the knowledge of
God.'[30] God is relegated to a remote role, given fuller expression in his
much-censured work of 1793 *Religion within the Limits of Reason Only*, and
man alone bears the burden of his own perfecting.

Practical considerations on education

Yet Kant was no impractical theorist; despite what might now seem as
idealistic utopianism, he recognized that his theories as outlined in *On
Education* would require considerable effort in application and even experimentation; moreover, it is uncertain whether Kant expected a complete,
literal realization of his projections. Indeed, by his own philosophy,
utopia is unrealizable since it must rest in a determinate world, and it is
possible, as the tenor of his lectures suggests, that, like Plato in the
Republic, he projected only an ideal at which we should aim. Certainly
Kant had no illusions that his theory of education was in any way complete; on the contrary, he made the point several times that both theory
and practice were seriously deficient in his day. 'The prospect of a theory
of education', he declared, 'is a glorious ideal, and it matters little if we are
not able to realize it at once.'[31] And here he developed what was to become a serious concern of German educational theorists after him, that of

converting the art of teaching (at its best) into a fully scientific procedure: 'the mechanism of education', he asserted, 'must be changed into a science'.[32] Given the need for a science of education, it necessarily follows that

> . . . experimental schools must first be established before we can establish normal schools [teachers' colleges]. Education and instruction must not be merely mechanical; they must be founded upon fixed principles; although at the same time education must not merely proceed by way of reasoning, but must be, in a certain sense, mechanical.[33]

By 'mechanical' he is referring to established predictable procedures such as science had already developed. And here it is interesting that Kant recommended not reason alone as a guide to proper action but also experiment because 'experience teaches us that the results of an experiment are often entirely different from what we expected'. In so arguing he showed the flexibility of his philosophy which allowed for an interplay between the phenomenal and noumenal worlds.

The institution of the school, too, was affirmed; despite Rousseau's theory in *Émile*, Kant had little patience with tutoring since it failed to cultivate moral responsibilities. Consistently he promoted the Philanthropinum as a model, pointing out in *On Education* that it had set an example that had stimulated 'many attempts of this kind to [educate similarly] children in other institutions'.[34] As early as 1776 he extolled its virtues in response to a request by his close friend the English merchant resident in Königsberg, Robert Motherby, for advice on a good progressive school for his six-year-old son.[35] Even stronger support followed in an article Kant published in the Königsberg newspaper on 27 March 1777 entitled 'To the General Public', which solicited subscriptions for the support of the Philanthropinum.[36] In this letter Kant argued that this institution was unlike all other educational establishments in Europe which, although well-meaning, are 'spoiled at the outset . . . because everything in them is working in opposition to nature'. His own pedagogical argument for instruction and character formation followed, with the pithy observation that 'it is useless to expect this salvation of the human race to come from a gradual improvement of the schools. They must be made over if anything good is to come from them.'[37]

By the time that *On Education* was published in 1803, a year before his death, Kant had become Europe's pre-eminent philosopher and had established a revitalized tradition of metaphysical idealism that was to dominate the nineteenth century. Indeed, all philosophy after Kant either follows or consciously rejects his position; none is indifferent. In education his influence was profound, especially in Germany. Kant's concern with morality and virtue as the overriding purpose of education dominated most subsequent theory, although it was not equally manifested in practice. Henceforth all serious theorists followed his lead in searching for the patterns of human nature, in particular the structure of the mind and the ways in which this orders our perceptions. They were also concerned with the two areas of intellectual and moral education and how these might reasonably be the subject of a science of education. This, in fact, was the life-work of a successor in his chair of logic and metaphysics at Königsberg, Johann Friedrich Herbart, whose ideas were to be drawn on heavily in the later nineteenth century. The other major contribution to the theoretical foundations of the new socially responsible and hopefully regenerative education was provided by the Swiss-German, Heinrich Pestalozzi.

Organic continuity and spiritual fulfilment: contribution of Pestalozzi

Early thought: man and nature

Throughout the French Revolution and the ensuing Napoleonic era, Pestalozzi was seen by many advanced thinkers as the educational hope of the revolutionary age; his schools attracted educational reformers, theorists and administrators from all over Europe; while Napoleon pointedly refused to accept his advice, Tsar Alexander I (r. 1801–25) gave him an audience to learn if his ideas could be used in Russia. His work drew the young Herbart who came to study his methods and to develop them, in turn, into the only rival system in Europe. Pestalozzi was working contemporaneously with Kant, although a generation younger, and was profoundly influenced by Kant's theories as they filtered through to him. Yet he was no uncritical follower; in fact he diverged from Kant and even asserted his intellectual independence (although the evidence does not fully support his claim). Pestalozzi's main departure from Kant is that he built his theory out of direct experience teaching children in the school, usually in unfavourable circumstances.

Johann Heinrich Pestalozzi (1746–1827) was born in Zürich, the son of a Protestant clergyman. He was educated in the local abbey school and in 1757 entered the Latin grammar Schola Carolina, going on in 1763 to the *Collegium humanitatis* of the university, where he became involved in the social-reforming movement of Swiss independence which was a manifestation of the Europe-wide revolutionary mood. Switzerland at the time was a loose confederation of thirteen German-speaking cantons, which had shaken free of the Holy Roman Empire in the fourteenth century and were now dominated by wealthy burgher oligarchies. In 1762 Pestalozzi joined the Helvetische Gesellschaft zu Gerwe, the radical Patriotic Society; owing to conflicts with authority on account of his political activism, he left the University of Zürich without a degree. However, he hated the formal, verbal education he had received and this made him a lifelong enemy of what he described as 'harsh and onesided schoolmasters' with their 'thousandfold arts of juggling words', 'this artificial method of schooling'.[38]

By this period (1763–6) he had read Rousseau and had immersed himself in the new spirit of nature-philosophy that Rousseau had stimulated. Central to this new movement was a concern with the imagination, a faculty that did not fit neatly into the Bacon–Locke taxonomy. These empiricists had identified judgement, reason, memory and sense perception as faculties that provide knowledge. What, however, of the imagination? This too was part of the Aristotelian inheritance which regarded the power of the mind to construct mental images or representations of reality as an essential aspect of the acquisition of knowledge. In the empirical scheme the faculties were content-related in that judgement and reason, for example, were regarded as appropriate to philosophy and mathematics, memory to history, and sense perception to geography. Other subjects were forced into these categories; since poetry was the only one that could be linked with the imagination, this faculty was pushed aside as fanciful and of no real intellectual value. The new Romantic movement, however, saw that an empirical analysis did violence to the organic wholeness of the world and began to propose a counter-philosophy whereby the world was seen as a unity, with man an integral part. So the medieval view of man outside nature – of the world as something to be conquered, to triumph over – which the empiricists had inherited and attempted to realize was opposed by the Rousseauian view of a holistic world in which the empirically fragmented understanding could be restored to a comprehensible unity by the power of the imagination. This conception of the world was later succinctly described in Haeckel's neo-logism of 'ecology' (*Ökologie*) which was, in time, to generate the concept of the ecosystem. Pestalozzi was an early sympathizer with this idea, and it is from such a viewpoint that his work should be interpreted.

Upon leaving university, then, and with the intention of getting into communion with nature, he went in 1767 to live in the village of Birr, near Berne, where he built his own house on a small estate which he named Neuhof ('New Farm'). In 1769 he married; the following year his son Jean-Jacques was born and Pestalozzi tried to raise him according to the principles of *Émile*. Pestalozzi's later student, the Baron Roger de Guimps, recorded that Pestalozzi wrote in his diary in 1774 that the aim was to 'teach him from the nature of things themselves . . . not by words. Leave him to himself to see, hear, find, stumble, rise again, and be mistaken. . . . What he can do for himself let him do . . . nature teaches better than men.'[39] At the same time, however, Pestalozzi was concerned about the condition of the rural poor whose economic inadequacy made them little better than serfs. At that time he became aware that education, if it were to cultivate the best in man, must first create economic independence and usable voca-tional skills. In old age he continued to assert the necessity of concern for all people, and especially the poor and disadvantaged, recognizing in each person that, 'however low his earthly condition, here too is one of our race, subject to the same sensations of alternate joy and grief, born with the same faculties, with the same destination, with the same hopes for a life of immortality'.[40] Accordingly, he opened Neuhof to state-ward orphans and in 1774 a few children arrived; by 1776 he had twenty-two, by 1778 they totalled thirty-seven. Seeking to provide an education appro-priate to working children, he taught them reading, writing and reckoning, and in addition the boys did farm work, the girls housework. As no philanthropic support was forthcoming, however, Pestalozzi was reluc-tantly forced to send the children back to the state office and to close down Neuhof.

Education according to nature: Leonard and Gertrude

Simultaneously, he was starting to put down his ideas and began the early pieces which over the next forty-odd years were to develop into a vast body of writing in many literary genres – essays, journalistic pieces, novels, instruction manuals, diaries, anecdotes – until by the end of his life he left sufficient materials to be edited in his *Sämtliche Werke* (*Collected Works*) in twenty-seven volumes. In 1780 came his first major work, a collection of meditative aphorisms entitled *Evening Hours of a Hermit*, which contains the essential ideas of his educational approach. Here we read that 'Man, driven by his needs can find the road to truth nowhere but in his own nature . . . obedience to your nature' is everything.[41] The following year these thoughts were expanded into a didactic novel on the plight of the poor villagers under the domination of unscrupulous landowners, entitled *Leinhard und Gertrud*. The plot is nothing more than a simple device on which to hang the parable: Leonard the tenant farmer has been ruined and brought to alcoholic degradation by his debts; his indomitable wife Gertrude struggles on and through her courage and honest convictions rehabilitates her husband and provides her family with an education that leads to vocational and economic self-sufficiency. In the process Gertrude illustrates how the good mother can make the home, as described in the *Evening Hours*, into the 'foundation of pure and natural education of mankind'.[42]

Industry, frugality and perseverance are at the heart of Gertrude's actions, and in everything she has a double motive: to make each activity positively educative; and to make the children aware of worthwhile ethical purposes in all their actions. So:

> While they were spinning and sewing, she taught them to count and cipher, for she regarded arithmetic as the foundation of all intellectual order. Her method was to let the children count their threads or stitches both forwards and backwards, and add and subtract, multiply and divide the result by different numbers. The children vied with each other in this game, trying to see who could be quickest and surest in the exercise. When they were tired, they sang songs, and night and morning Gertrude prayed with them.[43]

These activities were carried on throughout the day, every action having its moral component. The book was an instantaneous success when published in 1781. It was reprinted in 1783, 1785 and 1787, and spread the name of this new natural-order educator across Europe.

In the period of nearly twenty years from 1779, when the Neuhof experiment in education for the poor failed, until 1798, Pestalozzi turned completely to writing and produced some of his most depressed work, particularly the pessimistic *Investigations into the Course of Nature in the Development of the Human Race* (1797) which came at the end of his period of frustrations. Throughout those two decades there was much to concern any social reformer, particularly the spate of popular revolutions, many of which were quashed by reactionary governments. Even the French Revolution of 1789, so promising at first, degenerated into the extremist Jacobin Terror of 1793, although in 1795 the middle-class Directory took charge with one of its new generals Napoleon Bonaparte in command of what became the major front, in Italy, against the Coalition of Great Britain, Austria and Prussia. Napoleon's army defeated the Coalition in northern Italy, and as a consequence much of Europe bordering on France, including the Swiss cantons, came under French dominance. The French had already spread their revolutionary doctrines among the Swiss, who now seized the opportunity to rebel against their bourgeois oligarchies and form the democratic Helvetian Republic in 1798. Pestalozzi was reinvigorated; here was the chance to see social progress. He was given the editorship of a *Swiss Peoples' Newspaper* to help spread his educational ideas and in the same year (1798) accepted an invitation to establish a school for war orphans in the shattered town of Stans, near the canton capital of Berne, which had been ravaged by the invading French forces in their push south into Italy.

Theory into practice: Stans, Burgdorf, Yverdon

Pestalozzi received this offer from the newly appointed Minister for Education, Philipp Stapfer, an admirer of Kant's philosophy and its educational application. Kant's pedagogical lectures of 1776–7 and 1786–7 had now become widely diffused, and Stapfer saw a great similarity between the ideas of Kant and Pestalozzi. Meanwhile Pestalozzi had become well acquainted with Kant's ideas, particularly in the period beginning in 1788 when a young, ardent proselytizer for the Kantian philosophy, Johann Gottlieb Fichte, had taken a tutoring position at Zürich and, having met Pestalozzi, endeavoured similarly to enthuse him. Pestalozzi, however, resisted being drawn by Fichte or anyone else into statements of acknowledgement – for he was a fiery individualist despite his theories of social morality – and even went so far as to disclaim philosophical sophistication, recording as late as 1818 that 'I was little qualified for that [educational] task by the precision of my philosophical notions, but supported rather by a rich stock of experience, and guided by the impulse of my heart'.[44] The effort was unsuccessful: Stans was a Catholic town and Pestalozzi's approach too deistic and unconventional to be acceptable to the conservative clergy and townspeople.

He then moved on in 1799 to the town of Burgdorf, just north of Berne, where a school was already operating in the castle, remaining there until 1804. Here his educational ideas matured rapidly. Although originally in conflict with the existing teacher, the cobbler Dysli – since as was customary the two taught in the same room and Dysli's methods were strictly those of traditional verbal instruction – Pestalozzi, supported by the patriotic Society of the Friends of Education who were planning a national teachers' college to prepare teachers for the new Swiss republic, became the dominant personality. The castle was turned into an institute to develop a systematic practice of education based upon his increasingly popular theories, these being re-expressed in an optimistic treatise whose title, rather misleadingly, promised a sequel to *Leinhard und Gertrud*: this was the publication in 1802 of *Wie Gertrud ihre Kinder lehrt* (*How Gertrude Teaches Her Children*), which was not a novel but a series of fourteen educational essays. Here he was joined by a number of followers, Hermann Krüsi, Johannes Niederer, Johannes Buss and Joseph Neef, all devoted to finding the organic method of education. Niederer observed of the period that when Pestalozzi 'took over the castle and founded the Institute [his aims were] revolutionary.'

> By word and deed he wanted to tear down and build up again: tear down the whole school system as it had existed up to then, a system which appeared to him monstrous; then to build up a new school system in which he wanted to entrust the subjects taught to the basic elements and methods of nature. . . . The course of instruction had to be brought into complete harmony with the stages of development of human nature.[45]

In 1803 the revolutionary movement in Switzerland faltered, as it did in most of Europe; in the United States the revolution held firm, elsewhere reaction set in as Napoleon tightened his grip on the continent, while the Coalition did likewise in the territories surrounding him. The Helvetian Republic was dissolved in that year back into its autonomous cantons by Napoleon's Act of Mediation; the following year Pestalozzi's Institute at Burgdorf was closed and the castle converted into a military hospital. Pestalozzi moved to Hofwil, south of Berne, where the aristocrat Philipp Emmanuel von Fellenberg had a college providing a cultured liberal education for the upper classes of Europe. The original plan to co-operate was doomed from the start – they worked at opposite ends of the social spectrum – and within a year Pestalozzi withdrew to the French-speaking town of Yverdon at the southern end of Lake Neuchâtel where he had a standing invitation to establish a school in the old castle, by this time civic property.

At Yverdon he entered his most productive period, 1804–25, and although he had frequent differences of opinion with his staff (even the devoted Krüsi left him in 1816 after a disagreement) the school flourished, beginning in 1804 with seventy pupils and doubling its enrolment the following year. The school was fee-charging for boys; Pestalozzi opened it to girls and established a free division for the poor, all the time refining and putting his theories into practice, and from practice reworking his theories. Already at Burgdorf in *How Gertrude Teaches Her Children* he had developed what he considered the most fundamental of his pedagogical principles, the doctrine of *Anschauung*, a German term with a wide range of meanings, all centring on the idea of deep intuitive observation of mental phenomena as related to learning. By 1810 Burgdorf had become the focus of European attention as educators and administrators travelled there to observe the astonishing new theories and methods in action: from England came the philanthropic supporters of education Robert Owen and Andrew Bell, from Germany the young educational reformer Friedrich Froebel, from Prussia a group of students sent for their education, and a delegation of seventeen educators to observe the method for its possible application in their own country. By 1816, at Yverdon, Pestalozzi had begun to set down the most mature version of his educational ideas in a series of thirty-four *Letters on Early Education*, written in the period 1816–19 to his English admirer James Pierrepoint Greaves, who was at Yverdon from 1818 to 1822 to learn the theory in order to apply it in England. With the translation and publication of these *Letters* in English in 1827, Pestalozzianism spread into England and thence throughout the English-speaking world. In 1825, and now seventy-nine years of age, Pestalozzi left Yverdon after disputes with his staff, returned to Neuhof and wrote the aptly titled *Swansong*, dying there in 1827.

Theory of organic development and continuity

Pestalozzi made no single exposition of his approach to education; rather, it is diffused throughout his voluminous writings which collectively reveal a continued concern to realize the aim expressed in the early *Evening Hours of a Hermit* – that of making education follow nature. All his postulates are based on the concept of nature (*Natur*) and he accepted as axiomatic much of the Enlightenment thinking of Locke, Leibniz, and

Kant in particular, although he always avoided acknowledging specific influences. Moreover, he eschewed any kind of ontological theorizing; his concern was with establishing educational theory developmentally in the careful observation of children, and disadvantaged ones at that; not for him the scions of well-to-do families with supportive parents as Basedow had, or only fictional children for whom there could be no consequences for failure as Rousseau and Kant dealt with. Pestalozzi did, however, make certain definite metaphysical assumptions: that each individual has a nature that is inherently good, contains all of the necessary potential for intellectual and moral development, and stands in need of careful cultivation which is best achieved by a bond of love between, first, mother and child, later, teacher and child. Accepting the Kantian priority of living the good life in pursuit of virtue, he argued that 'actions which do not conform to the order of nature undermine our capacity to perceive the truth',[46] and from this axiom his entire educational position is developed, but he did stress that following the dictates of our personal nature, while a necessary condition for virtue, is not in itself sufficient, for we must see it in relationship to nature and society.[47] His life's quest was to seek for those 'laws to which the development of the human mind must, by its very nature, be subject,' and these, he added, 'must be the same as those of physical nature'.[48] This led him to another metaphysical assumption of the Enlightenment, that each individual is born with pre-existing faculties which give order to sensation-based experience. So he asserted that, although he preferred not to engage in debate 'about the knotty question whether there are any innate ideas, [the mother or teacher] will be content if she succeeds in developing the innate faculties of the mind'.[49]

The metaphor of natural unfolding, so extensively employed by Rousseau, was used by Pestalozzi to describe the child as 'being endowed with all the faculties of human nature, but none of them developed: a bud not yet opened. When the bud uncloses, every one of the leaves unfolds, not one remains behind. Such must be the process of education.'[50] In another context, he used the analogy of the final perfection of a tree which from a seed grows slowly and imperceptibly to a sapling, pushing out branches and leaves, until maturity – and hence purpose – is reached. Further, each child is born with a complete range of faculties, all of which need harmonious development since 'nature forms the child as an indivisible whole, as a vital organic unity with many-sided moral, mental and physical capacities; [moreover] she wishes that none of these capacities remain undeveloped'.[51] Here is the imperative for education, which seeks

to realize man's fullest potential: 'The faculties of man must be so cultivated that no one shall predominate at the expense of another but each be
excited to the true standard of activity; *and this standard is the spiritual
nature of man.*'[52] The educational problem, with which the bulk of his
writing is concerned, is how proper – not just effective – procedures for
ensuring the harmonious growth and development of this spiritual nature
can be achieved.

Pestalozzi focused his attention upon three major aspects of education:
intellectual development, moral growth and the teacher–pupil relationship. The first of these, intellectual development, rested in the Baconian
school of sense-empiricism, namely, the view that there is an external
world of reality which causes our experience; he accepted, too, the conventional organization of this reality into the traditional subject categories
of the curriculum: language, literature, mathematics, natural science,
geography, music and art, along with the associated performative skills
of reading, writing, calculating, singing, drawing, modelling and physical
activity. Where he made a significant departure, however, was in analysing
more intensively the constitution of the reality that causes experience and
in challenging the associated epistemology as expounded by Locke in
which the blank tablet becomes 'furnished' by its reception of sensations
and subsequent reflections upon them.

Anschauung: *intuitive observation of nature*

External reality, for Pestalozzi, has a more complicated structure than was
acknowledged by Baconian sense-empiricism. Nature is a complex,
divinely structured organic unity and is not simply a sequence of sensations which our senses, and in turn our mind, receive. On the contrary,
our apprehension is much more holistic and really to know the external
world it is necessary to look deeply into it. So he used the word *Anschauung* to express this process, and, it is essential to appreciate, the term
was carefully chosen since in German it does not have an explicit meaning:
it includes the notions of sense impressions or perceptions, observation,
contemplation, intuition, and the mind's awareness of its own processes
(the Leibnizian 'apperception'). It was the distinctive characteristic of
Bacon–Locke theory that mental processes could be analysed into these
separate components. As Pestalozzi quite rightly averred on many
occasions, he was no sophisticated philosophical theorist and this is revealed by his use of the one term *Anschauung* to cover the range of mental

processes which the sense-empirical school had postulated. As such, of course, the term lacked the precision that its separate components had; it does not, however, mean that his theory is any the less adequate. In fact, these faculties have no demonstrable existence; despite the whole tenor of empirical concern with objective knowledge, such processes remain purely metaphysical postulates. Pestalozzi sensed this and sought in the use of *Anschauung* to comprehend the dynamic interrelatedness, the essential unity, of human knowing. The fact that he was unsophisticated in the ways of the professional metaphysicians does not negate his position; it simply means that he was attempting within the conceptual limitations of his time to express the essential nature of learning.

Pestalozzi sought to discover how the process of *Anschauung*, of intuitive observation, penetrates to the essential structure of reality. His answer was that all reality, all nature, has three fundamental dimensions, those of form, number and language: all things in the world have shapes, they exist in quantities, and can be spoken about. This is the cognitive whole; everything is a development, in endless individual variations, of these three fundamentals. Here he seems almost to return to traditional Platonic metaphysics – although perhaps unknowingly – by separating essentials from accidentals. Any given object has a shape, but it is an accidental, or individual, shape of historically conditioned existence; at the same time, it cannot be a purely arbitrary shape without determining rules, but must be governed by an architecture of its essential nature. All phenomena are perceived by means of the senses, he claimed, and yield truth if what we receive is of essentials, error if of accidentals. So he wrote that

> ... all things which affect my senses are means of helping me to form correct opinions, only so far as their phenomena present to my senses their immutable, unchangeable, essential nature, as distinguished from their variable appearance or their external qualities. They are, on the other hand, sources of error and deception so far as their phenomena present to my senses their accidental qualities, rather than their essential characteristics.[53]

Anschauung: *educational application*

Although the doctrine of *Anschauung* is given no single comprehensive exposition, the best concentrated discussion occurs in Letters 7, 8 and 9 of *How Gertrude Teaches Her Children*; clearly, however, it goes beyond the naïve inductionist account of sense-empiricism as an explanation of knowledge. His argument was, implicitly, that all observation is already directed by a pre-existing pattern of assumptions and experiences and for him this is the coherent, ordered architecture of a divinely inspired nature. Through *Anschauung* we are able to put aside what he called 'one-sided, biased impressions made by the qualities of individual objects' and see 'the essential nature of things' in order to arrive at a 'clearer insight'.[54] Although much of the theory of *Anschauung* is expressed in this generalized metaphysical language, Pestalozzi did attempt to give concrete examples. So he developed what he termed exercises for 'eliciting thought and forming the intellect' and in his Thirty-First Letter to Greaves he stressed that he

> . . . would call them preparatory exercises in more than one respect. They embrace the elements of number, form and language; and whatever ideas we may have to acquire in the course of our life, they are all introduced through the medium of one of these departments.

The correct pedagogical procedure, he continued, is to ensure that

> The elements of number, or preparatory exercises of Calculation, should always be taught by submitting to the eye of the child certain objects representing the units. A child can conceive the idea of two balls, two roses, two books; but it cannot conceive the idea of 'Two' in the abstract. How would you make the child understand that two and two make four, unless you show it to him first in reality? To begin by abstract notions is absurd and detrimental, instead of being educative. The result is at best that the child can do the things by rote without understanding it; a fact which does not reflect on the child but on the teacher, who knows not a higher character of instruction than mere mechanical training.

Moreover, he emphasized that teaching should be effected by asking questions. As these procedures are followed, children's minds are enabled to build up abstract generalized concepts and they become 'perfectly aware not only of what they are doing but also of the reason why'.[55] In the Seventh Letter of *How Gertrude Teaches Her Children* he gives an exhaustive account of the way in which number concepts should be built up. The operation must always begin with objects, 'real, movable, actual things', and when counting, grouping, adding and subtracting up to ten are attained then the teacher can repeat the operations on a blackboard using dots or strokes in place of objects; only as a final step is, say, the number 3 written in place of three strokes. So with fractions: rectangles or squares should be subdivided by having the child fold paper or break up patterns of blocks and then see these on a chart prepared by the teacher;

the child is thereby enabled to become 'fully conscious of the visible relations of the fractions' built upon 'exact sense-impression, which leads by its clearness to truth, and susceptibility to truth'.[56] This leads on, he argued, to what he claimed is 'the highest, supreme principle of instruction in the recognition of *sense-impression as the absolute foundation of knowledge*'.[57]

He treats form similarly, beginning with an understanding of geometric figures as the basis; he even subordinates drawing to the act of measuring, giving an example of having the child discover 'the divisions into angles and arcs that come out of the fundamental form of the square, as well as its rectilinear divisions. . . . [Further] we show him the properties of straight lines, unconnected and each by itself . . . then we begin to name the straight lines as horizontal, vertical and oblique', and so on, leading to a thoroughgoing analysis of all of the elements of what is, basically, the draughtsman's approach to form. This then could be applied to drawing and, by extension, to the world of objects and of nature. Language was similarly treated in the Seventh Letter, the sequence being sounds, words, language. As *Leonard and Gertrude* also illustrates, the child is first taught to speak clearly and correctly with well-articulated diction (much more easily done in Italian or German than in English), and is then taught the letters of the alphabet that correspond to the vowels, adding consonants one by one to form syllables.[58] The method led on to the building of the longest words, which German allows more readily than English.

Pestalozzi argued that the entire curriculum should be constructed on the basis of analysing it into its essential elements and organizing a sequence of logically related structures, always guided by the cardinal principle of proceeding by graded steps. The method appealed to progressive educators in many places and was employed with considerable success, being a distinct advance over the usual rote methods. Years later Pestalozzi wrote to Greaves of its successful implementation by others such as

> My friends Ramsauer and Boniface who have undertaken the very useful work of arranging such a course in its natural progress from the easiest to the most complicated exercises; and the number of schools in which their method has been successfully practised confirms the experience which we have made at Yverdon of its merits.[59]

Pestalozzi recognized, however, that primary sense impressions could not always be provided; every learner (and teacher) is limited by the circumstances of time and place and so, if objects could not be used, then 'pictures should be introduced. Instruction founded on pictures will always be found a favourite branch with children, and if this curiosity is well directed and judiciously satisfied it will prove one of the most useful and instructive.'[60] Recognizing that, despite his emphasis on things before words, some learning must involve abstract principles, he suggested that these should be embodied in a factual statement, or a moral maxim, so that at least a verbal illustration could be provided.[61]

From intellectual to moral development

This, then, is the method of intellectual education, which, although by its very nature elusive of definitive description, was exemplified quite well in practice by Pestalozzi and profoundly impressed the many visitors to his schools, particularly at Yverdon. Although Pestalozzi accepted the empiricist concept of mental faculties that structure experience, chiefly in the Kantian version, he was seeking something deeper than a knowledge of the relationships of the external world; he was in quest of the divinely ordained meaning of life itself, the answer to which lies beyond empirical statements. His insistence on the greater priority of morality indicates this. For him, morality does not consist in observing mere conventional forms of behaviour, and he therefore went beyond Locke who saw it as habit formation; he followed in the path of Rousseau and Kant who considered it the highest form of human activity. Yet Pestalozzi's theory has an inbuilt conflict: while he recognized the need to accept a sensory component to knowledge, he was unable to effect a transition to the holistic position he was advocating, and this has led to his being categorized, quite incorrectly, as a sense-realist.

Pestalozzi's close linking of intellectual and moral education supplied the rationale for intellectual education, and an imperative to provide it for every person in society. Education he considered not as an ornament for the wealthy, nor as a utilitarian commercial advantage for the unscrupulous, but as the means whereby every person may be enabled to attain happiness, which he defined as 'a state of mind, a consciousness of harmony both with the inward and the outward world: it assigns their due limits to the desires, and it proposes the highest aim to the faculties of man',[62] this aim being 'the elevation of man to the true dignity of a spiritual being'.[63]

Morality, then, is the end of all education, and both parents and teachers should strive to inculcate it in their children and students. First they must themselves set good moral examples and therefore always regard themselves as learners along with their students. Second, the properly graded, *Anschauung*-based curriculum must lead the learner to see the essential structure of reality resting on a spiritual foundation, and all intellective activities should aim at cultivating such an awareness. Third, morality will emerge as the child's experiences in cognitive learning engender an affective awareness of the interrelatedness and interdependence of all phenomena in nature, of the underlying organic wholeness of life, and therefore the imperative for each person to enter into a sympathetic relationship with all persons and things. This simply cannot be achieved without an intellectual stimulation and progressive enlightenment of the understanding. To this end, the moral component requires the presentation and discussion of situations which will produce an *Anschauung* of morality, the methods of achieving this being the main theme of *Leonard and Gertrude*, particularly in the later chapters. The achievement of a true morality, in Pestalozzi's view, will issue as love for all creation when seen in proper perspective; love is a term that runs through all his writings, by means of which he linked Christianity with education: 'For the ultimate destination of Christianity, such as it is revealed in the sacred volume and manifested in the page of history, I cannot find a more appropriate expression than to say that its object is to accomplish the education of mankind.'[64] Christianity he saw not as dogma nor as sectarian doctrine but rather as a heightened, concentrated store of moral experience that assists in man's education.

The external systems – home, school, teachers, texts, curriculum – must therefore support these ends. The role of the teacher must be one of 'a continual and benevolent superintendence',[65] and, since the intellectual and moral autonomy of the learner is the goal, the student should be the agent of his own learning: 'let the child not only be acted upon but let him be an agent in [his own] intellectual education'.[66] Pestalozzi did not accept, therefore, the Rousseauian position of negative discipline; he firmly followed Kant in asserting that the child must be 'acted upon' with discipline:

> The animal is destined by the Creator to follow the instinct of its nature. Man is destined to follow a higher principle. His animal nature must no longer be permitted to rule him, as soon as his spiritual nature has commenced to unfold.[67]

In this respect, even physical punishment is sanctioned, although always avoided if possible, and never used if the system or the teacher is at fault.

By the time of his death Pestalozzi was the educationally dominant figure of Europe, having become the embodiment of the thought of Rousseau. His fame was even more widely spread by Fichte who, in his famous *Addresses to the German Nation* of 1808, urged the moral regeneration of Prussia after its defeat by Napoleon at Jena in 1806 and pointed to the work of Pestalozzi as the proper approach to education. Following the conceptual revolution in education achieved by Rousseau, Pestalozzi effected a practical revolution by showing how most of Rousseau's principles could be put into practice.

Systematic cultivation of virtue: pedagogy of Herbart

Moral growth in a real world: the problem identified

Meanwhile, another development of the theory of education as primarily a moral endeavour was being made by Johann Friedrich Herbart (1776–1841), stemming from the Rousseau–Kant position, but in reaction against it. Originally a disciple of Pestalozzi, Herbart sensed inadequacies in the theory underlying the method of *Anschauung* and ended up devoting most of his life to putting it on a sounder basis; his approach to education was to provide, conjointly with Pestalozzi, much of the theory for later nineteenth-century endeavour.

Herbart was born in Oldenburg, a city near the North Sea port of Bremen, his father being a prosperous merchant. In 1794 he went to the University of Jena where the German nationalist Johann Gottlieb Fichte (1762–1814) was currently teaching philosophy; Fichte's tenure lasted only for the years 1794–9, after which he was forced to leave by the conservative establishment because of his liberal ideas. Herbart, however, was exposed to, and influenced by, Fichte's idealistic philosophy, particularly the doctrine that the individual's own consciousness is part of the activity of knowing; such activity Fichte considered to be the force of the ego, and this remained an element of Herbart's thinking, along with another Fichtean idea, which stems from Kant: that of the priority of a moral component in consciousness in interpreting the world. Jena was the scene of disturbances during that period of the French Revolution;

8   Plate XLVIII from Basedow's *Das Elementarwerk* of 1770–2, showing the school laboratory at Dessau.

9   Schoolmaster and scholar
with hornbook, 1622.

13

A
In Adam's Fall,
We sinned all.

B
Thy life to mend,
This Book attend.

C
The Cat doth play,
And after slay.

D
A Dog will bite,
A thief at night.

E
An Eagle's flight
Is out of sight.

F
The idle Fool,
Is whipped at school.

An Alphabet of Lessons for Youth.

A WISE son maketh a glad father, but a foolish
son is the grief of his mother.

BETTER is a little, with the fear of the Lord,
than great treasure, and trouble therewith.

COME unto Christ, all ye who labour and are
heavy laden, and he will give rest to your
souls.

DO not the abominable thing which I hate, saith
the Lord.

10   A woodcut from the *New
England Primer* of 1690.

Herbart left for Interlaken in Switzerland where he took a tutoring position in 1797, and two years later he visited Pestalozzi, coming under the latter's pedagogical influence. In 1800 Herbart went to Göttingen where he completed his degree in 1802 and remained until 1809 as a lecturer in philosophy, becoming preoccupied with Pestalozzi's theories: in 1802 he wrote *On Pestalozzi's Most Recent Work 'How Gertrude Teaches Her Children'* and the *Idea of an ABC of Sense Perception*; in 1804 these were followed by *A Standpoint for Judging the Pestalozzi Method* and *The Aesthetic Presentation of the World as the Chief Business of Education.*

Following the consciously theorizing tradition – begun by Rousseau and followed through by Kant and Pestalozzi – which concentrated upon morality as the central concern of education, Herbart also recognized that mere instruction must have this higher purpose. So he asserted in the opening lines of *The Aesthetic Presentation of the World* that 'The one and the whole work of education may be summed up in the concept – Morality',[68] chiefly because this is the highest aim of humanity. Already Pestalozzi had impressed Herbart with the possibilities of *Anschauung* as the basis, and it was this that stimulated Herbart's interest in the 'aesthetic presentation' of the world, using the word 'aesthetic' in its original Greek sense of *aisthesis*, perception by the senses. How, from a perceptual encounter with the external world, can morality be cultivated? The answer itself is complex, and Herbart provided it in a series of major books over the ensuing thirty years. In *The Aesthetic Presentation of the World* he indicated the direction his work would take by considering Pestalozzi's method of 'training in acuteness and the first preparation for contemplative observation (*Anschauung*) and the work immediately following it, in short, the ABC of the senses, [as] the beginnings of the course of knowledge.'[69] Herbart pursued the course of a realist explanation of knowledge, going on to publish in 1806 his major work, *General Pedagogy Deduced from the Aim of Education* (later translated into English as *The Science of Education*).

By this time Herbart had gained a considerable reputation as an educational thinker in the innovating tradition and his work came to the attention of the Prussian Minister for Public Instruction, Wilhelm von Humboldt (1767–1835), who wished to implement Fichte's call for a moral regeneration of Prussia according to Pestalozzi's methods. In consequence, he appointed Herbart to the Königsberg chair (there were only two Prussian universities at the time, the other being at Halle) where it was hoped that new educational ideas could be introduced. Herbart took up his position in 1809 and remained there for the next twenty-two years, being exceptionally productive, writing a *Textbook of Psychology* (1816), *Psychology as a Science based on Experience, Metaphysics and Mathematics* (1824) and *The Application of Psychology to Education* (1831). Meanwhile, in an effort to reform German university education, von Humboldt had been instrumental in founding a third Prussian university at Berlin in 1810, to whose chair of philosophy Hegel was appointed in 1818. Hegel became pre-eminent as a German philosopher and upon his death Herbart considered himself heir-apparent. By 1831, however, the conservative reaction had set in, Herbart's ideas were unacceptable, and he failed to secure what was now the leading Prussian chair. Consequently, he left Prussia in disgust and returned to Göttingen, where, although he discontinued lecturing on pedagogy – concentrating on philosophy – he published a final summary of his educational ideas in 1835 as *Outlines of Educational Doctrine*. Like Pestalozzi, Herbart spread the same ideas throughout his books and no single one gives a complete account of his theory: and theory it rightly is, since, unlike Pestalozzi, Herbart worked entirely within the confines of a university, particularly within the teacher-preparation course he conducted, which was known as the Pedagogical Seminar.

Experiential construction of mind

The starting-point for understanding his educational thought lies in Herbart's concern to reconcile the Pestalozzian insistence on sense perception as the 'absolute foundation of knowledge' with the Kantian conception of the 'manifold' which is given meaning by the innate structuring of the mind. Herbart baulked at the Kantian model of the mind because of the dualism noumenon-phenomenon around which it was built, and so he set out to reconcile this into a unitary theory which accorded with common sense. In Herbart's view the external world consists of matter and form existing as ultimate particles of reality (*Realen*) which may be analysed by the method of contemplative observation (*Anschauung*).[70] Since for him the mind too is materially existent, he considered it as a simple *tabula rasa*, denying it any pre-existing faculties or other organizing powers. He developed this theory at length in the 1816 *Textbook of Psychology* and employed it throughout all his educational texts: 'It is an error, indeed,' he asserted, 'to look upon the human soul as an aggregate of all sorts of faculties . . . faculties are after all at bottom one and the same principle.'[71] Herbart's explanation was to postulate mind as the arena in which experiences of external reality – and he accepted a limited sensationism – come together. These experiences of ultimate reality (*Realen*) he termed presentations (*Vorstellungen*) and out of them he was able to construct a fascinating, and certainly the hitherto most plausible (and original), epistemology and corresponding psychology.

According to Herbart, mind is the structure of presentations that come together, in a random way, out of the aesthetic continuum of the external world. There are three possible relationships between presentations: they may be similar, dissimilar or contrary, and, as they link into bonds (*Schmelzungen*) or merge into fusions (*Complexionen*) or conflict with each other, so consciousness is sustained in a complex, or mass, of perceptive awareness; to this Herbart gave the term *apperceptive mass*. In this way, developing a theme expounded earlier by Herder, he explained differences among cultures since available experiences will vary considerably in the range of presentations possible for the individual; if the Kantian theory is correct, he argued, all races and cultures should be equal as a result of the innate organizing power of mind. Further, the way in which presentations come together and structure the mind allowed Herbart to account for individual differences both in experience and thought. Since the presentations are the structure of the mind, it follows that mind is in continuous process of being formed by continued association of presentations.

The ability of new presentations to bond in with existing structures depends upon a number of factors: whether the existing structures are sufficiently conscious for links to be effected and so recognized in apperception; whether the mind can distinguish the similarities between existing and new presentations in order that fusion can take place. This led Herbart to hypothesize that the effectiveness with which new presentations can be incorporated (that is, for learning to take place) depends upon the range of previous presentations, organized as concepts, that are available above what he termed the threshold of consciousness. At any given moment, moreover, consciousness has a focus at which ideas are marshalled; out of the mind a sub-group of concepts rises, if a visual illustration may be employed, like a cupola on a dome, and Herbart used the metaphor of *Wölbung* ('arching' or 'vaulting') to explain this. Out of the cupola, like a small spire, an even more concentrated group of concepts appears by a process of 'pointing', *Zuspitzung*, and it is to this focus of current interest that the new presentation must be bonded or fused (depending on whether it is a similar or dissimilar presentation). So building mind – that is, learning – depends on the readiness with which previous experiences can be summoned to consciousness, and the links that can be effected between existing concepts and new presentations.[72]

In his *General Pedagogy* of 1806 Herbart asserted that 'the mind is always in motion: at times the movement is very rapid; at others, scarcely perceptible',[73] and it was this that led him to postulate that the will, which drew from Fichte's concept of the ego as the driving force of the personality, is itself the product of the mind built out of presentations. And here he made his own venture into metaphysical assumptions: having discarded faculties, he postulated an alternative group of powers which order the mind, designated the five moral ideas. As mind is built, it develops a drive towards a moral perfection, and to do this it is guided by the emergence (rather mysteriously) of the five moral ideas of inner freedom, perfection, goodwill, justice and equity. Herbart elaborated on these ideas at length in his *General Pedagogy* but the general notions they contain may be easily summarized: inner freedom describes intuitive action towards the good; perfection is the condition of complete physical and mental health, existing within a highly developed rational culture which acts as a guiding force; goodwill, or benevolence, describes positive, beneficial interaction with other persons; justice enables us to avoid social conflict; equity sees that distributive justice takes place. In this way, moreover, he explained bad behaviour, or evil, as faulty development of the will; in children (and by definition bad adults are considered morally immature, that is, 'children') 'experience continuously accumulates confused masses' in their minds.[74] So, becoming a moral adult means that minds must be corrected of their confusions and this, of course, puts a premium on proper education: it is the process whereby a moral society can be built.

The educational task: pedagogical intervention

Herbart's educational theory was constructed on this metaphysical and epistemological basis, and his approach may be considered as one of intervention in the normal course of events in order to restructure the child's experiences in the direction of morality; in brief, his pedagogy intended to counteract the 'confused masses of experience' that build up in the child's mind. Behind this intention lies the metaphysical assumption that the world is an organized, coherent whole, sustained by moral purpose, and it is easy to appreciate his receptivity to the two converging traditions of science and Enlightenment philosophy. Herbart was impressed by

Newton and the mathematical approach to understanding the external, so-called 'objective' world; indeed, he used mathematical diagrams and algebraic equations in his works to explain ideas. He was also living in the period of scientific taxonomy, characterized by the widely adopted classification of Linnaeus in his *Philosophia botanica* of 1751, and in the table of chemical elements outlined by Lavoisier in his celebrated 1789 *Elementary Treatise on Chemistry* which put forward, in the idea of 'elements', a view akin to Herbart's *Realen*. Equally, however, the world was still conceived as needing a guiding purpose, and both mechanism and sensationism were rejected as explanations. Given the rejection of divine right and its replacement by contract theories of social organization in which the whole people exercise sovereignty, concern with legality based upon morality (rather than royal caprice or force) was a serious concern, and Herbart followed in the Enlightenment tradition in accepting the notion of a moral will that presides over earthly events.

Pedagogy is the term used by Herbart to refer to the process whereby the teacher deliberately intervenes, and to know how to do this most effectively each child must be carefully studied since 'educability is limited by . . . individuality';[75] this scrutiny must encompass the whole child – 'observation both of his thought masses and of his physical nature'[76] – since education is much more than 'instruction in the sense of mere information giving'.[77] Despite these cautions, the Herbartian pedagogy is still basically intellectual, as is emphasized in Herbart's three-stage sequence (similar to Kant's views) of government, discipline and instruction. The child must first be brought under control or government (*Regierung*) as a first step, by restraint and coercion if necessary, using punishment and rewards; then to a condition of discipline (*Zucht*) which means a disposition to conforming behaviour: only then can the stage of instruction (*Unterricht*) be entered into, this being the process of forming the will. Since the will is generated out of the interaction of presentations, this becomes a formal, cognitive process.

Instruction, in Herbart's view, is not, however, merely a process of building up in the mind of the child a taxonomy of data concerning the external world; it must follow the five moral ideas and the moral structure of the world so that all the child's intellectual processes are engaged. The teacher, then, has the important task of arousing in the child a 'many-sided interest' in order to bring about the most complete possible structuring of the mind in the cultivation of virtue. This had significant implications for the curriculum, which Herbart was careful to consider. There is no limit to the classification of possible objects of study, he observed: 'classify not objects, but conditions of mind'.[78] This is an important distinction because it defines the curriculum as that organized body of knowledge which is best calculated to relate to conditions of mind. There are six such conditions, which he identified in two groups – those given by social experience and those by object experience, translated in the *Science of Education* as, respectively, sympathy and knowledge. Our social experience, he argued, gives us sympathy with our society, with mankind in general and with the deity; our object experience gives us knowledge of the external world, the law and aesthetic relationships;[79] and it is these six conditions that offer scope for the development of many-sided interest and content for the curriculum. Object experience is found in the areas of mathematics, natural science and handicrafts, while social experience is gained from language, literature, religion and history; above both comes geography, that supreme integrator of all experience, and in making this assumption Herbart clearly saw geography in the same light as it was conceived by Alexander von Humboldt, Wilhelm's brother, and developed in the famous *Kosmos*, and not in terms of the traditional lists of place names and products.

The four-step methodology of teaching

Methodology is all important in Herbart's pedagogical theory, the task being to take the six areas of experience and present them to the mind in correct order, since faulty association causes error, and hence moral immaturity as well as immorality.[80] The methodological task, then, based upon the concept of *Anschauung*, is to make the child's ideas distinct and clear so that they can be properly organized in the apperception mass. As a first step, the formal curriculum of language and literature, history, geography, religious studies, mathematics, natural science and handicrafts has to be arranged into a structure of topics, sub-topics and individual units down to, ideally, the most elementary facts. Once this is done, the curriculum has to be age-graded according to the intellectual reach of the child and taught by a careful sequencing. The crucial methodological step in the Herbartian pedagogy was the individual lesson-plan, the basic unit of the instructional sequence. Since the mind is an active apperception mass with 'arching' and 'pointing' in continuous operation, the lesson-plan must conform to this process for maximum effectiveness. The child, if properly approached, will be able to enter easily into the procedure, as his plasticity (*Bildsamkeit*) is a characteristic feature; indeed, so concerned was Herbart with this concept of the capacity of the child for being 'moulded' by appropriate lesson procedures that he commenced his final work, *Outlines of Educational Doctrine*, with this notion: 'The plasticity [*Bildsamkeit*], or educability, of the pupil is the fundamental postulate of pedagogics.'[81]

This process of moulding via the lesson-plan is achieved by working in harmony with the two psychological processes of immersion or concentration (*Vertiefung*) and reflection (*Besinnung*), the latter being further sub-divided into three parts. Altogether, then, Herbart evolved a four-step sequence of instruction of clarity (*Klarheit*), association (*Umgang*), system (*System*) and method (*Methode*). The first step – gaining clarity through immersion in the object to be studied – is basically that of *Anschauung* taken from Pestalozzi: the object under consideration is looked at closely for every possible characteristic, not just its accidental features but its essentials. So, in a sequence of natural science lessons on, say, flowers, a particular flower would be studied not only for such features as colour, size and perfume but in respect of its structure of stem, sepals, calyx, petals, and so on; it would be investigated for its reproductive system and the fruit that subsequently develops, its relationship to the plant of which it is part, and so on. By this method of immersion (and it may be the subject of a number of lessons if the object has many features) the flower becomes distinct both as an object and as a corresponding mental idea. During the process the relevant concepts are brought to an apperceptive focus or 'arch' with a 'point'. After clarity has been achieved, the teacher's task is then to follow the three steps of reflection, in which are summoned above the threshold of consciousness related concepts – which the child would have acquired both by experience and from previous lessons – whereby this particular flower could be linked or associated with other flowers already studied and with other relevant ideas. Then in the third step, system, this association would be broadened, usually by intensive questioning so that latent ideas might be brought to consciousness, in order that the next level of generalization could be made, for example, that flowers are reproductive organs of certain classes of plants. In the final step, method, the learning achieved in the lesson would be sum-marized in a broad principle comprehending all three previous steps, which would serve as the introduction for the next lesson. The whole approach was taxonomic and ordered in the spirit of what was felt to be the scientific method of inductive inquiry.

By these means Herbart believed that a genuinely objective, scientific – and therefore 'exact' – view of the world could be built up in the learner, and error eliminated; morality would therefore develop as the learner acquired a properly constructed 'circle of thought' in which the will finds scope for adequate development. As increasing clarity of ideas occurs, as the mind is properly built, then goodwill ensues. Herbart thus provided for the attainment of abstract concepts by suggesting that the mind itself, being the active arena of presentations, comes into the possession of abstract ideas, especially the five moral ideas, simply through the re-structuring that takes place; to build up to abstract thoughts by his method is not difficult since, he pointed out, 'thought travels quickly, and only that lies far from reflection, which is separated by many intermediate concepts or by many modifications of thought'.[82]

Herbart's achievement: foundations for the future

Herbart's pedagogical writings were an impressive achievement and he made a number of distinct advances over existing theory. By far the most important was his rejection of faculty theory; his postulation of an active mind which needs a many-sided stimulation meant that all subjects are of value in the degree to which they contribute to the clarification of ideas of the human and external worlds. His metaphysics, however, was too fantastic to be entertained seriously, although this, as it happened, did not matter; despite his disclaimers, his psychology and pedagogy were quite easily detached from the metaphysics and the ethics; there is no necessary evident connection between cognitive awareness and moral insight and consequent ethical behaviour, and his ideas were not acted upon in this respect. But his model of the cognitive mind (if the moral dimension is removed) was extremely plausible and turned out to be highly attractive; moreover, the pedagogy of the four formal lesson-steps provided, in reasonable detail, the best explanation yet advanced of how people learn. In particular, the theory of the apperception mass, of the conscious mind, of the threshold, of arching, pointing and assimilation of new ideas, made mental processes understandable. Further, these concepts gave a new dimension to educational theorizing about whether the latent ideas of the mind are not innate but are the effects of previous experience that have not yet received consciously articulated form. In addition, he opened up an avenue of theoretical speculation that eventually led to Freudian psychopathology. Of major importance was the fact that his epistemology was equally adaptable to the sense-empiricist model: the presentations did not have to come from *Realen* but could equally be considered as simply sensations of the Bacon–Locke variety, and it was this interpretation that was generally followed.

By the time of his death in 1841 Herbart's thought was still only in limited academic circulation. Europe was in its period of extreme conservative reaction, and there was no more widespread interest in his educational ideas than in those of Pestalozzi; the bourgeois temper of the times favoured simple, practical methods that would preserve the existing order, not reconstruct it into a new moral world. Herbart, like Pestalozzi, was temporarily put aside; their theories, however, were not forgotten, and by the end of the century they were to provide, often fused together into various syntheses, the two most dominant systems guiding educational practice in the Western world. The practices of Herbartianism, as his applied thought came to be called, are still quite operative, even if often denied.

CHAPTER 8

An Age of Revolutions 1762–1830: Beginnings of National Systems

The thought of Rousseau was an articulate response to political, social and economic developments in Europe and the New World; while he stimulated a vigorous stream of educational theorizing, he also heightened awareness of the need for systems whereby new educational ideas could be put into practice. His *Considerations on the Government of Poland* stressed that properly organized systems of education could promote social change and the common good, form the national character and institutionalize popular government – all attractive ideas to both liberal and radical reformers. When revolution broke out in the United States and France, one of the major concerns of the French revolutionary government, and to a lesser extent the American, was the creation of systems of national education that could implement the new ideals and at the same time secure the republics on a permanent basis. This trend, moreover, spread: Prussia became anxious to create a system of state education, not for revolutionary purposes, but for purely nationalistic reasons; while in other parts of Europe the idea also met with limited success, particularly in Switzerland and Austria; it was resisted in England. Not all the credit should go to Rousseau; while he was the central figure of the revolutionary ethos, his significance lies as much in the stimulus he gave to others. Moreover, it was a two-way process: he drew from his milieu and expressed more effectively than anyone else what was being thought by many and, in fact, from the publication of *Émile* in 1762 until the outbreak of the French Revolution in 1789 there was a keen interest in national systems.

Towards a national system in France

From Émile *to the revolution*

From 1762 to 1789 educational theory in France consisted in a duel between the conservative Catholic Church and Enlightenment thinkers. Even before *Émile* was published, in response to the trends of rationalistic Enlightenment thinking FitzJames, Bishop of Soissons, wrote in 1756 that while science is valuable in furthering human affairs it needs direction, and to this end 'Christian doctrine alone is adequate . . . it is that which guides all sciences to fulfil their proper ends' within the divine plan.[1] In 1762 the church Assemblée du Clergé accepted that education might have a secular component, but insisted this must remain subordinate to religion, and throughout the following decades the Catholic Church in France produced a considerable conservative literature of education, including the attacks on Rousseau and alternative *Émile*s such as *Eusebio*.[2] It was essentially a reactionary movement; the initiative was with the radical innovators whose thinking was to become embodied in the educational documents, legislation and actions of the French Revolution.

The seminal document was the *Essai d'éducation nationale* (*Essay on National Education*), published earlier in 1763 by Louis-René de Caradeuc de La Chalotais (1701–85), attacking clerical control of education and making proposals for reform. Attorney-General of the Parlement of Brittany, La Chalotais was a bitter opponent of the Jesuits and led a provincial *parlement* committee of investigation into the order which when tabled in 1762 recommended their suppression. The *Essay* reveals a wide acquaintance with the educational thought and practice of the period, asserting that education in France was in an appalling condition because of excessive clerical control, authoritarian learning of irrelevant – chiefly Latin – materials to the detriment of sound vocational and artisan training, and fragmentation among competing congregations. Education, La Chalotais argued, should aim to remove ignorance and 'direct the studies [of the school] towards the greatest public benefit'.[3]

Prescriptions for his proposed new system of education hinged upon the conception of morality as issuing from natural law and being prior to revelation, which has a purely secondary, supporting role. Educational activities should be concerned, therefore, with the world of ordered knowledge, and La Chalotais accepted the encyclopedist approach of an integrated structure to the world; the task of education should be far more properly seen as one of vocational and civic efficiency with secular knowledge paramount; there are, he wrote, too many clerical colleges, too few skilled labourers and artisans. So he criticized the Brothers of the Christian Schools: 'they teach reading and writing to people who ought to learn only to draw and handle the plane and file.'[4] The thrust of the national system, he argued, should be for minimal book learning, especially of the formal, abstruse kind – 'it is contrary to nature that children should remain seated for five or six hours [a day]'[5] – and for maximum practical learning, free of religious doctrine. In the final paragraph La Chalotais concluded: 'I am convinced that this plan is correct, because it is founded upon the nature of the mind and upon the principles of human knowledge.'[6] The argument for a national system was not, of course, built around the case for republicanism, since the *Essay* was addressed to Louis XVI; instead, it was for a new society based upon the principles of natural law and a secular morality.

Further similar plans appeared over the next twenty years in increasing numbers;[7] in 1775, the year before he was dismissed, Anne-Robert-Jacques Turgot (1727–81), Minister of Finance, addressed a short *Memorial of Municipalities* to the king urging the replacement of the haphazard provisions for education with a balanced national system, still at no cost to the crown, but under the control of a Council of National Education which would coordinate and supervise a four-tier system of elementary schools, colleges, universities and academies, and oversee the production of appropriate textbooks, uniform educational policy and a balanced, socially relevant curriculum. Louis XVI dismissed Necker the following year – the year in which the American colonies revolted – and continued his own heedless drift towards revolution.

A decade of revolutionary provisions for education 1789–1799

The storming of the Bastille on 14 July 1789 commenced the French Revolution, which lasted until November 1799, when Napoleon (1769–1821) became First Consul for five years and then Emperor until 1814.

Throughout the decade of revolutionary government, education was a continued concern. The development of policy falls into two main phases: a turbulent first period from 1789 to the end of 1795; and a second, beginning with the Daunou Law of 25 October 1795, which brought a measure of stability until Napoleon imposed a more rigid and authoritarian pattern. These two phases, moreover, correspond closely to the political strength of the new republic: in the first period the revolution took its inevitable course of conflict as various domestic factions fought for dominance, and as the country as a whole had to confront the armed intervention of the European monarchies of the First Coalition, formed by Britain, Austria, Prussia and Russia; in the second, Napoleon became commander of the Italian campaign and began the series of military victories that put France on to the offensive and created conditions of domestic stability.

Throughout the first phase of revolutionary concern for education two complementary sequences were in operation: the dismantling of church schools as part of a policy of anticlericalism, and the substitution of an alternative national system drawn from a synthesis of the most acceptable ideas generated during the previous four decades. Attacks upon the church were easily initiated. Less than three weeks after the almost empty Bastille fell, a revolutionary decree by the National Assembly of 4 August 1789 abolished the church tithe revenues, thereby severely affecting fiscal viability. In July of the following year the *Civil Constitution of the Clergy* restructured the French church by centralizing it under the government, each diocese being coextensive with a civil administrative *département*, with provisions also for the election of bishops, priests and vicars on a proportional population basis by the laity, without reference to Rome, a fixed scale of stipends and the subordination of the clergy to the overall authority of the Procurator General-Syndic of the *département*. Despite resistance by more than half the clergy, the revolutionary factions continued their pressure against the church and on 18 August 1792 the brief-lived Legislative Assembly (October 1791–September 1792) suppressed all religious orders and teaching congregations and confiscated their endowments. Religious provisions for education ceased for over a decade until December 1803, when Napoleon allowed the return of the Brothers of the Christian Schools and the Ursulines. Catholic schools, however, were not closed; they simply went underground if anticlericalism was rampant, or, in the isolated rural areas which in general opposed the revolution, they carried on undisturbed.

Meanwhile, both the National Assembly and the succeeding Legislative Assembly had to grapple with the more difficult problem of providing for education. Despite all the theorizing over the previous half-century, nowhere was there any national system of education to serve as an example. The existing systems of the church orders and congregations, operating alongside the various civic and voluntary schools, whatever their deficiencies, made some provision, even if rapid industrial and technological development put an increasing strain upon them. Problems of finance, buildings, curricula, school sequences, textbooks, administration, supervision and teacher preparation and supply had all been either ignored or but lightly touched upon in the reforming literature; they had to be confronted and solved if revolutionary theory were to be translated into effective practice. At the centre of these problems was the main issue: what constitutes a 'national' system of education and what provisions are entailed?

A number of educational committees were convened to make recommendations, while individuals offered advice and made representations; in all, more than twenty separate submissions were received in the revolutionary decade. The first of importance was the *Mémoire sur l'éducation nationale française*, presented to the National Assembly on 11 December 1790 by the Abbé Yves-Marie Audrien of Grassins College, one of the colleges of the University of Paris. Audrien pointed out that 'there is no national education anywhere'[8] to serve as a guide and, after the observation that girls had been neglected in the past and needed more adequate consideration by the new republic, argued for 'three orders of education naturally established: the little schools, the small colleges or language colleges, and the great or senior colleges'.[9] The bulk of his proposal dealt with organizational matters but it had an essential theme to the effect that a proper system of national education would preserve the revolution – a theme, moreover, that had already occupied the thoughts of American educational planners. On 4 September 1791 the National Assembly resolved that 'a system of public instruction shall be created, common to all citizens and gratuitous so far as that part of education is concerned which is necessary for all men alike. Schools of various grades shall be supplied as necessary over the whole kingdom.'[10] The Assembly had before it, moreover, two more submissions, the *Travail sur l'éducation publique* by Honoré-Gabriel Riquetti, the Comte de Mirabeau, which was presented posthumously in the year of his death (1791), and the *Report* by Charles-Maurice de Talleyrand-Périgord (1754–1838). Both documents contained similar ideas. Talleyrand's, which was more comprehensive, recommended a general elementary education for all children, without charge, after which should come fee-charging district secondary and advanced *département* institutions, surmounted by a National Institute, a kind of research and higher-learning body. In general he recommended a modernized curriculum and the abolition of all existing institutions, with the *département* schools replacing universities. The most important provision was that, while education should be universally available, and its express purpose should be to make people 'better, happy and more useful',[11] it should not be compulsory.[12]

To consider these and other reports the new Legislative Assembly on 25 September 1791 appointed an educational Committee of Instruction with five members led by the Marquis de Condorcet (1741–94). Their report appeared on 20 April 1792 as the *General Organization of Public Instruction* and, following the plans of Mirabeau and Talleyrand, recommended a five-tier sequence of a four-year primary school, one to every 400 persons, teaching reading, writing, reckoning, civics and useful knowledge to all; a secondary school based upon contemporary sciences of mathematics, science, chemistry, natural science, ethics and social science; followed by either a technical institute for trade training or a *lycée* (a new term in the revolution) to provide former university-level instruction; and, at the top, a National Society of Sciences and Arts. This widely discussed report also specifically recommended against any compulsory enrolment.

Scarcely had Condorcet's report been presented than the Assembly was confronted with the threat of war by the First Coalition; its only educational action was to suppress religious orders and teaching congregations in August 1792. On 21 September 1792 government passed to the Convention and in December it considered two reports from the Committee of Instruction, the first recommending that elementary education be the responsibility of communes and a second, under the authorship of Gilbert Romme, which proposed a complete national system, with a dual scheme of compulsory primary schooling for boys and girls, and an advanced system of *lycées* for boys only. On 26 June 1793 yet another report was presented by a Committee under Joseph Lakanal, a former brother of the Doctrinaire congregation, which again urged a minimum primary education; on 28 January 1794 Alexandre Deleyre recommended separate secondary instruction in domestic education for girls. None of these schemes was adopted, Romme's was not even discussed, and by 1794, despite the many committees and reports, no national system was in being, the schools were languishing in the areas of effective revolutionary activity, and elsewhere there was a growing resurgence of religious schooling.

The Convention: a period of constructive legislation 1794–1799

The period of rule by the Convention saw the most turbulent phase of the revolution so far, and it had to deal with internal dissension as well as the external threat of the First Coalition; in January 1793 Louis XVI was executed after his attempted flight from the capital and in mid-1793, with the fall of the Girondins, the Jacobin Committee of Public Safety led by Robespierre launched the campaign of terror to eliminate opposition to the revolution. The excesses of the Convention period pushed religion aside, the new era being symbolized in the Cult of the Supreme Being and marked with a new calendar, proclaiming September of 1793 as the beginning of Year 1. In this spirit of extreme rationalism the Committee attempted to restructure education completely, although without any sense of clear direction.

To the end of the year 1793 there was nothing positive to show for half a century of theorizing on the new education for equality, while the church system had been ruined. By late 1794 the Convention, with the worst of the Terror over and its chief architect Robespierre executed in July, realized that the destruction had to stop and charged the Commission on Public Instruction to make inquiries and come up, yet again, with positive suggestions. One submission arrived on 6 October 1795 from the principal of the leading college of the University of Paris, Jean-François Champagne (1751–1813), who endorsed their efforts 'to reassemble the scattered debris of education' and urged the Commission to get the college system going again by establishing a wide-scale, liberal scholarship system for promising students.[13] In his account of the damage done to higher education, Champagne wrote to the Commission that 'all was torn down, nothing rebuilt . . . the teachers insulted, vilified, and hunted down . . . most of the colleges, the ancient dwelling places of youth and the Muses, were transformed into prisons [and] the teaching of the young in Paris came to an end.'[14]

Already French education had acquired a *de facto* centralization under the University of Paris. The secondary system of Jesuit colleges served the entire country and had been successful in providing educated leadership;

it was, after all, mostly from Jesuit colleges that the *philosophes* and after them the revolutionary generation came. When the order was expelled from France in 1764 their colleges were transferred to other orders and secular commissions. By this time these colleges provided a variety of curricula, although only a minority – the *collèges de plein exercice* – offered a full curriculum through to entry to the *maîtrise en arts*. In the best of the Jesuit colleges a full liberal arts education at university level in the upper four grades was provided; in many cases these colleges were constituent elements of the universities. Paris had thirty-eight such colleges of which Louis-le-Grand, under the principalship of Champagne, was the only one to remain open, in distressed condition, at the height of the Terror. We do not know how many colleges offering a range of instruction from incomplete secondary through to the bachelor's degree and licenciate existed at the outbreak of the revolution in 1789; rough estimates go up to 900, reliable ones from 320 given by Champagne[15] to 562 stated in the 1844 Report of the Minister of Public Instruction Abel-François Villemain. During the revolution, particularly in the years 1792–3, most of the colleges were raided for recruits, staff were dispersed, and the buildings requisitioned.

Unrest was also growing from within. As early as 1782 the *philosophe* Louis-Sébastien Mercier scorned their ossified Latin curriculum in his *Tableau de Paris*, observing that 'a hundred pedants try to teach Latin to children before they know their own language ... seven or eight years are spent in learning Latin, and out of a hundred pupils ninety come out without knowing it.'[16] The conservatives rebutted his charge by ridiculing the current fashion of ignoring good latinity and stuffing the heads of youth, as the Abbé Proyart of Louis-le-Grand wrote in 1785, with every new subject in order to produce 'prodigies of knowledge; really, little Encyclopedists'.[17] Students at Paris, the entire body studying philosophy, took the radical side and in 1789 petitioned against the excessive use by their professors of dictated lecture notes, which were 'written almost always without being understood, preserved without being read, initialled by the professor without being looked at, [and serving] as a step in our rise to the higher faculties'.[18] Now that printed books are available, they argued, the practice must cease. The *Petition*, moreover, objected to lectures being given in Latin. The following year more student complaints asserted that 'the fate of the nation depends on the reform of education' and urged a number of reforms including the abolition of corporal punishment.[19] By 1792 all Paris colleges except Louis-le-Grand were closed; outside the capital, colleges were closed or restricted, and few seem to have escaped the attentions of revolutionary committees. The élitist structure of the colleges and the education system as it existed was being attacked, and it was in this context that the Convention attempted its period of positive reforms.

These began in the last months of 1794, starting with the *Décret sur les écoles primaires* of 17 November 1794, which, based upon the Lakanal report, required the establishment of one six-year primary school for every town of 1000 inhabitants, for boys and girls, to teach reading, writing, arithmetic and the French language, and to 'inculcate republican principles, the Rights of Man and the French constitution'.[20] On 16 December of the same year they decreed secondary *écoles centrales*, to replace the Jesuit and other religious *collèges*, in each major town at the centre of a population of at least 300,000 people. Both decrees met with a limited success, and on 17 April 1795 a supervisory and inspectorial commission of five members, including Lakanal, was appointed to provide enforcement.

In the same period a large number of specialized, independent, advanced schools were established on the pattern of scientific societies and scholarly academies to meet emerging needs of society. So a number of schools were either founded or reorganized out of earlier institutes: the École des Armes concerned with military ordnance, and the military college, École de Mars; the medical school, École de Santé; the Conservatoire des Arts et Métiers, a school of technology; and the famous École Polytechnique. Early the following year (1795) further schools and government institutes were established, the Conservatoire de Musique, the École des Beaux-Arts, the Bureau des Longitudes and the École des Langues Orientales. A school was established for the preparation of teachers, the École Normale, the term *normale* being derived from the Latin *norma*, a standard against which other things are judged (originally a carpenter's square) and coming, perhaps, from the use of the term by Abbot Felbiger in Silesia who referred to his Austrian teachers' college in 1774 as a *Normalschule*.[21] Certainly the Paris École Normale was intended to set standards by which teaching competence could be judged. The intention was to scour France for students, one for every 20,000 persons, who after a four-month course in Paris would return to their local district and pass on their experiences in teacher preparation.[22]

By the end of 1795 in the remaining few days of office the Convention enacted the *Loi Daunou* of 25 October which included an education code that lasted until Napoleon's legislation. Generally, it provided for primary schools in villages and towns but not under village or commune control, administered instead by the larger local government unit of the canton, and, although the state paid part of the teacher's expenses, these were to be supplemented by pupil fees. It required also two central schools in each *département* with a six-year curriculum: for twelve- to fourteen-year-olds languages, art and natural history; for fifteen- and sixteen-year-olds science; for seventeen- and eighteen-year-olds belles-lettres, grammar, history and constitution. As a third tier the code followed Condorcet's recommendations and enacted a National Institute of Arts and Sciences with three streams: physical science and mathematics; literature and fine arts; moral and political science.

Gradually the various schemes for a national system of education merged into a composite pattern for which the state passed laws and established a uniform national Education Code, setting standards for teacher certification and student attainment by means of examinations. Boys and girls were to be provided for equally at canton and department level in a three-level system of primary, secondary and advancd institute, but with neither compulsion nor gratuitous tuition required; it was not until the *Loi Guizot* of 1833 that elementary education on a popular scale began to be taken at all seriously. The founder of the theory of Ideology, the Comte Destutt de Tracy (1754–1836), in his *Observations sur le système actuel d'instruction publique* (published in Paris in 1801), reflected a general French attitude to education when he wrote that 'in every civilized society there are necessarily two classes, one which works with its hands . . . the other with its mind . . . the first is the working class; the second is that of the intellectuals.' There is, therefore, he continued, a mandate for two totally separate systems of instruction which have no need of any common relationship.[23] Indeed, de Tracy summarized a dominant conviction which, despite the Convention's concern to oppose élitism, had been growing since the *Loi Daunou*.

The problem was serious: granted universal assent to the *école primaire*'s provision of instruction in literacy, what exactly would be the pattern of the secondary stage, to be given in the central schools, *écoles centrales*, which were to replace the old Jesuit-style *collèges*? What, moreover, was to be the character of the advanced educational schools and institutes which were to offer a liberal education as distinct from the specialized vocational foundations? Since the central schools did not flourish, a solution was found by working downwards; a move was made, then, to stimulate them by establishing liberal arts colleges which might give a lead to central schools as preparatory institutions. On 8 July 1797 it was proposed in the Council of Five Hundred that the confiscated endowments of ten former colleges, including Louis-le-Grand, now renamed Equality College, Collège Égalité, should be combined to establish a superior college to give a lead to the advanced-education tier. This was established, with an authorized complement of 800 students and designated the Prytaneum, a classical Greek revival from the original meaning of a public hall. Two years later it was found unwieldy and was divided among four campuses at Paris, Fontainebleau, Versailles and Saint-Germain. In addition to the Prytaneum, and to assist in stimulating the secondary schools, came another advanced, third-tier institution whose name also reflected the classical revival then emerging. This was the *lycée*, from Lyceum, Aristotle's school in ancient Athens.

Education under Napoleon: the Imperial University

Strictly speaking, the *lycée*, although proposed by Condorcet, was a development of the Napoleonic era, being first used in 1802 in its current sense. Napoleon, with a military disdain for indecision and vacillation, gave orders for education to be put on a regular, systematic basis. The task was given to Antoine-François, Comte de Fourcroy, who had been involved in revolutionary educational concerns for the previous decade and whose report to the Conseil d'État on 19 April 1802, incorporating a number of other reports, recommended a four-tier scheme: primary schools back under commune control, secondary schools provided by either communes or private bodies (chiefly religious groups were intended), *lycées* as advanced institutes to replace the central schools and, at the top, specialized vocational and professional schools.[24] By this time the curriculum had become more clearly defined: the primary schools should concentrate on literacy and numeracy from age six to twelve; the secondary on French, Latin, natural history, geography, mathematics, physics and drawing for four years; the *lycées* for ages sixteen to twenty on a liberal education, specializing in languages and science. Thirty *lycées* were to be maintained at state expense, for boys only, for which 6400 scholarships were authorized; by 1813 there was a total enrolment for all France of 14,492 students of whom only 3500 were scholarship holders,[25] usually orphans of army officers rather than talented youths, with a student body in the secondary schools, which served the *lycées*, of about 30,000.

The *lycées*, at this stage, had supplanted the former university colleges of liberal arts and offered a modern curriculum, the universities being necessarily superseded, Fourcroy observed in his report, as institutions which were 'no longer in accord with the progress of reason, and whose reform had been called for by half a century of philosophy and enlightenment'.[26]

Napoleon moved astutely in his years as consul although, as one of his ministers, the historian Baron Bignon, observed, Napoleon considered church resistance to state supremacy 'evidence of unendurable clerical ambition and medieval backwardness'.[27] Gradually, however, Napoleon established good relations with the papacy in a concordat of 16 July 1801 which recognized Catholicism as the dominant French religion and provided for new diocesan boundaries, new bishops (although the state had the right of nomination to the sees) and state retention of all confiscated church lands from the revolution; in return the state was to provide funds for church activities. Two years later the Brothers of the Christian Schools and the Ursulines were allowed to reorganize their schools; no other church schools were allowed, but private schools were tolerated on payment of a special tax. The concordat provided for religion to be reintroduced into the schools, and, following his penchant for uniformity, Napoleon authorized, without reference to the Vatican, a common school catechism which the bishops accepted with some misgivings. It was revoked on 22 July 1814 when Napoleon fell.

Having settled religious issues reasonably well, Napoleon continued to impose uniformity on education, indicating that 'My aim is to have a means whereby a lead may be given to political and moral conceptions',[28] and to effect this in a decree of 10 May 1806 the Imperial University was foreshadowed as a single, totally centralized state department of education:

> *Article 1.*   There shall be formed under the name of an Imperial University a body charged exclusively with public teaching and education in the whole Empire.[29]

It took nearly two years for this annunciatory decree to be drafted in detail, and on 17 March 1808 the law was promulgated, Title I setting out the intention:

> *Article 1.*   Public teaching in the whole Empire is confided exclusively to the University.
> *Article 2.*   No school, or any establishment for instruction whatsoever, may be formed outside the Imperial University or without the authorization of its head.

Article 3. No one may open a school, or engage in public teaching, without being a member of the Imperial University, and having a degree from one of its Faculties.[30]

The foundation of the Imperial University centred all executive authority in Napoleon himself through the Grand Master of the university and the executive body, the Conseil de l'Université. Louis-Marcelin de Fontanes was appointed Grand Master – in effect, president of the entire university. Under this new scheme a hierarchy of institutions was organized from primary schools up through private schools and colleges (both providing a secondary education) to *lycées* and academies. Despite Title XIII which allowed regulations to be issued for primary schools, almost nothing was done and they remained the concern of local communes, which did as much or as little as they cared. The emphasis remained on the higher levels, especially that of providing for the sons of the bourgeoisie, a group that by now had become a major political force in France and that Napoleon sought to cultivate. The *collèges* were local, commune-run secondary schools; similar private schools were termed *instituts*; both gave a curriculum based on French, Latin, science, mathematics, history, geography and religion. Above these in status but overlapping in curriculum were the *lycées*, which under Napoleon had changed character into quasi-military academies, organized into companies of twenty-five wearing uniforms, with life regulated by drum rolls and bugle calls. Entry to the *lycée* was competitive; 2400 scholarships were reserved for the sons of military officers and senior civil servants.

Two further centralized features are contained in the Imperial University decree: all higher learning in the universities and advanced professional schools was reorganized in thirty-four regional academies, each supervised by a rector; and henceforth all teachers throughout France were required to have state certification, this being rigorously enforced only at the secondary and higher levels. What happened, in effect, was that a corporate teaching body, *un corps enseignant*, was created by virtue of Regulation I.3 and all of Title XIV, of which Article 100 decreed that 'There will be established in Paris a residential normal school, designed to receive three hundred young men to be trained in the art of teaching the sciences and letters.'[31] This referred to the preparation of teachers for the higher levels, not primary, and a special institution was created, the École Normale Supérieure, whose award was the much-coveted *agrégation,* which means, quite literally, a 'joining together' in the symbolic unity of the *corps enseignant.* The *agrégation* gave entry to the prestigious post of teacher in a *lycée*; the degrees and diplomas of the advanced schools and academies provided an avenue of upward mobility in the growing civil service for the sons of the bourgeoisie, creating a French meritocracy and the new social concept of the 'career open to talent'.

Yet the religious issue was by no means settled; parents objected to the military character of the *lycée*, and the state responded by making conditions difficult for private church-oriented schools. Despite his concordat, Napoleon wanted no excessive religiosity; just enough, as it were, to legitimize state authority, as he explained to his Council of State in 1806: 'The end to aim at is that the young people should grow up neither too devout nor too sceptical; they should be made to fit the state of the nation and society.'[32] Even though opposition built up, it could not prevail against Napoleon's administrative strength and a compromise was effected: the elementary schools, left to the communes, continued to be taught by the *curé*, or by a teacher responsible to him, and in effect retained their pre-revolutionary character.[33] The issue had been waged over the secondary and advanced schools and it was with respect to these that the compromise was effected: the revolutionary zeal for the totally secular school, *l'école laïque*, was put aside by Napoleon, and religion, taught as a subject, was introduced into the secondary curriculum; at the *lycée* and academy level it was excluded on the grounds of academic freedom. During the administration of Napoleon's successor, Louis XVIII (r. 1815–24), this pattern was followed. Throughout his reign the church continued to press for control of the whole of education, arguing that a religious viewpoint should suffuse the entire curriculum; the liberals, for their part, resisted with equal determination. Some changes were effected: the *lycées* were renamed 'royal colleges' and non-Catholics allowed to opt out of the system and organize their own schools.

Throughout the years after Napoleon, French education remained unsettled, unaffected by the reforming thought of Rousseau and Pestalozzi for the time being: there had been enough ferment. None the less, the gains of the revolution remained; the reactionary era of Metternich and the Congress System did not completely put back the clock. Elementary education was still conservatively implemented, but this fact should not obscure the good work done, often with a deep sense of religious faith, by the communes, who frequently contracted elementary education to the teaching congregations, particularly the Brothers of the Christian Schools for boys, and for girls not only to the venerable Ursulines but also to the burgeoning number of female orders in the nineteenth century. In addition, voluntary societies began to appear, as in England, and one movement in particular enjoyed a brief period of prominence, the Société pour l'Instruction Élémentaire which, founded in 1815, introduced into France the monitorial system of mass instruction currently enjoying a vogue in England. It could not, however, compete with the Brothers of the Christian Schools. The communes, likewise, looked after their colleges often with a high degree of solicitude and slowly these distinguished themselves from the *lycées*, or *collèges royaux*, by taking on more of a technical character, in contrast to the latter's literary-scientific bent. Religious pluralism remained, and non-Catholics were allowed to open their own schools – which they did chiefly at the elementary level. By 1840 there were 677 Protestant schools and thirty-one Jewish, along with 2052 compromise 'mixed' schools supported by several confessions with separate curricula according to faith.[34]

By 1830, however, Europe was on the brink of revolution again; Metternich's diplomacy was not holding, economic expansion was increasing rapidly, new social classes were appearing in France, and anticlericalism was resurgent. Louis XVIII had unwisely appointed the Catholic bishop Denis-Luc Frayssinous to the Grand Mastership of the University in 1821 and this new 'minister for education' dismissed from their chairs many liberal professors, including the renowned Victor Cousin, and attempted to make religious education compulsory in the royal colleges. Louis XVIII died in 1824 and was succeeded by his incompetent brother Charles X (r. 1824–30). Meantime the Jesuits had been reinstated by Pius VII's bull *Sollicitudo omnium ecclesiarum* and although lacking their pre-revolutionary power were attempting to recover lost strength; they sided with the weak Bourbon regime, and the melodramatic coronation of Charles at Reims, in the manner of the *ancien régime*, raised to boiling-point liberal fears of a return to authoritarian monarchy; in July 1830 they staged a *coup d'état* when Charles, fearing liberal dominance, attempted to dissolve the Chamber of Deputies, part of the system of constitutional government that came after Napoleon and had sought, under liberal pressure, to sustain the gains of the revolution. Charles escaped to England in the turmoil and further revolutions broke out in other countries suffering post-Napoleonic repression. For the French, the connection between church and state was too close; the liberals demanded a new constitution and a number of social reforms which included a much greater secularization of education.

Prussia: education for the corporate state

Fichte: education for moral regeneration

During the Napoleonic period the Prussian state also moved towards a national system of education, not for the same ideals as the French revolutionaries, but as a defensive response to Napoleon's European dominance. Prussia had suffered severely from Napoleon's strategy of expanding France to its 'natural' frontiers: the Pyrenees in the south-west, the Alps to the south-east, the Rhine to the east and north – France of the 'hundred departments' – as well as controlling the rest of Europe as client states. Germany thereby became a divided nation: Prussia to the north, Austria in the south and the Confederation of the Rhine in the centre, bounded by the east bank. Of these three major regions only Austria, owing to its Habsburg history, had any national unity; the Confederation of the Rhine was a Napoleonic contrivance to bring together for administrative convenience the multitude of separate principalities, archbishoprics, counties, duchies, electorates, abbacies and free cities that emerged from the Peace of Westphalia of 1648; Prussia was a desolate marcher land on the Polish frontier inhabited by illiterate Slavs whom the Order of Teutonic knights had subdued in earlier centuries, beginning in the eleventh. This territory had been infiltrated by a landed class of resident squires – the German word is *Junker* – who enserfed the people and built up great estates. By a dynastic succession the territory passed to the Hohenzollerns and it was this Electorate of Brandenburg which became Prussia in the early eighteenth century. By the early nineteenth it was little more than a camp-follower of the Coalition powers, as dependent upon their military strength as it had been, in cultural matters, upon France during the eighteenth century. In 1806, in his campaign against the Third Coalition of Britain, Russia and Prussia, Napoleon smashed the forces of the latter two at the battle of Jena, and the following year, by the Treaty of Tilsit, Prussia lost much of its territory to the newly created Grand Duchy of Warsaw and was required to accept a French army of occupation as well as to pay a crushing financial indemnity. Scarcely was the treaty signed than Prussia's leading philosopher, Johann Gottlieb Fichte (1762-1824), in his celebrated *Addresses to the German Nation* (*Reden an die deutsche Nation*), called for a total effort of the entire population to build a new, corporate state on a new moral order; one, moreover, that would never again suffer such humiliation at foreign hands. Central to Fichte's call was the need to reconstruct the system of education on modern lines as the agency of corporate regeneration.

Fichte's fourteen *Addresses* were delivered in the great hall of the Academy of Sciences in Berlin in the winter of 1807–8 to capacity audiences, including French occupation officers, and created a widespread public enthusiasm, since he was, by now, one of Germany's established philosophers, having had a brilliant although stormy career at the University of Jena, and was at the time living in Berlin. He was, moreover, speaking to an audience of literati, Prussian nationalists who, having accepted the Enlightenment, now resented French dominance. The occupation officers, for their part, are reported to have allowed the *Addresses* since they were on education, assumed to be probably over the heads of most people, and because these Frenchmen were, anyway, as one opinion has it, 'connoisseurs of rhetoric'.[35] Fichte's *Addresses* certainly were, to pragmatic French ears, flights of literary eloquence; to the German middle classes they had a cogent appeal.

The basis of his argument rested in the postulation of a moral order or the 'sublime Will' which creates the determinate world, each person being an agency whereby the 'sublime Will' realizes its purposes. This concept is of the greatest significance in the development of German nationalist education, since every child, he argued in the *Third Address*, must be made to realize that he

> . . . is not merely a member of human society here on this earth and for the short span of life which is permitted him on it. He is also, and is undoubtedly acknowledged by education to be, a link in the eternal chain of spiritual life in a higher social order.[36]

The theme was pursued throughout the *Addresses*, the Prussian people being castigated for their moral failures; although it was widely recognized that children should be given a good education, especially in morals and religion, few received one and those who did were simply pursuing selfish ends:

> Education . . . has been brought to bear hitherto only on the very small minority of classes which are for this reason called educated, whereas the great majority on whom in very truth the commonwealth rests, the people, have been almost entirely neglected by this system and abandoned to blind chance. By means of the new education *we want to mould the Germans into a*

corporate body, which shall be stimulated and animated in all its individual members by the same interest.[37]

And in making his strident assertions Fichte recommended that no better model of education could be found than that of Pestalozzi, whom he had visited in Switzerland and who was currently enjoying his period of greatest success and popularity in Yverdon.

Foundation of the Prussian state system

Fichte alone did not stimulate Prussia; already the defeat at Jena had gone deep, and Frederick William III, incompetent as he was, recognized that a complete overhaul of the state was necessary, especially its education. When, for example, Napoleon closed the university at Halle in 1806, and a deputation of professors in 1807 urged the king to establish a replacement, he agreed enthusiastically: 'That is right! That is fine! The state must replace what it has lost in physical powers by intellectual ones.'[38] Indeed, changes were already under way, commenced by Heinrich von Stein (1757–1831), a Rhinelander who had been appointed First Minister by Napoleon, after Tilsit, to reorganize Prussia on French constitutional lines. Stein, however, was dismissed by Napoleon a year later for his excessive democratization of the country; he was followed by his associate Karl August von Hardenberg (1750–1822) who, an equally enthusiastic reformer, proceeded more circumspectly and enlisted the support of the Junkers, whom Stein wanted to curb. Under Hardenberg the Junkers destroyed the peasantry by emancipating and dispossessing them; they had, in consequence, to accept positions as day-labourers on the now even greater Junker estates. At the same time the army was reorganized and made into a significant element of Prussian society, offering an important career structure within the state service. Since Prussia lacked large towns and industrial capacity, the state and civil service increasingly provided a major area for employment for the emerging middle classes; to survive, Prussia had to become a bureaucratic meritocracy in which education was a necessary element.

Reform was initiated by one of Prussia's greatest scholarly figures, Wilhelm von Humboldt (1767–1835), who after serving in Rome as Prussian Minister (1801–8) was recalled to the Ministry of the Interior in Berlin to work on education. Immediately he dispatched a group of students to Yverdon to be enrolled in Pestalozzi's school and sent an inspection delegation of seventeen educational administrators to observe the methods of *Anschauung* in detail. Humboldt's main concern, however, was with secondary and higher education, especially as it was related to the cultivation of morality. Wilhelm, like his younger brother Alexander, was strongly influenced by the classical revival which had gathered momentum in the later decades of the eighteenth century under the stimulus of some of Germany's greatest scholars – Herder, Lessing, Goethe, Schiller. No one gave a better summary of the ethos of the movement than Hegel, while still the principal of a Nuremberg grammar school in 1809, in an address which referred to the value of teaching classical languages as being 'the profane baptism which shall give to the soul the first and in-alienable tone and tincture for taste and scholarship'. And, he added, the classics must not be read in translation, for this 'might well give us the content but not the form, not their aesthetic soul'.[39] During the early eighteenth century humanism had lost status and universities and schools generally declined; with Humboldt's positive advocacy, the classics were restored to a leading position through the restructured secondary schools and universities.

Throughout Prussia the three-year elementary school became standard-ized as either the *Volksschule* or the preparatory school and in the course of the following decades normal schools were established to provide teachers; between 1817 and 1840 thirty-eight were founded, all following Pestalozzian principles of teaching and providing a three-year post-elementary course.[40] The preparatory school led on, in the case of the privileged middle-class boy – for Hardenberg's reforms favoured this group – to the revived grammar school, now officially designated as a *Gymnasium*. This Greek term was deliberately revived to stress the classical ideal of *paideia* as the goal of education; the *Gymnasium* was to cultivate both mind and body. Consequently, the nine-year curriculum consisted largely of literature – Latin, Greek and German and their cognate studies of religion and history – with the addition of mathematics, the ideal of *paideia* being achieved through the cultivation of *Wissenschaft*, the scholarly, scientific, wholly detached approach to learning. Wilhelm von Humboldt left the Ministry on 23 June 1810 for duties in Vienna, where he remained until 1815, but his classical initiative was sustained and on 12 July 1810 a government rescript finally separated the occupations of pastor and school-master, making the latter autonomous. This decree, *Examen pro facultate docendi*, provided for boards of secondary-teacher certification, known as the *wissenschaftliche Deputationen*, which in due course were constituted out of the faculties of the established Prussian University of Königsberg, and the two new ones of Berlin and Breslau, their task being to examine teachers in the subjects they wished to profess.[41]

The *Gymnasium* was preparatory to the university which by now, under the influence of the philosophical tradition begun by Kant and sustained by Fichte, Herder, Schelling and others, and the classical revival, had developed into a new institution. A symbolic change was the renaming of the Faculty of Arts as Philosophy and its recognition as an autonomous body, no longer preparatory to the professional faculties. Indeed, there was disdain for vocational preparation: the university task was the pursuit of *Wissenschaft* and the creation of an intellectual élite to fill the offices of the bureaucracy, these being the 'educated bourgeoisie' – *Bildungsbürgertum*. Entry to the university required boys to have first completed the nine-year *Gymnasium* programme and to have passed the matriculation entry examination, the *Abitur*. Within the Prussian university the student was expected to devote himself to the 'creative enlargement of his spirit', to seek the underlying unity of knowledge, in conjoint study with his teachers, in order to move to the Fichtean ideal of attaining moral freedom. Not only did this provide for individual excellence; Humboldt believed that it would promote the ideal of national, corporate development. University ranks also became more ordered, with the three-level system being established. The beginner, designated literally a 'private teacher', *Privatdozent*, received no salary and was dependent on either private means or student gratuities; his task was to win acceptance as a lecturer and tenured, salaried appointment as either associate professor or regular *Professor*. Many German universities, particularly in the Confederation, had by this time become degenerate and indisciplined, and in the spirit of reform new Prussian universities were founded at Berlin in 1810, the first completely secular university in Europe, and at Breslau in 1811.

Yet this was only a limited achievement which reached the sons of the middle and upper classes, and even they had high failure rates: the requirement of three years' compulsory military service was moderated for those youths in the *Gymnasium* who at age sixteen had completed six years of the programme (nine years of schooling in all); they were allowed to 'volunteer' for one year's army service as an alternative. Most children went to the fee-charging *Volksschule* and stayed as long as their parents' means permitted; in addition, many were unsuited to the classical *Gymnasium*, and alternatives, of significantly lower status, were developed: the modified *Gymnasium*, *Progymnasium*, with a six-year course and the putatively less demanding subjects of history, geography, science and modern languages, and the *Realschule*. Technical education developed outside the framework of the classical revival and in the course of the nineteenth century Prussia, and, by example, Germany, established a wide range of technical schools, of which the best were the *Realgymnasien*, along with specialized technical schools, colleges, academies and even technical universities.

The spirit of creative reform did not survive the peace that followed the Congress of Vienna in 1815. By 1817 students in German and Prussian universities had formed student societies, *Burschenschaften*, which, looking increasingly inward to a shallowly conceived nationalism, disturbed both Hardenberg and his Austrian counterpart, and architect of post-Napoleonic Europe, Prince Klemens von Metternich (1773–1859). Metternich had already organized an intelligence-gathering network and in 1819 issued the notorious Carlsbad Decrees which marked the conservative reaction in Germany. By these decrees the press was heavily censored, universities more closely controlled and *Burschenschaften*, which were rather innocuous groups, declared illegal. The possibilities for liberal growth were immediately forestalled; Prussia entered a period of post-war economic stagnation owing to its industrial incapacity, and in the same year (1819) Wilhelm von Humboldt withdrew from public life, disappointed that the great process of corporate nation building, according to liberal constitutional principles, was not proceeding. Prussia, Germany, all of the continent, in fact, entered a period of reaction.

Hegel: the state as an instrument of divine purpose

In these 'quiet years' that followed, from 1819 until the July revolutions of 1830, the concept of the corporate Prussian state continued to be developed, although in a form that was interpreted to support, not liberalism, but the conservative, even totalitarian state. The chief exponent was Georg Friedrich Wilhelm Hegel (1770–1831) whose ideas dominated the nineteenth century and gave rise to many subsequent movements. Born in Stuttgart and educated in theology at Tübingen, Hegel held a succession of positions as tutor in Gern, *Privatdozent* in Jena, editor of a newspaper in Bamburg, principal of a Nuremberg grammar school in the years 1808–16, and Professor of Philosophy at Heidelberg, 1816–18. In 1818 he was appointed to the principal German chair of philosophy at the rapidly ascendant University of Berlin where he remained, the leading intellect in academe, commanding the attention of the government and the educated populace, until his death of cholera in the 1831 epidemic. At the time of the student unrest that led to the Carlsbad Decrees, for example, Baron Karl von Allenstein, Minister for Spiritual, Educational and Medical Affairs as this new subdivision of the Interior was called after 1817, arranged for Hegel to lecture to students, public officials and army officers on the philosophical understanding, and resolution, of political issues. From his first significant work, written at Jena and published in 1807, *Phenomenology of Mind* (*Phänomenologie des Geistes*), until his death, Hegel was the leader of German idealism, building on a Kantian foundation.

Hegel wrote on all aspects of philosophy, but his most popular theme, which captured the public imagination and influenced subsequent thinkers, including Marx, was the historical explanation of world events, his ideas being particularly accessible in his *Lectures on the Philosophy of History*, first edited, posthumously, by Eduard Gans in 1837, subsequently by his son Karl Hegel in 1840.[42] In a sense, Hegel's philosophy of history put the thought of Kant and Fichte into an evolving social and political context.

The purpose of the *Lectures on the Philosophy of History* was to answer the question: 'What is the ultimate purpose of the world?'[43] Man, as outlined in his *Lectures*, is confronted by the flux of current events, much of it severely disordered in the wave of revolutions and wars in which both individuals and states are in profound conflict. This condition, Hegel argued, is itself engendered by passion, which in the state of nature is one 'of injustice, violence, untamed natural impulses of inhuman deeds and emotions';[44] the necessary imposition of order is the task of the organized corporate state, which in its best expression is 'the moral whole'.[45] Indeed, Rousseau's concept of the popular will is inadequate since it is not necessarily an informed, disciplined will: 'What constitutes the state', Hegel argued, 'is a matter of trained intelligence, not a matter of "the people" '; the Constitution itself is 'not a matter of choice but depends on the stage of the people's spiritual development'.[46] This immediately raises the main theme of his lectures: history is the cumulative record of the spiritual development of mankind. Through history the 'world spirit' is expressed in a succession of states emerging and developing internally to points of high culture, each state in turn reaching 'the period of its bloom, its excellence, its power and prosperity';[47] at that point, when total harmony obtains, when social and political conflicts are resolved, the state, having reached a condition of freedom, has fulfilled its task. Its culture, however, is not lost; this itself becomes part of the heritage of the succeeding state which seeks to reach a condition of harmony: and so the historical record illustrates a sequential development, Sumer to Akkad, Assyria to Babylon, through Greece, Rome, medieval Christendom and Renaissance Europe up to the present period. In this modern period, for the first time in history, under the guidance of Prussian philosophy, 'the Germanic peoples [have come], through Christianity, to realize that man as man is free and that freedom of Spirit is the very essence of man's nature'.[48]

The notion that history illustrates the progressive development of the 'freedom of spirit' is the essence of the Hegelian position. The concrete objectification of the only genuine reality – which in his word is *Geist*, translatable as either spirit or mind – is the world of nature. So Hegel offered a metaphysical interpretation of the world, on the Kantian model, of noumenon–phenomenon, of spirit and matter. The origin is *Geist*, a vague, undefined creative force, existing in imperfect form as the idea-in-itself, and which seeks perfection through a process of creative evolution. Nature is the idea-outside-itself, the idea in concrete instances. Hegel added a further concept: the creative development of the idea-outside-itself, in nature, generates a condition of self-awareness, and it is really this which is history. It is an abstruse concept, yet important to the understanding of most subsequent social and political theory: history is the record of the idea-outside-itself achieving freedom. *Geist* or spirit, then, is the self-consciousness of the evolving idea, objectified as history. This brought him back to the state as the basic unit by which spirit seeks freedom, and he employed a further metaphysical concept – logical development. Spirit evolves by means of a relentless logical process for which he used the Platonic notion of 'dialectic'; the historical record is not one of an unbroken, smoothly ordered growth of various states; on the contrary, it is one of conflict and resolution towards the achievement of harmony. Built into every situation (*thesis*) in nature is an essential contradiction (*antithesis*) and history is the record of the dialectical interplay between thesis and antithesis which becomes resolved in the higher development of synthesis. Yet the synthesis, as a necessary condition of the progressive development of spirit, itself becomes a thesis with an inbuilt antithesis which must be resolved. History, then, is the objectification of spirit's development. Development implies a goal, which is freedom, the ultimate ideal of all action. Hegel popularized, for the first time, the notion of progress through the organized state. Man by himself is historically nothing: 'in world history, only those peoples that form states can come to our notice';[49] 'the state is the divine Idea as it exists on earth . . . the State is the definite object of world history proper'.[50] The state's role, therefore, is to provide spirit with a vehicle for its dialectical progress; the state is an instrument of divine will, of a creative theodicy. It must therefore be prior to the individual. If this is the interpretation to be placed upon the events of nature, answering the original question 'What is the ultimate purpose of the world?', then one further question necessarily emerges: what is the purpose of man? What is each individual's role in this schema? Hegel had a comprehensive answer: it is to understand this metaphysical interpretation of history and to seek freedom by assisting spirit's development,[51] and in the degree to which we can achieve this – and a lifelong devotion is needed to the study of the scriptures, classics and literature, the gymnasial and philosophical curriculum – so each person attains freedom. The individual must therefore be educated to see his role in allowing reason – the dialectical development of spirit – to continue, and thereby to attain the individual's highest goal of personal freedom: 'the insight to which . . . philosophy should lead us is that the actual world is as it ought to be'.[52]

Hegel's thought was acclaimed both in Berlin and throughout Germany since it provided a dynamic interpretation of world events; it put the era of revolutions into perspective and, moreover, comforted the bourgeoisie with the belief that they were serving divine purposes. It gave, of course, an imprimatur to the classical revival of the *Gymnasium* and faculties of philosophy. Most important, Hegel's *Lectures* provided a comprehensive theoretical framework within which much subsequent political and social theory proceeded. Quite obviously it was subverted to reactionary ends; none the less it gave the best dynamic explanation of metaphysics so far advanced. And it was easy, as Marx demonstrated, to accept the method without the content. After his death, Hegel's philosophy developed into Hegelianism, Right and Left. The Right Hegelians, the conservative faction, accepted the literal content of his philosophy; the Left Hegelians, of whom Marx was to become the most significant, rejected the content but accepted the dynamic explanation. Of course, Marx threw out the metaphysics of spirit and, in his celebrated metaphor, claimed to stand philosophy back on its feet (after Hegel had put it on its head) by seeing history as the dialectical development not of spirit but of matter, of the world of nature. In education, Hegel was of the first order of importance: his ideas dominated philosophy, and the bourgeois school curriculum, for the ensuing century.

The United States: education for republicanism

The Americans, meanwhile, had even greater problems of national identity: despite the term 'United States', unity was precarious and rested in little more than a common desire among the thirteen colonies to be free of British rule; the basis of union had yet to be established and, from the insurrection in 1776 until the Treaty of Versailles of 1783 which gave a settlement, no positive steps were taken. The Constitutional Convention met in 1787 to provide the revolutionary and interim government, the Continental Congress, with a constitution. The almost insurmountable problem was that the thirteen colonies had no desire to lose their various rights and privileges so dearly won over the previous century or longer. When the Constitution eventuated in 1791, with ten amendments, it was a compromise document that embodied much of the contract theory of European and American thinkers in untested form. At the same time, however, it contained some sophisticated ideas, notably that of providing checks and balances in government through the separation of the legislature, executive and judiciary; such a system was, however, workable only in a remote country: it would be inconceivable for any European state to be so restricted, given the proximity of belligerent neighbours and the need for quick, effective response.

At the time of the Convention there was already a growing lobby pressing for national involvement in education, and no person was more active or articulate than Benjamin Rush (1745–1813), signatory to the Declaration of Independence, a surgeon-general of the revolutionary army and a member of the Constitutional Convention. His intense concern to see education a coping-stone of the new society led him, in an excess of rhetorical enthusiasm, to utter one of American educational history's most celebrated metaphors, contained in an essay submitted to the American Philosophical Society's competition of 1795 for the best plan of national education, to the effect that children must be made into 'republican machines'.[53] The other great figures of the period – George Washington, Benjamin Franklin, Thomas Jefferson and Noah Webster, among others – all spoke on the need for national support of education and proposed various Bills or propounded schemes of education: Washington and Jefferson both submitted Bills to establish national universities; Rush and Webster published persuasive appeals. This educational concern focused largely upon higher education, especially the establishment of colleges and universities; elementary schooling was not so seriously considered. The Convention, however, was less concerned with the needs of education than with acting purposefully in relationship to the European powers, and the particularly sensitive issue of states' rights.

Because of the varying backgrounds of the colonies, for many of which education was an integral part of their differing cultures, education had remained a responsibility of the newly sovereign states. The Constitution as a federal document specified those areas for which authority had been delegated to the union government, although a system providing for amendments allowed for the growth of additional areas. Education was left as either a state or a local concern, and only seven of the original thirteen states, along with the new state of Vermont (1791), assumed state responsibility. In a significant number of the original states, and of those that were admitted subsequently, elementary and secondary education were not accepted as a function of state government, and in post-revolutionary America there was the curious paradox of a highly generalized recognition of the value, desirability and even necessity of education, especially as the instrument of republicanism, along with an equally widespread reluctance for any particular authority to assume responsibility. On the contrary, there was, for a variety of reasons, considerable resistance to centralized authority which can be explained, in part, by the historical development of the various states.

Colonial provisions for elementary schooling

Following the explorations of Drake, Gilbert and Ralegh in the Elizabethan era, English settlements were established along the east coast of North America, beginning with Jamestown, Virginia, in 1607; in the seventeenth century eleven such settlements were made, along with one by the Dutch in 1626, Nieu Amsterdam, which in 1664 became British under the name of New York; in the eighteenth century the then most southern colony, Georgia, was founded. All the colonies were tied directly to the crown and had limited local responsibility under various kinds of assembly. The immigrants were mostly free settlers, some having been given large grants of land in the colonies, others choosing to leave Europe for religious or political reasons; some were simply adventurers. There were marked religious differences between the colonies: in northern New England, where the Congregational Church was established, were the Puritan or Calvinist settlements of Massachusetts (1629), Connecticut (1639) and New Hampshire (1679); to the south were colonies of mixed population, Maryland (1632), Rhode Island (1638), New York (1664), New Jersey (1664), Pennsylvania (1682) and Delaware (1682), which were more eclectic and pluralist in religion; further south again were the more topographically open settlements of Virginia (1607) and North and South Carolina (1663) which had an established Anglican Church. This pattern was reflected in education to a considerable extent in that the prevailing religious beliefs determined the educational ethos of each region.

Because of the religious persuasions of the colonists and their predominantly Protestant beliefs, schools were established from the beginning, the first being required in an Act of 1642. The most famous reference is contained in a second Massachusetts Act, the 'Old Deluder Act' of 1647, which states that it is 'one chief project of the old deluder, Satan, to keep men from a knowledge of the Scriptures, as in former times by keeping them in an unknown tongue, so in these latter times by persuading from the use of tongues.'[54] It is thus necessary to sustain literacy, 'the use of tongues', and hence ability to read the scriptures.

> . . . it is therefore ordered, that every township in this jurisdiction, after the Lord hath increased their number to fifty households, shall then forthwith appoint one within their town to teach all such children as shall resort to him, to write and read, whose wages shall be paid either by the parents or masters of such children, or by the inhabitants in general.

The Act also provided for a grammar school in each town of 100 families or households. The requirements are quite simple and seem to have been complied with to some extent, and followed elsewhere, especially in neighbouring Connecticut. The Act did not, however, specify an elementary schoolhouse, nor did it make schooling compulsory. In effect, it meant that elementary and grammar schooling was available only to those boys whose parents were sufficiently energetic to see the Act enforced; girls were definitely not encouraged, and for the ensuing two centuries or more there was a continuing battle for women to receive equality of educational opportunity. Provisions for school buildings remained limited; in some communities there were requirements for simple timber schoolhouses to be built,[55] but often the school was held in the church itself or an associated meeting-house.

Throughout the colonial era of some 150 years this was the general pattern of elementary school provision, and the exercise of local option was extremely varied; even Massachusetts, which set the best example, has many records of prosecution of communities for non-observance of the two Acts of 1642 and 1647. There was, of course, a continuation of the English philanthropic impulse. As early as 1634 Benjamin Syms bequeathed money 'for the erecting of a very sufficient School house and the Rest of the Increase that are left . . . [for] Repairing the School' with the intention that it be employed 'to manteyne poor children'.[56] In 1706 the London-based Society for the Propagation of the Gospel in Foreign Parts, the SPG, which had grown out of the Society for the Promotion of Christian Knowledge, sent its first missionaries to the American colonies with a brief, among a very large number of charges, to 'encourage the setting up of Schools for the teaching of Children'.[57] Despite charity, however, colonial schools were generally fee-charging, some communities paying the teacher out of the community chest; the use of ministers' wives and widows as teachers points to a continued problem since elementary teachers were seriously underpaid, and it is always surprising to read in the records of communities' indignation at finding the worst types coming forward. Widows, therefore, seemed ideal cheap labour; otherwise, as in Europe, the job was doubled up on a person already employed; in Northampton, Massachusetts, in 1664 the town voted to a farmer, Mr Cornish, 'six pound towards the scoole and to tacke the benefit of the scollers provided that he teach Six months in the yeare together'.[58] Incentives were offered and in 1661 in Nieu Amsterdam the teacher received a yearly stipend plus a bonus

. . . for every child, whom he teaches the a-b-c, spelling, and reading, 30 st[yvers]; for teaching to read and write, 50 st.; for teaching to read, write and cipher, 60 st.; from those who come in the evening and between times pro rata a fair sum. The poor and needy, who ask to be taught for God's sake, he shall teach for nothing.[59]

The school year varied with the length of the seasons and the need for child labour: in 1682 the school's hours in Flatbush, New York, were required to 'begin at eight o'clock, and go out at eleven; and in the afternoon shall begin at one o'clock and end at four',[60] a common European pattern. Within the school the elementary curriculum was built around the alphabet learnt from a hornbook, basically a square wooden bat with a handle, on which was pasted the alphabet and usually below it the Lord's Prayer, the page being covered, for protection against wear, by a layer of transparent animal horn; later, battledores were introduced, these being usually a folded sheet of printed cardboard with simple moralizing sentences illustrated by woodcuts. Once able to read, the child usually went on to the Calvinist catechism and admonitions by an English Puritan, John Cotton (1584–1652), entitled *Spiritual Milk for Babes Drawn out of the Breasts of Both Testaments*, published in London in 1646. This had no competitor until the famous *New England Primer*, originally an English publication, began to be printed under its American title by 1690 (the exact date of the first edition is not known).[61]

The model for this primer – originally a primer was a book of private devotional prayers – was the introductory pages of *Orbis pictus* with its simple woodcuts illustrating the letters of the alphabet. The *New England Primer* usually had twenty-six woodcuts (or twenty-four at times when J and X were ignored), each followed by a rhyming couplet to illustrate the letters of the alphabet:

> A. In Adam's fall,
>   We sinned all.

> B. Thy life to mend
>   This Book [i.e. Bible] attend.

Enterprising New York printers took this English primer and issued innumerable editions with various titles, *The Columbean Primer*, *The New York Primer*, *The American Primer*, and changed the couplets and woodcuts, these at times reflecting political conditions. So, in the early seventeenth century, K was often illustrated by the monarch –

> King Charles the Good
> No man of blood

– but in American editions, after 1776, this was changed to

> Kings should be good,
> Not men of blood,

while Q observed that

> Queens and Kings
> Are gaudy things.

The primers were gradually enlarged to include catechisms reflecting the religious persuasions of the communities in which they were used, and included abridgements of Cotton's catechism, based on the 1643 revision of the Anglican faith determined by the Westminster Assembly, now retitled *Spiritual Milk for American Babes*; the element of grim didacticism, however, remained a prominent feature of their content.

There was very little change in elementary reading materials for fifty years or more after the revolution, with the exception of the introduction of spelling books. In an effort to standardize spelling, Thomas Dilworth in London published in 1740 his *New Guide to the English Tongue*, following a trend set by others of which one of the most popular was Thomas Dyche's *A Guide to the English Tongue in Two Parts* of 1709 which reached a forty-fifth edition by 1764 and its final edition in 1830. Dyche also published *The Spelling Dictionary* and *A New English Dictionary* which were widely used in England. Dilworth, however, was the author most adopted in the American colonies and his *New Guide* was very popular until Noah Webster published his famous speller, under the pretentious title of *The First Part of a Grammatical Institute of the English Language*, in 1783, later changing it to *The American Spelling Book* and then to *The Elementary Spelling Book*. Webster, as a dictionary writer, sought to standardize and simplify spelling in America; this he did very successfully, and by the time his *Speller* had finished its run it had sold twenty-four million copies. It was more than a list of words with 'correct' orthography; after the graded lists of words, it had sequences of graded reading lessons in fable and sentence form, and moral tales, and was illustrated with woodcuts. The reading material was, as expected, quite moralizing: 'Christ is a mediator between an offended God and offending man'; 'The love of whiskey has brought many a stout fellow to the whipping post.'[62] A major effect of Webster's *Speller* was to make spelling both a subject of the curriculum and a craze into which teachers and children plunged with enthusiasm. Spelling-bees, weekly competitions and even inter-school rivalry rapidly became a new educational vogue, and remained so throughout the nineteenth century and into the twentieth.

Writing was usually begun on slates, progressing to ruled cards and thence to printed copy-books in which spaces were left for the child to copy specimen lines. These copy-books were produced by engraving, first on copper plates, later on steel plates. The child was required to possess a bundle of turkey or goose quills, a penknife to cut them to points, a packet of ink powder for adding to water and a packet of sand which was sprinkled on the written passage and acted as a drying medium before the invention of blotting paper. Again the passages were the same kind as contained in the primers and spellers, but one anomaly remained: it was very difficult indeed for the quill pen to reproduce the engraved copper-plate specimens, and young hands, knuckles often prematurely thickened from work in the fields, laboriously attempted to develop this 'copperplate' writing style down through the nineteenth century. Basic arithmetic, or ciphering (from the Arabic *cifr*, zero) as reckoning had been called since arabic numerals supplanted roman in the sixteenth century, was often taught with an abacus or similar counting-frame and was quite simple.

It is not surprising, then, given the austere curriculum of the colonial elementary school, that children were restless and inattentive and that coercion was necessary. The cane, or ferule, was commonly employed, especially as it had strong ecclesiastical sanction as a means of purifying the soul. Other methods included whipping, the victim being tied to the whipping-post erected in front of many schoolhouses: in 1656 Harvard College prescribed for certain misdemeanours 'whipping in the Hall openly, as the nature of the offence shall require, not exceeding ten shillings or ten stripes for one offence';[63] while a century later the famous German teacher in Pennsylvania, Christopher Dock, wrote in the first indigenous American text on pedagogy, the *Schulordnung* published in 1750, that for 'cursing or swearing' they are to be put in a version of the stocks, 'the punishment seat, with the yoke on their neck', although this should be preceded by the milder 'slap with the hand, hazel branch or birch rod' as a first warning.[64] A lesser punishment recommended was the dunce's cap, or being seated on a dunce's horse in the corner, or wearing placards variously inscribed 'Lying Ananias' (the liar in Acts 5 : 1–11) or 'Idle Boy', while whispering and talking out of turn should be punished by a wooden bit being put between the teeth and laced back, like a tight horse bridle, behind the offender's head.[65] At the same time, positive rewards were offered such as commendatory cards, gingerbread, small tokens such as cheaply cast medals 'For Merit', and so on, and such toys as kites and spinning-tops.

Grammar schools, academies and colleges in the colonial era

Following the English and European precedent, the colonies established a limited number of grammar schools; the first reference is to Henrico

College in Virginia in 1619, followed by a 1643 mention of a 'faire Grammar Schoole' at Harvard, and the subsequent 1647 Massachusetts Bay Act which linked the grammar school specifically with university preparation. Usually the Old World pattern was followed, teachers often being brought across on contract, and textbooks imported from London, these again being standard works: Comenius' *Orbis pictus* was the most frequently used introductory Latin reader and remained in use until the late nineteenth century. The introductory text was followed by a first Latin reader, this almost invariably being the *Colloquia selecta* of Corderius (1480–1564), first published in Europe in 1564, this volume of selected readings remaining in publication well into the nineteenth century.[66] After these came the usual texts of the humanities curriculum – Caesar, Ovid, Virgil, Cicero. The ability to read such Latin authors, with some skill in Latin and Greek grammar, formed the entire matriculation requirement in the statutes of *c.* 1646 issued by Harvard College, the first university-type institution established in colonial America.[67] This was the end towards which the colonial grammar schools were to strive. Of these the Boston Latin Grammar School, still in existence, was made famous by the redoubtable Ezekiel Cheever (1614–1708) who taught there continuously for seventy years from 1638. Cheever's other claim to fame is his *Short Introduction to the Latin Tongue*, or *Cheever's Accidence*, which prepared boys for Harvard and other colleges as they were founded, and which was the only genuinely indigenous school textbook written and printed in America before the revolution.[68]

The grammar school followed the English model, especially since it often served as a preparation for Oxford, Cambridge or one of the European universities for sons of the wealthy, particularly in the southern plantation states of Virginia and the Carolinas; it was, however, clearly maladapted to the New World where there were no endowments, no well-entrenched groups of literati and very little perceived need for classical learning, apart from divinity and law. For colonial America a grammar school education, while respected as an ideal, was still considered highly 'ornamental' in a frontier environment, and in the mid-eighteenth century the English institution of the academy, both private and dissenting, began to be put forward as a more relevant kind of institution. One of the first such foundations was by the greatest of American 'practical' men, Benjamin Franklin (1706–90), who, himself with less than a year's formal schooling, became one of the most influential colonists of the eighteenth century. In 1749 Franklin wrote, as a prospectus for his academy, *Proposals*

Relating to the Education of Youth in Pensilvania in which he observed that while 'it would be well if they could be taught *every Thing* that is useful, and *every Thing* that is ornamental', it is wise to remember that 'Art is long, and their Time is short', and therefore the curriculum should select 'those Things that are likely to be *most useful* and *most ornamental*, Regard being had to the several Professions for which they are intended'.[69] The *Proposals* became a model for Franklin's new kind of secondary school, which was opened in 1751, and it set out ideas on buildings, staffing and, in particular, the curriculum which included writing, arithmetic, accounting, geometry, astronomy, English language, oratory, history, geography, chronology, morality and natural history – all subjects being recommended as a complete curriculum offering a genuinely liberal education. Franklin included in his *Proposals*, moreover, physical exercise, especially swimming, and with respect to natural history urged practical work in 'gardening, planting, grafting, inoculating, etc.', and field excursions. He also included classical and modern languages as specific preparation for certain occupations: 'all intended for Divinity should be taught the Latin and Greek, for Physick, the Latin, Greek and French; for Law, the Latin and French; Merchants, the French, German, and Spanish', while none should be compelled to learn languages unless they have 'an ardent Desire' to do so.[70] Yet, it is interesting to note, of the two programmes actually offered by Franklin's Academy, the English-language one was unsuccessful, while the classical-language programme flourished and in time developed into the College of Philadelphia in 1755 and, in turn, into the University of Pennsylvania.

Franklin's Academy was not the first; there are records of similar institutions earlier, although they seem to have been conducted in rented premises and private homes. Following Franklin's Academy, however, the number of such institutions increased; in Newark, New Jersey, in 1775 one offered 'an English School for the teaching of Reading, Writing, Arithmetick, and Bookkeeping in the usual and Italian methods', its prospectus observing that 'different rooms will be made use of for each branch of instruction' while 'boys are separated from girls'. This advertisement in the *New York Gazetteer* had the essentials of the typical academy: practical subjects, the innovation of separate rooms, provision for (and chaperoning of) girls, and board for out-of-town (especially rural) students.[71]

The academy movement continued to flourish after the revolution, offering especially such necessary utilitarian studies as navigation, surveying and, by the 1850s, civil and railroad engineering. By the peak year of 1855 Henry Barnard (1811–1900), editor of the *American Journal of Education*, reported their statistics: in the entire United States at the time he had identified 239 colleges, 6185 academies and 80,978 public elementary schools, with respective enrolments of 27,821 for colleges and 263,096 in academies.[72] In New York alone there were 887 academies; while many were limited operations, significant numbers were substantial institutions with neoclassical buildings, competent staffs and well-deserved reputations. There was, however, little state funding: state support was usually limited to grants of land, usually between 500 and 1000 acres, which could either be sold as building lots or rented, as a form of income; otherwise the academies had to finance themselves, chiefly through tuition fees; indeed, there was widespread opposition to funding them through public taxes. Within the range there was considerable diversity and several all-female academies are known: Science Hill, Kentucky, founded in 1815; Troy Seminary, 1821; Hartford Female Seminary, 1828 – all established by the Catholic Church. In the southern states military academies catered to the love of horsemanship and weapons training enjoyed by the rural squirearchy; there was also Colonel Dick Johnson's Choctaw Academy for Choctaw, Creek and Pottawatamie Indians in the period 1842–60.[73]

Above the elementary school, the secondary levels of the Latin grammar school and the more popular and numerous academies was the college system, itself the forerunner of the university. The settlement at Massachusetts Bay, dominated by Cambridge dissenters, moved quickly to establish a 'new Cambridge' and, in fact, later so named the site of their college. As an unidentified chronicler reported in 1643,

> After God had carried us safe to *New England*, and we had builded our houses, provided necessaries for our liveli-hood, rear'd convenient places for Gods worship, and setled the Civill Government: One of the next things we longed for, and looked after, was to advance *Learning* and perpetuate it to Posterity; dreading to leave an illiterate Ministry to the Churches, when our present Ministers shall lie in the Dust.

Further, the chronicle relates, that from among them

> It pleased God to stir up the heart of Mr. *Harvard* (a godly Gentleman, and a lover of Learning, there living amongst us) to give one halfe of his Estate (it being in all about 1700 [pounds]) towards the erecting of a Colledge: and all his Library . . . the Colledge was, by common consent, appointed to be at *Cambridge* . . . and is called (according to the name of the first founder) *Harvard College*.

This document gives further interesting details, describing, for instance, the contiguous erection of 'a faire Grammar Schoole for the training up of young Schollars, and fitting them for Academicall Learning, that still as they are judged ripe, they may be received into the Colledge of this Schoole', and the college's curriculum, based on Emmanuel College, Cambridge, from whence these settlers came, in '*Latine* and *Greeke*, and Disputations Logicall and Philosophicall'.[74] Once matriculated, students were bound by a set of regulations developed between 1642 and 1646 of which Article 13 required them 'never [to] use their mother tongue, except that in public exercises of oratory, or such like, [when] they may be called to make them in English'; Article 18 gave the requirements for the bachelor's degree, consisting solely of the ability 'to read the original of the Old and New Testament in the Latin Tongue, and resolve them logically', while for the master's degree Article 19 required that the candidate be able to write 'a synopsis or summary of Logic, Natural and Moral Philosophy, Arithmetic, Geometry, and Astronomy, and is ready to defend his theses or positions'.[75]

It took a full century before two more colleges were founded in the British American colonies. William and Mary was chartered in Virginia in 1693 as a 'Place of universal Study . . . for promoting the Studies of true Philosophy, Languages, and other good Arts and Sciences, and for Propagating the pure Gospel of Christ',[76] but instruction did not commence until 1729. The Statutes of 1727 made provision for a grammar school in which 'the Latin and Greek tongues be well taught' as well as an ancillary school 'to teach the Indian boys to read, and write, and vulgar arithmetick. And especially . . . to teach them thoroughly the catechism and the principles of the Christian religion.'[77] A similar charter was granted in 1745 to the Congregationalists of Connecticut to establish a 'Collegiate School at New Haven, known by the name of Yale College'.[78] In the ensuing thirty years, up to the Revolution, a further six colleges were founded: Princeton, New Jersey (1746); King's (later Columbia), New York (1754); College of Philadelphia (formerly Franklin's Academy) (1855); Brown, Rhode Island (1764); Queen's College (later Rutgers), New Jersey (1766); Dartmouth, New Hampshire (1769). By this time their studies were reflecting the changed curricula of European universities and the modernizing influences of the various academies and scientific societies.

National education: Americanization of the new generation

This was the general pattern of education prevailing in the American revolutionary period from 1776 to 1791 when the federal constitution was adopted, and it was due to the unevenness of provisions that some of the founding fathers – Washington, Franklin, Jefferson, Webster, Rush – vigorously urged federal support for education, chiefly, however, at the university level. There was a variety of motivations, but they all centred on Rush's concept of using education to turn the new generation into 'republican machines', and from this there developed the view that education must be kept completely within the United States. As early as 1785 Jefferson asked in a letter, 'But why send an American youth to Europe for education?' since nearly everything needed, except medicine and fluency in speaking modern languages, 'can be as well acquired at William and Mary College, as at any place in Europe'. Jefferson disliked England where, he warned, the student will learn 'drinking, horse racing, and boxing, these [being] the peculiarities of English education', although he was careful to point out that in continental Europe too there were dangers: the student might contract 'a partiality for aristocracy or monarchy' because of a fascination 'with the privileges of the European aristocrats'.[79] Jefferson might have mentioned along with William and Mary the other nine American colleges, although being in Paris at the time he might have been unaware of the tenth to be founded, the new 'University of Georgia', established by the General Assembly on 27 January 1785, four months earlier than his letter. This, the first American state university to be chartered, although not to be opened, was actually founded in the precise spirit of Jefferson's admonitions, that of 'suitably forming the minds and morals of [the state's] citizens'.[80]

North Carolina, chartered in 1789 and opened in 1795, seems to have been the first operating state university. In the year of its opening George Washington observed that 'with indescribable regret ... I have seen the youth of the United States migrating to foreign countries', and because this is a practice dangerous to the survival of the republic, 'the time is therefore come, when a plan of Universal education ought to be adopted in the United States'.[81] He also emphasized the need for a national university in 'the Federal city' to provide for the completely indigenous education of all American youth.[82] These were widely shared views, but they did not eventuate; Jefferson, for his part, did not entirely accept them, wanting his own state's College of William and Mary to be upgraded into the national university.

No national provisions for education at any level were made during the immediate post-revolutionary period; by 1791 only eight of the fourteen existing states specifically accepted education as a responsibility by virtue of the Constitutions adopted; the remainder left it to local initiative, or apathy. In 1795 the American Philosophical Society, developed out of Franklin's informal Friday night society called the Junto, offered a prize for the best plan for a national system of education and received a considerable number of entries, but this came to nothing. For the eight states which accepted educational responsibility, however, attempts were made to develop, if not national education, at least republican nationalistic versions, and the late eighteenth century was a period of school legislation. The tenor of the various Acts is quite uniform: in 1776 Pennsylvania in Section 44 of its Constitution required that

> A school or schools shall be established in every county by the legislature for the convenient instruction of youth, with such salaries to the masters, paid by the public, as may enable them to instruct youth at low prices; and all useful learning shall be duly encouraged and promoted in one or more universities.[83]

North Carolina, Georgia, Vermont and New Hampshire all made similar provisions. In 1790 Pennsylvania, in a revision of the educational provisions of its state constitution, initiated a new trend that required 'as soon as conveniently may be . . . the establishment of schools throughout the State, in such manner that the poor may be taught *gratis*'. So Delaware in 1792 similarly enacted and Ohio, admitted as a state in 1803, in Section 25 of its Constitution stipulated 'that no law shall be passed to prevent the poor . . . from an equal participation in the schools, academies, colleges, and universities within this State, which are endowed, in whole or part, from the revenues arising from the donations made by the United States for the support of schools and colleges',[84] although this did not exactly provide free tuition. In 1816 Indiana, admitted to the union that year, made it a 'duty of the general assembly to provide by law . . . [for the support] of schools'.[85] At this same time nothing was said about education in the Constitutions of New Hampshire, New Jersey, Delaware, Maryland, Virginia, South Carolina and Kentucky; nor were any provisions enacted by either Connecticut or Rhode Island which had no written Constitutions (relying instead on their colonial charters) until 1818 and 1842, respectively.

Ideal of equality: educational discrimination and disadvantage

All the existing constitutional provisions are seemingly very liberal; some state quite positively that 'schools are to be provided', others are more negative: 'none shall be prevented from attending' publicly endowed or funded schools. But that is a misleading interpretation of American educational provision in the republic-building enthusiasm of the immediate post-revolutionary period of 1776 to around 1830. The word 'all' turned out to refer, in the main, to white middle-class boys. There is a continuing American myth that Benjamin Franklin, possessed of a sense of iconoclastic humour, was not allowed to draft the Declaration of Independence for fear that he would interpolate a joke; as it was, the Declaration contains surely the grimmest of all jests in the opening lines of its second paragraph:

> We hold these truths to be self-evident, that all men are created equal, that they are endowed by their Creator with certain inalienable Rights, that among these are Life, Liberty and the pursuit of Happiness.

In his original draft, Jefferson had written the words 'sacred and undeniable', crossed them out and then written above them 'self-evident'. Whatever the precise meaning he intended, there was nothing sacred, undeniable or self-evident in the republican squirearchy's perception of equality for women, blacks, Indians and working-class white men; indeed, all were disadvantaged by the existing social structure which favoured the wealthy oligarchies of planters in the south, traders and industrialists in the central and northern states. The attitude of the establishment is best summed up in an exchange reported by Franklin in a letter in 1784; in Virginia, in colonial times, the Reverend Commissary Blair had sought from Attorney-General Seymour an endowment for a religious seminary in Virginia in order to provide clergy to care for the souls of the people. Replied Seymour to Blair: *damn their souls! make tobacco!*[86] Republican government was, in reality, oligarchic government; souls of women, blacks, Indians and poor whites were still to be damned as far as most government action was concerned, and the nineteenth century saw a long struggle by such disadvantaged groups, still not completely achieved, for the manifestation of that proclaimed equality.

There are some records of such disadvantagement in the eighteenth century: in 1740 South Carolina prescribed, in a statute, the enormous fine of £100 for any person 'who shall hereafter teach, or cause any slave or slaves to be taught, to write, or shall use or employ any slave as a scribe in any manner of writing whatsoever';[87] after the revolution the suppression of blacks from literacy and the ministry was quite active in the slave-owning states. In 1808 the importation of slaves into the United States was forbidden by Congress but by then their numbers had risen to such a magnitude that they were being, like cattle, bred for the market. Despite the many accounts of humane and considerate treatment on individual plantations and other establishments, the fact remains that legally they were accorded property status and their children were 'progeny', to be considered the disposable possessions of the slave owners. So any avenues to self-advancement and emancipation obtainable at the time through literacy and religion were blocked. In 1801 there is a record of a famous black clergyman John Chavis being licensed to preach by the Presbytery of Lexington in Virginia 'as a missionary among people of his own colour',[88] but his case was, in his own day, recognized as exceptional and it is more consonant with the temper of the times to read in 1823 of the Reverend Dougherty, a white Methodist parson in Charleston, South Carolina, who, for establishing 'a school for the black children', was set upon by an irate white mob one Sunday evening and dragged from his pulpit down to the pump where he was thrown into the trough: a mild but unmistakable chastisement for a man of the cloth, and a warning of worse to come if he persisted. The treatment for blacks was much more savage; apart from the prevalence of lynch-law, even the state prescribed severe penalties. In 1831 Virginia, despite the case of John Chavis, enacted that teaching negroes to read or write was illegal and for white teachers prescribed a fine of up to 50 dollars and/or up to two months' imprisonment, for the blacks or mulattoes being instructed, up to twenty lashes,[89] this being enacted similarly by Alabama in 1832 and South Carolina in 1834, while any black caught preaching was, by an 1831 Act of North Carolina, for each instance upon conviction before a magistrate to be punished by whipping 'not exceeding thirty-nine lashes on his bare back',[90] such punishment often resulting in the death of the victim.

Discrimination was almost equally practised against girls (although not with such manifest brutality), the aim being much the same, that of keeping them in accord with their station in life. Well-to-do families, of course, provided schooling for their daughters, often by private tutoring or else in select academies, but the aim was not so much to give them an education as to make them 'accomplished': in fact, the word accomplishment is the usual description of girls' schooling in the period. There were some notable advocates of women's right to an education, including the famous Englishwoman Mary Wollstonecraft, whose *Vindication of the Rights of Women* (first published in London in 1792 and republished in Philadelphia in 1794) was read in the United States, but there was no contemporaneous American woman of comparable significance. Benjamin Rush, however, stood up to be counted, writing in 1798 that if a genuine republic were to prevail then women must be equally admitted to 'all our plans of education for young men'.[91] These, however, are isolated and famous exceptions; far more typical and prevalent was the attitude that girls do not need an education, especially in literacy and numeracy; the household arts of sewing and cooking certainly, but these could as easily be learnt at home, and so save public funds. At base, apart from division of labour issues, was the problem of financing and the objection by many middle-class persons (the most taxable ones) to paying for unnecessary schooling. So in 1788 Northampton, Massachusetts, voted to be 'at no expense for the schooling of girls', and they were not admitted to public schools until 1802. In Boston, in 1790, girls were allowed into the town schools only in the summer months, and then only if there were places available; there was no effort to make such provisions. Slowly in the nineteenth century girls were admitted, but their struggle for equality and admission to colleges was to occupy decades to come.

The Bourgeois Epoch in Europe 1815–1900: Liberal Reform and Conservative Reaction

The bourgeois position: defence of privilege

The revolutionary ferment at the end of the eighteenth century, and the beginning of the nineteenth, reflected the tremendous range of problems that emerged in a period of dramatic change – problems generated by the convergence of rapidly accumulating scientific and technological knowledge, the quickening tempo of industrial development and its consequent mass urbanization, and the inevitable impact these made upon traditional social and political institutions and procedures. The Congress of Vienna in 1815 restored the French Bourbon regime and reinforced the Hohenzollerns of Prussia and the Habsburgs of Austria. It also permitted the Hanoverian house of George III (r. 1760–1820) in England to feel somewhat more secure from the earlier dread of an insurrection on the Paris model; but agitation remained and reached flashpoint at Manchester in August 1819 when a mass meeting of workers in St Peter's Fields was fired on by watching soldiers who killed eleven and injured many more. A nervous government removed the people's few civil liberties after this 'massacre of Peterloo' in a series of six repressive Acts of 1819, and the Prime Minister, Lord Liverpool, summed up the current bourgeois dilemma as he surveyed London anxiously from his window: 'What can be stable with these enormous cities? One insurrection in London and all is lost'.[1] And this was the nineteenth-century bourgeois attitude, which approved Metternich's repressive Carlsbad Decrees of September the same year, especially in education: how little could be conceded to the working classes to keep them assuaged, yet quiescent in the condition of servitude to which providence had properly ordained them?

Europe in the nineteenth century was dominated by Britain and France, the major industrializing powers; in the second half of the century Prussia (especially as it came to dominate northern Germany with the potentially rich Ruhr industrial region) and the United States became major competitors. Elsewhere the Scandinavian and German states were under Prussian hegemony; Austria, anxious to avoid Prussian dominance, moved eastwards to entente with Hungary and détente with Ottoman Turkey and exercised little European influence; Italy, Spain and Portugal remained intellectual, cultural and industrial backwaters; Greece, restive under repressive Turkish occupation, was in a pitiful condition when it gained independence in 1830 and began its slow struggle towards nationhood. In the east the Russian tsars held Finland, the Baltic states of Estonia, Latvia (Livonia), Lithuania and especially Poland in even more ruthless subjection than their own enserfed, savagely subordinated population. The notion of civil liberties and popular democracy was largely unknown among the illiterate rural masses of eastern and southern Europe. The revolutions of France and the United States, and the continued condition of incipient rebellion in England, were stimulated by massive discontent of the emerging middle classes and growing republican sentiment. It is important, however, to realize that modern political concepts such as 'democracy' and 'social class' existed at the time in only rudimentary form, and this serves to emphasize the fact that reform movements were necessarily inchoate and disorganized. Promoting awareness of such concepts was indeed a major contribution of Marx and the many others who raised political consciousness, chiefly in Britain, France and the United States.

Apart from the aristocracy, which had been seriously curtailed by the revolutionary era and, in the subsequent Napoleonic and then Congress periods, was subjected increasingly to constitutional controls, the bourgeoisie was the one coherent, economically powerful, and therefore dominant, social class in Europe at the beginning of the nineteenth century. It was, moreover, quite homogeneous throughout the West, sharing a relatively common culture, based upon Enlightenment ideals, although keeping these moderated by a firm alliance with the established church, Anglican in England, Catholic (and proto-Gallican) in France, Lutheran in Prussia, Anglican or Nonconformist in the various United States. The term bourgeois, French in origin, was used to describe the self-made, commercial, town-dwelling class that emerged in the latter part of the eighteenth century and became consolidated in the early decades of the nineteenth, providing the political basis of support for the restored Bourbon regime of Louis XVIII (r. 1814–24). The etymological origins are from the late Latin *burgus*, a borough; by the thirteenth century the English free man was referred to as a burgess; by the sixteenth century the French *bourgeois* appeared as a corresponding term; in the eighteenth it was given widespread currency in the title of Molière's *Le Bourgeois Gentilhomme*. It was in the early nineteenth century, however, that this term, which acquired such emotive political connotations, particularly from radical dissenters, received its pejorative meaning from the Comte de Saint-Simon who referred to the Restoration as 'un règne de vile bourgeoisie'.[2] Even the Germans adopted it in this sense in order to separate it from their own vernacular term *Bürgertum*, which had a more precise meaning of middle-class social rank as distinct from the *arriviste* class created by the French Revolution.

The religious position of the bourgeoisie was firmly conservative; indeed, alliance with the established churches was essential as a legitimizing process; the churches, for their part, having lost many medieval privileges and much aristocratic support, owing to the aristocracy's loss of status and wealth through both political and economic changes, were happy to enter into accord. Religion, moreover, was beginning to enjoy a renewed prestige and authority in the early nineteenth century as archaeological researches in the ancient orient found lost civilizations, scripts and languages. The nineteenth was a century of decipherment and gave a tremendous fillip to classical and biblical scholarship; the new science of archaeology, it seemed too, would prove the truth of the Bible, and this helped to confirm the study of the three classical languages of Hebrew, Greek and Latin as central to a genuinely liberal education. The conservative traditions of both religion and education received strong reinforcement, one consequence being the resurgence of the classical curriculum, exemplified in the grammar school, *lycée* and *Gymnasium*. The Western bourgeoisie embraced this institution wholeheartedly, even though it was already becoming anachronistic in an industrializing world: many middle-class boys were constrained to study the classics regardless of whatever future career they might follow.

For this *arriviste* class, therefore, a grammar school background became as essential as belonging to the established church as a mark of social and political legitimacy; for a bourgeois boy to receive a technical or scientific schooling was to confer the stigma of cultural bastardy. The result was that in England, France and Germany, and to a considerable extent in the United States, nineteenth-century bourgeois schooling followed the traditional conservative model of preparatory school, grammar school (or *lycée* or *Gymnasium*) and if possible humanities, liberal arts or philosophy at university. For middle-class girls, tutors were preferred, or else private boarding-schools; yet many bourgeois households of the early nineteenth century still followed Dr Samuel Johnson's advice of the eighteenth when he made the observation that he would 'sooner see a good dinner upon his table than hear his wife talk Greek', an attitude reinforced in English society when the law, as reported in the contemporary *Digest of the Law Respecting County Elections* of 1790, classified women with infants, idiots and lunatics as unfit for education since they were considered to 'lie under natural incapacities' and therefore were unable to 'exercise a sound discretion', or else 'are so much under the influence of others that they cannot have a will of their own.'[3]

The bourgeoisie, however, particularly in England and France, was subjected to considerable pressure, both from within its own ranks by radical reformers and from without by increasingly articulate and organized working-class movements. The extent of this pressure and the nature of the response altered with the progress of the century, which was characterized by such rapid and accelerating change that it is not possible to describe education, any more than any of its other features, in century-long generalizations. To maintain its dominance in government, commerce and industry, as well as the traditional agriculture, the bourgeoisie defended its newly won privileges successfully and, although the classical curriculum remained, it was modified by the demands of science, technology and industrialization. Within educated middle-class ranks from the beginning of the century there was an array of liberal activity concerned with the wider social good – although in general it endorsed a class-structured society – and it was from the efforts of such liberals that most of the reforming initiative stemmed. The educational character of the early nineteenth century can be conceived as a conflict between the bourgeois defence of privilege and liberal-led programmes of provisions for mass schooling.

Schooling the masses 1800–1850

The new radical philosophy: British utilitarianism

In an editorial of 16 August 1819 *The Times* of London commented on the demands for 'radical reform' made at St Peter's Fields by Henry Hunt, the chief speaker, and observed that this was a term 'in very bad odour', a statement indicative of the bourgeois attitude to the working classes. Labour agitation was a central feature of the nineteenth-century struggle for social reform, but the basis was laid down in the formulation of new social theories by middle-class thinkers, in particular Jeremy Bentham and James Mill. Hitherto, all social-reforming theory had a heavily moral character, especially with respect to education, resting upon certain metaphysical assumptions, as exemplified in the thought of Rousseau and Fichte: virtue and morality were their cardinal ideals and education, in consequence, should cultivate these, by means of the classics. Bentham attempted to sweep aside these theories as pompously verbose, untrue and, in effect, supports of bourgeois privilege. Only one criterion of social value and reform could be entertained, he argued, and he repeated the ideas of Francis Hutcheson of the University of Glasgow: the greatest good of the greatest number. These propositions made Bentham the major radical of the day and his utilitarianism provided a theoretical foundation for reform, in which education thereafter held a central position.

Jeremy Bentham (1748–1832) was born in London, the son of a lawyer, graduated from Oxford in 1763 and then studied law at Lincoln's Inn, being called to the bar in 1767. His professional preparation took place in the decade of Rousseauian doctrines of natural law and social contract, and these concerned him deeply. Throughout his large corpus of unfinished works, as well as his completed *Introduction to the Principles of Morals and Legislation* of 1789, he involved himself with problems of legislation and the public good. There can be neither natural law nor self-evident rights, he argued, otherwise these would prevail; the great mass of underprivileged and oppressed workers indicates that only a consciously created law can determine legal rights. Social privilege reinforced his viewpoint; the upper classes had control of parliament and the courts and could impose their will, which they did with a vengeance, as illustrated by the increase in the number of capital offences, which added up to more than 200 by 1808.[4] A reading of the *Newgate Calendar* for the period reveals instances of children of eight or nine years of age being hanged, and this kind of oppression – one law for the rich, another for the poor – was no uniquely British institution; in France Gustave de Beaumont reported to the Chamber of Deputies in 1843 the investigations of his Commission on Prison Reform which found that 'the labouring population almost exclusively fills our galley-hulks and prisons' while the 'man of wealth pays money, [and] remains at liberty under bond'.[5]

In considering the concepts of crime and punishment, Bentham sought to establish a sounder basis than aristocratic and bourgeois dominance and coercion. Punishment, in his mind, if over 200 offences were capital, could scarcely be related to the offence. The word 'crime' itself comes from the Latin *criminor*, to charge, accuse or complain of; clearly this definition of crime had survived as an instrument of oppression, while at the same time punishments, as the agents of effecting this, were capricious and intuitive on the part of judges. Bentham sought to have crime and punishment redefined in terms of social effects. Rejecting Rousseauian contract theory, Bentham accepted Hobbes's earlier position that sovereignty is absolute, but vested in the whole of society; the good, then, is what society considers desirable, and that must be the pleasurable, since nature has imposed on us the polarity of pleasure–pain. All actions, he asserted, following David Hume, are directed towards maximizing pleasure and minimizing pain; the public good is therefore the sum of those actions that most maximize pleasure for all people, and minimize pain, and the criterion should be the affirmation of the majority of the population: what most people enjoy doing must be the good. There are, of course, immediate objections: what is pleasure? Sensate appetition? Aesthetic delight? Intellectual achievement? Plato had taught of an ascending scale in which contemplation of the form of the good is the highest good; Aristotle had argued for the conscious intellectual cultivation of virtue as leading to the enjoyment of the good, *eudaimonia*, which is well above sensate appetition, *hedoné*. The bourgeois claim that poetry, opera and the salon are infinitely superior to bawdy ballads and the tavern was rejected by Bentham as mere dogmatic assertion, for which the educated Latin tag is *ipse dixit*; he therefore dismissed the bourgeois scale of values as mere *ipsedixitism*. There is no means of constructing any scale of values on the basis of intrinsic merit; we can only assign value on the basis of contribution to the social good.

Following the British empirical tradition, which by now was yielding impressive scientific results in the move to quantification, Bentham attempted to calculate units of pleasure content of given actions and proposed the 'hedonic calculus', an effort not as fanciful as might be imagined. The law, in fact, makes this effort continuously by constructing scales of punishment in the form of periods of detention and fines; salary scales and taxes are similar efforts. Bentham's complex investigations are not germane here; they did, however, focus attention on the traditional views of morality and virtue, crime and punishment, and therefore on education. A moral problem inevitably arises: can the public be mistaken in its beliefs and on occasion pursue the bad instead of the good? Bentham is not unambiguous here and this is the logical point at which his position is most attacked. Now certainly the public can enjoy cruelty on a mass scale, as the Roman colosseum and Spanish *corrida de toros* demonstrate; do blood sports, then, meet Bentham's criterion of a 'good'? And, if so, must we then accept a new conception of the good? His response, followed by the utilitarian school, is that the cardinal principle remains the greatest good of the greatest number; we must therefore put aside our own personal pleasures in seeking the common good. This makes education extremely important in that each person is in need of a widened vision; as this enlargement takes place, so perceptions of the good become more comprehensive, and practices, such as organized cruelty, will be seen to be against the common good.

Bentham's views on education were elaborated by the Scotsman, James Mill (1773–1836), who became a vigorous opponent of bourgeois privilege and its alliance with the established church. The son of a shoemaker in Forfar, north of Dundee, he attracted the patronage of Sir John Stuart who financed his studies in theology at the University of Edinburgh, where he was exposed to the classics and particularly Greek philosophy. In 1802, disliking preaching, he went to London as a journalist and there became a close associate of Bentham in the years from 1808 to 1819; in 1817 he published his monumental *History of British India* which secured him a post in the East India Office from 1819 until his death in 1836. It was in this period of contact with Bentham that Mill wrote his two significant – although short – pieces on education: an attack upon educational privilege in 1812 entitled *Schools for All, in Preference to Schools for Churchmen Only* and his article 'Education' written in 1815 for the fifth edition of the *Encyclopaedia Britannica* (1816–23). *Schools for All* was a defensive polemic against Anglican attacks upon the philanthropic schools for the London poor being conducted by the dissenter Joseph Lancaster and contained no educational theory; that was set out in 'Education', which gave the utilitarian position quite succinctly.

Mill had no intention of changing society to a classless structure; this can be ascertained from another article, on 'Government', one of a number that he wrote for the *Encyclopaedia Britannica*, in which he examined social structure and theories of political power, observing that 'most of the objects of desire and even the means of subsistence are the product of labour' and that the best form of government should promote these ends, thereby securing the 'happiness of the greatest number' as expeditiously as possible.[6] The bulk of the article was concerned with power and controls on its abuse. Mill accepted the threefold class structure of society, which was justified by the need for division of labour, and he called these classes the 'aristocracy', 'the middle rank' and 'that class of people who are below the middle rank'.[7] Of the greatest importance to his utilitarian philosophy and his educational theory is the assertion that the class of the middle rank is the origin of good morals, achievement, aspirations and taste; they are 'the chief source of all that has exalted and refined human nature'.[8] This enabled him to overcome the problem of the common 'good' being bad; following the Enlightenment doctrine of progress, he claimed that in society there is a continued emerging perception of good ends, introduced by the middle class. So, in the educational institutions provided for the middle rank, 'call it university, call it college, school, or anything else; there ought to be provision for perpetual improvement; a concern to make the institution keep pace with the human mind', for 'the grand distinction of Man' is 'that he is a *progressive* being'.[9]

Despite this emphasis, Mill was not proposing to reinforce bourgeois privilege; in a letter to David Ricardo on 23 August 1815 he declared that government was bad in Britain because 'the intellectual and moral parts of the mind among the leading orders [are] corrupted and depraved'.[10] The middle class he championed was not yet in a position of power; in any case, it was the taste, morality and achievement of this class that he put forward as a model for all to emulate, and moreover he offered the prospect of enlarging its ranks to wider membership. It is here that education becomes significant; for it will enable the boorish classes, both aristocratic and working, to achieve middle-rank standards: 'all the difference which exists, or can ever be made to exist, between one *class* of men, and another, is wholly owing to education'.[11] In support of this he adopted the Lockeian empirical psychology of the mind as a *tabula rasa*, built up of sensations, which become associated as ideas, organized by the three faculties which he called, interchangeably, 'qualities': intelligence, benevolence, temperance; it is the business of education to cultivate these.

Education – following utilitarian precepts which put complete faith in man's rationality, and the associated empirical doctrines – must therefore become a 'science' which can ascertain 'the ends, the really ultimate objects of human desire' and 'the most beneficent means of attaining those objects'.[12] With progress, Mill believed these will be determined, in time, by philosophers who will 'perfect this inquiry' and inform us 'what is the real object to which education is pointed'.[13] Clearly, if the notion of quantification of pleasures is accepted, it will be those resulting from middle-class taste that will prove capable of yielding the greatest, sustained quantity, as well as quality, of pleasures. To ensure progress towards an informed public he argued for instruction in literacy and complete freedom of the press, which meant the removal of censorship and abolition of the prohibitive newspaper tax of one shilling which prevented the ready circulation of reading material and the formation of popular political consciousness.

For Mill, education was just beginning to offer wider vistas for the mass of underprivileged society and he, like Bentham, was pioneering a new way. There will of necessity, he admitted, have to be social classes performing a variety of functions, but this should not preclude the widening of opportunities for social mobility that hitherto had been the right of a privileged stratum. Despite the logical difficulties in utilitarianism, which his son John Stuart Mill attempted to solve, giving the actual name 'utilitarianism' to the position early in the nineteenth century, the prospects were appealing to liberal reformers. The idea of solving endemic social problems – crime, poverty, class-conflict – by means of a simple test of public benefit became attractive, especially as it was consonant with the promising scientific theory of empiricism. Utilitarianism became increasingly accepted, especially in Britian, France and the United States, although in piecemeal form rather than as a complete system; in Prussia it was unable to prevail against the philosophies of Fichte and Hegel, and in England, indeed, it was vigorously opposed by the Church of England which feared it would undermine the social order. In particular, the church attacked the new system of mass instruction that the utilitarians, among others, were currently promoting as a step towards progress. It was in defence of schooling for the masses that James Mill wrote his pamphlet *Schools for All, in Preference to Schools for Churchmen Only*.

Education for the poor by mutual instruction: Lancaster, Bell and the monitorial system

Meanwhile, in the last two years of the eighteenth century, one of the greatest philanthropic ventures in education for the underprivileged ever undertaken in the West had begun in London and in the course of the first half of the nineteenth century, for nearly a full fifty-year span, was to spread across Europe, to Russia and to North America. This was Joseph Lancaster's method of 'mutual instruction' by monitors. It aroused bitter opposition from the Church of England, which alleged that the monitorial system, promoted by utilitarian philosophy, was godless, but their attack was more likely a reaction against the emancipation of the poor. The church, moreover, claimed an exclusive right to education, which of course it never fully exercised, and which was used by the government as an excuse not to follow the modest examples of France, Prussia and several of the United States in providing state assistance.

The story begins with the late eighteenth-century decline of the SPCK in England, caused by friction on the governing boards between the Anglican Church which wanted total ecclesiastical control of the society, and the philanthropic supporters who sought lay control. In this climate of dispute, independent charitable workers and societies modelled on the SPCK became more active. One of the most important movements was that led by the Rev. Robert Raikes (1735-1811), who opened in Gloucester in 1780 an Anglican parish 'Sunday school' for neglected poor children, which provided literacy and scriptural instruction, using, in the process, the more advanced children as monitors – that is, assistant teachers. Despite conservative protests, particularly by the zealous Sabbatarians who objected to any kind of activity on Sunday except prayer and divine service, and who were successful in having the Lord's Day Observance Act passed in 1781, Raikes popularized his ideas and methods in the *Gloucester Journal* which he edited, and these spread among other philanthropists and charitable workers. One of the greatest of these was Hannah More (1745-1833), who extended the Sunday-school movement to Cheddar; it then spread throughout the north-west and west of England.

Some time later, in British India, at the Egmore Male Military Academy in Madras, the Rev. Dr Andrew Bell (1753-1832), superintendent during the early 1790s, conceived the idea of teaching the first steps in learning to write by having the students trace letters of the alphabet in a sand-tray. The idea was not new; the novel departure lay in the introduction of the sand-tray (actually the tops of tables with a retaining rim nailed around all four sides) into the classroom and training the brighter or older boys to teach the others. In 1796 Bell outlined this system of possible mutual instruction as an effective, economical method of teaching elementary literacy and numeracy in his report to the academy board under the title *An Experiment in Education, Made at the Male Asylum in Madras, Suggesting a System by which a School or Family may teach itself under the Superintendence of the Master or Parent*. In these preliminary activities of Raikes and Bell the monitorial system had its modern origins. During the latter decades of the eighteenth century other Protestant, Nonconformist and Jewish societies were formed to provide charitable instruction, foremost among them being the Quakers, a religious sect founded around 1668 by George Fox, who considered themselves guided by an 'Inner Light' to do compassionate social acts; consequently, they were pacifists, refused military service and concentrated upon philanthropy, especially in education. By the year 1800 they were known formally as the Society of Friends, and had several famous members, including Joseph Lancaster (1778–1838) who organized and personally conducted a charity school in London.

Lancaster's school was in the Borough Road, Southwark, in London; it opened in 1798, two years after Bell's *An Experiment in Education* was printed in Madras. This report, however, did not reach Lancaster until around 1800 when he was already experimenting on similar lines with some children as teachers; Lancaster expressly acknowledged his debt to Bell in his first publication of 1802, *Improvements in Education*.[14] Lancaster's system was similar except that his own envisaged much larger enrolments, as the full title of his publication indicates:

> *Improvements in Education*, as it respects the industrious classes of the community, containing, among other important particulars, an account of the institution for the education of one thousand poor children, Borough Road, Southwark; and of the new system on which it is conducted.

The school started with an enrolment in 1798 that varied between 90 and 120, as Lancaster reported,[15] expanding to 300 in 1803 and to 700 in 1804, without any 'unpleasant effect upon the order of the school'.[16] In 1804 there were nearly 800 boys on the rolls and nearly 200 girls, thereby approximating the notion of 'one thousand poor children' in one institution, and '*without any adult assistant teachers*'.[17] The emphasis was on teaching boys; plans for additional accommodation for girls were made under the supervision of Lancaster's two sisters.

The monitorial system was described at length in *Improvements in Education*. The school taught only reading, writing and arithmetic, with the addition of needlework for girls, and while not promoting 'the Religious Principles of any Particular Sect' it sought to 'instruct Youth in useful Learning, in the leading and uncontroverted principles of Christianity, and to train them in the practice of moral habits, conducive to their future welfare, as virtuous men and useful members of society'.[18] Instruction was organized in classes, defined as 'any number of boys whose proficiency is on a par' but not exceeding ten per class; a monitor was assigned to each, 'the word monitor, in this institution, [meaning] any boy that has a charge either in some department of tuition or of order'.[19] There were a large number of monitors (Latin *monere*, to advise or counsel) all wearing embossed badges of rank, usually suspended from a collar chain. Monitors were the brighter pupils; they came earlier in the day to receive instructions and were ready to teach their classes when the day began. The monitors themselves were stimulated by an elaborate system of rewards; apart from having the authority and prestige of power, they accumulated points which were convertible into presents and small cash amounts. At the top of this command structure was the monitor-general. In addition, there were non-teaching monitors appointed to rule writing books 'by machines made for that purpose' as well as 'inspecting monitors', 'monitors of slates' and 'book monitors'.

Like most schools of the period it was conducted in a single large hall, down the centre of which were rows of benches and up to 100 long desks, each providing space for a class of ten, the front desks having raised edges so that dry sand could be spread on top for teaching beginners to write; behind them were the more advanced classes. Around the walls of the hall were 'stations', consisting of a post or wall-board on which some printed material could be hung, and a semicircle was painted on the floor, providing a line around which, on occasions, each class could be arranged. The general sequence of instruction was for the beginner to learn the alphabet by tracing the shapes in the sand from a letter printed on a card held up by the monitor. Once writing was mastered, the beginners moved back into the slate rows where they repeated the process, in as many days or weeks as it required each individual to become proficient (and this meant the continued restructuring of classes according to attainment); after slates came writing on cards, then in books. Numeracy and the four rules of arithmetic were similarly taught. Meanwhile, the more proficient children would be engaged in reading, and the ingenious

Lancaster bought two copies of each book required, cut them up and pasted each page to a sheet of card. Monitors would arrange these on posts or boards at each station and the children of a given class, standing in a semicircle, would read one after the other from the cards, going through the whole book over a period of time. So, in theory, the school consisted of classes of ten, under the solicitous eyes of monitors, moving from one activity to another, learning the skills of reading, writing and arithmetic by means of letter and number formation, dictation, spelling and group reading.

Following Quaker beliefs, Lancaster objected to physical punishment for failure to learn and instead used positive rewards, illustrating this when teaching the alphabet: 'the best boy stands in the first place; he is also decorated with a leather ticket, gilt, and lettered *Merit*.'[20] His accounts rendered to the society make interesting reading on this point. In the balance sheet for the end of the school year, in June 1801, for example, his entire budget amounted to £118.10s., and contained the usual items of tuition, his own salary and other expenses of £84.15s., and necessary supplies: coal for the fire, slates, reading books, spellers, hymnals, scriptural texts and 10,000 quills, these collectively adding up to £15.7s.10d. In addition, however, are these items:

- 11 Purses, lettered
- 7 Silver pens
- 6 Half-crowns, engraved 'Reward for Merit'
- 300 Toys, for premiums
- 1500 [Cardboard] Commendatory Tickets
- 130 Leather Commendatory Tickets, lettered 'Reward for Merit'
- 6 Excursions: to Wandsworth, Clapham, Sydenham, Norwood and Blackheath, with 50, 80 or 124 Boys at a Time, as a Recreation and Reward of Attention to their Learning.

This latter group added up to £19.3s.11d., thereby accounting for approximately 55 per cent of the maintenance budget, that is, excluding tuition fees.[21] Even more interesting is the fact that in that year he had an enrolment of 113 free scholars, and so he was providing instruction for approximately £1 per child. In addition, for those who could afford half-rate tuition, he accommodated more than an additional hundred. This modest expense was sustained: in his accounts for 1802–3 he taught 217 charity boys for a total of £228.1s.6d.; in 1803–4, 212 charity boys were taught for £223.7s.0d.; in both years the cost per pupil was slightly over

£1 each. These are the figures he gave in his annual reports to subscribers to account for their donations; in addition, he also enrolled fee-paying children who were, presumably, his private students and for whose fees no accounting was needed; this explains the discrepancy between his two sets of enrolment figures.

The charity funding was based upon the prevailing subscription system. In the beginning, Lancaster reported that he was assisted financially only by Elizabeth Fry although he attracted early support from the Duke of Bedford and Lord Somerville. Within the first five years Lancaster was receiving subscriptions from fifty major donors, five of whom were members of parliament and included William Wilberforce, as well as smaller occasional sums. In 1805 King George III visited the school and was so impressed that he subscribed £100, the queen £50 and the princesses £25 each.

Sectarian rivalry: Anglican provisions in the National Society

By the year of the royal visit, however, trouble was brewing on account of increasing Anglican opposition; in 1798 the established church opened several smaller schools practising Bell's theories in London, but with much less spectacular results, and moves were made to get rid of the Quaker competition. This, of course, was the period of the Napoleonic wars, and England was a major member of the Coalition Powers; Quakers were in any case suspect both for their pacifism and their Nonconformity. Lancaster became the target of an attack led by Sarah Trimmer (1741–1810), a person well connected with the Tory establishment, mother of twelve children and active SPCK worker after 1793, writing abridgements of both Testaments for the society. Her own attitudes were made clear in 1792 in her *Reflections upon the Education of Children in Charity Schools*, where she wrote that it would be wrong to educate the 'lower kinds of people' since that might make them socially mobile 'and disqualify them for those servile offices which must be filled by some members of the community', and that 'The children of the poor should not be educated in such a manner as to set them above the occupations of humble life, or so as to make them uncomfortable among their equals'.[22] In 1805 she attacked Lancaster by accusing him of plagiarizing Bell's theories; Bell was upset, since having come to England from India he was a friend of Lancaster and the two were sharing ideas. The Trimmer attacks, however, polarized the dispute, with the established church asserting its monopoly over charitable education, the debate being reported from an Anglican point of view in the *Quarterly Review*, from a Lancasterian in the *Philanthropist* and the *Edinburgh Review*.

Despite its cost – and monitors' monetary gains could, in cases, be as high as they were able to earn in factories – Lancaster's method of rewards was a major innovation in education; it was more effective and no more extrinsic to the learning process than the prevailing notion of punishment for failure to learn. Lancaster, however, was no businessman and his project failed financially, being saved from total ruin only through the intervention of several Quaker friends, notably William Allen the manufacturing chemist who put the finances on a sound footing. Lancaster became less prominent and Allen more influential after 1808 when the school was reorganized and incorporated into the newly formed Royal Lancasterian Institution, and that, in turn, as the Royal British System in 1810, and the British and Foreign School Society in 1812. Simultaneously, in 1811, the Anglican Church, earlier prodded by Mrs Trimmer (now deceased), founded a rival – and eventually larger – National Society for the Promotion of the Education of the Poor in the Principles of the Established Church, using the same principles of monitorial instruction. In 1811 the Anglican Church opened the attack when, at the invitation of the SPCK, the Rev. Dr Herbert Marsh, Professor of Divinity at Cambridge, preached a sermon on 13 June in St Paul's Cathedral, London, asserting that only the established church could properly discharge the task of educating the populace since the established religion is the national religion, and therefore 'national *education* must be conducted on the principles of the national *religion*'.[23]

James Mill was stung to immediate reply to this specious logic, and in answer to Marsh's sermon which appeared in the October issue of the *Quarterly Review* he published his celebrated utilitarian response in the *Philanthropist* the following year under the title *Schools for All, in Preference to Schools for Churchmen Only*. Disparagingly referring to the church as 'the establishment', Mill argued that far from being national it served only the interests of the dominating section of the nation which had 'totally neglected . . . the education of the lower orders'; indeed, 'while bishops and archbishops, and deans and rectors, and lords and gentlemen, looked on in apathy', Lancaster alone, acting in a spirit of Christian charity, 'proved that the education of the poor might be rendered incredibly cheap', and only when 'new schools were ready to spring up in every part of the country' now comes 'the cry that "the Church [is] in danger"'.[24]

The attack on Anglican hypocrisy suffused the entire long article; the church was criticized for its bigotry, sectarianism, complacency, narrow-mindedness and lack of concern for the poor, the disadvantaged and the vulnerable. Mill denied that the Church of England alone represents the true and only Christian faith and argued that in education only one thing matters, 'the question of utility'; that the poor and ignorant children be quickly helped by a useful education.[25]

The social evidence was all around in the rapidly growing cities where children, loosened from the regulative structures of traditional village life, were the victims of every kind of exploitation, crime and vice. Just as the majority of factory workers were juveniles, so they accounted for a significant proportion of the criminal class: Parliamentary Select Committees learned that in 1816, in Newgate Prison, 514 prisoners were under twenty, 284 under seventeen, 51 under fourteen; the youngest was nine; girls frequently ended up in brothels as young as eleven or twelve years, the average age being fourteen, and venereal disease was rampant.[26] The Nonconformist, and utilitarian, hope was that some improvement, both in morals and industriousness, might be effected for the growing mass of urban factory-fringe dwellers.

Fortunately, the conservative Anglican and Tory establishment was opposed by a strengthening Whig liberal opposition. Despite mutual acrimony, the monitorial movement, both Lancasterian and National Society, grew enormously and for the following thirty or so years, until the 1840s, it was the chief means of providing elementary schooling for the working classes, with the National Society, owing to its Anglican support, gaining a much wider following as its returns, from its foundation in 1812, indicate:[27]

	Schools	Enrolments
1812	52	8,620
1813	230	40,484
1820	1,614	approx. 200,000
1830	3,670	approx. 346,000

Not only was the method of both systems consonant with the concept of rewards, chiefly wages, for labour; it fitted in, from the bourgeois point of view, with the industrial character of the evolving society. On top was the middle, managerial, entrepreneurial class; beneath, the organized factory based upon mechanical power and the replication of standardized products. The mechanized monitorial school, in compliance with this system, was seen to prepare (and discipline) the future factory worker. In 1819 Henry Macnab wrote that Lancaster and Bell would be honoured by future generations for their invention 'with sentiments more elevated and spiritual than those due to the talents of a Watt and an Arkwright',[28] while Sir Thomas Bernard, the founder of the Society for Bettering the Condition and Increasing the Comforts of the Poor, applauded the system since 'the principle in schools and manufactories is the same . . . [it] is the division of labour applied to education'.[29]

Britain at this time was undergoing massive social and demographic changes: in the period from 1800 to 1850 not only did the population double from 8.9 million to 18 million but its predominantly rural population was transformed as the great urban concentrations, now numbering some 9 million, 50 per cent of the total, grew wildly on the inadequate sites of what had been really little more than rural service towns. At the end of the eighteenth century, Britain had only four major urban regions: London with a population of 750,000, Dublin with 150,000, Edinburgh with 80,000 and Glasgow with 36,000. Now a new set of circumstances prevailed which the country – and especially the comfortable bourgeoisie – was unable to comprehend, much less provide for adequately, and the result, in education, was the rapid expansion of the monitorial system throughout Britain; it was not until 1847 that it disappeared as it became upgraded into the pupil-teacher system. In the early decades, the monitorial system was even employed in grammar schools as a method of intensifying the teaching of particular subjects. Mill's theories, moreover, became widely adopted as more rational, even sanguine, views prevailed that throughout the industrializing world the masses needed some kind of basic schooling.

Extension of the monitorial system

Continental Europe had been largely cut off from Britain during the Napoleonic period. As soon as the wars ended, French liberals in 1814 formed the Society for the Encouragement of National Industry which sent a deputation to study Lancaster's Borough Road school. They were so favourably impressed that they persuaded the society to establish an educational division, which appeared in 1815 as the Société pour l'Instruction Élémentaire. The following year the French government issued an educational *ordonnance* of 19 February 1816 which required, in Article 14, that 'every commune shall provide a primary education for all children of the inhabitants, and in the case of the poor this shall be given gratuitously', and, in addition, required every canton to establish a Committee to Supervise and Encourage Charitable and Free Primary Education for the indigent.[30] The state provided a modest fund of 50,000 francs annually for the most deserving cases, and it was to this fund that the Society for Elementary Instruction applied for assistance. A translation of Lancaster's *Improvements in Education* by the Duc de La Rochefoucauld-Liancourt was published by the society under the title *Amélioration dans l'éducation des classes industrielles de la société*, being widely distributed and well received. As well, the society organized monitorial schools for children, adults and persons seeking appointment as principals of such schools. By 1817 they had established one in every arrondissement of Paris and in all the major industrial cities, and several in the larger centres of Besançon, Arras, Bordeaux, Poitiers, Nantes and Lyon. By 1820 there were 1500 monitorial schools which absorbed most of the 50,000-francs government primary-education grant.

In France, as in Britain, sectarian problems arose. Since the Society for Elementary Instruction was predominantly liberal and Protestant and looked favourably on the monitorial system because of its utilitarian and Quaker associations, it was attacked in France by the conservative, bourgeois forces which gained power under the Bourbon restoration. In alliance with the Catholic Church which sought to regain its pre-revolutionary privileges, the bourgeoisie made every effort to keep the monitorial schools to a minimum, and in this they were relatively success-ful. Even though there were 1500 monitorial schools, these were limited to the larger urban centres; in the same period most communes observed the *ordonnance* of 1816 by contracting out their primary schools to the Brothers of the Christian Schools, the Ursulines and other congregations; in the year 1820 the 1500 monitorial schools (the maximum reached) must be balanced against the total of 27,581 commune schools (of which fewer than 400 were for girls) with a total enrolment of 1,123,000 children,[31] the total population of France in that year being 30 million. Primary schooling was reaching only a fraction of the masses, and the teaching congregations still had control of most schools; despite this, the moni-torial system remained in operation until the 1840s when it was gradually changed as monitors were chosen from older children and thereby became in effect pupil-teachers, while the master increasingly taught the assembled school in certain hours as the methods of the Christian Brothers were adopted. The Brothers had long used what they termed the 'simultaneous method', which became common in the nineteenth century: the teacher taught all children the same lesson at the same time, in contrast to the usual technique of calling up each child individually to read or recite while the remainder of the class continued with separate learning assignments. The monitorial school halls in time developed a gallery of tiered benches at the end of the hall able to hold all of the enrolment. This gallery could be used for prayers and increasingly was used for mass 'simultaneous' instruction by the teacher, and in this way the monitorial method became upgraded into the nineteenth-century-style classroom. In France the monitorial schools were changed by an 1853 *ordonnance* which forbade classes of more than eighty children and which required set lessons in religion, reading, writing and arithmetic. Increasingly they adopted the same plan as the schools of the teaching congregations, with three one-hour lessons in the morning in religion, writing and reading followed by three afternoon one-hour lessons in arithmetic, reading and writing.[32] By the 1860s the French monitorial schools 'dissolved' into the new developments that were taking place.

Much the same story holds for the other European countries where the system was adopted. Forestalled in Prussia by the provision of elementary schools, and in Austria by the teaching congregations, it was adopted in Sweden, where in 1822 a society was founded which set up close on 500 schools by 1841, and in Denmark, where nearly 3000 schools were established by 1831. The system was employed in Switzerland, Italy, Spain and South America,[33] while philanthropic societies in England took it to the colonies, including Canada and Australia. Tsarist Russia became interested in the monitorial method, partly through the efforts of William Allen who urged it upon Iosif Gamel, a Russian scientist sent to England in 1813 to study industrialization, and in a personal audience with Alexander I in 1814 when the Tsar visited London. At this time England and Russia were diplomatically close and there was an enthusiasm in both St Petersburg and Moscow for 'things English'. One by one, after 1817, schools were established, and when the Free Society for the Establishment of Schools of Mutual Instruction was founded in St Petersburg in 1819 the movement spread rapidly to many of the major towns and cities.[34]

Yet even in Russia the spread of basic education for the lowest classes met with opposition both from the Orthodox Church, which was disturbed by the Quaker materials (in translation) sent over by William Allen, and from the Tsar's secret police who attributed the mutiny of the Semyonovsky Regiment to Lancasterian education of the soldiers. Thereafter the system was closely watched, its growth was checked and in the period 1827–30 the schools began to decline. In 1827 there were 213 Lancasterian schools in Russia;[35] after the 1830 July Revolution in Paris, with government reaction reinforced by Orthodox xenophobia, the instruction of the masses was actively discouraged, funds dried up and schools closed. Some lingered on; a few were still operating as late as 1858 when they were officially closed and declared obsolete by government decree.[36]

The system spread to North America too, being propagated by Lancaster himself from his arrival in the United States in 1818 until his death in New York in 1838. Even before Lancaster's arrival, however, monitorial schools were being opened and the first such school appeared in New York in 1806. In the larger cities many charitable societies were active, including the Sunday-school movement, and it was on to this philanthropic stock that the monitorial system was grafted. In 1814 a preparatory school was opened for the Academy of Raleigh, North Carolina, based on 'the highly approved mode of teaching children the first rudiments of Learning, invented by the celebrated Joseph Lancaster of London, by which one man can superintend the instruction of any number of scholars from 50 to 1000'.[37] In the same year a Society for the Promotion of a Rational System of Education appeared in Philadelphia, and through its efforts in 1817 a new society was organized, the Philadelphia Society for the Establishment and Support of Charity Schools, which published a manual of instruction on the monitorial method. By the early 1820s the Lancasterian movement was being taken up in earnest in the eastern states, beginning with Massachusetts and spreading westwards as far as the Mississippi River; in 1825 Lancaster went to La Paz, at Simon Bolivar's invitation, to organize schools in Bolivia; in 1829 he went to Canada to establish some pilot projects for the Canadian government; in 1829 the system was also established in Mexico. In every case it remained operative until the 1840s when, around the world, it became rapidly outmoded and declined.

Bourgeois concessions: dual systems of education

Britain: the independent, voluntary system

The revolutions that swept Europe in 1830 and ended the repressive era of Metternich's 'congress diplomacy' produced shock waves in Britain, leading to the election of a Whig government in 1830 as the aristocracy was compelled to share power with the rising industrial and commercial classes. The new liberal party brought in the First Reform Bill in 1832, providing, among other things, for the enfranchisement of male property owners whose annual rental capacity was at least £10. Twice the House or Lords rejected the Bill, while disturbances broke out across the country, and against this background William IV (r. 1830–7) was forced to enlarge the Lords with newly created peerages to give it a more liberal character and so have the Bill passed. In consequence, England's class structure began to change with the emergence of a commercial stratum of the peerage drawn largely from the great merchant bankers, members of the upper middle class which was growing in numbers and influence in the developing industrial regions, and reinforced by a lower middle class of small traders, manufacturers and businessmen which was continuously augmented throughout the century as the developing urban-industrial system created new occupations of clerical and sub-managerial type in the banks, railways, warehouses, shops and various governmental and private bureaucracies that became necessary as service industries. English radicals were discontented with the pace of political reform and in 1838 the famous People's Charter was drawn up by Francis Place and William Lovett, with its six demands – adult male suffrage, no property qualifications for election to parliament, salaries for members of parliament, secret ballots, equal-size electorates and annually elected parliaments – which highlight the prevailing system of an unrepresentative oligarchic parliament. The Chartist demands were resisted by the Tory faction and by many Whigs; however, by 1867 the pressure of this 'white-collar' class could no longer be denied and in that year the Disraeli government enfranchised the urban lower middle class, including those males who either owned property with an annual rental value of £10 or paid an annual rent of the same amount. The turmoil of the Paris Commune of 1871 and the industrial challenge of Prussia led to further reforms, with the secret ballot in 1872 and the extension of the franchise to male agricultural and mine workers in 1884; not until 1918, however, was the vote extended to women in Britain.

Against this background the existing educational institutions of preparatory school, grammar school and university continued to be used by both middle classes and aristocracy in the early nineteenth century, although they were modified and augmented as external pressures forced changes upon them. While commercial academies existed, they catered to a

minority business interest, and one that became prominent only in the last
third of the century; dominating all secondary schooling was the classical
curriculum, even though the grammar schools were often quite bad.
Early in the century even the historic endowed schools had a poor reputation, and it was in this context that Thomas Arnold (1795-1842) became
famous for his reform of Rugby School after his appointment as principal
in 1828 when middle-class boys were beginning to enter the grammar
schools *en masse*. For the following twelve years he opposed the tradition
of ritual bullying of the younger boys by older students and teachers. He
emphasized moral discipline, somewhat moderated the classical curriculum
with modern languages, and even encouraged field nature studies,
especially in geology. Arnold's reforms remained within the existing
system and his influence spread throughout the grammar schools, with
Rugby now the prime model for emulation.

Throughout the middle decades the grammar schools remained dominant, exclusive and expensive and their classical curriculum continued to
be remote from the needs of an industrializing, urbanizing society. Eton,
the leading endowed school by 1860, was only one of many living fossils;
at that time, as Oscar Browning, a famous master, later recorded, 'the
education was purely classical, little mathematics were taught and no
science', while 'modern languages did not form a part of the regular
curriculum'. Indeed, the programme rested almost entirely upon 'the
foundation of the Greek and Latin languages. . . . The school work, as it
was called, was absolutely rigid, confined to certain Latin and Greek
books read again and again until they were learnt by heart.' Defending the
school, he observed that 'Eton in those days was a very fine educational
institution; but she was out of touch with the age'.[38] In spite of this,
Browning went on to observe that the dominance of Eton alumni in later
life, 'apart from the advantages given to them by their birth', was due
'largely to the classical education which they received, an education which
it is quite impossible that mathematics or science could supply'.[39]

Likewise, in the first half of the nineteenth century, Oxford and
Cambridge were quite backward, in marked contrast to the progressive
developments of Edinburgh and Glasgow, and the infant foundations of
London (1836) and Durham (1837). In 1850 parliament set up a Royal
Commission of Inquiry into Oxford and Cambridge, as a result of much
public dissatisfaction. Oxford refused to cooperate, and would not even
admit the commissioners; the Chancellor, the Duke of Wellington,
advised parliament that the revised statutes of 1636 and the academic

system thereby instituted were still completely adequate. The commission, however, was not so impressed, and criticized the exclusion of the poorer sections of the community and of non-Anglicans.[40] Reforms followed at both Oxford and Cambridge, in parliamentary Acts of 1854 and 1856 respectively, removing religious tests for graduation and somewhat modernizing the curriculum at Oxford – more markedly at Cambridge, which recognized that the future lay as much with science and mathematics as with the classics.

The partial reform of Oxford and Cambridge came in a period of increasing public concern about education, with criticisms being more frequently heard of Anglican complacency and the grammar schools' conservatism. In 1861 the government was also forced by widespread complaints to inquire into the nine historic great public schools which still were financed, for a minority of the wealthy upper middle class and the aristocracy, by endowments of public lands made in previous centuries; so was empowered 'Her Majesty's Commission to inquire into the Revenues and Management of certain Colleges and Schools, and the Studies pursued and instruction given therein' under the chairmanship of the Earl of Clarendon. The report of this 'Clarendon Commission' was issued in 1864 and, while it vindicated the classics, observing that 'we are equally convinced that the best materials available to Englishmen . . . are furnished by the languages and literature of Greece and Rome', it was quite critical of the narrowness and ineffectiveness of an exclusively classical curriculum.[41]

The Clarendon Report stimulated further inquiry and in 1864 the Schools Inquiry Royal Commission was set up under Baron Taunton, 'to inquire into the education given in schools not comprised within the scope of [the Newcastle and Clarendon Reports]', the Newcastle Report of 1861 having dealt with 'popular education'. The Taunton Commission surveyed, chiefly by questionnaire, some 3000 schools of endowed, private and proprietary types, of which 705 were classical-curriculum grammar schools and nearly 2200 offered either a commercial or a non-obligatory classical curriculum. In their report the commissioners laid bare the problem facing the *ad hoc* growth of English secondary education by a middle-class voluntary system: it was inadequately and unsystematically financed. There was clearly a need to extend a comprehensive, modern, useful secondary education to a wider spectrum of the middle class and on a properly funded basis; they anticipated future developments in stating that 'We believe that recourse must be had to rates if this object is to be effectually attained', although they realistically observed that 'We are not, indeed, prepared to recommend that rates for secondary education should be made compulsory'.[42] Unfortunately, the Taunton Report, presented in 1868, was not accepted in its entirety; in 1869 parliament passed the Endowed Schools Act which made better provisions for supervising the finances of that privileged sector and allowed for some working-class access by means of a scholarship system. None the less, it retained the emphasis on a Latin curriculum and made no serious effort to cope with the lack of access for girls.

Even so, changes were occurring within the voluntary middle-class secondary system, and pressures were coming from many quarters, not only the liberal parliamentarians but from established scholars who urged the entry of the schools into the scientific era. Pressure for change came also from trades and professional associations and, most importantly, from within the schools themselves by a growing number of thoughtful reformers dedicated to the improvement of the schools and, significantly, to the professionalization of the vocation of teaching. Throughout the second half of the nineteenth century, parliament increasingly entered into the field of educational inquiry and legislation, not only at the secondary level but also with respect to popular, working-class provisions, and, from the Taunton Report of 1868 until the end of the century when the 'Balfour-Morant' Education Act of 1902 was passed, five major royal commissions were established and eleven education Acts passed which were focused upon two chief areas of the voluntary secondary sector: the modernization of the curriculum and the improvement of opportunities for girls and women.

Despite the observations and strictures of earlier royal commission reports, science was still the most neglected area of the curriculum – a problem heightened by the rapid progress being made in physics, chemistry and other sciences and the growing respect being accorded to empirical methods of inquiry. By mid-century this was championed by Herbert Spencer (1820–1903), who accepted the evolutionary theory published in 1859 by Charles Darwin in his *Origin of Species* and in his own evolutionary positivism defended the development of science and education as part of universal human progress. He argued the case in a number of polemical essays issued in 1861 under the title of *Education*, the most famous of these being 'What Knowledge is of Most Worth?' in which he attacked the prevailing classical education as 'the badge marking a certain social position'[43] and useful only to parasitic celibates since it did not cater for

the cardinal human needs of self-preservation and the rearing and discipline of offspring. 'Science is of chiefest value', he stated, since, 'whether
for intellectual, moral, or religious training, the study of surrounding
phenomena is immensely superior to the study of grammar and lexicons'.[44]
His opinions were supported by the vigorous T. H. Huxley (1825–95),
acknowledged as one of England's leading scientists. Self-educated,
Huxley trained as a medical practitioner, in 1851 was elected a fellow of the
Royal Society and until his death dominated English science, in the
process arguing for science education and serving on eight royal commissions.

In 1872, against this background of intense agitation, and with Britain
now seriously challenged for world leadership in industry by France and
Prussia, parliament established 'An inquiry with regard to Scientific
Instruction and the Advancement of Science' (of which Huxley was a
member) under the chairmanship of the Chancellor of Cambridge, William
Cavendish, Duke of Devonshire (1808–91). The Devonshire Report of
1875 was a scathing indictment of the obduracy of most grammar schools
in refusing to reform the curriculum; conducted on a comprehensive
scale, covering 128 endowed schools, it found that science was resisted in
large part because of 'the difficulty of finding time for a new study in an
already overcrowded curriculum' and because of 'uncertainty as to the
educational value of science'.[45] The report calculated that the schools had
a thirty-five-hour week of instruction and that even six hours of science
and six hours of mathematics, with twenty-three remaining for languages,
was considered unacceptable. None the less, the report made its mark, and
science increased its share of the curriculum, chiefly because it was able to
expand in the private and proprietary schools patronized by the commercial classes.

Twenty years later, the royal commission set up under James Bryce to
determine the best means of providing an integrated system of secondary
education reported in 1895 that great progress had been made: the
endowments were better managed, curricula had been reformed, a professional body of teachers had appeared, organized into a number of
guilds and unions, and there had been significant improvement in provisions for girls. Unfortunately, the commission reported, there was still
no genuinely integrated system – which they defined as 'an organic
relation between different authorities and different kinds of schools which
will enable each to work with due regard to the work to be done by the
others, and [without] waste both of effort and money'.[46] The secondary

schools, it confirmed, remained the privileged preserve of the middle class and 'the classical languages are taught more extensively then ever', although there was some improvement: they were now taught 'less as if they were dead, and more as if they still lived'.[47]

In the same period the university monopoly of Oxford and Cambridge was broken with the chartering of the new civic universities. The first of these, the University of London, was conceived by dissenters as the apex to their system of academies, since they were barred from Oxford and Cambridge; it gestated throughout the 1820s and the first college was finally opened, to the indignation of the establishment, the *John Bull* magazine commenting on 7 May 1827 that it was nothing more than 'a humbug joint-stock subscription school for Cockney boys, without the power of granting degrees or affording honours or distinctions, got up in the bubble season'.[48] In 1829 King's College was added; slowly, further secular, forward-looking university colleges with open admission appeared, mainly in the bustling cities of manufacturing England: London was fully chartered in 1836 and added further constituent colleges later; Durham came in 1837; St David's in Lampeter, Wales, acquired degree-granting rights in 1852; in the 1840s colleges opened in Sheffield and Birmingham and in 1851 in Manchester, 1871 in Newcastle and 1872 in Aberystwyth, Wales; Yorkshire College (Leeds) was founded in 1876. By then, colleges also existed in Bristol, Nottingham and Reading. In the final decades of the nineteenth century many university colleges were upgraded to full university status: the federated Victoria University at Manchester in 1880, breaking up into the independent institutions of Manchester and Liverpool in 1903, Leeds in 1904; Wales was chartered in 1893, Birmingham in 1900, Exeter in 1901, Southampton in 1902, Sheffield in 1905, Belfast and Bristol in 1909.

Britain: provision for popular education 1833–1900

Parallel to the middle-class voluntary pattern was something resembling a system of schools for those classes of the 'lower orders' who were either unwilling or incapable of providing for themselves. This, however, is quite a different story – that of a relatively small number of reforming liberals battling a combination of indifference, hostility and at times determined opposition. Indeed, so slow was the progress of popular education that it took until the end of the nineteenth century for a basic, elementary-school system to come into operation, with only minimal provisions for academic mobility, by means of scholarships, across to the middle-class schools which led to the advanced and professional occupations. The fundamental problem of the bourgeoisie, throughout Europe, was their inability to accept working people as equally deserving of access to the possibilities of the good life. As late as 1888 the Royal Commission 'to inquire into the working of the Elementary Acts [of previous decades] in England and Wales', known as the Cross Commission, reported evidence from one chief inspector that it was doubtful whether it would be good to give a talented working-class boy a scholarship to the university and thereby 'lift him out of his own social station, and put him in one which is not congenial to him'.[49]

There is no doubt that the growth of the working class created problems on a scale never encountered before. Between the censuses of 1811 and 1881 the total population of England and Wales increased two and a half times from 10 to 26 million. Moreover, the labour force moved, permanently, from the rural to the urban sector; in 1801 one-third of all workers were in agriculture, in 1851 only one-sixth were on the land.[50] The bulk of the new class of urbanized workers were dependent on industry – manufacturing or service – for a living and were outside the provisions of the Poor Laws originally designed as parish charities on a minor scale. One index of the scale of change is the fact that the total population of the ten major cities of England and Scotland increased from 1,494,000 in 1800 to 4,460,000 by 1850.[51] These increases accelerated in the second half of the century: not only did Britain's agricultural workforce show a continued decline in absolute numbers but the population increased from 26 million in 1881 to 37 million in 1901 (including Scotland), with the ten major cities more than doubling to a total of 10,947,000. Such growth created tremendous problems: housing, sanitation and public health, water supplies and transport all invariably took priority over education.

Popular education for the first half of the century was provided chiefly on the monitorial model by a voluntary system, dominated by two groups – the large National Society and the smaller British and Foreign School Society – but it was becoming increasingly obvious that problems generated by efforts to school the masses were growing faster than the voluntary provisions. In 1833 the government entered the field of English education directly by providing a grant of £20,000 to assist with school buildings; thereafter, public education was increasingly regulated by the government, although, as compared to the voluntary system, parliament instituted fewer royal commissions and intervened much more by legislation and executive actions. As early as 1802 the Health and Morals of Apprentices Act provided for a twelve-hour day with no night shifts for child workers, but it was poorly enforced and easily circumvented. The Factory Act of 1833 was the first real step forward, forbidding the employment of children under nine years of age and limiting those aged nine to thirteen to nine hours a day, six days a week, with two hours schooling, in addition, to be provided in the factory. This last provision was a farce and in many factories the 'teacher' giving this instruction – often a mill-hand – signed the required register of attendance with his mark. At the same time, it was reinforced by further reforms including the 1833 emancipation, and deportation, of black slaves, the 1834 and 1840 Chimney Sweepers Acts giving those exploited children some protection, and the 1842 legislation prohibiting the employment of women and children underground in mines.

The 1840s was a period of real progress in English popular education, initiated by parliament's creation in 1839 of the Committee of the Privy Council on Education with James Kay (1804–77) as its first secretary and a grant of £500,000. The plan was to establish a normal school in order that 'a body of schoolmasters may be formed, competent to assume the management of similar institutions in all parts of the country. In such a school, likewise, the best modes of teaching may be introduced, and those who wish to improve the schools of their neighbourhood may have an opportunity of observing their results.'[52] James Kay took the initiative and attempted to set up such a normal school, but was frustrated by religious squabbles. Undeterred, in 1840 he opened one privately in the London borough of Battersea, where, to fulfil the notion of 'the best modes of teaching', he introduced the methods of Pestalozzi and Fellenberg. Caught up in the disputes surrounding Lancaster and Bell, however, and unable to continue financing the school, Kay reluctantly handed it over to the Anglican Church which continued to operate it in relatively unaltered form.

Kay continued his crusade to improve English popular education and in 1846 inaugurated a major advance with the development of the pupil-teacher system, whereby monitors were to be replaced by older, apprentice teachers. In February 1842, upon his marriage, he changed his name to Kay-Shuttleworth and under that name framed the resolution of the Committee of Council on Education in 1846 to provide 'annual grants of money . . . towards the stipends of apprentices in elementary schools' and for 'indentures of apprenticeship to be prepared' for pupil-teachers at least thirteen years of age who were signed on for a five-year period.[53] The scheme developed well, and in the following decade teachers' colleges were founded by the Church of England to provide further professional training, Queen's scholarships being available to those pupil teachers who had successfully completed their apprenticeship.[54]

By mid-century it was clear that state intervention was increasingly necessary, despite the efforts of the Anglican Church which continued to lay claim to popular education and, unable to provide sufficient schools, sought at least to staff and control all of the training colleges. In 1856 the Privy Council's Committee on Education was enlarged to include an administrative Department of Education and two years later the government set out to assess 'the state of popular education in England' by establishing a Royal Commission under the chairmanship of Henry Pelham, Duke of Newcastle, whose committee presented the Newcastle Report in 1861. It had as its background a decade of education Bills defeated in parliament by denominational disputes, from 1847 to 1857; the government now sought to assess the situation and determine future needs. In a heavily statistical report, one figure is outstanding: it was discovered that in England and Wales 2,535,462 children were receiving some schooling, generally between the ages of six and eleven, and this is supported by the increasing literacy rate which reveals that by 1844 67 per cent of males and 51 per cent of females could sign the marriage register. The number in school, however, was still only a fraction of the total population of England and Wales which in 1858 was given to the commission, by the Registrar-General, as 19,523,103. The result was that the government approved further grants for education but avoided the explosive issue of public taxation or rates for the education of the working classes, or compulsion to attend school, noting specifically that 'any universal compulsory system appears to us neither attainable nor desirable'.[55]

The Newcastle Report, however, led the government to issue in 1862 a revision of the Code of Regulations used by the Committee of the Privy Council on Education, which changed the basis on which grants were made to various bodies to provide popular schooling. Instead of a simple capitation grant, this Revised Code, as it was titled, had a variable scale of grants depending on the number of children enrolled, and a sliding scale of payments for the total number of days in the year each child attended. In addition, pupils were assessed by inspectors' tests of attainment in the three subjects of reading, writing and arithmetic; for each pupil who successfully passed the tests the school received a further grant. This combination of *per capita* and achievement grants became known as 'payment-by-results' and was responsible for effecting considerable improvements in popular literacy and numeracy. The standards scale provided inexperienced teachers with a clear set of goals, the achievement of which led to tangible rewards. At the same time, its limitations were criticized by a member of the Newcastle Commission, Matthew Arnold (1822–88), eldest son of Thomas Arnold, and one of England's most energetic school inspectors in the period from 1851 to 1883. The system of payment-by-results had been devised by Robert Lowe, head of the Department of Education, in order to meet the brief that the system be as economical as possible; as he stated in the House of Commons in 1863:

> I cannot promise the House that this system will be an economic one and I cannot promise that it will be an efficient one, but I can promise that it shall be one or the other. If it is not cheap it shall be efficient; if it is not efficient it shall be cheap.[56]

His proposal was attacked in the House and Matthew Arnold opposed it on the grounds that it was a mechanical approach whereby teachers would have an incentive to drill the children only in the three subjects. And that is exactly what happened. In 1867 the three basic subjects were augmented with history and geography to widen the curriculum, but Arnold continued his opposition. He was successful in moderating only some of its excesses; the system remained the basis for funding English popular education until the end of the century.

Many poor children, however, remained out of schools, and in the towns were either employed in factories if the inspectors were lax or worked at various activities, in many instances merging into the large class of urchin and vagabond children. In agricultural regions many remained in the fields, and not until 1873 did parliament pass the Agricultural Children's Act which forbade their employment under the age of eight years. To provide for the urban urchins the ragged-school movement was created in the 1840s, being formally brought together in 1844 by John Pounds in the Ragged School Union, another philanthropic body using volunteer teachers as well as the monitorial method, which by 1870 had 132 schools with an enrolment of some 25,000 poor children.[57] Alongside these were the continuing Sunday schools and various other benevolent-society schools; collectively, they made little impact. Government compulsion, of the kind already enacted in Massachusetts (1852), the

District of Columbia (1864) and Vermont (1867), was clearly necessary to bring all children into school. After studying the success of similar educational provisions in France and Prussia, Matthew Arnold observed in his Report to the Council of Education for 1867 that 'throughout my district I find the idea of compulsory education becoming a familiar idea with those who are interested in schools'. English society was changing: in the same year the Second Reform Bill enfranchised the English urban lower middle class, and the following year (1868) the Trades Union Congress brought together in more organized political form the various craft unions; it has been estimated that the class of white-collar workers doubled in the 1860s and doubled yet again in the 1870s to keep pace with the needs of the industrial economy.

In 1870 parliament grasped the nettle when William Edward Forster, Vice-President of the Council of Education, introduced England's Elementary Education Bill which acknowledged 'a demand from all parts of the country for a complete system of national education'. Forster's speech pointed to the inadequacies of English popular education: although 1,500,000 children between the ages of six and twelve were receiving government-funded schooling, 'only two-fifths of the children of the working classes are on the registers'.[58] The Bill was enacted, with considerable amendment, chiefly the dropping of the compulsory-education clause, but it did provide for the establishment of local school boards with authority to raise funds for elementary schools and to charge fees to parents. The religious issue between Anglicans and dissenters remained a matter of serious contention, especially since the Catholics, like most Anglicans, considered state schools to be godless, while Nonconformists feared Anglican dominance. So the Act included the compromise Cowper-Temple clause providing for no specifically denominational religious teaching. Subsequently, the school boards, of which there were some 2000, were given power in 1876 to require compulsory attendance if they wished, and in 1876–80 most of them did so; in 1880 parliament made it mandatory for school boards to require compulsory attendance at elementary schools, but not until 1891 were fees abolished. In 1882 the Elementary School Code was extended to provide for an additional, seventh grade, and scholarships to endowed grammar schools were created for promising children so that some educational mobility for the working class became possible.

In the last two decades of the century, education for all classes had become an essential feature of government activity. The Royal Commission on Technical Education of 1882, under Bernhard Samuelson, confirmed that England was being overtaken by the industrial superiority of Prussia, France and the United States and recommended the introduction of technical and scientific education into the secondary schools. This Samuelson Report highlighted the end-of-century needs: the redefinition of the elementary school; the revision of the curriculum throughout the entire school system, especially with respect to industry and manufacturing; the encouragement of educational mobility; and the provision of teacher training. By the time the report was tabled, these issues had become urgent; while some 97 per cent of the population were now minimally literate, the Catholics especially, and to an extent the Anglicans, were unhappy with many provisions. The government therefore appointed, in 1888, another Royal Commission, under Lord Cross, 'To inquire into the working of the Elementary Education Acts, England and Wales'; this committee was divided in its views and issued majority and minority reports. The majority, including the Catholic Cardinal Manning and the Anglican Bishop Temple, felt that school buildings were adequately provided, the inspectorate sound, the pupil-teacher system satisfactory and denominational training colleges appropriate but in need of increased numbers, while compulsory education to age eleven was sufficient. Their criticisms concerned the lack of adequate finance to the voluntary, church-run schools and provisions for the entry of more women into teaching. The minority disagreed and urged the abolition of the pupil-teacher system and the adoption of the Scottish system of teachers' colleges providing teacher preparation after completion of secondary school; they also objected to sectarian religious instruction and to any rate support for voluntary schools. Both factions agreed on the need to abandon payment-by-results.[59] Despite these criticisms, by the end of the century England had approximately 2500 school boards with some 1,900,000 elementary children enrolled, while the alternative voluntary system, chiefly Anglican, had 14,500 elementary schools with an enrolment of 1,200,000. Much was still to be done, however, especially in providing equal opportunity for working-class children. By this time, in fact, Scotland had surpassed England; as early as 1868 the Argyle Commission had reported on the need for compulsory elementary and secondary education, now that the great Clydeside industrial areas had developed, and in 1872 parliament enacted that school boards be created in Scotland with powers of compelling elementary- and secondary-school attendance.

One further development was in the education of girls and women, which was closely related to teacher training. Women were still heavily disadvantaged, few occupations being open to them outside domestic service; the careers of nursing and teaching were the first to become available on a wide scale. In reporting to the government on the training of pauper children in 1841, an Assistant Poor Law Commissioner, Edward Senior, wrote in his report that the schoolmasters and school-mistresses in the pauper schools were 'usually very incompetent, and are frequently persons who have been unsuccessful in some other calling';[60] the pupil-teacher system was a step towards changing that situation. In 1843 the governesses in private homes organized their Benevolent Institution as a first step towards professionalization; in 1848, with support from the men of King's College, London University admitted the female Queen's College, concerned chiefly with preparing women teachers, although they were not allowed to take London degrees until 1878; Bedford College, also federated to London, followed in 1849. In 1874 the Cambridge women's college, Girton – a redevelopment of an earlier college at Hitchin of 1869 – was founded, and this was followed by Newnham; at Oxford, Lady Margaret Hall opened in 1879; more colleges were founded at Cambridge, Oxford and London, but not until the twen-tieth century did Oxford and Cambridge permit women to qualify for degrees; hitherto their curriculum still contained much that was, in the terminology of the day, 'ornamental', such as piano playing. But the need was there and, with teacher preparation as a vocational goal, women in England, late in the nineteenth century, gained some limited access to higher education.

France: church–state conflict in education

In France educational development took another course. Two major factors exercised a determining influence from the beginning: one was the centralization of education by Napoleon within the Imperial University; the other was the revolutionary ideology of equality, and, even though the reactionary restoration of the Bourbon, Louis XVIII, put a check on working-class demands, it could not suppress them. France, like Britain, was both industrializing and urbanizing rapidly and increasing in pop-ulation too, but the pace of change was not as fast – or painful – as in Britain. Whereas Britain's population increased 300 per cent in the cen-tury, from 9 to 32 million, France's was barely half that at 144 per cent, from 27 to 39 million. The major French cities, however, grew at approximately the same rate as Britain's, both Paris and London recording 600 per cent increases throughout the century, but in 1900 Paris was only half the size of London; and, similarly, the largest French cities, Marseille and Lyon, were smaller than Liverpool, Manchester, Birmingham and Glasgow. The demographic effect was that France retained a greater rural agricultural population, dispersed over a much more extensive area, and this meant that change was not so accelerated. The great technological agent of nineteenth-century social change was the railway, which provided rapid, efficient, cheap transport for the first time ever; in a sense it was a mechanism of unification more powerful than ideology, and it was because of the smaller territory and denser populations of Britain and Prussia that they were able to forge ahead of France, where the effects were not felt until later in the century.

Following the July riots of 1830 and the flight of Charles X to sanctuary in England, after a short period of turmoil in the capital Louis-Philippe, Duc d'Orléans, was proclaimed king. A range of reforms were introduced, including the restoration of a limited franchise to men over twenty-five years of age owning property to the value of 200 francs. Under the Minister of Education François Guizot, who held office in 1832–7, parliament enacted the *Loi Guizot* of 28 June 1833 which vested authority and responsibility for the family and its religious upbringing in the father, gave the parish priest the right to supervise the school education of children, and, to ensure this, obliged every commune (there were now more than 30,000 of these) to provide an elementary school to which indigent children were to be admitted free. It was this last provision that placed these schools chiefly under the control of the religious congregations, with a small minority supported by the monitorial Société pour l'Instruction Élémentaire. Nothing further was done for the elementary education of French children for the next forty years: they were solely dependent on the basic religious and literacy programme provided by the commune, and their parents' ability to pay.

Secondary education was the centre of attention, since it functioned as a legitimizing process. At the top of the social system were the surviving landed aristocracy, now shorn of real power, but with their prestige largely undiminished and living a self-contained life of outwardly legitimist, conservative, Roman Catholic character, strongly supporting the revived Jesuits. Next came the *haute bourgeoisie*, styled the *notables*, who dominated the high administrative offices and bureaucratic decision making and who, owing their position to the Napoleonic democratization and bureaucratization of France, supported the centralized University and sent their sons to the new *lycées*. At a third level were the *petit-bourgeoisie*, such as salaried professionals and senior teachers in *lycées*, colleges and academies, as well as self-employed businessmen; these identified, as much as possible, with the *notables*. Below were the skilled artisans, and beneath them the unskilled urban and rural workers. The last two groups received little educational provision for most of the nineteenth century; the secondary school was the area of interest and conflict, dominated by struggles between church and state (which paralleled those between the conservatives and liberals) in which the Jesuits played their traditional role.

When restored on 7 August 1814, the Jesuits were restricted to eleven colleges and were forbidden to wear their distinctive habit or to use the name of the society, this being Louis XVIII's compromise with the Gallicans and anticlericalists. Their college retained the ten-year programme, commencing when the boy was eight years of age, but early in the Metternich era they had somewhat reformed their curriculum according to a *Plan d'études* – the Study Plan. Latin remained the foundation of studies, leading on to Greek and French; in addition there was philosophy and a small amount of history, geography and mathematics; to this, since they catered to the upper class, they added the accomplishments of fencing, drawing and music; yet everything was pervaded by a Catholic interpretation, and great emphasis was placed on religious studies, prayers and retreats. Even this modest enterprise aroused opposition and in the gathering storm before the July 1830 revolution, by an *ordonnance* of 16 June 1828, the Jesuits were again restricted, their eight seminaries closed and their colleges, by now eight in number and designated as belonging to a 'non-authorized' congregation, put under the control of the University. After the July riots, for the next eighteen years, until the next major revolution of 1848 which led to the foundation of the brief-lived Second Republic (1848–52), the Jesuits, seen as ultramontanist and enemies of the state, were forced into exile, and they re-established themselves in a college in Spain, two in Savoy, three in Switzerland and one in Belgium.[61] In exile the society issued a reformed *Ratio studiorum* in 1832 which, while continuing to emphasize the *studia humanitatis*, gave greater prominence to the vernacular and enlarged the total share of history, geography and mathematics in the curriculum to six hours per week. The Jesuits' chance to return to France came in 1850 when the *Loi Falloux* provided what seemed a workable compromise between conservative

Catholics, on the one hand, and the coalition of liberal Gallicans and anticlericalists on the other.

Meanwhile, from 1830 to 1850, the period of the July Monarchy, the conservative bourgeoisie, in reasonable agreement with the liberals, maintained secondary education in a steady state. Although numbers of schools fluctuated throughout this period, their relative strength can be gauged from the totals of 1848 when there were 48 Napoleonic *lycées*, 312 municipal *collèges* and 1016 private schools. The *lycées* and *collèges* were generally liberal, the private schools conservative and often avowedly Catholic. In addition, various congregations and orders conducted 127 *petits séminaires*.[62] In all the schools the classics were dominant, and efforts were made to sustain bourgeois control. Yet this was not left unchallenged and in 1848, when the revolution brought in a more liberal government, the new Minister for Education, Hippolyte Carnot, attempted to liberalize education with a Bill for free compulsory elementary education for all boys and girls, and to develop a more republican system of egalitarian schools. He did not get far; the conservative backlash occurred in late 1848 and the reactionary Armand de Falloux was appointed Minister for Education (1848-9). In this period, both conservatives and liberals were in alliance against working-class agitation, *déclassement* (social mobility) was threatening and it provoked the politician Adolphe Thiers to exclaim, 'reading, writing and reckoning, that is all that should be taught; as for the rest, it is superfluous'.[63]

Under the new minister the *Loi Falloux* of 15 March 1850 supported the church more than any Act since the *ancien régime*; it favoured the congregations, put the commune schools under definite control of the *curés*, centralized their control on a *département* basis, and closed the normal schools. It took one forward step: all communes of more than 800 inhabitants were required to maintain a girls' school. It allowed private secondary schools to remain open, these being generally conservative anyway; the public *collèges* and *lycées* were unaffected. The overall aim of the *Loi Falloux* was to counter socialism with a new emphasis on religion and a traditional curriculum. In 1850 Louis-Napoleon abandoned the Second Republic and declared himself emperor of the Second Empire, and France entered a quiet era until the third great revolution of the century in 1870. In education, the conservative reaction was strengthened by the appointment of Hippolyte Fourtoul, who, during his period as Minister for Education from 1850 to 1856, attempted to dismantle the state University, although without success. Fourtoul gave the Catholic Church strong support; the Jesuits returned yet again and bishops petitioned the society to establish schools, especially since their programme of the *studia humanitatis* with its goal of producing the 'finished power of utterance' – the Renaissance and Reformation ideal of eloquent piety – was so attractive.

France: conservative–liberal conflict in education

Throughout the Second Empire economic and industrial change was occurring inexorably, populations growing, urbanization the pattern of the future; Britain was ahead in manufactures and trade as the Great Exhibition of 1851 in London, and later the London Exhibition of 1862, demonstrated to the world. Pressure mounted in France for a more relevant education to take account of the realities of science, technology and business growth, and Fourtoul's ministry was forced to respond. Yet the stance of the church and the conservatives was firm: the classics and Latin versification were still considered the best preparation for the industrial age. Compromises had to be reached in secondary education, while concessions had to be made in elementary education, this being the task of Fourtoul's assistant, Jean-Baptiste Dumas, who was responsible for the concept of *bifurcation*. According to this notion, all children were to receive a common elementary education (although, since the schools were still fee-charging and teachers were either in congregations or underpaid lay persons, no great doorway was opened up); beyond this there was to be a two-branch (hence 'bifurcation') system offering alternative classical and science curricula, the intention being to provide candidates for law, teaching and the bureaucracy with a classical training, and those going into medicine, science and the government technical institutes with a scientific one. At the elementary level the monitorial system was phased out in 1853 with an *ordonnance* limiting class sizes to a maximum of eighty, and the pupil-teacher system and the Christian Brothers' 'simultaneous' method became standard.

Bifurcation was resisted by the conservatives who argued that it would be dangerous to let students study science before their minds had been formed by the system of classical values. Throughout the 1850s an uneasy compromise existed, and the final qualification that marked the successful conclusion of the secondary course, the externally examined *baccalauréat*, could be gained in either programme. Yet science did not take hold as strongly as its supporters had anticipated, and in 1863 the Minister for

Education Victor Duruy (incumbent 1863-9) officially abolished bifurcation and merged science into a predominantly classical, but widened,
curriculum; Latin versification was de-emphasized. Efforts were also made
to develop technical schools to cater for industrial needs; a commission
for Professional Education, L'Enseignement Professionel, stressed in its
report of 1864 that 'the goal of modern education . . . can no longer be to
form men of letters, idle admirers of the past, but men of science, builders
of the present, initiators of the future'.[64] In 1865 the Commission de
l'Enseignement Technique, the Commission on Technical Education,
under the chairmanship of Eugène Rouher, surveyed provisions in
Britain, Germany and France, and, finding their own country deficient by
comparison, recommended more state support.

Conditions had not improved for the workers, however, and throughout the Second Empire many children worked long hours in mines,
factories and fields without any education, often badly treated, and un-
protected by the law. France's only factory law (of 1841) had been easily
circumvented by unscrupulous employers; some factories complied with
the requirement that children receive one hour of instruction a day by
establishing *écoles de fabrique* (factory 'schools'), others released children to
the commune school for an hour; most ignored the law, for there were no
inspectors to enforce it. In 1867, as part of its investigations, the commission for Professional Education recommended, unsuccessfully, that
the minimum age for child workers be ten, with a six-hour day for the ten-
to thirteen-year-olds, a ten-hour day for thirteen- to sixteen-year-olds, and
part-time *école de fabrique*, or equivalent, education to continue to age
sixteen. The bourgeoisie objected to spending money for the education of
'other people's children', as it was commonly expressed; working-class
agitation increased, and in a period of tension leading up to a war with
Prussia the republicans of Paris rose in revolt in September 1870 and
formed the Paris Commune. In 1871 the Third Republic was created, with
universal male suffrage, and a new period of educational provisions ensued.

The Third Republic was anticlerical and the decade from 1871 to 1881
saw the church on the defensive, while the Society of Jesus was openly
attacked from the days of the Paris Commune when some Jesuits were
executed for their alleged ultramontanism; uncontrolled mobs massacred
others. Nevertheless, in the period 1870-8, still acting under the support
offered by the *Loi Falloux*, the Jesuits actually opened thirteen new
colleges in response to conservative demand. By this time the traditional

French universities had become decadent, and the Napoleonic re-structuring had, ironically, weakened them, since the teaching of the sciences and technologies was concentrated in new institutions, symbolized in the 1868 foundation in Paris of the École Pratique des Hautes Études (School of Advanced, Applied Studies), which promoted research and teaching in mathematics, physics, chemistry, natural science, history and philosophy. Having lost control of the state universities, now subsumed under the omnibus University of France, the church pressed for the right to establish Catholic universities which would act as both seminaries and advanced institutions of learning within a framework of Catholic religious belief. In 1875 this right was granted; by 1879, however, the anticlerical tide began to prevail and although Catholic universities were not forbidden (actually they never advanced past Catholic faculties in existing universities) they were the object of a Bill introduced into parliament in March 1879 by Jules Ferry, the new Minister for Education (1879–81), to forbid any independent institution to use the word 'university' in its title and, therefore, to award degrees. Even though the Bill in 1880 failed to pass the conservative Senate, Ferry implemented it the following year by *ordonnance*. The Jesuits, the prime target, refused to disband their faculties; the government determined to close them down and in cases the bailiffs had to pick the locks on the doors of the buildings in which the priests had barricaded themselves before they could be forcibly ejected. Twenty-seven colleges were closed, 10,000 students dispersed, and the Society of Jesus lost its final attempt to maintain Catholic orthodoxy in French education. The state pressed on and in 1882 the *Loi Ferry* made primary education in France compulsory and secular, establishing municipal school commissions to supervise the enactment. Henceforth, all French children went to school, and by the end of the century literacy was almost universal for both males and females. The struggle to secularize the schools lasted another two decades; in 1886 the *Loi Goblet* provided for the replacement of religious by lay teachers, and in 1904 all congregations were prohibited by law from conducting schools. Throughout the 1870s and 1880s a tremendous volume of educational regulations and reforms appeared as the Third Republic moved France into the urban, industrial era. The schools, however, still reflected the social divisions of French society, and equality of opportunity was still largely denied to the working classes.

Prussia: education for service to the corporate state

By a curious paradox it was Prussia, which was late in entering the industrial era, that was used by Britain, France and the United States as an example of how education should be organized to cope with the challenging conditions of the nineteenth century; by the later decades of the century Prussia had become a mecca for educational administrators throughout the West; in addition, its universities attracted students from abroad, particularly Russia and the United States. Indeed, the stimulus to found universities with advanced research facilities in the United States, in distinction to the existing American college which was often a university in name only, came from a late-century desire by Americans to move the apex of their educational system from Prussia to their own country. The paradox to be explained, then, is how Prussia first developed a wide-ranging system of education producing a high level of general literacy as well as a specialized structure of higher schools and institutions that other nations saw as worthy of emulation.

Events of the first decades of the nineteenth century provide the basis for an answer. The Prussians themselves had an ethnic identity as Protestant Anglo-Saxons, surrounded by Catholic France and Austria to the west and south, Orthodox Russia to the east, and Catholic Slavs of various kinds to the south-east; and as part of that identity they had the tradition of philosophic leadership established by Kant, Fichte and Hegel. The Prussians believed that they were the leading proponents of the *Zeitgeist*. The teaching of Fichte, which was readily accepted, held that, since the state is everything, the individual has to subordinate his individual will or ego (*das Ich*) and find expression in the corporate state; the concept of the 'corporate' was easily interpreted to mean a class-structured society with well-defined status levels and appropriate class roles. Moreover, to resist the surrounding pressures, Prussia was forced to harness its collective energies to a common goal, and this demanded an informed, literate common population. In contrast to Britain and France, even though Prussia's rate of population increase was comparable with the rest of Europe, its rural/urban distribution remained constant throughout the first half of the century, the rural sector accounting for more than 70 per cent. Education, then, was necessary for nation building, and, since in default of industrial capacity the agricultural sector had to become more productive, Prussia was stimulated to develop highly efficient, specialized schools of forestry, agriculture, mining and kindred activities which later in the century were developed into the famous system of technical universities.

In addition, Prussia was impelled to take the political initiative among the German states. Given its position between two traditional enemies Russia and France, and the unreliability of Austria as an ally, now weakening rapidly and dreaming of past Habsburg grandeur, Prussia, if it were to exercise the role Hegel had predicted for it, had to assume Germanic leadership. One of the settlements of the Congress of Vienna in 1815 had been the reorganization of the petty states as the German Confederation; throughout the period 1815–48 Berlin increased its authority over the Confederation, especially when it formed the *Zollverein* (Customs Union) in 1834 and, by establishing a kind of common market, created an economic unity that was dominated from Berlin. From then on, Prussia moved resolutely, as a matter of policy, to absorb the various German states, particularly during the premiership of Count Otto von Bismarck in the 1860s. By 1871, with the defeat of France, the annexation of Alsace and Lorraine, and most of the German-speaking regions incorporated, modern Germany had been created out of twenty-two states and three free cities.

From the days of Stein and Hardenberg, education was an essential element of Prussian political policy; it could not be left to haphazard voluntary provisions with feuding charitable societies and social classes as in Britain; nor could it be the object of church–state conflict as in France. As early as 1810 teaching was made a secular activity. All Prussians were to receive the compulsory three-year elementary instruction in the *Volksschule*, which provided for some 90 per cent of the population; the system reinforced social stratification, since only the bourgeoisie (*Bürgertum*) could progress beyond the preparatory school to the nine-year *Gymnasium*, or to the alternatives that were developed in the 1830s and 1840s to moderate its rigorous curriculum: the six-year *Progymnasium*, the *Realgymnasium* and the *Realschule*. Up to 1848, the schools were still in process of development, but Prussia led the world in literacy rates, which as early as 1841 approached 90 per cent and increased to 100 per cent by the end of the century.[65] Elementary education was extended upwards in the course of the century, the *Volksschulen* added grades and progressively abolished fees to parents as the state provided funds; in 1868 the law required an eight-year *Volksschule* curriculum with compulsory attendance; in 1888 fees were entirely abolished.

Simultaneously, the élite secondary system which provided for bourgeois attainment, *Bildungsbürgertum*, was receiving its main stimulus from state legislation. As early as 1812 the grammar school certificate, the *Maturitätsprüfung*, was required for entry to the civil service, while admission to the university required the passing of a similar standard examination set by the university itself, the *Abitur*. Entry to the civil service was highly competitive, and within the bureaucracy, by a regulation of 1843, a university degree was required for advancement to the highest positions. To be an official, a bureaucratic functionary, became a proud Prussian distinction, conferring the prestige of *Bildungsbürgertum*. As the strict educational requirements stimulated competition, the *Gymnasium* with its classical curriculum flourished, and mid-century Prussia suffered the phenomenon of an 'unemployed, overeducated' class.

Changes had to come, especially in the period 1850–70 when Prussia began its first phase of serious industrialization. At the beginning of the century all of Germany (excluding Austria) had a population of approximately 25 million; by the time of the empire in 1871 it had increased to 40 million, and some 50 per cent of the people lived in urban environments, dependent upon secondary industries and service occupations for a living. As in Britain and France, the factory and the railway were important agents of change, and there was a demand for literate workers and an educated managerial class. This created a dilemma for the autocratic state since, while skilled workers were needed to compete with France and Britain and maintain hegemony over the German territories, at the same time the revolutions of 1848 were seen as the work of educated – and therefore dangerous – liberals. Hence the government sought to dampen the growing enthusiasm of Prussian teachers who, following the ideas of Pestalozzi learned in the flourishing normal schools and university-based pedagogical seminaries, were beginning to make such significant changes in the classroom that visitors from other countries were coming in increasing numbers to study them. The normal schools had, in fact, been doing very well, and from the time of Wilhelm von Humboldt numerous teacher-training institutions of the Pestalozzi type had been founded in Prussia and, by emulation, in other German states. By mid-century Prussia had forty-five normal schools and most universities had a pedagogical seminar, the most highly regarded being at Leipzig and Jena. Since teaching itself was an avenue of upward mobility, although only as far as the lower levels of the bourgeoisie, and with extremely low salaries, it offered security and status and attracted a plentiful supply of recruits. The corpus of German educational theory and philosophy, derived from Rousseau and developed by Kant, Fichte, Hegel and Herbart, was intellectually respectable; the pedagogy of Pestalozzi was sound and attractive; and the normal schools quickly became part of the Prussian state system. The most prominent of the new style of teacher-educators was the director of the Berlin Normal School, Adolf Diesterweg (1790–1866), who gave strong leadership to the emerging profession after his appointment there in 1832, until his forced resignation in 1847 for his critical, nonconforming attitudes. Despite this, the following year he founded the German Teachers Union, Allgemeiner Deutscher Lehrerverein. It was precisely this sort of activity that aroused the hostility of the Berlin government to liberal education, and after the revolution of 1848 it attempted to solve the problem by moving all normal schools to rural areas by a Regulation of 1854 which also created a single grade of elementary school with a curriculum restricted to religion, reading, writing and reckoning, and which banned all German literary classics from the elementary classroom.[66]

In the same period the secondary schools were reorganized as pressures grew in the 1850s to modify the rigid classical programme of the *Gymnasium*. This prestige institution retained its exclusive character with its rigorous, nine-year curriculum, following three years of preparatory school in the tradition established by Hegel and Fichte; alongside it had appeared the five-year *Progymnasium* which offered a less demanding, intermediate-level education in classics, modern languages and other studies. Plans for reform led to the development in 1854 of a new Order of Studies; in 1859 this was further revised. The most important feature of the 1859 plan was the development of the *Realgymnasium*, taking its title from *Realien*, 'realities' and, by extension, the so-called 'exact sciences'. Latin was curtailed but still offered; Greek was eliminated; and the curriculum was to be concerned chiefly with German language and literature, the sciences of physics, chemistry and to a lesser extent biology and geology, and the studies of geography and history. At a lower level still were the expanding *Bürgerschulen*, the municipal city and town schools which substituted French and science for Latin and Greek. This proliferation of schools created serious problems: the schools were unsystematic since they were independently funded and conformed to no overall plan of national development; voices of criticism were increasingly raised. The problem, of course, was the rapid pace of industrial, economic and social change; it was simply not feasible for a systematic overall plan to be developed at that time in Prussia any more than in Britain or France.

The greatest pressure for change in the secondary schools was from the proponents of science who argued that the classical curriculum, whether offered wholly (Latin and Greek) or in part (Latin only), in any institution, *Gymnasium*, *Progymnasium* or *Realgymnasium*, was obsolescent and that a forward-looking approach was to construct the curriculum entirely on the foundations of German, mathematics and science. Their argument had considerable force. The *Realgymnasium*, which attempted to bring the curriculum into the nineteenth century, had generally remained wedded to the humanities, merely substituting modern for classical languages, and in fact had made no serious encounter with the sciences. A new kind of secondary school was proposed: the *Realschule*. This had appeared in the early decades of the century as a version of the *Bürgerschule* and was regarded as an inferior *Gymnasium* with a watered-down programme. By 1870, however, the *Realschulen* had gradually gained acceptability, and their programmes were now accepted for matriculation into the university faculties of mathematics, science and modern languages; but the state's refusal to allow students acquiring qualifications by this route to teach in other than *Realschulen* made these schools a closed, lower-grade stratum of education. The *Realschulen* teachers fought back and in 1876 formed a Society of *Realschule* Masters, Realschulmänner-Verein, which in the following years argued for parity for the scientific curriculum. In 1892 the Emperor Wilhelm II ordered a commission of inquiry into the condition of secondary education in the Reich. A new Order of Studies, in a decree of 1900, finally recognized the *Realschulen* as having matriculation status and civil service employment opportunities equal to the *Gymnasium* and *Realgymnasium*; this coincided with a second period of German industrial growth which began in the mid-1890s.

The Chancellor of the German Reich from its foundation in 1871 was a Prussian, Otto von Bismarck; under him Prussia became the dominant power in Germany and its example widely followed. By the end of the century the Prussian school system became the German norm and spread with modifications across the borders into the Scandinavian nations, Holland, and even south into Italy, Austria-Hungary and various Balkan states. The reform of the elementary school, still the only kind of education open to the mass of the people, became increasingly necessary by 1870. The law of 1868 establishing an eight-year programme was a first recognition, and in 1870 the energetic Friedrich Schneider became Director of Primary Education and initiated a series of far-ranging reforms, prompted by economic pressures from without and organized teacher pressure from within. In 1872 the elementary schools received an upgraded curriculum, with an emphasis on real-life studies, and church influence was almost totally eliminated from Prussian education, although in Catholic states it still retained control of a separate system of schools. Despite the heavily bureaucratic state and the sham democracy of universal male suffrage, in which Germany was ruled chiefly by decree and regulation rather than parliamentary legislation, the liberal forces continued to grow and teachers' associations became very active, partly as a result of the continued traditions of scholarship within the normal schools and pedagogical seminars. Indeed, by the 1860s German professors of pedagogy were increasingly talking of a science of education, particularly after Tuiskon Ziller (1817–82), professor at the University of Leipzig, in 1865 published *Foundation of the Doctrine of Educational Instruction* (*Grundlegung zur Lehre vom erziehenden Unterricht*) as a text for the pedagogical seminar. The *Foundation of Doctrine* picked up the theme of moral development initiated early in the century and revived the dormant educational thought of Herbart; it stimulated the foundation in 1869 of the Society for Scientific Pedagogy which published a monthly journal and a yearbook. Against this background of increasing educational concern, and the growing professionalization of teachers, Schneider reformed teacher training on the systematic lines suggested by the educational theory of Herbart and reconstructed the elementary curriculum in the 1870s to include German, religion, arithmetic, geometry, history, geography, natural science, art, music, needlework and physical training. Even though it was possible for very talented boys to transfer by scholarship across to the secondary-school system, this was not common, and to provide further educational opportunities an extension to the *Volksschule* was made; in central places the higher-grade *Mittelschule* (middle school) was established.[67]

By the end of the nineteenth century, despite the misgivings of many, including Professor Wilhelm Rein of the University of Jena who exclaimed in despair, 'Have we not now higher and lower burgher schools, upper real-schools, real-gymnasiums, and real-schools, middle schools, pro-gymnasiums, real-progymnasiums ... ?',[68] it was clear that Germany had achieved a comprehensive system of schools with a reasonable degree of articulation. Certainly it was still highly class-structured and chiefly served the interests of the bourgeoisie and the bureaucratic state. None the less universal literacy was achieved for girls as well as boys; for the masses there were the vernacular *Volksschule* and the advanced *Mittelschule*: for the better-off there were really three basic secondary curricula which provided a comprehensive range of training for the needs of the modern industrial state – the classical curriculum of the *Gymnasium*, the Latin and science curriculum of the *Realgymnasium*, and the modern languages and science curriculum of the *Realschule*, all leading on to the university. Although all equal in law, the universities still had separate faculty matriculation requirements, with theology demanding Greek, and medicine and law requiring Latin. In addition the army had its own specialized technical schools, similar to those of the French, and further technical institutes appeared. Yet there were still many inequalities: women continued to be discriminated against and the German sentiment that girls should be trained for the three Ks – *Kirche, Kinder, Küche* (church, children, kitchen) – still prevailed. Women had few rights in law and were under almost total male control all their lives; on marriage they simply exchanged paternal for husbandly authority. Girls were admitted to the *Volksschule* throughout the nineteenth century and, since the convents (*Klosterschulen*) had closed down, some secondary schools were opened, but they were few; the first German universities to admit women were Heidelberg and Freiburg in the state of Baden in 1901; not until 1908 did Prussian universities follow.[69] In general, despite decrees of equality, the classics remained the means whereby social mobility could be carefully controlled. Unlike France and Britain, where the development of dual systems aroused the strong antipathy of sectors of the working class and stimulated them to respond by forming socialist societies based upon utopian or Marxist theory, in Germany the dual system was accepted more passively. The state itself was ruthless in suppressing opposition that had developed in the 1840s under the influence of socialist activists, of whom Engels and Marx were two of the most prominent, and in 1849, in the reaction that followed the 1848 revolutions, Marx, whose Prussian citizenship had already been revoked in 1845 while in exile, was expelled from Germany and his radical newspaper, *Neue Rheinische Zeitung*, published in Cologne, was closed down. In the wake of the repressions, many liberal Germans emigrated, chiefly to the United States but also to South America and Australia. Thereafter socialism had little following in the nineteenth century, and the dual system of education prepared dutiful members in the service of the corporate state.

CHAPTER 10

Science and Education: Towards a New Pedagogy

The concept of organic holism in education

Early nineteenth-century conflicts in science and philosophy

At the threshold of the nineteenth century the religious-classical tradition in the West was confronted by the growing scientific challenge. The strength of the classical position was that it offered a secure basis for the continuity of social life; by contrast, science lacked any necessary grounding in faith and appeared to provide nothing more than mechanistic explanations and the continuing fragmentation of knowledge: it is not surprising that the churches resisted demands for a scientific foundation to the curriculum. In the course of the century, however, as science became associated with material productivity in the consolidating capitalist economy, so it became more acceptable. Enthusiasts for educational reform, accepting the millennial promises of science, saw it as the means of effecting progress in education in two ways: by basing the curriculum on the sciences, and by a reconceptualization of teaching as a form of scientific activity. Throughout the nineteenth century the phrase 'science of education' occurred with increasing frequency, and educators became preoccupied with the quest to make education scientific and hence predictable. Just as science acquired its applied arts of technology, education was to have its applied art of pedagogy.

The story, however, is much more than a simple struggle between a conservatively religious viewpoint and an innovating, scientific enlightenment. By the late eighteenth century, science was divided into two major positions on the religious issue – between the supporters of natural theology who believed that science would confirm the idea of the designed earth as an expression of divine order, and their opponents who rejected such theological explanation and in general chose to interpret the earth in materialist and mechanistic terms. This period, moreover, saw the emergence of a third significant viewpoint, the concept of the earth as an organic whole, and this position developed two separate emphases: on the one hand there were those, such as Pestalozzi and Froebel, who saw the organic world as divinely ordained; on the other were those, such as Alexander von Humboldt and Charles Darwin, who avoided any reference to divine links, seeking to avoid religious controversy. The chief exponent of religious-scientific enlightenment was Joseph Priestley (1733–1804), the discoverer of oxygen, who attempted to put science into a holist framework by rejecting the mind-matter dualism on the grounds that it does not explain how the mind and body interact and proposed instead a unitary theory of the whole person reacting within a context. He considered knowledge to come from the totality of experience, past and present, as it is reconstructed from antecedent as well as current experience, everything issuing from nature, itself of divine origin and secured in revelation. So Priestley, who was vitally interested in education, saw an important role for history and therefore the humanist curriculum in contributing to a balanced scientific understanding. Priestley, a Unitarian dissenter educated at Daventry Academy, published these ideas in 1788 in his *Lectures on History and General Policy*, a work set at Warrington Academy in England, in some Cambridge colleges and in various academies in the United States.

In strong opposition to Priestley's concern for history was the French chemist Antoine Lavoisier (1743–94) who argued that the progress of exact science depends, as Bacon had claimed, on attending only to the evidence of the senses, the 'facts of nature', and for this it is necessary to sweep aside all previous notions and to dispense with history. So thoroughly did Lavoisier pursue this policy that he failed to mention in his *Principles of Chemistry* the earlier contribution of Priestley to the discovery of oxygen. Like Newton, he combined the Cartesian concern for mathematics with a search for rational principles, and in the main thrust of his work provided a definitive statement of the scientific method based on Bacon's inductive approach of sense-empiricism, a method that, once divorced from the idea of divine order, posed the kind of threat most feared by the church.

In education, meanwhile, learning theory was increasingly being based on a sense-empiricist, Lockeian model, although a small group of thinkers, following the lead of Rousseau and Kant, were searching for a theory of knowledge that would include both rationalism and empiricism, this approach receiving its strongest expression in Germany in the work of the famous 'Weimar Circle', located both in the court city of Weimar and the university of nearby Jena, which included Johann Wolfgang von Goethe (1749–1832) as well as Johann Gottfried von Herder (1744–1803), Friedrich Schiller (1759–1805), Johann Gottlieb Fichte (1762–1814), Friedrich von Schelling (1775–1854) and the brothers von Humboldt – Wilhelm and Alexander. Collectively they evolved the concept of *Natur-philosophie*, which attempted to reconcile the empirical and rationalist positions, along with the discoveries of science, into a coherent, value-laden theory. In *Naturphilosophie* they opposed the mechanistic and materialist science of the French, exemplified by Lavoisier, and stressed the need to comprehend the unity and harmony of nature among the phenomena. Herder, who published in 1784 the first volume of his important *Ideas on the Philosophy of the History of Mankind* (*Ideen zur Philosophie der Geschichte der Menschheit*), accepted the existence of a divine pattern underlying nature; at the same time, emphasizing the role of empiricism, he argued that even reason is developed through experience: '[Reason] is not innate in man, but acquired: and according to the impressions he has received, the ideas he has formed, and the internal power and energy, with which he has assimilated these various impressions with his mental faculties, his reason is ... stunted or well-grown, as is his body.'[1] Moreover, Herder considered language to be the link between man and nature, providing the means for the 'progressive improvement of the human mind', although, reacting aginst sterile wordiness, he cautioned that language must be a continually inventive process aided by imagination.

Contributing to the concept of *Naturphilosophie* was the poet-philosopher Schiller whose prolific output included the seminal *Letters on the Aesthetic Education of Man* (*Briefe über die ästhetische Erziehung des Menschen*) of 1794–5, which drew together much of the Weimar group's

SCIENCE AND EDUCATION 331

thinking and had a profound influence upon the innovative stream of early nineteenth-century German education. By 'education' here, Schiller was referring to enlargement of vision and the fulfilment of human potential, and his work provided a powerful stimulus to the organic-nature educators, chiefly Pestalozzi and Froebel. The Thirteenth Letter dealt with the problem in an educational context, and Schiller argued that the extremes of both rationalism and empiricism lead to an unbalanced world-view, because each yields only a part of total reality: rationalism gives an austere set of propositions; empiricism, through total reliance on the senses, leads to materialism and hedonism. To correct this, Schiller put the case for an education from infancy involving creative play in a total environment. Although he did not directly challenge the faculty theory of the mind, he stressed the complete involvement of the child in creating knowledge: perception is the starting-point of awareness; to aesthetic experience (Greek *aisthetikos*, perception by the senses) is added a rational understanding in which the imagination plays as important a part as logical reason. In this way, said Schiller, each person constructs an image of the world for himself.

The school of Naturphilosophie

The nature philosophers set the intellectual pace of the late eighteenth and early nineteenth centuries and were accompanied by a moderate scientific school, as developed by Priestley, which attempted to construct a holistic science built upon both rational and empirical foundations, concerned with providing an organic view of nature and man's relationship. This school of thought developed throughout the early decades of the nineteenth century and reached its apogee in the work of Alexander von Humboldt and William Whewell. Whewell (1794–1866), professor and twice vice-chancellor at Cambridge, concentrated upon philosophical explications of science, presented in two massive three-volume publications, *History of the Inductive Sciences* (1837) and *Philosophy of the Inductive Sciences* (1840). Whewell argued that the mind itself plays an active role in creating knowledge out of the data of sense experience, while history provides a framework within which ideas are formed as integrators of experience. He did make one lasting contribution: in the *Philosophy* of 1840 Whewell used the 'art/artist' relationship to coin the term 'scientist' on the analogy 'science/scientist'. The task of the scientist, he argued, is to use historical and antecedent knowledge as a method of 'conceptual colligation'; that is, the binding together of empirically gained experience into knowledge, or science.

The peak of this development was reached in the work of Alexander von Humboldt (1769–1859), who shared the humanist interests of his elder brother Wilhelm, and already as a young mining superintendent had opened what was probably the first trade school for workers in Germany. Throughout a long and varied career as one of Europe's leading scientists, he not only contributed to numerous advances in science but helped create the intellectual climate in which the early stages of an attempt to make a scientific application to education occurred. Like Whewell, he argued for a basic modification of the Baconian notion of scientific method as it had emerged over the preceding two centuries, questioning its emphasis on the study of objects or 'facts' and drawing attention instead to the importance of the mental concepts that make such study meaningful. Relying to a large extent on Kant's teachings in this respect, Humboldt went on to suggest that general concepts are not innate but are built out of human experience in the context of nature and in the course of history. Accordingly, he saw man, nature and knowledge as a dynamically interrelated whole, and this was the beginning of later holist thinking about the ecosystem. The imagination, shunned by the hard-line empiricists, he considered to have as vital a role in developing complete knowledge as the cognitive processes.[2]

The current need, he argued, was for an understanding of the dynamic world-complex and, opposing both the increased compartmentalization of the new sciences and their growing separation from the humanities, he outlined in *Kosmos* a new science of the universe, providing as well an account of the historical development of ideas about the world, leading to his own concept of what he called 'the community of nature'. The aim of science should be to contribute to the generalization of knowledge with regard to 'continuous, active natural processes' by showing how dynamic elements form an integrated whole; this, he asserted, is a more useful way of proceeding than the Baconian method of sense-empiricism which consisted of an 'attempt to classify and examine the individual elements'.[3] What is essential in Humboldt's approach is that man and society must be seen as integral with nature; he was totally opposed to the dualist view that man is outside nature, and the correlative inference that nature is there to be exploited. In an age before ecological crises of increasing frequency and magnitude, he sounded warnings of problems ahead. Quite obviously Humboldt's theory of total awareness, and the involvement of social conscience in matters of environmental action, were in diametrical opposition to the exploitative approach of emerging industrialism and the heady excitement of scientists who considered their methods able to make nature yield up its secrets for man's conquest. Unfortunately his scientific thought did not receive full recognition, and the English translators generally missed the essential argument and interpreted *Kosmos* in traditional empirical terms.[4]

Educational reform: Pestalozzi's holism applied

At the beginning of the century, innovations designed to meet the needs of the new industrial society, such as the monitorial method, drew on mechanical, factory analogues. In *The Madras School, or Elements of Tuition* of 1808, Bell had argued for the 'economy of labour, time, expense, and punishment' of the monitorial system, observing:

> . . . like the steam engine, or spinning machinery, it diminishes labour and multiplies work, but in a degree which does not admit of the same limits, and scarcely of the same calculations as they do. For, unlike the mechanical powers, this intellectual and moral engine, the more work it has to perform, the greater is the facility and expedition with which it is performed, and the greater is the degree of perfection to which it is carried.[5]

The method had its critics, of course, but it provided one avenue of development. Following an entirely different course were the holistic educators, led by Pestalozzi, whose views of the child and human nature were in the same organic tradition as Priestley, Whewell and Humboldt. The early education of the Humboldt brothers had been influenced by the ideas of Rousseau, whose approach, though not effecting immediate changes in schooling, had inspired the intellectuals of his time, especially in the literary sphere, to a concern for feelings and emotions that provided a basis for the holist movement.

Pestalozzi's work, especially in the years at Yverdon (1804–25), became the first serious Western expression of education interpreted as science. The method of *Anschauung* was the pedagogical application of a scientific holism, and Yverdon became an important educational centre. The Catholic countries – Portugal, Spain, Italy and Austria – were not interested; their schools, dominated by church doctrine and the teaching congregations, saw *Anschauung* and *Naturphilosophie* as unacceptable. The methods of Pestalozzi flourished in the Anglo-Saxon and Protestant environment that stretched across northern Europe from Britain to Holland, Scandinavia and Prussia. In Prussia the method became established in the normal schools in the 1830s and 1840s under the influence of Adolf Diesterweg; in Holland the Haarlem Normal School adopted Pestalozzianism under the stimulus of Prinse, whom Kay-Shuttleworth visited to study the method in operation. Quite early, various British reformers sensed the promise of the method, particularly with respect to mass schooling. In 1813 William Allen published accounts of Pestalozzi and Fellenberg in his journal *The Philanthropist*, which stimulated Robert Owen and Andrew Bell to visit Yverdon in search of assistance in their own charitable exercises. Pestalozzi's ideas were introduced to Britain chiefly through the separate efforts of Henry and Elizabeth Mayo and James Pierrepoint Greaves. Having studied Pestalozzi's methods at Yverdon between 1818 and 1822, Greaves translated Pestalozzi's letters on the method of *Anschauung* into English in 1827 as *Letters on Early Education*, and so the doctrines became more accessible.

Various persons in England had already developed an enthusiasm for Rousseau. There was a growing literature based upon naturalistic education which stimulated the foundation of a number of private schools, where the theories of Pestalozzi were welcomed as a timely development. Several stood out, such as the Pestalozzian Academy, South Lambeth, in London, and Alcott House in Surrey, but the most prominent was Cheam School, also in Surrey, taken over in 1826 by Henry Mayo, who had earlier studied Pestalozzi's methods at Yverdon in 1819–22, when Greaves was there. Mayo was helped by his sister Elizabeth who published in 1829 a formal textbook on the method of *Anschauung* entitled *Lessons on Objects*, which spread the ideas even further and, in the process, changed them significantly in the course of its sixteen editions over the ensuing thirty years. Elizabeth Mayo organized a sequence of lessons on objects of experience to which children should be introduced, thereby dealing with one of Pestalozzi's three categories: the grammar of form, chiefly applicable to natural science. The basic idea was to gather a large number of everyday objects and to show their qualities and interrelationships. So Lesson XI, for example, commences:

Bread.
Ideas to be developed in this lesson: edible, wholesome, nutritious.

Qualities of Bread.
  It is: porous,
        absorbent,
        opaque,
        solid,
        wholesome.
  It is nutritious,
        edible.[6]

Given the increasing numbers of normal schools in the 1840s and 1850s, this book, and others like it, met a real need in providing a syllabus of instruction, meaningfully related to the environment, and sequentially developed through a progression of carefully elaborated lessons. However, although it was relatively easy to develop a superficial text based upon external knowledge, it is doubtful that Elizabeth Mayo was conversant with the *Naturphilosophie* from which Pestalozzi drew his position; it is obvious that the young pupil-teachers in training would not have the remotest idea of the holistic scientific world-view underlying the 'object' lesson. Object-lessons proliferated, children were encouraged to bring objects into the classroom (leaves, insects, fruit, stones, and so on) and gained nothing but a catalogue of external features; the method flourished throughout the nineteenth century, the objects increasingly reduced to illustrations on wall-charts.

Friedrich Froebel: *education and* Naturphilosophie

Meanwhile, a determined effort to develop a systematic exposition of Pestalozzi's pedagogy in accordance with *Naturphilosophie* and holistic science was being made by his former student, Friedrich Froebel. Born in Oberweissbach, in the forest region of Thuringia and close to Jena, Froebel (1782–1852) later recalled that the forest environment profoundly influenced him and created the attitudes that drew him to the University of Jena in the years 1799–1801 when *Naturphilosophie* was at its height and Schiller was lecturing there. After a short period as a forester's apprentice he developed a desire for a teaching vocation and in 1805 went to Yverdon to study Pestalozzi's method, becoming converted to the master's theories, particularly the methodology implied by *Anschauung*. Clearly, Froebel wrote, 'objects have form, size and number, and these must be taught',[7] while language is essential as the 'pivot' or connection between 'the mind and the outer world'.[8] Yet, even while with Pestalozzi, he sensed an inadequacy in the theory of *Anschauung* which he later identified as a lack of philosophical coherence, and he raised the problem explicitly: 'What is the value of the methods advocated by Pestalozzi? Above all, what is the purpose of education?' The answer he proposed came straight from the holistic school of science and *Naturphilosophie*: man must be educated to see nature as a complete, integrated, purposeful system with himself an integral part, to recognize that 'It is all a unity; everything is based on unity, strives towards and comes back to unity.'[9] The problem with Pestalozzi's method, he concluded, is that it has 'no organic connection between the subjects of instruction'.[10] Following the thought of Schiller, he argued that 'It is intended that man should recognize Nature in her multiplicity of form and shape, and also that he should understand her modes of being and come to a realization of her unity. So in his own development he follows the course of Nature and imitates her modes of creation in his games.'[11] Accordingly, Froebel put forward the doctrine of play as the chief means by which the child constructs an interpretation of reality: 'Every person forms his own world for himself,'[12] he wrote, almost exactly quoting from Schiller's Thirteenth Letter *On the Aesthetic Education of Man*.

It took Froebel some twenty years to develop the views expressed in his masterpiece, *Die Menschenerziehung*, commonly translated as *The Education of Man* (it should be noted that *Menschen* means 'mankind' and should be given that more general force). In between he experimented, unsystematically, with various activities in his quest for knowledge. In 1811 he went to the University of Göttingen where he wrote a short essay entitled *Sphära* (*The Sphere*) in which he argued for the symbolic unity of all matter and form in the perfection of the sphere; the following year he went to the University of Berlin to study crystallography, a science that readily illustrates an underlying regularity in nature; in 1814 he was employed in the Mineralogical Museum of the University of Berlin. Then, in 1816, he made his first serious efforts in education by opening the Universal German Institute at Keilhau, with six boy students, all his nephews. The apparently contradictory title was intended to signify that the students would be educated to become German first, then, by an expanded educational vision, universal in outlook; above all, he aimed to avoid the parochialism and vocationalism in current German schools which functioned as 'state-machines', 'cutting out and shaping' citizens on an assembly-line, as he wrote in a letter to Karl Krause in 1828. Froebel was keen on the industrial metaphor; earlier, in *The Education of Man* he asked, rhetorically, 'must we go on stamping our children like coins instead of seeing them walk among us as the images of God?'[13] Keilhau prospered; within three years he had sixty students, and for the rest of his life, some thirty-two years, he became immersed in reforming education along progressive, naturalistic, scientific lines, his position receiving its mature expression in *The Education of Man*, which he applied over the suceeding quarter of a century.

The fundamental ideas of *The Education of Man* draw together the developing organic tradition. Everything is seen as bound together in an essential unity with a divine source; the purpose of everything is to realize its essence, and education is the process by which that is effected for man. Froebel argued for two worlds, man and nature, but he did not put man above nature as an exploiter; in a later context, the *Pedagogics of the Kindergarten* of 1840, he placed man within nature: 'he is both a part and a whole. On the one hand he is a member of the created universe and on the other his is a complete being, since his creator's nature, which is a unity in itself, lives in him.'[14] Education must be permissive in order to assist the unfolding of processes of natural self-realization. He considered life and education to be organically continuous and strenuously rejected Locke's view that the child at birth is a blank tablet: it is emphatically not 'a piece of wax or a lump of clay which can be moulded into any shape we choose' but like 'young plants and animals [to which] we give space and time, knowing that then they will grow correctly according to inherent law'.[15] Following Rousseau, Froebel saw most problems arising out of interference with natural processes. Like Schiller, he saw play and active engagement with the environment – he called it productive activity – as both the content of the curriculum and the means of implementing it; a proper education would allow 'the child's powers and aptitudes and his physical and mental activities [to] be developed in the order of succession in which they emerge in his life'.[16]

From these views, and his experiences in the Universal German Institute, he developed a theory of education from infancy to adulthood, traversing the same terrain as *Émile* but with a surer touch and more intimate knowledge of the developing child. The early years of life he discussed in *Pedagogics of the Kindergarten* where he urged a relaxed approach to the new-born child – no restrictive swaddling or other constraints, simply mother and baby in a caring, nurturing relationship; the years of infancy and childhood are dealt with in *The Education of Man*. The educational task is to create good schools offering a natural education, and we might note his very interesting and innovative definition of a 'school' as 'the endeavour to make the pupil conscious of the essential nature of things and of himself. It is the endeavour to teach him the relationships which exist within the material world and which link that world and himself to the ground of all being.'[17] Teaching becomes a new kind of occupation; it loses its traditional character of imparting pre-existent knowledge, whether badly or well, and becomes one whose 'function is to point out and make intelligible the inner spiritual nature of things'.[18] In making this assertion he contrasted such an ideal vision with contemporary practice in 'the sort of school where a tailor sits enthroned on his worktable while the children below recite their ABC, or [one in which] an old woodcutter in a dark room in winter drives in the explanation of the small Lutheran catechism [in the same manner] as he does his wedge in wood-splitting'.[19]

Froebel followed the Pestalozzian analysis of reality in language, form and number, calling them instead language, nature and mathematics. All subjects of the curriculum should be organized within these three categories in order to provide understanding of their nature as well as their content. Given the usual curriculum, to be taught in the vernacular because it best expresses the national ethos, he argued for the threefold division because each is essential to a complete understanding of nature and man. Nature itself should be studied in its manifold variety, as directly as possible through activity methods and play, and from this the child will learn of such fundamentals as form, energy, substance, sound and colour in various combinations and relationships. Mathematics is important for the same reasons advanced by Plato in the *Republic* – because it links the phenomenal world, the objects of perception, with the noumenal, the objects of intellection. The third category, language, links mind and nature; it is the 'pivot' between mind and the outside world. In proceeding this way, a genuine religiosity would be inculcated, he believed, in that the child will come to 'see God clearly revealed in all his works'.[20]

Underlying his argument is the fundamental premiss set out earlier in *The Education of Man* which guided all Froebel's thought and practice: 'an eternal law pervades and rules all things'. From this he derived the subsidiary postulates of unity, divine order, and the purpose of man as self-realization. Therefore, he argued: 'Education becomes a science when the educator in and through himself practises the science of life – when he recognizes this eternal order of things and understands its cause and its coherence, when he knows life in its totality.' From this, further educational inferences are drawn:

> Educational theory consists in the principles derived from such insight, which enable intelligent beings to become aware of their calling and achieve the purpose for which they are created. The art of education lies in the free application of this knowledge and insight to the development and training of men so that they are enabled to achieve their purpose as rational beings.[21]

Here is the first expression in the Western educational record that education is capable of becoming a science, and pedagogy a technology. Froebel's conviction that he had developed something akin to a science of education led him to denounce current practices as negative and deleterious, since 'existing educational methods . . . blunted – I might even say destroyed – any attempt in the schools to promote true knowledge or give any genuine scientific training'.[22] Here we find him considering education as a science in the tradition of divine design linked with organic holism and *Naturphilosophie*, and it was from this position that he at last recognized the inadequacy of Pestalozzi who 'was too crudely empirical' and 'not scientific enough' in that he was 'not guided by essential reality and its principles and . . . failed to recognize or value science in its divine nature'.[23]

The organic-development school: a garden for children

Over the ensuing decade (1828–38), while teaching in Switzerland, first at the village of Willisau and then at an orphanage in Burgdorf, Froebel concentrated on finding a means of reorganizing the school along the lines of organic, natural development. In 1838 he began publishing a *Sunday Journal* in which he set out his ideas in short pieces, and these began to arouse the notice of progressive educators. In this period he returned to the Platonic concept of the perfection of the sphere, expressed earlier in 1811 in *Sphäira*, along with other mathematical forms as the symbols of the interconnected unity of the world. It had occurred to him that the creative play of the child by which it comes to understand the world would be facilitated by means of a series of geometric objects in which pure form is dominant: the sphere, cube and cylinder. These he called 'gifts' (*Geschenken*), of which the first two are elemental: the first gift is a set of six balls in the colours of the spectrum, red, orange, yellow, green, blue and violet; the second is a cube, cylinder and sphere; they were usually constructed of wood although stuffed cloth balls were also used for very young children. The gifts were meant as more than playthings: Froebel believed that as the child handled them it would become aware that they symbolize the building blocks of nature. So, along with these two gifts, he devised a sequence of didactic objects also known as 'gifts', numbered from three to ten and consisting of wooden cubes cut up in such a way that they could be pulled apart into rectangular prisms and then reconstructed, triangular prisms, solid and hollow cylinders, half-cylinders (arches), flat board shapes of various kinds (parallelograms, rhombuses, quadrants, sectors, circles and semicircles), bundles of wooden rods and flat wooden rings. With these gifts the child could play at building and counting and thereby come to an understanding of the essential forms underlying phenomena, both natural and man-made; this would cultivate form and number (or nature and mathematics). Complementary activities in language were devised, beginning with what naturally appeals to children, songs and nursery rhymes, able to be expressed in simple games, all with a didactic purpose. These were published in 1843 as *Mutter- und kose-Lieder*, ('Mother and Love Songs'), translated into English later as *Mother's Songs, Games and Stories*. Each of the short songs, forty-five in all, gave an action for the child to perform with hands or body in pantomime fashion. Accompanying the verses were simple musical scores to which the words could be sung; later in the century the teacher was urged to play the accompaniment on the piano.

The *Mother's Songs* were not completed in Switzerland; nor were the gifts fully developed; in 1840 Froebel returned to Germany, briefly to Berlin and then to the village of Blankenburg where he worked at the task of developing his new approach to education. Even a new name for the institution was needed: 'school' had acquired too many negative, coercive connotations over the previous centuries. Froebel wanted to make a fresh start in education, and to emphasize his natural-growth concept he called the school literally 'a place where small children can be fully engaged [in creative activity]', which in the German compound form was *Kleinkinderbeschäftigungsanstalt*. Obviously it was too long and clumsy; a shorter, pithier description was necessary and in 1840 he hit upon the metaphorical 'garden for children': *Kindergarten*. This was to be the new school, from the first to the final grades, in which children could grow, develop and mature naturally. Froebel now had an evocative concept, Germany in the period was moving towards the extension of education, and the theories of Pestalozzi were well received; here was the opportunity to present a more scientific development of Pestalozzian ideas. He plunged into this during the ensuing decade, propagating the articles in the *Sunday Journal*, and travelling around Germany urging the replacement of the school by the kindergarten. At that time, Froebel saw the kindergarten as an institution offering the totality of educational experience; the gifts and mother songs were simply the early foundations on which further developmental sequences were to be built, and he developed more kits of objects and related tasks known as 'occupations' which included building, modelling, sewing, paper weaving, and so on, often planned to occupy the child for several weeks at a time. From a beginning in spatial relationships and sensory experience the child was to be brought to a cognizance of coherence in the world, and to comprehend the integrality of the material and spiritual worlds by means of mathematics and language as the instruments of assisting an intuitive awareness of the essence of nature. Behind it all was an ultimately religious purpose: to see god, exemplified in Christ, as the author of all unity and the final end to which man strives.

By 1850 the kindergarten idea was gaining strength and Froebel attracted the patronage of the Baroness Bertha von Marenholtz-Bülow, a member of an aristocratic family connected with the Humboldts. Froebel's own kindergarten was moved, under her guidance, from Blankenburg to Marienthal, while the Baroness actively promoted the kindergarten in articles and talks. Froebel by this time was growing old – he was sixty-eight in 1850 – and becoming less effective. At the same time, his reforming theories were interpenetrating the normal schools which themselves were causing serious concern to the reactionary government after the 1848 revolutions. Prussia was industrializing, the ideas of Pestalozzi and now Froebel were seen as too challenging; social responsibility was in conflict with Bismarck's demand for public subservience; holistic naturalism was the enemy of industrialization and burgher capitalism and, in a wave of reaction, a decree of 7 August 1851 by the Minister of Education closed Froebel's schools on the grounds, in the words of the decree, 'that kindergartens form a part of the Froebelian socialistic system which is calculated to train the youth of the country to atheism'. Although the allegation of atheism was unfounded, there is no doubt that the government sensed the dangers of a socially responsible form of education.

Froebel died in 1852 and the decree of prohibition was not rescinded until 1860. Meanwhile his ideas and literature spread through northern

Europe to England, where the first Froebelian schools were established in 1851 by German refugees of 1848, Johannes and Bertha Ronge. Although these stimulated interest in Froebel, it was not until the 1870s and 1880s that his ideas received further application when the rapid expansion of mass education created a demand for more systematic theory and practice: in England the Froebel Society was founded in 1871, in Germany the Pestalozzi-Froebel House was established in Berlin in 1881; in the United States one of the the earliest Froebel schools was founded at Watertown, Wisconsin, by another 1848 refugee from Germany, Frau Karl Schurz, and in 1860 a short-lived private kindergarten was opened in Boston by Elizabeth Peabody, while in 1868 a Froebelian teachers' college was also founded there; in 1873 the first public kindergarten, which successfully established the idea, was opened in St Louis. By this time, profound limitations had been discovered, stemming from inadequacies in Froebel's own theories, especially concerning the understanding of the relationship of mind and nature. Unsophisticated as he was, Froebel uncritically accepted prevailing faculty theory and, although objecting to the idea of the mind as a blank tablet, actually followed Locke's theory of knowledge: 'To receive the external world man has his senses. To give material expression to the world of his mind he has his physical powers and attributes. To grasp the unity of the spirit he had his intuition, his heart and mind, his spiritual awareness.'[24] Unfortunately, his remarkable insights into the unity of nature, the totality of the personality, and learning through complete interaction in the environment were not carried to completion; Froebel proposed what was essentially an empirical model of the mind receiving experiences and interpreting these by means of separate mental faculties. It was a relatively easy process for his works to be interpreted in this light, as in fact they were: as exercises in training the senses, the physical powers and the intuition, considered as logical cognition. Gifts and occupations became routinized in a large number of expository works and, like Pestalozzi's, his ideas were subjected to the demands of the orderly, government-inspected classroom. Only at the introductory level of schooling was the creative-play approach retained, and the word kindergarten became restricted solely to what, in his view, would be a contradiction in terms, the 'pre-school' years. None the less Froebel effected a considerable change in attitudes to education and his attempt to identify it with organic, holistic science was not lost, although it was swamped beneath the rising tide of later nineteenth-century mass education. From his time on, the dictum of Schiller that he popularized has continued to inspire and guide many progressive educational re-formers: 'Come let us live for our children.'

Positivistic science and utilitarian education

Developments in science: holism to positivism

Holism was dominant at the beginning of the nineteenth century when science, evolving out of the philosophical tradition, had not yet achieved autonomy; even mathematics were used as proof of a divine governing order. Science, moreover, was still not being pursued in any systematic way, despite the scientific revolution of the seventeenth century and the foundation of a number of academies and societies. By the end of the eighteenth century England's Royal Society had reached an all-time low, while the Jacobin Terror in France dismantled many of the scientific institutions and even executed Lavoisier who, at the time, was working on the metric system. Against this background the *Naturphilosophie* of the Weimar Circle and the University of Jena dominated European scientific thought, and this occurred, among other reasons, because science was not yet intimately related to industry and the development of technology. For the first half of the nineteenth century most science was a rather desultory affair with no greater purpose than 'uncovering the secrets of nature', as it was commonly expressed, while the parallel industrial revolution was very much an empirical operation, discoveries and appli-cations being gained from practical experience by manufacturers and engineers.

The continuing growth of manufacturing industry throughout the first half of the century stimulated an increasing interrelationship between science and industry in the interests of technology and led from holism to positivism, as the industrial revolution triggered irreversible processes that accelerated production, leading to an economy that required con-tinuing market growth. Industrialization created mass production on an expanding scale; both machinery and manufactured goods had to become increasingly predictable in quality and reliable in productive output; the pressure, in turn, was to make larger machines utilizing more efficient forms of energy as well as new materials and processes. There could now be no stopping; the factories created large urban populations which in turn became necessary markets for the manufactured goods, although the exploitative approach of early, crude capitalism did not appreciate the close connection between well-paid workers (with adequate purchasing power) and a high volume of manufactured products. Given the efforts to pay the lowest possible domestic wages, the industrializing nations sought overseas markets as well as sources of raw materials, and the latter part of the nineteenth century saw these economic activities develop into international wars as the powers grabbed for colonies.

Science was drawn increasingly into the service of industrial processes; the great urban masses now had to be provided for by industrial means and that meant, equally, the technologizing of agriculture and other primary industries. There was, of course, no coordinated effort to harness science to industry; it simply happened in a random way as needs emerged. The French *écoles* of the Napoleonic period, for example, were established to provide for military purposes in engineering, bridging, fortifications and munitions; Napoleon even offered prizes for useful discoveries. This paved the way for the foundation of various kinds of technical institutes designed to train boys and men for the various specialized activities of an industrializing society, and as industry became more developed so technical or 'mechanics" institutes appeared. Britain led the way: in the eighteenth century it had only the amateur Manchester Literary and Philosophical Society founded in 1781; in 1800 the Royal Society established a related technical institute, the Royal Institution of Great Britain, and in the second decade various other provincial societies, on the Manchester model, were founded at Liverpool (1812), Leeds (1818) and Sheffield (1822); more followed, the London Mechanic's Institute and the Glasgow Mechanics Institute, both 1823. By the middle of the century Britain had 600 such institutes and scientific and quasi-scientific societies, with more than 100,000 members, all concerned with technological studies related to industrial manufacturing processes, chemistry, geology, mines, engineering, building, surveying, metallurgy, and so on. A similar process was repeated in France, Germany, the United States and, to a lesser extent, other industrializing nations of Europe.

Concurrently, scientists began to organize themselves into new societies, and as the industrial enterprises sought their assistance scientists were stimulated to apply their efforts to useful ends; in particular, chemistry and metallurgy, which showed the most ready application, developed rapidly. Early in the century the Prussians held the lead, their societies being dominated by the conception of holism; as early as 1810 the great

German biologist at Jena, Lorenz Oken (1779–1855), published the *Lehrbuch der Naturphilosophie* (*Textbook of Holistic Science*) and in 1817 began publication of the world-famous scientific journal *Isis*. When the repressive Carlsbad Decrees of 1819 required him to submit the journal to official censorship, he resigned his chair rather than do so. Oken went to the University of Basle and then Zürich; he then convened the first German Science Congress (Deutscher Naturforscher Versammlung) at Leipzig in 1822; expanded by Alexander von Humboldt in 1828, it was held annually thereafter, although with increasing bureaucratic control as membership was enlarged by the growing number of teachers and researchers in various government institutes, *technische Hochschulen* and universities. By the 1850s and 1860s Germany had taken the lead in founding scientific societies and research institutes; it published the greatest number of journals in the vernacular and German became the leading language of scientific scholarship. The German example spread and in 1831 the British Association for the Advancement of Science was founded, in 1839 the All-Italy Association for Science, in 1848 the American Association for the Advancement of Science; belatedly, in 1872, the French Association for the Advancement of Science.

All of this changed the nature of science, since its practitioners, as the century wore on, industry burgeoned, research became more costly and laboratories more lavishly equipped, became institution-dependent. Robert Boyle's seventeenth-century experiments with the kinetic theory of gases were conducted with home-made apparatus rigged to the staircase of his lodgings in Oxford High Street; after the 1850s such practices were impossible in most areas. In an age of political repression after the revolutions of 1848, neither industries nor governments wanted holistic, socially responsible science; industrialists wanted profits, governments wanted conformity; scientists, mechanics and technologists accepted these conditions in return for employment and research facilities, and this was reinforced by a system of rewards and honours: fellowships of closed-circle academies, peerages and knighthoods for some, medals struck by scientific societies by the score, and numerous prizes, culminating in the bequest of Alfred Nobel (1833–96), inventor of dynamite, of the five annual prizes in physics, chemistry, medicine, literature and peace promotion. Scientists surrendered their consciences in return for patronage, and the spirit of Oken's stand against governmental interference disappeared. In the second half of the century scientists disavowed values; activity was increasingly fragmented into specialist institutions, scientific and technological workers were cut off from each other, and the maintenance of a unified world-view was rejected.

Given such isolation, and increasing specialization, scientists escaped any obligation for social responsibility by accepting the idea of completely value-free theory: the consequences of application had to be borne by others. So came a vigorous return to Baconian empiricism: the world is merely a bundle of particulars; knowledge comes from sensation and induced generalizations; scientific method is one of inductive objectivity; science deals only with value-neutral facts. Metaphysical constructs and religious presuppositions were seen as hindrances to logically valid induction and had to be cast aside. This attitude received its first wide-ranging expression in Auguste Comte's six-volume *Cours de philosophie positive*, published in the period 1830–42. Comte (1798–1857) accepted the doctrine of progress and applied it to science: in mankind's historical progress, man first made religious interpretations of phenomena; increasing sophistication led to progress to metaphysical explanations; finally enlightenment with a positive understanding was achieved, by the method of pure inductive reasoning. Science and the experimental method, he argued, are the ultimate, and correct, avenues to knowledge and truth. Positivism flourished: it was exactly what scientists wanted; it suited exploitative capitalism, and even Darwin's theory of evolution, first presented in 1859 in *Origin of Species* and completed in 1872 in *The Descent of Man*, was converted by Spencer to the doctrine of social Darwinism which appeared to demonstrate bourgeois superiority in the struggle for survival. Positivism reached its highpoint in the position that true science denies all intermediate constructs; knowledge comes directly from observations. Although opposition to positivism existed, particularly among religious conservatives, most of the 'advanced' Western nations easily effected a role separation, accepting the benefits of positivistic science and technology on weekdays and keeping moral scruples for Sundays.

Educational consequences: shift to pedagogical empiricism

Given the circumstances of the times, widespread application of organic education was impossible, and the approaches of Pestalozzi and Froebel remained limited to individual pioneering schools conducted by visionaries and patronized by the avant-garde well-to-do; general application had to be made through inexpensive derivations such as textbooks and charts, and mass-produced kits of objects, gifts and occupations. Too many factors militated against holistic education: the theory and practice were demanding; the philosophy of nature-unity was in conflict with the dominant ethos of man as master of nature; teachers needed a high degree of dedication and training; and the faculty theory of Bacon and Locke still provided the basis for theories of learning and of scientific method. The systems were, moreover, very costly in terms of staffing and facilities, since classes had to be small and intensively conducted, in stark contrast to the available resources of the period. In mid-century the pupil-teacher system was still evolving out of the monitorial method in some countries, while in others teacher training was given as an alternative to a complete secondary education; those available for teacher training were young, relatively uneducated and unsophisticated, drawn from the working and lower middle classes, for whom teaching was primarily a vocation offering steady employment and a modicum of social mobility. The wealthy objected to paying taxes for social services, and especially for schools; organic education was perceived as anti-capitalist and heavily socialistic, since it stressed the doctrines of love and common humanity, symbolized in Froebel's kindergarten by the large circle painted on the floor around which the children were to assemble every day, holding hands, as a means of inducing the sense of commonalty. The antipathy of the governing class was well expressed in England by Robert Lowe when he introduced the system of payment-by-results in the Revised Code of 1862; Lowe had an absolute horror of democracy and the theory of human equality and said in the Commons, 'if this house means to maintain the great power and influence which it exercises over the executive government it must beware of putting itself on too democratic a foundation'.[25] Lowe saw the ideal form of education as thoroughly competitive and meritocratic: for the lower classes functional literacy in the three Rs was sufficient; for the leaders a scientific education was needed, on the evolving positivist pattern. Despite his classics education at Oxford, he condemned an education based on what he considered a dead past.

The same forces that changed science, and scientific and technical education, to a positivist character also influenced the emerging national education systems, for the demand of the stratified industrial society was for greater instrumental competence by the workforce, not as whole persons but as 'operatives'; it was to meet such pressures that the various compulsory education Bills of Europe, beginning with the Prussian law of 1869 and followed by those of 1880 in England and 1882 in France, were enacted. Similar Acts were passed in the United States between 1850 and 1918, the year when Mississippi finally required compulsory attendance, and throughout most of the other nations of western Europe and their colonies. This initiated an era not only of mass education but of mass teacher training, when governments in general sought the most efficient methods at the least possible cost, and for these purposes the holistic approach was unappealing.

The solution came from Prussia, where the tradition of pedagogical seminars in universities made famous by Kant in the eighteenth century remained in operation, despite effective governmental action in making it conservative and amenable to control. Two universities led the field, Leipzig and Jena, chiefly because of the dominating personalities of their respective professors of pedagogy, Ziller and Stoy. Of these Tuiskon Ziller (1817–82) pioneered the way, putting forward systematically the first persuasive case for education as a science with its associated technology of pedagogy, in his publication of 1856, *An Introduction to General Pedagogy* (*Einleitung in die allgemeine Pädagogik*).[26] In this he argued that teaching should not be considered as an intuitive art, as Pestalozzi and Froebel suggested, but as a technology – as an application of scientific principles according to a predictable method. The question was: what are the scientific principles? Froebel's *Education of Man* was obviously not scientific as that term was understood in the 1850s, despite his assertions, and Ziller turned to the neglected work of J. F. Herbart whose teachings over a thirty-year span reached a summation in the *Outlines of Educational Doctrine* of 1835. Herbart's work constituted an alternative to the systems of his contemporaries Pestalozzi and Froebel, but at the time his ideas were unpopular. With the movement towards empiricism and positivism from mid-century onwards, and with the associated rejection of metaphysical interpretations, Herbart's work was revived by Ziller as an adequate theory of education and pedagogy once it was detached from its complicated metaphysics of *Realen*. Ziller demonstrated that Herbart's psychology of education could stand independently. Of course Herbart had intended his educational theory primarily to serve the cultivation of virtue; that view was easily discarded. The five moral ideas (inner freedom, perfection, goodwill, justice, equity) were metaphysical constructs, and their removal in no way altered the effectiveness of the theory of perceptions and apperceptive mass, or the instructional procedures of pedagogical intervention whereby the teacher reconstructs the confused random experiences of the child by means of structured lesson sequences, each lesson following the 'natural' psychology by which the mind forms 'correct' ideas: clarity, association, system and method. Herbart had, after all, allowed for a theory of knowledge as a taxonomy of external relationships in an objectively real world, precisely what positivism was asserting.

In 1865 Ziller re-expounded Herbart in this fashion – although he was apparently not aware that he was presenting a positivist interpretation – in *Foundation of the Doctrine of Educational Instruction* (*Grundlegung zur Lehre vom erziehenden Unterricht*). Here the new factor is the notion of 'instruction' (*Unterricht*) which implies a mechanist pedagogy. The work was a tremendous success and became the basis of much mass teacher training in Prussia. It did not – indeed, could not – make too great a departure from conventional morality, since no one was prepared to assert that schooling should have a completely secular character; on the contrary, it was thought necessary to inculcate morality among the lower orders. So Ziller developed a Hegelian-type curriculum which was designed for the compulsory eight-year *Volksschule* and was based on a study of the eight great culture epochs of European history, one to be studied each year, in succession, as 'centres of concentration':[27]

1 Epic fairy tales	5 Kings of Israel
2 *Robinson Crusoe*	6 Life of Christ
3 History of bibilical patriarchs	7 History of the Apostles
4 Judges in Israel	8 The Reformation.

The entire curriculum, on an integrated basis, was to be contained within these centres, which were organized into a sequence of graded lessons, each one conforming to the four-step system of instruction.

The further popularization of Herbart's theory occurred in the pedagogical seminar at the University of Jena under two professors: Stoy, and his successor Rein. Karl Volkmar Stoy, twice at Jena, in the period 1842–65 and again in 1874–85, kept reasonably close to an orthodox interpretation, although he went against the current trends of later nineteenth-century science and industry; none the less, he continued to popularize the theory and Jena, like Leipzig, became a place to which educators travelled from abroad to study the world's latest advances in scientific pedagogy. Wilhelm Rein, a former student of Ziller's at Leipzig, suceeded Stoy in 1885 and was responsible for the final removal of Herbart's metaphysics by developing in cooperation with two teachers at the nearby Eisenach Normal School an eight-volume study (planned for the eight-year *Volksschule* curriculum) entitled *Theory and Practice of*

Folk-School Instruction according to Herbartian Principles (Theorie und Praxis des Volksschul-Unterrichts nach Herbartischen Grundsätze).[28] This was the most influential of the growing stream of Herbartian manuals of teaching method that were written to meet the needs of the rapidly expanding normal schools, and it set the style for the positivist presentation of the lesson by redeveloping the four steps of Herbart into five steps with a seemingly scientific character, corresponding, more or less, to the empiricist doctrine of inductive reasoning. Basically, Rein subdivided Herbart's first step into two, and renamed the succeeding three steps, as follows:

Herbart		*Rein*	
		Preparation	(*Vorbereitung*)
Clarity	(*Klarheit*)	Presentation	(*Darbietung*)
Association	(*Umgang*)	Association	(*Verknüpfung*)
System	(*System*)	Generalization	(*Zusammenfassung*)
Method	(*Methode*)	Application	(*Anwendung*).[29]

Herbartianism was now flourishing, having shown considerable flexibility by incorporating within itself the stereotyped features of Pestalozzianism and Froebelianism such as formalized object-lessons, by now reduced to illustrations in textbooks or on wall-charts, and the 'occupations', degraded into mechanical craft exercises in paper folding and cutting, and such activities as shop work and needlework that were clearly preliminary to work on the factory assembly line. Educational reformers, however, did not see it in that way; many were ecstatic that the new educational order was arriving: Cecil Reddie, for example, founder in 1889 of Abbotsholme School in England, visited Rein in 1893 and could not believe his good fortune in finding so valuable a method. As he recalled on studying the practice school at Jena, 'We saw for the first time what teaching was and for a full fortnight we sat five mortal hours, [each day] one after the other, and drank in that which is creating modern Germany.'[30] The five-step lesson methodology became the basis of the teacher-training curricula of the normal schools in the United States where it enjoyed a tremendous degree of popularity due to three men in particular, Charles de Garmo, Charles McMurry and his brother Frank, all of whom studied Rein's methods in Jena and elsewhere in Germany, and in turn popularized it at home, De Garmo at Illinois State Normal School, Charles McMurry at Northern Illinois Normal School, Frank McMurry at Teachers College, Columbia University. There was also a considerable following of equally persuaded educators of national importance: William

T. Harris, the United States Commissioner for Education (1889–1906); Francis W. Parker, Superintendent of the Quincy, Massachusetts, Board of Education (1873–80), and then Principal of the Cook County Normal School in Chicago; and John Dewey, professor at Chicago and one of his country's promising educational theorists at the end of the century.

Throughout the developed regions of the Western world, Herbartianism flourished, but it was in the United States that it took strongest root, in part because of the relative absence of well-established, competing conceptions and practices of education, but chiefly because its seemingly scientific character accorded well with the technological, inventive, 'practical' ethos of an America self-consciously trying to build a new, progressive society. Yet, at the very moment of its greatest successes, Herbartianism was vigorously attacked as being anti-educational, as the antithesis of everything that the school should be doing. The opening attacks were made in 1892 by Joseph Rice; these were followed by John Dewey who became increasingly critical of the supposedly scientific character of Herbartianism and by the end of the century, and in the first decades of the twentieth, led such blistering attacks upon the doctrine that it became seriously discredited in the United States and elsewhere. In order to understand these attacks by Dewey it is necessary, first, to turn to the development of educational systems in the United States during the nineteenth century, which had been following a different course from those in Britain, France and Prussia.

Scientific education achieved: American Herbartianism

Development of higher education in the United States 1830–1900

American education in the nineteenth century, like European, was dominated by the colleges and universities, and the emergence of a system of popular education was a slow and difficult process, harassed on all sides by privileged intransigence and deliberate obstruction. In the early decades of the nineteenth century the United States had only the beginnings of a system of higher education, and it was in building this that most energy was expended; those who laboured to create popular provisions were a tiny minority. The civil war of 1860–6, moreover, brought to a head long-standing ideological differences and resulted in a fractured society with two socio-cultural value systems that were reflected in state provisions for education.

In the first half of the century, higher education developed along the lines of the college system that had emerged in the colonial era; in the year of the revolution (1776) there were nine colleges, which provided the model for further foundations in the next period of development from 1776 to 1812 when new colleges were founded, and existing ones, Harvard, Georgia and North Carolina, were upgraded to university status. From 1812 until 1860, universities as well as colleges were increasingly founded, although in the case of universities the change was more in terminology than in character and reflected a desire to keep pace with Europe. Usually these new universities and colleges were uncertain of their role in society and, in the absence of clear directions in which to proceed, they maintained the *status quo ante*, offering, generally, curricula dominated by the classical tradition. In the 1820s, however, two major developments occurred that were to have a profound influence on the subsequent development of American higher education. The more crucial of these was the Dartmouth College Decision of 1819, a judgement by the Supreme Court of the United States that ended a period of litigation commenced in 1816. The issues in this very complex matter concerned the power of the state of New Hampshire to change the status of the college, by legislation, to that of a university, and thereby to gain control: the intention was to found a state university, not *de novo*, but by taking over an established institution. Chief Justice John Marshall, in his judgement, ruled that the proposed state action would violate the Constitution of the United States.[31] The result was momentous: it preserved the right of private corporations to found and maintain institutions of education free from subsequent state control, and from this two major consequences flowed. First, it established, in education, the principle of adversary litigation – which meant that thereafter a great deal of subsequent educational activity was challenged in the courts, with the result that, unlike other countries where internal development came by means of regulations and edicts, in the United States reformers have often had to face long struggles through the courts. Second, it meant that the establishment of state universities through the takeover of private colleges was henceforth impossible, and this gave a tremendous fillip to the foundation of independent colleges and universities. So followed an era of college foundation by every sectarian body jealous of its individuality and distinction; by the outbreak of the civil war some 516 colleges had been founded in sixteen states and, of these, 182 survived to permanent status.[32] Altogether, as Barnard's statistics show, there were some 239 colleges in 1855.

The other major development was that science had begun to challenge the classical tradition in education. As in Europe, its early progress was slow, and the beginnings consisted in seemingly innocuous activities, chiefly the publishing of literature and founding of societies. The first major publication was the *American Journal of Science*, founded in 1818 by New England's first professional geologist, Benjamin Silliman, which became a vehicle for popularizing technology and what Benjamin Franklin had called 'useful science'. Technology was further stimulated by Jacob Bigelow, teaching at Harvard, in his extremely popular *Elements of Technology* of 1829. It was, in fact, technology rather than science that first took root in American higher learning, generally in specialized institutions such as the Franklin Institute in Philadelphia, (founded 1824) and the Rensselaer School (later Polytechnic) in Troy (1825). By the 1830s, as in England, mechanics' institutes burgeoned and the demand increased for higher technical education. As the frontier moved westwards and states were founded throughout the nineteenth century, it was in the central regions – the 'Middle West' – of the great Mississippi–Missouri plain that the need for technical and technological higher learning was greatest, as is illustrated by the request of the legislature of Illinois in 1853 for the Federal Congress to provide for 'a system of Industrial Universities, liberally endowed in each state of the union, cooperative with each other, and with the Smithsonian Institute at Washington'.[33] The request was framed in a wider context which saw 'the spirit and progress of this age and country [requiring] culture of the highest order of intellectual attainment in theoretic and industrial science'. This was the temper of the times; America's exhibit at the Great Exhibition in London in 1851 was quite modest, but in 1853, the year of this resolution, America staged the Crystal Palace Exhibition of industry and commerce in New York in an attempt to compete. Throughout the 1850s the effort was sustained, and in 1859 Senator Justin Morrill, from Vermont, introduced his famous Bill for 'An Act donating Public Lands to the several States and Territories which may provide Colleges for the Benefit of Agriculture and the Mechanic Arts', which eventually became law in 1862. So was created a fund for establishing the famous American 'land-grant' colleges which, in the course of time, were to become rivals to the older, well-established colleges and universities of the east. The Morrill (Land-Grant)

Act of 1862 signalled the entry of the federal government into education, not by direct funding, but by providing federal land, which could be either sold or leased to provide revenue to support mechanical and agricultural higher education, and this stimulated state governments to take similar action.

From 1865, when General Lee, commander of the Southern Confederate Army, surrendered to General Grant on 9 April, until the end of the century, higher education in the United States entered a new era of contending forces and confusion in ideas and goals. Throughout the second half of the century the system of higher education split into two sectors: a small group of older, wealthy and traditional colleges and universities, supplemented by a few state universities, on the one hand; on the other, a vast number of institutions of a wide range of concerns and competencies, all characterized by an absence of prestige *vis-à-vis* the former group. In this respect American higher education was in contrast to Europe and Britain, where there were fewer universities, all under more or less direct state control.

Throughout the 1850s and 1860s concern for the future development of American higher education grew into a continuing debate over the purposes of higher learning. Concessions had to be made, and even Harvard and Yale established separate technical institutes in 1847, the Lawrence Scientific School and the Sheffield Scientific School, respectively. The Morrill Act benefited particularly the growing midwest colleges, some of which grew into strong institutions: Illinois, North Carolina, Tennessee, Missouri, Georgia, Minnesota, Wisconsin and Iowa, in particular. In the midwest, of course, the owner-farmers and businessmen of the burgeoning new townships wanted practicality. The colleges, however, were creations of a previous era and looked back to a religious and classical tradition that, strong in Europe, was equally entrenched in the United States, where in general the presidents of the hundreds of small colleges were the minions of parochial boards of trustees representing the conservative tradition. So few were the great university reformers that they towered above the flat academic landscape, such as the first to urge the nation to build universities for the future, Henry P. Tappan (1805–81), President of Michigan 1852–63, who earlier had been forced to resign from the University of the City of New York and in 1863 was required to do so at Michigan, although in 1875 the Board of Regents had the courage to recognize their injustice and commend Tappan's achievements. A similar fate befell professors and presidents in many universities that sustained a highly conservative view of the higher learning, and this attitude kept controversial appointments to a minimum.

At Michigan in 1851, Tappan, who had visited Prussia, strongly recommended German universities as a model for the United States because they avoided the (English) system of collegial tutoring and were 'purely universities', complete with libraries, and

> ... having professors of eminence to lecture on theology and medicine, the philosophical, mathematical, natural, philological, and political sciences, on history and geography, on the history and principles of Art, in fine, upon every branch of human knowledge. The professors are so numerous that a proper division takes place, and every subject is discussed. At the University every student selects the courses he is to attend. He is thrown upon his own responsibility and diligence.[34]

These views were propounded even more vigorously in his lecture of 1858 on the idea of the university in which he listed the main elements as scholars, books and freedom; indeed, the features he indicated – specialist professors, a wide range of topics, electives, academic freedom – were to provide the main avenue for development in the second half of the century.

By the 1860s American colleges were in a dilemma: science, technology and industry had to be served; the utilitarian demands of the relatively uneducated electorate had to be met; the conservative tradition could not be lightly discarded. The colleges were inadequately prepared for all these tasks, even for the traditional role of transmitting the cultural heritage, since American college teachers commonly carried high teaching loads by the classroom method of the 'recitation' (questions, answers, explanations) covering a number of subjects in the curriculum. Overseas, university teachers were more specialized: in England they had tutorial functions, involving the systematic discussion of topics with a few students at weekly intervals; in the rest of Europe they usually lectured to large classes or supervised intensive seminars. To compensate for deficiencies at home, students from the United States went increasingly to Prussia, the country of first choice, for advanced university training, and throughout the period from 1870 to the first decades of the twentieth century German universities exercised a strong influence. Many forward-looking American educators commended the advantages of the Prussian universities in enthusiastic reports such as the 1874 treatise *German Universities: A Narrative of Personal Experience* by James Hart, then Professor of

English Literature at Cincinnati. In this extremely influential book – effectively, an American guide to study in Germany – Hart stressed the progressivism in the German notions of *Wissenschaft, Lehrfreiheit* and *Lernfreiheit.* He defined *Wissenschaft* as 'knowledge in the most exalted sense of the term, namely, the ardent, methodical, independent search after truth in any and all of its forms, but wholly irrespective of utilitarian application'; *Lehrfreiheit* as the right of 'the professor or *Privatdozent* [to be] free to teach what he chooses, as he chooses'; and *Lernfreiheit* as 'freedom of learning, [which] denotes the emancipation of the student from *Schulzwang*, compulsory drill by recitation'.[35]

After 1870 many of the smaller colleges declined or disappeared entirely, while the larger, more adaptable institutions were forced to accommodate, often in uneasy coexistence, all three trends: science, industry and utility; specialization and research; and the cultural tradition. The elective system was the most controversial development since it challenged the set-piece curriculum based upon the classics and humanities. In his inaugural lecture of 1871 President Noah Porter of Yale denounced electives as 'the certain evil of breaking into the common life of the class and the college'; for students still without the ability to choose wisely he saw no alternative but the compulsory, traditional curriculum 'which is truly liberal' and best fits students for 'the work of life'.[36] The elective system was intended to break the monopoly of the traditional curriculum; prompted by the movement towards positivism and specialization and the desire to be value-neutral, scientists in particular wanted to be free of religious controversy and to pursue their separate interests; other academics wanted equally to escape conservative dominance and assert, on the German model, a right to academic freedom. The movement to electives gained its greatest support when Charles William Eliot, President of Harvard, endorsed it in 1885 in his *Educational Reform* as providing genuine 'liberty' in education.[37] Eliot introduced the elective system at Harvard, along with a number of other innovations such as admitting blacks and students of poor families if they had the requisite academic promise, but not women. Harvard was a pacesetter; at Yale, by contrast, President Porter forbade the eminent sociologist William Graham Sumner in 1879 from setting Herbert Spencer's *Study of Sociology* as a text because, written in a 'pamphleteering style . . . it attacks every Theistic philosophy of society and of history' and was therefore unsuitable for the unformed minds of undergraduates.[38]

None the less, in the late nineteenth century the American university achieved a distinctive identity, and this was shared by a small number of great historical institutions along with several state universities chiefly from the midwest, and augmented by newer private foundations including Chicago, Cornell, Stanford and Johns Hopkins. Of these, Johns Hopkins is especially interesting in that it was established in 1876 by an unfettered bequest from Hopkins, its Quaker benefactor, providing for a university. The trustees decided that it should be a completely graduate institution on the German model which would locate the apex of the American system of higher education within the nation, and so make studies abroad unnecessary. By the end of the century most leading universities had organized themselves into two divisions, undergraduate and graduate, the former offering bachelors' degrees, usually on a compromise core/elective curriculum, while the graduate schools were modelled upon the German ideals of *Wissenschaft, Lehrfreiheit* and *Lernfreiheit*. One survey of twenty-four leading universities in 1896 revealed the changes effected: approximately 25 per cent of students were enrolled in natural sciences, 25 per cent in social sciences (including history and psychology) and 50 per cent in humanities, this last group being heavily scientific and philological.[39] The pressure was to attain respectability by becoming scientific, and, as then understood, this meant a positivist and quantifiable approach, even if the subject did not warrant such treatment.

Universities and colleges remained the preserve of the privileged classes, mostly white males, to the extent that in 1907 a philosopher, R. M. Wenley, writing in the *Educational Review,* complained that 'the universities tend to become the prey of the *bourgeoisie* [turning out] an immense number of identical spools, all fitted to find place in a huge, undifferentiated *bourgeois* stratum'.[40] In the years 1908–10, however, university education in the United States became the subject of intense scrutiny and reassessment and entered a new era of development in which previously neglected issues had to be confronted, especially social matters relating to the excluded groups, chiefly women and blacks. Some early provisions had been made for girls to receive a university education, but not with any vigour. Female academies were founded early in the nineteenth century, such as the Troy Female Academy of 1821 which under Emma Willard taught 'scientific housewifery'. Other such academies existed, but not until late in the century were women admitted to universities; coeducation was not generally favoured, and they were generally under tremendous disadvantage. In 1848 at Seneca Falls, New York, was convened the 'First Convention on the Rights of Women' which issued a document, parodying the Declaration of Independence, observing that 'the history of mankind is a history of repeated injuries and usurpations on the part of man toward woman, having in direct object the establishment of an absolute tyranny over her'.[41] Even the liberal Charles Eliot in 1869 kept women out of Harvard because 'the difficulties involved in a common residence of hundreds of young men and women of immature character and marriageable age are very grave [and] the necessary police regulations are exceedingly burdensome'.[42] In 1879 the National Educational Association resolved that the federal government should 'look to the feasibility of donating a portion of the public domain for the endowment and maintenance of at least one institution in each State and Territory for the higher education of women'.[43] In the last two decades, some of the universities yielded and admitted women; others allowed the affiliation of separately established women's colleges, thereby confirming the status of women in many places as the ladies' auxiliary of the human race. Opinions were divided; whereas the progressive case was stated in 1902 by President Nicholas Murray Butler of Columbia that 'coeducation is a dead issue, . . . why discuss the matter further', President G. Stanley Hall, psychologist and founder of the child-study movement, stated in 1904, 'it [is] established that mental strain in early womanhood is a cause of imperfect mammary function which is the first stage of the slow evolution of sterility'.[44] The serious university education of women had to wait until the twentieth century, and in general the higher education of women, as in Britain and Europe, was centred on preparation for teaching in the developing normal schools.

Popular education in the United States 1830–1900

The revolutionary upheavals that shook Europe in the late 1820s were expressed in the United States in a popular agitation that led to the election in 1828 of General Andrew Jackson, champion of the people. With his inauguration in 1829, introducing the era of 'Jacksonian democracy', the hopes of the common person were raised and expectations were voiced for educational provisions for the working classes. Entry to higher education was achieved solely through the system of secondary-level academies which flourished from the mid-eighteenth century until the mid-nineteenth; in the year 1855, according to the *American Journal of Education*,[45] there were some 6185 with an enrolment of 263,096 and, although some were supported by state grants of land, all were fee-charging and accessible only to a small section of the well-to-do. The bulk of the people in the first decades of the century had only the rudimentary elementary schools. On 7 October 1829 the *New York Free Enquirer* reported a Delegation of Working Men of Philadelphia submitting to candidates for state election matters for social reform of which education headed the list, and questioning them on their support for 'An equal and general system of Education' based upon provision of 'an open school and competent teachers for every child in the state, from the lowest branch of an infant school to the lecture rooms of practical science, . . . and [for] those who superintend them to be chosen by the people'.[46] The next year the Boston Working Men's Party resolved to oppose 'all attempts to degrade the working classes' and proposed 'that the establishment of a liberal system of education, attainable by all, should be among the first efforts of every lawgiver who desires the continuance of our national independence', and that the law should provide for 'the more extensive diffusion of knowledge, particularly in the elements of those sciences which pertain to mechanical employments'.[47]

Pressure increased and during the 1830s elementary schools were increasingly founded and maintained, usually as fee-charging establishments, often on monitorial lines, in many cities and townships. In 1826 Josiah Holbrook (1788–1854) had the idea of a public drive 'to establish on a uniform plan, in every town and village, a society for mutual improvement and the improvement of schools';[48] the idea caught on and in 1831 a steering committee was convened in New York to organize a National Lyceum. By 1835 the lyceum movement had spread rapidly with some 3000 town and village societies and 100 county organizations whose supporters included many prominent liberals, such as Oliver Wendell Holmes, Horace Greeley and Abraham Lincoln. Not that they went unopposed; public schools meant public taxes and the *Philadelphia National Gazette* in its issue of 12 July 1830 argued that it 'is beyond the province and power' of government to provide public schools and that 'education in general must be the work of the intelligence, need and enterprise of individuals and associations',[49] thereby following up an article of two days before, in the same gazette, on the theme that education 'must cost to everyone, time and money'.[50] This, indeed, was the core of the issue – who is to pay? – and the privileged answer was 'the user'. The 'user-pays' principle was rejected; the popular demand was for a sharing of the financial burden by the whole community, and the crusade for the common school, into which the lyceum movement developed, was to spend the rest of the century attempting to secure a national consensus for community-based support of schools. The story is long, complex and textured with litigation every step of the way, but the general outlines are clear: it was a movement that began in the populous east and spread westwards; it was, moreover, one that came to incorporate the doctrine of compulsory and secular, as well as free, instruction, based on the premiss that education is a national investment in which all are involved and from which all persons, whether directly or indirectly, draw benefit, even if simply from living in a cultivated, enlightened society.

Education was a state responsibility under the federal constitution, and as a consequence of the agitation of the 1830s Massachusetts took the lead in establishing the first state board of education in 1837, acting on a recommendation of Governor Edward Everett that 'provision ought to be made for affording the advantages of education, throughout the whole year, to all of a proper age to receive it'.[51] The first secretary of the board was Horace Mann (1796–1859), a lawyer from a Massachusetts Calvinist family. Mann was an outstanding choice; his belief, as he recorded in his Twelfth Annual Report of 1848, was that 'Education . . . , beyond all other devices of human origin, is the great equalizer of the conditions of men, – the balance-wheel of the social machinery'.[52] During his incumbency he laboured without respite, travelling throughout the state to promote the cause of the common school, until ill health caused his premature retirement in 1849. In 1843 he visited Prussia on behalf of the board and returned full of enthusiasm for what he had seen, determined to implement the best features he had observed, chiefly those relating to state rather than county funding, and free tuition, so as to create maximum uniformity in order to raise the standards of the lower sections and to provide avenues of upward mobility. In addition, he urged the establishment of normal schools on the Prussian model. In 1838 neighbouring Connecticut followed Massachusetts's lead, and established a state board with Henry Barnard (1811–1900) as secretary. Despite a stormy career, Barnard succeeded in proselytizing the cause of the common school and equal opportunities. In 1855 he founded, and edited, the *American Journal of Education*, and he became, in turn, President of the University of Wisconsin and then of St John's College; finally, in 1867, the first United States Commissioner of Education. Their examples were followed throughout the other states, where boards of education with superintendents were created, these being adopted in counterpart offices in cities and counties.

In 1852, in retirement, Mann saw his initiatives come to fruition when

11 Clapham School, built 1810 to house 200 pupils, and conducted on the Madras System invented by Dr Andrew Bell.

12   Borough Road School in London's East End, *c.* 1839, illustrates the Lancastrian monitorial system whereby brighter pupils received instruction they in turn passed on to other children. A scale of rewards applied for the monitorial boys who could exchange points they accumulated for the toys seen hanging from the rafters.

the state of Massachusetts enacted the first compulsory education law which, by Section 1 of the Act, required all children between the ages of eight and fourteen years to attend a public school for at least twelve weeks a year, if schools existed, six weeks of which were to be consecutive.[53] This modest Act specified penalties for noncompliance which put pressure on school boards to provide facilities. Three years later, in 1855, in the *American Journal of Education*, Henry Barnard reported his survey of educational institutions and, in addition to the 239 colleges and 6185 academies in existence, he cited 80,978 elementary schools. In 1800 the United States population was about 5 million; in 1855, owing to continuing immigration from Europe, especially after the revolutions of 1830 and 1848, it had increased to some 30 million, with a large Irish immigrant element demanding funding for separate Catholic schools. The achievement was impressive; the United States, now fully extended to the Pacific coast with the addition of the states of Texas and California in 1845 and 1850 respectively, and the territories of Oregon (1848) and Utah and New Mexico (1850), had one elementary school for every 370 persons. Massachusetts, however, was ahead of the times, and elsewhere legislation for compulsory education came slowly: in the District of Columbia in 1864, Vermont in 1867; fourteen states passed such legislation in the 1870s, ten in the 1880s, and the rest either in the 1890s or, in the case of Texas and ten southern states, between 1905 and 1916. Catholic agitation, moreover, was regarded as contrary to the spirit of the common school and the forging of a single nation, by now a growing ethos, especially since the great waves of immigration, as well as the unstable borders with Mexico and Canada, created pressures towards cultural homogeneity that at times verged on xenophobia.

Despite legislation, it was a long time before compulsory education was fully implemented; again it must be stressed that its impact was chiefly upon white, middle-class males. Blacks and Indians were largely ignored and had to depend on charitable, federal and self-help agencies; in many states there was a covert, but deliberate, policy of not enforcing attendance laws. Immigrant groups were severely disadvantaged, and throughout the second half of the century and well into the twentieth they were subjected to intense pressures to assimilate under the conception of the 'melting-pot', a concept popularized in Israel Zangwill's play *The Melting Pot* of 1908 which summarized fifty years of immigrant experience. American nationalists feared the cultural impact of new arrivals, especially religious and racial divisions, and Zangwill's play, set on Ellis Island in

New York where the Statue of Liberty stands and immigrants first dis-
embarked, welcomes them

> . . . with your fifty languages and histories, and your fifty blood hatreds and
> rivalries. But you won't be long like that, brothers, for these are the fires of
> God you come to – these are the fires of God. A fig for your feuds and your
> vendettas! German and Frenchman, Irishmen and Englishmen, Jews and
> Russians, into the crucible with you all! God is making the American![54]

The crucible is the vivid image of the melting-pot, the pressure was to
succumb to Anglo-conformism, and those who failed to acquiesce were
not forced to attend the school. A famous social worker of the late nineteenth century, Jane Addams, reported in the *Journal* of the National
Education Association in 1897 that 'too often the teacher's conception
of her duty is to transform him into an American of a somewhat snug and
comfortable type'; she worked among Italians, and because of the parents'
lack of interest in schooling the boys usually avoided attending, with no
fear of retribution, in order 'to sell papers and black boots, to attend
theaters, and, if possible, to stay out all night'; 'it is a disgrace', she
remarked, 'that we allow so many Italian boys thus to waste their health
in premature, exciting activity'.[55] She reported that the same system applied
to young Greeks and Turks under the *padrone* system, whereby so-called
'sponsors' brought boys in to use as menial workers from ignorant
Mediterranean families who 'unknowingly sent thousands of youngsters
into quasi-slavery in the United States'.[56] As late as 1914 Florence Kelley
in the *Child Labor Bulletin* wrote of the practices in Maine where children
of ethnic minorities were allowed to work in factories and canneries under
the age of fourteen, despite the law; everyone knew of it, and nothing
was done – 'the factory inspector lives in Augusta, and the nearest
Justice of the Peace is twenty-eight miles away, and the roads are often
bad'.[57] It is indicative of the attitudes of the bourgeois manufacturing
class that, even though the first federal anti-child-labour legislation in the
Palmer-Owen Bill of 1914 was passed by Congress, organized business
appealed and had it rejected by the United States Supreme Court. It
was with opposition such as this that educational reformers had to
contend.

The common-school crusade sought to provide not just a system of
elementary schools but a ladder of educational opportunity, and this
meant extending the public-school system upwards by providing alternative institutions to the private academies. Out of this was generated

the American 'high' school, a unique institution in the nineteenth century that was to become a prototype for other countries in the twentieth. The origins of the word itself are obscure, and there are suggestions that it may have come either from Scotland or from Prussia, where *Hochschulen* were being founded – although 'high schools' in Prussia were actually post-gymnasial schools of the 'higher' learning (that is, technical universities and institutes). The term was first used in the United States in 1824 when the private English Classical School in Boston, founded in 1821, changed its name to the English High School. In 1827 Massachusetts passed a law requiring 'each town or district within this Commonwealth, containing fifty families, or householders', to establish a school to provide instruction in 'orthography, reading, writing, English grammar, geography, arithmetic, and good behaviour'; in every town or district of 100 families or householders the school was to offer, in addition, United States history, single-entry bookkeeping, geometry, surveying, algebra; further, every town or district of 4000 inhabitants was also to provide Latin, Greek, history, rhetoric and logic.[58] Under the secretaryship of Horace Mann this law was well enforced, and the three levels of schools, although not specifically designated in the Act as 'high schools', were, in fact, the origins of this new development. Throughout the 1840s and 1850s such high schools appeared slowly and inconspicuously, usually as upper extensions of the elementary school and often taught in the same building, and taxes were collected for their partial support. They were, however, relatively few in number and offered no real challenge to the academies, which in the 1850s and 1860s were at their peak, before their decline after the civil war.

The academies did not disappear immediately but by the first decades of the twentieth century still existed in very small numbers as exclusive, independent, private secondary schools, often residential, and with a wider and more socially 'ornamental' range of activities. The academy declined as the new democratic ethos and greater state control encouraged the growth of the high school. The new industrial and economic era demanded the upward extension of the school; however, the federal government was reluctant to become financially involved, and education was still the focus of much sectarian controversy. Throughout the 1870s and 1880s liberal Bills introduced into Congress to provide a national system of education were frustrated by states'-righters, church groups arguing against state control, white racists who feared aid to blacks, Indians and disadvantaged minorities, and the usual opponents of centralized bureaucracy: in 1870 the Hoar Bill was rejected, in 1872 the Pierce Bill, in 1879 the Burnside Bill, then between 1882 and 1890 all five Bills introduced by Henry Blair. The high school itself was not immune either. In 1872 three taxpayers in the township of Kalamazoo, Michigan, objected to paying property taxes for the maintenance of the high school and filed a complaint. The case went to the Supreme Court of Michigan which gave a decision on 21 July 1874 in favour of the defendants against which the complainants did not appeal. The decision legitimized a *de facto* acquiescence by thousands of uncomplaining taxpayers over a preceding period of thirteen years by giving legal force to the collection of these taxes. The precedent was established and thereafter the high school became an accepted level of state educational provision, and although its curriculum was still fixed and formal by the end of the century the elective system was in partial application, as in the colleges.

Formal teacher education: era of the normal schools

In the parallel movement of training teachers, the United States followed European, especially Prussian, developments. Throughout the nineteenth century innovations came from abroad and often conflicted with conservative local practices. At the beginning of the century the monitorial system was something of an exception; clearly it offered an opportunity to provide cheap, predictable schooling of a basic kind for large numbers. Even so, Europe exercised a fascination and the European origin of a practice often gave it an advantage; the educational history of the United States in the nineteenth century was in large part one of following Europe, chiefly Germany and England, at a respectable distance. The new pedagogical theories of Lancaster, Pestalozzi and Froebel were adopted to a limited extent; but, as in Europe, only derivative, applied versions were received, not the original, vital practices. Jefferson's friend, Joseph Cabell, a member of the board of school commissioners in Nelson County, Virginia, not only corresponded with Lancaster on the possibilities of the monitorial system but was alert to every promising new approach. In 1803-6, while in Europe, he went to Yverdon to study the new methods of Pestalozzi to assess their suitability and persuaded one of Pestalozzi's assistants, Joseph Neef, to establish an Yverdon-type school in Philadelphia. In this way, along with a growing literature on his method, various interpretations of Pestalozzianism became diffused, although it was neither universal nor dominant. Similarly the methods of Froebel were carried by a wave of German refugees in the 1850s from post-1848 repression.

The theories of Pestalozzi and Froebel became attractive in the 1840s and 1850s as the common-school crusade and the lyceum movement made headway and the first normal schools were established to supplement the teacher training previously given within the academies which offered one-year courses. The initiative was taken by Massachusetts under the prompting of Horace Mann who, in the first year of office, had secured from a private benefactor, Edmund Dwight, a donation of 10,000 dollars for the purpose of 'qualifying teachers for our Common Schools'.[59] Three normal schools were opened in Massachusetts – the first such public institutions in the United States – at Lexington and Barre in 1839, at Bridgewater in 1840. This seemed the way of the future and other states followed: Connecticut and Michigan in 1849, Rhode Island in 1852, Iowa in 1855, Illinois in 1857, Minnesota in 1858, Pennsylvania in 1859. Some states, however, such as New York, continued to use the academies or colleges, and, although by 1900 all states had institutions for training teachers, not until 1910 was this entirely conducted in normal schools.[60]

It was within this developing system that the new Prussian science of pedagogy was applied, particularly in the final quarter of the century, and it was to Pestalozzian and Froebelian literature that normal schools turned for a body of theory and related method. By the middle of the century derivative Pestalozzian texts such as Elizabeth Mayo's *Lessons on Objects* were coming to dominate the field, along with other second-order interpretations. One of the most influential came from Canada's famous educator Egerton Ryerson (1803–82), appointed superintendent of schools in 1843, for what was then Upper Canada, the English-speaking territory centred on Toronto. The monitorial system had been introduced into Upper Canada in 1816, and to upgrade this Ryerson toured the United States and Europe for eighteen months between 1844 and 1846 and on his return founded Toronto Normal School on the Pestalozzian lines he had observed in Prussia. By an 1850 Act this school was strengthened and Ryerson began issuing aids, apparatus and specimens to schools as object-lesson materials. While on holiday in Toronto, Edward Sheldon, super-intendent of the Oswego city schools in New York, saw the Pestalozzian materials and introduced them into the schools within his jurisdiction in 1858. In 1861 Oswego established a normal school with Sheldon as principal to train teachers on Pestalozzian lines; in 1865 the National

Teachers' Association, founded at Philadelphia in 1857 to provide a professional structure for teaching, endorsed the object-lesson and the Pestalozzi method; this stimulated their spread, especially as Oswego Normal School had become a national centre of interest.

By this time, with the civil war over and reconstruction the mood of the times, the increasing tempo of Western industrial development was felt in the United States where circumstances favoured positivistic science and capitalist industry and commerce as much as in Europe. Americans found the doctrine of progress attractive and for a time the philosophy of Hegel enjoyed a great vogue in academic circles, receiving its most popular expression in the work of Josiah Royce (1855–1916), who, educated at Berkeley, Leipzig and Göttingen, returned to take his doctorate in 1878 from the new Johns Hopkins (f. 1876) as one of its first and most distinguished graduates. After a period back at the University of California Royce was appointed to Harvard in 1882 where he remained to expound his famous americanized version of Hegelianism as Absolute Idealism which attempted to counteract growing positivist doctrines.

Ideal of progress: a scientific pedagogy

In general, however, Americans were persuaded to regard science as the moving force, and in keeping with the mood of the times education became increasingly linked with scientific development. The doctrines of Herbart, enjoying a tremendous revival at Leipzig under Ziller, and at Jena under Stoy and then Rein, were studied by scores of American scholars and administrators who saw in them the new scientific spirit applied to education. Herbart's original work of 1806, the *General Pedagogy* (*Allgemeine Pädagogik*), was translated in 1892 under the title *The Science of Education*, and in the hands of a small group of dedicated exponents the thought of Herbart himself was transmitted into quite another pedagogical theory, that of 'Herbartianism'.[61] In the United States five books were outstanding: Charles de Garmo's *Essentials of Methods* (1889) and his translation of the German text of Karl Lange as *Apperception* (1893); Charles McMurry's *The Elements of General Method* (1889) and, with his brother Frank as co-author, *The Method of the Recitation* (1897); and *The Herbartian Psychology Applied to Education* (1897) by John Adams, a brilliant Scottish thinker who held the chair of education in the University of London. Along with a number of other books in similar vein, these works formed the core of theoretical pedagogy texts in the normal schools from the late nineteenth century into the early decades of the twentieth and registered huge sales, most running into tens of thousands.[62]

As the dates of these textbooks indicate, Herbartianism began to flourish in the United States in the last decade of the nineteenth century, some twenty years or so after it had been revived in Prussia by Ziller, Stoy and Rein, and during this interval the doctrines were significantly changed. American Herbartianism was two steps removed from the thought of Herbart: the original doctrine had been formulated within the framework of holist *Naturphilosophie*, in which the cultivation of ethical character remained integrally related to the entire philosophical conception; in the Prussian revival of the 1870–90 period Herbart's doctrine lost its metaphysics, although Rein made efforts to retain its holist emphasis and concern with ethical character; in the American interpretation, however, all holism was lost and the superficial features of the psychology of apperception masses and sequential instruction were annexed to the new conceptions of positivistic science. The change was so complete that what is now called Herbartianism would have been disavowed by Herbart himself.

In *Outlines of Pedagogics*, the 1893 English-language abridgement and translation of Wilhelm Rein's eight-volume *Theorie und Praxis des Volksschul-Unterrichts nach Herbartischen Grundsätze*,[63] and the version available to American readers, the shift from the original Herbartian doctrine can be readily discerned: the metaphysics is entirely gone, the epistemology and ethics remain. An implicit metaphysical theory exists, of course, as a realism of the ordered structure of a material external world, while in its epistemology knowledge is derived by putting together the separate fragments of our experience of this external world. The Herbartian doctrine of the mind as the ground in which active ideas are organized into apperception masses was retained as a major element, but with a significant change: Rein responded to the scientific development of the mid-century by noting that knowledge had accumulated so rapidly that individuals, especially young ones, are incapable of effecting meaningful interrelationships alone; 'the constructive activity of the youthful mind is overestimated, if one assumes that it would of itself establish the connections between the manifest circles of ideas'.[64] Indeed, children can only come, through their own efforts, to 'broken, disconnected pieces or bits' of knowledge whereas their need is to achieve 'large connected masses'.[65] And here he sustained the original Herbartian position that 'the ethical culture of the will must be regarded as the highest purpose of education'.[66] As apperception masses are built into connected systems, so the individual becomes aware of the totality and wholeness of the world, and his necessary relationships within it; this produces moral character.

This view implied a moral role for both instruction and the teacher: these two agencies between them form the ethical character of the child, and Rein minced no words here: 'The aim of instruction, accordingly, coincides directly with the aim of the formation of character.'[67] The curriculum must itself contain the manifold extent of the external world and be presented by procedures as harmonious as possible with the psychology of the apperceiving mind. The manifold world Rein conceived in Hegelian fashion as one of culture epochs, from which a corresponding curriculum can be built around religious and secular history, literature, art, music and languages as the expression of man's spiritual development, and natural science as the realm of the external environment, these between them comprising what he termed the 'circle of thought'. Instruction should aim at extending the child's vision as fully as possible by arousing a 'many-sided' interest, presenting this by a graded sequence of instruction. Rein's thought operated within the holist conception of *Naturphilosophie* with its focus upon effecting the most thoroughgoing correlation of studies and meaningful relationships within the culture-epochs curriculum, but it included some profound shifts in emphasis of which American readers, ignorant of the original Herbartian *corpus* and raised in a different cultural milieu, would be unaware. In view of the exploitative character of the Western capitalist economy, readers by the late century were ready to accept the division between nature and man in Rein's separation of the natural sciences from the study of man and his disposition (*Gesinnungsstoff*).[68] Rein put man outside the world of nature and reinforced the dualism of body–mind in the curriculum of mass education.

Charles de Garmo identified the crucial issue for education in an industrial society when he wrote in the *First Yearbook of the National Herbart Society* of the 'vast enterprise' of building and equipping schools, of training, certifying and paying teachers for the task of extending 'the benefits of education to all the people'.[69] De Garmo himself was instrumental in bringing German educational thought to America, chiefly in *Essentials of Method* (1889) and *Herbart and the Herbartians* (1895), and he was active, along with the McMurry brothers, in founding the Herbart Club in 1892. This was reorganized in 1895 as the National Herbart Society for the

Scientific Study of Teaching and became a national association for the dissemination of Herbartianism. It was, however, the kind of Herbartianism expounded in the McMurry books, *The Elements of General Method* (1889) and its sequel, *The Method of the Recitation* (1897), which became widely disseminated and with its claims to present a truly scientific pedagogy seemed to usher in at the turn of the century the educational millennium.

The general theory of McMurry Herbartianism was set out by Charles McMurry in the first volume, *The Elements of General Method*. At a cursory reading it seems similar in ideas and spirit to Rein's work, but it contains, on closer inspection, profound shifts of both interpretation and emphasis. Herbart's own doctrine, conceived within the holist view that man is part of nature and learns by organic interrelationship, saw 'mind' as the structure of ideas of the apperception mass and definitely not as a separate entity with powers or faculties by which sense experiences are received, interpreted and structured. In *The Elements* Charles McMurry instead accepted, without critical analysis, the separation of mind and nature; it seems that he was unaware of the tradition of holism and Herbartian thought based in *Naturphilosophie* and simply accepted the mechanistic world-view associated with the positivist position. So we read in *The Elements* that 'Nature should not appear to man as an inextricable chaos, but as a well-ordered mechanism, the parts fitting exactly to each other, controlled by unchanging laws, and in perpetual action and production'.[70] Given this clockwork conception, it is not surprising to find him writing that, since 'the command early came to men to subdue the earth, and we understand better than primitive man that it is subdued through investigation and study', natural science is the means whereby 'all the forces and bounties of nature are to be made serviceable to us, and it can only be done by understanding her facts and laws. The road to mastery leads through patient observation, experiment, and study.'[71] Here is the exploitative approach of the late nineteenth-century West: the world exists for man to conquer; science and education are instruments for that purpose.

Serious consequences must flow from this viewpoint, and in education they did. McMurry accepted the Baconian theory of knowledge, fundamental to the nineteenth-century position: that mind is detached from the ordered external world; understanding is achieved through sense experience organized by the various mental faculties. So he wrote freely throughout of having 'sense perception sharpened', of the 'training of the senses and of the observing power', of 'the apperceiving faculty', 'the aesthetic faculty', 'the imagination' and even of the will as 'no isolated faculty'.[72] At the same time, McMurry was sensitive to criticisms of the widespread doctrines of formal discipline which held not only that the mind is composed of separate faculties but that the justification for including various subjects in the curriculum is that they discipline the faculties: history disciplines memory, Latin and Greek the concentration, mathematics the reason, and so on (there were an infinitude of expositions of both faculties and appropriate subjects). Disavowing any excessive allegiance to this position, he wrote that education must seek to go beyond confining attention 'exclusively to the acquisition of certain forms of knowledge and to intellectual training, to the mental discipline and power that come from a varied and vigorous exercise of the faculties' to 'a better result in [the] child than mere knowledge, intellectual ability, and power'.[73] This provided the ethical dimension.

McMurry was quite aware that, if the dualisms of man/nature and body/ mind are accepted, the source of values has to be determined externally, and he asserted that, since the religious core had gone, values must come from a secular and scientifically determined position. So he accepted Rein's view that the aim of education is to build character, by means of an expanded apperception mass; the morally good person, then, is produced by the process of education that reorders the confused data of the external world into meaningfully related structures and systems. This means that the curriculum has to be comprehensive and far-ranging. Despite his belief in the progressive scientific approach, McMurry had not not advanced at all from the conservative position of Aristotle or Comenius.

Having separated man from nature, and mind from body, McMurry's educational exposition in *The Elements of General Method* followed a predictable course. Since there is a fixed, unchanging external world, man, as part of it in one sense, must also have a fixed, unchanging nature, and once this is properly understood, by discovering the laws governing human nature, a psychology of instruction can be determined. This is why Prussian Herbartianism became relevant to the mass training of teachers in the late nineteenth century, for the Herbartian model of the mind and the psychology of learning was explanatory and plausible enough to be adapted to the positivist position. In fact, deprived of its metaphysical and epistemological framework, the Herbartian theory of apperception masses and the explanatory psychology of association of ideas fitted extremely well. Indeed, the sequences of instruction developed by Rein of preparation, presentation, association, generalization and application seemed to parallel, in schoolroom fashion, the procedures of the scientific laboratory. Once mind was detached from body, moreover, teaching consisted in disciplining the child to sit still while the mind made the meaningfully active engagement with learning.

The totality of the movement towards positivism can be gauged by the emphasis in *The Elements of General Method* given to induction and apperception. The basic assumptions in this regard follow Rein – that the child is incapable of correctly receiving and interpreting experience, much less in acting intelligently upon it. McMurry accepted the Pestalozzian-type object-lesson as a valuable means of studying nature through the senses but inevitably the individual's experiences would be partial, he asserted, and, if expanded vision and hence ethical character were to be achieved, then it is necessary to 'clear up all confused and faulty perceptions',[74] so that true concepts might be formed 'out of the raw products furnished by the senses and other forms of intuition'.[75] Object-lessons are valuable because through them 'a child becomes conscious of . . . the direct action of his senses and of his mind upon external nature or inner experience'.[76] All the time, the teacher, using the Herbartian psychology of apperception, must be guiding the perception and leading to the formation of 'correct' results, working by the processes of logical induction to assist the otherwise confused mind of the child to 'the formulation of the general truths, the concepts, principles, and laws which constitute the science of any branch of knowledge'; to organize the contents of knowledge in 'well arranged textbooks' and ensure that they are 'stored in the mind in well arranged form'.[77] The apperception mass of each child, McMurry wrote, is different because backgrounds vary; the task is, by means of a curriculum of many-sided interest, by sequentially organized lessons, to develop common apperception masses. The essence of the position was to produce an identity of outlook among the mass of the population; the image of the industrial system demanding uniformity and interchangeability is dominant. The morality and character being sought was a conformity of wills and predictability of behaviour; there was no intention of accepting individuality or personal autonomy.

In *The Method of the Recitation* this Herbartian system of mass schooling received its practical exposition; the book was basically an exposition of the five-step lesson method with some illustrative examples. But it went further than *The Elements of General Method*: it proclaimed pedagogy as a science of instruction, asking the question 'Is there any essential, natural process upon which a uniform method of treating the varied school subjects can be based?'[78] Indeed there are, it answered, 'fundamental laws [which . . .] lie deep and must be searched out by patient examination and labor'.[79] These laws, of course, were the burden of the preceding volume, and *The Method of the Recitation* showed how they can be applied, defining scientific pedagogy as the 'mastery of the general truths of a subject'.[80] Quoting Kant's dictum *Anschauungen ohne Begriffe sind blind*, 'percepts without concepts are blind', the McMurrys argued for the validity of the inductive system in producing generalizations as necessary conditions for thinking and expressing thought, for classifying knowledge, and for assisting the apperception of new experiences. This was the mature development of the Herbartian position, late in the nineteenth century: it had moved across to a metaphysics of an external, ordered, unchanging world providing the data of sense experience. The mind receives, orders and interprets these experiences, and, with the schoolmaster's assistance, properly constructed apperception masses are built which become progressively structured into systems of generalizations or 'truths'. In the degree to which this process follows the 'fundamental laws', so is education effective and scientific.

Here, then, was the imprimatur for the school: it has a necessary task, as the McMurrys declared, a 'mission . . . to correct and widen such observation' which the child has gained by faulty means from experience, and *The Method of the Recitation* showed how this is to be done, by a detailed examination of the five formal steps. Of these, the first four were claimed to be inductive, the fifth, deductive. The first step, preparation, is a questioning procedure by which the teacher 'directs all attention to past related experiences' to a concrete problem.[81] The second, presentation, ensures that 'new thoughts are united with old'; it is a step of synthesis.[82] The teacher must be skilled in the art of questioning; the 'object' being talked about must be brought into the classroom if possible; otherwise, if it is abstract, large or remote, then models, maps, photographs, lantern slides, newspaper or magazine clippings should be utilized. The children should talk as fully as possible on the topic. The third step, association, sees that the various separate ideas elicited are fused into 'general notions', and this can be done by means of multiple examples, comparisons and abstractions. Then comes the fourth (the final step of the inductive process), generalization, whereby a definitive statement is made summarizing all of the preceding.[83] The statement may come from a book;

it may, in the case of a moral judgement, be summarized in a maxim; at all costs, mere verbalization must be avoided. The fifth step, application, is deductive; the experience gained from the generalization is amplified into principles, comparisons, and a further review of previously learned knowledge in the light of the new learning.[84]

Central to this approach were the new doctrines of interest and correlation, and much was made of these in all Herbartian writing. By interest was meant the need for the teacher to appeal to the full range of possible concerns of the child's mind and, if these were lacking, to stimulate 'interest' in the wider world, itself a very worthy aim in a period of burgeoning activities and knowledge, especially as the school drew upon large segments of the community that had highly limited experience; it was, in effect, a necessary socializing function of the school and one that was discharged with zeal. Likewise, correlation was intended to ensure that the entire curriculum was interrelated, thereby reflecting the external world it expressed; it was the procedure of showing knowledge as 'a network of connections'; of the 'natural scientific order or sequence of topics upon which the systematic framework of [each] science rests'.[85] Unfortunately, all too often, interest became converted into the practice of motivation, often extrinsic, while correlation became an artificial forcing of relationships.

The method of the recitation was intended to apply to the entire curriculum, and it had the effect of encouraging teachers to accept an external, systematically structured curriculum on the model of the great taxonomies of knowledge of the various sciences and technologies being developed in the same era. Teaching now became, indeed, a technology rather than an art; it was a method of reproducing in the child's mind the paradigms of knowledge that were believed to contain scientific knowledge. 'Laws', 'general truths', 'valid inductions', 'universal generalizations' became the concern of the school; the teacher's role was one of restructuring 'faulty' perceptions and building appropriate and 'correct' conceptions. Given the failings of human nature and limitations on resources, it is not surprising, despite the McMurrys' admonitions, that dozens of mechanical textbooks appeared and the classroom was given over to verbalizing and memorization. Everything came from the teacher, all had first to pass through his or her mind, and the efficacy of the system was necessarily limited by that consideration. In *The Method of the Recitation*, however, these limitations were not discussed; instead, the text ended with a triumphant assertion that education had arrived as a science, with pedagogy as its technology, built upon the basic 'laws underlying the processes in teaching': the laws of induction, apperception, aim, self-activity, absorption, reflection, interest and correlation.[86] These 'laws' were suspect indeed. The 'law of induction' stated that 'The order of steps in the acquisition of knowledge is: (a) individual notions; (b) general notions'.[87] The 'law of apperception' was defined as stating that 'New thoughts can be comprehended only by the help of old thoughts; also, new emotions (and volitions) are dependent both in quality and strength upon old emotions (and volitions).'[88] It was, then, upon the basis of such a 'scientific' approach that education was elaborated in the late nineteenth century, and in the early decades of the twentieth this became widely diffused throughout many nations as the basis of teacher training, curriculum construction and teaching method. Nineteenth-century education entered the scientific era of the twentieth.

CHAPTER 11

The New Era in Education: I. Utopian and Progressive Movements in Europe

Pathways to progress: ideologies of the future

Educational thought and practice on an allegedly scientific, Herbartian model did not, however, enter the twentieth century unchallenged; on the contrary, there was an equally powerful movement of dissent that had been growing throughout the nineteenth century and that became a major force in the early decades of the twentieth. It is not strictly accurate to speak of a movement in the singular except at the level of generalization, for it included many positions that were sceptical of, or even hostile to, the new 'scientific' pedagogy, but in general they shared a central value – namely, a belief in the need for the reconstruction of society. This concern, itself part of the Western intellectual tradition, had its immediate springs of action in nineteenth-century socialism and new perceptions of social responsibility. To many avant-garde thinkers at the turn of the century it was manifest that so-called progress had to be redirected in more bene-ficent ways; scientific empiricism, social Darwinism and exploitative capitalism were charged with the oppression of the mass of the people by allowing the growth of profoundly antagonistic social classes which the two-track school system served and perpetuated. The clockwork Herbart-ian method was no unquestioned triumph of education; it was seen by many as a means of maintaining the servitude of the workers, creating uniform minds to do the mechanical, interchangeable tasks developed by a ruthless industrial-commercial system. Towards the end of the nineteenth century various theories, founded upon a multitude of ideas – socialist, religious and morally scientific – gathered strength and political effectiveness as a serious opposition that called for a reconstruction of society in which a radically new theory and practice of education would be an essential element. In all of them, there was a utopian tincture.

Early utopian socialism: Robert Owen and the cooperative movement

The socialist movement has its modern origins largely with the indefatigable Robert Owen who in an 1827 issue of his *Co-operative Magazine* first used the word 'socialist'. Born in Wales, in Newtown, Montgomeryshire, the son of a saddler, Robert Owen (1771–1858) catalysed early nineteenth-century social conscience through his lifelong dedication to the reconstruction of society – moral, social and industrial. With a genius for mastering the complexities of both social mobility and industrial success, he rose from shop-boy at nine – his brief schooling finished – to draper's apprentice, and by the age of eighteen was master of his own drapery business, in the year of the French Revolution. Moving from textile retailing into manufacture, he became head of his own cloth factory in a company partnership in New Lanark, Scotland, by the age of twenty-eight.[1] That was in the year 1799, at the height of the Napoleonic Wars, when manufacturers were making astonishing profits; unlike most of them, however, he had a strong conscience and in the second decade of the century became deeply absorbed in trying to understand the social consequences of the industrial revolution, especially after 1813 when the cessation of hostilities and the ensuing slump sent demand plunging.

Owen's immediate response to the trade depression, which hit the working classes hardest, was to write a series of four economic tracts entitled *A New View of Society* whose subtitle, *Essays on the Principle of the Formation of the Human Character, and the Application of the Principle to Practice*, indicated his belief that the problems of the period were not due simply to fluctuations of the business cycle but were much more profound, arising from the economic structure of society itself. In calling, therefore, for both social and moral reconstruction, he was indeed making radical proposals. He was not seen, however, as a dangerous radical at the time; in fact, when his four essays appeared, two in 1813 and two in 1816, they were received as a promising attempt to moderate some of the excesses of early industrialization and crude capitalism. The root of the problem, as he saw it, was that man had been degraded to the position of 'a secondary and inferior machine'[2] in a social system dominated by the greed of the manufacturers who, by pursuing the 'narrow principles of *immediate gain*',[3] are 'capable of raising a formidable opposition to any measure which they imagine will affect their interests'.[4] The task he set himself was to oppose the 'blind avarice of commerce'[5] by persuading government, manufacturers and workers that the cure for economic and related social ills required first the recognition that, in the words of the Dedication to the Fourth Essay of *A New View of Society*, 'the true origin of that misery may be traced to the ignorance of those who have formerly ruled, and of those whom they governed'; he proposed, therefore, 'to sketch the outlines of a practical Plan of Government, founded altogether on a preventive system, and derived from principles directly opposed to the errors of our forefathers'.[6] Throughout the pages of *A New View of Society* and in a number of more carefully argued tracts over the next thirty years, Owen spread his reforming ideas. These can be reduced, in essence, to three simple words – loving, sharing, caring – which inspired workers, social reformers and utopian visionaries, and which were increasingly opposed by the bourgeois establishment and the Anglican Church as the full implications became apparent.

Owen was, of course, writing in the reforming utopian tradition which had flourished both in eighteenth-century France, where it became an established literary genre,[7] and in England where, in addition to the literary tradition established by More and Bacon, a number of practical experiments were in operation.[8] The immediate sources of Owen's vision were the ideas of Rousseau, Pestalozzi, Bentham and Mill, which he combined in his own creative synthesis. Following the utopian perfectibilist theorizing of his own day, Owen asserted that man could control his own future if only he would rid himself of the three cardinal vices of competition, rewards and punishments and realize that the supreme value is happiness of the total population; he called it 'the single principle of action' and defined it, in his own italics, as '*the happiness of self, clearly understood and uniformly practised, which can only be attained by conduct that must promote the happiness of the community*'.[9] Throughout his writings he was an uncompromising proponent of utilitarianism, asserting that 'government, then, is the best, which in practice produces the greatest happiness to the greatest number; including those who govern, and those who obey'.[10] Here is an essential part of his plan: the rulers themselves must come to recognize and appreciate that their own good rests upon that of the workers; it is, in effect, good business practice to have happy, well-treated employees. Owen put this into practice by using the most enlightened management techniques in his own factory at New Lanark, paying the highest wages for the shortest hours, offering good meals and clean accommodation, refusing to employ children under ten years of age, and providing supervised infant and primary schools for the workers' children and evening schools for the adults.

During the years 1813–19 Owen promoted his ideas on social reform and in 1816 opened his factory school which was conducted according to his new theories. Like all utopian theorists, he saw a new educational theory and practice as being essential to his plans, and he set out the central tasks of education, and their relationship to society, in a *Report to the County of Lanark* of 1820, commissioned by a committee of Lanark councillors considering the problems of poverty and urban unemployment. The *Report* anticipates much economic theory of the later decades of the century, and many of the human problems of the twentieth. Central to his argument was the belief 'that manual labour, properly directed, is the source of all wealth, and of national prosperity',[11] and should, therefore, be considered a 'natural standard of value' instead of the gold and silver currently used as standards. If this were done, the contributions of individuals employed in the production process could be more equitably assessed and the workers given a fair return, proportional to their labour which created it; as things stand, he wrote, manufacturers do not share equitably, their warehouses are glutted and unemployed operatives are destitute. The solution to the problem was to balance production and consumption more evenly, and, in particular, not to encourage unnecessary luxury and conspicuous consumption; people should produce only as much as they can reasonably consume, he argued, in an era before the manipulation of desire became a skilled occupation of advertisers.

The essence of Owen's proposal was to settle the unemployed workers in cooperative communities, because 'union and mutual co-operation . . . is a more advantageous principle on which to found the social system, for the benefit of all', than individual interest.[12] He suggested that areas of good soil and climate be chosen, and communities of 300 to 2000 established, with 800–1200 the optimum range. The town plan should be symmetrical, enclosing a central parkland containing the main public buildings, including a school with playgrounds. The social organization

including recommendations for communal eating, which was more economic in terms of space and food preparation, while the dormitory habit-
ations were designed as large four-storey terraces on the new urban-
planning models just coming into vogue. The most interesting feature is
the notion that everyone should remain whole in their working lives and
not become specialized process-workers:

> ... instead of the unhealthy pointer of a pin, – header of a nail, – piecer of a
> thread, – or clodhopper, senselessly gazing at the soil or around him, without
> understanding or rational reflection, there would spring up a working class
> full of activity and useful knowledge, with habits, information, manners and
> dispositions that would place the lowest in the scale many degrees above the
> best of any class which has yet been formed by the circumstances of past or
> present society.[13]

Production would then be related to needs and consumption: meaningless
overproduction could be regulated by abandoning mechanical for spade
agriculture, and, since everything would be produced for communal
benefit by cooperative teams, there would be neither waste nor shoddily
made rejects. Social distinctions would remain, based upon the concepts
of production and management (Owen did not foresee any total egalitarianism), but the workers would be infinitely happier, would indeed
'remain well satisfied with their own station in life' and not envy the
stresses of managerial functionaries.[14]

Owen's emphasis on proper education as the key to good government
makes the *Report to the County of Lanark* a reforming treatise as much on
education as on government, economics and social organization. The
school itself should be a common institution, all children being compelled
to attend with no exceptions of sex, class or competence. Compulsion is
necessary, he argued, because none has the capacity to become self-made
and because, anyway, education is primarily an experience of social interaction. Existing educational practices are bad because, based as they are
upon competition, rewards and punishments, the education gained is
demoralizing;[15] the educational aim of the good society should be, he
emphasized, 'to *remoralize and conserve*'.[16] For this he recommended two
levels of schooling, an infants' division for the two- to six-year-olds (the
origin of the modern infants' school) and another for those aged from six
to fourteen. The ideas of Rousseau and Pestalozzi are implicit throughout
the educational argument,[17] especially in his recommendation of dis-
cussion-based lessons devoted to meaningful activities on the object-
lesson model. Earlier, in the period up to 1812, he had been attracted to

the possibilities of the monitorial method and had discussions with both Lancaster and Bell, and contributed considerable sums to them as benefactions. But the monitorial method was not suited to the cultivation of whole persons and had been criticized earlier in *A New View of Society* when he observed that in the national schools of the Anglican Church the children learnt by rote; such sole dependence on memory he derided as 'this mockery of learning'.[18] Education should be constructive and engage the whole child; books and memorization were rejected in favour of 'useful knowledge' acquired 'through the means of sensible signs, by which their powers of reflection and judgment may be habituated to draw accurate conclusions from the facts presented',[19] these 'signs' being the illustrated charts and objects on which object-lessons were based.

Concurrently with this *Report* Owen had such a system in operation in his New Lanark factory, and it was upon its practices, and successes, that his theory drew. Established in 1816 after his exploration and rejection of the monitorial method, the school was organized into two divisions, for infants and older children, with an additional evening division for adults. The method was based upon object-lesson conversations stimulated by the children's curiosity; formal lessons, especially arithmetic, came from Pestalozzian manuals in which abstract concepts of the four operations were illustrated graphically on diagrams of squared paper. In 1819, after three years of operation, H. G. MacNab wrote in *The New Views of Mr Owen of Lanark Impartially Examined* that this was 'the most valuable establishment in education to be found in this or any other country'.[20] There were many novel features that contrasted with prevailing practices, all built around conversational methods and actual experiences with an absence of external rewards and punishments. One of the most innovatory was group dancing, which was enjoyed by the children but objected to by Owen's business partners. Through his London contacts, Owen had taken William Allen, Lancaster's benefactor, into partnership and it was Allen, the Quaker, who saw the devil in dancing and raised such objections, gaining the support of several other London partners, that Owen was forced to hand over the management of the school to his partners, whose moral code eliminated the progressive, innovatory practices and reorganized the school on the monitorial system in 1824. Thereafter it degenerated into a repressive lock-step regime.

In that year, after other difficulties as well as those connected with the school, Owen left for America where he set up a new utopian society at

New Harmony in Indiana,[21] staying there for five years, and returning to Britain in 1829. Immediately he plunged again into the task of social reconstruction. Already his efforts had been largely responsible for the landmark 1819 Factory Act, and the Factory Act of 1833 included many of his ideas; in 1833 he also organized the militant workers into the National Consolidated Trades Union which had hopes of a new social order. The employers opposed the union and after a bitter struggle lasting barely a year Owen lost leadership of the working-class movement. The New Harmony venture failed, although many similar communal, utopian ventures were tried on the American new frontier in that century. None the less, Owen left an indelible imprint on the social conscience of Britain and was succeeded by others who sought to implement his educational and social ideals. Owen himself continued to write ceaselessly in the cause of socialism, and new books and reprints of former publications appeared nearly every year from 1834 until his death, in his birthplace, Newtown, in 1858. His thought remained utopian and optimistic, and the titles of his books reflected this, such as the 1841 *Signs of the Times, or, the Approach of the Millennium* and one of his journals, published in his last two years, *Robert Owen's Millennial Gazette*.

Millennial hopes, however, were not easily dashed, and Owen's ideas were taken up in the Co-operative Movement of the 1830s which organized workers for their collective good, originally in groups for buying food and other necessities, but extending into associated welfare projects including medical care and education. Schools, in effect, were mooted at the Second Co-operative Congress of 1831 and several were established based upon the best of Owen's reconstructionist teachings; altogether three or four were founded in London and one in Salford, near Manchester. They were ambitious in curriculum, excessively ideological in aim, and too expensive for workers; by the end of the 1830s they seem to have disappeared.[22] In the 1840s a second Owenite development occurred – the Rational Religion schools, which attempted to indoctrinate children in Sunday classes in the socialist views of the Universal Community Society of Rational Religionists. By 1842 the society was conducting twelve Sunday schools as well as nine full-time day schools.[23] These schools adopted Pestalozzian methods, attempting to go beyond literacy to a study of the world in its manifold aspects through all the organized subjects. They, too, were excessively ambitious and disappeared with the decline in the early 1840s of the Rational Religionists.

The early socialist movement in France: Fourier and Saint-Simon

Contemporaneously with Owen, socialist ideas were developing strongly in France as a natural consequence of the utopian literature of the eighteenth century and the hopes that had been born in the Revolution. Claude-Henri de Rouvroy, Comte de Saint-Simon (1760–1825), began his serious writing late in life, around 1814, and became particularly active after his meeting in 1816 with Comte, by whom he was profoundly influenced. In particular, Saint-Simon was attracted to the concept of positivism and its application to the rational organization of society, a view already expressed in his early work of 1803, *Letters of an Inhabitant of Geneva*. His thought, diffused throughout a stream of political and proto-socialist writings, developed to his mature position: that the inevitable conflict of social classes must lead to a new political ideology and a superior form of society, one apparently similar to Plato's Republic (although there is no explicit reference to that original utopia). Briefly, he envisaged a society organized in a hierarchy of talent, controlled by three chambers of authority; chambers, in the parliamentary sense, of invention, examination and deputies, which would be concerned, respectively, with the initiation of ideas, their assessment and their execution. Education was central to the scheme and would be supervised by the chamber of examination.

Saint-Simon's ideas attracted a ready following and after his death these devotees, the Saint-Simonians, developed and extended the socialist import of his ideas in *The Doctrine of Saint-Simon*.[24] In many respects this widely influential exposition followed the master, although in several aspects it made a significant departure, chiefly in the rejection of positivism on the grounds that it was an insufficient basis for general theory and decision making; science and technology were considered inadequate, and stress was placed upon the role of history, political experience and ideology, the historical events of the eighteenth century being seen as having created, of necessity, conditions for revolution, itself a conflict between the 'two opposing camps' of the conservative, medieval-minded regime of authority and the 'partisans of new ideas'.[25] The progress of history, they argued, led inevitably to conflict and from that encounter a new social order would arise, as successor to the *ancien régime*; the historical sequence was a progression from class antagonism to universal association with the return of alienated property to the community as a whole and the institution of a new, just society based upon the rule of law. Yet the Saint-Simonians did not argue for full equality; their theory envisaged a new state with hierarchical grading according to merit. Education had an integral role to play as a mechanism for securing common morality and canons of approved social behaviour on the one hand, and, on the other, as a sorting, selecting device to determine intellectual capacity and to fit each person into an appropriate vocational position. So *The Doctrine* observed that 'general or moral education' must be universal in order to ensure 'the initiation of individuals into society, the inculcation into individuals of sympathy and love for all, the union of all wills into one sole will, and the direction of all efforts towards one common goal, the goal of society'. In addition, 'special or professional education' has as its purpose 'the transmission to individuals of special knowledge needed to accomplish the various kinds of sympathetic or poetic, intellectual or scientific, material or industrial work to which they are called by the needs of society and by their own ability'.[26] In their detailed prescriptions the limitations of science were stressed, chiefly that science is unable to provide moral guidance; each individual, therefore, should have his 'faculty of feeling' cultivated by moral education.[27] Beyond this, special education ensures that each person will be required to perform his or her role in society 'on the basis of individual ability and talent' and, 'since the various functions and professions will be assigned on the basis of ability, they will be exercised more perfectly'.[28]

Meanwhile, an equally influential socialist utopia was being promoted in Paris by François-Marie-Charles Fourier (1772–1837), a recluse and eccentric whose thought had an enduring impact on the nineteenth century. He published his first book in 1808 propounding his ideas on the reconstruction of society and continued writing nearly every day until his death. His ideas were akin to the Stoic doctrine of an underlying design to the world, of man's need to discover it and thereby live in harmony with nature. Fundamental to all his many writings is the belief that nature is of central importance, in effect a divine plan. Within man, he believed, are thirteen passions which, if repressed, are the cause of all social difficulties but, when released, allowing society to be dominated by the laws of *attraction passionnelle* (literally, 'passional attraction'), will transform the world into a utopia.[29] The fantastic elements cannot be considered here; it is sufficient to observe that his economic analysis and predictions were similar to Robert Owen's. Like him, Fourier believed that the solution would be found in an arcadian utopia of agricultural communities, which he called *phalanstères* (that is, communities for phalanxes) and which would be of similar size to Owen's cooperative villages.

Within the phalansteries, education would be a major preoccupation, the aim being to rear children who would be free of repressions and could grow into healthily adjusted adult members of these cooperative, wholesome communes.

Fourier's chief educational ideas, which exercised a major influence on socialist theory, are Rousseauian in origin; it was assumed that the child is born good, whole and endowed with a large number of instincts, thirty in all, which lead along the path of natural harmonious development; it is the intervention of a faulty civilization that inhibits healthy growth and development. Education in the phalansteries would therefore aim to allow the instincts to unfold in natural sequence. Arguing that 'there is no problem upon which people have gone more astray than upon public instruction and its methods',[30] he considered existing school practices to be so dangerous that they should be abandoned immediately and replaced by harmonic education whereby natural instincts would be cultivated by means of craft activities. The aim most certainly is not 'to create precocious little *savants*, intellectual primary school beginners', he wrote in 1838 in *Théorie de l'unité universelle*; the educational task is to follow the path of nature by organizing children's activities in such a way that there is 'an integral play of the faculties and attractions of the soul, combined with the integral exercise of the faculties of the body by means of proportional gymnastics'.[31] More important than the three Rs are cookery and opera, because the former cultivates the senses of taste and smell, the latter, sight and hearing. Like Rousseau, he did not deal with the mechanics of formal literacy; his focus was entirely romantic and poetic. Thus Fourier continued the position of romantic naturalism initiated by Rousseau.

None of these early socialist thinkers, who collectively provided the reconstructionist impulse, envisaged any basic change in the theory of knowledge; their reforms were social and economic rather than metaphysical and epistemological. Owen, Saint-Simon and Fourier all manifest a naïve rationalism which considered that the right path had only to be pointed out and society would follow; their educational theories were all based upon the current positivist epistemology of sense-empiricism with its associated faculty psychology. Owen held this position uncompromisingly in *A New View of Society* when he wrote, in italics:

Can man, when possessing the full vigour of his faculties, form a rational judgment on any subject, until he has first collected all the facts respecting it which are known? Has not this been, and will not this ever remain, the only path by which human knowledge can be obtained?[32]

Saint-Simon was an avowed positivist, and even the Saint-Simonians, although they diverged from absolute faith in science, maintained the faculty approach by assuming that each person has the three faculties of sympathy, rationality and material activity, for which the curriculum should provide the corresponding curriculum studies of fine arts, science and industry.[33] Fourier's concept of instincts, too, is close to that of faculties, although he did see the need for organic, whole development from within.

The socialist movement: Marx and scientific socialism

Socialism flourished in the 1840s, and these utopian theories provided hope for many. To the modern mind, disillusioned by a flood of twentieth-century dystopias, as written by Huxley, Orwell and Zamiatin, for example, these early works might seem ingenuous and impracticable; but to a suppressed workforce with little social security, twelve- to sixteen-hour working days, a life expectancy of often no more than thirty or forty years, and crowded into vast urban ghettos, these were inspiring in their vision of a promised land, and in the periods of repression after the revolutions of 1830 and 1848 there was considerable emigration to the United States in an effort to turn the dream into reality. Already in the early eighteenth century that new nation had been host to the religious utopians, Shakers and Perfectionists; later Owen stimulated the secular cooperative-village movements, first at New Harmony and then in a number of similar communities from the Atlantic seaboard as far inland as the Mississippi. The followers of Fourier established colonies on the phalanstery pattern under the banner of Associationism, and the fact that most failed, as did the Owenites, led in the 1840s to a wave of political realism, particularly among Germans expelled in the wake of the repressions after the abortive revolution of 1830.

Many German political activists and social reformers went into exile in neighbouring countries, chiefly Belgium, France, Switzerland and England, where they continued their efforts to achieve a more equitable society. By the mid-1840s a more strongly coordinated workers' movement was growing across western Europe, and a literature of working-class political consciousness appeared alongside the utopian literature, a seminal example being Wilhelm Weitling's *Guarantees of Harmony and*

Freedom of 1842. Meanwhile, a number of German exiles in Paris had formed a political action group called the League of the Just, of which Weitling was a member, and in 1846 they convened a meeting in Brussels to develop a strategy for working-class activism; the following year they reorganized themselves as the Communist League, having been joined by Karl Marx (1818–83) and his close associate Friedrich Engels (1820–95), who were charged with preparing its political rationale which they presented in February 1848 as the *Communist Manifesto*. The opening words were emotionally charged and ominously prescient:

> A spectre is haunting Europe – the spectre of Communism. All the Powers of old Europe have entered into a holy alliance to exorcise this spectre: Pope and Czar, Metternich and Guizot, French Radicals and German police-spies.[34]

Marx had been inspired by utopian visions, and this *Manifesto* reflected the hopes held by the new communists for a millennium in which, as a result of an inevitable historical process, the bourgeoisie would be vanquished by the workers who would assume control of society; indeed, the closing words of the first section triumphantly assert that the 'fall [of the bourgeoisie] and the victory of the proletariat are equally inevitable'.[35]

One of the most interesting features of the *Communist Manifesto* is Marx's analysis of what he termed the Critical-Utopian Socialists, and he referred to Owen, Fourier and Saint-Simon, the three major originators, as being part of the historical evolution of communism. They provided, however, only limited theories and he contemptuously dismissed them as still continuing to 'dream of [the] experimental realization of their social Utopias'[36] without having any effective basis for action. The true basis was to be the new 'scientific socialism' now proclaimed by Marx and Engels, scientific in the sense that it drew upon the study of the dialectics of historical development. Paradoxically, both retained utopian elements in their own thought; in a later essay, *Socialism: Utopian and Scientific*, published in German in 1880, in English in 1892, Engels examined the distinction at length and argued that, to be effective, socialist theory had to be placed upon a scientific basis. The historical-philosophical method of Hegel he considered a necessary intervening step, but it was the genius of Marx, he argued, that provided 'two great discoveries, the materialistic conception of history and the revelation of the secret of capitalistic production through surplus value. . . . With these discoveries, socialism became a science.'[37] Engels was referring to Marx's monumental three-volume *Das Kapital*, first published in German in 1867, 1885 and 1894 respectively, the final, incomplete volume being edited posthumously by Engels. In this great contribution to socialist thought, Marx reversed the Hegelian philosophy by assigning priority to the material world; although he retained the general notion of some kind of progressive evolution, he saw this as an evolution of man in society rather than of some divine spirit. Marx identified three forms of society – feudal, capitalist and socialist – each with its own characteristic 'mode' of production; the current nineteenth-century mode of production, capitalism, was transitional because it contained the inherent causes of its own decline. In his view, capitalism had separated man into two classes: the capitalists, who own the means of production; and the mass of workers, the proletariat, who are forced to sell their labour for bare subsistence. Everything in a capitalist mode of production exists on a 'commodity' basis, and the sale of these commodities gives wealth to the producers. The proletariat does not share in this wealth; instead, the capitalist class keeps this 'surplus value' as profit which builds up the store of capital. Inherent in this system is the need for capitalist enterprises to grow bigger, to eliminate smaller competition and mechanize their factories increasingly; this in turn widens the gulf between the two classes in a series of confrontations between the frustrated, underprivileged workers and the ever-wealthier and ever-decreasing number of capitalists, until the workers unite, overthrow the system and replace it with a socialist and eventually communist mode of production.

In the second half of the nineteenth century, chiefly as a consequence of Marx's writings, socialism acquired a corpus of 'scientific' and therefore 'respectable' theory; indeed, Engels even claimed that socialism is part of 'the positive science of Nature and history'.[38] The socialist initiative had been checked in the repressive 1850s and thereafter the slower growth of the European economy, which entered a cycle of booms and depressions, forced the socialist movement to proceed more cautiously. In 1875, to consider a new strategy, the German Social Democratic movement sent Marx a provisional outline of its ideas for discussion at a convention to be held in Gotha, near Erfurt. Marx's commentary on the doctrines to be discussed, the *Critique of the Gotha Programme* (1875), was a major document on the organization of the socialist initiative. Here he rejected Owen's doctrine that 'manual labour, properly directed, is the source of all wealth', and asserted emphatically that 'Labour is *not the source* of all wealth. *Nature* is just as much the source of use values . . . as labour, which itself is only the manifestation of a force of nature, human labour power.'[39]

This opening comment is significant in that, while claiming scientific status for his materialist interpretation of history, Marx had diverged from current positivist science, which saw man as external to nature and dominant over it; in Marx's view, complete domination of nature could be achieved only by the proper control of social forces themselves. The relationship between man, nature and production was to become a matter of the greatest importance to subsequent socialist thinking, especially on education. Indeed, in the *Critique of the Gotha Programme* Marx made the observation that socialism needed a moral transformation to become fully effective.

For the final decades of the nineteenth century socialism was chiefly concerned with organizing itself to attain its goals; the ideology was well settled by then and, despite Marx's contempt, utopian socialism remained a major element. Significantly, however, little was said on education, and, although Marx vehemently rejected any dependence on state provisions for schools in the *Critique of the Gotha Programme*, the fact remains that the socialist movement tacitly accepted the steady entry of the state and its continuing enactment of compulsory-schooling laws as well as the correlative provisions of buildings, grants and other aspects of a support system. The socialist preoccupation was with political organization and resources, and, as membership grew rapidly from the increasing number of trade unions, the movement gained in strength and political influence. Trade-unionism could no longer be opposed, except in tsarist Russia, and it was generally free of repressive legislation in most Western nations by the 1880s. Simultaneously, unions became nationally coordinated, in Britain with the first meeting of the Trades Union Congress in 1868, France with the Confédération Générale du Travail of 1895; international organization followed in 1895 with the International Co-operative Alliance and in 1913 the International Federation of Free Trade Unions. By the end of the century socialism had achieved considerable acceptance as it adopted a more moderate programme accommodated within the institutional framework of democratic procedures; one index is the formation in London in 1884 of the socialist Fabian society (named after the Roman general Fabius Maximus Cunctator who defeated the Carthaginians by avoiding pitched battles and so wearing them down) which, based on a policy of gradualism, attracted some of the leading intellectuals of the day: George Bernard Shaw, H. G. Wells and Sidney and Beatrice Webb. Drawn into the socialist camp were many teachers, who organized themselves into unions, for educational progress and equity as well as for professional purposes. Moreover, by the turn of the century socialism as a marginally respectable political ideology gave the impetus to the formation of parliamentary wings, such as the Labour Party of Great Britain, founded in 1906. Throughout Europe socialist parties of various complexions increasingly contested elections and came to form governments as well as vigorous oppositions. This initiative, both formally organized, and informally diffused through the public conscience, began to demand more of schools and the process of education than the minimal provisions for attendance and instruction that the masses were given under the dual systems obtaining in most countries.

Moral regeneration: religion purified

The socialist drive of the nineteenth century had not only to contend with capitalist industry but also to fight against the conservative policies of established churches, usually in league with the bourgeoisie, and the century was marked by a sequence of Europe-wide conflicts as the churches fought to retain authority and their traditional control of education. Anticlericalism was rising in many countries; in Lutheran lands, however, the church was supported as an agent of the state, especially in Sweden, Norway and Denmark. In Germany difficulties came from the Catholic regions, especially since Pope Pius IX had promulgated in 1864 the contentious *Syllabus of Errors* which, in its condemnation of every modern development – liberalism, rationalism, science, the concept of progress, contemporary styles of living – was astonishingly out of touch with the times. In 1870, to override the authority of the bishops who were potentially vulnerable to state dominance or even could be in connivance with government, the same pontiff proclaimed the doctrine of papal infallibility: when pronouncing *ex cathedra* (from the throne, with authority) on Catholic faith and morals, the pope cannot be in error. The implications, even to many devout Catholics, were horrendous; it meant that the coercive moral authority of Rome was now absolute. These developments further heightened tensions and in many cases increased the resolve of states with Catholic populations to curb the authority of that church, now more ultramontanist than ever, particularly with respect to education. In Spain, where by a concordat of 1851 the church had secured the teaching of Catholic doctrine in all schools, secular and parochial, there was little deviation, although liberals resisted the arrogation of such extreme papal authority. In Italy, however, the developing nationalist state annexed the papal territories in 1871; the government of Prime Minister Francesco Crispi, in the period 1887–96, was violently anticlerical and enacted measures to make religious instruction optional in state schools and to curb the activities of the teaching congregations. It was the middle regions of western Europe – France, the Low Countries, Austria-Hungary – where the state–church conflict was greatest. Bismarck's May Laws of 1873–5 put priests under state control; elsewhere prolonged struggles between the emerging liberal, democratic governments and the conservative Catholic Church produced much bitterness and division, which became institutionalized in the growth of religious political parties and laid the foundations for continuing social division, especially in education, well into the twentieth century.

Against this background there were increasing efforts to rise above such conflicts, not by renouncing religious belief, but through attempts to purge religion of its occult and mysterious elements – in effect, to rationalize it so that divisiveness would disappear. In the nineteenth century groups with less concern for scriptural authority became more widely followed, such as the Society of Friends (Quakers) and Unitarians, which had a nominal Christian allegiance, although the latter intellectualized themselves out of any real theological position. In keeping with the increasing secular mood, more 'rational' forms of religious belief were favoured and in the United States the philosopher Ralph Waldo Emerson (1803–82), deeply influenced by the natural philosophy of the English Romantic poets, Coleridge and Wordsworth, promoted transcendentalism, the doctrine that each person contains the entire means of achieving complete religious experience, and that, more important, this is a sufficient guide for ethical conduct. This line of philosophical-ethical-religious theorizing led all the way to the development of agnosticism professed by T. H. Huxley and the deliberative mysticism of William James so well expressed in *The Varieties of Religious Experience*, the Gifford Lectures for 1901–2.

These developments in religious attitude greatly affected education, not only by supporting anticlericalism and the secular-education movement, but also by giving a qualitative element to the counterculture which now sought to find a way between the dogmatic inflexibility of established religion and the extreme godless positivism that characterized so much of science and the associated Herbartianism in education. For many, it was not sufficient for morality, ethics and social values to be tacked on as an afterthought, in the belief that these would somehow emerge in the process. It was unfortunate for the socialist initiative that Marx had so stridently denounced utopianism and had stressed historical materialism; or, at least, that he was interpreted in such a way, especially since his more humanly sensitive writings, chiefly the Paris Manuscripts of 1844, had not become widely disseminated. In this moral vacuum of the late nineteenth century there was a proliferation of efforts across Europe to find a non-dogmatic source of religious values, and none caught on with the same vigour as the new syncretistic movement of Theosophy which symbolized, for many, a promising way forward into the new era and a valid foundation for education and the schools of the future.

Theosophy, meaning 'knowledge of god' (Greek *theos*, god; *sophia*, wisdom), was founded in New York in 1875 by the Russian-born spiritualist Helena Petrovna Blavatsky (1831–91), in association with Colonel H. S. Olcott, as an attempt to realize deeper truths of religious experience than was possible with traditional faiths. By this time, Asia had become much better known to Europeans and the development of new academic disciplines, particularly psychology and anthropology, stimulated by biology, geology and the Darwinian evolutionary ethos, led to the new study of comparative religion which focused upon the systematic classification of the varieties of religious manifestation in so-called primitive cultures as well as advanced ones in order to find interrelationships and, perhaps, universal elements. Madame Blavatsky moved to India in 1878 and re-established the Theosophical Society in Adyar, near Madras, in 1882. The society then burgeoned throughout the Western world with a large number of branches, teaching its composite doctrines, drawn heavily from the Vedic scriptures, of the transmigration of souls, the mystic union of all mankind and the potential validity of all forms of religious experience as they contribute to knowledge of the divine. Sectarianism and dogma were eschewed and Christian revelation was denied. The chief following consisted of avant-garde intellectuals.

After Madame Blavatsky's death the leadership was assumed by Annie Besant who was responsible for much of Theosophy's European success. One of her early associates was Rudolf Steiner (1861–1925), leader of the German branch, who broke away in 1907 and founded in 1913 his own Anthroposophical Society (Greek *anthropos*, man) which, like transcendentalism, looked within man alone for spiritual truth. Near Basle in Switzerland Steiner built a most imposing central headquarters complex known as the Goetheanum (which indicates a *Naturphilosophie* link) and concerned with fostering individual spiritual development. In the early twentieth century, Theosophical and Anthroposophical supporters played a significant part in the new, anti-Herbartian, progressive-education movement; significant, not because of numbers, but because of the spiritual intensity of their efforts. The established churches had become moribund in their educational thought and practice and in the twentieth century, as conditions changed dramatically, the churches, especially the Catholic, became even more reactionary, and educational experiment and innovation were exercised by other groups.

The new science of psychology: physiological origins

While early twentieth-century education was to be greatly influenced by the doctrines of socialism and non-revelatory and ethical religious syncretism, it was also affected by the new science of psychology. Taking its name from the Greek, as did every other new subject that sought academic and intellectual respectablity in the classical revival of the eighteenth and nineteenth centuries, psychology developed as a branch of philosophy, especially through the influence of Kant. The quest was for an understanding of the essential self, as its etymology implies (Greek *psyche*, soul; *logos*, study or science); an alternative term 'pneumatology' (Greek *pneuma*, breath, spirit) fell into disuse after the eighteenth century, although a concern with the nature of the soul and the dualism postulated by classical Greek and later Christian teachings remained central to early psychological thought.

In the nineteenth century the purely verbal, speculative approach of earlier thinkers was supplemented by the beginnings of the experimental, observational method, the pioneers of which were the German scholars Gustav Theodor Fechner (1801–87) and Hermann von Helmholtz (1821–94). Both worked from the biological and physiological standpoint, attempting to relate structure and function, and Fechner in particular, a devotee of *Naturphilosophie*, sought to discover a means whereby the spirit or soul could be accounted for in mechanistic or quantitative concepts, devoting much of his time to the measurement of sensation. Psychology attracted students, and experimental laboratories appeared in increasing numbers, particularly in Germany, where in the later decades of the century the most internationally acclaimed exponent was Wilhelm Wundt (1832–1920), who founded the first specific psychology laboratory, equipped with the growing number of metal measuring instruments, which led to William James's epithet of 'brass-instrument' psychology.

13   Froebel's kindergarten, *c.* 1880.

14 Immigrant children saluting the American flag in the Mott Street Industrial School,
c. 1889.

Wundt's approach, based on dualist presuppositions, was concerned with traditional philosophical issues: the relationship of sense experience to brain activity and the phenomenon of 'mind'; the connections between mind and brain. To gain access to the mind Wundt pioneered the analysis of experiences reported, introspectively, by the subjects under investigation, although his answer to the question of how sensations and perceptions become meaningfully related recalled the speculations of the classical philosophers. Plato had talked of the two processes of the mind, *dianoia* and *noesis*, which give 'intellectual intuition', and Aristotle wrote of 'congenital discriminative capacity',[40] while later explanations, varying from theories of divine illumination to the more mechanistic ideas of La Mettrie, generally suggested some kind of dualism, a ghost within the machine.[41] Wundt described a process called 'creative synthesis'; somehow, he concluded, there are within the mind 'integrative powers' which resolve sensations into emotions and concepts, and he pressed into slightly different usage the term apperception to describe the unknown process by which ideas are brought together into conscious awareness. Now the use of the word 'apperception' recalls the thought of Herbart, which in effect laid the groundwork for a psychology free of faculties. However, with the advent of positivism the 'scientific' educators of the later nineteenth century adapted Herbartianism to include the faculty psychology of Baconian sense-empiricism; and the work of Wundt did not resolve this issue.

In the later decades of the nineteenth century the infant science of psychology gave some attention to education, but the possibilities of any widespread application were not envisaged, the main concern being to solve immediate problems. The original stimulus was given by Édouard Seguin (1812–80), a Paris physician and a Saint-Simonian, and it was his concern for humanity that led him to work in a state hospital with severely mentally defective patients and to attempt by motor training to improve their general effectiveness. His work, an early application of functional psychology, met with a certain limited success. Following Seguin came the widely recognized work of Alfred Binet (1857–1911), a physiologist who became director of the Physiological Psychology Laboratory of the University of Paris. Required to help with the classification of retarded children for medical and educational treatment, he conducted experimental investigations into the thought processes of children and adults and developed scales of mental effectiveness which paved the way for the concept of intelligence testing, a practice first seriously adopted in the

First World War for the screening of recruits to the United States army. The specific psychological study of children, however, was largely the achievement of Granville Stanley Hall (1844–1924), an American who had studied under Wundt.[42] Although a conservative, especially with respect to the education of women, Hall wanted to make a scientific study of the patterns of child growth and development and in 1882 established a child-study laboratory at Johns Hopkins where he was guided by the prior conception of recapitulation (that the individual repeats the evolutionary experience of the human race in his development). Although this theory was later discredited, Hall initiated the child-study movement and upon being appointed President of Clark University in 1889 made this a central feature of the institution. His stimulus marked a significant concern with pursuing child-centred as opposed to school-centred educational procedures. Hall, however, was still a laboratory scientist; the next development was to study the psychology of learning and to relate it to education in real-life contexts.

The new era in sight: Maria Montessori and the progressive movement in Europe

Maria Montessori and the search for a progressive science of education

During those closing decades of the nineteenth century, when educators were seeking to establish a science of education, whether derived from a Herbartianist standpoint or using methods of laboratory 'brass-instrument' psychology, Maria Montessori, who in the twentieth century was to win European and then world acclaim as one of the greatest of both scientific and progressive educators, and who evolved her methods from actual experience in teaching, was receiving her early training. Born in the year that modern Italy was founded, into a well-to-do family in Chiaravalle on the central Adriatic coast, Maria Montessori (1870–1952) went with her parents to live in Rome at the age of twelve and so received her secondary and higher education in the recently designated capital of the new nation. Her interests were human and biological, and so medicine, particularly social medicine, became the focus of her ambition, although no woman had ever been admitted to a medical faculty in an Italian university. After considerable difficulty and much conservative opposition, overcome by useful family connections, she was admitted to the University of Rome from whence she graduated in 1896 as Italy's first woman physician. For the succeeding two years she carried out medical research along with her internship, becoming interested in mental and nervous disorders, especially the new science of anthropology, exemplified in the work of both Lombroso and Sergi at Rome, and concerned with relating bodily structure to mental function. In 1899 she accepted a lecturing appointment in Anthropology and Hygiene at the Royal Women Teachers' College (Regio Istituto di Magistero Femminile) until 1904 when she was appointed Lecturer in Anthropology at the University of Rome, a position she held until 1916. She became interested in the preparation of teachers, which was now a demanding task, since the compulsory-education legislation of 1877 initiated by the *Lex Casati* of 13 November 1859 was intended to force the nation to catch up with the more advanced regions of Europe. In the years 1899–1901 she was also appointed director of the Orthophrenic School, an institution for feeble-minded children in Rome – a position she accepted as part of the social challenge around her, in the same spirit that led her to demand entry for women to medical faculties and to represent Italy at world feminist congresses at Berlin in 1896 and at London in 1900.

Italy in the late nineteenth century was severely handicapped after centuries of disunity and foreign domination; the bulk of the population remained illiterate and the region south of Rome was one of the poorest in Europe. Social issues at the beginning of the century seemed insuperable and, despite massive emigration to the United States and Argentina, the cities of Rome and Naples along with other large centres held huge underprivileged populations in ugly ghettos. In the years 1907–8 Maria Montessori was drawn by her deep concern for social reform to work in one of these, the San Lorenzo quarter of Rome, which had a large, seriously disadvantaged population in abandoned tenement houses, parents unemployed, children unschooled and unruly. In a resettlement plan, the buildings were to be made more habitable and the children given some modest care.

Maria Montessori had already been influenced by Wundt, Seguin and Binet, and had followed Seguin's example while in the Orthophrenic School in Rome treating retarded children by beginning with motor training and attempting thereby to influence mental development. She had also read the work of Giuseppe Sergi, one of her medical professors, entitled *Educazione e Istruzione* (1892), which followed Binet and Wundt and also incorporated the latest data from physiology and anthropology, and her disappointment with this led Montessori to develop her own approach. In San Lorenzo came the chance to apply her methods with the mentally subnormal to 'normal' children; although suffering no obvious physical or intellectual handicaps, these slum children had little of the socialized behaviour that teachers need as a preliminary to classroom instruction. Montessori thereupon used the behaviourist approach of the Orthophrenic School and attempted to teach the children by identifying a number of necessary skills and desirable behaviours and then concentrating on producing these.

From the beginning of the experiment Montessori made major breaks with established practice. Coming to the classroom as a physician and social worker, Montessori had no stereotyped model of traditional teaching behaviour. There was to be no 'school' in the accepted sense in San Lorenzo; instead, learning was to occur in a 'Children's House', Casa dei Bambini, and this was not a periphrastic camouflage: she determined to provide a genuine alternative to the traditional school. The Children's House was designed with smaller-scale furniture and cupboards; the child was not forced to conform to adult sizes; the real-life needs of the children were identified and given age-related gradings. Such simple but necessary tasks as buttoning and lacing their clothes, preparing meals and setting the table were considered essential learning activities. Reading, writing and counting were taught early on, brightly coloured blocks of wood which the child could handle being used for counting; reading began with large alphabetic letter cut-outs which, when memorized, could be arranged in simple words on tables. Montessori started without a clear prior theory, and as a trained medical psychologist proceeded with the primary, manageable tasks demanded of the children by the society in which they were to function. Slowly the exercises were developed and more activities and apparatus added to train the sense perceptions of the child, and what was to become famous as the method of preceding all abstract mental operations with concrete experiential activities (even to the extent of solving quadratic equations on pegboard with large numbers of coloured pegs) was first systematically developed in the Casa dei Bambini at San Lorenzo and, in the years immediately following, at other locations.

Maria Montessori had read exhaustively in the educational literature of Europe from Comenius and Locke to Rousseau, Pestalozzi and Froebel. She was, moreover, a devout Catholic raised within the fold of Thomist orthodoxy and her own thinking was guided by the famous dictum of

Aquinas that 'there is nothing in the intellect that was not first in the senses'. Although she accepted the faculty theory of Aristotle and the modern sense-empiricists, her own inclinations led her in the holist direction and in 1912 she published her first major educational book in this tradition, *Il Metodo della Pedagogia Scientifica applicato all'educazione infantile nelle Case dei Bambini*, translated almost immediately into English as *The Montessori Method: Scientific Pedagogy as Applied to Child Education in the 'Children's Houses'*. The book was a tremendous success and was published in numerous editions, and in more than twenty major world languages, over the ensuing thirty years. This was followed in 1913 by *The Advanced Montessori Method* and in 1914 by *Dr Montessori's Own Handbook*. Her fame spread rapidly and in Italy a society was established by philanthropic liberals, first under the title Amici del Metodo (Friends of the Method), then as Opera Montessori (The Montessori Foundation, or Society), to promote the methods and underlying pedagogical theory in the schools of Italy. Montessori Foundations and Societies appeared throughout Europe and Britain and spread across to America.

Montessori's 'scientific pedagogy'

In the first edition of *Scientific Pedagogy* of 1912, Maria Montessori set out her approach with its assumptions and procedures, which remained essentially unchanged over the ensuing forty years. There is no doctrinaire theory of education; rather, she acknowledged her indebtedness to Rousseau, Pestalozzi and Froebel and sought to develop that holist tradition in twentieth-century terms, using the best available advances in medical and psychological science. It was for this reason that Montessori talked of 'scientific' pedagogy; if not 'brass-instrument' science it was certainly a 'white-coat' approach. This was vividly illustrated by her ready acceptance of an analogy made by the Dutch geneticist Hugo de Vries (1848–1935) who, among other contributions to biology, developed the concept of genetic mutation. On meeting him in Amsterdam in 1917 Montessori was flattered by his suggestion that her approach to the child paralleled aspects of his theory of the development of plants, and she continued to quote de Vries, and use his analogy, throughout her life. In understanding this biological approach it is important to remember that Montessori followed in the tradition established by Rousseau; like him, she saw the adult enfolded within the child and capable of either good or ill depending upon the experiences of childhood and adolescence. Like

Rousseau, Montessori accepted the European cultural tradition that the cultivated adult is the goal of all educational procedures, the aim being to help the child arrive at this final state of civilized adulthood as comfortably and easily as possible. Her writings all bear this imprint: she habitually spoke of the child as a developing organism following innate natural laws, of processes of continuous and intense transformation as the child struggles to realize its latent adulthood. Within the child, on the basis of her observations and analysis, she postulated a fund of self-generating activity manifested in streams of mental and physical energy. The child was conceptualized, however, not as a miniature adult, but as a different being, an incomplete personality that struggles – even if unaware of the end result – to realize its latent potentialities. She used the biologist's concepts of saltation and metamorphosis, the former (from the Latin *saltatio*, a dance, or leaping movement) indicating sudden spurts of growth whether physical or mental, the latter describing the profound changes that result, such as puberty. She frequently referred to the child as an 'absorbent being' that readily soaks up the experiences of the environment and incorporates them within its personality. By contrast she saw the adult world (in the manner of a taxonomically trained scientist) as ordered, systematic and desirable; knowledge for her, as Thomism taught, is awareness and understanding of the connections of external events, for she held to a correspondence theory of truth. The newly born child has no innate ideas or knowledge but only the capacity to learn and to actualize its potential, and the task of education is to provide the most favourable conditions for this.

Two fundamental assumptions determine the entire process of education in Montessori's view: first, the necessary goal of every child is entry into the realm of knowledge, designated as 'culture'; second, human culture is best acquired through natural processes of biological and psychological growth, development and maturation. The science of pedagogy is therefore derived, she argued, from knowing the nature of the child and adolescent and assisting it to follow its natural processes in the most positive and rewarding relationship possible as culture is acquired. All education should assist this; the school and the formal curriculum should consist of specific, intentional activities designed to secure such educational attainment. The classroom, then, assumes crucial significance; it is, in effect, what Montessori termed a 'prepared environment' in which positive learning takes place. Its activities must always lead to the realization of potential; as we fail to learn, so comes the natural punishment which she defined in *Scientific Pedagogy* as the loss of 'the consciousness of [our] own power and greatness, which constitute the quality of manhood'.[43]

Maria Montessori did not enter into the philosophical debates about the relation of metaphysics and epistemology to education. She was trained, as a scientist, in the late nineteenth-century tradition of sense-empiricism and accepted this, with reservations. While she did not criticize the theory that sense impressions are organized into a coherent pattern of knowledge by the powers of the mind, she did, of course, object to a materialistic interpretation and always brought to bear a social, even socialist, conscience, asserting that science alone, in a narrow positivist sense, offers no real solutions; true science, she said, must go beyond 'mechanism' – that is, the routine application of knowledge – to a spiritual approach in which the scientist is required to find 'a way leading to an understanding of the profound truths of life, . . . [of finding] out how to raise the veil covering its fascinating secrets'.[44] In practice, this meant that the teacher must attempt to understand the complexities of the child's unsteady, but dynamic, growth to adulthood. The child's restless urge to grow means that it already possesses the drive to know, to compare, to classify, to judge, the impulse of endless curiosity and the quest for independence. The pedagogical task is to structure the classroom as a prepared environment within which order, and hence meaning, can be given to the child's existing experiences and impressions. Since the curriculum too must always anticipate the child's innate impulses, it must be worked out well in advance as a series of developmental tasks that will, with the best of timing, enable the child to achieve the necessary growth and hence success. The teacher is not in any strict sense a 'teacher'; rather, Montessori always considered the teacher to be a director of learning experiences, and, since she regarded it chiefly as a woman's occupation and was a staunch and active campaigner for women's emancipation, the usual Italian term in her works is *direttrice*, 'directress'.

An essential part of the prepared environment and the anticipatory curriculum is the range of educative materials. These were developments of the Pestalozzian *Anschauung* objects and the Froebelian 'gifts', with the difference that Montessori demystified them. For Pestalozzi the grammars of form, language and number have a spiritual dimension; for Froebel the 'gifts' are mystically charged. Like Froebel's gifts, the Montessori materials are objects to be handled, but they have no mystic significance in themselves; they are purely the means to understanding and effectively engaging in the external world. So the Montessori materials include a vast range of objects, chiefly made of wood (plastic in modern versions), which the child must use as part of the learning sequences. Coloured blocks, counters, beads, building kits, rods and pegboard shapes are all to be available to help the child count and develop concepts of numeracy; they also provide opportunities for creative play. Reading and writing are preceded by having the child handle alphabetic cut-out letters. The materials should also include everyday objects; at lunchtime, for example, the children should set the table with real cutlery and dishes, and they should wash up afterwards – all in the spirit of Pestalozzi's *Leonard and Gertrude*. The classroom must always contain stimulating apparatus, objects, toys and literature in order to capitalize on the child's inner, irrepressible drives to be active, to learn about and cope with the adult world. Montessori strenuously objected to her materials being considered mere toys; certainly they may provide fun in their handling and may be used for recreational play; they must, however, always have as their *raison d'être* a potential for assisting learning. The director of learning must constantly monitor the child's growth and development by providing the appropriate materials, and be ever alert to the imminence of saltation, watching for what Montessori called 'sensitive periods' (a term she adopted from de Vries) when a sudden jump or spurt of development in a new direction occurs.

The method is totally child-centred, and Montessori even considered her approach to be one of liberating children as an 'oppressed class';[45] she was, consequently, charged with neglecting the social and moral development of the child. In the newly formed Soviet Union of the early 1920s the Montessori method was rejected for this reason; in his *Education in Soviet Russia* of 1926 Scott Nearing reported that Montessori was spurned by the Russians because they claimed that in their new socialist utopia 'the [educational] material selected comes from the community and not a cupboard'.[46] For her part, Maria Montessori argued that social growth occurs when children interact in the prepared environment of the classroom. She believed in an age range of several years in each class so that the older children could assist the younger ones with the materials, the older ones giving the benefit of experience, the younger ones learning that cooperation requires seeking assistance as well as giving it. Moreover, if the classroom environment is challenging and stimulates the child, social and moral growth are fostered, as learners seek to solve problems collectively. As far as possible all learning should proceed by discovery methods and even though the adult teacher knows the answers in advance this does not lessen the excitement the child feels when it solves problems on its own or as a member of a cooperating group.

Despite the rejection of the Montessori method by the Soviet Union, it swept the globe in the years after the First World War. In 1919 Montessori visited London, was honoured with a civic reception and gave a teacher-training course which she repeated every second year in England until the outbreak of the Second World War. Britain was particularly impressed by her pedagogy; in 1923 the University of Durham awarded her an honorary doctorate in philosophy; George V received her at Buckingham Palace in 1927. In her native Italy, the Minister for Public Instruction, the philosopher Giovanni Gentile, recommended her method in 1923 to the newly ascendant Mussolini who made it the standard method of all Italian schools. In Austria, where societies established the *Haus der Kinder* on the model of the Casa dei Bambini, it spread rapidly. Even in Australia the method was officially adopted for state infants' schools in New South Wales. In the United States there was tremendous initial enthusiasm; as early as 1913 she was invited by Alexander Graham Bell, whose wife was president of the newly formed Montessori Educational Association of America, to settle in the United States and propagate her method; however, despite her enthusiastic reception there, she returned to Europe. Societies sprang up everywhere in Europe, especially in Holland and Scandinavia; they appeared in Africa, India, Japan and South America, and in 1929 the Vatican officially approved her method, thereby encouraging its adoption by Catholic schools and teachers' colleges. At the same time, a wider movement was developing and established the International Montessori Congress, which acted as the periodical convention of the various national societies. The congress met around the world: Helsinki in 1925; Nice, 1932; Amsterdam, 1933; Rome, 1934; Oxford, 1936; Copenhagen, 1937; Edinburgh, 1938. Yet in the turbulent 1930s the Montessori system was also attacked: in 1933 the Nazis closed all such schools in Germany, the Fascists followed suit in Italy in 1934, and Spain in 1936; Austria was forced to close the schools in 1938 after the Nazi occupation. After the war, Montessori continued to receive wide international recognition, especially in Europe, India and Pakistan, receiving a standing ovation when she addressed UNESCO in 1949; in the same year the French awarded her the Legion of Honour and she was nominated for the Nobel Peace Prize, and was nominated again in 1950 and 1951. She died in 1952.[47]

Maria Montessori had a profound influence on education in the twentieth century, especially in Europe, where she represented a continuation of the best in the bourgeois tradition, carrying forward the ideas of Comenius, Rousseau, Pestalozzi and Froebel that were cherished as major advances in educational thought and practice. She did not seriously challenge those values; rather, possessed of a sense of the need for social reform, she worked from within the system. Earlier, in 1918, Pope Benedict XV wrote a commendatory foreword to a new edition of *Scientific Pedagogy*, which included an apostolic benediction, and the method thereby gained wide acceptance in Catholic lands and provided the Catholic Church with a modern approach to education. Her method seemed to meet the new demands for a human interpretation of scientifically based education, and its inclusion of non-empirical values gave it an appeal not only to Catholicism but to other religious sects as well as to Theosophists, humanists and even agnostics. At the same time, the circumstances were propitious in that the nations of Europe were expanding their educational systems and there was great pressure for humanitarian and scientifically valid approaches. Not that her work was universally acclaimed: apart from the totalitarian objections on the grounds that her method made children too individualistic, it was criticized in the United States by progressives too. Yet the method offered a major and more attractive alternative to the prevailing Herbartianism. Clearly, as large state educational enterprises had to be constructed and teachers trained *en masse*, the Montessori system, which stressed the role of the child as active learner and the teacher as director of learning experiences, seemed infinitely more attractive to most progressives than the Herbartian system which stressed the role of the teacher as expositor and the child as dependent memorizer.

Europe: the independent progressive movement

Throughout the 1920s and 1930s Maria Montessori was, for many, the chief exponent of European progressive education. Certainly she was the best known and most popularly followed, as Montessori teachers' colleges – state, Catholic and private – were founded by the score and her many pedagogical books, all redevelopments of the original theme of *Scientific Pedagogy*, became virtually undisputed manuals of progressive instruction. Yet this recognition should not detract from the widespread resolve of many others to reconstruct the school and even, perhaps, society. In the years leading up to the First World War there were very few progressive schools in Europe; most were in England, where middle-class enthusiasm for voluntary provisions favoured the multiplication of independent schools which, if privately owned rather than the instruments of a church or society, could engage in progressive activities. The chief constraint was finding parents who sought a progressive school and were prepared to pay the necessarily expensive fees. Almost inevitably such schools were fully residential, and this kept their costs high; the early progressive schools of Europe therefore reached only a small group; the children of relatively well-to-do, avant-garde parents. In several cases, some parents who could not find a suitable school started one of their own, as did the philosopher and radical activist Bertrand Russell with his second wife wife Dora at Beacon Hill between 1927 and 1932, Dora continuing it alone after that. The history of Western education is in large part the record of creative innovation in the face of a conservative tradition, and it is in this light that the schools of Basedow, Pestalozzi, Fellenberg and Froebel must be interpreted; by the end of the nineteenth century and the beginning of the twentieth, however, progressivism became more urgent as the state increasingly legislated school codes, levied taxes, provided schools and trained teachers. In Britain, it was the advent of state intervention and a bourgeois fear of proletarian anarchy, as Matthew Arnold expressed it in 1869 in *Culture and Anarchy*, that stimulated many progressive education ventures.

European progressivism did not grow out of socialism, Marxism or other working-class movements; rather, it developed chiefly from those sections of society concerned with religious and spiritual renewal who saw possibilities that might be incorporated from aspects of socialist and scientific thought. Generally, by the end of the century, labour and socialist movements preferred to work through the provisions made by the state, and modern progressive-school origins are to be found in a very small number of private ventures, mainly in England, of which the most prominent was Abbotsholme in Derbyshire, founded in 1889 by Cecil Reddie (1858–1932).[48] Reddie was originally a socialist who in 1883 had joined a radical society known as the Fellowship of the New Life, and Abbotsholme was projected as an ideal school to implement the anarcho-socialist ideals of the Fellowship; by the time it eventuated, however, Reddie had renounced socialism. The school flourished, as did the Bedales School founded in 1893 by one of Reddie's teachers, John Badley. These two, and a few other schools such as Alexander Devine's Gordon Boys' Home at Manchester and Badminton Park Girls' School at Bristol, made up the total of visibly prominent progressive schools in England at the turn of the century. They were all in startling contrast to the prevailing schools – the private and endowed preparatory and grammar schools with their hierarchical codes of authority and massive deference to a traditional curriculum and pedagogy; or the state board schools with their meagre utilitarian curriculum taught by the Herbartian method (if they were fortunate), with some attempted leavening of the lower grades with a weak, little-understood following of the Froebelian kindergarten. The few innovative schools were progressive because they stressed individualized learning with considerable practical activity such as shopwork, excursions, library and laboratory lessons, while the teachers were expected to exercise a supervisory role of caring for and nurturing the psychological growth of each child. The pupils, for their part, were given the opportunity to discuss the school's procedures with the staff and, to a limited extent, participate in school government. There was, however, no serious questioning of the curriculum itself, nor of the traditional goals of middle-class accomplishment set out so persuasively in Rousseau's *Émile* and sustained as an ideal thereafter. Montessori provided a twentieth-century modernization of that early progressive doctrine.

Continental copies of Abbotsholme were carried into Germany by Hermann Lietz (d. 1919), who established three boys' *Landerziehungsheimen* – country boarding schools – between 1901 and 1904, for six- to twelve-year-olds at Ilsenburg, for thirteen- to sixteen-year-olds at Haubinda, and for seniors, sixteen to nineteen, at Bieberstein.[49] These expanded to eight schools in time, and his teachers moved on to found their own schools on this model which, like Abbotsholme, stressed individual instruction and, in particular, the project system. Innovating masters founded further schools on what became known as the 'English model' in Holland, Belgium, Switzerland, Germany and France, although in France there were very few of distinction, perhaps only the École des Roches.

Meanwhile other activists were turning to social reform by means of education, one of the most prominent being Mrs Beatrice Ensor, an inspector of girls' 'domestic science' schools who around 1911 helped organize a group of reformers. The publication of Montessori's *Scientific Pedagogy* in 1912 provided the group with considerable stimulus and they assumed the title New Ideals in Education; chapters quickly formed and in 1914 their first annual conference was held, continuing until stopped by the war in 1939. Simultaneously, Beatrice Ensor was a member of the Theosophical Society and was responsible for having it organize a section known as the Theosophical Fraternity in Education, which was to be affiliated with New Ideals in Education and was to propagate Montessori doctrines. The Theosophical Society established a number of such progressive schools, beginning with the Arundale School in London in 1915, although after Mrs Ensor's resignation from the Theosophical Society in 1925 they faded from the innovative scene. The Theosophists, however, made yet another major contribution to progressive education by means of Rudolf Steiner, who, after founding his own Anthropo-sophical Society, published in 1914 a short treatise *The Education of the Child in the Light of Anthroposophy* and in 1919 opened his first school, the Freie Waldorfschule near Stuttgart.[50] This rapidly achieved distinction and attracted many students, 1000 in the first five years; this and further foundations flourished until suppressed in 1938 by the Nazis. After the war they were reopened and today there are over 200 Steiner schools throughout the world.

There were, in addition, numerous other progressive movements and schools in Europe in the 1920s and 1930s, most of which were distingui-shed by some particular characteristic, such as Franz Čizek's school in Vienna which attempted to provide a complete education on the basis of free expression in art and craft activities, also closed by the Nazis in 1938; there was the equally specialized approach of the Eurythmic movement founded by Jacques Dalcroze which sought to educate through the medium of expressive action. In 1921 the Dalcroze school in Hellerau, a suburb of Dresden, was visited by Alexander Sutherland Neill (1883–1973) who wished to study this new approach based upon arts, craft, music and dance; upon, that is, the principle of making education grow out of creative engagement with meaningful activities. In 1923 the Dalcroze school moved to Sonntagberg in Vienna and Neill returned to England, where he opened England's most controversial progressive school, Summerhill, at Lyme Regis on the south coast; in 1927 it moved to Leiston, in Suffolk, where Neill conducted it until his death in 1973. Neill's school was distinguished chiefly by its attempts to establish a high degree of student involvement in school government and decision making, this having been exemplified earlier in the Little Commonwealth school near Dorchester run by Homer Lane for a group of philanthropists headed by the Earl of Sandwich.[51] Lane, an American, had been associated with the earlier work of student self-government conducted in Detroit by W. R. George with juvenile delinquents, and known as the Junior

Republic movement. Equally specialized was the school for young children established in the disused Malting House at Cambridge in 1924 by Susan Isaacs, who offered a psychologically based approach as an alternative to that of Montessori.

These many efforts, of which only a few of the more prominent are catalogued here, were not completely random but came together in a worldwide movement, formally initiated in 1921 as the New Education Fellowship. The origins of this were also with Beatrice Ensor, who founded in 1920, within the framework of the Theosophical Fraternity in Education, a journal (of which Neill was an early assistant editor), *Education for the New Era*, which carried as its subtitle *An International Quarterly Journal for the Promotion of Reconstruction in Education*. In that optimistic early post-war period, when the League of Nations was seeking to promote international harmony, fourteen nations were represented at the foundation conference in Calais; Maria Montessori and A. S. Neill attended. The journal *Education for the New Era* was adopted as one of three publications sponsored by the NEF, the others being the French *Pour l'Ère Nouvelle* and the German *Das werdende Zeitalter*, although Germany was excluded from participating at Calais. The NEF spread around the world to twenty-eight countries in the 1920s, and efforts were made to hold bi- or triennial conferences.

Throughout the 1920s the NEF promoted the goals of progressive child-centred education and the Montessori approach in particular; later in the decade the NEF, owing to the Montessori stimulus, increasingly became concerned with the impact on education of the new science of psychology as a growing volume of psychological literature, still chiefly laboratory-based, became available. The Great Depression of 1929 and the rise of fascism in Italy and Germany, and Stalinist terror in the Soviet Union, checked the progressive movement considerably; there was a worldwide reaction against what was increasingly seen as indulgent permissiveness in an era racked by poverty, disease, inequality and incipient world war. The NEF reacted defensively by modifying its aims. Whereas at the Calais conference of 1921 the list of aims stressed 'supremacy of the spirit', individuality, innate interests, individual and social responsibility, cooperation, coeducation, worthy citizenship and individual dignity,[52] the 1932 conference at Nice listed concern for 'the complexities of our times', the operation of social and economic forces in human affairs, the 'emotional and intellectual needs of different children', social life and cooperation, national heritage and human culture.[53] By then the West was in turmoil and progressivism was increasingly checked. The dreams of social reconstruction turned sour as totalitarian systems took control in Italy, Spain, Germany, Austria and the Soviet Union, and the West moved inexorably towards the war which was the complete negation of everything progressive education stood for.

CHAPTER 12

The New Era in Education: II. Progressivism in the United States

A radical American philosophy: John Dewey and the doctrine of experimentalism

The progressive movement in Europe was basically individual and voluntary, pursued by enthusiastic reformers in private schools supported by various kinds of philanthropic foundations, societies and committees, while at a more general level it came together in the loose confederation of the New Education Fellowship. The movement had no common philosophy, nor did it seek to make radical changes to the existing conceptions of knowledge, and, while it drew inspiration from the socialist tradition, both 'utopian' and 'scientific', aided by religious and scientific movements, it did not challenge the concept of bourgeois culture. In *Culture and Anarchy* Matthew Arnold had expressed the same convictions as James Mill earlier in the century: the middle class is the bearer of real culture; it is the repository of 'the best which has been thought and said' in the world and which leads us to pursue perfection. So reform of society is a process of striving towards gradual inner educative development.

Simultaneously, in the United States, progressive approaches to education were being developed which took a quite different turn, and it is misleading to refer to the European and American movements as 'progressive' without being aware that these terms have quite different connotations. The American approach was founded on a totally different philosophy which rejected the correspondence theory of truth and belief in a fixed external world; it was, moreover, first propagated by university professors and then taken up by teachers and their professional associations in the public scools. Its aim was the radical transformation of society. There were many devoted enthusiasts, of whom two were dominant, William James and John Dewey, although their efforts depended upon the support of the teachers, who formed in 1919 a Progressive Education Association that paralleled the New Education Fellowship. In the 1920s and 1930s the progressive movement in America strongly influenced educational development.

Holist psychology applied to education: contribution of William James

American progressivism, like that of Europe, began with a great psychologist, although one of entirely different temperament and intellectual cast from Maria Montessori. This was William James (1842–1910), whose two-volume *Principles of Psychology* (1890) was a radical departure from the European school in which he had been trained and made a tremendous impact by providing a modern, persuasive interpretation, in psychological terms, of the holist thought of the early nineteenth-century philosophers and educators, and, surprising as it may seem, of aspects of Herbart himself. Born in New York City, James came from a comfortable family and studied medicine at Harvard. He was not drawn to practise as a physician, however; the laboratory was his interest, with anatomy, physiology and psychology the chief areas that attracted him, and his professional life was spent teaching at Harvard.

James has to be understood in relationship not only to the developing science of psychology but also to changes in philosophical thought in the late nineteenth century. The emerging studies of evolutionary theory applied to biology, geology and anthropology stressed the principles of relativism and impermanence in all earthly processes, and the cherished belief in the stability of both the social and natural orders of existence increasingly gave way to more limited conceptions of 'permanence'; life was being reassessed as a moving continuum of change. Such an attitude was further reinforced when in physics the entire framework of Newtonian 'absolute' laws and eternal principles was challenged by the notion of relativism introduced by the Michelson-Morley experiments in the United

States, in 1881, on the velocity of light rays. These stimulated a succession of explanations, issuing in Einstein's *General Theory of Relativity* of 1915 which showed, among other things, that mass varies with velocity and that, even in physics, there are no independent absolutes. These issues, meanwhile, were receiving philosophical consideration in the work of Charles Sanders Peirce (1839–1914), an American eccentric who worked chiefly for the United States Coastal and Geodetic Survey. Son of the nation's foremost mathematician of the day, Professor Benjamin Peirce of Harvard, Charles Sanders, much to his own disappointment, never held an academic position. Nor did he publish much; most of his influence came from discussions and letters and occasional learned papers. After his death his scattered documents were brought together, beginning in 1931, as the *Collected Papers of Charles Sanders Peirce* and *Chance, Love and Logic*, and from the 1930s onwards his thought had increasing impact. In his own day, he corresponded consistently with James, and it was Peirce's philosophical interpretation of the new conceptions of relativity that provided the stimulus for many of James's writings.

Peirce's central idea appears in the *Collected Papers* in the passage,

> Consider what effects, that might conceivably have practical bearings, we conceive the object of our conception to have. Then, our conception of these effects is the whole of our conception of the object.[1]

Written in 1878, this pronouncement had a major impact upon Western thought in that it seemed to rule out metaphysical considerations, putting stress upon the observation of effects or consequences. Peirce used the Greek word *pragma*, meaning a 'deed' or 'act', in the name of his new philosophy – pragmatism (the doctrine that valid knowledge comes only from consequences of actions). Knowledge, he held, is constituted only by the pattern of relationships obtaining in any given situation; there can be no external reality that a situation reflects, nor is there any antecedent truth that events confirm; there can only be the flux, or continuum, of acts, which we observe and on which we make temporary judgements, relative to that moment. Such, at least, was the interpretation given to Peirce's new ideas by James, even though Peirce was apparently not trying to construct a full philosophical system but, in effect, merely a logic, initiating what later became the movement of linguistic analysis – that is, the clarification of ideas by concentrating upon the statements made about objects and their observable consequences.[2] James appropriated the doctrines as a new philosophy, much to Peirce's annoyance, and published them in

Pragmatism: A New Name for Old Ways of Thinking in 1907, not, however, before Peirce had disowned James's interpretation and coined the new term 'pragmaticism' to distinguish his system of logic from the Jamesian interpretation. James's ideas prevailed, however, and he gave the alternative name of 'radical empiricism' to his interpretation of knowledge as coming only from observed consequences, and therefore as relative to, and valid only for, specific situations. In 1912, two years after his death, James's collected thoughts on consciousness and experience were published as *Essays in Radical Empiricism*.

Both Peirce and James were responding to the late nineteenth-century questions: given the advance of science, where then do values reside? what can we make of the earth and ourselves? how can truth and knowledge be identified in a universe if it is in ever-changing, impermanent, unknowable flux? James made a challenging, affirmative stand, and, since he continually developed his theories over the years, the following outline of his position is a composite portrait, drawn from his views on religion, psychology and philosophy. Central to all his work is the descriptive approach; only by the careful analytic description of events, he argued, can any essential understanding be reached. Beginning with his first major work, the *Principles of Psychology*, James rejected the dualisms of the past, asserting that there are neither dualisms nor pluralities in the world; there is only one interrelated continuum of experience of which each of us is self-consciously aware. There is neither mind nor body, subject nor object, except as linguistic descriptions of the temporary focus of awareness. Certainly we give these focuses names, both of objects and conditions, but to give a name is an act of linguistic convenience. The words 'rain' or 'snow' or 'hail' indicate, not separate realities, but useful descriptions of transient and continuous phenomena. So, further, we describe ourselves, and we must be careful of using inherited (that is, historical) terms such as body and mind, and the concepts they describe, as if they were realities. Where does body end and mind start? We can know, he argued, only our own mental states, always changing, idiosyncratic and selective, and these only by introspection. Thinking itself is no disembodied act of an ethereal 'mind'; on the contrary, it is the functioning of a whole person. In so writing, he moved away from the fashionable structural or physiological psychology towards an uncompromising functionalism. James believed that there is more to man than mere automatic mechanism, and he sought that leading force.

In the 1890s, then, James became interested in the qualitative aspect, or imperative, of life. If we can know for certain only our introspective states as we experience the continuum of events (that is, the realm of experience), then traditional metaphysical and religious explanations are unacceptable because they are simply historically conditioned sequences of linguistic labels. Yet, if we deny mechanism, or dualism, there must be *some* imperative, and in a celebrated essay of 1897 entitled *The Will to Believe* James postulated something close to an absolute: the force within each person that makes us deny mechanism and assert our moral will. Each person, he said, necessarily has a 'will-to-believe', an attribute that provides a motive for action and engagement with the experiential continuum. (Upon hearing of this, Peirce, in a letter to James, described the concept as 'suicidal'.[3]) James pursued the idea as the only consistently acceptable course open to man and examined it more thoroughly in *The Varieties of Religious Experience*, published in 1902. Again the descriptive method is used to impressive effect. All societies, he wrote, appear to have experiences that can be termed 'religious', but if we are to understand such experiences they must be divested of ancillary features: historical accretions, ritualized liturgy and fossilized dogmas. Ultimately, of course, this search for an inner essence led to very little except the intuition that there is a something to life greater than a mechanistic explanation, and, while James would have denied a ghost in the machine, he maintained that the totality of experience and our own understanding of experience require us to exercise the will-to-believe that an inexpressible infinite exists.

The core of James's philosophy, then, was in the notion of experience as the central, knowable reality, and it was to this end that he appropriated Peirce's pragmatism. So he denied the correspondence theory of truth which holds that our experiences become true as they correspond to an external, objective world. James turned that theory around and asserted that, if anything, it is the external world that should correspond to our experience of events. That is, man's experience, always of the moment, contains truth; and such 'truth' is obviously not some reified concept such as Platonic 'justice' but, literally, the verification of experience. As has often been said of his approach, there is no such thing as abstract truth; there can only be concrete instances of verification or 'truth-making'. In 1904, in his essay *Does Consciousness Exist?*, his various ideas were synthesized into something approaching a general theory. There are, he continued to assert, no parts of anything, no external qualities or separate perceptions: there is only the realm of pure experience, the totality of possible events of the universe to which we have access as wholes. Our consciousness may abstract linguistic labels, and an apple, for example, may be seen as red and round, felt as a mass, tasted as a sweet fruit and chewed with a kinaesthetic awareness, but each of these is only a transient focusing on one aspect or feature, not in any sense an independent part, of what is an indivisible whole. His philosophy was firmly based on a belief in a holist experiential nature in which, with a will-to-believe, we can enjoy life as an aesthetic and moral quest.

Apart from challenging both unthinking, conservative religious interpretations, as well as the nihilistic, mechanist explanations of scientific positivism, James offered an entirely new conception of education, which is implicit in all his writings, and which, as a retrospective of a set of lectures first delivered to an audience of teachers in Cambridge, Massachusetts, in 1892, he set down in print as *Talks to Teachers* in 1899. The book was an overwhelming success and came as a timely counter to the rising tide of Herbartianism. *Talks to Teachers* draws together all James's ideas into a specifically pedagogical focus, and it must have been a stimulating and encouraging message for teachers perplexed by the growing attempts to make education a science, with pedagogy its technology. There is, he said, no science *per se* of education; rather, 'psychology is a science, and teaching is an art; and sciences never generate arts directly out of themselves. An intermediary inventive mind must make the application, by using its originality.'[4] The stimulus to teachers was the awareness of their creative role. Following his psychological theory, James posited the 'stream of consciousness' as the essential aspect of the child; the total child comes to school, he wrote, and is in constant motion as its consciousness directs activity. The school's task, therefore, is to harness that activity, or behaviour, towards positive, morally good ends which come together in the ultimate value of freedom.[5] Education should produce the free personality, which is characterized by as complete a cultivation of the will as possible. He was in total opposition to the system of latter-day Herbartianism in which the child's will was bent to meet the needs of pre-existing correspondence theories of knowledge, reality and morality.

The pedagogical procedures he suggested were, of course, more demanding on the teacher. Having denounced rote learning – and he criticized both English and German schools for their preoccupation with narrowly conceived conformity – James asserted that education really 'consists in the organizing of *resources* in the human being, of powers of conduct which shall fit him to his social and physical world'.[6] This means that teaching is fundamentally concerned with helping the child to develop a wide receptivity to the experiences around him, to appreciate the significance of these and their potential interrelationships. There is, then, an important shift of emphasis; teaching is not the imparting of facts and pre-existent paradigms of knowledge, no matter how skilfully organized; it is, instead, the guidance of the total behaviour of the reacting child. Everything, said James, is reaction to the continuum of experience; the child, then, must be helped to organize his reactions so that they come together as good habits, and habits James defined as 'tendencies to act characteristically when certain ideas possess us, and to refrain character- istically when possessed by other ideas'.[7] That is, to act with a moral will; and this involves the search 'to find the right idea or conception for the case'.[8] The good educational environment is therefore one in which the learner is assisted to see the realm of experience, and his own involvement therein, as a unity; reaction means learning to organize one's stream of consciousness so that all possible ramifications of actions are appreciated, alternative choices considered, and appropriate responses made, based upon a decision as to the best conception for the case. It was, of course, a nature-based, holist view of education providing a means of intelligent interaction with experience; it was completely hostile to Herbartianism, which analysed the external world into a series of logically structured 'facts' to be learned. James was also opposed to the Montessori method, which assumes a fixed external world.

To help teachers understand his approach James provided an inter- mediate model, not of the mind, but of the thinking processes. The individual's stream of consciousness at any given moment, in his view, comes to a temporary focus as impressions are assessed in their mutual relationships; clearly, we attend to these as a total act of thinking and responding behaviour, and to describe this he used the traditional term 'association'. He even used the word 'faculties' to refer to the powers of dynamic association. Indeed, it is impossible to talk about mental behaviour without using such terms as mind, memory, cognition, faculty, idea, association, and so on; it is, however, quite faulty, he argued, to reify these because of their linguistic labels. Such terms should always be used with caution, not as denoting separate pre-existent entities, of which 'mind' is the most dangerous, but as ways of referring to active processes. So, he emphasized, 'The "faculty" of memory is thus no real or ultimate explanation; for it is itself explained as a result of the association of ideas.'[9] The most that James would do was to stress the role of association which is, ultimately, controlled by the will-to-believe. We can learn nothing about education, or teaching, he stressed, from the contemporary fad for 'scientific or brass-instrument child-study' in which many enthusiasts – and G. S. Hall must have been in his mind – 'are taking accurate measurements of children's elementary faculties' by exhibiting to the child 'a series of letters, syllables, figures, pictures, or whatnot, at intervals of one, two, or three seconds', and, as a result of the tabulation of statistical compilations, produce a rating scale against which an individual mind may be assessed 'according to the strength or feebleness of its faculty as thus made known'. And to stress his holist conception of learning he wrote, in the same context, 'Now I can only repeat here what I said to you when treating of attention: man is too complex a being for light to be thrown on his real efficiency by measuring any one mental faculty taken apart from its consensus in the working whole.'[10] The educational need, he went on, is to realize that in real life we are always engaged in total situations, hardly ever in exercises such as those in the child-study laboratory with its concentration upon 'incoherent and insipid objects'.

James was not an educator; his task as a psychologist in these lectures was to show how education and teaching might fruitfully be approached. He stimulated the new educational movement of applied pragmatism, known as experimentalism (of which John Dewey was to be the major exponent), and, consequently, greatly influenced the progressive-education movement of the first half of the twentieth century. In the work of William James the utopian movement of the nineteenth century in its manifold diversity reached a brilliant summation, for he brought together much of the intellectual questing of that era, uniting in a superb synthesis the philosophical, religious and scientific impulses to achieve greater human and social effectiveness. William James's influence upon education has been profound, not the least because he sustained the link with holism and the conception of education as intelligent response to a total interconnected universe within which we have all of our manifest, and possible, existence.

American reactions to Herbartianism

The ordered conception of the world, transmitted by the newly developed Herbartianist pedagogy, then, was challenged in the 1890s at the same time that it was enjoying its greatest vogue. Herbartianism seemed to be sweeping everything before it, and in that last decade neither Peirce nor James had made any perceptible impact upon the schools. The various

Herbart societies in Germany were reflected in the Herbart Club established in the United States in 1892, which was reconstituted as the National Herbart Society, issuing its first Year Book in 1895; and in 1902, as the ultimate expression of the scientific movement, it adopted the grand title of the National Society for the Scientific Study of Education. In 1909 it was to drop the word 'scientific' from its title as the earlier enthusiasm for precision began to wane under various attacks, beginning with those of Joseph Rice and culminating in the work of John Dewey.

This campaign was directed against the continuation of nineteenth-century repressive classrooms, as caricatured in Charles Dickens's *Hard Times*. In setting up as a paediatrician, Joseph Rice went to Jena and Leipzig in the years 1888–90 to study pedagogical theory and what he saw appalled him; in 1892, back home, he accepted a commission from *The Forum*, a New York magazine, to write on American education. To gather information for this, he visited thirty-six cities and held discussions with 1200 teachers, and in the process discovered that those Dickensian tormentors of childhood, Gradgrind and M'Choakumchild, were alive and well and oppressing a wide spectrum of America's children, as exemplified in the statement of one school principal that children were not to turn their heads in class for the reason: 'Why should they look behind when the teacher is in front of them?'[11] Rice's articles were read with enthusiasm, sales of *The Forum* rose rapidly, and the American public, as well as its teachers, became increasingly aware that the scientific millennium had not yet been achieved, nor was the Herbartian pedagogy to usher in any utopia.

Questioning the tradition: the school as a social laboratory

In this period the opposition advanced by William James was being more systematically developed by John Dewey (1859–1952) who, throughout the early decades of the twentieth century, was to dominate much educational thought in the United States and to achieve international recognition and acclaim as the chief architect of the concept of social reconstruction. Born in Burlington, in rural Vermont, John Dewey received the usual middle-class education of the period, including classics, and for his liberal arts degree at the University of Vermont he studied, among other subjects, both Latin and Greek. Given the classical revival of the century, and the dominance of German philosophical idealism, he also came into close contact with Hegelian philosophy and courses in the history of Western civilization. Upon graduation in 1879 he taught in a Pennsylvania high school for two years and then, in 1882, enrolled for graduate studies in the still-innovatory Johns Hopkins University in Baltimore, where he presented a doctoral thesis entitled 'The Psychology of Kant' in 1884. Although no copy is known to survive, this set the direction of his thinking: the same year he published a paper on 'Kant and the Philosophic Method' in the *Journal of Speculative Philosophy* and in the following decade remained interested in the European idealist tradition, publishing papers and reviews on Kant, Leibniz, Hegel and T. H. Green. This is highly significant, for these scholars, along with Spinoza, were responsible for introducing the coherence theory of truth into philosophic discourse.

Traditionally, since Plato and Aristotle, epistemology had been dominated by the correspondence theory, which assumes that there is an external world of fact and that the more closely our beliefs and ideas correspond to that world the more they can be said to be true. During the scientific revolution of the seventeenth century developments in mathematics had provided a model for the coherence theory, which judges the truth of ideas by their ability to be placed in an integrated system; this sustained the quest of idealist philosophy as developed by Spinoza, Leibniz and Kant. The intellectual history of the nineteenth century may be seen, in one of its major aspects, as a conflict between these two rival metaphysical positions: clearly, coherence gave support to the classical revival and its associated religious revival; on the other hand, correspondence was the belief of positivists and scientists. Dewey, like Peirce and James, was born into a world in which these were metaphysical alternatives. It was Peirce's distinction that he attempted to resolve the conflict by proposing a third possibility, pragmatism, which dispensed with *a priori* metaphysical assumptions and emphasized 'practical bearings', and James followed this lead. Dewey, as a young lecturer in philosophy from 1884 until 1894, first at the University of Minnesota, and then at Michigan, became interested in the problems.

From 1894 until 1904 Dewey was at the University of Chicago, and during that time he became deeply involved in questions of education, social theory, and their relationships to philosophy. One reason for going to Chicago was that his contract allowed him to lecture on pedagogy and conduct experiments to discover an educational form more consonant with the times. Sensitive to Rice's criticisms and influenced both by the philosophical ideas of Peirce and by the psychological ideas of James, Dewey's early experiments were simple and reasonably cautious when seen in retrospect. At that time he had the support of Francis Wayland Parker (1837–1902), who had already established a national reputation as a progressive educator. Having started as a teacher in New Hampshire, Parker moved to Dayton, Ohio, as assistant superintendent and then travelled to Germany to study the 'new pedagogy'. On his return in 1875 he was appointed Superintendent of the Quincy School System in Massachusetts and made it one of the most advanced in the United States, drawing large numbers of visitors to see the new methods in operation, based upon object-lessons, excursions, and what he called the 'new education' founded on real-life learning. Parker, already sensing changes in the educational climate and expressing them in the most interesting forms of the period, accepted in 1882 the challenging position of Principal of the Cook County Normal School in Chicago where he further developed the 'Quincy System' (he always disclaimed this appellation) in the training of teachers.[12] Here the best of Pestalozzi, Froebel and Herbart were synthesized into a new pedagogy, and it was in the practice school attached to the Normal School that Dewey became acquainted directly with the new 'scientific' thrust of education. Responding to the excitement of science and the stimulation given by the new doctrines of pragmatism, Dewey decided to make the school an area of scientific experiment.

This concern with a science of education received its first explicit expression in 1897 when Dewey secured the cooperation of a group of parents who wanted a better education for their children. With the approval of the university which gave its moral support, Dewey opened an experimental – later called 'Laboratory' – school attached to the Department of Philosophy, Psychology and Pedagogy (of which he was head), with two teachers and sixteen children. From the beginning, he wanted to test the new pragmatist theories, especially the educational psychology of James. The general procedures of the school are recounted in *The School and Society* (1899). His criticisms of standard practice, and his own inclinations, are well summarized in the opening paragraph of the second chapter:

> Some few years ago I was looking about the school supply stores in the city, trying to find desks and chairs which seemed thoroughly suitable from all points of view – artistic, hygienic, and educational – to the needs of the children. We had a great deal of difficulty in finding what we needed, and finally one dealer, more intelligent than the rest, made this remark: 'I am afraid we have not what you want. You want something at which the children may work; these are all for listening.' That tells the story of the traditional education. Just as the biologist can take a bone or two and reconstruct the whole

animal, so, if we put before the mind's eye the ordinary schoolroom, with its rows of ugly desks placed in geometrical order, crowded together so that there shall be as little moving room as possible, desks almost all of the same size, with just space enough to hold books, pencils, and paper, and add a table, some chairs, the bare walls, and possibly a few pictures, we can reconstruct the only educational activity that can possibly go on in such a place. It is all made 'for listening' – because simply studying lessons out of a book is only another kind of listening; it marks the dependency of one mind upon another. The attitude of listening means, comparatively speaking, passivity, absorption; that there are certain ready-made materials which are there, which have been prepared by the school superintendent, the board, the teacher, and of which the child is to take in as much as possible in the least possible time.[13]

His intention was to make the school an institution where the advances of the century could be directly transmitted to the coming generation with such excitement still intact, not dead and formalized into the external curriculum of the Herbartian lesson methodology. Not that Dewey was yet directly criticizing Herbartianism; his concern was to attack the lifeless pedagogy. There are, however, further implications, and *The School and Society* gives evidence: passivity, listening and 'the dependency of one mind upon another' are all, *ipso facto*, undemocratic. Pragmatism seemed to Dewey, as to many others, to be a democratic philosophy that challenged traditional authoritarian theories by defining truth as what the collective experience of society verifies and thereby affirms. If knowledge is relative and truth both contingent and emergent; if there is only the whole child (free of faculties, apperception masses, blank tablets and body–mind dualisms) in interaction with an environment of continually changing experience; then, surely, it is dishonest and immoral not to say so, and not to educate the child accordingly. So the school should be, basically, an institution with the essential characteristics of 'the workshop, the laboratory, [with] the materials, the tools with which the child may construct, create, and actively enquire'.[14] The school flourished, especially with Parker's encouragement, and began to gain a reputation for its innovative approach under both its official title of the University of Chicago Laboratory School and its more popular designation of the 'Dewey School'. In 1896, meanwhile, the Cook County Normal School ceased operations and was reopened privately in 1899 as the Chicago Institute of Pedagogy by Parker with the philanthropic support of the wealthy Mrs Emmons Blaine; in 1901 it merged with the pedagogical section of the University Department of Philosophy, Psychology and

Pedagogy as the University of Chicago School of Education. The following year Parker died and Dewey became the sole progressive educational leader. In irreconcilable conflict with President Harper on matters relating to his administration of the Laboratory School, chiefly because he could not get university funds for the merged Chicago Institute of Pedagogy which remained unendowed, Dewey resigned in 1904. The following year James McKeen Cattell secured him an appointment to Teachers College, Columbia University, in New York, where he remained until his retirement in 1930 and where all of his seminal work was written.

Reflective thinking: scientific method applied to learning

Dewey's first major book on the new pedagogy of experimentalism, as it was now being called, was *How We Think* (first edition 1910), which came as an effort to counter the Herbartianist psychology of the apperception mass and the pedagogical methodology of the five normal steps with a psychology of classroom procedure based upon a pragmatic approach. Already the Herbartianist position was being modified and reinterpreted away from the rigid version being propagated by the McMurrys. In 1897 a professor of education in the University of London, John Adams, a Scot by birth and education, had published the influential *The Herbartian Psychology Applied to Education*, which gave a far more dynamic and intelligent analysis of Herbart than that coming from the American Herbartians. Now Adams had read Herbart in the original German texts, particularly *Psychologie als Wissenschaft* and *Lehrbuch zur Psychologie*, and it was from the latter work that Adams drew his educational applications. Bypassing the intermediate interpretations of the Jena school and the American commentaries and translations based in turn upon them, he was able to appreciate the greater vitality of the original Herbart, and expounded this in the pithy summary that the whole quest of Western epistemology up to the time of Herbart was 'to explain ideas by the mind' whereas Herbart's great contribution was 'to explain the mind by ideas', to recognize that 'the ideas really make up the mind'.[15] Adams stressed the principle of dynamic associationism, and it was this approach that Dewey followed in his own psychological explanations, using the Jamesian notion of the continuum of experience as the ground in which ideas come together in association. Dewey found this an inadequate psychology, and it was not until the Gestalt theory of the late 1920s came through, from the work in Germany of Wertheimer, Köhler and Koffka, that he was able to revise *How We Think* in the 1933 edition by taking account of the presupposition of holist perception. In the 1910 edition, however, he used the associationist approach to analyse the processes of thinking and to effect a pedagogical linkage.

Dewey was forced to begin with a metaphysical assumption, the basic postulate of 'continuity'. When do we really think? he asked, and his answer came readily: when we are challenged. And challenges, as already pointed out, are part of our life. So came his next question: *how* do we think? His answer offered two alternatives: either by accepting the views of others or by involving ourselves in a process of critical inquiry. The former approach he rejected as characteristic of the slave: the democratic man must reach genuine, personal solutions. So, following what he believed to be the scientific method, Dewey set out a five-stage sequence which in the 1910 edition he termed the Complete Act of Thought.

We think, in the full sense of the word, when challenged by a problem that stimulates us to seek a solution. The next step is to gather data about the causes of the problem. Next we think out an orderly sequence of steps towards a solution, or, in the words of the scientist, construct a hypothesis, and then test it by application; if this yields a confirmation, the problem is solved. If the hypothesis is not confirmed, we go back to the data, using the failed hypothesis as one more element, and construct a new hypothesis, taking into account our former experience and proceeding as before. Laboratory science often has to reconstruct hypotheses many times before final solutions are reached, and this is equally true of human life in general. The need is to maintain continuity, the forward drive of life in a ceaseless interaction with the environment. In the 1933 edition of *How We Think* Dewey used the simple example of a person taking a walk along a country path, being obstructed by a ditch, and using the processes of reflective thinking to find a solution. The end result, he observed – and had it printed in italics – was that

> *The function of reflective thought is, therefore, to transform a situation in which there is experienced obscurity, doubt, conflict, disturbance of some sort, into a situation that is clear, coherent, settled, harmonious.*[16]

Dewey proposed the method of reflective thinking, with its five steps of problem, data collection, hypothesis, testing and confirmation, as an alternative to the five Herbartian steps of preparation, presentation, association, generalization and application. Whereas Herbart provided a method of instruction for the teacher, Dewey put forward a method whereby the teacher could help the child solve the kinds of real problems that life presents.

A systematic theory of education: Democracy and Education

Not only did the first decades of the twentieth century witness exciting scientific advances; they were also a period of profound economic, social and political turmoil. The socialist drive of Marx had lost its impetus and the workers' parties had opted for cooperation with capitalism in an attempt to deal with the serious depressions of economic and industrial growth, although the mass of workers remained seriously disadvantaged in Europe where the forces of oligarchic repression were still strong. Wars between the great powers were waged continuously throughout the age of imperialism from 1890 to 1914 as they fought for Africa, Asia and China and drifted towards the Great War of 1914–18. In large part, wars occurred, Dewey wrote in *The Christian Century* in 1923, because they were the sole means available for legitimately solving international disputes.[17] Unable to shake off his Hegelian training, Dewey recognized the inevitable dialectical origins of conflict and the necessity of conflict in human existence, since with its resolution comes the aesthetic experience that he termed 'the moment of passage from disturbance into harmony [which] is that of intensest life',[18] but he also proposed that these should, in the case of destructive conflicts such as war, be eliminated wherever possible, and that all conflicts be resolved by the experimental approach of scientific problem solving, or what he called 'the method of intelligence'. It was, in fact, this attitude that had already led him to argue that a properly educated population is the best means of minimizing conflict, from local to international level.

To explain his views on how problems could best be avoided and, if unavoidable, properly handled, Dewey had already written in 1916 his greatest work on education, the famous *Democracy and Education*, in which he put the reconstructionist case for the fully educated democratic society as the only acceptable form of social organization and government. *Democracy and Education* is a long, complex and rich work, and its impact upon teachers, coming as it did in the middle of the European war (the United States did not enter until 6 April 1917), was enormous; no other work has ever so profoundly influenced American education, and it is still in print. Dewey wrote in a society that was itself struggling with violent internal problems of bitter racism and unassimilated ethnic minorities which seemed ready to shatter the precarious social unity in a replica of the European conflicts; despite the liberal rhetoric of the common school, America was not well educated, nor was it a genuine democracy. The wealthy commercial and industrial oligarchies held the reins of power and controlled the ladders of social mobility, and while ever the educational system sanctioned the competitive ethos and kept the common people in subjection, America would fail to realize her promise, both to become the first genuine democracy and by example to stimulate the rest of the world. So *Democracy and Education*, despite its dry prose and analytic method, was an exciting manifesto of a possible new era.

It was against prevailing practices that Dewey reacted vigorously in *Democracy and Education*, arguing that education at the beginning of the twentieth century was almost totally meaningless: it was the training of slaves. The aims of virtue and moral character were imposed from above and built out of a dubious, empty metaphysics; the curriculum was an overwhelming corpus of totally lifeless information. The child as an integral human being was violated; mind and body were separated as abstractions and the body suppressed, violently if necessary. Everything was directed towards cramming the 'mind' with vast amounts of largely verbal formulae, masquerading as knowledge, devoid of real content and imposed by a necessarily authoritarian teacher, and quite removed from the experiential context within which it was originally created. Traditional education is based on the learner's dependence on the mind and will of another. How, under these circumstances, could the young become participating, constructive members of a democracy committed to extending the potentialities of the good life to everyone? *Democracy and Education* sought to provide an answer to that provocative question. The basis of all democratic education, he argued, should be scientific, in the rigorous sense of the word. The school, following his early example at the University of Chicago, must become a social laboratory where children learn to subject the received tradition to the pragmatic tests of truth; the accumulated knowledge of society must be demonstrably seen to work. Moreover, this has to be a continuing process: the school has to develop in the child the necessary competence to solve current problems and to test future plans of action according to the experimental method. This book, in which his revolutionary doctrine was put forward, immediately became the centre of educational interest across America and stimulated wide discussion and some quite bitter reaction.

The basis of Dewey's theory of education is not metaphysical in the traditional sense; instead he began his argument from an anthropological and psychological position. Life, he claimed, seeks its own sustenance, which is secured by man through the medium of the organized society. Education is fundamental to this process because it enables the individual to maintain continuity by learning the techniques of survival and development from the accumulated experience of his group. As life becomes more complex, education becomes more 'formal' and 'intentional' and is largely directed towards ensuring that the young come to accept the morality of their society. At this point, two paths are possible: either to see that such morality – in the full sense of the ways of society – is closed, fixed and unchangeable, or to ensure that it is kept open, tentative and subject to revision in the light of continued social experience. Only the latter path should be admissible in a democracy which is based, by definition, on a deep commitment to belief in the inner worth and equal dignity of all persons.

Educational implications flow from this assumption. The child must be allowed to retain its dominant characteristic, plasticity; children must be encouraged to follow this 'natural' proclivity to seek, inquire, explore, to become immersed in the environment and to learn by experience. This leads, Dewey said, to growth; the most desirable form of our behaviour is the disposition always to react to new situations with flexibility and curiosity. Education should encourage the individual to respond creatively. The opposite is to respond with a set solution, a prejudice – to impose a static, established attitude or belief upon a new situation. This latter approach, he asserted, is exactly what schools fostered: they closed children's eyes by imposing upon them predetermined views of the world and previously developed solutions. Children were taught, by means of a preordained curriculum, to see the world as fixed, finished and ordered; their only possible accomplishment would be to see how much of it they could memorize.

Dewey reconciled the priority of social continuity with the need for the flexibility of the individual by arguing that the collective experience of a democratic society should be seen as a resource for solving future problems. This is how he viewed history and all learning organized as 'subject matter' – a taxonomy of previous solutions. So the child should see school subjects as bodies of material with possible relevance for future action; subjects should not be revered and memorized simply for their own sake. Nor should school learning be purely verbal. Dewey recognized that symbolic and written material does have the ability, if properly used, to extend the meaning of our experience, but too often it is a dry, rote-memory form of encyclopedic recitation, often having no meaningful connection with real-life experiences.

Activity is one of Dewey's key terms; he considered it the dominant human characteristic. Man is constantly acting to maintain the continuity of life, because checks upon continuity – and hence survival – are part of the order of nature. Dewey's view of life as a sequence of challenges, heavily reinforced by the pace of industrial development in the early decades of this century when nothing seemed either certain or predictable, did not lead him to despair about the progress of civilization; on the contrary, he argued that the machine must be accepted because it is the instrument by which people can be freed from slavish routine occupations and allowed to enjoy a life of purposeful, creative activity. This led him to suggest that education should be consonant with society, at that time a developing industrial democracy. Education, as well, should be a democratic process of conjoint activity, guided by the highest form of solving problems yet devised: the scientific method. So as early as the Chicago years Dewey conceived of the school as a laboratory rather than a sit-stillery, and learning as experimentation and search into the unknown rather than passive absorption of external 'facts'; he unscrewed the desks from the floor and put in laboratory benches; the teacher's table disappeared and children were encouraged to stand, walk about and talk together as they studied real-life issues. Over the years a wide literature on 'activity' learning appeared along with the associated 'project' method.

In accordance with his arguments in *How We Think*, and the psychological ideas of William James, Dewey was resolutely opposed both to the dualism of traditional metaphysics (mind–body, subject–object, being–becoming, and so on) and to the tendency to make abstractions substantive. So in *Democracy and Education* he criticized such abstract concepts as mind, intelligence, interest, attention and discipline, arguing that it was belief in a substantive existence for these and many other terms that had led to the bad features of traditional education. We have no 'mind' as a self-contained separate entity; we are engaged always as total, reacting persons. As we work towards the scientific solution of problems, we act intelligently and are thus engaged (or 'interested', from the Latin *inter est*, that which is between the doer and the activity),[19] we attend and we control our behaviour. So Dewey believed that if schools based their activities on scientific inquiry a great deal of compulsion and coercion would disappear and artificial, external motivation would be unnecessary.

This would lead in turn to the disappearance of one of democracy's greatest enemies: the dualism, inherited from the Greeks, of leisure and labour. Nothing is intrinsically liberal or illiberal: anything that helps solve problems is potentially liberating and is not the province of any special class of studies. On the other hand, anything that hinders creative activity, as does much of the traditional humanities curriculum, is potentially illiberal.

How, then, does the individual acquire morality and a proper set of values? Again Dewey found the answer within his democratic, scientific theory; indeed, his rejection of an external value-system imposed from above as advocated by traditional metaphysics was the cause of much church opposition to him. Dewey argued that morality is learned within a social context by observing appropriate rules, which emerge from shared experience. The teacher is also a cooperative learner, but older and wiser, whose role is to help the child learn the values of democratic participation, not by imparting information, but by inquiry into problematic situations. Again, in a truly democratic society, he argued, education should be controlled by the state with schools provided for all, regardless of sex, religion, race or social class; any other system is divisive, inhibits the learning of democratic values and therefore has no genuine educative function.

Dewey was aware that the term 'values', like so many that we use, is an abstraction; in practice, there is only the act of valuing, which he saw as being achieved through the scientific method. Learning occurs when, faced with the necessity to choose between alternative courses of action, we become involved in constructing hypotheses that anticipate the consequences of particular ways of acting. In his view, a complete act of thought requires us to anticipate the consequences implied for others, for the wider community and for the environment, as well as for ourselves. Not that every hypothesis will achieve this objective; if it did, Dewey said, we would be living in a finished world. We must accept the fact that our hypotheses may be imperfect, that solutions to problems, even if they work – and so meet the pragmatic test of truth – may be only partial. We must always be aware of the tentative nature of our conclusions and the limitations of our understanding. We are, in effect, entitled to make mistakes, but if we are to secure and maintain democracy we cannot be negligent. Genuine morality comes from remaining flexible, alert and creatively responsive to new challenges, and transmitting this quality to the young is the highest purpose that can be given to education.

Experimentalism in controversy: objections to the theory

With the publication of *Democracy and Education*, Dewey gained national prominence and provided a strong position for educational reformers, particularly those concerned with the working classes. By the time that the Progressive Education Association (PEA) was founded in the United States in 1919, and the New Education Fellowship (NEF) of Europe held its first conference in 1921 in Calais with over a hundred delegates from fourteen countries, Dewey had been acclaimed as a philosopher and educational theorist of world standing. For his part, Dewey remained a university academic and a continuing stream of reforming, progressive literature came from his pen. Indeed, he sustained his intellectual output to the end of his long life, answering the many controversial issues that his position aroused, for he was by no means universally acknowledged as an educational messiah. Attacks came from many conservative quarters: his philosophy of pragmatism drew the scorn of academic philosophers; his moral views aroused the ire of the churches; his problem-solving, child-centred conception of education (criticized as 'soft-pedagogy') gained the hostility of Herbartianist and traditionalist teachers, particularly those in private and church-supported schools who saw standards under attack. Against a continuing opposition Dewey persevered in his quest to formulate a complete educational philosophy, and it is his achievement that he produced the only significant, comprehensive, fully independent theory of education since Plato and Aristotle.

The controversial status of Dewey is probably best illustrated by the outcome of his being invited to deliver the Gifford Lectures in 1929. Adam, Lord Gifford (1820–87), left a bequest for a foundation to be established for a biennial lecture series to be given in Scottish universities 'for promoting, advancing, teaching, and diffusing study of natural theology, in the widest sense of that term'. The series started in 1888 and Dewey's lectures, given at the University of Edinburgh, were published under the title *The Quest for Certainty*. Dewey was highly critical of traditional dualist approaches to religion and philosophical attempts to understand what to him was the hypothetical concept of a reality greater than experience; philosophy, he said in the first lecture, has been dominated, ever since classical times, by the obsession 'that the office of knowledge is to uncover the antecedently real, rather than, as is the case with our practical judgments, to gain the kind of understanding to deal with problems as they arise'.[20] The published text enjoyed a large number of reprintings and had an impact in radical philosophical circles on the theory of ethics and logic; in the *Oxford Dictionary of the Christian Church*, however, first published in 1957, Dewey's name is conspicuously absent from its list of 'notable Gifford Lecturers'.[21] Also absent is the name of William James whose *Varieties of Religious Experience* were the Gifford Lectures for 1901-2. Dewey was adamant throughout his life that there is no reality greater than experience; and the verification theory of truth is nowhere better set out than in these lectures, which reveal his mastery of the Western intellectual tradition – scientific as well as philosophical. He dismissed Kant as having produced only an 'alleged revolution' in that he made explicit what was implicit in the classic tradition', namely, 'that knowledge is determined by the objective constitution of the universe', 'a shift [merely] from a theological to a human authorship'.[22] The concluding chapter, 'The Copernican Revolution', is an exciting, fast-moving argument, too complex to discuss in detail here, which rejects both realist (correspondence) and idealist (coherence) approaches to knowledge. We must abandon such quests for certainty because they lead nowhere, he argued; all we can 'know' is what we can experience: 'There is [only] a moving whole of interacting parts; a center emerges wherever there is effort to change them in a particular direction.' This 'center' has to be mind, but a 'mind . . . no longer a spectator beholding the world from without and finding its highest satisfaction in the joy of self-sufficing contemplation. The mind is within the world as a part of the latter's own on-going process.'[23]

Such a position was of little comfort or assistance to insecure, inept or ignorant schoolmasters; over the centuries in Europe teachers had worn academic gowns which symbolized their being clothed in authority, the necessary extension of such authority being the taxonomy of ordered knowledge and a pedagogy drawn from an exact psychology. Herbartianism allowed even the meanest teacher to come into possession of power; Dewey's challenge to that was attacked by conservatives. Moreover, his philosophical approach itself was considered by many philosophers to be unsound: by insisting upon verification as the criterion of truth, Dewey, they argued, had confused the fact of an event with an individual subject's discovery of it. In the often repeated charge of his critics, he had failed to observe proper logical procedures and had 'psychologized' philosophy. This was a major obstacle to Dewey's wider acceptance; allied to it, especially as far as education is concerned, is the problem of external knowledge, the realm of facts as we commonly understand them, that is, of 'common sense'. Now Dewey's position, by ruling out certainty, and therefore any absolute knowledge, seemed to fly in the face of our daily experience. For instance, could it not be said that the law of gravity operates independently of our experience? Common sense would say yes; Dewey pointed to the continuing discoveries in science that had upset previously held 'immutable truths', even the concept of gravity: those experiences we like to consider absolute have only, in his words, a 'warranted assertability' of belief.

A further issue of the greatest relevance to education was the question of antecedent knowledge, namely, the organized bodies of knowledge, ordered systematically and stored symbolically, usually in language, but also in various other notations – mathematical, musical and, nowadays, electronic codes – from which the traditional curriculum has been formed. Again, Dewey argued that the only reality is immediate experience, regarding symbolic and vicarious experience as only of potential value in the degree to which it can be meaningfully (Peirce would say 'practicably') incorporated in immediate experience, that is, in the solution of current problems. In *The Quest for Certainty* Dewey did not denigrate symbols and their function in storing vicarious experience but asserted that 'the invention or discovery of symbols is doubtless by far the greatest event in the history of man. Without them, no intellectual advance is possible; with them, there is no limit set to intellectual development except inherent stupidity.'[24] However, Dewey stressed what he called the 'fallacy' of considering 'independence from any specific application' as being 'equivalent to independence from application as such';[25] the touchstone must always be specific application to immediate experience, and we sense here again both the positivist tradition with its emphasis on direct experience, and his Kantian background, the assertion that *Anschauungen ohne Begriffe sind blind*. So education, like all other aspects of human activity, must be governed by the awareness of contingency and the emergent, by the need to remain flexible and responsive to continued novelty in our lives.

The problem of the status of stored, symbolic knowledge and of the verification theory of truth remained widely disputed among philosophers and educators. Dewey attacked the sense-empiricist position as merely 'sensationalist'[26] and yet himself was partly within that tradition, since he accepted the immediate and the material as the conditions of our experience. Ideas, symbols, vicarious experience for him are all part of a mysterious realm of potentiality; Dewey did not see them as equally coexisting in experience. He gave recognition to the most important set of all possible ideas, collectively designated as 'history', in the opening chapter of

Democracy and Education, 'Education as a Necessity of Life'; none the less, he always regarded history, the totality of man's consciousness of previous experience, as having no real, independent status. Even if his arguments against this position could be accepted (and there would be no universal assent), Dewey left himself open to the criticism that he still kept within the positivist camp. Problems emerge, in his view, from without, from the environment; man is largely outside nature, and ideas are only resources that are available to be called upon. Dewey did not advance to the view to which his position logically could have taken him, and which would have strengthened his argument considerably – that man and ideas are just as much part of the continuum of experience. He did not come to realize that ideas are not merely, as he described them, 'objects of thought',[27] but are part of the totality of experience and so help to generate problems; their existence is as real as man himself; man is not outside nature, solving problems, but is within, as one element of the continuous flux of events. Similarly, he considered symbolic knowledge to be only potentially available, and not a permanent part of the whole environment; likewise, he still held to a sense-empiricist position by regarding experimentalism as a method external to man, and capable of being employed as needed.

American progressivism in practice

The reforming impulse in American education 1890–1918

While Dewey was the pre-eminent philosopher and spokesman of social reconstruction, he must be seen in context as only one of a large number of social and educational reformers, many of whom, although not so intellectually sophisticated, none the less exerted considerable pressure for educational change. The development of American progressivism occurred in three main stages – from the late nineteenth century to the First World War, from 1919 to the Great Depression of 1929, and in the decade of the 1930s up to the Second World War – and Dewey played the greatest individual role in that first period, when the progressive movement was beginning to take coherent form. Throughout the nineteenth century, American education had been influenced only minimally by the counterculture; socialism had made very little headway and the various millennial groups such as those at New Harmony and Oneida had kept to themselves, contributing virtually nothing to educational reform. Yet as the century wore on there was a continuing reaction against the bourgeois bookishness of formal schooling and the classical domination of the high schools, academies and colleges. In a frontier society proclaiming the virtues of honest work it was the height of hypocrisy to put a premium on latinity and an effete literary curriculum, and this objection was increasingly raised in the latter part of the century, as the case for the inherent dignity of manual labour and a practical education was put forward. Such early reformers as Parker at Quincy stressed the practical curriculum, and the great American industrial exhibition of 1876, the Philadelphia Centennial – the nation's answer to the London and Paris Exhibitions – was staged under the theme of 'Education and National Progress'. The most striking exhibit of practical education was the Russian contribution, based upon the methods of Victor Della Vos, Director of the Moscow Imperial Technical School.[28] This stimulated an American response and in the following years manual and vocational workshop instruction was increasingly introduced, the ideas of Della Vos being first adopted at the Massachusetts Institute of Technology in 1876. Already higher technical education had appeared in the foundation of the Rensselaer Polytechnic Institute in 1824, Harvard's Lawrence Scientific School and the Sheffield Scientific School in 1847, Dartmouth's Chandler School of Science and Arts in 1851 and the Massachusetts Institute in 1861. With the Moscow example, technical and scientific legitimacy moved into the schools as well. In 1879 Calvin Woodward opened a Manual Training School at Washington University in St Louis, the first in the United States.

Problems ensued as the conservatives defended the literary and mathematical tradition while innovators promoted the merits of manual and mechanical education, the latter position being supported both by the American Federation of Labor, founded in 1886 as the successor to the National Labor Union of 1867 and the Knights of Labor of 1869 to represent working-class interests, as well as by the National Association of Manufacturers which sought better-trained tradesmen. The ideology of experimentalism that John Dewey promoted sought to reconcile the need for abstract thought and the traditional organization of knowledge with demands for practical application and verification of theory in practice. The difficulty many teachers felt with Dewey's early thought, however, was that, apart from being abstruse, it was not sufficiently explicit and prescriptive. The attainment of the American teaching force in the first two decades of the twentieth century was minimal, and Dewey made demands that very few could meet. By the year 1900 all forty-five states had normal schools of some kind, yet Massachusetts, still the educational pace-setter, required only a high-school diploma and two years of teacher training; all other states required less. Indeed, even though by 1911 most states had teacher-certification laws, by 1921 only four states required formal teacher training for certification; fourteen states gave credentials on the basis of four completed years of secondary schooling (usually after eight years of elementary schooling), while thirty states made no academic requirements at all for the award of a teacher's certificate.

Simultaneously with Dewey's early work, many progressive educational experiments were being undertaken by various reformers, all concerned to change society through the school, all influenced by separate elements of nineteenth-century progressive thought; since their approaches varied according to the relative emphasis given to the respective elements, the results were correspondingly different. At one extreme were those who stressed an individualist approach, of whom the outstanding examples were Marietta Johnson and Helen Parkhurst. In 1907 Marietta Johnson began a free, privately supported experimental school in Fairhope, Alabama, which was in essence an attempt to develop Rousseau's ideas in institutional form through the approach of 'organic education'. The institution was called the Organic School and its emphasis was upon the unfettered growth of the child's interests and capacities, with no external constraints of teacher dominance, fixed syllabuses or examinations. Yet problems abounded as Marietta Johnson attempted to reconcile organic growth with the need to ensure that it followed the directions of attaining adult competence. Less doctrinaire was the approach of Helen Parkhurst who, as a sixteen-year-old beginning teacher in a Wisconsin log-cabin school in 1904, with forty pupils, developed a system of individualized instruction on a 'contract' basis which made the children the agents of their own learning. She became attracted to the contemporaneous ideas of Montessori and integrated them into her own plan; indeed, she worked with Montessori to gain experience in developing her own system which was adopted in 1920 in the Massachusetts high school of Dalton, Helen Parkhurst's birthplace. The system, thereafter known as the Dalton Plan, spread rapidly throughout Britain, Europe and the Western colonial world as a promising form of progressivism since it met the major criterion of making pupil interest, self-motivation and activity the dominant factors in education.

Contemporaneous with these two individualist approaches was a more socially oriented method developed by school superintendent William Wirt in Gary, Indiana, beginning in 1907. Gary was being developed as a company town by the United States Steel Corporation and the thirty-year-old Wirt seized the chance, in a brand-new community, to attempt to develop a new type of school that would incorporate the socialist and progressive thought of the period, including that of Dewey, by integrating learning and labour, the abstract and the applied, the individual and the social. So he designed the Gary school system as one in which each component school had only one-half of its accommodation in formal desk-furnished classrooms, the other half being in various activity spaces: auditorium, workshops, laboratories, gymnasium, playground and library. Although the formal Indiana state curriculum was followed, the Gary schools avoided a compartmentalized subject approach and instead adapted the curriculum to a system of units of work based on broad social themes. Since only half the students could be engaged in classroom work at a time, the schools were organized into two divisions known as 'platoons', and by this method various aspects of learning were timetabled, the auditorium being used for assemblies where students could discuss matters of concern to the whole enrolment, the gymnasium, shops and laboratories being used for projects involving social cooperation, while the library and classrooms were reserved for individual learning needs. The 'Gary Platoon School' approach was extremely innovative for a public system in the 1910s and, quite predictably, aroused considerable controversy. In 1915 John Dewey, with his wife Evelyn, published *Schools of Tomorrow*, which put forward various models, such as Marietta Johnson's Organic School and the Gary System, and recommended these to the progressive-minded. The latter approach was further helped by the publication in 1916 of *The Gary Schools* by Randolph Bourne, and a second work in 1918 under the same title by Abraham Flexner and Frank Bachman which served to strengthen the reputation of the system. By 1929 more than 200 city systems in forty-one states had adopted the platoon-school approach in various interpretations.[29]

Progressivism in action 1919–1929

By the end of the First World War, American public education had become the world pacesetter as moves were made to extend teacher education and to base the curriculum upon the latest methods. Already various communities and school boards had demonstrated a willingness to experiment with new approaches; the time was now ripe for further initiatives to be taken in extending the progressive ideas of Dewey and his collaborators. In 1919 Stanwood Cobb, a teacher at Annapolis Naval College, formed the Association for the Advancement of Progressive Education with an initial membership of eighty-five and a seven-point charter of aims for improving the elementary school:

1 Freedom to develop naturally,
2 Interest the motive of all work,
3 The teacher a guide, not a task-master,
4 Scientific study of child development,
5 Greater attention to all that affects the child's physical development,
6 Co-operation between school and home to meet the needs of child-life,
7 The progressive school a leader in educational movements.

Following the example of the European movement, the New Education Fellowship, which had its own journal *Education for the New Era*, the American Progressive Education Association (PEA), as it was later called, founded a quarterly journal in 1924, *Progressive Education*, to disseminate ideas on the seven points. In so doing, it introduced American readers to the work of the European innovators and experiments in progressivism, including Reddie's work at Abbotsholme and the principles of Lietz's *Landerziehungsheimen*.

Simultaneously, teacher preparation was becoming upgraded throughout the 1920s. Teachers College, Columbia, seized the initiative and strove to become the nation's leading school of teacher education. This college had been chartered in 1892 in affiliation with New York's Columbia University, and under the foundation dean James Russell it prospered when Dewey joined its staff in 1905. Russell gathered together all the best people he could, the historian Paul Monroe, the psychologist William Thorndike, the social theorist Harold Rugg, the curriculum theorist William H. Kilpatrick and the apostate-Herbartianist Frank McMurry, who early in the twentieth century had been converted to functionalist psychology. A new body of educational theory, based upon their pioneering work, was assembled under the broad headings of history of education, philosophy of education, psychology applied to education and general methodology, and it increasingly supplanted the more limited and prescriptive pedagogical theories developed in the nineteenth century. While all of these were important in the work of upgrading teacher education, William Heard Kilpatrick (b. 1871) was by far the most influential, with a national reputation as the deviser of the project method. Kilpatrick arrived at Teachers College in 1909 as a graduate assistant completed his doctorate in 1912, and remained there until his retirement as Professor of Education. In 1914 and 1916 he published two books, both highly critical of the European concept of progressivism, *The Montessori System Examined* and *Froebel's Kindergarten Principles Critically Examined*. His objections were based on a pragmatist approach and he rejected Froebel and Montessori for their 'fixed-in-advance' concept of knowledge. Kilpatrick was no highly original educational thinker; he was chiefly an expositor of experimentalism and of Dewey's ideas, the most famous such exposition appearing in the *Teachers College Record* in 1918 under the title 'The Project Method'. Using a concept of C. S. Peirce, that of 'purposeful activity', he repeated his objections to European educational thought as knowledge fixed-in-advance and, because of the subject-matter approach, compartmentalized into static, unrelated elements. He argued that learning should instead be organized in relation to purposeful activity, and in the school this should be a project, defined as a broad, real-life integrative theme. This article, 'The Project Method', was highly successful and over the ensuing decades some 60,000 reprints were distributed.[30] In 1925 it was expanded into a book, the *Foundations of Method*, which became both a worldwide standard manual of the Deweyan method applied in specific classroom form and an influential teachers' college text.

Towards the end of the 1920s the Teachers College group had come to dominate the professional preparation of teachers on progressive lines and in 1927 they 'absorbed' the Progressive Education Association by winning election to most of its offices. John Dewey was elected honorary president, and the secretariat moved to Teachers College where it remained; henceforth the PEA was almost an agency of the college and Teachers College the acknowledged centre of progressivism. Yet even at that moment of seeming triumph, the progressive movement was beginning to be challenged from within. Throughout the 1920s it had no real inner cohesion, and its doctrines, although based upon Dewey, were in fact much more diffuse; there was, for example, genuine confusion about the respective emphasis to be placed on child-centred or society-centred education, and this was forcefully brought out in the work of two of its most vigorous members, both professors at Teachers College, Harold Rugg and George Counts. In 1928 Rugg published an important book, *The Child-Centered School*, which, like Dewey's *Schools of Tomorrow*, was a survey of developments. (Rather curiously, Rugg claimed a kind of

copyright over the phrase 'child-centered school' as his own neologism.)
This book illustrates one extreme of the progressive movement which
endeavoured to fulfil the seven aims of the Progressive Education Association's manifesto. At the same time, this point of view was being attacked
by many progressives, including Dewey himself, on the grounds that it
was too onesided and needed to be balanced by the cultivation of a social
morality. The most vociferous critic of child-centred education was
George Counts, who was deeply concerned with the dominance of the
American school system by the well-to-do middle class, and the failure to
provide adequately for the ethnic, racial and disadvantaged minorities. As
early as 1922 he wrote *The Selective Character of American Secondary Education*; in 1927 he published two more critical exposés of the bourgeois
maintenance of inequalities in *The Social Composition of Boards of Education*
and *School and Society in Chicago*. Counts was the most forward-looking of
the Teachers College group; he was aware that democracy was under
threat and, moreover, that the economy of the United States was danger-
ously overheated: Europe had widespread unemployment, farm incomes
were falling everywhere, the stockmarkets were rising alarmingly. On
24 October 1929 the New York Stock Market crashed overnight, and the
Great Depression spread to Europe and then around the world as all the
advanced industrialized economies collapsed. A decade of immense social
misery and disaster ensued.

American progressivism and social conflict 1929–1939

The depression decade of the 1930s had a profound effect upon American
progressivism, as indeed it had upon almost every facet of life all over
the world. Throughout the 1920s the rise of Italian fascism, German
Nazism and Soviet communism dominated international events. These
totalitarian regimes had an influence on the remainder of the West;
Europe was in trance and the United States was politically polarized. In
1933, in a national mood of both despondency and hope, Franklin D.
Roosevelt took office as president, promising a 'New Deal' for the people.
Various measures were taken to stimulate the economy, chiefly reform of
the banking and agricultural systems and the creation of government-led
employment with various public projects such as the Tennessee Valley
Authority reclamation and hydroelectrification schemes, the National
Industry Recovery Act and the Works Progress Administration. By this
time many middle-class Americans had developed strong isolationist

feelings *vis-à-vis* the outside world, while the bewildered and angry workers began to look towards socialism and leftist policies for solutions.

American teachers by the early 1930s had become increasingly organized into unions, the major nationwide federation being the National Education Association which in 1931 had a membership of 216,188.[31] In that year the total American population was some 120 million, and the United States Bureau of Education estimated an enrolment of 24 million children in elementary schools but less than 3 million in high schools; by including the seventh and eighth elementary grades with the four high-school grades (ninth to twelfth), the Bureau estimated that 3,130,000 were receiving a 'secondary' education. Altogether there was a total teaching and educational administration force of something approaching one million, so that the NEA claimed a quarter of the nation's teachers as members, while further unions held the allegiance of other teachers; administrators belonged to their own organizations. By 1935 there were 1,105,921 teachers in the United States,[32] and it was clear that already they were professionally well organized and, owing to the journals and yearbooks of their societies, increasingly better informed. As part of a campaign to inform teachers further about the social issues of the time, and indeed to stimulate them to action, George Counts in 1932 addressed the PEA annual conference on the theme 'Dare Progressive Education be Progressive?' and later in the year published this in a pamphlet *Dare the School Build a New Social Order?* This signalled the beginning of a move by the radical faction of the PEA to take political initiative, and the mood spread to the NEA. The journalist Lincoln Steffens observed at the time that 'all roads in our day lead to Moscow',[33] and many American radicals openly admired the egalitarian experiments of the Soviet Union, as yet still not in the period of Stalinist terror. Counts urged teachers to free the schools from the grip of the middle class, and considerable numbers of teachers took out socialist or communist party membership; in 1935 the American Federation of Teachers, which had been formed in 1916 as an affiliate of the American Federation of Labor, had a fully communist membership of its New York branch, Local Number Five. Many of these were either angry visionaries disturbed by the inequalities in American education, or else doctrinaire utopians who saw the Marxist vision producing the new social order and the Soviet Union as the bulwark of freedom confronting the growing totalitarian horrors of Nazism and fascism; many who accepted the Marxist analysis of the capitalist oppression of the working class saw the 1930s as evidence of the collapse of capitalism from within.

Already reaction to progressivism had set in during the 1920s and various opposition groups had formed, chiefly led by academic philosophers who put the case for a traditional position, bolstered by social-Darwinist attitudes. The Catholic Church rejected progressivism and on 31 December 1929 in an encyclical *Divini illius magistri* Pope Pius XI denounced such education, wherever it existed around the world, making European and American progressives the targets of his attack. The encyclical, translated as *On the Christian Education of Youth*, was a strongly worded case for the historical teaching mission of that church and for a conservative traditional approach to the process of education itself, advising that 'greater stress must be laid on the employment of apt and solid methods of teaching';[34] further, the essential depravity and sinfulness of man was stressed, and hence the necessary function of the church in effecting salvation. The encyclical commented specifically on state legislation for education in the Oregon School Case of 30 May 1929 heard before the United States Supreme Court, criticizing compulsory school attendance as a state violation of parents' natural rights, while it attacked the progressive movement in the passage declaring that

> Every method of education founded, wholly or in part, on the denial or forgetfulness of original sin and grace, and relying on the sole powers of human nature, is unsound. Such, generally speaking, are those modern systems bearing various names which appeal to a pretended self-government and unrestrained freedom on the part of the child, and which diminish or even suppress the teacher's authority and action, attributing to the child an exclusive primacy of initiative, and an activity independent of any higher law, natural or divine, in the work of his education.[35]

This encyclical restrained Catholic schools, and Catholic teachers in state schools, in conscience from supporting progressivism, and put them into alliance with philosophical conservatives, the various chambers of commerce and similar organizations, and political right-wing groups.

Throughout the 1930s many moderate progressives, recognizing limits to the ability of education to reconstruct society, attempted to sustain the viability of the movement and to steer a middle course. Consequently, in 1933 the Teachers College Columbia group, led by Dewey, prepared the Yearbook of the National Society of College Teachers of Education on the theme of living properly in a world transformed by science and technology. Dewey was opposed to Marxism because its historicist assumptions about the inevitability of the march of dialectical materialism denied the method of critical and social intelligence. He was joined in writing the yearbook by six others, and they produced the major progressive exposition of the decade which argued a three-point programme for action: the widening of adult education to produce a more educationally conscious public, the stressing of social history and social issues in the school curriculum, and an increase in both student and teacher participation in educational administration.[36] Reflecting the times, the progressive emphasis had clearly shifted from an individualistic child-centred concern to a socially responsible approach. In 1934 this was followed by a new journal, the *Social Frontier*, also issued out of Teachers College and edited by a board composed of Dewey, Bruce Raup, Harold Rugg, Boyd Bode (of Ohio State University) and Kilpatrick, and this continued to present to American teachers an interpretation of progressivism as moderate, socially responsible, but not radically revolutionary. At the same time, however, conditions worsened as the world moved closer to war and the depression continued. By 1938 America still had 10 million unemployed and, with the horrors of Stalinism being recounted, the Left lost impetus. The *Social Frontier* lost circulation and in 1939 was taken over by the PEA under the new name of *Frontiers of Democracy* as an additional publication to its official organ, *Progressive Education*.

In that decade, however, the American progressive movement effected significant changes in the schools of the nation, and even the Catholic Church and conservative factions could not remain unaffected. When the first issue of *Progressive Education* appeared in April 1924, its inaugural president, Charles W. Eliot, President of Harvard, had written in a congratulatory *Foreword* that 'the Progressive Schools are increasing rapidly in number and in influence and the educational public is becoming more and more awake to their merits. They are to be the schools of the future in both America and Europe.'[37] While he was reasonably correct about their influence, the PEA itself was not to survive. In 1932 it forged international links with Europe by becoming the United States section of the New Education Fellowship, but by 1940, with Europe at war, progressivism in its more extreme doctrinaire versions had lost its appeal, and between 1945 and 1955 the PEA tailed off and was disbanded. It had, however, fulfilled its original mission, as one recent scholar of its history has observed, to effect a transformation of the school.[38]

CHAPTER 13

The Rise of National Planning 1870–1939

The dynamics of change

Throughout the first four decades of the twentieth century, Western educational thought was dominated by utopian and progressive aspirations for a new era in education, and although European and American conceptions differed there was a high degree of unanimity on the need for concerted action to ensure that education became universally available as a means of both personal development and preparation for responsible social involvement, civic and vocational. Accompanying these hopes was the conception of the school as a transformed institution, no longer built on the model of the grim factory or squalid prison of nineteenth-century industrialism, but a centre of creative, cooperative learning. Much progressive thought was given to structure as well as function, and in some experimental ventures the school was reorganized architecturally. Unfortunately, imagination always soars beyond the reach of practicality and there was no possibility that utopian aspirations could be fulfilled on any wide scale. Experimental schools were limited to a tiny sector of European society in only a few countries, Britain, Germany, Switzerland, northern France and the United States, which were, in the period, the pacesetter nations of the industrial West. Elsewhere, economies were weak and there was little realistic basis on which minimal mass education could be built, much less the shining images of the new era. There were a multitude of impediments; not only did the dominant nations control most of the productive power of the West – indeed, of the world – but there were cultural forces, both religious and social, that resisted change. In most of underdeveloped Europe education was closely linked with the conservative established churches – Catholic in central, eastern and southern Europe, Orthodox in Russia and the Balkans – and the populations were predominantly rural peasantry with neither an appreciation of, nor a desire for, urbanization, industrial development and the social turmoil that had inevitably accompanied these processes.

Throughout the early twentieth century all the Western nations were engaged in building systems of education. In the first instance, the four leading nations accepted the intervention of the state in education, and the initial era of compulsory elementary school legislation of the 1870s and 1880s was extended in the twentieth century to what came to be termed 'secondary' education as well as 'further', 'technical' and 'adult' education for the working classes. The established bourgeois system of preparatory and grammar schools leading on to college and university was considered adequate, and little effort was made to change this except by providing minimal ladders of upward mobility for the few clever youths who would be allowed to climb above their station and thereby, it was hoped, be drawn off as potential leaders of any working-class unrest. The essential characteristics of this movement were that the national state became the major provider of education and educational planning became an increasingly greater concern of government; in the twentieth century this activity reached the point at which educational expenditure became one of the largest calls on the domestic budget. Governments had become mindful of the disciplinary effects of mass schooling upon the population. The schools mirrored the prevailing industrial system, the buildings generally reflected the same architectural style and in them children received the appropriate training for the factories of their adult life. Even the curriculum reflected this, and one of the major reasons for retaining the dual system was that it prepared the future industrial worker in basic literacy and related skills, while the humane, cultured studies were taught separately in the bourgeois schools for the working-class children's future masters.

At the same time, political developments in the early nineteenth and early twentieth centuries had altered the boundaries of the great European powers and throughout that period subject peoples emerged to attain independence: Belgium in the west, Finland, Estonia, Latvia and Lithuania in the Baltic region, Poland, Czechoslovakia and Hungary in eastern Europe, all became separate nation states, while in the Balkans, as Ottoman power declined, Romania, Yugoslavia, Bulgaria and Greece wrested independence from the Turks and turned instead to fighting each other in a long series of border disputes. Concurrently, the long-established states with arrested development – Scandinavia, Italy, Spain and Portugal – attempted to catch up with the pacesetters. Further east, Russia, since the time of Peter the Great, had been attempting to westernize and join the orbit of European culture and commerce. In all these states, education was basically to be a recapitulation, speeded up as much as possible, of the developments that had already taken place in the dominant nations. Outside the pacesetters, and the peripheral states of Europe, a new wave of 'Western' nations – the overseas colonies of the European powers in Africa, Asia, South America and Oceania – now sought to westernize their educational practices.

Within Europe, in the various new nations that had been formed with the independence of submerged ethnic minorities, education was seen as the key to national and cultural identity, although in many cases linguistic and religious divisions created serious difficulties, notably in Belgium and in the new hybrid states set up after the First World War following the collapse of the Austro-Hungarian and Ottoman empires in central and south-eastern Europe. Czechoslovakia, formed in 1919 out of eastern Austria-Hungary in accordance with the Versailles Treaty, was ethnically diverse, with a population of approximately one-half Czechs, one-quarter Germans, one-eighth Slovaks, and the rest Poles, Jews, Magyars and Ukrainians. Similarly, Yugoslavia, also formed in 1919, was the consequence of a century-long process of changing coalitions of various Slavic groups in the region, Slovenes, Croats, Dalmatians, Serbs, Montenegrins and Macedonians, whose precarious union had been prompted by a desire to be free of Austro-Hungarian hegemony in the north and Ottoman rule in the south. In all these states except Belgium, there had been little industrial development and there were large peasant numbers, so the task of nation building and providing even minimal systems of schooling was to be extremely difficult. In the two multicultural nations of Czechoslovakia and Yugoslavia the difficulties were exacerbated by the language problem, and even today education is not fully available; in 1974 in Yugoslavia only 83 per cent of the population were reported by its government to be literate, while Greece and Bulgaria reported 84 per cent and 90 per cent respectively. Most of the others claimed 100 per cent,[1] which means, in effect, that elementary education had been in force long enough for the older section of the population to have received at least rudimentary schooling.

In the long-established but underdeveloped nations of Italy, Spain and Portugal – all societies with a long history of civilization and culture – a lack of natural resources had limited their ability to industrialize and compete in the nineteenth century. Moreover, whereas the advanced Western nations were largely Protestant, with even France asserting a high degree of religious autonomy, these southern European states were strongly dominated by Roman Catholicism, their existing educational systems being largely under the control of teaching congregations. Impetus to change in all these nations came from reforming liberals who envisaged an industrial economy and a secular state independent of clerical influence. Italy had the basis for industrial development in the Lombardy region, but the liberals had to pay the price of a rupture with the Vatican and the pursuit of a policy of vigorous anticlericalism to modernize the country, while in Spain and Portugal the process was to be much slower; indeed in both these countries the nineteenth century was marked by tragic conflicts between reactionary and liberal forces that are still being played out. Italy and Spain still have only 90 per cent literacy each, and Portugal is the lowest in Europe at 66 per cent.[2]

The developed nations: educational pacesetters

The United States

In statistical terms the United States in the early twentieth century was the world's educational pacesetter; by the year 1900 it had instituted the eight-year elementary school, available to most white children in nearly every state. While it is true that compulsory legislation was not enacted by the southern states until the period 1906–18, this in large part was intended to disadvantage blacks and some of the lowest socio-economic sections of society; it did not prevent the spread of literacy and a basic education among the bulk of the white population. Racist and élitist arguments were advanced against compulsion, centring on an assumption that blacks are inferior in intelligence, cognitive ability and industrious application. As late as 1914 compulsion was opposed also because it was considered an interference with parents' freedom of choice, un-American in spirit, leading to the growth of government power, and unnecessary since most children attended school anyway.[3] Despite such views, thirty-three states enacted compulsory-attendance laws between 1852 and 1900, while the remaining states – the subdivided state of Dakota, the territories of New Mexico, Arizona and Oklahoma and eleven southern states – so legislated between 1900 and 1918, Mississippi being the last. In that initial period of compulsory legislation from 1870 to 1900, when the total population increased from 44 to 76 million, elementary-school enrolments rose to some 16 million, while high-school and college enrolments moved up to 750,000, the post-elementary sector comprising close to 5 per cent of the nation's total educational enrolments. In 1900 American schools held 22 per cent of the total population, a world record at the time. Illiteracy had been cut from an estimated 20 per cent of the population over ten years of age (since children learning to read and write are not counted) to approximately 11 per cent. The statistical increase continued, with elementary enrolments expanding to 18 million in 1910, 20 million in 1920 and 24 million in 1930, but decreasing to 20 million in 1940 owing to the lowered birth rate during the depression. High-school enrolments, however, increased much more rapidly, from half a million in 1900 to one million in 1910, to one and one-half million in 1920 and reaching a peak of seven million in 1940, when the total population had reached 132 million. In addition, there were large numbers in continuation, apprenticeship, evening and adult-education programmes.[4]

Of equal significance to the sheer size of school populations is the proportional increase in the high school and college sector from less than 5 per cent of the total educational enrolment in 1900 to 10 per cent in 1920 and 42 per cent by 1940. Now in part this was due to a change in the organization of the school sequence itself, since the elementary school in the nineteenth century, as in Europe, was the sole institution for the bulk of the people, planned as an eight-year sequence; the high school was a four-year programme for a continuing minority. In 1870 80,000 students were enrolled in high schools and 60,000 in colleges; this indicates a close link between the two, the high school acting, in effect, as a college preparatory institution, chiefly for boys. As the high school became more popular in its own right, various school boards shortened the elementary school to six years and increased the high school to six years, producing the 'six-plus-six' system. As a result, the statistics of elementary/high-school numbers are not always easy to determine. One further development is worth noting, however: the high school had poor holding power up to 1940 and so one further development occurred, the American phenomenon of the 'junior high school' which occupied three years in between a six-year elementary period and a final three-year senior high school period, thereby producing the 'six-three-three' sequence.

Throughout the developmental period, from 1900 to 1940, regardless of the various organizational patterns, 'eight-four', 'six-six' or 'six-three-three', the American high school followed the elective system and, since these schools were financed by local property taxes, they were community-based and community-run. The American high school became a multilateral comprehensive school, catering for a wide range of abilities and interests. By the nature of its local property-based funding, the school caused as much social divisiveness as it sought to cure, since communities varied enormously in their tax-raising capacities. In 1946 a searing indictment of this system was published by three American professors, Lloyd Warner, Robert Havighurst and Martin Loeb, in *Who shall be Educated? The Challenge of Unequal Opportunities*, which compared the school to a conveyer belt on a factory assembly-line, designed for 'sorting and ticketing and routing children through life'. In American education, they charged, the undemocratic European dual system continued in operation, carefully disguised within the framework of the comprehensive, multilateral community school.

Throughout the early decades various other indictments were made, chiefly by the Catholic and Lutheran churches which attempted, with partial success, to run their own school systems. The public schools were strongly influenced by the Deweyan progressive philosophy, especially at the lower-grade levels, and this the churches could not accept, particularly after Pius XI's encyclical *On the Christian Education of Youth*. At the same time, there was increased criticism from conservative thinkers who considered that American education had become weak, unscholarly and excessively concerned with meeting social and community, rather than intellectual, needs. Of these, the most vocal was Robert M. Hutchins, President of the University of Chicago in the 1930s and author of the influential *The Higher Learning in America* (1936), which took a strongly European dualist position and excoriated American education for its soft-pedagogy, Left-leaning teachers and lack of intellectual rigour and discipline. Conservatives were unhappy with the increasing expansion of school enrolments at higher levels, particularly since ever larger numbers of women and blacks were being admitted. It was, of course, very difficult to counter women's demands for an education, and in general pressure was more indirect in the form of public opinion and parental attitudes. The public institutions, elementary, high school and college, however, being community supported, could not have discriminatory policies; girls were admitted and from the nineteenth century the schools were coeducational. Catholic and private schools, unless they were very small, kept the sexes segregated on the European pattern and also exercised greater authority over the curriculum.

For blacks the situation was quite different, in that they were deliberately excluded from the public schools and comprised the bulk of illiterates at the beginning of the century. During the civil war they had been emancipated in 1863 by Lincoln and in the period of reconstruction were given citizenship in 1868, males being enfranchised in 1870 by President Grant. It was now legally impossible to prevent their seeking to become educated, but, given the nature of community organization of schools, the white power-élite was able to gerrymander school-board boundaries to keep white and black populations separate; the latter, being economically weak, had poorer schools. None the less, blacks pushed forward, founded schools and colleges and in the twentieth century moved, slowly, towards equality. The record is difficult to summarize, since practices varied from state to state; generally, all states practised racism and discrimination, the north more covertly than the south. Reacting against black mobility, the state of Kentucky legislated in 1904 against racially mixed schools, public or private, on pain of a daily fine of 100 dollars for each day of convicted violation.[5] In the more liberal states segregation was less overtly enforced; it had, however, a *de facto* if not a *de jure* reality and throughout the 1920s and 1930s blacks slowly brought test cases before the courts which they defined, not as enrolment in separate but 'equal' institutions, but as admission to the patently superior white institutions. In a landmark decision of 12 December 1938 in the 'Gaines Case', brought by a black, Lloyd Gaines, against the University of Missouri, the Supreme Court of Missouri ruled that he must be admitted to that all-white university since he wished to study law, and no such course was available at the black university. While the court observed that the state was free to establish a separate black law school for Lloyd Gaines if it so chose, none the less it ruled as legal and constitutional the fact that a black could, otherwise, be admitted to a white school. Unfortunately, as events in America have proved, communities do not always accept unpleasant court decisions and it took another sixteen years, till 1954, for the Supreme Court, in the celebrated case of *Brown* v. *Topeka*, to rule that separate schools were inherently unequal.

Throughout the early decades of the twentieth century American education came, slowly and often reluctantly, to provide equality of access for its black population. Women, white and black, were admitted to schools in larger proportions, although in higher learning they were often restricted to private women's colleges since there was still much opposition; indeed, not until 1920 did they gain the vote. Yet the fact that progress was made must not obscure divisiveness within that society. Power and wealth remained concentrated in the hands of a tiny minority: at the outbreak of the First World War 2 per cent of the population had 60 per cent of the income of the nation; just two men, John Pierpont Morgan and John Rockefeller, between them had 20 per cent of the nation's wealth, and the wealthy, the stratum termed the 'power-élite' by C. Wright Mills, sent their children to private, highly privileged schools. The overwhelming majority of the population went to public schools; the Catholic and Lutheran church schools accounted, in this period, for barely 10 per cent.

By the end of the second decade liberal pressure had mounted for central coordination and in 1918 Congress established a Federal Department of Education. One of its first tasks, owing to the increasing demand for post-elementary learning, was to appoint a commission to report on what secondary education should be, given that in 1890 one person in 210 of the total population went to secondary schools, in 1910 one in 89, in 1915 one in 73. The commission produced the famous statement on 'Cardinal Principles of Secondary Education', listing seven: '1. Health. 2. Command of fundamental processes. 3. Worthy home-membership. 4. Vocation. 5. Citizenship. 6. Worthy use of leisure. 7. Ethical character.'[6] The list attempted to balance individual and social needs, cognitive and ethical attainment, basic skills and aesthetic activities; moreover, it pointed the way to the general future development of American education. Despite the setback of the Great Depression, the seven cardinal principles guided the policies pursued in American education throughout the 1920s and 1930s.

Britain and its colonies

Education in Britain remained dominated by English thought and practice, and, although the Scots and Northern Irish gained some local concessions, in all of Britain there remained a high degree of uniformity. By the beginning of the twentieth century it was becoming clear that state subvention in education had to be markedly raised above minimum support. In 1886 the Cross Commission investigated workers' elementary education and issued a report in 1888; in 1895 the Bryce Commission reported on secondary education. Between them these two commissions stimulated further government action, issuing in 1902 as the Education Act which recognized that there was no real 'system' of education in Britain but, on the contrary, a patchwork of offerings by a number of uncoordinated authorities. The 1902 Act was developed as the progressive 1904 Public Elementary School Code which declared that 'the purpose of the Public Elementary School is to form and strengthen the character and to develop the intelligence of the children entrusted to it'.[7] A range of desirable qualities were suggested, including the cultivation of habits of observation and clear reasoning, knowledge of the facts and laws of nature, awareness of the ideals and achievements of mankind and of the literature and history of the United Kingdom, the ability to use language as an instrument of expression, a taste for reading, experience of manual and practical work and physical training. In addition, a ladder of mobility was included. The new code enjoined teachers 'to discover individual children who show promise of exceptional capacity, and to develop their special gifts so that they may be qualified to pass at the proper age into Secondary Schools, and be able to derive the maximum of benefit from the education there offered them.'[8]

To effect these intentions the Act of 1902 abolished local school boards and replaced them with local education authorities (LEAs) which were to supervise elementary education. In addition, new secondary-school regulations were issued in 1904 to empower LEAs to provide such schools, in limited numbers, for promising children up to the age of sixteen, with a curriculum consisting of English, history and geography, an ancient or modern language, mathematics, science, physical exercise, drawing, singing and household studies. Fees were to be charged for tuition, but LEAs were authorized to offer up to 25 per cent of the enrolment as free places to deserving cases. This was the situation until 1917 when, in an effort to standardize practices throughout such schools, the externally examined School Certificate was introduced. Even so, the majority of working-class children, excluded economically and socially from the private, privileged school sector, still had only the LEA elementary school, in some cases with two secondary grades at the top; the minimum leaving age remained at twelve years. In 1917 a *Report on Post-War Juvenile Employment* recommended raising the minimum leaving age to fourteen; the following year the Education Act of 1918 made new provisions that were to remain until the next major upgrading in the Education Act of 1944. The 1918 Act, introduced by the historian, H. A. L. Fisher, demonstrated a manifest social conscience, linking extension of the franchise to providing educational opportunity and facilities for all future voters. Elementary education was to be provided for all up to the age of fourteen, part-time day-continuation schools were to be organized, health and welfare of children were to be better cared for, and a more integrated national system was foreshadowed. Yet the Act had a sting in its tail: it was not providing better education for working-class children 'in order that they may rise out of their own class, always a vulgar ambition', but that their lives may gain some qualitative enrichment in their spare time, as 'a refuge from the necessary hardships of a life spent in the midst of clanging machinery in our hideous cities of toil'.[9] The English working class, a full century after Lancaster and Owen, was still expected to know its station in life.

Throughout the 1920s, however, world developments influenced Britain and advances in educational thought and progressive practice, especially in the educational applications of psychology, could not be ignored. In 1924 the Board of Education, of the Labour-majority parliament, set up a consultative committee under the chairmanship of William Henry Hadow to consider 'The Education of the Adolescent'. The Hadow Report of 1926 made several significant recommendations, including the principle of two stages of education in the child's life – 'primary' and 'secondary' – thereby putting forward the notion of an education for the working classes similar to that given to the privileged sector. An essential element was the extension of the minimum leaving age to fifteen, so that the five or six years of primary schooling, up to age eleven, would be followed by four years of secondary. By the time the report was tabled a Conservative government was in office and the report was set aside; a Labour government was returned in 1929 and presented these recommendations in a Bill, but the minimum-age clause of fifteen was defeated. None the less, the Hadow Report was the basis for much upgrading of the secondary school in the 1930s, as much as could be effected during the Great Depression, and it was followed in 1931 by a second part of the report, dealing with the primary school. This recommended some major progressive ideas as the basis for the school of the future, including the use of experience-centred activities rather than subjects as the foundation of the curriculum, ability streaming on the basis of intelligence quotients, maximum class sizes of forty, and general acceptance of current developments in progressive psychological and pedagogical thought. However, the times were difficult, and the Hadow Report recommendations, although well received, had to wait for implementation until the significant Education Act of 1944 which restructured English education along the present lines. This Act maintained a separation between private schools, variously aided by government grants, and the state schools which were in two streams: a common primary school, separating into academically advanced grammar schools and less demanding 'secondary modern' schools.

Outside England, similar patterns obtained. For Wales, the Westminster parliament in 1889 passed the Intermediate Education Act which provided a new kind of day school as a bridge between the minimum elementary schools and the few grammar schools; by 1895 there were thirty such intermediate schools giving a minimum secondary education, and in 1896 a Central Welsh Board of Education was established to administer them; in 1899 this was abolished and Wales was brought under the authority of the Board of Education in England. Scotland was treated similarly. In 1872 an Education (Scotland) Act was passed requiring compulsory schooling, and local boards were authorized, a Scottish Education Department appearing in 1885. In 1908 the Education (Scotland) Act brought the disparate schools and boards together in greater unity and the Act of 1918 paralleled the English Act of the same year. Thereafter, apart from local differences, education in Scotland was on the same basis as that in England, although administered by the independent Scottish Board of Education.

In Australia and New Zealand the mother country was followed closely throughout the nineteenth century. The separate colonies began with private schools, generally denominational with serious differences between Anglicans, Protestants and Catholics; public schooling began, on a minimal basis, with colonial boards of education, and compulsory elementary legislation came at the same time as in Britain and the rest of Europe, beginning with Victoria in 1872, followed by Queensland (1875), South Australia and West Australia (both in 1878) and New South Wales (1880). New Zealand enacted in 1878. Thereafter these sovereign states, as they became, continued to look to Britain for models of further legislation and practice which they copied, unimaginatively, at a safe distance.

In Ireland the religious issue continued to poison relations with

England; the Catholic Irish population remained subordinate to the Anglo-Irish Anglican establishment. Catholic emancipation had been proclaimed in 1829 throughout the United Kingdom, and, following the waves of popular protest and revolution that swept Europe in 1830, the liberal Whig government at Westminster included in its Reform Bill of 1832 a grant of £30,000 towards popular education in Ireland – before, in fact, anything had been given for similar purposes in England. At that time, there was no popular Irish education, only the officially acknow-ledged SPCK schools and the clandestine hedge schools. This grant was to help fund an Irish national system, non-denominational in character, with common textbooks for Catholic and Protestant child alike, with the express purpose that, by the children's studying together, bonds of understanding and amity would be forged, as well as mitigating the appalling level of illiteracy. To meet religious needs, one day a week was to be set aside for each faith to have separate instruction by the clergy who had the right of access. The Irish bishops gladly joined the scheme, having received papal approval, and 789 national schools, with an enrolment of 107,042 children, were opened the first year. At the end of the first two decades, in 1851, the numbers had increased to 3501 schools with an enrol-ment of just on 500,000 girls and boys.[10] The instruction was entirely in English, while the local Erse was allowed to decline. Literacy rose correlatively and in 1851 some 53 per cent of the population were estima-ted to have been able to read and write in English.

Administration of the Irish national system was entrusted to a Board of Commissioners, representing the several denominations, and varying in number at any one time from between seven and thirteen, and their task was to dispense the subvention, £120,000 by 1849, to various qualifying schools. The Christian Brothers of Ireland refused to join in the scheme but the various women's teaching congregations, notably the Presentation Order and the Ursulines, cooperated enthusiastically. The system, how-ever, did not develop as planned, since Catholics and Protestants could not agree. Many Protestants belonged to the establishment and sent their children to private schools; among the working classes there was strong residential segregation, over the first twenty years separate sectarian populations in the schools became the norm, and by 1851 there was, in effect, *de facto* segregation. The Commissioners sanctioned the arrange-ments and throughout the second half of the century the Irish bishops increased pressure on the Board for an independent Catholic national system. Although this did not eventuate, they certainly made the *de facto* segregation permanent. In 1892 Westminster abolished fees for these schools and required compulsory attendance, which proved hard to enforce. Despite this, by 1901 the nation had a literacy rate of some 86 per cent; in that year the Irish marriage registers recorded only 13.2 per cent of men and 10.7 per cent of women signing with marks.[11]

Parallel with this was the establishment of a modest system of inter-mediate schools when the Intermediate Education Act was passed in 1878 providing grants for intermediate and technical education to both private schools and national boards; beyond this, grammar schooling remained private, either Protestant or Catholic. University education made some gains, and the first Catholic university of Dublin opened in 1854 with Henry Newman as first rector until 1858; this was replaced in 1883 by the Jesuit-run University College of Dublin, in 1908 renamed the National University of Ireland, incorporating the three constituent colleges of Dublin, Cork and Galway. Once established, this system of state-funded national elementary schools, intermediate schools (with agricultural and technical versions), private grammar schools and university colleges continued into the twentieth century, almost unchanged to the present.

In the Catholic-majority south the Irish remained opposed to British domination and a series of disturbances beginning with the Easter Rising of 1916 led to the Government of Ireland Act in 1920, conferring a kind of 'dominion' status on the south. In 1922 southern Ireland gained recognition as the Irish Free State while the largely Protestant north remained within the United Kingdom as Ulster; in 1937, the south became the independent Eire, the Republic of Ireland. The former educational system remained unchanged in Eire except for the disappearance in 1923 of the Intermediate Education Board. The government tried to revive the native language of Erse, but this has proved difficult, despite such artificial practices as requiring it for university matriculation and certain civil service appointments. The national system of direct grants to boards continues, and these are largely administered by the church; the schools remain dominated by religious orders or conducted by lay teachers in Protestant areas. There is a small system of secondary schools, but these are neither compulsory nor well attended. To this day in Ireland there is strong *de facto* separation of the Catholic and Protestant communities, as a result of the national system which was expressly designed to produce the opposite effect.

In Canada, Britain had another difficult problem caused by the in-corporation of the former French territories in the domains. By the Constitutional Act of 1791, the French region of 'Lower Canada', centred on Montreal, was separated from 'Upper Canada', centred on Toronto, or York as it was then called. Then followed the tragic division of the new nation, the Catholic Church being supported in Lower Canada and the Protestant churches in Upper Canada and the Maritime regions of New Brunswick, Prince Edward Island and Nova Scotia. No church was officially established, although they all received grants of land as endowments to provide funds. As in the Australian colonies, the Anglicans claimed to be 'established' because of the English situation; this was bitterly refuted in Canada too, and the Protestant sects had to share both funds and responsibility for education. After 1791 the various regions developed separately but in 1841 Britain administratively reunited Upper and Lower Canada and in 1845 a Common School Bill was enacted to authorize school boards. In 1846 these were operating in Upper Canada under the administrative genius of Egerton Ryerson who had been superintendent of schools there since 1843. Under Ryerson the progressive methods of the day, both European and American, were introduced, including a normal school in 1846 at Toronto; by that year, of the 198,434 children in the province of school age, some 110,002, 55 per cent, were in attendance. Fees were gradually reduced; by 1865 they were almost entirely abolished and 85 per cent of children in the future Ontario were in school.[12]

Meanwhile, in Quebec, under the Act of 1845, a system similar to that in France was chosen, but using the parish instead of the commune. Confessional schools became the norm until an Act of 1859 established for all Canada a Council of Public Instruction which introduced public, provincial systems. In Quebec this was initiated under the premiership of P. J. O. Chauveau, who, as Minister of Education too, sought to eliminate parochialism, although, as in other Catholic countries, Chauveau had to contend with the bishops who sought to keep the schools under church control. In 1867 Britain granted Canada independence under the British-North America Act and education became a responsibility of the separate provinces, four at the time: the renamed regions of Ontario and Quebec, along with New Brunswick and Nova Scotia. Educational development thereafter was pursued separately as new provinces were founded (Manitoba, 1870; British Columbia, 1871; Prince Edward Island, 1873; Saskatchewan and Alberta, 1905; Newfoundland, 1949), but with a high degree of similarity and much greater dependence on nearby American models than on those of Britain.

France

To understand educational change in France under the Third Republic (1875–1940), it is necessary to reconsider the claims of the Catholic Church to the divine mandate of *magisterium ordinarium* – that is, the right to teach the faithful through an eternal office of receiving and interpreting the scriptures – since this influenced developments in all the Catholic regions of Europe as well as in the New World. In the nineteenth century, with industrial and economic developments and rising nationalist demands in Europe, the Holy See recognized that an even more serious threat confronted it than the doctrinal schism of the sixteenth century. The nineteenth century was seeing the deliberate proclamation of godless doctrines of all kinds, and, in the struggle to survive the ruthless economic and political battles of the period, the emerging states were placing nationalism and modernity before religion.

In the face of these developments the papacy fought energetically to retain its *magisterium*, and in those troubled years of working-class unrest and bourgeois reaction, ever-growing industrialization, technologization and the positivistic-materialist outlook, between 1830 and 1900, it had a formidable task. Gregory XVI (r. 1831–46) moved to strengthen papal authority over Catholic Europe by developing the first tenets of the theory of infallibility, and by objecting to current liberal thought in a series of encyclicals that denounced 'mixed' marriages, popular insurrections in Poland, religious indifference, the interference of the German state in church affairs and Protestant Bible societies. Two encyclicals are important, *Mirari vos* of 1832 against liberalism, and *Singulari nos* of 1834 attacking the increasingly popular ideas of Félicité-Robert de Lamennais (1782–1854), a follower of Rousseauian thought who, while a priest, argued for the restriction of the church to spiritual matters and for its abandoning of politics. In *Singulari nos* Gregory fulminated against all liberal doctrines, including the 'academies and universities [which] resound with new and monstrous opinions, and no longer secretly or obscurely . . . attack the Catholic faith, but publicly declare against it a horrible and impious war'.[13] Gregory was succeeded by an even more determined pope, Pius IX (r. 1846–78), who, acting more diplomatically, signed concordats with the various Catholic states by which they recognized the exclusive right of the church to conduct schools, the most important being concluded with Spain in 1851 and Austria in 1855. Papal opposition to liberalism, socialism and positivist science was vigorously expressed in a stream of encyclicals from his first on 9 November 1846, *Qui pluribus*, against communism, reaching a crescendo in his twenty-second, *Quanta cura* of 8 December 1864, which had, as an appendix, the *Syllabus of Errors*. *Quanta cura* restated the conservative case of the church and listed as dangerous modern errors the developments of pantheism, naturalism, rationalism, indifferentism, socialism, communism, secret societies, Bible societies, clerical-liberal societies, civil and mixed marriages, liberalism and non-recognition of the civil power of the pontiff.[14] In 1868 Pius IX convened a Vatican Council of some 700 bishops which, against considerable minority opposition, took a stronger line against modernism and in 1870 passed two contentious resolutions, the primacy of the pope and the doctrine of papal infallibility.

The council had to break up, leaving its work unfinished, when the war of 1870 struck a further blow at the papacy. Throughout the 1860s there had been moves to unite the Italian states under a single sovereign, which the papacy resisted, seeking to hold its temporal possessions – hence the final 'error' denounced in the *Syllabus errorum*. Ignoring the Vatican, Sardinia and Piedmont formed the kingdom of Italy and in 1860 Garibaldi sailed from Genoa with his 'Thousand', landed in Sicily and in a swift campaign liberated the Spanish Bourbon-ruled Kingdom of the Two Sicilies – Sicily, Calabria and Benevento – up to the southern border of the papal states. A new Kingdom of Italy under Victor Emmanuel (r. 1861–78) was proclaimed in 1861. A French army contingent continued to help garrison the papal states, but with the defeat of France in 1870 in the Franco-Prussian war General Cadorna of the Italian army invaded and annexed them to Italy. Pius IX declared himself a prisoner of the Vatican and neither he nor his successors Leo XIII (r. 1878–1903), Pius X (r. 1903–14) and Benedict XV (r. 1914–22) ever left the precincts. It was Pius XI (r. 1922–39) who concluded the settlement condordat of 1928 with Mussolini, whereby the papal state – now reduced in area to the land in Rome, the Vatican, on which its buildings stand – was accorded sovereign status. During the period of self-incarceration the papacy disadvantaged itself severely, and in its determination to assert authority imposed enormous strains of conscience upon Catholic states, often polarizing political parties within them, particularly in France, Belgium, Italy and Spain. Governments were forced to accept Vatican directives in areas of social, political and educational policy, or else to turn to the extreme of self-determination which generally issued as anticlericalism.

France was caught up in this problem as early as the period of its compulsory-education legislation, and in the early years of the Third Republic it turned anticlerical, asserting the primary authority of the state. From 1872 onwards came a stream of reforming moves, at first directed at secondary and higher education, such as in 1880 when the appellation 'university' was forbidden to all but authorized institutions. In 1881 came the first *Loi Ferry* which provided free primary education throughout France, and in 1882 the second *Loi Ferry* which made such schooling compulsory. Steady progress was made: illiteracy declined, and the elementary teaching force increased from 64,000 teachers in 1877 to 100,000 in 1893 and 125,000 in 1913;[15] by a law of 1889 teachers were required to be trained in *département* normal schools and to receive their salaries directly from the state. Secondary education was regulated, although the provisions of the Second Republic still applied, the privileged sector going to the *lycées* and various *écoles pratiques, hautes écoles* and universities.

At the same time, the rural areas remained conservative and closely attached to the church; the educational reforms coming from Paris were related to the temper of the industrial north, and French education remained unevenly distributed between north and south. In the south it was rudimentary among large sections of the peasantry who were suspicious of too much schooling, their attitudes being strongly reinforced by the parish clergy. Women lay teachers were particularly discriminated against; in one memoir of the period around 1887 a teacher recollected from her experiences in a Médoc village, in the rural south near Bordeaux, that she and her companions were overcharged in the shops, abused and given poor accommodation with the remark that 'a cowshed would be good enough for these hussies', while in some areas the people refused to sell them any food at all. She attributed this to the 'religious fanaticism' of the rural areas, and the fact that they had replaced 'nuns whose school had been secularized'; as a result they received 'abuse of all kinds: blasphemous education, atheistic education, Godless schools'.[16] Similarly, the leader of the *petit bourgeois* radicals, Georges Clemenceau (1841–1929), later prime minister 1906–9 and again 1917–20, in 1894 criticized the Catholic countryside for its opposition to the state school, and the plight of the teacher for whom 'the country squires are his enemies; with the priest there is latent hostility; with the Catholic schools there is open war. . . . They steal his pupils; they crush him in a hundred ways, sometimes with the connivance of the mayor, usually with the co-operation of the big influences in the commune.'[17]

Such religious conservatism remained in the rural areas but in urban France the secular spirit continued, positivism in particular became a fashionable philosophy, and in 1902, with the radicals becoming more aggressive, the elections were fought on the clerical issue; in 1904, by a law of 7 July, religious congregations were prohibited from teaching and private schools were to be phased out by 1914, although the Great War prevented that from happening. Slowly France modernized and secularized as the state-school system became extended and working-class socialism gained considerable ground, although at the price of bitter confrontations with the government in a series of nine major strikes between 1898 and 1913. In 1906 Clemenceau had to mobilize 20,000 troops, and violent clashes with the striking miners occurred; again in 1907 troops were called to riots in the southern vineyards, but they sided with the strikers and mutinied. In this period of social unrest, education received little attention before France was plunged into the First World War, when, despite its final victory on the Allied side, it lost 1,385,000 soldiers dead and sustained further great losses of civilian deaths and injuries. One consequence of the war was a recognition of the inadequacy and inefficiency of technical schooling and the excessive concern with formal bookish curricula in the established system. In 1919 the *Loi Astier* was passed to reform intermediate-level technical education, leading in 1921 to the establishment of trade schools (*écoles de métiers*). In the ensuing two decades, no further significant changes were made; there were administrative improvements, but in general French education retained its totally centralized administration with a stratified system of highly competitive schools. Like England, it maintained a basic primary education for all children which in 1933 was extended to a minimum leaving age of fourteen with abolition of all fees; further educational progress to either technical or secondary schools, or the *lycée*, was highly competitive. The position in 1927 was described by Albert Thibaudet as one in which every social class had access to higher education, 'but law and medicine are closed to all but those with private means. The same is almost true for would-be engineers or higher civil servants, [while] . . . the traditional core of the army is still to be found among some 20,000 noble and bourgeois families.' Social mobility, as everywhere in the Western world, was possible through schoolteaching, this being 'the one career recruited almost exclusively from the portionless *boursier*. Eight or nine out of ten students in the *École Normale Supérieure* are supported by state bursaries won against strong competition.' The rich and well-to-do families avoided teaching; it was the exclusive preserve of the 'new educated'. The traditional pattern of French society is well summarized in his final paragraph:

In Paris the strongholds of the intelligentsia are the *Académie française*, the *Institut*, literature, journalism, the Bar. The universities come a bad second, and the teacher counts for nothing. But in the provinces teachers are the intellectual elite, and in the villages, with the curé out of the way there is only the village schoolteacher left.[18]

With the same unpreparedness as when it entered the First World War, France went into the Second World War in 1939, with even more disastrous results, capitulating to Germany in June 1940. Acting under pressure from the occupying power, the Vichy regime made some changes, and as soon as France was liberated in late 1944 a commission under the chairmanship of Paul Langevin and, subsequently, Henri Wallon, was established to plan the reconstruction of French education, the June 1947 report of this commission being known as the Langevin-Wallon Plan. Again, the French analysis revealed technical insufficiency, and the plan proposed radical reforms: the abandonment of the sterile formalism of the bourgeois tradition with its emphasis on excessively cognitive attainment, and a stress instead on 'the diversity of individual aptitudes, the equality of all children in respect of education, to allow each, in the interest of all, fully to develop his personality'.[19] Despite these fine sentiments, French education did not shake off its encyclopedic formalism and excessive concern with status, inherited and acquired, and the two separate paths these imply: the higher professions for the well-born, lower professions for the hard-working *capacités*. The problem was well analysed in 1966 in the *Revue française de sociologie* by Pierre Bourdieu, professor at the École Pratique des Hautes Études, in an article 'L'École conservatrice'. In that and other studies,[20] Bourdieu showed that in France 'the educational system reproduces all the more perfectly the structure of the distribution of cultural capital among classes'[21] – that is, that the dominant *notables* and *grande bourgeoisie* still retain their privileged position, while below them are the middle and lower classes whose children, if talented (*capacités*), may rise part of the way up the social scale; all this not in spite of the educational system but because of it.

Germany and Belgium

Like Britain and France, Germany had developed most of the infrastructure of a national educational system by the beginning of this century, but, whereas the English had shown considerable receptivity to the progressive movement, neither the French nor the German government was interested in progressivism within the state system: the external features of Pestalozzi, Froebel and Herbart were applied to the extent that they supported the conservative tradition. Generally, in Germany the twentieth century saw few innovations, chiefly because that nation was crippled by the Great War of 1914–18 and the subsequent burden of reparations imposed in 1919. By 1920 the country was in a disastrous condition and in education was excluded as an international pariah from the 1921 NEF Conference at Calais. Throughout the 1920s under the Weimar government (1919–30) it staggered on with impossible inflation under Allied occupation of the Ruhr, its industrial heartland; when regeneration came in the 1930s under the Nazi regime, its educational system was reorganized as part of a programme of total mobilization for war.

Despite the difficulties of the Weimar period, a few changes were made to the nineteenth-century imperial model of education. The dual system continued, and the bourgeoisie had a sequence of preparatory schools (*Vorschulen*) which led on to the classical *Gymnasium*, the *Realgymnasium* or the *Realschule*, while a fourth similar institution had been established for girls, the *Lyzeum*, which was a state replacement for the *Klosterschule*. For the mass of the working class there remained the *Volksschule*, which offered an eight-year curriculum, and the parallel, slightly advanced inter-mediate-level *Mittelschule*, which provided a five-year curriculum for grades four to eight. Beyond these were part-time continuation schools, *Forbildungschulen*, which led to advanced technical and trades training in the *Fachschulen* and the *technische Hochschulen*. In a gesture to improve the status of the *Volksschule* and *Mittelschule*, male teachers were permitted in 1900 to serve only the first year of compulsory military service and then transfer to the officers' reserve, thereby enhancing their social standing in a highly class-conscious society, and giving also an indication of the role education was seen to serve in the state. In the Weimar period an effort was made to democratize this under the federal Constitution of 11 August 1919 which required the twenty-six states (*Länder*) to introduce a single common elementary school for all children, thereby abolishing the separate *Volksschule* and *Vorschule* for the two social classes and introducing, in their place, the new common four-year elementary *Grundschule*. These were to be administered by the individual *Länder*, but there was little effective central control. Apart from the *Grundschule* the schools remained as before, and it seems that little real selection by merit occurred and that the highly structured, middle-class-dominated system continued unchanged. A slight opening-up occurred in the *Grundschule* for children who failed to transfer to the selective *Gymnasium/Realschule* part of the system in that some states provided a special 'German higher school', *deutsche Oberschule* or *Aufbauschule*, at the eighth-grade level which concentrated on a university-matriculation programme.

Generally the same German pattern was followed throughout Austria, although by a concordat with the Holy See of 1855 Austria recognized the authority of the church in education. State provisions were made, chiefly by regulation, and in 1869 universal free education was decreed. However, funding and enforcement were to be left to individual local authorities spread throughout the fifteen crown lands, each with its own legislative assembly.

Germany had exercised a tremendous influence on much Western education in the late nineteenth century, when its innovations attracted the interest of visiting administrators and theorists from North America and particularly from neighbouring countries in Europe: the Low Countries, Scandinavia, Austria-Hungary, Poland and Switzerland. The Netherlands, where elementary education was made compulsory in 1878, developed virtually the same system. Switzerland, too, especially in the German-speaking north, followed the German example, and in the 1874 constitutional revision a unified public-education system was introduced with compulsory-attendance laws, although this caused continuing internal dissension among the separate ethnic communities for more than a decade.

Belgium was a more complex case, since it had been artificially created in 1815 by the Congress of Vienna out of the Habsburg section of the Netherlands. The Dutch, being in effect in occupation, developed the schools on their own pattern and introduced Dutch as the official verna-cular. Belgium, however, was a mixed population comprising, in the north, Calvinist, Dutch-speaking Flemings and, in the south, Catholic French-dialect-speaking Walloons. It was, moreover, rich in raw materials, particularly coal, and throughout the history of Europe had been a major centre of skilled trades. The Belgians revolted against Dutch control in the general uprisings of 1830 and gained a precarious independence. Education became involved because the nation was forced to maintain the same developmental pace as its four neighbours, England, Germany, the Netherlands and France, and that required a better-trained workforce; in addition, it had to forge a national identity. The result, however, was that difficult decisions had to be made in mid-century, since the demands of identity, national independence and modernization ran counter to the current pressure from the Vatican for conformity to the faith. This deeply troubled the Catholic Walloon community of this small nation of some four million people and led in 1879 to the *guerre scolaire*, the 'war of the schools'.

Early Belgian politics had been dominated by the bourgeois parties elected under the system of the *régime censitaire* which required a property qualification for the franchise and thereby kept the working class out of politics. In 1848 there were popular demands for widening the franchise to the *capacitaires*, those with three years' middle schooling, but this was refused. Additional pressure for reforms came from both sides: the extremist Flemings demanded their own language exclusively in all areas that concerned them, including their home region of Flanders, in Flemish army regiments, the University of Ghent and the law courts; the Catholics wanted greater political participation and the preservation of their rights which the government was eroding through a series of legislative and administrative acts which made the continuation of church-run primary and secondary schools more difficult. The working class was numerous, generally illiterate and largely made up of peasants and exploited coal-miners; because of the country's tragic record of mine disasters, socialism was making headway among the miners. When expelled from both Germany and France in 1845, in fact, Marx went to Brussels in the period 1845-8 and there composed the *Communist Manifesto* and organized the left-wing Association Démocratique.

The government formed by the Protestant Centre Liberals, led by Charles Rogier, but dominated by the Minister of Works Walthère Frère-Orban, attempted to steer a middle course during this period. By the 1870s, when the era of universal schooling was under way in Europe, they designed on the German and French models a secular state system whereby the church would be excluded from all participation, a centralized government department of education would be created, and teachers would have to be trained in state normal schools and meet state certification requirements. Administration was to be delegated to local communes. The Catholic community, strongly ultramontane, refused to cooperate with this Bill of 1879 and raised an enormous fund to open an independent Catholic primary school in every province. The clergy, moreover, faithfully following the directives of Pius IX, denied the sacraments and absolution to any Catholic parent who sent a child to the state schools or to any Catholic who taught in them; in Belgian parish churches the prayer was read at every Mass, 'From Godless schools and faithless teachers, good Lord deliver us'.[22] The king, Leopold II, was forced to sign the 1879 Bill on 18 June and Belgium was badly fractured, the newly formed Socialist Party of 1879 forging an unlikely, and obviously impermanent, alliance with the Catholic Right against the Centre, bourgeois Liberals. As a mark of displeasure, the Vatican refused to send representatives to the celebrations for Belgium's fiftieth anniversary of independence; in 1880 Frère-Orban retaliated by breaking off diplomatic relations with the Holy See. The new pope, Leo XIII (r. 1878–1903), however, was an astute diplomat who recognized the growing strength of both nationalism and workers' movements of the Left and saw that if the church were to hold its *magisterium* it could not continue to oppose the trends of the times. Leo was responsible for the Vatican's becoming seriously engaged in supporting some features of modern developments, especially in the great encyclical of 15 May 1891 on the condition of the working class, *Rerum novarum*, 'Of New Things'.

The Belgian Catholics were not easily mollified. The Bill of 1879 they called the 'law of disaster' (*loi de malheur*). In 1884 the elections resulted in a landslide Catholic victory, and they retained government to the end of the century, their election being largely due to the 1883 extension of the franchise to include the *capacitaires*, those with a minimum secondary education. Continued working-class agitation led to universal male suffrage in 1894, and in 1898 French and Flemish were accorded joint official-language status. The school issue, fought as the *guerre scolaire*, was not so easily resolved. When the Catholics came to power under Jules Malou they restored diplomatic relations with the Vatican and returned the school situation to the *status quo ante*, only to find, in the meantime, that the communes had, reluctantly, to accept the *loi de malheur* and create the beginnings of a secular, state-supported system of education.

Eastern Europe: insurgent nationalism

Much of European politics was dominated in the early twentieth century by the efforts of repressed bourgeois minorities, driven by nationalistic and liberal ideals derived from western Europe, to assume leadership of independent states in eastern and Balkan Europe, free from occupation and control by the great powers of Germany, Russia, Austria-Hungary and Ottoman Turkey. Power conflict had already emerged in earlier centuries, as expansion and national development led to border disputes, particularly in the richer agricultural plains. To strengthen their hold on the occupied lands, the four great powers maintained a policy of strict subjugation and, in cases, the attempted annihilation of subject-minority cultures. So, from the Baltic Sea in the north to the Aegean in the south there was a string of marcher lands, populated by restive, oppressed minorities: Finns, Estonians, Letts, Poles, Bohemians, Moravians, Czechs, Slovaks, Ukrainians, Romanians, Bulgars, Croatians, Slovenes, Serbs, Macedonians, Montenegrins, Dalmatians, Albanians and Greeks. All were integrated, if small, cultures, each possessed of its individual history, language, literature and a strong sense of identity, and none was prepared to be assimilated into the dominant culture of the occupying power. Moreover, all of their emerging bourgeois factions now looked to the West and saw their future in similar development. Educational demands in the nineteenth century, however, were significant factors in the emergence of an insurgent nationalism; while minority communities can live peaceably with larger neighbours when life proceeds by the oral tradition, the development of formal literacy and the spread of the school are much more threatening and added to the turmoil in the period 1870-1918 which resulted, when the map of Europe was redrawn in 1919 at Versailles, in the formation of a number of new states: Estonia, Latvia, Lithuania, Poland, Ukraine, Romania, Bulgaria, Transylvania, Czechoslovakia, the Kingdom of the Serbs, Croats and Slovenes, and an expanded Greece. Some of these had only a precarious existence after the Second World War and were reabsorbed into Russia, either as buffer zones again, under the euphemism of the Soviet 'Union', or else as tightly controlled Soviet satellites. Only three maintained full independence – Yugoslavia, Greece and the newly established small state of Albania.

In education, friction became manifest in the nineteenth century when Bismarck expanded the Prussian school system into its Polish regions of Poznan and Silesia and allowed only the German language as the medium of instruction. The problem was exacerbated by the fact that Poland was almost totally Catholic and had built its educational system on a network of Jesuit colleges. Simultaneously, across the border the Russians were pursuing a similar policy, based on the Orthodox Church, and had even embarked on a campaign to eliminate the Polish language and culture by actively impeding the Catholic Church, banning private schools and establishing Russian state schools. Poles in both Germany and Russia looked south to their separated compatriots in Galicia, incorporated into Austria, where Poles had the right to run their own schools and their two universities of Cracow and Lvov. Ironically, the Austrian leniency towards the Polish Galicians, which was extended to their other fourteen subjugated minorities, was to be a major factor in the rise of nationalism and demands for independent states. Throughout the early twentieth century this only heightened ambition among the Polish urban middle classes for independence; in secret, they maintained their national culture until the opportunity came, in 1919, for the re-establishment of their nation, partitioned since 1772–95.

Throughout central Europe, the Catholic Church remained in undisputed religious authority and in the realms of Habsburg Austria continued to run most of the schools, the elementary ones through various teaching congregations. Secondary schools were mostly Jesuit colleges, secured through the concordat with Rome in 1855. In 1867 the expedient of the Dual Monarchy was devised to maintain power, but Austria remained dominant over Magyar Hungary. There was, by this time, a clear need to begin modernization of the state, and in 1869 free, elementary (but not compulsory) education was decreed for all of the empire, extending the school throughout Austria, Hungary, the Tirol, Bohemia, Moravia, Slovenia, Croatia and Dalmatia. These were all Catholic lands, and Latin was widely used in education but not as a vernacular. While the Austrians accepted the local vernaculars in the schools, the Hungarians promoted a policy of compulsory Magyarization which they imposed upon their subject minorities, the ability to read and write Magyar being made a precondition for enfranchisement. The result was the same as that among the Poles: demands for independence and separation emerged, among the Slovenes, Croatians and Serbians a pan-Slav movement gathered strength, and in 1868 Croatia gained a limited autonomy within the empire. At the same time, Turkey was becoming relatively weaker, and in the Russo-Turkish War of 1877–8 the settlement of San Stefano gave independence to Serbia, Montenegro and Romania. The Romanians turned to Germany and built an educational system closely modelled on Prussia; Montenegro, small and impoverished, made little progress; Serbia, landlocked but with potential for growth, continued to push pan-Slavism and moved to build up its educational system, enacting compulsory elementary legislation in 1888. By the 1890s all the Balkan states had minimum elementary-school systems in operation; all, of course, had a restricted secondary system as a legacy of the religious era, Catholic everywhere except Serbia, Montenegro and Macedonia which were Orthodox. By the early twentieth century, the elementary school became standard in the cities and larger towns, although secondary schooling was very limited indeed, being restricted to the well-to-do minority.

Southern Europe: reaction and the modern era

Spain and Portugal

Education in Spain in the twentieth century was tragically backward, under the dominance of the Catholic Church which was able, more than anywhere else in Europe, to block the influx of modern ideas and practices and sustain a quasi-feudal society. Modern Spanish history begins when Napoleon's brother Joseph became King of Spain and, as part of imperial policy, began the construction of a centralized administration on the French model. A state Ministry of Education was set up and universities and schools brought under government control; in addition, in order to establish a secular system, the municipalities were authorized to provide schools. At this time, most education in Spain remained in the hands of the teaching congregations, and although the Jesuits had been expelled in 1767 by Charles III their colleges still existed, staffed by other congregations, as the only secondary schools, fee-charging, and catering mainly for the wealthy. Joseph Bonaparte made little headway; in 1813 Ferdinand VII (r. 1808–33) was restored and a period of reaction followed which initiated more than a century and a half of intermittent civil war.

Ferdinand VII looked to the church for assistance, bringing back the Jesuits in 1822, and a decree of October 1824 ushered in an era of severe intellectual repression, dominated by the Catholic Church, which, claiming sole possession of the truth, promulgated the doctrine that 'error has no rights', and as late as 1875 taught, in schools as well as from the pulpit, that voting for liberals was a mortal sin.

After the Carlist era, a coalition of radical socialist and republican groups in 1868–73 made efforts to reform education. It decreed free primary education and the expansion of state schools based on municipalities, recalled persecuted liberal teachers and in 1870 expelled the Jesuits and sequestrated their property. However, instability continued, and the restoration rule of Alfonso XII (r. 1874–5) began another reaction. He abolished free schools, restored the Jesuits and passed laws permitting only Catholics to teach in schools and universities; all textbooks were to be censored by church authorities, university lecturers were to submit outlines of lectures for approval, and Catholic dogma was to be a compulsory subject. Education continued in this condition until another brief burst of republicanism (1931–3) attempted to modernize Spain.

From 1870 to the first decade of the twentieth century efforts to reform Spanish education were led largely by two men, Sanz del Rio and his student, Giner de los Ríos.[23] Sanz del Rio (1814–69) was to become the central figure among a group of intellectuals seeking to modernize Spain; as a student of philosophy Sanz travelled throughout Europe in the 1840s, studying at Paris, Brussels and Heidelberg where the contrast with the regimented, priest-ridden Spanish universities inspired his determination to reform Spanish universities both by writing and from his chair of philosophy at Madrid.

An important member of Sanz's Philosophical Circle at Madrid was Francisco Giner de los Ríos (1839–1915), Professor of Law at the university, and later to be recognized by the poet Antonio Machado as the 'educator of Spain'. In 1876 Giner founded the Institución Libre de Enseñanza (The Free Educational Institute) as a private university college in protest against state and clerical domination of education. Here he introduced the best of English humanism and German organization, his Institución becoming so successful that in 1884 he opened a preparatory day school with an enrolment of 200 boys. According to Machado, Giner's own teaching method was highly personal; following the ideas of Froebel, he taught in a familiar, almost loving kind of way, using where possible the Socratic method of questioning, in an attempt to extend his students' interests and understanding. Giner opposed dogmatic and catechetical instruction, arguing that the child is in no position to know its own mind on such matters, and recommended a generalized approach to religion in schools. In imitation of progressive European practices, Giner introduced excursions and visits to museums, galleries and the countryside as an integral element of his approach. He stressed that he had developed neither a system nor a method, simply an approach to education incorporating the best that was currently being practised abroad; none the less, he stimulated considerable interest, and other schools, primary and secondary, were founded on his example.

Contemporaneous with Giner was the significant work of Santiago Ramón y Cajal, Professor of Histology at Saragossa, who led a campaign against those sterile methods of the university which emphasized right up to the reforms of 1931–3 the use of memorized textbooks in science. Like

Giner, Ramón urged students to travel abroad, to study science in the field and experimentally; to further this he began agitating in 1897 for reform of elementary education, and overseas study for promising young Spaniards. His efforts led in 1907 to the formation of the Junta para Ampliación de Estudios (Society for Widening the Scope of Studies) composed of twenty-one selected members pledged to build contacts outside the country and to engage in an active programme of selecting students for travelling scholarships. Despite conservative opposition to everything Giner did, the Junta kept functioning, even receiving a state grant to the scholarship fund.

Spanish education changed slowly, and under Giner's influence Spaniards attended various world congresses of education which were sources of new ideas. At the same time, the reforms of Sanz, Giner and Ramón were resisted: the church wanted science to be taught by memorization from censored textbooks, religion from textbooks and catechism, religion to be stressed as the basis of all learning, and any widespread popular education such as had been introduced across the border under the *Loi Ferry* of 1881–2 to be rejected. The church opposed the extension of public literacy and the general education of girls; it supported illiteracy on the grounds that ignorant persons could not be exposed to heretical, liberal or socialist doctrines and so would remain in a 'state of grace'. Throughout the first three decades of the twentieth century no real effort was made to provide schools for the people, the problem being compounded by the emerging middle class's refusal to let their children enter teaching because of its lack of social respectability.

Not until the Second Republic was proclaimed in 1931 was an effort made to deal seriously with the educational needs of the country. With a population of nearly 24 million, 50 per cent of the people were totally illiterate and there were no schools for their children; in all Spain there were less than a million students altogether in schools and universities. The teaching congregations had 350,937, made up of 128,258 boys and 222,679 girls; the state 'system' held some 400,000. Further, 57 per cent of teachers were completely untrained and without qualifications.[24] Under the guidance of the prime minister, Don Manuel Azaña, the Constitution of 1931 decreed the separation of church and state, the dissolution (yet again) of the Society of Jesus, the sequestration of their property, and a prohibition on all orders and congregations from teaching. The educational annual budget was immediately increased from 6.5 to 25 million pesetas and a loan opened for 600 million pesetas to provide schools to meet the requirements of the compulsory-education laws which, for the first time in Spanish history, compelled the attendance of children aged seven to ten. Acting quickly, the Second Republic had opened 2580 schools by the end of 1932, a further 3990 by the end of 1933. School enrolments increased to 55 per cent of eligible children; in addition 5000 regional libraries were established and all elementary schools received a school lunch programme to mitigate the worst effects of the depression on the childern. Teachers received a 50 per cent salary increase. In 1933 the government passed the Law on Confessions and Congregations, which specified a definite timetable for the removal of religious teachers from the schools as secular teachers were trained to replace them. To help the poor, illiterate rural peasants, travelling schools were established, *missiones pedagógicas*, which took travelling shows of art, craft, music, lantern slides and similar activities to the people in order to widen their horizons and, in many cases, to improve their vocational skills.

On 11 September 1933 the Azaña government was toppled by a reactionary monarchist-Catholic-rural oligarchy coalition and Spain again plunged into crisis. Immediately the ambitions of the republican liberals were thwarted: the education budget was slashed, the school lunch programme for the undernourished peasant and worker children was abolished, the *missiones pedagógicas* withdrawn. Spain moved towards the tragedy of the civil war of 1936–9 in which the reactionary conservative party of the Falange Española Tradicionalista led by Francisco Franco was successful, placing Spain under more than thirty years of fascist repression. Education, and the liberation of the people, was still a long way off in 1939.

Meanwhile, the educational history of Portugal throughout the nineteenth and twentieth centuries is a comparable record of reactionary oppression of the people by conservative royalists and ultramontanists. By 1834, under Maria II, the country had an estimated 90 per cent illiteracy, but, with the establishment of municipal schools under central-government stimulus, by 1841 half the boys of school age (seven to ten) were reported as being in school;[25] in addition, there were 270 private elementary schools. The secondary school situation was much poorer; the *liceu* (modelled on the French *lycée*) was the sole institution, catering for the wealthy classes. In 1836 it was decreed that one should be established in each urban district capital, and two in Lisbon. Fee-charging and exclusive, these *liceus* were to offer a reformed curriculum in three divisions: humanities, consisting of history, geography and literature; languages, comprising French, English and German; science, made up of chemistry, physics, algebra, geometry and natural history. In addition, specialized college-preparatory studies were to be offered in classics, rhetoric and philosophy. By 1844 these plans had proved to be too ambitious and the curriculum had to be narrowed; science was largely eliminated and modern languages restricted to major institutions in the larger cities.[26] These state *liceus* were designed as feeders to tertiary institutions providing professional personnel. In 1836–7 institutions on the model of the French *écoles polytechniques* were established – the Escola Politécnica in Lisbon and the Academia Politécnica in Porto – while a large number of *hautes école*-type institutions were founded: medical schools, naval and military academies and *conservatórias de artes e ofícios* (arts and crafts). In the course of the next few decades these were followed by technical colleges and literary institutes. By 1860, teachers' normal schools had been founded, and in the period from 1870 to 1910 the tiny supply of trained teachers trebled.

In the second half of the nineteenth century there was some improvement in education, stemming from a determined middle-class liberal drive to follow English and French examples. This progress was comparable to the situation in those two countries: the state elementary schools, co-existing with church schools, favoured the urban, upper half of the population, from whose sons came those selected to progress through the *liceus*, or the Jesuit colleges, to the advanced institutes and the university to fill the professional ranks required by a moderately industrializing, urbanizing society. To keep pace with developments in the late nineteenth century the curriculum of the *liceus* had to be revised and after 1860 science was restored and a five-year programme instituted; in 1895 the curriculum was again updated and the full course lengthened to seven years. Industrial, commercial and technical institutes were opened too. The universities – still, as in Spain, Jesuit-dominated and ultramontanist in sympathy – remained conservative, even reactionary, and contributed little to intellectual life.

Portugal in 1900 was at the watershed in its provision of education for the working classes, who still had very few possibilities open to them, especially in rural communities. Not until 1910 did this situation change, when political conflicts led to the abolition of the monarchy and the proclamation of a republic. The new republican government separated church and state, and in 1910 all religious orders (which chiefly staffed the schools, hospitals and charitable institutions) were expelled, the Jesuits being a special target of abuse. In 1926 a military coup led to the installation of General Carmona as president, with Antonio Salazar de Oliviera as Minister of Finance. Salazar became prime minister in 1932 and maintained an absolute, fascist dictatorship until his collapse of a stroke in 1968. At his death he left Portugal the least-educated nation in Europe.

The educational history of the First Republic and the Salazar dictatorship is one of a halfhearted domestic effort. In 1911 free compulsory elementary schooling was enacted for all children, girls as well as boys, between the ages of seven and ten, but by 1927 there were still only 8500 teachers and 7000 schools, and the illiteracy rate was only marginally reduced, to 68 per cent. In 1911 two more normal schools were built, and slowly the network of basic elementary schools was extended, but not until 1940 was illiteracy reduced to 55 per cent; in 1960 it was reported by the Lisbon government to be 34 per cent,[27] with the current prescribed minimum of schooling still at only four years. The provision of secondary-education facilities was even poorer. In 1927 these extended to only 32,000 students in a country of nearly 7 million; in 1940 the total was 74,000 for nearly 8 million; in 1950 it was 95,000. The gains are real, but quite inadequate in relation to the internal development needed for Portugal to achieve comparability with its European neighbours.

The West in turmoil: challenge of totalitarianism 1919–1939

Italy

Meanwhile, events took an ominous turn in Italy and Germany, where the doctrines of fascism began to redefine the process of education as a means of building the corporate totalitarian state, using the schools as agents. In Italy Benito Mussolini (1883–1945) formed in 1919 the Fasci di Combattimento, literally a 'combat union' of political activists, many of them war veterans, demanding a number of reforms. By 1921 this movement became a political party of the Right, Partito Nazionale Fascista, with an inchoate policy that generally favoured bourgeois dominance and opposed communism. Taking as their device the ancient Roman badge of senate authority, the *fasces*, a bundle of rods symbolizing strength by unity, the Fascist Party developed a programme based upon hierarchical and total governmental authority, typified in its party motto *credere, obbedire, combaterre* ('believe, obey, fight'). With much of Europe in post-war turmoil, Italy, even though one of the victorious allies, was equally effected; Mussolini became head of the government because he seemed to promise a genuine national revival. As part of his policy he set about reforming the schools in 1923 in a grand movement known as the *Riforma fascistissima*, by which the moral, intellectual and productive powers of the nation were to be brought together in the creation of a new, pacemaking European nation. Italy, however, was still a seriously underdeveloped nation after centuries of misrule and foreign dominance and in the 1920s was quite unable to effect the great development Mussolini had planned for it.

Up until 1861, when the new Kingdom of Italy was proclaimed, education was random and uncoordinated; religious congregations gave the bulk of instruction to the poor, while some orders conducted prestige schools for the wealthy. In addition, there were municipal schools, seminaries, the historic universities and the learned societies and academies which had all continued to flourish as the agencies of the leisured classes, with their traditional concern for the *studia humanitatis*, now called *litterae humanae*, unchanged. Even science in the Italian academies was conducted with a humanist interest. The first major development in educational reform was the formulation of a school code in 1848 by the Minister of Public Instruction in the Kingdom of Sardinia, Carlo Boncompagni di Mombello (1804–80), who attempted to eliminate church involvement. This code was reorganized by the new minister Count Gabrio Casati (1798–1873) in 1859; when Italy was proclaimed as a single kingdom in 1861 the *Lex Casati* became the education law for the new territories and remained the basis of Italian education until the *Riforma* of 1923.

The aim of the *Lex Casati* was threefold: to decrease illiteracy by extending the elementary school; to make wide provisions for secondary education; and to revive Italy's earlier pre-eminence as a source of humane and scientific culture. Although the state held nominal authority, in the case of elementary education this was delegated to the provinces, which in turn passed it on to the communes – these, of course (especially in the south), having the least resources. Despite such difficulties, of the 8000 communes in the nation by 1876 only 96 were without a boys' four-year elementary school, 358 without one for girls.[28] In that year, of the estimated 3 million children aged six to twelve who were covered by the law (out of a total population of 28 million) there were 1,931,617 on the school registers; in addition, there were 112 state normal schools and the teaching strength had increased from 30,000 to 47,000.[29] Moreover, the secular component had become much larger, at 84 per cent, while teachers in church schools belonging to congregations or in holy orders made up the remaining 16 per cent. In secondary education the state played a more dominant role and established, by the *Lex Casati*, the standard institution of the five-year classical gymnasium, *ginnasio*, followed by a three-year advanced course in the *liceo*, thereby providing for the privileged bourgeois minority a twelve-year span of schooling: four years' elementary, five *ginnasio*, three *liceo*. Through the establishment of the standard secondary school as the classical *ginnasio-liceo* sequence, the humane and scientific culture was continued. All *licei* and *ginnasi* were funded by the state, and at the same time private *ginnasi* were permitted, these generally being church schools. Since the technical needs of the country – long a world leader in most of the skilled arts, crafts and technologies – had to be met, versions of the German *Realschule* were established as technical schools and institutes, but these lacked prestige. The *Lex Casati* was introduced by the anticlerical government of Francesco Crispi; given the annexation of the papal states by Cadorna and the self-incarceration of the popes in the vestigial Vatican thereafter, all governments, as targets of papal hostility, reciprocated with anticlerical policies, which led to the increasing secularization of education. In 1870 an administrative regulation made religion an optional subject of instruction in state schools and this was confirmed by law in 1888; in 1904 the *Lex Orlando* omitted religion altogether.

Throughout the later decades of the nineteenth century the *Lex Casati* continued to provide an organizational and administrative basis for education in Italy, but it became evident quite early that many communes were not equal to the task of providing the four-year elementary schools; illiteracy remained a major problem, particularly in the south. Moreover, among the rural communities the elementary school had very little holding power and those children who attended frequently had only one or two years of instruction. Simultaneously, throughout the period, secondary education in the *ginnasio-liceo* sequence was not going well. These schools were difficult of access to the working class, had a largely bourgeois clientele and, despite their avowed concern with the *litterae humanae*, developed into competitive cramming institutions preparing boys for the restricted number of vocational positions, or for entry to the universities. In 1910 a partial reform was effected with the addition of a modern stream to the *liceo* curriculum so that students could follow either a classical course with some science, or a scientific course with some classics. The universities remained unchanged, and there matters stood until the Fascists came to power.

Italy, alone in the twentieth century, had the distinction of having a world-ranking philosopher as the first Minister of Education in the Fascist government. This was Giovanni Gentile (1875–1944), who held the chair of philosophy, in turn, at the universities of Palermo, Pisa and Rome before entering Mussolini's cabinet in 1922. Already Gentile had distinguished himself by writing on the philosophy of education, producing in 1900 *Il concetto scientifico della pedagogia* (*The Scientific Concept of Pedagogy*) and in 1914 the two-volume *Sommario di pedagogia come scienza filosofica* (*Summary of Pedagogy as a Philosophical Science*). He resigned from the government in 1924 after attempting a thoroughgoing reform of the educational system, to become president of the National Fascist Institute of Culture, while continuing to lecture at the University of Rome, and in this dual capacity produced what fascism had previously lacked: an articulated, theoretical justification of the movement. He was assassinated by partisans in Florence in 1944.

Gentile continued the Hegelian idealist tradition in philosophy; his position, briefly, is that the only ultimate reality is the pure act of thought, *atto puro*, gained by the individual in contemplative reflection. Stressing the idealist position, he saw man as fundamentally composed of spirit, which seeks self-actualization. This process is, moreover, essential to each person's humanization, although this cannot be achieved individually, since to become human means, necessarily, to develop a social and hence a moral conscience. This, then, is his argument for the necessity of the process of education, which he termed pedagogy (*pedagogia*), and it is essential to note the distinction between *pedagogia* and *educazione*: the former refers to process, the latter to product; process is the essential feature. Since the bond between all persons is spirit, and since communication is necessarily achieved by community of spirit, the process of communication is all-important. There are two basic resources available to assist *pedagogia*: one is the teacher, who must be a person of humane culture; the other is the humane tradition itself, preserved in the *litterae humanae*. So the good teacher is one who, already enlightened by this tradition, enthusiastically merges his mind with the learner in a common voyage of discovery. The *litterae humanae* are, of course, the traditional humanities, which include science in the degree to which it offers contemplative reflection in distinction to being simply a collection of techniques for application; the *litterae humanae* are, necessarily, preserved in writing. Therefore, for Gentile, language is the basis of all education: learning the alphabet, as a first step, confers a 'baptism of reason' which allows access to the *litterae humanae* and thereby the great dimensions of genuine education: that transcendence of time and space whereby the fullest development of the spirit can be effected and humanization achieved.[30] Pedagogy, especially in the training of teachers, he saw not as a collection of classroom strategies or a set of psychological maxims but as the study of the philosophy and history of the process of education which enables the individual student teacher to come to understand the essentially dialectic character of the pedagogical process. The Montessori method, it might be noted, was considered compatible with this position.

Given these views, Gentile argued for a largely common curriculum based upon linguistic studies, chiefly Italian, Latin and Greek, and extending to history, geography and further studies as they assist humanization. Although an idealist, he did not regard religion, in the confessional dogmatic sense, as having educative value; indeed, he considered confessional instruction to be non-educative because it represents only a sectional interest and serves, not to join people together, but to divide them. Instead, history is the supreme study for uniting people, since, taking a Hegelian stance, he believed that it illustrates a dialectical development; in so theorizing, he was able to account for the moral dimension. Clearly – and he took a similar position to Fichte – the individual can effect self-realization only through society, which in its most developed form is the corporate state; even further, the state is immanent in the individual will:

> *We* are the State, all of us who feel ourselves organized and unified by a fundamental law, as a people possessed of independence; and all the defects of the State cannot but be our defects. . . . The State has a *raison d'être* insofar as there is something to be guaranteed; and in reality it guarantees all the economic activities of a people, by law against the enemies within, and by defense against enemies abroad; and thus it guarantees also all the moral personalities (chief among them, the family) to which human economic activity gives rise.[31]

He wrote this in 1907 in *Per la scuola primario di stato* (*On the State Primary School*) and never changed this position. Here, then, is the justification for the state's having charge of the provision of education.

In 1923, from this position, Gentile launched the *Riforma fascistissima* or, as it is equally known, the *Riforma Gentile*. The main purposes were to stress the state role by centralizing administration and planning, and to achieve uniformity with nationwide procedures of evaluation by means of an *esame di stato* (state examination) that would certify satisfactory completion of elementary education and competence to proceed to the secondary levels; to renovate the secondary curriculum by emphasizing qualitative attainment rather than cramming and memorization; and to provide a range of possibilities for working-class children to proceed to secondary education. Gentile kept to a conservative humanist position and retained the *ginnasio-liceo* sequence intact for the most intellectually competent; at the same time, he introduced an equivalent of the *Realschule* in the form of the *liceo scientifico*. For girls the *liceo femminile* was introduced but was a total disaster; it attracted almost no enrolments, and had to be abandoned. The major innovations were two: the upgrading of teacher education by introducing the three-year *istituto magistrale superiore*, and for those children limited to the elementary school the *scuola complementare* which offered two years of continuation studies. All these schools were to be guided by Gentile's philosophy.

In the years immediately following, the hopes of the *Riforma Gentile* were not realized; Gentile was primarily a scholar and philosopher concerned with education and culture, while Mussolini and the Fascist Party were seeking cruder goals. In 1923 the Fascists established a one-party state, and the moral idealism of Gentile had to go, while throughout the 1920s Mussolini waged a campaign to bring the schools under strict state control. In the first instance, this was effected by organizing Italian youth in a number of political, paramilitary organizations in order to speed the process of 'fascistization' (*fascistizzare*). Along with the adult organization, the Fasci di Combattimento, and the subsequent Partito Nazionale Fascista, a youth organization was founded in 1919 which in 1923 was reorganized as the Avanguardie studentesche dei Fasci Italiani di Combattimento (Student Vanguard of Italian Combatants). Throughout the 1920s these youth organizations became agencies of 'fascistization' and concentrated on out-of-school military-type activities: drill, parades, paramilitary training, physical fitness and political indoctrination, reinforced by ceremonies, uniforms and the quasi-mystical cultivation of bonds of obedience, brotherhood, patriotism and duty, expressed in such maxims as 'it is better to live one day as a lion than a hundred years as a sheep'. Teachers were encouraged to join as supervisors, to attend drills, camps, excursions or displays, and demonstrate moral support for the fascist cause.

In a decree of April 1926 the collective movement was renamed Opera Nazionale Balilla (National Balilla Organization), which took its name from a Genoese boy-hero, Balilla, who led an insurrection in 1746 against the Austrians. Within this ONB was a range of three sub-divisions, the Balilla itself for eight- to fourteen-year-olds, the Avanguardisti for fourteen- to eighteen-year-olds, and for eighteen- to twenty-one-year-olds the Giovani Fascisti (Young Fascists). By 1930 this was again restructured with further organizations for university students, Gruppi Universitari Fascisti (University Fascist Groups), and workers, Opera Nazionale Dopolavoro (National Afterwork Society). Even these organizations showed the strains of maladministration, and in 1927 they were brought together as the Gioventi Italiana del Littorio (Society of Young Italian Lictors), the title 'lictor' being that of the ancient Roman officer who carried the *fasces* as the emblems of office and who executed sentence on persons convicted by magistrates of offences against the state. Only through participation in these youth organizations (GIL) could membership of the Fascist Party itself be obtained and, consequently, any effective participation in power be achieved.

Throughout the 1930s, at the same time that the Nazis were using youth groups similarly in Germany, the fascist state in Italy attempted to integrate the various youth organizations, now the GIL, into the system of state education and, in effect, to 'fascistize' the entire curriculum and organization of Italian schools. This meant possible conflict with the church, and Mussolini was careful to avoid open hostility and sought rapprochement with the Vatican. In the celebrated Lateran Accords of 1929 he healed the breach caused by annexation of the papal states in 1860 with an agreement that Catholic doctrine would be taught in all schools by priests; by 1935, religion was a subject in which a pass was necessary for progression through the grades. Yet Mussolini had no intention of surrendering youth to the church, as he made clear in the Chamber of Deputies in May 1929 when tabling the Lateran Accords:

> A regime different from ours, a demo-liberal regime, a regime of the kind we despise, might deem it useful to renounce the education of the young. *We cannot.*
> In this domain we are intransigent. Education must belong to us. Children should be reared in our religion, but we must integrate their education, give them a spirit of virility, power, conquest.

He went on in this speech to affirm the 'moral' character of the fascist state and, using a Gentile-type argument, asserted that the church itself is but part of the greater fascist state: 'The Fascist state fully revindicates its ethical character: it is Catholic, to be sure, but it is above all Fascist – exclusively, essentially Fascist.'[32]

To effect this, all teachers, including university professors, after 1931 had to swear an oath of allegiance to the fascist state; only eleven professors out of 2000 refused. In 1933 all elementary schools were put under state control and the entire process of formal schooling subjected to fascistization whereby only approved textbooks were to be used and teachers had the task of producing fascist personalities that recognized a primary duty to the state; teachers were required to present a fascist interpretation of history and literature, although other subjects were not so susceptible. Yet the programme was by no means effective; the Catholic Church offered some resistance, tempered by appreciation of concessions gained under Mussolini, and the teachers were only half-hearted in their membership of the GIL and in their concern for a fascist presentation of the curriculum. There was, in effect, too much depth to Italian culture, and too much sense of a greater history, against which fascism seemed a blustering *arriviste*. By 1939 there was, in fact, a profound sense of shortcoming in the entire fascist educational programme of the 1930s, and in 1939 the Minister for Education, Giuseppe Bottai, admitted as much in observing that the *Riforma Gentile* had not been effective, that the secondary schools remained largely bourgeois and still dominated by the traditional aims, content and method of the *litterae humanae*.

So, in 1939, Giuseppe Bottai attempted yet another reform, in a thoroughgoing fascist direction, of Italian education. The express intention was to realize Gentile's ideas of the schools as the means of producing the genuinely fascist state – a state in which the students would recognize and act upon a sense of conscious duty and patriotism. He called for a new humanism whereby the students would build a fascist society, a new state, out of the collective will of the 'people'. Recognizing that the corporate state needs division of labour, and a wide range of abilities and varied training, and that to achieve this a greater degree of mobility must be secured, he promulgated a School Charter which reorganized the system again. A common ten-year elementary school, called the 'Elementary Order', was proclaimed for all, with four stages: beginners started at age four in the two-year *scuola materna* (mother school) and went in sequence to the three-year elementary school, the two-year labour school and the three-year artisan school. Then followed the optional secondary programme, called the 'Intermediate Order', begun by fourteen-year-olds: a three-year sequence in either the general humane-studies 'unified middle school' (*scuola media unica*) or the specialized professional technical-preparatory school. After this sequence, students could, if they survived the continuous selecting process, go on to the 'Upper Order' of either the *liceo classico* or the *liceo scientifico* or the *istituto magistrale* from the *scuola media unica*; from the professional school they could proceed to the advanced *istituto tecnico*. A fourth 'University Order' was provided for graduates of all these 'Upper Order' institutions to receive advanced, specialized training. Much of this, however, was still only a reorganization of existing structures, except for the major reform of the *scuola media unica* which provided a genuine opportunity for working-class children to obtain a secondary education.[33] Scarcely had the School Charter been effected, in 1939, than Italy entered the war, in the course of which the nation was severely ravaged. Fascism was destroyed, but so also was much of the country, and educational development continued to be arrested.

Nazi Germany

Concurrently with fascism, the much more threatening movement of Nazism was developing in Germany. However, the Nazis did not come into formal power until 22 January 1933 when Adolf Hitler (1889–1945) became chancellor and was able to move towards a totalitarian state; eighteen months later, on 2 August 1934, with the death of the aged President von Hindenburg, Hitler was declared president and chancellor and began to implement in earnest his policy of *Gleichshaltung* – the harmonizing of state and party by eliminating all opposition. The Nazi regime lasted little more than a decade and had too short a period seriously to alter the pattern of education. Most of its educational effort was directed at the formation of a special Nazi character for German youth by means of the various youth leagues, in particular the Hitler Youth (Hitlerjugend) and the League of German Girls (Bund der deutscher Mädchen).

Throughout the 1920s the Nazi party had grown slowly while the Weimar government struggled with the crippling provisions of the Versailles Treaty and the crushed economy; the Great Depression of 1929 and the unbelievable inflation was fuel to Nazi rhetoric and in the early 1930s the Nazis came to power in a country in which the workers and lower middle class welcomed them. Long conditioned to an obedience mentality, the people saw firm leadership as a salvation, especially since on both potential military fronts they had hostile nations: a bitter and vindictive France in the west, the now frightening spectre of Soviet communism in Russia to the east.

No break was made by the Nazis with the Weimar pattern of education except that the local authority of the *Länder* was revoked and every educational institution, pre-school to university, put under central control of the Reichsministry of Education. The universities had their top administrators appointed by the Reichsministry, instead of their being elected by the staff; teachers were made public servants and were required to join the National Socialist Teachers' League (Nationalsozialistisches Lehrerbund). One further major change was a reversion to the Weimar pattern of the élitist, selective system of schools. Girls were to be discouraged from intellectual activities: the various schools – *Gymnasium*, *Realschule, technische Hochschule*, and so on – were plainly boys' schools, the Nazis argued, which girls, going against the grain of their natural femine inclinations, had infiltrated, perhaps under insidious pressures of various kinds. According to Hitler's express wish these schools were to be kept for boys wherever possible, and for girls a new type of school, the unified secondary school, was created, which stressed domestic and maternal arts and crafts: housewifery, needlework, cooking, babycare and mothercraft. In addition, the universities were largely closed to them. A decree in 1934 set a university-entrance quota of 10 per cent of all places for girls, with preference to be given to those wanting to enrol in faculties of domestic science and thereby to qualify as domestic-science teachers, hospital workers and other kinds of appropriately 'female' occupations. The derisive appellation of 'pudding matriculation' soon spread to describe this entrance to university.[34]

Hitler had failed to complete his own schooling and had a pronounced mistrust of academics and intellectuals. In 1932 he lectured Hermann Rauschning, a prominent party member – and later apostate from Nazism – on the evils of universal education, which he described as

> ... the most corrosive and disintegrative poison ever devised by liberalism for its own destruction. There can only be one education for each class and each separate grade within it. Complete freedom of education is the prerogative of the elite and of those whom it specially admits. All learning must be subject to continuous supervision and selection. Knowledge is an aid to life, not its central purpose. And, so being consistent, we shall bestow upon the broad mass of the lowest class the blessings of illiteracy.[35]

While the schools had to be maintained, they were not encouraged to stress intellectual excellence; on the contrary, there was sustained pressure on them not to penalize boys for absences or failure to reach prescribed standards if they had been away on Hitler Youth activities; instead, such boys were to have their grades made up to appropriate levels. Similarly, the universities were the target of Nazi suspicion, if not outright hostility. Many undergraduates enthusiastically supported Nazism and belonged to the Hitler Youth organization. Professors were often sceptical and reserved but generally swore oaths of loyalty to the regime, doubtless intimidated by the SS and SA. A few resigned in protest – the distinguished philosophers Eduard Spranger and Karl Jaspers, the theologican Karl Barth and the scientist Julius Ebbinghaus. Most remained in their posts and, given the pressure of terror, responded by stressing the practical, applied, 'relevant' aspects of their disciplines.

Books were the special target of the Nazis, and as early as 1933 they prepared their own *index librorum prohibitorum*, chiefly Weimar school texts and anything else contrary to their racist, *Volk*-worshipping policies, and held a nationwide book-burning spectacular at which university and school academics were required to attend, in their ceremonial robes; warehouse stocks of such texts were sent to be pulped. A new curriculum was introduced to implement a policy of Nazification among all children, with the core of studies built around those subjects most amenable to indoctrination, chiefly history, geography, literature and biology. History was now to stress the Hegelian argument for German supremacy; geography was to illustrate such history and, in addition, to put the case for territorial expansion (*Lebensraum*) to bring together all of the German *Volk*; literature was to express the *Volk* ethos; biology to deal with genetics, racial purity, sex and the Darwinian thesis of superiority by natural selection. At the centre was to be the study of Hitler's *Mein Kampf* (*My Struggle*) which teachers were expected to consider as a manual for indoctrination in Nazism. Hitler saw physical fitness as the supreme educational activity, and it received major emphasis at all levels of the curriculum, often being integrated with community and social-service projects. Mathematics remained relatively unchanged, except that specific problems often had values built in. Religion was excluded by 1937 in a series of manœuvres that left the church powerless. There was little problem in the Protestant north but in the Catholic south, particularly Bavaria, the church sought to keep religious instruction in schools. In 1933 a concordat was signed with the Vatican and as a token of compliance, and also as part of the centralization of authority, Hitler dissolved all schools that taught no religion (*Sammelschulen*) and made religious instruction compulsory. In 1935, however, it was made non-examinable, and in 1937 it was timetabled for the last period of the day, often being deliberately made to clash with youth-league outdoor activities.[36]

The main thrust of Nazi educational policy was in the youth-league area. These organizations had burgeoned in the 1920s, and by 1932 there were 10 million total enrolments, including a large number in the Catholic Youth Association; there were only, however, 107,956 in the Hitler Youth. To change this, Catholic Youth and most other organizations were declared illegal in 1936; only two were permitted: the Hitler Youth (HJ) and the League of German Girls (BdM). Both the HJ and the BdM, like the Italian Balilla, focused their energies on outdoor paramilitary activities in two divisions, for ten- to fourteen-year-olds and fourteen- to eighteen-year-olds, through excursions, camps, public projects, rallies, parades, marches, gymnastic displays and evening ceremonials. Uniforms, badges, banners and military bands all played an important part; boys were invested with the symbolic dirk, as bearers of weapons in defence of the Reich and the Führer, for whom they were to lay down their lives if necessary. The mystical amalgam of brotherhood, racial destiny, historic people (*Volk*), and so on, was promoted, and their oath, like that of Italian Fascist Youth, was 'believe, obey, fight'. Girls could join the HJ but were guided where possible into the BdM which stressed activities such as nursing and first-aid. With the ethos of male superiority, the initials BdM were given such derisive ascriptions as *Bald deutsche Mütter* (German mothers-to-be) and *Bund deutscher Milchkühe* (German milking cows).[37] In 1936 these organizations had an enrolment of 5.4 million from Germany's total population of a little over 60 million.

Within the Nazi Party itself attempts were made to establish élite schools for future leaders, institutions combining features of the military academy and the political-leadership college. The first three were created in 1933, on the Führer's birthday, and dedicated in his honour as National Political Institutes of Education (*Nationalpolitische Erziehungsanstalten*), or 'Napolas' for short. They were intended to form the highest level of the state system inherited from the Weimar era, and the first three were established in the former military-cadet academies at Potsdam, Plön and Köslin. The intention was to select the finest boys on the criteria of health, fitness and 'Aryan' physique and intelligence (in descending order of importance) in the third or fourth elementary grade, around the tenth or eleventh year of age, and put them through an intensive, exacting course which, at the end, would produce a supply of future officers for the armed forces and senior officers for the government. These grew slowly: by 1935 there were fifteen; by 1938 twenty-one; by 1943 they reached a final total of thirty-nine; given their short existence of ten years, their efficacy was limited. In 1936, moreover, they were taken over by the SA and used as institutions to train future officers of the SA 'Brownshirts'.

One other system of élite schools was founded in 1937, as a rival to the Napolas; these were the Adolf Hitler Schools (*Adolf Hitler Schulen*). The first AHS appeared at Krössinsee and had a planned six-year curriculum for boys aged twelve to eighteen. Again, these were based on a combination of an exacting military academy and a political-formation school. The intention was also to supply a cadre of top-level Party functionaries who would, after six years in the AHS, serve further terms in the labour corps and an armed service before being selected for final intensive training at the age of twenty-five in the advanced courses known as the *Ordensburgen* or training centres. For these, three huge pseudo-Teutonic castles were built at Krössinsee in Pomerania, Sonthofen in Upper Bavaria and Vogelsang in the Eifel.[38] Since the total sequence took fourteen years, none of the original intake reached the mature *Ordensburgen* stage, and, to begin these, young men were directly recruited at first. By 1942 only eleven AHS had been built, with a headquarters at the *Akademie* of Brunswick, and neither they nor the Napolas made any significant contribution to the élitist training of German youth.

Even though war seemed virtually inevitable by 1938, Nazi policies had led to a decline of the schools: the armed forces complained of low academic standards among recruits; teachers were in short supply and were poorly trained. As a result of Nazi anti-intellectualism and pressure on the universities, including the expulsion of Jews from all government positions (which included university positions), the higher learning was seriously impaired and university-student enrolments dropped a startling 50 per cent from 127,920 in 1933 to 58,325 in 1939.[39] In a desperate attempt to solve the problem, the secondary schools had a year removed from the curriculum in 1939 and all young people were compulsorily enrolled in the HJ and BdM (thus swelling their ranks to 10 million in 1939) for a year of pre-military training. To refuse was a criminal offence. Meanwhile, the teachers' colleges were instructed to accept student trainees with only the junior leaving certificate, the *mittlere Reife*, instead of, as hitherto, the higher matriculation level of *Abitur*. By 1939, however, it was too late to change the pattern of schooling, and after 1945 the defeated and partitioned nation had to be 'denazified' and have its educational system restructured, this time on two models, one Western, the other Soviet.

CHAPTER 14

The Socialist Millennium: The Soviet Union 1917–1940

The tsarist heritage

The chief characteristic of educational development in the early decades of the twentieth century was the advent of the state as the major source of educational provision, leading to expansion on a scale never previously experienced as governments throughout the Western world were forced to recognize that the working classes had come to share in political power, and that their increasing educational aspirations had to be accepted as legitimate and, consequently, to be provided for. All Western governments at the beginning of the century, however, remained predominantly representative of conservative forces, and even in the 1920s, when fascism and Nazism came to power allegedly representing the interests of the working classes, these movements turned into brutally oppressive, ultra-rightist totalitarian states. Meanwhile, the establishment of a communist government in Russia after the Bolshevik Revolution of 1917, and the formation of the Soviet Union in December 1922, was considered everywhere as the most momentous event of the twentieth century, although attitudes to the emergence of communism varied enormously. Working-class and radical movements welcomed it as the arrival of the socialist millennium, the vindication of Marx's scientific, historically based socialism, and the harbinger of a succession of worldwide workers' revolutions which would create the new moral order. The conservative Right, defending the notion of social inequality, viewed communism with greater alarm than it did fascism and Nazism, because communists expressly sought to overthrow existing regimes and establish everywhere new governments based, in the words of the *Communist Manifesto,* upon the dictatorship of the proletariat.

Central to the communist programme of reconstructing society was a belief in the need to create a new moral order, to achieve which the process of education had to be entirely reconceived. No sooner had the dust cleared in the first days of revolution in Petrograd than the Bolshevik government appointed Anatoly Lunacharsky as People's Commissar of Education, to preside over, not a Department of Education, but a Ministry of Enlightenment. Throughout the 1920s and 1930s, as other governments modified and adapted their systems of dual education, Russia was the scene of a tremendous range of educational experiment – much of it wasteful, ill thought-out and conflicting, but none the less attracting a continued stream of international visitors, curious to see how the world's greatest educational experiment was faring in its breathtaking task of creating a new kind of person in a new kind of society. For that was the avowed goal of Soviet education in the decade after the 1917 revolution: nothing less than the creation of the 'new Soviet person'. Yet the early Bolshevik educators found, to their dismay, that the reform of education was not to come so easily, and that the Russian tradition was more tenacious than they had realized. To appreciate the Soviet experiments and experiences of the 1920s and 1930s, then, it is necessary to consider the Russian educational background.

Early educational history: the Orthodox tradition

The Russian nation began as settlements of Slavs in the central areas of the great Eurasian plain as early as the third century AD. By the ninth century a major centre had been established at Kiev which was probably the greatest city in the world at the time, with other cities at Moscow and Novgorod in the north. At this time the Byzantine Emperor Michael III dispatched as missionaries the brothers Cyril (826–69) and Methodius (c. 815–85) to evangelize the illiterate Slavic peoples to the north of his realm. The efforts of these Orthodox monks to convert the Slavs of the western border regions led them to record the Slavic languages for the first time, using a phonetic script based on the capital letters of the Greek alphabet, their work giving rise to both the standard Cyrillic script (still used in Russia and Yugoslavia) and the strongly Orthodox character of Russian Christianity. After the mutual excommunication of Greek patriarch and Latin pope in 1054, the Slavs were cut off from European Latin Christendom and developed a separate religious culture; throughout the Mongol occupation of the thirteenth, fourteenth and fifteenth centuries the Slavs maintained their Orthodox faith, often in the face of Tartar persecution. In 1328 Moscow became the seat of the Russian Orthodox patriarch and in the ensuing centuries remained a centre of a rigid conservatism, while Kiev, where a second metropolis developed, remained closer to European influences.

Isolated from religious controversy or the influx of new Western ideas, the Orthodox clergy in Russia remained conservative and generally illiterate, and it was not until the Lutheran revolt and the Catholic Counter-Reformation of the mid-sixteenth century sent repercussions into Russia that the Orthodox Church was moved to stir from its lethargy. In 1551 the great Council of the Hundred Chapters, the Stoglav, was called to consider the divisions within Latin Christianity, and the increasing challenges from both Catholic and Protestant sources in Europe. Its declaration, the Hundred Chapters, from which the Council took its name, called for efforts to reform the clergy and increase its level of literacy (though with little apparent effect). In 1591 the English traveller Giles Fletcher wrote in his account *Of the Russe Common Wealth* that the common people 'excell in no kinde of common arte, much lesse in any learning or litterall kinde of knowledge',[1] while their clergy 'are men utterly unlearned, which is no marveille, forasmuch as their makers, the bishops themselves (as before was saide) are cleere of that quality, and make no farther use at al of any kind of learning, no not of the scriptures themselves, save to reade and to sing them.'[2] Yet this indifference to learning had its dangers, especially as the Jesuit Catholic Reformation drive into Poland was spilling across the border into Russia with increasing effect. Reacting to this, the energetic Metropolitan of Kiev, Peter Mogila (1597–1646), stirred the clergy to some action and to counter the Jesuits founded in 1631 a college on their pattern, in Kiev, 'to teach free knowledge in Greek, Slavonic and Latin, at the same time preserving the truths of Eastern Orthodoxy'.[3]

Mogila's college at Kiev was only a partial response to the problem; by the end of the seventeenth century, Russia, with a largely illiterate, conservative clergy ministering to an illiterate, equally conservative peasant population, was challenged by the Latin classical tradition as the language of educated European discourse. In addition, in the north, chiefly the Baltic regions, it was subjected to German pietistic Protestantism, in the western regions to Catholic evangelism; in its own heartland it clung to its Orthodox tradition.

The tsars look west: Peter the Great to Catherine 1700–1800

Having no defined borders, the country had been historically subject to all kinds of invasion, cultural as well as military, and it was this weakness that Peter the Great (r. 1682–1725) attempted to correct. After his celebrated tour of the West in 1697, which took him as far as the Dutch Netherlands and England, Peter came to appreciate the educational backwardness of his people. Peasants and townspeople were completely unschooled apart from the few boys who were recruited into the church for the necessary offices requiring literacy; the nobility disdained formal learning as 'clerical', and what education they had, in the sense of moral and social formation, came from the *Domostroi*, a conventional book of courtesy. Peter was determined to bring Russia into the modern era of the West and as a first step decreed the abolition of those symbols of Eastern conservatism, beards and kaftans, which were to be replaced by the shaven chin and the shorter European jacket. Only the clergy were allowed to retain beards and floor-length robes. These were only symbols; in 1701 he established the Moscow School of Mathematics and Navigation; in 1715 on the banks of the Neva, where it remains to this day, the Naval Academy of St Petersburg. In 1703 the Moscow Mathematics College and the first Russian newspaper *Moskovskie Vedomosti* (*Moscow News*) were founded. Young Russians were sent abroad to study the sciences and technologies of the West; scholars were imported, particularly from Germany, to teach their skills. Throughout the last twenty-five years of his reign, Peter's reforms were all of a technical, vocational nature; he saw the West as a source of techniques for application.

The nobility were reluctant to follow the reforms and Peter resorted to coercion: he required nobles to be literate before they could marry, which meant that estates and inheritance provisions were tied up. His ukase of 28 February 1714, which announced these literacy requirements, also ordered that 'students should be sent from mathematical schools [as teachers], several into each *gubernia*, to prelates and to renowned monasteries to establish schools [in arithmetic] . . . for the children aged between ten and fifteen of the nobility, of government clerks, and of lesser officials.'[4] It seems, however, that very few of these cipher schools were established, and, despite a continuing effort to get the churches to establish elementary schools for the children of the nobility, the spread of basic literacy and numeracy was slow. Peter therefore decided to take over the four existing church schools, which provided a purely religious training for interns. By ukase in 1721 he abolished the patriarchate, constituted a Holy Synod as governing body of the church and appointed a layman as head; straight-away, the church became a department of state and its schools the basis of a state system of education. The next year, in January 1722, he further organized the nobles in his famous Table of Ranks, in which every male member of the nobility had a rank in one of fourteen grades in the naval forces, the army or the civilian sphere; appropriate to each rank was a uniform, title and code of behaviour. All nobles were obliged to render a compulsory period of state service, and life was regulated by promotion through the Table of Ranks. So Peter formed the great Russian civil service and placed considerable centralized authority in the tsar's hands; the Table of Ranks, along with a subsidiary table of thirty grades for the non-nobility, chiefly peasants, lasted until the revolution of 1917.

Despite resistance by the nobility, Peter continued his modernization of Russia, founding in 1724 a European-style academy in St Petersburg under the direction of the German philosopher Christian Wolff. The enacting ukase of 28 January clearly distinguished a university from an academy and pointed out, rather realistically, that a university would be useless 'simply because there are no elementary schools, gymnasia or seminaries [in Russia] where young people could learn the fundamentals before studying more advanced subjects to make themselves useful'. An academy, as a place 'wherein languages as well as other sciences and important arts could be taught, and where books could be translated', clearly would be of value.[5] Peter was close to the mark; the historian Klyuchevsky reported only some fifty elementary schools in provincial and sub-provincial towns, and a similar number of garrison schools for soldiers' children.[6] In addition, Peter founded a number of specialized technical schools for navigation, medicine, artillery, engineering, and various forms of industry. He died in 1725 and was succeeded by a sequence of undistinguished monarchs until Catherine the Great came to the throne in 1762. In those reactionary years, only three major educational events took place: in 1727 the higher theological academy known as the Kharkov College, later upgraded to a university, was founded; in 1731 the Corps of Cadets was organized at St Petersburg; and in 1755 the University of Moscow, Russia's first, was founded. The stimulus for the university came from Michael Lomonsov (d. 1765), who had studied with Christian Wolff at Marburg in the 1730s after Wolf had left the St Petersburg Academy of Sciences, and as a result the new University of Moscow had a pronounced German character. Lomonsov himself wrote texts in physical chemistry and in Russian grammar, his grammar being a standard text for decades.

Catherine II (r. 1762–96), an even more enthusiastic westernizer than Peter, was particularly influenced by the French Enlightenment. During her reign the splendour of St Petersburg reached its peak; artists and scholars, including even Voltaire, visited the court, and for a while the ideas of Locke and Rousseau were eagerly accepted. Catherine's educational adviser Ivan Betskoy (1703–95) was an enthusiast for Rousseau and the ideas of *Émile*, which appeared in a Russian translation in 1770. There was a climate of reform aimed at the nobility and the minuscule official and middle classes; Betskoy proposed an intermediate rank of intellectuals in Russian society between the two existing classes of aristocracy and peasantry, and during Catherine's reign graduates of universities actually gained a foothold on the lowest (fourteenth) level of the Table of Ranks, while those with master's degrees were placed in the twelfth to tenth grades. Peasants, however, held no civil rights, had no access to the law and were illiterate, enserfed and brutally treated. Educational reform was not planned for the lower 95 per cent of the population.

Catherine's enthusiasm did not go far in practice, and the notion of implementing Rousseauian education remained only a courtly topic of conversation; at the same time, however, she further consolidated the educational plans of Peter the Great. In 1775 she decreed the establishment of local Boards of Public Assistance in each *gubernia* (province) to set up and maintain schools in all towns and the large villages. Then in 1782 Catherine brought in the Serbian, Jankovitch de Mirievo, as director of the growing system of schools and in the same year founded the Commission for the Establishment of Schools whose task it was to equip them, basically with teachers and books. Thus Catherine, perhaps unwittingly, completed the triangle (Holy Synod, Commission and Boards of Public Assistance) which was to spend the next century or so in a struggle for educational power. The enactment in 1786 of the National Schools Statute created two grades of schools: the Commission retained control over the four-grade major schools, while the local Boards of Public Assistance were given control of the simpler one-grade minor schools. In general most educational provision was for boys, but around this time some education, chiefly domestic, was being introduced for girls. Already in 1764 a school for noble and middle-class girls had been set up in St Petersburg as the Smolny Institute by the Educational Society of Noble Girls, and this was a significant forerunner; in 1783 the St Petersburg Normal School was founded, and it accepted girl students. In 1786 the 113 *Statutes for Public Schools in the Russian Empire*, with the Austrian influence of Abbot Felbiger in evidence, were published. Yet under Catherine II there remained no efficient, single centralized authority. Education remained in the hands of the various authorities, each responsible in some manner, often vague, to the tsar. As yet the three bodies – Holy Synod, the local School Commissions and the Boards of Public Assistance – all held semi-autonomous authority, and there were no direct lines of communication to the crown. The church was now spurred to action, and there was a considerable expansion in numbers of church schools, from 26 in 1764 to 150 in 1808.[7]

The bourgeois epoch: reaction and repression 1801–1900

Catherine's son Paul I (r. 1795–1801) was deranged, weirdly mystical and totally reactionary against the wave of popular Europe-wide reform at the end of the eighteenth century; he was strangled in an officers' palace coup and succeeded by his son Alexander I (r. 1801–25). Despite enthusiasm for the young prince, Alexander proved to be equally reactionary in the Napoleonic and Congress eras, although he did attempt to create a permanent national system of schools. In 1802 he decreed the abolition of the School Commissions and created the Ministry of Public Education, the purpose of which was to control all educational and quasi-educational institutions. In addition, a new elementary- and secondary-school system was inaugurated and three universities established on German models. Yet the reforms were not effective, each of the various educational authorities clung tenaciously to power, and when in 1817 Prince Golitsyn became Procurator of Holy Synod, and thereby Minister of Public Education and Spiritual Affairs, further reaction ensued. There was a marked return to religious orthodoxy, heavy censorship was imposed, and the universities were purged of liberals.

Throughout the early nineteenth century Russia came almost to an educational standstill and under Alexander's successor, Nicholas I

(r. 1825–55), whose reign spanned the excessively troubled period of the 1830 and 1848 revolutions, education was more tightly restricted than ever. In 1828 an earlier regulation prohibiting peasants from sending their children to secondary schools was revived and rigorously enforced; they were restricted to whatever local parish school may have been available, while the secondary schools were open solely to the children of nobles and officials. The universities were becoming receptive to the French socialist theories of Saint-Simon and Fourier, and the German historicist theories of Hegel and Fichte, both sets of ideas being propaedeutic to Marxism. In 1835, however, the universities lost autonomy, their curricula were heavily censored, and staff appointments had to be approved by the Ministry. Yet again the Russian intelligentsia were divided in their allegiances: the traditionalists became even more ardently Slavophile, looked to the Orthodox Church and asserted a separate, Slavic destiny for Russia; the westernizers responded to the powerful attractions of European thought, institutions and social developments. Some, like the philosopher Alexander Herzen (1812–70), exiled for radicalism soon after graduating from Moscow University in the period 1835–43, left Russia in 1847 for England where he attempted to produce, in his philosophical writings, a synthesis of the two approaches. At the same time Russia was slowly industrializing, not on the same scale as Britain, France or Germany, but enough for an industrial proletariat to develop from an estimated 170,000 in 1815 to some half a million in 1855, leading to the emergence of the populist Narodnik movement (*narod*, people or nation).[8]

The second half of the nineteenth century saw the rapid growth among Russian intellectuals of the doctrines of *narodnichestvo*, which, while diffuse and emotional, centred on the feelings of 'the people'. The major exponent was Nikolai Chernyshevsky (1828–89). A strongly materialistic positivist, he was exasperated by the slow pace of liberal reform and advocated radical destructive revolution as necessary for effecting any meaningful social change. In 1863 he published his celebrated nihilist treatise, *Chto Delat? (What is to be Done?)*; this led him to be exiled to Siberia in 1864 where he remained until within a year of his death. Unlike the nobility, who regarded Western learning as a decorative embellishment, many intellectuals, exposed to the stimulation of European liberal and radical thought, now sought to arouse in the Russian people a consciousness of their plight.

Some slight thaw was promised when in 1864 Alexander II (r. 1855–81) created local elective councils, the zemstvos, which assumed some responsibility for education, although, being dominated by landowners, the zemstvos were not sympathetic to education for the peasants. On 26 June 1864 Alexander II promulgated the Elementary School Code to further religious and moral understanding and to promote useful knowledge; it recognized the independence of the three major educational authorities, along with a new body, the zemstvo boards. Education now was under the control of a variety of powers: the Ministry of Public Education, the Ministry of Public Domains and Internal Affairs, Holy Synod and the zemstvo boards. The following December the Secondary School Code was published, a milestone in educational development, under which two types of secondary school on German models were established, the classical gymnasium and the real gymnasium. Scarcely had this been enacted when a solitary disaffected student, Karakozov, attempted to assassinate Alexander II in April 1866 by firing a pistol at him in the street. The whole weight of reaction fell upon the *narodniki*, the underground press and anything that remotely resembled liberal, not to mention radical, thought. Dimitri Tolstoy was appointed Procurator of Holy Synod and Minister of Education (1866–80) and, in the era of repression that followed, yet another attempt was made to stamp out subversive thought by restricting education. The gymnasia established in 1864 were made more difficult of access in 1871; they alone had the right to matriculate students to the universities, and girls were forbidden to attend the latter. Some circumvented the regulation in the late nineteenth and early twentieth centuries by going to Swiss and German universities.

The second attempt on Alexander's life was successful in 1881 by the bomb-throwing terrorist group of Narodnaya Volia (The People's Will), and even more reaction followed. The newly formed political police, Okhrana, infiltrated the schools and universities, and the government of Alexander III (1881–94) tried to stifle popular education with two decrees of 1884 and 1887. In 1884 the state, already in control of three of the four educational agencies, moved to take over the zemstvo schools. The new emphasis was upon educating only children of the nobility and the upper bourgeoisie, and excluding the peasants from education. Further action came on 18 June 1887 in a document known in Russia as the 'Ordinance on the Cook's Children'. By this decree, attendance at gymnasia would be limited to

. . . only such children as are in the charge of persons presenting sufficient guarantees that the children are properly taken care of. . . . The gymnasia and progymnasia, therefore, shall be freed from the attendance of the children of drivers, footmen, cooks, laundry-women, small traders and other persons similarly situated, whose children, with the exception perhaps of the exceptionally gifted ones, should not be encouraged to abandon the social environment to which they belong.[9]

The zemstvos resisted the move, chiefly from a determination to retain their power. With the zemstvos threatening to withdraw their financial support of the schools if the ordinance went through, the tsar withdrew the decrees.

Nicholas II, who succeeded Alexander in 1894, made further moves to crush the growing independence of the zemstvos, requiring them to forward all their decisions through specified bureaucratic channels for approval, and proscribing much of their educational activity. The zemstvos for their part began actively campaigning against the government and in their successive congresses passed resolutions of solidarity against any encroachment upon, or restriction of, their power. In 1902 they merely condemned the government, in 1903 they passed a resolution calling upon all governmental decisions on education to be first submitted to the zemstvos for approval, and in 1904 they formed the Union of Liberation (Soyuz Osvobozhdenia) which sought a Constitution for all Russia. Clearly the resolution was indicative of the mood that was arising in all kinds of dissenting groups.

Russian education in the early twentieth century 1900–1917

By the turn of the century Russia had become chronically unstable. The new tsar, Nicholas II (r. 1894–1917), ruled only by repression in alliance with a now outdated aristocracy still organized according to the Petrine Table of Ranks. The lower bourgeoisie, workers and the vast population of peasants were totally alienated; Nicholas's coronation in 1896 was marked by the massacre of a thousand demonstrators at Khodinka Meadow. The obsolescence of the system is illustrated by the fact that in the year 1900 the peasantry still made up, in the official census, some 94.5 per cent of the population, the lower urban classes 2.5 per cent, merchants less than 1 per cent, the parish clergy 1 per cent and the only recognized social class, the nobility and officials, less than 1.5 per cent.[10] Meanwhile the industrialization of Russia continued, slowly, in St Petersburg, Moscow, the oil regions of the south and the Black Sea ports, the industrial labour force having increased from the half-million of 1855 to 1.5 million by 1900. This led to political trade-union organization on the Western model, chiefly expressed in the Social Democratic Workers' Party founded in Minsk in 1898, broken up by the Okhrana and re-formed in exile. The most vigorous member was Vladimir Ilyich Ulyanov (1870–1924) – later called Lenin – who was exiled to London and Geneva from 1900 to 1905 but through his newspaper *Iskra* (*The Spark*) kept trying to ignite the flames of popular insurrection. In 1903 the Social Democrats held an exiled conference in London and split into two factions, the Mensheviks ('minority') who urged the peaceful evolution of communism according to Marx's historicist predictions, and a majority of Bolsheviks (*bolshii*, major) who sought to spark the revolution through the active intervention of the Party vanguard. In 1905 a peaceful demonstration marched through St Petersburg calling for constitutional reforms and a representative congress of the people; the tsar, informed by Okhrana spies in advance, took alarm and ordered the troops to fire on the crowd, many of whom were massacred on Bloody Sunday, 9 January old-style, 22 January according to the Western reformed calendar. The tsar knew only the policy of repression, the Bolsheviks declared open war on the regime, and the ensuing twelve years saw Russia become further divided.

Belatedly, the tsar realized that Russia had to move into the twentieth century, and a policy of minimal concessions was adopted. Throughout the later decades of the nineteenth century Russia had been attempting an imperialist policy, trying to expand east into Asia, west into Europe, south-west into the Balkans. It fared disastrously and in 1856 lost control of the Danube estuary after the Crimean War, was stalemated in the west by the insurgent nationalism of the European minorities and the strength of the major powers, and humiliated in the east by Japan in the Russo-Japanese War of 1904–5. Part of the problem was the lack of modern resources throughout the country and this led to the period of minimal reform. In education, some significant advances were made. By now the zemstvo schools were in a powerful position and had been able to challenge the church schools, chiefly, according to one authority, because they were superior in the two matters of teacher training and teacher salaries.[11] To meet this growing competition, the government produced yet another plan to control all education. Authority was now to be exercised by three main bodies, Holy Synod, the central Ministry and the local zemstvos, the Ministry of Public Domains and Internal Affairs having passed its schools over to the Ministry of Education. In a new drive for control the Ministry of Education promulgated a decision in 1906 to introduce a scheme of rapid development of universal education.

This was formally enacted by the Universal Primary Education Law of 3 May 1908, which laid down certain minimum provisions for education. All children, of both sexes, living within a two-mile radius of a school and aged between eight and eleven, were to be given a compulsory four-year primary education, although, since neither teachers nor schools were available, a ten-year period was set for the introduction of this decree. Teachers were to be provided at the ratio of one for every fifty pupils, and all instruction, texts, writing materials and required equipment were to be furnished freely by the schools.[12]

This ukase imposed a great burden on the local authorities, and the central government expected, through their hoped-for default, to be provided with a pretext for taking over the schools; like many previous efforts, this also failed. Turning to an alternative procedure the government sought control by further bureaucratic devices, and in this it was successful. The Minister for Education, Kasso, published the Ordinance of 2 February 1914 which controlled the zemstvo schools more tightly without destroying them. Under this ordinance the Ministry assumed the right to appoint and dismiss zemstvo teachers, it required all correspondence to pass through the school district inspector, it empowered itself to reverse zemstvo decisions, forbade the zemstvos to interfere in the educational and instructional provinces of the school, and declared all school property to belong to the government.[13]

This time strong efforts were made to secure compliance with the ordinance, and the government was now strong enough to force the issue, since the bureaucratization of Russia had proceeded simultaneously in other areas, and the country had become more amenable to such control. A large number of school inspectors were appointed to enforce the ordinances that came in increasing numbers in the period immediately prior to 1914 and that, according to one educator, 'sought to make provision for every minor contingency in the life of the secondary schools and left no margin for the individual endeavours of an independent educational staff'.[14] The inspector became a hated figure, and one contemporary writer records that his visits became 'not so much inspections as veritable punitive expeditions, to which pupils and teachers alike looked forward with fear and trembling'.[15] Whatever emotions the inspector and central bureaucracy aroused, by 1914 educational standards had been raised considerably; the schools offered a variety of curricula to a wide number of children from all social classes, and after centuries of struggle the Ministry had become all-powerful.

By 1914 four types of primary schools existed and literacy was up to 40 per cent. Lower primary schools in outlying areas gave instruction in reading and writing; in more populous regions there were one-class schools with a four-year curriculum in literacy, numeracy, religion, history, geography and natural science, along with two-class schools which gave an additional two years by adding on geometry, physics, zoology and hygiene. Beyond this, for those who could afford the fees, there was a terminal four-year upper-primary school which gave a fuller elementary education but did not offer all the necessary courses leading to the secondary entrance examinations. The secondary schools had been opened to all, regardless of social class, and according to Ignatiev it seems that some peasant children attended them. Although private control of secondary schools had been made so difficult that all but the most ardent were discouraged, in the public system a wide variety existed, divided into gymnasia, which offered a curriculum of classical languages along with religion, Russian, literature, Latin, mathematics, physics, history, geography, French, German, natural science, logic, psychology, law, writing, drawing and physical training, and 'real schools', which had a non-classical curriculum with less religion and Russian literature and greater emphasis upon mathematics, geography, natural science, modern languages and mechanical drawing. In addition, by 1913 there were 203 commercial schools along with special gymnasia for girls which offered both a seven-year course, and an eight-year course of teacher training if required. By 1914 there were 873 gymnasia and 92 'junior' pro-gymnasia for girls (enrolling altogether 383,577 pupils),[16] in which the emphasis was on modern languages and needlework. Very few girls went on to universities, for which a formal matriculation requirement had to be met, given at the end of the gymnasium or real-school course and known as the Statement of Maturity (*Attestat Zrelosti*).

Into the age of enlightenment

On the eve of the revolution

It was the Great War that hastened the end of the tsarist regime. The largely illiterate Russian army was no match for the technically trained Germans; for many Russian peasants, their wartime experiences gave the first inklings of a world that existed beyond their own village. Even worse was the fact that, while there came a belated recognition of the need for education, the educational system was deteriorating even more rapidly; inflation had already ruined teachers' salaries in relation to the rest of the community, and primary school teachers were not exempt from the draft.

Kasso was forced to resign at the end of 1914 and was replaced by the progressive Count Paul Ignatiev. Knowing he had support by the people, Ignatiev made bold efforts to reform education, many of his ideas being based upon Dewey's notions of the school and society. Above all, Ignatiev saw that the old class stratification of Russia was at fault. Scarcely had he assumed power than he called a conference of educational curators in renamed Petrograd for the week of 20–7 February 1915, where he stated his purposes: 'We must serve the needs of the population. Educational matters must be viewed solely in the light of the claims of life.'[17] Despite the urgency, Ignatiev sought to build an educational system around the cooperation of both public and private interests – one that was considerate of parents' wishes and allowed for an increase in local authority. Many of his reforms, however, remained at the ordinance level, and in his two years of office he was unable to effect any significant amelioration of the tragedy that was befalling Russia. By now the army was sadly beaten, the generals commanding what amounted to semi-autonomous groups with little integration in an overall strategy. At home there was mounting opposition from high officials towards Ignatiev's reforms, especially his liberal tendencies, and intrigue against him increased. Ignatiev resigned on 27 December 1916.

Under his successor, Kulchitsky, former Curator of the Educational District of Petrograd, education languished, routine was neglected, school morale declined, disciplinary problems in schools increased, and in some secondary schools strikes occurred. During its brief reign the provisional government made a few changes in the administration of education, attempting to transfer more power to the local authorities, but little was achieved. In a spirit of animosity towards the upper classes the provisional government had sought to decentralize education further, and, at a time when great control was needed, effort became widely dispersed. By then, however, the same malaise was afflicting all of Russian corporate life and on 25 October 1917, old-calendar (7 November of the Western calendar), it was a relatively simple matter for the Bolsheviks to assume control of the government.

Bolshevism came in on an excessive wave of utopian idealism, and needed for its continued success a period of consolidation. Foremost among the instruments available for this purpose was education, yet the system the Bolsheviks inherited was completely unsuitable: unorganized, controlled by various bodies and separated into a dual system of European-type upper- and lower-class schools. In the next few years the Bolsheviks concerned themselves with the task of determining policy and creating a new school system. The task proved difficult and instead of taking a few months, as they thought it would, it followed an agonizing, conflicting course for the next twenty years.

The Commissariat of Enlightenment: early Bolshevik changes

It seems clear, from the evidence available, that the Bolsheviks had definite ideas on the reform of the educational structure, even before they were in control of the government – the administrative pattern, at least, along with certain fundamental principles of policy that had been developed in earlier meetings.[18] Within weeks of their taking over, a set of official documents on educational policy was published, their first decree of 24 December 1917 stating:

> On the 25th of October, 1917, the entire state power was taken over by the Government of Workers and Peasants. The latter has given over all the Ministries to the People's Commissaires. The Ministries are re-named People's Commissariats.[19]

This document set out the fundamental principles of the new educational policy: universal compulsory education; expansion of education at all levels – kindergarten, college, university and home education being specifically mentioned; provision for scientific and experimental work; and the intensification of school-building and teacher-education programmes.

In addition, a new administrative hierarchy was established. In line with the ideological premiss of popular government by local authorities, people's soviets (*soviet*, 'council' or 'counsel', equally) were established. As the US Commissioner for Education stated in his 1918 *Report*, 'The dictatorship from above, so characteristic of prerevolutionary Russia, gave way to a new order of things, "the democratization of education".'[20] Control of the schools was vested in local Departments of People's Education, as set out in a further decree:

> The direction of affairs connected with people's education, such as primary

education and self-instruction outside the academic walls, with the exception of higher education, is entrusted to Departments of People's Education, appropriately organized in Executive Committees: Regional, Provincial, County and Volost.[21]

These formed a pyramid, resting upon the smallest units, the volosts. At the top was the People's Commissariat of Enlightenment (Narodni Komissariat Prosveshcheniya),[22] also translatable as 'Department of Education', whose initial syllables gave the acronym Narkompros by which it was generally known. This was the highest integrating body; in reality it became an all-powerful centralized authority exercising complete control over the direction of education. The State Commission was composed of the People's Commissar, Anatoly Lunacharsky, as chairman, his assistant, the five members of the Commissar's Collegium, the chief clerk of the commissariat, three representatives of the teachers' union, two representatives of the trade unions, one representative of the Bureau of Labour, and one representative of the Central Culture Organization. Their duties, by this decree were, among other things,

The formation of a general plan of People's Education in the Russian Socialist Federal Republic, and the establishment of fundamental principles governing people's education, as well as those of school reconstruction; the co-ordination of cultural activities in the localities; the drafting of a budget and the distribution of funds appropriated for common federal cultural needs; as well as other matters of fundamental significance submitted for consideration to the State Commission by the Commissariat's Collegium.[23]

Section 8 of the same document empowered the State Commission to 'call and convene, periodically, an All-Russian Congress of Education, to which it submits a report of its activity, and to whose consideration it submits for discussion questions of great importance coming within the jurisdiction of the State Commission.'

By the middle of 1918, less than twelve months after taking control, the new pattern of administration began to emerge. In June 1918 Lunacharsky issued his first annual report, the opening words of which asserted that his policy in the first year was to ensure that 'power . . . be kept by educating the masses', and that 'only a high level of public education could make possible a conscious governing-by-the-people'. The new administrative forms were set out: the church was disestablished and religion eliminated from the curriculum; private ownership of schools was abolished and all power vested at the local level in the newly created volosts. There was only the Unified Workers' School, based upon a continuous grade or 'ladder' system, with ascending divisions of lower primary, primary, upper primary, pro-gymnasia and gymnasia. Two types of schools were established at the secondary level, equal in access and social standing – language-oriented 'cultural' schools, and non-language 'technical' schools – while specialization before the age of sixteen was prohibited. These secondary schools had eight-year programmes organized into two four-year periods. In addition, fees were abolished, spelling was reformed phonetically, and a hot-meal programme commenced. In teacher training a dual system was introduced, with one-year normal schools for the preparation of elementary teachers and teachers' institutes for training higher-elementary teachers. Universities were granted autonomy; new departments and faculties were added. Textbook control was carried out, ostensibly because of the need to revise those books 'that inculcated in the minds of the young generation the supremacy of the Tsar of All the Russias'.[24]

These were all simple administrative changes. The serious problem had yet to be faced: what is the nature of genuinely communist education? How can the state, or people, provide schools and educational experiences that will produce the kind of personality so desired by the new order? In his first report Lunacharsky set out the leading principles of Soviet education as then understood, with an emphasis upon work as the primary basis of the school: 'The labor character of the school consists in the fact that labor, pedagogical as well as, in particular, productive labor, will be made the basis of teaching.'[25] However, there were profound sectional differences of opinion, and much early theorizing about education was confused and contradictory.

The clearest feature of this thinking was the total rejection of the old type of education. In a paper read to the First All-Russian Congress of Teacher-Internationalists on 2 June 1918, Panteleimon Lepeshinsky, one of the original 'People's Will' radicals, and a member of the Collegium, argued that the school had been destroyed as a servant of the ruling classes, and sought to justify the historicity of the process. The schools were eliminated, he asserted, not by a group of individuals, 'but by the elemental force of life itself. . . . History had paved the way for such a destruction, and it had become a pressing necessity of the present revolutionary period.' He also strongly denounced the link between the ruling classes and the church in fostering this servitude, and gave this as the reason for removing education from church control. The new school, he said, should be a place 'from which religious services and teachings are absolutely barred'. In this speech he argued that the new Soviet school must be

... compulsory and accessible to all, regardless of sex and social distinctions; it must be a school where tuition, books, and so on are free; and lastly, we conceive of the school as a labor unit. The school must be homogeneous in the sense that it is of uniform type, with a definite minimum amount of instruction – in the sense of uniformity of aims and problems grouped between two chief centers of gravitation – and in the producing of an harmonious individual with regard to his social development; and finally, in the sense of establishing an organized connection between the various school grades and unimpeded promotion of students from lower grades to higher.[26]

In this paper Lepeshinsky went on to elaborate the features of the new school. In all, six features can be distinguished:

1. The school must produce an early fusion of productive labor and academic instruction.

2. It must aim at all-round development for modern society, that is, polytechnical education.

3. Manual labor must be an integral part of school life.

4. The school should be a productive commune, both producing and consuming, based upon the principles of school autonomy and collective self-determination in the process of mental and manual labor.

5. The widest possibilities must be offered for the full play and development of creative forces – self-activity, creative and artistic activity.

6. Character development must proceed in accordance with bringing the child up as a 'social creature', and 'to produce an understanding of social labor: first, at the present time, then, labor in past history, and last, labor's problems in the near future'.

In another document, *Self-Education of the Workers*, Commissar Lunacharsky attempted to justify the six principles upon which the new schools of Russia were to be based. All of these rested upon the school as a 'collective' of some sort, and the truly socialist state would be created, in part, by organizing the schools on a socialistic basis in which the schools would have a 'collective' character, displayed in the production and consumption of group needs.

The new school was directed against the merchant classes as well as the nobility. Hence, in *Self-Education of the Workers* Lunacharsky wrote that

... the motto of the new school must be: 'to live is to work'. We must therefore take [this] as the starting point of our pedagogical system, as the chief subject of our teaching, aiming at the increase of technical knowledge. Our

students must feel themselves part and parcel of the work of the community.
. . . We must never lose sight of the fact that the chief aim of education is the
knowledge of the various forms of human culture, which, in its turn, includes
all forms of mental and manual activity.[27]

In their drive to create a socialist utopia, the Bolshevik educators went
further; not only were they determined to destroy the bourgeoisie by a
new form of worker-education, but they knew that they would have to
attack its social roots too. Already the family had been singled out as the
prime bourgeois institution, antithetical to a true socialist society,
Lunacharsky being emphatic that women 'must cease to be enslaved by
the proletarian kitchen and the proletarian nursery'.[28] Zlata Lilina, head of
the Petrograd Education Department, was even more vehement in her
attack during the Educational Conference in Petrograd in 1918, declaring:

We must exempt children from the pernicious influence of the family. We
have to take account of every child, we candidly say that we must nationalize
them. From the first days of their life they will be under the beneficial influence
of communistic kindergartens and schools. Here they shall assume the ABC of
Communism. Here they shall grow up as real Communists. Our practical
problem is to compel mothers to hand over their children to the Soviet
Government.[29]

Lunacharsky was more reserved in his polemic, but nevertheless he too
affirmed his belief that 'the attention paid to child welfare and the education of the young in connection with the organization of proletarian
elementary schools will lead to the transformation of working-class
family life'.[30] This programme was never fully implemented; the government was preoccupied coping with 7 million war orphans. The desire to
communize life, however, remained strong, and during this period a
variety of decrees and resolutions were produced to weaken the bonds of
family life: the *Code of Laws Concerning the Civil Registration of Deaths,
Births and Marriages* of 17 October 1918 asserted that 'Parental rights are
exercised exclusively for the benefit of the children. In case of abuse the
court is entitled to deprive the parents of their rights.'[31] Religious doctrines
of the sanctity of the marriage union were weakened by the *Decree on the
Introduction of Divorce*, 19 December 1917, which made mutual petition
sufficient grounds for annulment, and the compulsory civil registration
of marriages requirement of 20 December 1917.[32] Abortion was legalized
on 18 November 1920 when the Soviet government decreed that it would
'permit such operations to be performed freely and without charge in

Soviet hospitals, where conditions are assured of minimizing the harm of the operation'.[33]

The ideological problem: lack of a Marxian theory of education

Lenin himself made no significant contribution to educational theory, and like the other Bolsheviks he was unable to draw much out of Marx's writings. It was *Capital*, read in conjunction with various other passages in Marx's economic and political writings, that guided Lenin's interpretation and the general development of Bolshevik revolutionary thought. The problem remained, however, in this effort to transform society, that early Soviet leaders received little guidance from Marx or Lenin on educational theory or reform. *Capital* belongs to the late period of Marx's thought and contains neither a theory of education nor any indication of how education is related to the process of implementing the transition from the bourgeois mode of production to the 'higher' mode of socialist production. In the *Communist Manifesto* of 1848 workers were urged to make educational policy dominant in the new order, but little more was said. Lenin followed Marx's reasoning that by themselves the workers could not effect the transition to socialism; on the contrary, they stood in need of intellectuals like himself, and Lenin interpreted this as the rationale for the Communist Party: the Party should serve as the guiding instrument of the socialist people.

As later historical research has shown, however, Marx in his early years in Paris actually did write seriously on man and society, and on issues relevant to education, in his *Economic and Philosophical Manuscripts* of 1844, known as the *Paris Manuscripts*, which appear to have become lost in the second half of the nineteenth century. In these Marx developed his important doctrine of alienation (*Entfremdung*), which since the recovery of the *Paris Manuscripts* in the 1930s has greatly influenced social and political thought. The section on 'Alienated Labour' deals with work as an aspect of man's relationship to nature, that is, to what he termed the 'sensuous exterior world'. Taking Kant's view that man achieves full self-expression by engaging in creative production with the world, Marx argued that, as the products of labour become objectified in commodities, man becomes estranged from himself. This is the tragedy of the capitalist mode of production. Unable to sustain creative engagement with the world, cut off from the products of labour, workers are forced to fall back on non-working hours for solace, reduced to the only thing they can call their own: the appetitive animal functions. It is small wonder that the proletariat is in a condition of continued barbarism. The historically evolving remedy for this is communism, which Marx defined as

> . . . the complete and conscious return of man conserving all the riches of previous development for man himself as a social, that is, a human being. Communism as completed naturalism is humanism, and as completed humanism is naturalism. It is the genuine solution of the antagonism between man and nature, and between man and man. It is the true solution of the struggle between existence and essence, between objectification and self-affirmation, between individual and species. It is the solution to the riddle of history, and knows itself to be this solution.[34]

It seems that the provocative arguments of the *Paris Manuscripts* were unknown to most socialist and revolutionary thinkers. The controversy still continues about whether Lenin knew of their existence, or at least of the concept of alienation;[35] if he did, it seems that his acquaintance was not through the *Manuscripts* themselves but by means of their key ideas, expressed in similar terminology in subsequent writings by Marx. The *Manuscripts* were not rediscovered in German until 1932, translations into other languages came later, and they did not become generally available in Russian until the 1950s. Without the *Paris Manuscripts* no Soviet educator had sufficient theory to formulate a genuinely Marxist approach to education.

The socialist school as an experimental laboratory

This lack of explicit Marxian educational direction was reflected as early as 1918 in the tentative nature of Bolshevik thinking and action. At the time when he was expounding the ideological basis of the new school, Lepeshinsky made it clear in the paper read to the First All-Russian Congress of Teacher-Internationalists on 2 June 1918 that a great deal of experiment would be necessary:

> What is most needed is not merely world propaganda, but deeds. With this object the Commissariat of Education is organizing experimental schools. It would be an error to assume that here, in the capital, there is a tendency to introduce bureaucratic methods in the management of schools. We wish to impose nothing upon the people, and when we draw up certain plans, it is chiefly because the population itself, in the person of the organs of local soviet administration units, requires from us a general outline and suggestions.[36]

At the same conference four days later on 6 June Lunacharsky issued the *Declaration of the Principles of the Socialist School*,[37] establishing six principles:

1. Socialism is the maximum imaginable realization for our epoch in the collective life of humanity, of an intelligently directed coordination of labour – mental, physical, organizing, and executive.

2. The best possible system is a free, uniform, compulsory, and secular school based upon self-reliance and self-activity, which passes each individual through a complete cycle of knowledge.

3. The school must be a laboratory for the preparation of those social forms which are most appropriate for the contemporary cultural epoch; the struggle for existence becomes changed into an organized cooperation for making human nature follow the commands of man and for the attainment of new truths.

4. The school must be based on selection by intellectual ability.

5. The bourgeois tradition is destroyed by polytechnization, that is, the unification of the mental and manual.

6. The state becomes no longer omnipotent and the subjugator of society but is more simple and more dignified: that is, it becomes a protector.

Already a fundamental difficulty had emerged – how to impose nothing on the people and yet to ensure the emergence of a socialist society. The solution was to argue in historicist terms, the underlying Hegelianism being strikingly apparent in the *Declaration of the Principles of the Socialist School*. Within a week of the conference the first experimental school was announced on 19 June 1918, its aims being to make biological and sociological studies of children of school age, to study the relationships between physical education and formal education, to investigate the possibilities of an extensive organization of vocational schools, and to make experimental investigation of various other methods of educational work, including social and aesthetic education. On 1 September the Institute for Child Study was announced, with the aims of making a 'thoroughgoing study of all questions connected with prescholastic bringing-up and of creating a staff of trained instructors for the solution of urgent problems of today regarding state, social, universal and free education of children of pre-scholastic age'.[38] The confusion in educational thought of the period reached a highpoint with the Education Act of 16 October 1918. In its preamble the Act stated:

The personality shall remain as the highest value in the socialist culture. This personality, however, can develop its inclinations in all possible luxury only in a harmonious society of equals. We, the government, do not forget the right of an individual to his own peculiar development. It is not necessary for us to cut short a personality, to cheat it, to cast it into iron moulds, because the stability of the socialist community is based not on the uniformity of the barracks, not on artificial drill, not on religious and aesthetic deceptions, but on an actual solidarity of interests.[39]

Thus they raised the question of the uncoerced merging of diverse wills into a cultural unity; the problem lay in securing a genuine 'solidarity of interests' capable of providing a basis for action. It also raised the issue of the treatment of deviation and dissent.

A decade of luxuriant experiment

Throughout the Bolshevik revolutionary period, Russia was fighting a series of counter-revolutionary battles that drew to a close in a final combat with the Poles. In the Treaty of Riga, on 18 March 1921, the new nation found itself at peace in Europe for the first time since 1914; by the end of 1921 the country badly needed a respite. Already industry was severely reduced to an estimated 15 per cent of immediate pre-war capacity.[40] Farms were depleted, the people were facing a severe famine, the peasants uncooperative and hostile to the urban masses; the country was restless with vast numbers of displaced persons including 7 million orphaned and displaced children known as *besprizorniki*.[41] In an attempt to eliminate the chaos and to get the new social scheme working, a halt was called and the New Economic Policy inaugurated. Foreign loans were sought to provide working capital, and a return to partial free enterprise decreed; this period saw the commencement of the second phase of Soviet educational policy, marked by the government's determination to achieve the millennium in the shortest possible time. The twenties and early thirties were years of conflict in Soviet education, and the fundamental issue was that of reconciling the individual and the larger collective, at the same time ensuring steady growth towards the communist state.

To emphasize the labour basis of education, a coeducational ten-year school was planned, its activities to be built around the concept of poly-technization. This was intended to be much more than vocational training; it stemmed from an educational outlook that saw society as based on shared, productive work, culture being the sum total of this work. Through polytechnization Soviet educators hoped to achieve a balance between the liberation of the individual and the necessary cohesion of society, since they were charged not only with the formal educational training of children in basic skills but also with the creation of culture; the whole tradition of the communist era lay ahead of the people, not behind them, they asserted. The concept of polytechnization – although not the word – had appeared in Marx's writings, from whence Lenin brought it into Soviet usage. Marx had looked back to Robert Owen as the originator of the principle of productive labour through a combination of work and learning in the New Lanark factory. In Volume 1 of *Capital* he wrote:

> As we can learn in detail from a study of the life work of Robert Owen, the germs of the education of the future are to be found in the factory system. This will be an education which, in the case of every child over a certain age, will combine productive labour with instruction and physical culture, not only as a means for increasing social production, but as the only way of producing fully developed human beings.[42]

Marx gave the idea greater precision in a memorandum prepared for the Geneva Congress of the International in 1866 where he distinguished intellectual education and physical training from 'polytechnical training which gives instruction in the general scientific principles of all production processes and at the same time initiates the child and young person into the practical use and operation of the simpler tools in all occupations'.[43] In May 1917 Lenin continued the theme in *Materials Relating to the Revision of the Party Programme*, recommending 'Free and compulsory general and polytechnical education (familiarizing the student with the theoretical and practical aspects of the most important fields of production) for all children of both sexes up to the age of sixteen; training of children to be closely integrated with socially productive work.'[44]

Educators of the period were preoccupied with the task of producing a new Soviet culture through polytechnical education. Thomas Woody, for example, who visited Russia in 1918 for several months and then spent a year there in 1930, reported his conversations with Stanislav Shatsky, director in 1930 of an orphan school for *besprizorniki* known as the 'Colony of the Cheerful Life'. Shatsky's educational philosophy was founded on just such a picture – of the school as the creator of culture:

> Our aim is to build true culture. No nation has done so yet. True culture must be founded on the good of all. School, educational philosophy and political life must all be united. No true educational philosophy can be founded in a predatory society. The uniformity and order of a disciplined, collective society

is better than the chaos and waste that are inevitable in a 'free' and indivi-dualistic one. To lay the educational bricks in building socialism is the high duty of current pedagogy.[45]

Polytechnization did not mean that the formal, traditional curriculum was put aside, for Marx himself had included 'intellectual' education as a component; the task was effectively to integrate, or reconcile, the two approaches. So overseas progressive practices were borrowed, and Shatsky saw no inconsistency in freely adapting the educational ideas of John Dewey, while in places the Dalton Plan was used, each student working at an individual self-imposed pace – which, it was hoped, would cultivate self-reliance. Lenin's wife Nadezhda Krupskaya (1869–1939), one of the five members of the collegium of Narkompros, was an early enthusiast for both Dewey and the Dalton Plan. At the Third All-Russian Congress of Education she accused the Russians of lacking self-reliance, of not being able 'to set ourselves a definite goal, to work towards it, according to a plan, to take into consideration the difficulties which are waiting. Finally, we don't take into account individual working capacity; we don't know how to select people and to give them definite assignments.'[46] Krupskaya favourably reviewed Evelyn Dewey's *The Dalton Laboratory Plan* in 1922 in the journal *Na Putyakh k Novoy Shkole* (*On the Road to the New School*); in 1923 books on the Dalton Plan by Helen Parkhurst and Evelyn Dewey were translated into Russian, and enthusiastic committees set about assessing the suitability of the method.

At the same time, there was no universal acceptance. The mass of Soviet teachers (in December 1922 Russia imposed the Union of Socialist Soviet Republics upon the previous Tsarist Empire) were minimally trained and largely indifferent to either ideology or innovatory pedagogy; they remained solidly conventional and conservative throughout the decade of luxuriant experiment. Innovation and experiment were the preoccupation of the reforming vanguard, which itself was quite divided, many of them being suspicious of American ideas and methods. Shatsky, who conducted experimental schools on Narkompros grants, was cautiously reserved; he rejected European forms of education, claiming that none of them was, for him,

. . . as significant or interesting as what came to us from America. But, if Dewey and Tolstoy have exerted an influence, their idea of 'free education' is untenable. From my experiences I know that there is no free child; there is only a child, reflecting different training influences of environment. Therefore, behavior of the child should receive considerable social correction. It is here that we must correct the theory of Dewey.[47]

Concurrently, numerous other approaches were being tried – especially in Petrograd and Moscow, where the innovatory vanguard was chiefly located – all drawing heavily from America which alone had rejected the dual bourgeois/working-class educational system and concentrated on a single comprehensive school where student self-activity methods were emphasized. In particular, the Deweyan laboratory approach, as developed by Kilpatrick in the 'project method', was enthusiastically adopted as the 'complex method', often in combination with the Dalton Plan. The American radical Scott Nearing made a careful study of the Soviet application of the method, and reported:

> Instead of beginning with books, they had begun with life – the life of the village in autumn. They were observing it, analyzing it, discussing it. The teacher read something about it from books. The children were not so far along. So they used the autumn for their books, studied it with great enthusiasm and in a month they had learned a great deal about the things that were happening all about them.[48]

In 1928, in *The New Schools of New Russia*, Lucy Wilson reported that by then the complex method was almost universal in elementary schools and existed in many high schools, especially under the guidance of abler teachers.[49] Confirming this, Nearing stated that he 'did not go into a single school where some form of it was not in operation'.[50] The innovators also turned to the infant science of educational psychology which, under the influence of positivism, was attempting to achieve some useful application in the area of mental testing and measurement. This was known as the 'pedology' movement, defined by the Rector of the Second University of Moscow, Albert Pinkevitch, as that science 'concerned with the psychological and physical development of the child from birth to maturity, [which] studies the biology and psychology of human growth'.[51] Under the stimulus of Pavel Blonsky the measurement and testing programme grew until by 1926 he had tested the intelligence of 10,000 children in Moscow and in 1927–8 had organized a programme to measure the intelligence of every child entering school in two of the six educational districts of Moscow.[52]

In addition to such active methods of formal learning, the schools were organized as centres of pupil participation in social and political organization. Students were encouraged to participate in school government, and a system of political party youth groups was instituted, known as the Komsomols, or Young Communist League (Kommynisticheskii soyuz Molodezhi), as early as 1918. In 1922 this had become the senior youth group, beneath which were two junior organizations – the Little Octobrists for those aged eight to eleven and the Young Pioneers for those ten to fifteen. In July 1923 Krupskaya recommended the Komsomols in a speech during Children's Week because it

> ... instils in its members collective instincts and accustoms them to share joy and grief, teaches them to make the interests of the collective their own, to regard themselves as members of the collective. . . . [It] enhances children's communist consciousness by helping them to realize that they are members of the working class which is fighting for mankind's happiness, members of the huge army of the international proletariat.[53]

In the *Teachers' Gazette* in 1927 she wrote that 'the school and the Young Pioneer movement pursue one and the same aim: to bring children up as fighters for and builders of a new system. The goal of the Young Pioneer movement is to bring up a new youth which will achieve socialist, communist construction.'[54]

The organization of Soviet education by 1927, a decade after the beginning of the new system, was based on efforts to achieve the two values of individuality and collectivity. Student discipline was exercised through committees and persuasion rather than physical coercion, and studies were based upon three broad 'complexes' of social life, the whole of school life being permeated by political ideals with junior versions of the Communist Party extending down into the schools. In theory the entire nation was engaged in the transition from capitalism to socialism and was in process of creating a new society and a new socialist culture. The justification for such an organization of the educative process was that the desired learning outcomes, as Nearing reported them, 'will be naturally acquired along the plan indicated, by the methods of teaching applied to active work; if the school understands how to profit by every occasion to permit the students to put in practice – in socially useful activity – the theoretical knowledge they have acquired'.[55] An even more enthusiastic evaluation of a decade of experiment was recorded in Pinkevitch's important publication of 1929 *The New Education in the Soviet Republic*, in which he went to some length in the Preface, to acknowledge the value of American examples:

> ... the mere enumeration of the names of Hall, Dewey, Russell, Monroe Judd, Thorndike, Kilpatrick and many others, known to every educator i

our country, is a sufficient reminder of the tremendous influence which American education has exerted upon us. In spite of the undoubted differences in ideology which divide soviet from western educational leaders, mutual understanding and recognition of scientific attainments are indispensable. Even in order to condemn one must understand. We have found in the works of American pedagogues and pedologists a rich source of materials. Let us but recall the Dalton Plan, the project method, standard tests, and measurements. All of these innovations have been introduced into our country, even though in their fundamental assumptions they may not be acceptable to us. We, however, do not resort to wholesale condemnation. On the contrary, we study carefully and transplant upon our soil whatever of value we may find elsewhere. And today, I wish to repeat, the most valuable source of such materials is found in the writings of American scientists.[56]

Yet, by then, all was not well. There was profound disagreement among educators over the relative weight to be given to the cultivation of individuality on the one hand, collective social consciousness on the other. Moreover, the experimental approach had led to considerable chaos in the schools; the English Fabians, Sidney and Beatrice Webb, who observed at first hand, wrote that

> The whole decade, 1921–30, was a period of luxuriant experiment, when the lessons of other countries were ignored; discipline was neglected; the pupils were supposed to govern the school; the teachers did as they liked, whilst the inspectors favoured one system after another. The result has been described by foreign observers as a 'joyous bedlam', in which the pupils learned all sorts of things, and the cleverest among them not a little, but seldom the formal lessons common to other countries.[57]

Krupskaya in 1927 acknowledged the enormity of the pedagogical problem of promoting individual development in a socialist country:

> The Soviet system of education aims at developing every child's ability, activity, consciousness, personality and individuality. That is why our methods differ [from those of the bourgeoisie]. . . . The bourgeoisie tries to bring up its children as individualists who set their ego above all else, who oppose the masses. . . . We are for the all-round development of our children – to bring them up not to choose the collective but on the contrary to constitute its force and raise it to a new level. We believe that a child's personality can be best and most fully developed only in a collective. For the collective does not destroy a child's personality, and it improves the quality and content of education.[58]

The middle twenties were, at the same time, a period of profound political struggle. Lenin died early in 1924 and it was not until Stalin triumphed over Trotsky in 1928 that a new centre of power was definitely established and attention was diverted to a reintensification of efforts to introduce a thoroughgoing socialist order. About 1927 the beginnings of educational change can be distinguished: the schools became more consolidated, and there was a gradual return to former methods. Once the original burst of enthusiasm was spent, teachers lost interest in new approaches, and many looked around for guidance. In general, the decline of the complex methods occurred for much the same reasons as the loss of impetus of progressive education in the West. Nearing reported:

> The 'complex system', or unit problem system, succeeds very well for the first three or four years. The children like it, and the teachers are able to handle it effectively. Then some form of specialization becomes necessary because of the intricate nature of the problems that have to be handled. The old method was to let the child specialize – geometry, ancient history, physical geography, mechanical drawing. The aim of the Soviet school authorities is to keep classes at work on unit problems, but under the direction of a number of teachers who are specialists in particular fields.[59]

The growing failure of this method, as the mastery of organized bodies of subject matter became increasingly necessary, was paralleled by a rejection of such techniques as the Dalton Plan. On the same visit Nearing was told by the principal of one school: 'we have abandoned the Dalton Plan. It produced too much individualism by setting up each student to do his own task. We want the students to learn group work. That is what they will be called upon to practice when they get out into the world.'[60]

The millennium modified: the Stalinist era

A decade of educational reaction: the bourgeois return

In the first decade, then, Soviet educational policy went through two clearly defined stages: an early period lasting only a few years and marked by confusion, disorganization and a search for a definite policy, followed by the 'romantic' period of 'luxuriant experimentation' in the twenties.[61] Then, with the political ascendancy of Stalin, a new era began, characterized by the abandonment of one innovation after another and the reintroduction of traditional methods. The changes at first came slowly; the complex method gradually gave way in the higher grades to a formal study of subject matter, and the Dalton Plan was modified to the 'brigade' system in which children worked in groups of four, five or six towards collective goals. In 1928, after a seven-year period of relatively free enterprise, the New Economic Policy was replaced by the first Five-Year Plan which had three major emphases: collectivization of agriculture, increased development of industry and destruction of religion. The effects of this plan upon the school were immediate; it required the schools to improve and increase the output of technically trained people, and it inaugurated a systematic campaign to eliminate religion from the environment of children.[62]

The first major changes came in 1931, when Andrei Bubnov succeeded Anatoly Lunacharsky as People's Commissar for Education. Despite the legal autonomy of each of the six republics, there was a high degree of conformity to central authority and the decrees that followed in the next few years were rapidly implemented. In 1931 the project or complex method was finally abandoned; the modified brigade system of the Dalton Plan was abolished the following year. By a decree of 25 August 1932 from the Central Committee of the Communist Party, the official pattern of teaching in the elementary and secondary schools was to be the *urok* ('lesson') system and in the universities the 'lecture' method.[63]

There was a high level of agreement that the methods of experiment in the previous decade had been wasteful, and the Russian educator Vladimir Samarin stated categorically that 'it had harmed a whole generation of school children, both intellectually and morally'.[64] Curricula became fixed and many practices previously considered bourgeois were reintroduced. Samarin reported at the time on the reintroduction in the 1930s of conservative tsarist methods:

> The standard lesson had been made the sole and mandatory form of instruction. Examinations had been introduced, as had a system of grades, ranging from 'very poor' to 'excellent', and later a numerical system ranging from 'one' (lowest) to 'five' (highest). Much greater demands than before were now made on the students with respect to discipline as well as academic achievement. Textbooks were widely used, and standard texts began to appear, one after another, in all subjects.[65]

The movement gathered momentum, and increasingly testimony began to appear from all quarters, as teachers and educators pointed out the inadequacies of the experimental methods. The stage was now set for the discrediting of the entire scientific and psychological movement. It came as no surprise when on 4 July 1936 the Central Committee of the Communist Party banned the use of pedological methods in the schools in a decree 'On the Pedological Distortion of the System of the Narkompro-sov'.[66]

At this point the revolution had come full circle in education, and formal schooling had almost completely returned. As Beatrice King observed in 1937, Soviet educators were faced with 'the task of discovering methods which should be adequate to the demands of the cultural and economic life of the country', and Soviet educators turned to this with a will.[67] Now they sought a method of education that would cultivate essential skills and knowledge while at the same time producing mentalities at one with the party ideal and leading to action in accordance with the needs of group solidarity.

In the West, in Britain and the United States particularly, there was a mixed reaction to the volte-face. In the United States, the reversal from progressivism to formalism was hailed by the conservatives as a victory for their side, while the progressives denied defeat. As George Counts commented in *The New Republic*:

> Each group has claimed at one time or another that Soviet experience has supported its position. Thus the progressives have maintained that immediately following the Revolution, Soviet educators examined the educational practices of the world and decided in their favor, introducing the Dalton method, the project method, free activity on the part of children, pupil government in an extreme form, and so on. The conservatives, while originally discounting this apparent triumph of progressive ideas in Russia, have more recently agreed that these ideas were weighed in the Soviet scales in the nineteen-twenties, as their opponents had maintained, but were found wanting. In support of their argument they point to the resolution of September, 1931, and to subsequent resolutions of the Central Committee of the Communist Party, which seemed to mark the deliberate abandonment of progressive methods all along the line and the restoration of discipline and authority in the school. As a matter of fact Soviet education, if examined fundamentally, is farther removed today from education in capitalistic countries, whether progressive or conservative, than at any other time since the Bolsheviks rose to power.[68]

Beatrice King argued that the changes were due simply to the increasingly stable social conditions in Russia. Her observations led her to the conclusion that much of the apparently new order was a recombination of old elements, and that the Russians were simply reverting to their old ways in again insisting on a rigorous form of education and the improvement of quality. In addition, she noted a new emphasis on the individual which was designed to exploit competitive desires and so raise production.[69]

By 1936 the international situation was extremely grave; fascism and Nazism were growing rapidly and Hitler was turning Germany into a war machine. Education on experimental progressive lines was a luxury the Soviet Union could not afford; the need was for rapid industrial productivity and firm social discipline. Already, in an address to the graduating class of the Red Army Academy in May 1935, Stalin had given a forewarning, urging the people to new efforts of production: 'Technique without people who have mastered it is lifeless. But technique in the hands of people who know how to use it, can and ought to produce miracles.' In the same speech, Stalin produced his new slogan, 'Cadres decide everything' (*Kadri reshayut vsye*).[70] Whether by design or coincidence, the following August his idea was exemplified by a coalminer in the Donets Basin, Alexei Stakhanov, who, according to Russian sources,

> ... in one shift cut 102 tons of coal, although the normal requirement was 7 tons. He thus exceeded the requirements fourteen and one-half times. Stakhanov thereby initiated a mass movement among industrial and agricultural workers to raise both production rates and output to new and high levels. In his honour, the new movement is known as the Stakhanov Movement.[71]

This occurred during the second Five-Year Plan when the collectivization of the farms was being pushed ahead ruthlessly by Stalin in a campaign including wholesale slaughter of the peasants (kulaks) who resisted the bureaucratic organization of rural life. Stakhanovism spread rapidly and, under the decrees of the Central Committee, into education itself. As the country became geared to ever higher production, and the need for a continued improvement in standards was felt, the schools were forced to respond by turning to systematized subject teaching. The notion that the individual should work for the greater good was more clearly promulgated, and the principle of the working-cadre method, whereby production was to be pursued through group organization, was put into practice. The Soviet Union had returned to the bourgeois system, although class distinction was now to be based on merit as well as privileged birth.

Anton Makarenko and the practice of collective education

In the 1930s, when Soviet education reverted to a traditional approach, the thought and practice of Anton Semyonovitch Makarenko (1888–1939) became especially prominent and widely followed; indeed, in the Stalinist period of the late 1930s Makarenko's procedures seemed to be the most effective means yet devised of harmonizing individual and collective education by integrating learning and labour in an all-round polytechnical education. His ideas were published, serially, over a decade, and constitute a significant corpus of writing[72] which continues to exert an influence upon Soviet education; not with respect to intellectual education, in which it followed with complete orthodoxy the formal approach of the 1930s, but in the sphere of moral formation and the development of communist personality.

Anton Makarenko was born in the small Ukrainian town of Belopole, in the province of Kharkov, the son of a painter in a railway workshop.[73] In 1904 he was admitted to a one-year course of teacher training and after some years as a successful teacher secured admission in 1917 to an advanced course at the Poltava Teachers' Institute. After a brief period of military service he was reappointed to the railway school at Kruikov where he received his own schooling and two years later, in September 1919, became director of the school in Poltava. Makarenko had become critical of current education as early as 1905 when he spoke vigorously in support of workers' rights during the period of widespread uprisings that led to the formation in that year of the Union of Liberation (Soyuz Osvobozhdenia). Although never a ringleader, his continuing agitation for reform brought him in 1920 to the notice of the Provincial Department of Education; as a result of an interview with the head of that department, Makarenko accepted the disciplinary challenge to back his words with action by assuming direction of a colony of delinquents near Kharkov. During the seven years that he directed this institution, called the Maxim Gorky Colony, Makarenko struggled to develop his educational methods aimed at producing the communist ideal of the 'New Soviet Person'.[74]

In that period Makarenko continued to be criticized for his opposition to official 'experimental' educational policy. However, on 20 October 1927 he became director of a new orphans' colony founded that year in Kharkov as a memorial to the assassinated chief of the secret police, Felix Dzerzhinsky. This was the Dzerzhinsky Commune, and Makarenko, now secure from interference, conducted its educational policies by the same methods that he had developed in the Gorky Colony, remaining in charge until 1 July 1935. In that year Stalin was in the middle of the great purges that reached into most aspects of Soviet life, eliminating opposition of every kind. During this period Makarenko suddenly emerged as a 'genuine' Soviet educator and was relieved of his directorship of the Dzerzhinsky Commune so that he could travel the countryside lecturing on his methods, arousing enthusiasm and encouraging emulation by other teachers. He did so for nearly four years in his official capacity as Assistant Director of the Department of Labour Colonies of the People's Commissariat of Internal Affairs for the Ukraine, in the course of which he delivered, in an endless number of talks, the substance of an important book on Soviet education, first published in January 1938 under the title *Problems of Soviet School Education* (*Problemi Shkolnovo Sovietskovo Vospitaniya*). He died in 1939.

The essence of Makarenko's educational theory lies in his concept of the primacy of the collective rather than the individual. Education's major concern should be the subordination of individuality to the common good, a philosophy he reached during a period of some sixteen years in the children's colonies, and that he developed throughout his works, since collected into seven large volumes, of which the most important are *A Pedagogical Poem* (*Pedagogicheskaya Poema*), generally known in English-speaking countries as *The Road to Life*; a second, similar account of the Dzerzhinsky Commune in quasi-fictional form, called in Russian *Flags on the Battlements* (*Flagi na Bashnyakh*) and known in English as *Learning to Live*; and his celebrated *Book for Parents* (*Kniga dlya Roditelei*). All these have had a wide circulation, and *The Road to Life* alone had reached one and a quarter million copies in the Russian language by 1948.

In the Russian language there are three words that can be translated, according to context, as 'education': *prosveshcheniye*, *obrazovaniye* and *vospitaniye*. The first means 'enlightenment'; the second means 'shaping' or 'formation'; the third includes 'discipline' and also 'self-discipline'. It is important to bear in mind that Makarenko habitually used the last term, *vospitaniye*. The fundamental purpose of education, Makarenko believed, is to create a person thoroughly imbued with communist morality, and, since the family may be a pernicious influence, the school must be the primary agent. The aims of education, moreover, must not be determined *a priori*, but should come from the social needs of the people themselves. Central to the new communist morality was the cultivation of a particular type of character – and Makarenko always stressed character and morality rather than cognitive and intellectual attainment as the purpose of education. This should be achieved, he argued, through the conjoint operation of a programme of discipline in all phases of life: formal instruction in school subjects, guidance in social and political thinking, and the operation of school factory workshops, occupying around half of the time, in which all students are compulsorily engaged in making products for sale to the community. His own colonies specialized in making tables and chairs, cameras and electric hand-drills.

In his general theory Makarenko followed Marxist-Leninist orthodoxy but in his daily methods showed himself an uncompromising behaviourist. He rejected the current psychological belief in individual differences (apart from obvious cases of congenital or accidental brain damage), rejected the term 'juvenile delinquent' and refused to accept the record files of children transferred to his care. Every child was seen as a person to be absorbed into the collective of the school, and, since he considered everyone to be solely the product of experience, the way in which the school is organized is of paramount importance. The school he defined as a collective with the goal of producing a communist morality, achieved by maintaining a definite military-academy-style system, or regimen (*rezhim*) as he called it, which is conducive towards the development of discipline. He was careful to distinguish discipline from the processes of reward and punishment, arguing that discipline has a moral quality and, while demanding submission to the collective, must be seen by each person as benefiting both the collective and the individual.

It is his insistence on regimen – that is, a highly structured, predictable school routine – that gives his work such a strongly behaviourist quality, although he preferred to use for this concept of conditioning the word 'tradition'. Throughout all his writings this is a central element: the collective tradition, or regimen, acts as a positive reinforcement of children's behaviour, for, indeed, the child who willingly enters into the spirit of the school finds rewards liberally built into the system. Makarenko opposed physical coercion and in general argued that punishment in its most effective and appropriate form consists in restructuring the relevant situation in such a way that the transgressor comes to see how collective norms have not been met. Essentially, by exerting group pressure and actually involving each child in behavioural tasks, Makarenko took definite steps to promote moral growth.[75] The next stage is for the individual to effect a transition from the primary collective to the wider Soviet society, a troublesome business in any culture. His claims for success were at the level of anecdote and individual testimony, and throughout his works he cited numerous instances of former students who effectively entered into Soviet life as good citizens. Nor did he try to cover up his failures: these too were recorded.

In the strictest interpretation of Marx's theory of alienation, as given in the *Paris Manuscripts*, man does not need a programme of formal schooling; indeed, this is itself an alienating process. We develop our nature through interaction with the environment, and it is this activity that is our education. Since this is necessarily a constantly evolving affair, it is quite impossible to set up a curriculum in advance. Makarenko's thinking and writing, however, showed no awareness whatsoever of the concept of alienation, and his successful attempts to make the school a productive enterprise proceeding conjointly with book learning are more easily seen as an intuitive interpretation of more general features of the labour principle. One of the conflicting elements in his approach is the fact that he separated his school into two apparently exclusive operations: formal classroom instruction and social, moral learning. In all his writings he gave only the slightest attention to formal teaching and learning, devoting his serious interest to the procedures of developing a communist morality. At the same time his own work contained numerous instances of morally indefensible and contradictory actions. In *The Road to Life* the most striking example is the faking of food orders to obtain rations for the Gorky Colony in a period of widespread famine; in the same book, a similar situation occurs in connection with finding the finance to commence the operations of the furniture factory in the colony – which, it might be noted, proceeded like a typical capitalist enterprise.

In many respects, Makarenko's work appears, in the context of the broad sweep of educational history, to lack theoretical depth and to be highly limited. Yet he has been passionately defended and in the Soviet Union great significance has been found in his thought. Certainly he was sufficiently comprehensive in some respects: he gave a clear aim for education, accepted a straightforward view of the world and a simple correspondence theory of truth. Had he followed a genuinely Marxist approach, however, his view of the teacher's role would have had to be moderated, for, as learning by productive labour proceeds, new views and outcomes are continually created and the teacher cannot have so omniscient and authoritarian a role as Makarenko assigned. In fact, Makarenko's acceptance and encouragement of the division of labour in the commune's factory is a thoroughgoing means of producing alienation, and the authority of the teacher remained, even if cloaked by a seemingly non-directive strategy.

The highly specific nature of the colonies in which Makarenko's theories were generated must be considered, and his assertion that his methods are transferable to outside society should not be accepted at face value. Indeed, he did work with a captive group, in the full sense, and expulsion of the colonists – a real threat that was occasionally used – meant starvation in the early days or, in the later years, transfer to a more stringent institution. The superficial features of military paraphernalia should not deflect critical inquiry, for the constant pressure of regimen does not necessarily involve these symbols, but military and paramilitary institutions, such as his, find it difficult to dispense with them. It is no etymological accident that religious orders call their garb a 'habit'; from the earlier word for dress (Latin *habitus*) came the secondary meaning of mental constitution, settled disposition, and hence custom, and all organized groups – religious orders, armies, public servants, and so on – find that an external garb, which necessarily expresses itself in certain levels of ceremonial ritual, conduces to predictable outcomes in behaviour and thinking.

If Makarenko's educational theory has strength anywhere, it rests in his concept of the collective and his general methods of moral development by means of the conditioning process. Serious reservations must be expressed with respect to the generation of values and the development of any creative criticism or growth under Makarenko's system. The continued preoccupation with meeting rigid external goals, as expressed in daily behaviour, and with maintaining the subordination of the individual to the collective appears to provide for no kind of innovation. Indeed, in his system there seems to be no provision for the institutionalization of change or reform, much less for criticism. As such, his theory of education is coercive and maladaptive. It cannot, of course, be denied that he was preoccupied with a time of emergency; none the less Makarenko appears to have been claiming that he had actually developed a universal method, much as he cloaked this under the guise of an artless teacher's practical experiences. Moreover, his approaches fail to convince that a progressive development in moral growth takes place from the earliest stage of egocentricity to respect for the rights of others and the pre-eminence of justice.[76] Does Makarenko's system, in fact, provide the means for a wider moral growth beyond the primary collective? Or does an excessive concern with conforming to the collective keep moral growth arrested

15   Maria Montessori pictured while visiting a school organized on the Montessori principles of teaching, *c.* 1935.

16   An orphans' colony at Tsarskoye Selo in the Soviet Union, 1920.

and at a non-generalizing stage? With respect to cognitive and affective experiences his theory is totally deficient. Yet Makarenko cannot be ignored, having achieved in the Soviet Union a 'venerable founding father' status, and his works are still studied as a significant contribution to Soviet educational thought.

In the late 1930s, particularly after 1936, polytechnization in the Soviet Union was increasingly reduced to a classroom study of science and technology, and productive labour disappeared from the day schools, being retained only in residential institutions. The curriculum reverted to the traditional subject-centred European kind, teachers regained their customary authority, and the process of education took on a highly prescriptive character. By 1940 the Party had become all-powerful, and, while the working people had become significantly emancipated, the socialist millennium had in no way arrived. Life continued to be a matter of unremitting toil and application for most people, and the devastations of 1941–5 in the Second World War only increased the problems of development. With the war over and reconstruction under way in the 1950s, population surges made the 1960s equally difficult, and the Soviet Union remained a class society, still with marked inequalities of access and achievement. Khrushchev attempted reform in 1958, through a decree 'On Strengthening the Relationship of the School with Life and on the Further Development of the System of Public Education in the Country';[77] however, this was subverted and after a few years of halfhearted implementation it was a dead letter. The new society remained stratified, and the people learned that their revolution, and the education system, had simply replaced the tsars with the *apparatchiki* of the Communist Party.

CHAPTER 15

Patterns of Development: Significant Trends and Issues 1945 to the Present

Western supremacy: challenge and response

The communist challenge: sovietization of Europe 1946–1956

Throughout the war years, from 1939 to 1945 – even though the greatest combatants, the Soviet Union and the United States of America, did not directly enter until 1941 – education was subordinated to the utilitarian role of assisting the various war efforts. Schools, colleges and universities were disrupted, funds reduced to a minimum, textbooks became scarce, and teachers and young students were often assigned to the armed forces or the supply factories. With the cessation of hostilities the long slow process of reconstruction commenced. Learning from the experience of 1919, the victorious Allies exacted no retributive reparations; indeed, reverse 'reparations' were provided under the Marshall Plan of 1947 which had the West send supplies and finance to speed the rebuilding of Europe. Concurrently, in a mood of optimism, the Western and Soviet powers masterminded a new version of the defunct League of Nations, which in a Washington meeting of 1942 had been carefully devised as a post-war instrument 'to safeguard peace and security'. On 26 June 1945 in San Francisco fifty nations signed the Charter of the United Nations Organization, which then established a large number of ancillary economic, social and political commissions. In 1946 it created UNESCO, the United Nations Educational, Scientific and Cultural Organization, with headquarters in Paris, as its commission charged with coordinating scholarly and cultural development and seeking peace through international understanding.

Educational advancement was held back, however, by a decade of sustained hostility, 1946–56 – the Cold War – when the Soviet Union initiated a campaign to challenge the world-dominant position of the United States. Denouncing the Marshall Plan as 'dollar imperialism', the Soviet Union under Stalin's leadership began a campaign to bring eastern and central Europe under its control: as democratic governments were restored in the newly liberated countries, they were infiltrated and subverted by communist parties with Moscow allegiances. The Baltic republics, Estonia, Latvia and Lithuania, all occupied in 1939, never regained their freedom; the USSR occupied East Germany in 1945, and other eastern nations fell to Soviet dominance: Bulgaria and Albania in 1946, Romania and Poland in 1947, Czechoslovakia in 1948, Hungary in 1949. The complete sovietization of eastern Europe was frustrated in 1949 with the assertion of independence by Yugoslavia in 1948 and the defeat of the Left in Greece in 1949. Elsewhere, the communist offensive was sustained, particularly in Korea and Indo-China, while in China, on 1 October 1949, a victorious Mao Tse-tung proclaimed the People's Republic under the leadership of the Communist Party. Throughout all these regions the USSR imposed its policies and, in cultural matters, its particular version of Marxist-Leninism, and an educational system that expounded it. Generally, its metaphysics was a form of material realism, its epistemology a version of the correspondence theory of truth, its expressed values centred upon the solidarity of the people and the authority of the collective will. The educational system, theoretically based upon the common school, sought to promote these values, and the ideas of Makarenko and other authoritarian educators dominated both theory and practice.

Historical materialism, as the official Marxist-Leninist philosophical dogma, lent itself easily to a continuation of the traditional forms of education in Russia. Despite the common school, and the abolition of intelligence testing, a dual system of education was easily maintained by the method of housing allocations. The *apparatchiki* inhabited the spacious, well-provided suburbs in the cities and towns where their children attended schools that were better financed, equipped and staffed, even though nominally following the same curriculum – a procedure similar to

that employed in the United States where community-school-zone demarcation lines separated the privileged from the masses. In the Soviet system
the stress remained upon post-war reconstruction, and a deliberate effort
to overtake the United States was promoted. The educational consequence
was the presentation of knowledge as organized bodies of subject matter,
to be mastered systematically, with a stress upon cognitive attainment by
traditional methods – as it remains in the USSR to this day – modified by
tested, predictable, empirical findings. Throughout the Soviet Union
educational research, largely concentrated in the area of the psychology of
learning, was located in their pedagogical institutes, or teachers' colleges,
and followed strictly orthodox lines.

Soviet psychology had its great founder in the physiologist Ivan
Petrovich Pavlov (1849–1936), whose laboratory researches on dogs led to
the discovery of the phenomenon of classical conditioning, and thereby of
instrumental conditioning, which led to the concept of second-signal
learning, that is, the substitution of 'signals' such as language for direct
experience. Ever since the 1936 resolution of the Central Committee of the
Communist Party condemning the 'pedological distortion of the system
of the Narkomprosov', Soviet theorists had imposed on themselves the
difficult problem of how to explain the learning process. Clearly, they
had to reject a traditional dualist body–mind interpretation, since this
presupposes the autonomy of a non-material realm; further, they could
not accept pure materialism which reduces persons and events to mechanical functions, and in this latter respect the conditioning theories of
Pavlov had to be denied in their basic form. A more subtle form of
Pavlovian theory, known as 'act psychology', was proposed by one of the
world's greatest psychologists, Lev Semenovitch Vygotsky (1896–1934),
and published posthumously in 1936 as *Thought and Language*.[1] Central to
Vygotsky's argument is the linking of thought and language, not in
traditional terms by seeing language as the expression of thinking or,
conversely, thought as 'silent speaking' – which therefore assumes, in his
words, a mechanical relationship – but as a unity, expressed as 'word
meaning'. In his theory, which was crucial to advancing educational
psychology and, indeed, to a general theory of the development of
humanity, words are generalizations; each word 'is a verbal act of thought
and reflects reality in quite another way than sensation and perception
reflect it'.[2] Here was a promising way forward, moving beyond positivism and crude empiricism towards holism. Yet it was not orthodox
Marxism; it was suppressed on publication in 1936 in favour of an

alternative, allegedly 'Marxist' position and did not reappear until 1956 in the 'thaw' that followed Stalin's death in 1953.

This alternative led to the most astonishing intellectual occurrence in recent world intellectual history, and stemmed from the work of Trofim Denisovitch Lysenko (1898–1976), a Ukrainian agricultural scientist. Lysenko, along with many doctrinaire communists, rejected bourgeois science, especially the genetic theories of Mendel, which hold that biological characteristics are transmitted by genes inherited from parents and changeable only by mutation. Since this theory denies the influence of environment, and since Marxist historical materialism stresses the evolutionary character of the world and human experience, Lysenko argued that so-called 'genetic inheritance' is not a valid Marxist explanation and proposed the thesis that acquired characteristics can be transmitted to offspring. This was a modern version of the ideas of the French biologist Jean-Baptiste de Lamarck (1744–1829) which had been displaced in the nineteenth century by those of the Austrian monk Gregor Mendel (1822–84). In reverting to Lamarckism, Lysenko outraged Western scientists and many Soviet ones too; at the same time his bizarre theories and faked experiments suited the Politburo which had the task of developing official policy. Lysenkoism had profound political and social implications and clearly reinforced the educational approaches of Makarenko. The war years quietened the debate; once the war was over the debate was renewed and in an astonishing act, in 1948, the Central Committee of the Communist Party declared it orthodox.[3] Lysenko had been supported by Stalin as early as 1935; thereafter, for thirty years, until his work and theories were finally discredited and overthrown, Lysenkoism dominated all Soviet science, especially educational psychology.

The ideological basis was well expressed by Makarenko in the phrase 'man must be changed'; the process of correct change was to be sought in understanding the process of historical materialism and the ways in which human endeavours could be employed to realize the teleological course of such a process. Throughout the 1950s, right up to the fall of Lysenkoism in February 1965, when Lysenko was dismissed as Director of the Institute of Genetics of the USSR Academy of Sciences, Soviet education was under such dominance, and, while psychologists endeavoured, in the words of one such worker, 'to uncover the mental properties of man and the laws of his mental development'[4] as they are revealed in the historical evolution of class society towards social unity and 'classlessness', the entire educational enterprise was directed towards the Makarenko ideal of the common collective consciousness, and the school was seen as a major agent in the cause of overtaking and then defeating reactionary capitalism. When in December 1957 the Soviet Union launched *Sputnik* (literally, 'fellow-traveller' to the earth), it seemed that the new Soviet era had indeed materialized and that their post-war educational policies were successful.

Meanwhile the confrontation with the West had built up in 1948–9 with the Soviet blockade of Berlin and the Allied response of the airlift; in 1950 it was transferred to Korea. Defensive alliances were formed: NATO, the North Atlantic Treaty Alliance, in 1949; SEATO, the South-East Asian Treaty Organization in 1954; CENTO, the Central Treaty Organization, in 1955. The Soviet Union and its satellites responded in 1955 with the Warsaw Pact, while the Soviet Union sought to extend its hegemony over China, Asia and Latin America as well by encouraging leftist movements. After Stalin's death in 1953 there was some liberalization of the regime under the leadership of Nikita Khrushchev as First Secretary of the Communist Party. Khrushchev's denunciation of Stalin as the developer of a vicious 'cult of personality', in a secret speech to the Twentieth Congress of the Communist Party as early as 25 February 1956, initiated a new period in Soviet–Western relationships and a new era of internal Soviet reforms, among which significant efforts were made to improve education.

Western response: rising expectations and conservative backlash 1946–1957

Meanwhile, the Western allies were preoccupied with their own problems. Success in the war had strengthened their conviction that democracy is the best of all possible political forms and market-place capitalism, on the Keynesian aggregate-demand model – which requires deliberate government intervention to stimulate production, demand and employment, and therefore implies an ever-expanding economy – the best of economic theories and practices. With this conviction they set about strengthening capitalist economies throughout their own territories, domestic and overseas, to which they gave the description the 'free world'. It was inevitable, as these two 'worlds', capitalist and communist, came into post-war conflict for world dominance, that education should be centrally involved. Clearly, if the development of an expanding economy was the prerequisite of successful capitalist democracies, the school – at all levels – had to become an agent of that deliberate process. Society, moreover, in the capitalist system, was regarded as necessarily class-structured, and the dominant middle classes saw no need to alter the existing conception of education, which had evolved as the means of enabling a privileged order to hold power. It was classical Greece that first developed educational theory of a kind that rationalized this process, as the etymology of their word 'aristocracy' (from *aristos*, the best, and *krateo*, to rule) so clearly reveals. Throughout the nineteenth century the expanding industrial economy in the West had broken the power of the aristocracy and allowed the emergence of a new *arriviste* class which accepted the existing educational pattern of the dual system and even became excessively zealous adherents. Some ladders of social mobility were provided to enable a limited number of talented children from the working classes to climb from the basic schools. Yet the main development in education was for the new meritocracy, the urban industrial bourgeoisie, to appropriate the conservative tradition to themselves – at the same time preserving the aristocracy as a legitimizing symbol of their own membership of the power élite. So the classical double entendre of the 'liberal arts' was revived: while these offered intellectual liberation from the tyrannies of time and place, they were also appropriate only for the privileged. Liberal education and élitism became linked and have remained so to the present day. Even when the grammar-school curriculum was expanded to take account of modern developments, the sciences and mathematics were still treated as potentially 'liberal studies', although the highly restrictive enrolments of these schools meant that liberation was available, by definition, only to the few already chosen.

In post-war Western society that approach was sustained, and the nineteenth-century arguments for the necessity of social classes, of appropriate 'stations in life', remained dominant. Yet there was, at the same time, recognition of the possible need for more secondary schooling; already in the early twentieth century, as the industrialization of the West and the demands of the factory system multiplied their effects throughout the economies of Europe, creating warehouses, railways, post offices, banking and commercial organizations and requiring a literate working class, the West became a school-dependent society. While factory hands and artisans could still be trained by customary craft procedures, the greatly increased range of new occupations – mostly clerical – created by the industrial revolution and its insatiable appetite for paper documents meant that schooling (but not education) for the masses had become necessary. The returning servicemen and women of the armed forces, after 1945, and those who laboured in the supply factories, however, had interpreted in a different way the rhetoric of a war for freedom and democracy; the West entered a period of rising working-class expectations, which were reflected in their desire to see that their children received a better education than they themselves had been given. So, in various Western societies, secondary education was expanded, although no profound social revolutions occurred. In Britain the Education Act of 1944 and in France the Langevin-Wallon Plan are conspicuous examples; in the United States, Harvard University, long a pacesetter in American educational thought, established in early 1943 a University Committee on the Objectives of a General Education in a Free Society 'to consider the problem of general education in both the school and the college',[5] which came in response to that growing demand for better and wider public education. In the famous study *General Education in a Free Society* (1945) this committee concluded that, in contrast to 1940 when of the 25 million in schools only little more than 7 million were in the secondary sector, in post-war America there would be an unprecedented surge in demand for secondary and higher education and that 'the high school is morally obliged to adapt itself to every kind of student'.[6]

Such humane optimism was not fully accepted in the United States, much less in élitist Europe; moreover, post-war reconstruction and development tempered utopian demands. The Cold War played into the conservatives' hands and in Western nations the dominant classes were generally reactionary in education, as exemplified in one of the darkest episodes of American educational history: the 'Red scare' campaigns of the 1930s and their revival in the 1950s under Senator Joseph McCarthy with the Congressional inquiries into alleged communist activities of Americans. The sovietization of eastern Europe in the late 1940s was a profound challenge to the West which responded, as already noted, with the defensive alliance of NATO – in effect, a ranging of Western armies outside the rim of the 'iron curtain', as Churchill had described the communist frontiers in August 1945. By the early 1950s the West was on the defensive, even though its production was greater than in the Soviet bloc, and the American mood became paranoid with fear of communist subversion of schools and universities. Throughout the Great Depression of the 1930s there had been bitter conflict within the teaching ranks between Left and Right: the former generally accepted Deweyan experimentalism and progressivism for educational practice and the doctrines of social reconstructionism as the goal of their endeavours; the latter, often in church and private schools, leaned towards conservative thought and practice. In the 1950s, with the Right becoming dominant, progressive education increasingly became the target of hostile attack; cynicism spread rapidly, stemming from the belief that progressivism was 'soft-pedagogy' and that when Hitler, Mussolini, Stalin and Franco outlawed all progressive practices they knew that national strength, prosperity and survival depended, as Pius XII expressed it, on 'apt and solid methods of teaching', that is, the conservative tradition, rigorously enforced. Throughout the West, and most dramatically in the United States, there was suddenly a proliferation of books analysing the threat to Western democracy and assigning the cause, in part, to the subversive forces of progressivism in the schools. In the United States, Admiral Hyman Rickover and Professor Arthur Bestor became national figures overnight for their attacks on progressivism and their defence of the conservative tradition. The Progressive Education Association, moreover, was in decline, and progressivism was equated with subversion. Bestor's book *Educational Wastelands* (1953), subtitled 'The Retreat from Learning in our Public Schools', is a brilliantly polemical conservative attack on progressivism. The pace of innovation and experiment was slowed down; in many authoritarian countries it was eliminated, and as the world moved into the 1960s education had entered a new era – one dominated by a deliberate Western concern to respond to the Soviet challenge by reconstructing the schools as an agency of national planning.

Era of scientific positivism

The West on the offensive: education for development 1957–1967

Western response to the communist challenge changed dramatically in the second post-war decade; from a position of conservative reaction it moved on to the offensive. While there was no wholesale abandonment of the dual system in Europe or the European colonies, possibilities for social mobility were increased, the greatest gains occurring in the United States. After the 1954 Supreme Court ruling that school segregation of races was unconstitutional, the slow and often violent movement towards integration commenced and blacks gained greater access to higher learning, receiving, in the process, the landmark Civil Rights Bill of 1957. Throughout the United States the high school became the norm of educational aspiration, and colleges and universities were opened to wider enrolments than ever before. In Europe the pace was slower, but the signs of change were there, indicated, in just one significant instance, by a paper presented in 1958 to the Fourth World Congress of Sociology by Ralph Turner entitled 'Sponsored and Contest Mobility and the School System'[7] which expressed the new wave of social concern for, and sociological investigation of, the role of education in modern society. The perception of events in the late 1950s and early 1960s was of competition for survival, and the new concept of education for national development gathered momentum, leading, first, to a reappraisal of education, not as a liberalizing process on the traditional model, but as a form of investment that could be expected to pay dividends; second, to the attempted application of technological innovation and scientific techniques of management and prediction so that returns on investment could be secured at optimal levels.

The concept of education as investment burgeoned in the early 1960s as the Western world moved to meet the communist challenge. Yet this new resolve to assert the strength of democracy and its institutions was not motivated entirely by economic and political considerations; it had as well a moral component, as exemplified in the election in 1961 of John Kennedy as President of the United States. After the assassination of Kennedy in 1963, his successor Lyndon Johnson attempted to sustain the Western democratic initiative by authorizing American resistance to communist subversion in Indo-China with a naval engagement in 1964 in the Gulf of Tonkin that heralded direct American entry into the Vietnam War, already in continuous operation for more than twenty years. To emphasize the moral side, President Johnson signed a second Civil Rights Bill into law in 1964 and projected, as an answer to the communist challenge, the vision of the 'Great Society' built upon the concept of educating all of the people to enter, productively, into the free-market economy. This was the essential point: freedom, democracy and capitalism go comfortably together and will necessarily prosper in the degree to which education turns out persons capable of using their talents productively.

Nowhere is this new concern for education as economic investment better expressed than in Mark Blaug's introduction to his collected readings of 1968, *Economics of Education*. Blaug observed that 'the economics of education with its concept of human investment', which was barely in existence before 1958,[8] had emerged to replace 'old-fashioned' short-term approaches and would transform educational planning: 'it is now realized', he asserted confidently, 'that improvements in the quality of the labour force can have dramatic effects on economic growth.' The world-wide movement to consider education as a major area of investment now raised serious national questions as to the source of finance, the limits of expenditure and planning for 'the optimum combination of pupils' time, teachers, buildings and equipment'. Blaug's comments reflected the new approach: 'All of these peculiarities [of financing, calculating cost-effectiveness and allocating resources] make it difficult to appraise the efficiency with which resources are allocated in the education industry and raise the question whether the traditional apparatus of economists is, in fact, applicable to schools and colleges.'[9] Given this new conception of education as an 'industry', the section headings of his two-volume collection of articles, written variously between 1959 and 1968, show the trend of thinking during the decade: 'The concept of human capital', 'Cost-benefit analysis of educational expenditures', 'The manpower-forecasting approach', 'Educational planning in developing countries', 'Mathematical models in educational planning', 'International migration of human skills', 'Productivity and efficiency of education', 'The finance of education'.

Around the world, governments responded enthusiastically, and as early as December 1961 some twenty Western nations formed the new Organization for Economic Co-operation and Development, OECD, to promote economic growth through the best possible utilization of science, education and manpower. Expanding to twenty-five nations by 1968, the OECD continued to play an active role in development education. However, the investment-planning era subsided when it was realized that the economic and industrial concepts could not be applied as easily as had been thought. Despite the recognition that diminishing returns set in very quickly and that development education is not so readily implemented, governments, school boards and other authorities had learned that the economics of education must be carefully considered as a major determining factor in future plans, especially those involving reforms and innovations.

The application of techniques of scientific and technological management was in essence a continuation, although at a greatly accelerated pace, of the scientific movement in education that had begun in the nineteenth century in the area of psychology. Initially, the educational applications of psychology in the work of the Herbartians had developed out of philosophical theory; early in the twentieth century, however, such pioneer researchers as Wundt, Hall and Binet attempted to emulate the physical sciences by developing techniques of empirical investigation and seeking quantifiable results, but such 'scientific' areas grew slowly. Even throughout the 1930s educational psychology was concerned largely with investigating the concept of intelligence and cognitive processes, and related educational applications such as mental testing, ability grouping, grading and prediction.[10] Simultaneously, the Stanley Hall movement of child growth and development study was pursued as a correlative attempt to discover how students could best be streamed, grouped and graded through the various school and curriculum sequences. Social psychology was still primitive, growing slowly as an offshoot of psychological studies, and dealing with such issues as the alleged lower intelligence of blacks and coloured races. Underlying all these empirical studies was a preoccupation with measurement and prediction. Educational theory was still dominated by armchair methods: the 1950s were marked by the appearance of a wide literature of critical analysis, but little of it based upon extensive fieldwork and empirical inquiry. By the end of that decade, significant changes were under way as education was increasingly penetrated by behavioural studies, chiefly individual psychology, social psychology and the newly popular discipline of sociology. Gaining strength from the worldwide movement towards quantification and technological application, psychology in the Western nations had made great progress in its investigation of cognitive processes and learning theory, especially in the area of conditioning. By the late 1950s cognition and conditioning had been put together in the theory of 'programmed' learning, which seemed to offer a new era in education.[11]

This movement, which in effect was a continuation of the medieval desire for a faultless logical 'method', so well exemplified in the sixteenth-century quest for a *ratio* or *ordine*, reached its most developed form in the work of Burrhus Frederic Skinner (b. 1904). Throughout the 1950s and 1960s Skinner championed the psychology of behavioural conditioning and published a stream of articles on the modification and control of human behaviour through carefully graded programmes of reinforced-learning sequences, using, in the process, the term 'teaching machine', which designated the simple box in which the paper programmes, in serial presentation, were mounted on rollers. The publication of his mature views in 1971 in *Beyond Freedom and Dignity* created a furore. In this work championing the organization of society around methods of conditioning by reinforcing desired responses, he was presenting the autumn harvest of the nineteenth-century positivist quest to control everything by 'scientific' planning. To continue the metaphor applied by Santayana to the excesses of late nineteenth-century idealism, despite the brilliance of the autumn, the harvest remained one of dead leaves. Yet the idea was appealing, and ignorant of the lessons of history – because in true positivist fashion history was ignored as irrelevant – numbers of educational psychologists followed Skinner's lead with replication experiments. So ensued a decade in which the proliferating technology of communications went from the crude 'teaching machine' of 1960 to the more sophisticated presentation a decade later of computer-assisted instruction. The further development and miniaturization of electronic devices has made computer and machine technology increasingly accessible, and the belief that the machine has a major role to play in education has continued with the widespread use of radio, film and television programmes, satellite transmission, micro-teaching made possible by videotaping and, more recently, electronically assisted gaming and simulation approaches.

As the machine, its associated technology and related theory burgeoned throughout the 1960s, so the study of education, particularly in universities and teachers' colleges, changed; increasingly normative studies based upon philosophy, general theory and tested practice declined and were replaced by the newly fashionable scientific, research-based approaches. Along with such economic aims as education for investment and productivity went the application of the more complex technology of the expanding marketplace economy. Normative studies, it seemed, were no longer needed; values came from the interchange between demand, production and consumption, and the two disciplines that contribute value-theory to education – history and philosophy – also declined; many of their practitioners, eager to participate in the new educational crusade of the 1960s, attempted to follow in the path of scientific positivism. So philosophy of education in many places succumbed to the positivist trend of the age, eschewed its traditional metaphysical concerns and, especially in English-speaking countries, became preoccupied with logical analysis of terms, concepts and slogans.[12] This, of course, was a necessary function – which indeed Socrates and Plato recognized as an important role of philosophy – and it probably exercised a beneficial effect in purging the educational lexicon of the demons, phlegms and phlogistons of previous eras. Unfortunately, it neglected – even disdained – its customary theory-building, forward-looking function. When educational philosophy showed any concern for axiological matters, it was largely in the area of moral growth and development and was allied closely with experimental psychology,[13] although in

Germany and parts of Europe some concern remained with general theory of education.[14] In one of the most significant philosophical research projects on moral education in this period, sponsored at Oxford by the Farmington Trust, its chief investigator John Wilson wrote in the report, published in 1967 as an *Introduction to Moral Education*, that 'it is now recognized that the findings of natural science not only may but must be brought into the political arena'.[15]

This attitude is exemplified in the lifelong researches of Jean Piaget, chiefly at the Jean-Jacques Rousseau Institute of the University of Geneva, which he has reported in a considerable literature, probably best summarized in his *Psychologie et pédagogie*, published in 1969. As early as 1935 Piaget argued that moral education consists in learning, by the maturation of the individual's intelligence, the appropriate 'forms of behaviour capable of developing the critical attitude of mind, objectivity, and discursive reflection' which result in 'a real exercise of the principles of behaviour and not solely in a submission to external constraint'.[16] Originally working from a Kantian viewpoint, Piaget became increasingly interested in how children develop concepts of time and space – that is, purely abstract concepts – and from this he was led to study moral concepts. As late as 1965, in writing *Psychologie et pédagogie*, he argued that the relationships between philosophy and moral education are largely psychological, and that the central task remains to gain an understanding of 'the nature of intelligence or knowledge, the role of experience in the formation of ideas, and the mechanism of social or linguistic communications between adult and child'.[17] This, it should be noted, continued the educational inquiries of Montessori and Vygotsky. More recently, working from a similar position, Lawrence Kohlberg at Harvard University has undertaken experimental researches in order to elucidate the relationships between cognitive growth and moral development.[18]

Dramatic dissent: the radical challenge 1967–1973

Throughout the 1960s, however, the general development of the West – and its educational activities in particular – met with growing resistance and criticism, and the later years of that decade introduced a period of social and political turmoil. The challenge of the 'new frontier' proclaimed by President Kennedy and sustained by President Johnson as the 'Great Society' had lost pace and credibility as the United States became enmeshed in the Vietnam War. The idealistic component of those programmes was cynically rejected by the new generation of young students who considered themselves dupes of what they derided as the 'military-industrial complex': they considered education for development to be a continuation of nineteenth-century capitalist exploitation of the mass of society. Progressive education was also rejected as a more subtle form of capitalist indoctrination. At the moment that America was seeming to seize the development initiative from the Soviet Union in winning the 'space race' by landing Neil Armstrong on the moon on 21 July 1969, with all the industrial-technological achievement that implied, it was becoming a society increasingly divided within itself. Throughout the West widespread reaction and dissent seriously disrupted education, especially at the college and university level. From the radical extreme there came a new wave of Marxist and leftist consciousness expressed in demands for the reconstruction of society and for new forms of education, rejecting vehemently the industrial-capitalist technological culture that had been emerging.

These demands constituted a second, alternative stream of educational development that opposed the mainstream of scientific positivism applied to education. This movement of radical dissent, although virtually unfunded and unsupported, gained such worldwide following that it brought about a polarization. The immediate antecedents of this form of dissent were in nineteenth-century socialist movements culminating in the thought of Marx, and in the 1970s the Western world paid heavily for its conspiracy of silence on socialism and the aspirations of the counterculture. Twentieth-century dissent, it must be observed, while drawing from the socialist tradition, did not depend on it entirely; indeed, it stemmed from a diversity of sources including Christian, liberal and democratic movements within the capitalist system. Generally, however, the most conspicuous educational dissenters have had socialist connections, such as the social-reconstructionists in America in the 1930s, epitomized by George Counts, and the Christian-socialist historian in Britain, R. H. Tawney, whose treatise *Equality*, first published in 1931, remains widely read.

After the Second World War the growing strength of the dissenting movement was expressed in a series of provocative writings on equality, beginning with the 1946 American publication by Lloyd Warner and Robert Havighurst, *Who Shall Be Educated?* This theme was taken up increasingly, especially in Britain and the United States, and by the 1950s it had generated a considerable literature. Throughout the 1960s, however, when the world was ravaged by escalating conflict and the disparity between the industrially developed nations and the Third World became a more urgent issue, the liberal position was undermined as two polarities emerged: the conservative, reactionary Right typified by the *Black Papers* of 1969 in Britain; and an increasingly radical Left which drew its inspiration from Marxist thinkers such as Marcuse, and from portents of Euro-American liberation apparently foreshadowed in the Great Proletarian Cultural Revolution in China. These developments were examined in a more insistent literature of concern, chiefly sociological in origin. As early as 1958 the notion of equality and justice had been presented to British readers in *The Rise of the Meritocracy* by Michael Young, and this was now followed by a huge volume of sociological research, typified at its most critical in the work of Pierre Bourdieu reported in 'L'École conservatrice' of 1966.[19] By the late 1960s the positivist framework of educational theory was being critically rejected in a new wave of subjectivist thinking, of which notable examples appeared in *The Social Construction of Reality* by Peter Berger and Thomas Luckman,[20] and a revival of the phenomenological philosophy of Edmund Husserl of the 1920s and 1930s, which was opposed to the positivist view of empirical knowledge and the notions of objective and value-free research.

Simultaneously, throughout the 1960s a revisionist historiography, especially in the United States, had a major impact on the use of history as a contributory discipline to educational theory. Responding to the radical arguments, historians increasingly began to reassess the standard histories, which now appeared to them as little more than mythopoeic rationalizations of the conservative tradition and justifications for the privileged system. When teacher training began as a mass movement in the late nineteenth century, the extension of schooling to the masses was seen as part of the march of European progress; early historiography both perceived and described this development in such Hegelian terms, and this interpretation, transmitted through the twentieth century, provided a historicist justification for the desirability of sustaining the conservative tradition, moderating it slowly by modest increments of scientifically proven achievements. In the 1960s, stimulated by the world convulsions, American educational historians began to rewrite the history of education from a socialist perspective in terms of such concepts as class conflict, racism, sexism, bureaucratic defence of privilege and the reactionary policies of the entrenched power-élite.[21] As in all reforming movements, hindsight helps to discover pedigrees, and American historical revisionism found a worthy progenitor in Merle Curti's 1935 book, *The Social Ideas of American Educators.*

It is not possible to consider here the complex interplay between revisionist educational research and theory on the one hand, and the revisionist historical presentation on the other; what clearly happened is that by the late 1960s educational theory was in a confused state as the positivist research procedures of the post-war era were increasingly challenged by phenomenological and hermeneutic approaches to explanation. At the same time, action too was becoming more overt; the schools ceased to be quiet oases of academe, especially at the college and university level, as radical students sought more appropriate ways of implementing educational justice and reconstructing society on a more egalitarian basis. Both the Western and Soviet systems were rejected, and inspiration for the radical reform of society was found in the so-called developing nations: those that belonged neither to the 'First World' of capitalism nor to the 'Second World' of challenging communism. The Second World War had weakened the Western hold on its Afro-Asian colonial settlements, and while the Cold War continued in Europe the newly independent colonies moved vigorously to establish separate identities, strongly influenced in many cases by the Marxist doctrine of class struggle and the invincibility, and moral righteousness, of the sweep of historical materialism. In an attempt to establish political solidarity against the reassertion of either capitalist or communist dominance, in 1955 twenty-nine African and Asian states held a conference in Bandung, Indonesia, where they denounced many of the practices of the developed nations and identified themselves as a 'Third World', from the French phrase, 'le Tiers-monde'. The most influential participant was the People's Republic of China which, now free of external domination, was beginning, in the words of its chairman of the Central Committee of the Communist Party, Mao Tse-tung, 'to walk on two legs'; to be independent, that is, of foreign pressures. Hoping to reduce the nation to satellite status, the Soviet Union in 1960 abruptly withdrew all support, including credits, technicians and technology. Instead of collapsing, China moved ahead in the 1960s, almost entirely alone, learning to use its own resources. The example was morale-boosting for many nations of the developing Third World, and in the late 1960s it seemed to many Western radicals to offer a paradigmatic solution to the moral crisis engulfing the West. Throughout Europe and America – North, Central, South – there was a wave of radical enthusiasm for the Chinese way, especially for the form of Marxism that the Chinese termed 'Marxism–Leninism–Mao Tse-tung thought' and for the social revolution that had first broken out in 1966 as the Great Proletarian Cultural Revolution. The central doctrines of this revolutionary movement were the egalitarian reconstruction of society, and the establishment of a new system of people's education whereby everyone was to gain equal access to the schools.

The Chinese approach to education suddenly became the subject of world attention, and many radicals within the West argued that it was the path to salvation for the rapidly decaying capitalist system; many socialists, such as the European movement of Modern Leftism, regarded Soviet communism as state capitalism and therefore a co-equal enemy.[22] The appealing feature of Chinese education in the late 1960s was its cathartic character: it offered a purgation of mankind's ills. In late 1965 in Shanghai the Cultural Revolution was launched by the young Red Guards, under Mao's stimulus, to tear down the old order and create a new society, as the complete title of the movement indicates: 'a full-scale revolution to establish a working-class culture'.[23] By 1966 it had reached a peak of destruction and closed many of the colleges and universities of the nation for four years. The ideological aim of the young radicals, as of Mao himself, was to effect successfully that transformation of society the Bolsheviks had failed to achieve in Russia in the 1920s. Many of the external features of the Soviet experiment were adopted, chiefly the unified school, designated 'primary' and 'middle', which offered a complete education of up to ten years. Thereafter, progression was to various technical or higher-education institutes, which could be entered only after each middle-school graduate had completed three years of 'productive labour' in either factory or field. This was a novel feature designed to eliminate social classes and prevent their reappearance. All young people, at the age of sixteen, were to be assigned, and were expected to accept cheerfully, a position in the workforce. Then, at the end of that period, a committee of fellow workers decided on each student's future career, assigning them to farm, factory, technical institute, college or university on the basis of political enthusiasm and achievement: in the Chinese phrase, on the basis of each student's degree of being both 'red and expert'.

In Mao's view, the Soviets had failed to create a genuinely classless society because they had neglected two vital areas: to ensure, first, that young people formed 'correct' philosophical attitudes and, second, that these were cultivated by the successful application of the principle of polytechnical education. In the Soviet Union the study of Marxism, after the disastrous Lysenko era and the fall of Khrushchev, became completely separated from daily life; the Soviet economy became one of state capitalism in active competition with the outside world; schools and universities relegated ideological instruction to the political youth-league activities of the Komsomols, while the daily curriculum followed procedures indistinguishable from those of conservative Western countries. The Chinese Cultural Revolution sought to change all that. Its fundamental doctrine was set out in Mao's essay of July 1937, *On Practice*, subtitled 'On the Relation between Knowledge and Practice, between Knowing and Doing'.[24] Here Mao put forward the Marxist metaphysical position that man's interaction with the external world is a two-way process: our ideas are formed as we enter into engagement with the external world. The philosophical and hence educational task is to ensure that each person is led to interact with the external world in such a way that 'correct' ideas are formed of 'phenomena, the properties and laws of nature, and the relations between himself and nature; and through this activity in production . . . to understand, in varying degrees, certain relations that exist between man and man'.[25] In its essential metaphysics the argument closely followed correspondence theory, but with a difference: by engaging in practical activity, that is, praxis, and by being aware of the dialectical development of historical materialism, each individual comes to see the necessary interrelatedness and interdependence of all persons. It follows that polytechnical education, expressed by Mao as 'productive labour', is the proper way of ensuring that practice is effective. The formal textbook curriculum is actually deleterious; only by direct engagement in conjoint work experience can our knowledge of the external world be made operative, that is, part of social reality. These ideas were promoted by the Cultural Revolution; institutions of higher learning dominated by Red Guards set up revolutionary executive committees to ensure that learning and labour went in close relationship and that correct social ideas were formed. The aim, in short, was to ensure that the entire new generation of China became both red and expert.

American involvement in Vietnam, meanwhile, by 1968 symbolized for many all that was wrong with Western capitalism; the brutal Soviet repression of the liberal regime in Czechoslovakia in August 1968 showed that nothing humane could be expected from Soviet-style communism; the Chinese Cultural Revolution promising total social reconstruction seemed to Western radicals the way ahead. And, of course, the limited flow of information coming out of China concealed the savage fighting that had occurred; moreover, there was a Western radical willingness to accept repression of 'reactionary elements' for the sake of the necessary transmogrification of society. In that period, independently of China, radical revolts spread across the college and university campuses of the world, beginning with student disorders in Berkeley, California, in 1964 and the French city of Nanterre in 1967, demanding social, political and educational reforms, which were seen as inextricably linked. Riots erupted in Paris in May 1968, nearly bringing down the de Gaulle government; simultaneously in New York the radical Students for a Democratic Society (SDS) was formed at Columbia University and disrupted much university life, while on Kent State University campus in Ohio government troops shot four student protestors dead and wounded many others; in the Federal Republic of Germany an SDS leader Rudi Dutschke suffered an assassination attempt, and violence was unleashed. Throughout 1968 and 1969 there was a rapid spread of student revolts, particularly in the advanced Western industrial nations – chiefly France, Germany, Italy, Japan and the United States – but also in some Second and Third World countries, such as Africa, India, Pakistan, South-East Asia and Latin America; in Singapore and Malaysia they paralysed urban life; in Indonesia they were instrumental in bringing down the government. Even the repressive totalitarian regimes did not escape, and campuses erupted in Spain, Hungary, Czechoslovakia, Poland and Greece, among other places. The turmoil spread even into the secondary schools in some cases, although their forms of activism were generally more internally expressed in the questioning and defiance of established procedures and moral norms.

Clearly, by 1970 a new wave of radical social consciousness had emerged which, calling itself Modern Leftism, and drawing from this context of revolution and despair, rallied Western radicals to the new cause of educational dissent, rejection and alternativism. One of the many accounts appeared in 1971 in Richard Gombin's *Les Origines du gauchisme* which appeared in English in 1975 as *The Origins of Modern Leftism*. Here we find the continuation of the socialist, reforming initiative of the nineteenth century in late twentieth-century dress. Disillusioned with the Soviet Union, which Modern Leftism saw as failed Marxism, their demand was for a new society, with an appropriate alternative system of education, in contrast to the Soviet Union, all of the eastern bloc and allied regimes such as Cuba, where education had been returned to the conservative tradition. Indeed, the volte-face by the allegedly utopian regimes of communism was seen by the Modern Leftists as a problem: a true socialist (and therefore genuinely moral) society cannot come until an authentic socialist consciousness is created, and this cannot be done by making adjustments to the conservative tradition; a radically new form of education was needed. Gombin made the point in his preface that 'Systematic leftism takes the form of an *alternative* to Marxism-Leninism'. To understand the argument, it is necessary to read his text, but the gist can be put simply and briefly: it is that 'the present epoch is characterized by the irruption of the masses into the domain of *real* life'[26] and that, far from being a movement to be put down, it is one that must be accepted, and institutionally accommodated by society; it requires a wholesale reconstruction of society, and the provision of an alternative education, cultivating a genuinely new common consciousness. This was the motive force behind the student disorders of the late 1960s, which in watered-down and often ill-understood form quickly spread across the campuses of the world in the early 1970s, expressing itself as sit-ins, moratorium marches, demands for relevance, students for a democratic society, and environmentalist movements.

Now, while these student revolts dominated the popular press, and created fear and resentment among populations at large, they accounted for only a very small part of the educational enterprise, which continued to operate by more conventional, placid procedures. Yet the disorders did seem to represent the symptoms of significant social malaise. While it is impossible to generalize on their causes, governments and similar authorities have tried to explain them away as the consequences of external influences, Western democracies pointing to subversive Marxist doctrines, communist regimes assigning them to bourgeois revisionism and moral decadence. It is interesting to note that only rarely were these radical events conceded to be specifically educational in essence. Indeed, governments generally asserted that student protests are totally foreign to the character of education and that students should desist from using their colleges as locales for fighting what are fundamentally political battles and return to their proper role of academic study, with the implicit, and often explicit, assumption that this should follow the traditional model. Student radicals, for their part, consciously or not, generally reject this, and assert the fundamental premiss that all life is educational; that, indeed, it is idle – if not completely stupid – to attempt to develop a process of education in isolation from the world around them.

At the same time there was also a powerful verbal campaign against traditional education which sought both to stimulate action and to justify it. This might be called the radical rhetoric, and it reached deluge proportions in those years and exerted considerable pressure upon education. Like the campus demonstrations, it would be difficult, if not impossible, to catalogue this literature of radical rhetoric: it must exist in thousands of separate tracts. Much of it, of course, was simply occasional journalism of uneven quality, shallowly conceived and polemically expressed, which disappeared quickly from view, although several of its authors achieved periods of international prominence in the early 1970s, chiefly Ivan Illich, Paulo Freire, Paul Goodman, John Holt and Jonathan Kozol; more recently, Sam Bowles and Herbert Gintis.

These dissenters drew their arguments from the socialist and Marxist tradition; they considered alienation a paramount cause of human problems and identified the school as an agency promoting alienation chiefly because it divorces learning from living. They all, therefore, put forward the extreme position that the school in its traditional form must go, and it is this basic premiss that explains the titles of their works: Goodman's *New Reformation*, Holt's *Freedom and Beyond*, Freire's *Pedagogy of the Oppressed*, Kozol's *Death at an Early Age* and, above all, the archetypal title and argument, Illich's *Deschooling Society*. All these polemical works, published in various editions before 1971, were highly emotive arguments against the whole trend of Western development: its materialism, class divisions, extremes of inequality (often based on race, sex and religion) – above all, its dehumanization of the mass of the population. Their arguments, and those of their innumerable followers, generated a strong conviction that the school either had to go or else effect a major transformation, and this had practical consequences in stimulating the foundation of large numbers of 'alternative' schools. Generally, these appeared in the developed democratic countries, often with astonishing variations of approach, seeking to provide what were believed to be substantially better forms of education. It is not possible to categorize such alternative schools and approaches to education under a single label or even under a few; they are so diverse, and frequently so mutually exclusive in their procedures and rationales, that many must be studied as individual experiments whose activities have, perhaps, simply been catalysed by the new literature of dissent. And many, of course, were really only respectable continuations of the progressive schools of the earlier decades of the century.

The deschooling movement

When *Deschooling Society* was published in 1971 it had a profound effect upon Western educational thought, shocking many professional educationists out of their complacency. For Ivan Illich (b. 1926) questioned, in the most dramatic form, the need for the formal institution of the school. The most widespread response to his treatise was outrage, leading to rejection, but, despite this, *Deschooling Society*, more than any other work of the radical rhetoric, was responsible for making educators in the early 1970s look more closely at their arguments for the school and their practices, and to move towards improvement.[27] For this reason, then, Illich's argument for 'deschooling' society deserves to be considered as a significant innovation in Western educational thought, even though we still lack any reasonable historical perspective in which to assess it.

A great deal of Illich's thinking followed a Marxist interpretation of history, and he asserted that the school is so vicious and antihuman an institution that it must immediately – or as soon as practicable – be disestablished, just as the Catholic Church was separated from the state last century in many countries. For Illich 'school' is a generic term, encompassing all institutions from kindergartens through to colleges and universities, public and restricted, and at base all of these form part of a gigantic integrated system that has as its purpose the 'processing' of people for employment in different vocations. In his view, it most emphatically does not prepare individuals for a meaningful life. Moreover, the school, seen in this generic way, has a monopoly through its control of certification. Almost every vocation in modern life requires a certificate, ticket, diploma or degree of some kind before it can be practised, and behind these formal qualifications there is a required course or curriculum (and, although Illich never made this explicit, the Latin etymology of the word 'curriculum' as a 'race', or 'course to be run', helps bring out the idea).

As part of this processing activity, and chiefly because the school serves a market-place economy, knowledge itself, which once was generated in real situations, becomes processed and packaged into what Illich called 'commodities', with the consequence that it becomes remote and eventually meaningless. Illich generally used commercial metaphors, particularly that of the school's holding a 'knowledge stock' from which the curriculum is drawn; he might have added that, just as modern supermarket products are rendered as inert as possible, chiefly through added preservatives, to give a longer 'shelf-life', so too has this happened in the curriculum. Individuals in the advanced technological societies are compelled to take part in this ritual of schooling, and this in itself has created serious pressures. Schools are unbalanced social institutions and hold much in common with penitentiaries, armies, convents and monasteries in that they have large, relatively homogeneous sub-populations held together by rigorous discipline and, if necessary, coercion. So the need for social control is pressing, and, in the case of the school, already maintained at vast expense, additional costs are incurred in financing research devoted to finding ways of improving this control. As a consequence, much effort in educational research – particularly in psychology and sociology – is directed towards sugar-coating the pill of compulsion, towards finding the best possible strategies for ensuring that children keep to the relentless grind of acquiring as big a share of knowledge stock as possible with the least possible distress or complaint. Children, according to Illich, are conditioned to accept these as the right and proper values of education and as the role of its institution, the school, and these pressures to conform make up what he called the 'hidden curriculum'. Even in the advanced societies, however, this is not working, and in the United States particularly schooling is showing signs of considerable distress. When this approach to education is imposed upon developing societies, such as we find in Latin America – as Illich and his mentor Paulo Freire, the exiled Brazilian reformer, insisted – the problems become much more acute.

Mankind, in their view, is in crisis, and the school, with its alienating forms of education, heightens this. Deschooling is the destructive phase: what constructive steps can be taken? Make learning completely informal, Illich argued. Put it in its rightful place as the consequence of people being curious, active, alert and fluid, and engaging in the complementary activities (he did not, like Dewey, call them problems) of individual and social life. In the first instance this involves a radical change in public attitude; society itself must recognize the need for drastic change and act to implement the conviction that access to learning situations must be provided for, and kept open to, every person throughout life. This in turn means acceptance of the fact that people learn 'real' and meaningful knowledge by informal and random means and not via the formalized ritual of schooling.

In Illich's educational theory, education is conceived as a process of engagement in living. There is no room for concepts of superiority among people; there are only differences (although he never specified where these come from). These differences lead us to live our lives in different ways and to seek various forms of fulfilment. All are equally worthy – the jukebox and the chamber group – if they satisfy our need for involvement. Questions of value are relative and personal; we have no right to impose our conceptions on others. The curriculum itself, in the traditional sense, is totally abolished. The content of learning is completely a matter of personal need; it is drawn from life activities themselves, and is gained in the environment of objects, models, peers and elders. Teachers, of course, continue to exist, but their role is completely altered. Illich would call them 'educators' because the idea of a 'teacher' is too authoritarian and subject-centred. But there is serious intent to the change of name: it implies a radical change of function to one of assisting the individual to satisfy his felt learning needs; that is, to one of providing help in the achieving of learning tasks initiated by the learner himself. The state's role is no longer actually to provide education, because there are no schools; however, as an expression of a freely educated population, it will provide a maximum support system. Moral growth, again, remains a totally personal achievement, but Illich was largely silent about this. We are forced to make our own deductions, obliquely, from his work.

Beyond the rhetoric: the problems of modern society

In general terms, there were two types of response to the radical challenge – or three if we include the silent majority that had remained indifferent, pursuing customary procedures secure in its ignorance. Of the two active responses, the more dramatic was a conservative counter-offensive that stressed the enduring values of established practices and led to an equally polarized expression of belief. In the United States the conservatives formed the Council for Basic Education, and throughout the 1970s there was continued criticism of the progressive and radical influences, with allegations that these have led to widespread lowering of standards, indiscipline in the classroom and lack of commitment to abiding intellectual and moral values. In Britain a group of authors published the conservative position in 1969 and 1971 in *The Black Papers on Education*, while in the United States the leading educational conservative, Robert M. Hutchins, argued the same case in his article in *The Center Magazine* for January 1973, 'The Schools Must Stay'. Like the radical rhetoric, the conservative-backlash literature is extensive, wide-ranging, generally polemical, and often equally vacuous in its proposed solutions to a serious problem.

Concurrently a second response to the radical challenge, more responsibly evolutionary than revolutionary, has been attempting to take account of the pressures of the times. This is represented by the efforts of social theorists and sociologists to appreciate the rapidly changing nature of society and propose suitable forms of institutional adaptations. Much of their stress is on understanding the various forces that led to such disturbance in the schools and colleges and among students: the phenomena of urbanization and social change; of educational provisions and social mobility; of class and culture conflict, and its relationship to educational achievement; of roles and interaction patterns in school.[28] In addition, a growing interest in the sociological study of philosophical issues, stimulated by Berger and Luckman's *The Social Construction of Reality* (1966), has led to a considerable interest in the problem of the relativity of knowledge and the socially determined nature of the curriculum. Yet this response, like the conservative backlash, is still not taking sufficient account of the deeper forces of social and cultural change pressing upon the entire process of education. It is, essentially, a cosmetic approach that seeks to make a better accommodation of child and curriculum to society as it exists.

The profound disturbances of the 1960s, leading to the deschooling arguments of the early 1970s, however, were not manufactured by the radicals; both the disturbances and the rhetoric were symptoms of much deeper problems within not only Western society but the entire world order. Clearly, the pattern of the 1960s could not last, as many critics acknowledged, and in late 1973 it ended with the dramatic collapse of the world economy, foreshadowed by mounting energy and environmental crises, and precipitated by the Arab–Israeli conflict in the so-called Yom Kippur War. Throughout the 1970s the world economic order, already questioned as early as 1958 by John K. Galbraith in his best-selling *The Affluent Society*, faced the additional threat of global population explosion, rising discontent in the Third World, increasing illiteracy despite past efforts and mounting unemployment among the affluent, developed nations.

Paradoxically, dissatisfaction with education throughout the decade from the mid-sixties to the mid-seventies occurred, not as a result of neglect or indifference, but, on the contrary, during a period of the greatest deliberate concern with education ever known. Since the Second World

War, governments had poured funds into education on a scale so vast that in Western nations the school, in its various manifestations, had become the greatest single charge on domestic expenditure, while at the same time the preparation of teachers and the scholarly and scientific study of education had burgeoned into some of the largest areas of academic activity. In fact, this very expansion contributed in no small measure to the ferment: ever-increasing expenditure was not accompanied by equal returns, if judged by the economic criteria employed by governments; growing academic investigation of education by a proliferating number of contributing sub-disciplines – philosophy, history, psychology, sociology, measurement, politics and planning, administration, economics – led to theoretical fragmentation, and to debate and dispute rather than agreement and consensus. Moreover, the rapid expansion of universities and colleges in this so-called 'development era' meant that staff, and hence researchers, were recruited from a much wider social spectrum. Traditionally, academic staff had mostly come from the privileged sector, while those who were able to climb the ladder of social mobility were expected to eschew their humble origins and at least take on a privileged coloration; in the sciences this was more easily effected because of the dominance of positivism, which, being 'value-free', meant that academics and researchers regardless of their social origins were constrained not to make critical social comments. Positivism, in effect, as the union-card of the socially mobile, imposed a *de facto* vow of silence. In the era of development and rising expectations, this broke down, and a justifiable pride in unprivileged, or even disadvantaged, origins led to growing divergencies of academic and theoretical positions. After more than three millennia of deliberate educational activity and continuous theorizing, by the mid-1970s we had become more uncertain and divided than ever before in our history.

Much of this new research, moreover, was instrumental in challenging conventional historical explanations of the process of education as the road to opportunity and greater equality. Tawney's *Equality* of 1931 opened the way to a revisionist attitude that was pursued throughout the first post-war decades, influencing researchers in the social sciences as much as those in educational inquiry – in particular, economists, sociologists and political theorists. Collectively, their researches showed the goal of greater opportunity, equality and human welfare based on improvements in education to be illusory. In the United States, President Johnson's commission of inquiry into educational opportunity, chaired by James

Coleman, reported that the power of education to effect change and to distribute life chances more equitably was much less effective than generally believed.[29] This Coleman Report stimulated further educational investigation, and in 1972 a team led by Christopher Jencks launched a full-scale attack on the belief that education, *per se*, has any significant contribution to make towards equality or democracy. In their report, *Inequality*, the conclusions confirmed the earlier work in Britain of Douglas, Ross and Simpson that 'middle-class pupils have retained, almost intact, their historic advantage over the manual working class'.[30] In his highly controversial work Jencks concluded that, if equality is to be sought, then it must be by means outside the educational system, and therefore 'we will have to establish political control over the economic institutions that shape our society'.[31] And in arguing that educational activity must increasingly move into the political arena Jencks expressed a rapidly growing sentiment.[32]

At the same time, many other inquiries were being made into the dynamics of Western society, and it was becoming clearer that two centuries of increasing opportunities for the working classes had in no way diminished the power of the privileged; on the contrary, privilege was as well entrenched as ever, although more carefully concealed than before. Thorstein Veblen's blistering attacks on 'conspicuous consumption' in his *Theory of the Leisure Class* of 1899 simply resulted in a movement towards inconspicuous consumption, which has as its recent development the deliberately concealing techniques of the modern corporation and the transnational conglomerate. A growing body of recent research in politics and economics indicates that the privileged classes, and especially their top-echelon élites, have in fact retained their privileges and power relatively intact; the dominance of British life by those from English 'public schools', examined by Tawney in *Equality* in 1931 and confirmed in his fourth edition of 1952, was corroborated by Guttsman in 1968 in his careful study of *The British Political Elite*.[33] Moreover, the economic advantages of the élites, first attacked in Veblen's *Theory of the Leisure Class* and examined much more systematically in C. Wright Mills's *The Power Elite* of 1956, was confirmed for Britain in 1962 in Richard Titmuss's *Income Distribution and Social Change* and for the United States in the same year in a study by Robert Lampman for the National Bureau of Economic Research entitled *The Share of Top Wealth-Holders in National Wealth 1922–1956*.[34] When the British Association for the Advancement of Science met in conference in 1975, its proceedings reported that the economic advantages of the privileged were now possibly even more secure, owing to the rapid growth of transnational corporational organizations, assisted by international tax havens and the almost instant electronic facilities for the transfer of funds.[35] This also had the frightening implication that national governments were losing the power to control their own economies, thus posing the gravest threats to moderate and social-reforming governments.

Meanwhile the privileged sector had begun to recognize the extent of the threat to its position, and reaction began to increase, stimulated by what were presented as 'crises' of various kinds, but all deliberately manufactured to justify taking the offensive: the 'energy crisis', the 'crisis of law and order', even the 'crisis of democracy'. Taking advantage of the wave of anxiety that swept the world during the economic slump of 1973–4, the huge transnational conglomerates, controlling not only the forces of production but also the communication media, launched an attack upon social welfare and the demands for participatory democracy that had been strengthened in the previous decade. The media were able to play their part by sustaining a mass anxiety, while the banking sector, by restricting credit, was able to heighten that anxiety as workers found their newly achieved affluence suddenly undercut. The reactionary rhetoric of the *Black Papers* and the Council for Basic Education rapidly achieved the status of fact, and, in frightened response, school boards and parents were increasingly influenced by the widespread movement of 'back-to-basics'. The new rhetoric argued that parents could ensure the life chances of their children, and so act responsibly, only if they saw to it that the schools concentrated upon the traditional elements of literacy and numeracy, a systematically organized 'realist' curriculum – now that 'positivism' was eschewed as pejorative – leading on to vocational training in various kinds of technical colleges and institutes.

The move to the extreme Right in national as well as international politics was not completely clandestine; in May 1975 a Rockefeller-funded convention assembled, in Kyoto, leaders of the largest transnational sectors of business and industry from the United States, Europe and Japan, in what became designated as the Trilateral Commission, to consider the crisis posed for privilege and the private business sector due to the upsurge in popular demands for participatory democracy. Clearly recognizing that growing populist feelings, the rising pressure of consumerism, ecological and environmental concerns and demands for more relevant education were presenting the most serious threat ever, the Trilateral

550 A HISTORY OF WESTERN EDUCATION

Commission responded with counter-charges of the 'ungovernability' of societies if democratic processes continued to grow: 'an excess of democracy means a deficit of governability,' the Kyoto meeting observed.[36] Their report was published the same year under the chilling title *The Crisis of Democracy*, and it led Sam Bowles to write a critical commentary entitled with savage irony 'Can the Trilateral Commission Make Democracy Safe for Capitalism?'.[37] One of the major recommendations of the Trilateral Commission was that governments should reverse the expansion of higher education and redesign the curtailed education 'programs so as to be geared to patterns of economic development and future job opportunities' and, in addition, should 'lower job expectations'.[38] Both as a consequence of the considerable influence of this commission – and it was attended by many of the senior members of the subsequent Carter administration in the United States[39] – and as a response to the same international trend that alarmed the privileged sector, educational developments throughout the Western world were arrested and subsequently subjected to negative growth. By 1980 this was a world trend; and it is an important index of political developments – and hence attitudes towards state support of education – that in 1970, at the height of the democratic upsurge, every nation in western Europe except Spain had at least a socialist component in government; in 1975 these began to topple, and in 1980 Norway alone had such a component.

An increasingly authoritarian move to the Right now characterizes all societies, the West as well as the Soviet and Third World blocs, and the future is both highly uncertain as well as menacing: the faltering world economy of 1980 seems to be typified as much by repression as depression. We do not know what lies ahead, but a reassessment of the world order is inevitable. Education will certainly be much more conservatively treated by governments, and no longer will uncritical faith be placed in its alleged efficacy for achieving whatever tasks are entrusted to it. At this point the historical narrative is forced to break off: the future lies within the realm of speculation.

The task ahead: towards a coherent theory of education

Educational issues of the future: equality and responsibility

Such speculation, however, can gain considerable assistance from the historical perspective, where significant trends can be discerned. Clearly, much discontent with education stems from disenchantment with former promises, which arose in part from an excessively romantic doctrine of social progress inherited by the early twentieth century and later, in mid-century, from unrealistic predictions about the capacity of science. Unfortunately these false expectations became the basis of wide aspiration; the world disorders of the early 1970s led to a heightened dissatisfaction with education and to a widespread cynicism concerning its ability, in its traditional form, to cope with problems that seemed to be increasing exponentially. The literature of dissent against privilege, drawn from a long record of class conflict and division and reaching a crescendo in the radical rhetoric of the past two decades or so, simply underlines a growing frustration with inadequate programmes of reform. The developing ethos of this century has issued in demands for popular, participatory demo-cracy, and for greater social equality. Revolution in the active, violent sense is a symptom of impatience with the slow pace of change, often of rage at the politics of reaction. The message is clear: the working classes demand access to the privileges previously reserved to themselves by minority élites. Further, education is clearly believed – despite the argu-ments of Jencks and others – to be a means of providing this access. The whole social-reforming thrust of this century has been towards greater equality, and this has been especially identified as a task for education. If the movement to equality is checked, then the schools, and the process of education identified with the privileged élite, are likely to be interpreted as an obstacle to reform and attacked in overreaction. Put simply, if the privileged system cannot be made accessible to the people, and the con-servative tradition restructured in relevant and responsible form, then the system and its tradition are seen as disposable. The problem of moving towards greater social and educational equality has been a major trend of the post-war decades and will continue to dominate the future. Our problems will be those of determining what Maurice Kogan called the 'hard' or 'soft' options: the 'hard' approach overcompensates the deprived and disadvantaged with lavish provisions for advancement; the 'soft' offers minimum legal access and leaves the individual to strive and succeed by personal effort.[40] Rhetorical rage or revolutionary violence; either way, these in the future will stem from frustrated expectations and will, in the long run, be settled by political, not educational, processes.

At the same time, another major trend in education is a growing movement in all areas of theory away from an enchantment with positivist claims for rationality and objectivity. There has always been an awareness that complete knowledge cannot be attained because of limitations in our measuring instruments, or the difficulty of analysing data fully, with the result that only a hypothetical absolute objectivity has been postulated which the researcher must strive to reach. This, of course, was associated with a dualist theory of mind–matter, or subject–object, exemplified in the correspondence theory of knowledge, and in all educational psychology of the nineteenth century and much of the twentieth. It has chiefly been historians and sociologists who have argued that such an approach is false, that, as James and Dewey wrote at the beginning of the century, mind and matter form a unity, and 'mind' cannot objectively observe the external world of 'matter'. All observation includes the observer as part of that being observed. This is now having a profound influence on modern scientific thinking, which is entering a post-positivist phase,[41] and in educational theory this seems the most promising way of reforming education in the direction of equality, relevance and responsibility.

Of course, educational research and theory, as much as in all other areas of human endeavour, are still constrained to proceed by the methods of empiricism, but it is essential that these be moderated by the recognition that we cannot detach our minds from our collective experience or from the problems in hand. We cannot simply 'search for the facts' and 'let the facts speak for themselves'. That is the way of the objectivist fallacy. In the emergence of all human problems there is always a necessary historical component, and we would be wise to heed the failure of Francis Bacon, in his grand design for 'The Advancement of Learning' of 1605, to sweep away all past theories. Historical experience is part of our present consciousness and contains a necessary moral component. So, in developing educational theory, it will not do to list a series of positivist researches that lack any conscious design and sense of human, social purpose. We must proceed by the method of recognizing the interrelatedness of all phenomena, including mankind. The future, especially in the realm of human conflict, is not as fully determined by education as romantic utopian visions have suggested; clearly one significant achievement of

17 Parisian students marching to the suburb of Billancourt, May 1968, in a declaration of solidarity with the striking Renault workers.

18 Free school in South London, *c.* 1970.

educational theory over the past twenty-five years has been the recognition that education, and the school, are part of a much wider social and political process.

Into the post-positivist era

The history of Western education illustrates the considerable lag that occurs between the development of new ideas and their absorption into practice; this is particularly the case in the modern era, when both thought and practice remain heavily influenced by nineteenth-century positivist approaches. Traditional empirical research has yielded valuable insights and provided a useful data-base for illustrating the mechanics by which activities proceed; at the same time it has fragmented knowledge and led away from a unified view. The accelerating trend since 1950 has been to model educational research and theory on the obsolescent methods of the empirical sciences, in the belief that, because of continuing scientific research, answers to problems will eventually come. Yet the radical ferment of recent decades caught virtually all educational authorities totally unprepared, and it is characteristic of the inadequacy of the positivist approach that it dismisses radical 'disorders' as being of no lasting significance, chiefly through a lack of conceptual ability to understand them. The fact that must be faced is that it is the confused state of contemporary educational thought and practice that must be dismissed, not the radical warnings. The situation as we approach the end of the twentieth century is that we have still not achieved a coherent theory of education.

Fortunately, in the past two decades science has begun to make a significant change of direction, and the leading thinkers have abandoned positivism and the methodology of naïve sensory empiricism. Obviously, increasing environmental crises over recent decades have made us realize how fragile and interdependent the earth is; the publication of *Silent Spring* by Rachel Carson in 1963 led to the first widespread public knowledge of what 'ecocrisis' really means. Clearly, her work was built upon a preceding tradition, but one that had been submerged by the dominance of positivism. Now that we are forced to realize that all future human endeavours are constrained by the delicate balance of the world ecosystem, the positivist analyses have to be replaced. One influential thinker of the late twentieth century, Kenneth Boulding, popularized the phrase 'Spaceship Earth' to heighten our awareness of the total integration and interdependence of all earthly activities. 'Ecology', as a biological term describing the study of relationships of plants and animals to their environment, was devised in the nineteenth century by Ernst Haeckel, and the German term he used, *Ökologie,* is derived from the classical Greek *oikos,* meaning a home or household. Ecology now embraces all of the earth including mankind; nature can no longer be seen as 'out there', available to be exploited. It contains mankind; we are within nature, totally. Positivism taught of a dualism: that man – or at least his mind – is outside nature, existing as a sure instrument to isolate phenomena, analyse, develop techniques of control, and so exploit. Modern eco-conscious science is now moving towards the position of 'social empiricism',[42] which, while accepting that we know through the evidence of our senses, emphasizes the subjectivity of such knowledge – or its 'social construction' – and the position that we can never clear our minds of previous concepts and discover the 'pure facts'. Our minds are in continuous engagement with the totality of the earth's *oikos* and necessarily include our own conceptual history, which is therefore an integral part of our assessment of situations and our decisions to act. Science is already effecting that recognition; industry is reluctant to; educationists, generally, do not yet know that the position exists.

The way ahead: education for the new moral world

In 1970 Alvin Toffler wrote in *Future Shock*: 'what passes for education today, even in our "best" schools and colleges, is a hopeless anachronism ... our schools (despite their rhetoric of preparing for the future) face backwards towards a dying system, rather than forwards to the emerging new society.'[43] His observations are no longer denied; yet, like so many futurologists, he failed to emphasize the conceptual revolution in education that has yet to occur. And so this final section of the volume, and of the trilogy, concludes with an assessment of the basis on which future action must proceed.[44] For it is clear that educational thought and practice must move beyond its present obsolescent positivist phase, catch up with current developments in science, and develop a coherent theory for the future.

Neither the radical nor the conservative positions can have the last word, because neither offers a solution to current problems; rather, their continued existence is a symptom of a deeper disorder within the world and underlying education. It does not seem feasible for us ever to develop a radical alternative to the process of education *per se*; certainly we shall continue to evolve strategies of teaching and learning, especially as electronic developments occur; certainly the curriculum will continue to respond to changes in needs and in knowledge; certainly we shall continue to improve all aspects of administration, student evaluation and support systems. Yet, for all these improvements, the process of education must retain its central purpose since society began, namely the humanizing of each new generation. The term 'humanizing' has been deliberately chosen in preference to 'socializing' because the latter can be interpreted to mean mere social conformity; equally we must avoid narrow concepts such as 'instructing' or 'teaching'. Education retains, as its central purpose, the utopian aspiration of producing genuinely human persons; indeed, the present task, difficult as it may be, is to find a way ahead in education, not in negative 'alternative' versions, but in a single positive conception that draws together the many disparate, worldwide concerns, enthusiasms and actions.

Clearly, the intellectual tradition cannot be discarded; we are constrained by much of its structure, institutions, processes and achievements. In a word, by our history, since history is not merely a record of the past, much less the past itself; history is present consciousness of collective human experience and is therefore as much a part of our world as the objects of perception. The search for genuine improvements in education must lie within the limits of our experience as we bring it to focus upon problems in an emerging world; to do this is scientific in the best sense of the word, since it is experience alone that provides the data of hypothesis formulation. If we accept the premiss that the function of a genuine education is to humanize each person, then we find that the problems we seek to overcome were accelerated in the nineteenth century when the conditions that might have made for a fuller social life for all, in the tradition of Western utopian aspirations, were subverted by the polarization of industrial society into antagonistic classes. Since then, a vast literature has been produced around the seminal Marxist concept of 'alienation'.

Here, then, are the springs of contemporary unrest. Even if some simple dissatisfactions with education may be nothing more than localized irritations, there remains a wider concern with global implications still mostly expressed negatively, to which solutions must be found. While the problem can be described as one of universal alienation, the Marxist explanation must be reassessed. Marx believed that alienation results from the separation of the worker from the products of his labour; many today would agree, and consider that society is better in so far as production is more evenly distributed and distress and poverty alleviated. In the twentieth century, however, we are alienated because the approach of natural holism was subverted, and subsequent social and educational development became dominated by positivism and the exploitative approach. Even in the abundant Western world there is an emptiness of the spirit, which thoughtful persons are sensing and seeking to correct. Our task is to return to that point in our experience when holism was the promising way ahead; having spent a century following positivist-capitalism, imposed by the dominant class which held most wealth and devised the dual school system, we now recognize that it has led us to class warfare, social division, the threat of ecocatastrophe on a global scale. *Naturphilosophie* teaches that we are all co-equal members of the earth with its limited resources and its single, interconnected structure of relationships. Each one of us belongs to the unitary system and we become human in the degree to which we effect that realization and are enabled, by virtue of our experience, to enter creatively and constructively into the interconnected affairs of life. Genuine education must try to realize the holist goal in each person and to eliminate, as much as possible, the sources of alienation. Life must be fostered as continuity with each other and with the environment, and in the realization that the highest good is to seek our own and others' fulfilment, as part of a unified, collective endeavour.

The holist conception, of course, also forces upon us profound moral realizations; the unity of man means the recognition of illiteracy, poverty, distress, underdevelopment and tyranny around the globe, those original founding concerns of UNESCO in 1946. Educational theory, then, as part of the current collective experience available for the solution of future problems, has an important part to play in assessing the development of education this century and attempting to reconcile competing, separate strands into a coherent body of knowledge. Clearly, the task of educational theory is to go beyond the immediate and local to a wider synoptic view of our achievements, and limitations, to the more significant purpose of finding a promising pattern for the future; to effect, as it were, the conceptual revolution, with its change from economic to cultural rationality, that our time is generating.[45]

Increasingly, modern thought is using the concept of the paradigm to describe the conceptual framework within which experience is interpreted as 'reality'. Even though the paradigm becomes an increasingly distorting mirror of experience and common sense as challenges keep altering its various elements, we struggle to see the picture whole and properly proportioned, until the point is reached where the paradigm can no longer contain the disparate elements: suddenly, new elements are incorporated and come together in what we interpret as a new pattern of relationships, that is, in a new paradigm, by a process described by Thomas Kuhn, rather evocatively, as a 'gestalt-switch'.[46] We are, it appears, at such a moment now, and the condition of educational theory and practice over the past twenty-five years or so shows that, indeed, around the world there has been a universal recognition of the need for reconceptualization of education. Once this is appreciated, the tremendous energy expended recently in a search for 'alternatives' in education can be more readily understood. The world quest for alternatives in education appears as evidence of a mass recognition, even if at a still subliminal level, of the imminence of 'gestalt-switch'.

Already educational progressivism this century made a great step forward by recognizing nature within man, and it led to remarkably humane advances in education when it sought to enlist the child's own unfolding nature in the interests of organic fulfilment. It did not, however – and this is where as a doctrine it is still limited – effect the realization that mankind is *within* nature, and that any attempt at separation is artificial and disastrous, both for the environment and mankind. That is why the current versions of European progressivism exemplified in the thought of Montessori and Piaget, and their many applications, remain a limited approach to those seeking the wider humanization of mankind. For a while unitary pragmatism with its doctrines of experience taught by James and Dewey seemed an attractive avenue and led to the tremendous enthusiasm of American progressivism, which, however, had petered out, not just in disillusionment but in conceptual exhaustion, by the early 1950s. The task ahead is to transcend the persisting, destructive doctrines of nineteenth-century industrial capitalism, with its theory of mind over nature, of the external world as the object of man's exploitation. The necessary correlative is that other people also become the objects of exploitation, and that we have seen happen on a global scale. Our deepest concerns, then, must be to eliminate those fateful dualisms of mind–body, mankind–nature, subject–object, which have hindered the fuller development of our cultural tradition, and at the same time to avoid the conceptual shallowness of pragmatic problem-solving activity that does not include all the noetic history of humanity as part of immediate experience. The way ahead is surely to fulfil Robert Owen's vision of the 'new moral world', reconstructed now on the basis of the recognition of the totality of mankind as part of nature, and therefore to develop a new unitary theory of knowledge and morals in the interest of producing a genuinely humane world. This, surely, is the highest purpose we can assign to education.

Notes

Chapter 1

1 For a fuller discussion of Erasmus and sixteenth-century humanist educational theorizing generally, see the preceding volume to this, *A History of Western Education*, Vol. 2: *Civilization of Europe: Sixth to Sixteenth Century* (1975), chapter 11.

2 Regional and city population statistics are in R. R. Palmer, *Atlas of World History* (1962), pp. 193–4, where the demographic sources are also listed.

3 Ibid. p. 194. The twenty cities are London, Bruges, Antwerp, Brussels, Amsterdam, Lisbon, Seville, Barcelona, Madrid, Rome, Naples, Palermo, Milan, Venice, Florence, Cologne, Hamburg, Berlin, Vienna and Prague.

4 The educational arguments of Luther and Melanchthon are set out in Vol. 2 of the present work, chapter 12 *passim*.

5 Friedrich Paulsen, *German Education: Past and Present* (1906), trans. T. Lorenz (1908), p. 32.

6 Ibid.; quoting from F. Eulenberg, *Die Frequenz der deutschen Universitäten von ihrer Gründung bis zur Gegenwart* (Leipzig, 1904).

7 Palmer, op. cit. p. 193.

8 Collected in *Melanchthons Werke*, ed. R. Stupperich, Vol. 1: *Reformatorische Schriften* (Gütersloh: Gerd Mohn, 1961), pp. 215–71. They are also collected in *D. Martin Luthers Werke* (1883), Vol. 26, pp. 195–240.

9 See Paulsen, op. cit. pp. 58 ff.

10 Ibid. p. 65.

11 Paulsen (op. cit.) gives for the north Stettin in Pomerania (1543) and Joachimsthal in Brandenburg (1607); for the south Württemburg (1559), Ansbach (1582) and Coburg (1605).

12 Translated, with an introduction, by Paul Monroe, *Thomas Platter and the Educational Renaissance of the Sixteenth Century* (1904).

13 See Vol. 2 of the present work.

14 Monroe, op. cit. p. 117.

15 Ibid. p. 122.

16 Ibid.

17 Ibid.

18 Ibid. p. 158.

19 See the present work, Vol. 2, chapter 10.

20 A. M. Stowe, *English Grammar Schools in the Reign of Queen Elizabeth* (1908), p. 9.

21 See A. C. F. Beales, *Education Under Penalty* (1963), pp. 26 ff. and *passim*.

22 The account is given fully in ibid.

23 Ibid. appendix 4, pp. 273–4.

24 Ibid.

25 Proclamation, 18 October 1591; cited in P. McGrath, *Papists and Puritans* (1967), pp. 146–8.

26 Ibid. pp. 255–6.

27 See Stowe, op. cit. pp. 10–11. Stowe's numerous and lengthy appendixes contain a considerable amount of information. Appendix A lists the schools known in the period, with the necessary supporting information.

28 Ibid. p. 125.

29 These terms are discussed in Carlo Cipolla, *Literacy and Development in the West* (1969), chapter 1 *passim*.

30 *The Workes of Sir Thomas More* (London, 1557), p. 850.

31 Quoted in Stowe, op. cit. p. 154.

32 Consilium Tridentinum, Session IV, 8 April 1546. Collected in H. Bettenson, *Documents of the Christian Church*, 2nd ed. (1963), p. 368.

33 *Injunctum nobis*, November 1564; Bettenson, op. cit. p. 375.

34 A fuller examination of Jesuit educational theory and practice is set out in the present work, Vol. 2, pp. 425–31.

35 See W. H. E. Johnson, *Russia's Educational Heritage* (1950), p. 21.

36 A detailed study of the Jesuit college will be found in A. P. Farrell, *The Jesuit Code of Liberal Education: Development and Scope of the Ratio Studiorum* (1938).

37 See generally H. C. Barnard, *The French Tradition in Education: Ramus to Mme Necker de Saussure* (1922). This quotation, p. 2.

38 The publishing history of *Gargantua and Pantagruel* was as follows: 1532,

Book II (*Pantagruel*); 1534, Book I (*Gargantua*); 1546, Book III (*Le Tiers Livre*); 1548, Book IV (*Le Quart Livre*), chapters 1–11; 1552, Book IV, complete; 1562, Book V (*Le Cinquième Livre*); 1567, Books I–V, *opera omnia*.

39 From the translation by Jacques Le Clerq, *The Five Books of Gargantua and Pantagruel* (1936; repr. 1944), II. 8, pp. 190–4 *passim*.

40 Quoted in Barnard, op. cit. p. 18.

41 Set out fully in ibid. pp. 19 ff.

42 The text is in the *Index*, ed. Bréchillet-Jourdain, MDCCLXXII, 354; quoted in Barnard, op. cit. p. 20, n. 1.

43 Quoted with source in ibid. p. 23, n. 1.

44 Ibid. p. 28.

45 Ibid. pp. 80 ff.

46 Quoted in ibid. p. 88.

47 Quoted in ibid.

48 Bettenson, op. cit. p. 303.

Chapter 2

1 There are many monographs on this topic. A compact introduction is Patrick Moore, *Watchers of the Stars: The Scientific Revolution* (1973).

2 Ibid. p. 149.

3 Galileo, *Dialogue Concerning the Two Chief World Systems: Ptolemaic and Copernican* (Florence, 1632), trans. W. Drake (1953), pp. 55–6.

4 R. W. Gibson (ed.), *Francis Bacon: A Bibliography of His Works and of Baconiana to the Year 1750* (1950).

5 The variant endings are determined by the fact that *organon* is the transliteration of the Greek word which ends in -*on* in the nominative singular; *organum* is the Latin equivalent which ends in -*um* in the same case.

6 Bacon, *Novum Organum* (1620), Book I, aphorisms 11–18; trans. R. J. Ellis and J. Spedding (*c.* 1858), pp. 62–3.

7 Bacon, *The Great Instauration*, Proemium (first published 1620, with *Novum Organum*); trans. in Bacon, *Selections*, ed. M. T. McClure (1928), pp. 20–2.

8 Bacon, *The Advancement of Learning*, ed. G. W. Kitchin (1915), p. 28.

9 Bacon, *The Great Instauration*, p. 32.

10 Ibid. p. 24.

11 Bacon, *New Atlantis*, ed. A. B. Gough (1924), Preface.

12 Ibid. p. 35.

13 Ibid. p. 44.

14 Ibid. p. 37.

15 Ibid. p. 44.

16 Ibid. p. 39.

17 *Novum Organum*, I. 97, p. 122.

18 Ibid. My italics.

19 A fuller account of the Italian academy movement is given in the present work, Vol. 2, pp. 234–41.

20 On this, see Frances Yates, *The French Academies of the Sixteenth Century* (1947), p. 3.

21 Ibid. for a footnote reference to the Accademia dei Filleleni, p. 6, n. 3; A. F. Didot, *Alde Manuce et l'hellénisme à Venise* (Paris, 1875).

22 For a fuller discussion, see Yates, op. cit. chapter 1 *passim*.

23 Following the comprehensive treatment given by J. H. Randall, *The School of Padua and the Emergence of Modern Science* (1961), p. 46.

24 Ibid. pp. 31, 55.

25 Ibid. p. 56, n. 32, referring to evidence in Galileo Galilei, *Opere*, ed. Nazionale, IV. 520.

26 Quoted in Martha Ornstein, *The Role of Scientific Societies in the Seventeenth Century* (1938; repr. 1963), p. 75.

27 Quoted in ibid. p. 75, from *Lynceographia* (1612).

28 Giovanni Tozzetti, *Notizie degli aggrandimenti delle scienze fisiche accaduti in Toscana nel corso di anni LX del secolo XVII*, 4 vols (Florence: Bouchard, 1780); quoted in Giorgio Abetti, 'L'Accademia del Cimento', in *Celebrazione della Accademia del Cimento nel Tricentenario della Fondazione* (Presso la Domus Galilaeana, 1957), pp. 8–9.

29 Ornstein, op. cit. p. 88.

30 *Celebrazione*, p. 9.

31 Ornstein, op. cit. p. 78, n. 34.

32 Following Frances Yates, op. cit. chapter 2, pp. 14 ff.

33 French text, pp. 319–20 in appendix I to Yates, op. cit.

34 Ornstein, op. cit. p. 225.

35 On this see Yates, op. cit. pp. 292–7.

36 Harcourt Brown, *Scientific Organizations in Seventeenth Century France* (1934), pp. 17 ff.

37 Ibid. p. 30.

38 Pierre Pellisson and Pierre-Joseph d'Olivet, *Histoire de l'Académie Française*, ed. C. Livet (Paris, 1858), I. 256; quoted in Yates, op. cit. p. 292, nn. 2 and 4.

39 Ibid. p. 292.

40 The historical movement towards the formal foundation of the Académie des Sciences can be traced through Harcourt Brown, op. cit.

41 Ibid. p. 8.

42 Ibid. p. 14.

43 Because their first Rule was based on that of St Francis of Assisi and on the notion that they were founded by St Francis of Paola (1416–1507), the *Ordo Fratrum Minimorum* is often mistakenly considered Franciscan and so

Mersenne has frequently been erroneously described as a Franciscan or a Minorite.

44 Quoted in Brown, op. cit. p. 37.

45 Boulliau, *Fonds Dupuy*, 18. f. 21; quoted in Brown, op. cit. pp. 64–5.

46 Descartes, *Discourse on the Method of Rightly Conducting the Reason and Seeking for Truth in the Sciences*, Part I.

47 Ibid.

48 Ibid.

49 The dream is in Baillet, *Vie de Descartes* (1691); trans. in N. K. Smith, *New Studies in the Philosophy of Descartes* (1952), pp. 33–9.

50 Descartes, *Philosophical Letters*, trans. A. Kenny (1970), pp. 26–7.

51 Descartes, *Philosophical Letters*, p. 28.

52 Descartes, *Discourse on Method*, Part II, in *Philosophical Works* (1967), p. 92.

53 Ibid. Part III, p. 101.

54 Descartes, *Principles of Philosophy*, Part I, principle VIII, *Philosophical Works*, p. 221.

55 Descartes, *Principles of Philosophy*, Part I, principle XXX, *Philosophical Works*, p. 231. This argument was presented earlier in the *Meditations on the First Philosophy* (1641), p. 191.

56 Descartes, *Principles of Philosophy*, Part I, principles IX, XXXIX–XLI, *Philosophical Works*, pp. 222–35.

57 Descartes, *Letter to Mersenne*, April 1630, p. 11. Stated again in *Principles of Philosophy*, Part I, principle X, *Philosophical Works*, p. 222.

58 Brown, op. cit. p. 67.

59 Quoted from Desmolets, *Continuation des mémoires de littérature et d'histoire*, II. 2 (Paris, 1776), p. 323; in Brown, op. cit. p. 67.

60 Quoted from *Fonds français*, 13027, f. 119, 5 February 1658, by Brown, op. cit. pp. 78–9.

61 6 December 1658, Huygens, *Œuvres complètes*, II. 287; Brown, op. cit. p. 87.

62 Thévenot, *Autobiography* (1662); quoted in Brown, op. cit. p. 136.

63 Ibid. p. 145.

64 Articles in Ornstein, op. cit. pp. 160–1.

65 Discussed in detail in ibid. pp. 198 ff.

66 See particularly W. K. Jordan, *Philanthropy in England 1480–1660* (1959), pp. 279 ff.

67 G. H. Turnbull, *Hartlib, Dury and Comenius: Gleanings from Hartlib's Papers* (1947), p. 59, n. 1.

68 Robert Boyle, *The Works*, ed. Thomas Birch; facsimile reprint of the 1772 London edition edited by Douglas McKie (1965), pp. xxxiv, xl.

69 The controversy surrounding the real nature of the invisible college is reported in Boyle, op. cit. p. vii, n. 7. See also M. Purver, *The Royal Society* (1967), pp. 193–205.

70 Sprat's *History* is available in a facsimile reprint edited by J. I. Cope and H. W. Hones (1959).

71 For the question of the accuracy of Sprat's *History*, and the general debate, see Purver, op. cit. chapter 1, pp. 9 ff.

72 Sprat, *History*, p. 18.

73 Ibid. XVI, p. 35.

74 *Novum Organum*, aphorism XCIX: quoted and discussed in Purver, op. cit. p. 49.

75 Purver, op. cit. p. 96.

Chapter 3

1 Rabelais, *Gargantua and Pantagruel* (1944), Book II, chapter 8, pp. 190–4 *passim*.

2 A fuller account will be found in Armand L. Gaetano, 'G. B. Gelli and the Rebellion against Latin', *Studies in the Renaissance* (1966), Vol. XIII, pp. 131–158.

3 Quoted in ibid. p. 142; Savonarola had written: 'In questa nostra lingua le più atte e più difficil cose di filosofia, non manco facilmente e perfettamente che qual si voglia scrittore latino.'

4 Ibid. p. 144.

5 On this topic, see Paul Grendler, *Critics of the Italian World 1530–1560* (1969), chapter 5, pp. 136–61; this particular point, p. 155.

6 Paul Grendler, 'The Rejection of Learning in Mid-Cinquecento Italy', *Studies in the Renaissance* (1966), XIII, pp. 230–49, 236.

7 Grendler, *Critics of the Italian World*, p. 240.

8 Ibid. pp. 245–6.

9 Ibid.

10 Michel de Montaigne, *Œuvres complètes*, ed. Albert Thibault and Maurice Rat (1962), p. 172; '. . . et le surnom de magister n'avoir guire plus honorable signification parmy nous'.

11 Ibid.

12 Ibid. p. 165.

13 Ibid. 'De l'expérience', p. 1041: 'Quand la raison nous faut, nous y employons l'expérience.'

14 Ibid. 'De l'institution des enfants', p. 172.

15 Andreae, *Christianopolis*, ed. Held (1914), 173, cap. xxvi; quoted in J. W. Montgomery, *Cross and Crucible: Johann Valentin Andreae (1586–1654)*, *Phoenix of the Theologians*, Vol. 1 (1973), p. 63, n. 170.

16 Ibid. p. 146.

17 Ibid. p. 152. See also the modern parallel described by Paul Tillich of 'ultimate concern', ibid. p. 133.

18 Campanella, *City of the Sun*, coll. in F. R. White (ed.), *Famous Utopias of the Renaissance* (1946; repr. 1955), p. 162.

19 Ibid. p. 171.

20 Ibid. p. 204.

21 Comenius, *Labyrint světa a ráj srdce*, ed. and trans. Count Lützow (1901); also trans. Matthew Spinka (Chicago: National Union of Czechoslovav Protestants in America, 1942).

22 Spinka (trans.), op. cit. pp. 218–19.

23 Quoted in Montgomery, op. cit. p. 151.

24 Ibid.

25 An exhaustive bibliography of Comenius' writings is given in Matthew Spinka, *John Amos Comenius: That Incomparable Moravian* (1943).

26 A facsimile reprint to celebrate the tercentenary of the publication was issued in 1957, *Opera didactica omnia*. All references are to that edition, cited hereafter as *ODO*.

27 The influence of the Jesuit edition was acknowledged by Comenius, *ODO*, Vol. 1, p. 253.

28 A recent translation is E. M. Eller, *The School of Infancy* (1956).

29 'Homini utpote μικροκόσμῳ omnia inesse': *Didactica magna*, XIX. v. 41; *ODO*, Vol. 1, p. 109.

30 Ibid. XXII. vi. 14; *ODO*, Vol. 1, p. 129.

31 Ibid. XXVII. 2; *ODO*, Vol. 1, p. 165.

32 The most relevant of Comenius' writings on the subject have been collected by R. F. Young, *Comenius in England* (1932).

33 The standard English translation is E. T. Campagnac, *The Way of Light* (1938).

34 Quoted in Charles Webster (ed.), *Samuel Hartlib and the Advancement of Learning* (1970), p. 2.

35 'To the Kings most Excellent Majesty, the Humble Petition of Samuel Hartlib Senior', *Hartlib Papers*, VII. 19 (c. 1660); cited in Webster, op. cit. pp. 5–6.

36 The record is a Hartlib retrospective, contained in the same petition above, ibid.

37 The term is applied by Webster in his valuable essay introducing the collection of readings, ibid.

38 Samuel Hartlib, *A Description of the Famous Kingdom of Macaria, Showing its Excellent Government* (1641), coll. in Webster, op. cit. p. 81.

39 Quoted in ibid. p. 35.

40 John Milton, *Tractate of Education*, para. 4.

41 Ibid.

42 Ibid. para. 5.

43 See Webster, op. cit. pp. 50–2.

44 William Petty, *The Advice of W. P. to Mr Samuel Hartlib, for the Advancement of Some Particular Parts of Learning* (1648), p. 4.
45 Ibid.
46 *Didactica magna*, XVIII. 35.
47 John Dury, *The Reformed School* (1650), ed. H. M. Knox (1958), p. 38.
48 Ibid.
49 Ibid. p. 40.
50 Ibid.
51 Ibid. p. 48.
52 Ibid. p. 28.
53 Ibid. p. 55.
54 Ibid. p. 57.
55 Comenius, *Analytical Didactic*, ed. V. Jelinek (1953), pp. 3 ff.
56 For these recovered books and English translations, see *John Amos Comenius on Education*, ed. Jean Piaget (1957), pp. 115 ff.
57 This edition is now extremely rare. The copy consulted is in the Bibliothèque Nationale, Paris.
58 *ODO*, Vol. 1, p. 455: 'Fervet jam per omnes Europae angulos Pansophicum et melioris Didacticae, studium. Quod si nihil etiam plus praestiterit Comenius, quàm quòd tantum stimulorum segetum in omnium sparsit animos, satis fecisse putandus est.' The English translation is in J. W. Adamson, *Pioneers of Modern Education in the Seventeenth Century* (1905; repr. 1971), p. 85.

Chapter 4

1 See H. C. Barnard, *The French Tradition in Education* (1922), pp. 44–5.
2 This account follows ibid. pp. 52 ff.
3 H. C. Barnard, *The Port-Royalists on Education* (1918), pp. 27 ff.
4 Following ibid. pp. 19 ff.
5 Saint-Cyran, *Lettres chrétiennes et spirituelles* (1645), Vol. 2, pp. 228 ff. This document, and a collection of Port-Royal primary sources in English translation, is collected in Barnard, *The Port-Royalists*. This quotation, pp. 57, 59.
6 Pierre Coustel, *Les Règles de l'éducation des enfants* (1687); Barnard, *The Port-Royalists*, p. 69.
7 Coustel, *Règles*; Barnard, *The Port-Royalists*, p. 150.
8 Pierre Nicole, *Essais de morale*; Barnard, *The Port-Royalists*, p. 159.
9 See R. N. Coe, 'The Idea of "Natural Order" in French Education', *British Journal of Educational Studies*, II, 2 (May 1957), p. 145.
10 Jacqueline Pascal, *Règlement pour les enfants: Constitutions du Monastère du Saint Sacrement*; Barnard, *The Port-Royalists*, p. 226.
11 Barnard, *The French Tradition in Education*, pp. 100–2.

12 Ibid. p. 106.
13 *Edict of Fontainebleau*, October 1685 ('Revocation of the Edict of Nantes'); coll. and trans. in S. Z. Ehler and J. B. Morrall, *Church and State through the Centuries: Historic Documents with Commentaries* (1954), pp. 208–13.
14 Maurice Ashley, *A History of Europe 1648–1815* (1973), p. 74.
15 The history is in W. J. Battersby, *St John Baptist de la Salle* (1957).
16 Quoted in H. C. Barnard, *Education and the French Revolution* (1969), p. 4.
17 Battersby, op. cit. p. 306.
18 M. Fleury and P. Valmary, 'Les Progrès de l'institution de l'instruction élémentaire de Louis XIV à Napoleon III', *Population*, XII (1957), pp. 80 ff.
19 C. Cipolla, *Literacy and Development in the West* (1969), p. 61.
20 Ibid., discussing late sixteenth-century figures for the Narbonne area which would be similar to those for late seventeenth-century France, given that the intervening century was one of economic stagnation.
21 J. W. Adamson, *Pioneers of Modern Education in the Seventeenth Century* (1905; repr. 1971), p. 215.
22 H. C. Barnard, *Madame de Maintenon and St Cyr* (1934), p. 40.
23 Molière, *Les Femmes savantes* (1672).
24 Fénelon, *Traité de l'éducation des filles* (1687); coll. and trans. in *Fénelon on Education*, ed. H. C. Barnard (1966), p. 1.
25 Ibid. p. 23.
26 The standard account is H. C. Barnard, *Madame de Maintenon and St Cyr*.
27 Ibid. *passim*; also, H. C. Barnard, *The Port-Royalists*, p. 35, which is followed here.
28 A detailed account of this appears in C. H. Haring, *The Spanish Empire in America* (1947), chapter 11.
29 See A. H. de Oliviera Marques, *History of Portugal*, 2nd ed. (1976), Vol. 1.
30 Friedrich Paulsen, *German Education: Past and Present* (1908), p. 82.

Chapter 5

1 The figure of 281 is given in A. M. Stowe's detailed investigations reported in the appendix tables in his *English Grammar Schools in the Reign of Queen Elizabeth* (1908). See also Notes, p. 560, Chapter 1, n. 27, above. Since then, A. L. Rowse, *The England of Elizabeth: The Structure of Society* (1950), p. 503, gives the number of endowed schools as 360. See also D. Cressy, *Education in Tudor and Stuart England* (1976).
2 From the researches of Lawrence Stone, *The Crisis of the Aristocracy 1558–1641* (1965), p. 684.
3 Taken from the investigations of Nicholas Hans, *New Trends in Education in the Eighteenth Century* (1951), p. 20 and *passim*.
4 Archdeacon Kennett, 'The Charity Schools for Poor Children Recommended

in a Sermon', May 1706; quoted in M. G. Jones, *The Charity School Movement: A Study of Eighteenth-Century Puritanism in Action* (1964), p. 14, n. 1.

5 See W. K. Jordan, *Philanthropy in England 1480–1660: A Study of the Changing Pattern of English Social Aspirations* (1959); these statistics, p. 283.

6 Ibid. p. 294.

7 Ibid. pp. 279–91. See also Lawrence Stone, op. cit. p. 684, for comments; also, Lawrence Stone, 'The Educational Revolution in England 1560–1640', *Past and Present*, XXVIII (1964), p. 44.

8 Stone, *Crisis*, p. 687.

9 Ibid. pp. 687 ff.

10 Stone, 'Educational Revolution', p. 66, table X: 'Admissions to St John's and Caius College, Cambridge, 1630–39 and 1690–99'.

11 Five Mile Act, 17 Charles II, cap. 2; in H. Bettenson, *Documents of the Christian Church*, 2nd ed. (1963), pp. 416–18.

12 Recorded and discussed in H. McLachlan, *English Education under the Test Acts: Being the History of the Non-Conformist Academies 1662–1820* (1931). See also Irene Parker, *The Dissenting Academies* (1914).

13 McLachlan, op. cit. appendix.

14 Quoted by V. H. H. Green, *British Institutions: The Universities* (1969), p. 45.

15 Ibid.

16 Ibid. p. 47.

17 John Wesley, 'Scriptural Christianity', Sermon 4, preached at Oxford, 24 August 1744; in *The Works of John Wesley* (1872), Vol. 5, p. 47. The Journal entry is ibid. Vol. 2, p. 48.

18 Hans, op. cit. p. 54. See also pp. 54–62 *passim*.

19 A wide-ranging descriptive catalogue of dissenting-academy manuscripts and printed texts is given in McLachlan, op. cit. appendix I, pp. 275–311.

20 Ibid. pp. 295–6.

21 Ibid. pp. 288–9.

22 Hans, op. cit. p. 118.

23 Ibid. p. 69.

24 Ibid. p. 65.

25 Set out in detail in ibid. pp. 63–116.

26 Richard Altick, *The English Common Reader* (1957), p. 19.

27 Ibid. p. 26.

28 Ibid. p. 30. Altick's figures are in agreement with the major statistical population figures including Roger Mols, *Introduction à la démographie historique des villes d'Europe du 14e au 18e siècle*, 3 vols (1954–6).

29 W. L. Sargent, 'On the Progress of Elementary Education', *Journal of the Royal Statistical Society*, XXX (1867), pp. 127–8.

30 King's tables are reproduced in many places; they can be found conveniently in Phyllis Deane, *The First Industrial Revolution* (1969), pp. 8–9.

31 Cited in Christopher Hill, *Reformation to Industrial Revolution* (1967), p. 46.
32 Ibid. p. 256.
33 See Jones, op. cit.
34 Jenyns, *Free Inquiry into the Nature and Origin of Evil* (1757), quoted in Samuel Johnson, *Works*, XIII, p. 226; quoted here by Altick, op. cit. pp. 31–2.
35 Ibid.
36 Jones, op. cit. pp. 153 ff.
37 Ibid. p. 98.
38 Ibid. pp. 79–80.
39 Ibid. pp. 97–8.
40 Victor Neuberg, *Popular Education in Eighteenth-Century England* (1971), pp. 36–7.
41 John Durkan, 'Education in the Century of the Reformation', in D. McRoberts (ed.), *Essays on the Scottish Reformation 1513–1625* (1962), p. 149.
42 S. J. Curtis, *History of Education in Great Britain* (1963), p. 578.
43 *First Book of Discipline*, Part 5, in *John Knox's History of the Reformation in Scotland*, ed. W. C. Dickinson (1949), Vol. 2, appendix VIII, pp. 295–6.
44 Ibid.
45 Ibid. pp. 301 ff.
46 Curtis, op. cit. p. 528.
47 Jones, op. cit. p. 179.
48 For this, see H. Trevor-Roper, 'The Scottish Enlightenment', *Studies on Voltaire and the Eighteenth Century*, LVIII (1967), pp. 1953–66, on which this section depends.
49 Ibid. p. 1640.
50 Following ibid. pp. 1639 ff.
51 This section depends upon A. J. Roderick (ed.), *Wales Through the Ages*, 2 vols (1959–60). For popular Welsh education, see chapter 11, Mary Clement, 'The Campaign against Illiteracy', pp. 78–85.
52 J. Gwynn Williams, 'Wales and the Commonwealth', in Roderick, op. cit. p. 72.
53 Jones, op. cit. p. 293.
54 Ibid. p. 296.
55 Ibid. p. 310.
56 Clement, in Roderick, op. cit. p. 93.
57 Jones, op. cit. p. 222.
58 Quoted in Green, op. cit. p. 32.
59 See Jones, op. cit. pp. 219 ff.
60 See the map showing the distribution and commentary in R. D. Edwards, *An Atlas of Irish History* (1973), p. 137 and pp. 137–9 *passim*.
61 Jones, op. cit. p. 232.
62 Ibid. pp. 233 ff.
63 For this topic, see D. P. Dowling, *The Hedge Schools of Ireland* (1935), and

D. H. Akenson, *The Irish Education Experiment: The National System of Education in the Nineteenth Century* (1970), chapter 2.

64 Jones, op. cit. p. 235.

65 *Petition, A Humble Proposal for Obtaining His Majesty's Royal Charter to Incorporate a Society for Promoting Christian Knowledge among the Natives of the Kingdom of Ireland* (1730); text reproduced in and quoted from Jones, op. cit. pp. 233–5.

66 Ibid. p. 238.

67 G. A. Cranfield, *The Development of the Provincial Newspaper 1700–1760* (1962), p. 53.

68 John Wesley, *Works* (1872), Vol. 4, pp. 307–8; quoted in Jones, op. cit., on whom the foregoing account is based.

69 Jones, op. cit. p. 253.

70 Ibid.

71 Friedrich Paulsen, *German Education: Past and Present* (1908), p. 136.

72 Ibid.

73 Ibid. p. 27.

74 A. W. Ward, *Collected Papers*, Vol. 1 (Historical, i) (1921), pp. 195–207 *passim*.

75 Paulsen, op. cit. p. 122.

76 Ibid.

77 The account of Francke follows Paulsen, op. cit. pp. 127 ff., and J. W. Adamson, *Pioneers of Modern Education in the Seventeenth Century* (1905; repr. 1971), pp. 237–57.

78 Adamson, op. cit. p. 241.

79 Ibid. p. 247.

80 *Nützliche Vorschläge von Aufrichtung einer mathematischen Handwerker Schule bei der Stadt Halle*; see Hans, op. cit. p. 216.

81 Paulsen, op. cit. p. 128.

Chapter 6

1 Cited in Henri Brunschwig, *Enlightenment and Romanticism in Eighteenth-Century Prussia* (1949), p. 7.

2 Hobbes, *Leviathan* (1651; 1955), p. 82. In illustration, Hobbes added, 'the savage people in many places of America . . . live this day in that brutish manner' (p. 83).

3 Locke, *Essays on the Law of Nature*, trans. W. von Leyden (1954), pp. 123–8, 133. These essays were written in Latin in 1664 and, although not published in Locke's lifetime, their ideas were the basis of the two *Treatises*.

4 Locke, *Of Human Understanding*, Book I, chapter 1, section 2, in *The Works* (1823), I. 2. 1.

5 Ibid. II. 1. 1–4.

6 Ibid. II. 22. 1–3.

7 As Bronowski and Mazlish point out, 'This view remained an outstanding doctrine of science from the time Locke wrote, in 1690, for well over two hundred years. It lasted, although attacked by Kant and Hegel on philosophical grounds, until the emergence of Heisenberg's uncertainty principle and Einstein's relativity physics led to a new scientific view: the view that the observer plays an essential part on the discovery of nature'. J. Bronowski and B. Mazlish, *The Western Intellectual Tradition* (1963), p. 235.

8 Locke, *Of Human Understanding*, II. 37. 24–5.

9 Aristotle, *Posterior Analytics*, II. xix. 99b; *De anima*, III. iv. 429b.

10 Aristotle, *De anima*, III. 433b; II. 415a.

11 Locke, *Of Human Understanding*, IV. 14 *passim*.

12 Ibid. IV. 17 *passim*.

13 See John Passmore, *The Perfectibility of Man* (1970), p. 159 and chapter 8, pp. 149–70 *passim*.

14 Locke, *Some Thoughts Concerning Education*, cap. 216.

15 Ibid. 32.

16 Ibid. 1.

17 Ibid. 134.

18 Ibid. 135.

19 Ibid. 147.

20 Ibid. 101–2.

21 Ibid. 66.

22 Ibid. 81.

23 Ibid. 33.

24 Ibid. p. 66.

25 Locke, *Some Thoughts Concerning Education*, cap. 201.

26 Ibid. 70.

27 This view is also proposed by Passmore, op. cit. pp. 161–2.

28 See Hugh Trevor-Roper, 'The Scottish Enlightenment', in *Studies on Voltaire and the Eighteenth Century*, LVIII (1967), p. 1639 and *passim*.

29 See A. J. P. Taylor, *The Course of German History* (1945; repr. 1961), p. 18.

30 This series of quotations all from La Mettrie, *L'Homme machine* (1747); coll. and trans. in I. Berlin, *The Age of Enlightenment* (1956), pp. 269–70.

31 D'Alembert, *Preliminary Discourse to the Encyclopedia of Diderot*; in Diderot, d'Alembert *et al.*, *Encyclopedia*, trans. and ed. N. S. Hoyt and T. Cassirer (1965), Introduction, p. xxiv.

32 Ibid. pp. xxiv–xxv.

33 *Encyclopedia*, s.v. 'College'; Hoyt and Cassirer, op. cit. p. 36.

34 Ibid. p. 40.

35 Ibid.

36 See E. W. Marvick, Chapter 6, 'Nature versus Nurture: Patterns and Trends

in Seventeenth-Century French Child-Rearing', in Lloyd de Mause (ed.), *The History of Childhood* (1974), pp. 259–301 *passim*.

37 Montaigne, 'De l'institution des enfants', *Œuvres complètes*(1962), p. 172; also, Fénelon, *Traité de l'éducation des filles*, trans. Barnard (1966), p. 23.

38 Comenius, *Orbis sensualium pictus* (1672), plate CXX and pp. 244–5.

39 Marvick, op. cit. pp. 269–71.

40 Rousseau, *Émile, ou De l'éducation* (1964), II. 76. Throughout, Rousseau will be quoted from the Garnier text (translations by the present author), with book and page numbers provided. Other translations will be separately acknowledged.

41 Ibid. I. 10.

42 *Discours* (Amsterdam, 1755), p. 111; quoted in Franco Venturi, *Utopia and Reform in the Enlightenment* (1971), p. 76.

43 In Rousseau, *Œuvres complètes*, ed. B. Gagnebin and M. Raymond (1959–64); both quotations in Venturi, op. cit. pp. 77, 85. The quotation on p. 85 reads: Rousseau took 'Genève pour modèle des institutions politiques à fin de la proposer en exemple à l'Europe'.

44 Rousseau, *Émile*, I. 7.

45 Ibid. I. 10–11.

46 Ibid.

47 Ibid. I. 12.

48 Ibid. I. 44.

49 Ibid. II. 63.

50 Ibid.; a similar phrase occurs in *Considérations sur le gouvernement de Pologne* (1962), chapter 4, p. 353, 'la bonne éducation doit être négative'.

51 Rousseau, *Émile*, II. 81: 'Ne donnez à votre élève aucune espèce de leçon verbale; il n'en doit recevoir que l'expérience.'

52 Ibid. II. 103.

53 Ibid. II. 105–10.

54 Ibid. III. 86: 'qu'il n'apprenne pas la science, qu'il l'invente'.

55 Ibid. III. 191.

56 Ibid. III. 210: 'Je hais les livres; ils n'apprennent qu'à parler de ce qu'on ne sait pas.'

57 Ibid. IV. 245.

58 Ibid. III. 224.

59 Ibid. IV. 278.

60 Ibid.

61 A concept developed by Fernand van Steenbergen, *The Philosophical Movement of the Thirteenth Century* (Edinburgh and London: Nelson, 1955), chapter 4; see Vol. 2 of the present work, p. 148.

62 *Du contrat social* (1962), I. 1. 236.

63 Ibid. II. 6. 258: 'Sans doute il est une justice universelle émanée de la raison

seule, mais cette justice, pour être admise entre nous, doit être réciproque.'
See also J. B. Noone, 'Rousseau's Theory of Natural Law as Conditional',
Journal of the History of Ideas, XXXIII, 1 (January–March 1972), pp. 23–42.

64 *Du contrat social*, II. 6. 258.

65 Noone, op. cit. p. 27, refers to 'innate feelings' which suggests the same idea.

66 Rousseau, *Émile*, IV. 335.

67 See also Noone, op. cit. p. 27.

68 Ibid. pp. 27 ff.

69 Rousseau, *Considérations sur le gouvernement de Pologne*, IV. 353.

70 Ibid.

71 *Considerations on the Government of Poland*, in *The Minor Educational Writings of Jean-Jacques Rousseau*, ed. and trans. W. Boyd (1910; repr. 1962), IV. 354; pp. 97–9.

72 Discussed at greater length in C. E. Elwell, *The Influence of the Enlightenment on the Catholic Theory of Religious Education in France 1750–1850* (1944), pp. 32 ff.

73 Ibid. p. 149.

74 Brunschwig, op. cit. p. 26.

75 Issued in facsimile (1972) from the edition of Theodor Fritzsch as *J. B. Basedows Elementarwerk*, 2 vols.

76 Basedow, *Ausgewählte Schriften* (Leipzig: H. Beyer, 1880), p. 119.

77 D. Treadgold, *The West in Russia and China: Religious and Secular Thought in Modern Times*, Vol. 1: *Russia 1472–1917* (1973), p. 119.

78 R. Herr, *The Eighteenth-Century Revolution in Spain* (1958; repr. 1969), p. 63.

79 J. R. Spell, *Rousseau in the Spanish World before 1833* (1938; repr. 1969), p. 55.

80 Ibid. pp. 72 ff.

81 Ibid. pp. 72–6.

Chapter 7

1 See George Rudé, *Paris and London in the Eighteenth Century: Studies in Popular Protest* (1952).

2 Text cited here is from H. S. Commager (ed.), *Documents of American History* (1963), coll. in Williams (ed.), *Revolutions 1775–1830* (1971), pp. 44–51.

3 Locke, *Second Treatise of Government*, VII. para. 87; also, VIII. 95: 'Men being . . . by nature all free, equal and independent'.

4 Tom Paine, *The Rights of Man* (1791); coll. in Williams, op. cit. pp. 110–11.

5 Hartley, *Observations on Man*, I. i. 2, prop. XIV (1810); quoted and discussed in J. Passmore, *The Perfectibility of Man* (1970), pp. 165–6.

6 A beginning exists for France in F. B. Artz, *The Development of Technical Education in France 1500–1850* (1966).

7 Leibniz, *Reflections on Knowledge, Truth and Ideas* (1684), in *Leibniz Selections*, ed. P. P. Weiner (1951), p. 285.

8 Leibniz, *New Essays concerning Human Understanding*, trans. A. G. Langley (1896; repr. 1949), p. 43.

9 Ibid. pp. 43–4, 71.

10 Kant, *Prolegomena to any Future Metaphysics that will be able to present itself as a Science* (1783), trans. P. G. Lucas (1953), pp. 5–9.

11 Kant, *Kritik der reinen Vernunft*, 1st ed. (A) 1781, 2nd ed. (B) 1787; trans. N. K. Smith, *Critique of Pure Reason* (1952), A 51, B 75. See also A 258, B 314.

12 The foregoing analysis is indebted to John Macmurray, *The Self as Agent* (1957), *passim*.

13 See E. F. Buchner, *The Educational Theory of Immanuel Kant* (1904; repr. 1971), p. 16 and *passim*.

14 The most accessible translation is by A. Churton, *Immanuel Kant: Education* (1960). An unscholarly presentation, it lacks an *apparatus criticus* but is taken from Kant's *Vorlesungen über Pädagogik*, edited by Theodor Rink (1813).

15 All following citations are from the Churton translation, checked against *Über Pädagogik*, and are given with a dual reference, first by Kant's chapter and section, followed by the Churton pagination. This quote, I. 29; p. 27.

16 Ibid. II; *passim*.

17 Ibid. I. 3; p. 3.

18 Ibid. I. 9; p. 15.

19 Ibid. I. 17; p. 16.

20 Ibid. V. 102; p. 108.

21 Ibid. IV. 67; p. 69.

22 Ibid. I. 12; p. 11. I. 10; p. 9.

23 Ibid. IV. 68; p. 70.

24 Ibid. IV. 75; p. 80.

25 Ibid. IV. 70; p. 74.

26 Ibid. IV. 71; p. 76.

27 Ibid. V. 81; p. 86.

28 Ibid. I. 16; p. 15.

29 Ibid. I. 7; p. 7.

30 Ibid. VI. 105; p. 111.

31 Ibid. I. 8; p. 8.

32 Ibid. I. 14; p. 14.

33 Ibid. I. 20; p. 21.

34 Ibid. III. 59; p. 60.

35 Kant, *Letter* to C. H. Wolke, 28 March 1776, in *Kant: Philosophical Correspondence 1759–99*, ed. and trans. A. Zweig (1967), pp. 83–5.

36 Collected in Buchner, op. cit. pp. 242–5.

37 Ibid. pp. 242–3.

38 Pestalozzi, *Evening Hours of a Hermit* (1780), coll. and trans. R. Ulich, *Three Thousand Years of Educational Wisdom* (1954), p. 482.

39 Roger de Guimps, *Pestalozzi: His Life and Work* (repr. 1890), p. 5.
40 Pestalozzi, *Letters on Early Education (Addressed to J. P. Greaves)* (repr. 1898), Letter XXXII, 25 April 1819; quotations all from the reprint of 1898; this quote, p. 166.
41 Trans. Ulich, op. cit. p. 481.
42 Ibid.
43 Pestalozzi, *Leonard and Gertrude*, trans. E. Channing (1910), p. 95.
44 Pestalozzi, *Letters on Early Education*, Letter VI, 31 October 1818; p. 30.
45 *Pestalozzi im Lichte zweier Zeitgenossen: Henning und Niederer* (Zürich, 1944); trans. in M. Heafford, *Pestalozzi* (1967), p. 44.
46 Pestalozzi, *Evening Hours of a Hermit*, trans. Ulich, op. cit. p. 483.
47 Ibid.
48 Quoted in G. L. Gutek, *Pestalozzi and Education* (1968), p. 85.
49 Pestalozzi, *Letters on Early Education*, Letter XXIX, 4 April 1819; p. 148.
50 Ibid. Letter III, 7 October 1818; p. 16.
51 Pestalozzi, *On the Idea of Elementary Education (Über die Idee der Elementarbildung)*, trans. and quoted in Heafford, op. cit. p. 47.
52 Pestalozzi, *Letters*, V, 1818; p. 27.
53 Pestalozzi, *How Gertrude Teaches Her Children*, trans L. E. Holland and F. C. Turner (1894), p. 80.
54 Ibid. p. 81.
55 The foregoing quotes all from Letter XXXI, 17 April 1819; pp. 155–7.
56 Pestalozzi, *How Gertrude*, p. 138.
57 Ibid. p. 139.
58 Ibid. p. 92.
59 Ibid. p. 120.
60 Pestalozzi, *Letters*, XXVIII, 27 March 1819; p. 144.
61 Ibid. p. 145.
62 Ibid. XXXII, 25 April 1819; p. 164.
63 Ibid. XVI, 31 December 1818; p. 79.
64 Ibid. XXXIV, 12 May 1819; p. 177.
65 Ibid. XXI, 4 February 1819; p. 101.
66 Ibid. XXIX, 4 April 1819; p. 146.
67 Ibid. IX, p. 51.
68 Herbart, *The Aesthetic Presentation of the World*, trans. H. M. and E. Felkin (1892), p. 57.
69 Ibid. p. 73.
70 Herbart, *General Pedagogy* (1806); trans. H. M. and E. Felkin as *Science of Education* (1892; repr. 1896), p. 134.
71 Herbart, *Outlines of Educational Doctrine* (1835), trans. A. F. Lange (1901), p. 15.
72 A more comprehensive explanation will be found in the most important of

recent monographs on Herbart, H. B. Dunkel, *Herbart and Herbartianism: An Educational Ghost Story* (1970). See chapter 8, pp. 123–50.

73 Herbart, *Science of Education*, p. 126.

74 Ibid. p. 127.

75 Herbart, *Outlines*, p. 4.

76 Ibid. p. 22.

77 Ibid. p. 23.

78 Herbart, *Science of Education*, p. 132.

79 Ibid. p. 133.

80 Ibid. p. 127.

81 Herbart, *Outlines*, p. 1.

82 Herbart, *Science of Education*, p. 125.

Chapter 8

1 FitzJames (1756): 'La doctrine Chrétienne est la seule qui se rapporte par elle-même à la vie future. . . . C'est elle qui dirige toutes les autres sciences à leur véritable fin; sans elle tout ce que l'homme peut connaître de plus curieux, lui devient plus nuisible qu'utile.' Quoted in C. E. Elwell, *The Influence of the Enlightenment on the Catholic Theory of Religious Education in France 1750–1850* (1944), p. 138.

2 Developed at length in ibid.

3 La Chalotais, *Essay on National Education*; coll. and trans. in François de la Fontainerie, *French Liberalism and Education in the Eighteenth Century: Writings of La Chalotais, Turgot, Diderot and Condorcet on National Education* (repr. 1971), pp. 41–2.

4 Ibid. p. 60.

5 Ibid. p. 54.

6 Ibid. p. 157.

7 See H. C. Barnard, *Education and the French Revolution* (1969), *passim*.

8 Audrien, *Mémoire*; coll. and trans. in R. R. Palmer, *The School of the French Revolution* (1975), pp. 97–105.

9 Ibid. pp. 99–100.

10 Translated and cited in Barnard, op. cit. p. 58.

11 P. Chevallier *et al.*, *L'Enseignement français de la Révolution à nos jours* (1968), p. 24.

12 Talleyrand, cited in ibid. p. 24.

13 Champagne, Letter to the Commission on Public Instruction, 6 October 1795; in Palmer, op. cit. pp. 157 ff.

14 Ibid. p. 158.

15 Champagne's figure of 320 is in Palmer, op. cit. p. 12; that from Villemain is cited in Fontainerie, op. cit. p. 7.

16 Mercier, *Tableau de Paris*, chapter 81; Palmer, op. cit. p. 79.

17 Abbé Proyart, *De l'éducation publique*; Palmer, op. cit. pp. 82–3.

18 *Petition to the Rector and Professors of the University of Paris by the Students in Philosophy* (late 1789); Palmer, op. cit. p. 88.

19 Student letter (Paris, 1790); Palmer, op. cit. p. 94.

20 Barnard, op. cit. p. 167.

21 Felbiger, *Allgemeine Schulordnung für die deutschen Normal-, Haupt- und Trivialschulen*.

22 Barnard, op. cit. pp. 153–4.

23 Destutt de Tracy, *Observations sur le système actuel d'instruction publique* (Paris: Panckouke an IX, VIII–82 [1801]), pp. 2–5.

24 Following Barnard, op. cit. pp. 204 ff.; also p. 202.

25 Palmer, op. cit. p. 197.

26 Comte de Fourcroy, *Report to the Conseil d'État of the Consulate*, 19 April 1802; Palmer, op. cit. p. 198.

27 Baron Bignon, *Histoire de France depuis le 18 Brumaire*, 11 vols (Paris, 1829–); repr. 2 vols (Paris, 1842). This quote 1842 ed., Vol. 2, p. 201; quoted in Peter Geyl, *Napoleon: For and Against*, trans. O. Renier (1949; repr. 1965), p. 41.

28 Napoleon, Council of State Papers; Geyl, op. cit. p. 133; quoted from Hippolyte Taine, *Les Origines de la France contemporaine* (1890), Vol. 6, p. 157.

29 This decree of 10 May 1806 and the subsequent ones of 17 and 24 March 1808 are in Palmer, op. cit. pp. 219–32.

30 Ibid. p. 223.

31 Ibid. p. 227.

32 Taine, Vol. 6, p. 165; in Geyl, op. cit. p. 134.

33 A good account of this function of the *curé* will be found in John McManners, *French Ecclesiastical Society under the Ancien Régime: A Study of Angers in the Eighteenth Century* (1960), pp. 85–98, 147–9.

34 R. D. Anderson, *Education in France 1848–1870* (1975), p. 17.

35 The phrase is by A. J. P. Taylor, *The Course of German History* (1948; repr. 1961), p. 39.

36 Fichte, *Third Address to the German Nation*, trans. R. F. Jones and G. H. Turnbull (1922; repr. 1956).

37 Ibid. para. 9, p. 14. My italics.

38 Quoted and translated by D. F. S. Scott, *Wilhelm von Humboldt and the Idea of a University* (1960), p. 7.

39 Ibid. p. 5.

40 Paulsen, *German Education: Past and Present* (1908), p. 244.

41 Ibid. pp. 199 ff.

42 An accessible abridgement is Hegel, *Reason in History: A General Introduction to the Philosophy of History*, ed. and trans. R. S. Hartman (1953); in which see pp. xli–xlii.

43 The following quotations from Hegel's *Lectures in the Philosophy of History* are from the translation by Hartman in *Reason in History*. This quote, p. 20.

44 Ibid. p. 54.

45 Ibid. p. 49.

46 Ibid. pp. 57, 60.

47 Ibid. p. 30.

48 Ibid. p. 24.

49 Ibid. p. 51.

50 Ibid. p. 53.

51 Ibid. p. 45.

52 Ibid. p. 47.

53 Benjamin Rush, 'Of the Mode of Education Proper in a Republic', coll. in *Selected Writings of Benjamin Rush*, ed. D. D. Runes (1947), p. 92.

54 *Records of the Company of Massachusetts Bay*, II. 203; coll. in E. W. Knight and C. L. Hall, *Readings in American Educational History* (1951), p. 62. This extensive collection of primary sources is hereafter cited as K & H.

55 *Statutes at Large of Virginia*, ed. Hening, I. 336–7 (1642); K & H, p. 9; C. Johnson, *Old-Time Schools and School-Books* (1904; repr. 1963), pp. 6–8.

56 Copy, Virginia State Library; K & H, pp. 58–60.

57 *Instructions to the Clergy of the SPG* (1706); C. F. Pascoe, *Two Hundred Years of the SPG 1701–1900* (London: SPG, 1901), pp. 837–40; K & H, p. 24.

58 Johnson, op. cit. p. 4.

59 Instructions to Evert Pietersen, a teacher in Nieu Amsterdam (1661); K & H, pp. 16–17.

60 D. J. Pratt, *Annals of Public Education in the State of New York from 1626 to 1746* (1872), p. 57; K & H, p. 17.

61 See Johnson, op. cit. chapter 3, pp. 69–99.

62 Ibid. p. 183.

63 *Harvard Regulations*, 21 October 1656; K & H, p. 67.

64 Dock, *Schulordnung* (1750); K & H, pp. 34–5.

65 Johnson, op. cit. pp. 44–5.

66 For a wider treatment, see Vol. 2 of the present work, pp. 415–16.

67 *Statutes of Harvard* (c. 1646); coll. in R. Hofstadter and W. Smith, *American Higher Education: A Documentary History*, 2 vols (1961), Vol. 1, p. 8. Hereafter cited as H & S.

68 Johnson, op. cit. p. 14.

69 *Papers of Benjamin Franklin*, ed. L. W. Labaree *et al.* (1959), Vol. 3, pp. 397–421; coll. in T. R. Sizer (ed.), *The Age of the Academies* (1964), pp. 70–1.

70 Ibid. p. 84.

71 *Rivington's New York Gazetteer*, 23 March 1775; K & H, p. 181.

72 *American Journal of Education*, I (1855), p. 368.

73 Sizer, op. cit. p. 34.

74 Reproduced in S. E. Morison, *The Founding of Harvard College* (1935), pp. 432–433; H & S, Vol. 1, pp. 6–7.

75 *The Laws, Liberties and Orders of Harvard College* (1642–66); H & S, Vol. 1, pp. 61–2.

76 *Charter of William and Mary* (1693); H & S, Vol. 1, pp. 33–9.

77 *Statutes of William and Mary* (1727); H & S, Vol. 1, pp. 39–48.

78 *Yale Charter* (1745); H & S, Vol. 1, p. 49.

79 Jefferson, Letter from Paris to J. Bannister, 15 October 1785; K & H, p. 192.

80 R. and G. Watkins, *Digest of the Laws of the State of Georgia* (1800), pp. 299–302; K & H, pp. 192 ff.

81 *Writings of George Washington* (US Government Printing Office, 1940), Vol. 34 (ed. J. C. Fitzpatrick), pp. 149–50.

82 Ibid. Vol. 11 (ed. J. Sparks), pp. 14–16.

83 *Federal and State Constitutions, Colonial Charters and Other Organic Laws of the United States*, ed. B. F. Poore, 2 vols (US Government Printing Office, 1877).

84 Ibid.

85 Ibid.

86 Letter, Franklin to Messrs Weems and Grant, 18 July 1784; in J. Sparks (ed.), *Works of Benjamin Franklin* (Boston: Hilliard, Gray, 1836–40), Vol. 10, pp. 109–11.

87 *Statutes at Large of South Carolina*, ed. D. J. McCord, Vol. 8, p. 413; K & H, p. 661.

88 General Assembly of the Presbyterian Church in Virginia, *Acts and Proceedings* (1801), p. 7; K & H, p. 662.

89 *Supplement to the Revised Code of the Laws of Virginia* (1833), cap. 186; K & H, pp. 664–5.

90 *Laws of North Carolina* (1831-2), cap. IV; K & H, p. 665.

91 Benjamin Rush, *On the Mode of Education Proper in a Republic*; in *Selected Writings*, ed. Runes (1947), p. 95.

Chapter 9

1 V. R. Lorwin, 'Working Class Politics and Economic Development in Western Europe', *American Historical Review* (1957), p. 341; quoted in S. G. Checkland, *The Rise of Industrial Society in England 1815–1885* (1964), p. 328.

2 Cited in G. Rudé, *Europe in the Eighteenth Century: Aristocracy and the Bourgeois Challenge* (1972), p. 106. See also *The Doctrine of Saint-Simon: An Exposition*, ed. and trans. G. G. Iggers (1958; repr. 1972), p. 211: 'the hotheaded convictions which often make an egotistic bourgeois seem like a devoted citizen'.

3 Samuel Heywood, *Digest of the Law Respecting County Elections* (1790), p. 158; this quote, and the preceding one, from B. Turner, *Equality for Some: The Story of Girls' Education* (1974), p. 46.

4 See J. J. Tobias, *Crime and Industrial Society in the Nineteenth Century* (1967; 1972), p. 232.

5 Gustave de Beaumont, *On Prison Reform*, 7 September 1843; coll. in *Tocqueville and Beaumont on Social Reform*, trans. S. Drescher (1968), pp. 61–2.

6 James Mill, 'Government'; coll. in E. A. Burtt (ed.), *The English Philosophers from Bacon to Mill* (1939), pp. 857–94; this quote, p. 858.

7 Ibid. p. 888.

8 Ibid.

9 'Education' (1815); in *James Mill on Education*, ed. W. H. Burston (1969), p. 112.

10 James Mill, *Correspondence of David Ricardo*, No. 109, Mill to Ricardo, 23 August 1815; Burston, op. cit. p. 30.

11 Mill, 'Education'; Burston, op. cit. p. 71.

12 Ibid. p. 61.

13 Ibid. p. 67.

14 Lancaster, in D. Salmon (ed.), *The Practical Parts of Lancaster's Improvements and Bell's Experiments* (1932), p. xxiii.

15 Lancaster, *Improvements in Education*, 3rd ed. (1805), p. 1.

16 Ibid. p. 7.

17 Ibid. p. 8.

18 Ibid. p. 25.

19 Ibid. pp. 40, 37.

20 Ibid. p. 13.

21 Ibid. These accounts are in the old sterling system of pounds (£), shillings (*s.*) and pence (*d.*).

22 Sarah Trimmer, *Reflections upon the Education of Children in Charity Schools* (London: T. Longman, 1792), p. 7.

23 *Quarterly Review* (October 1811), p. 289; cited in Burston, op. cit. p. 186.

24 Mill, *Schools for All*; Burston, op. cit. pp. 122, 124, 125.

25 Ibid. p. 168.

26 Select Committee on Police ,1816–18, Chairman H. G. Bennet, MP; cited in Tobias, op. cit. p. 88.

27 P. Monroe (ed.), *A Cyclopedia of Education*, 5 vols (1911–13): s.v. D. Salmon, 'National Society, England', Vol. 4, p. 384; M. E. Sadler and J. W. Edwards, *Special Reports on Educational Subjects* (1898), Vol. 2, p. 446.

28 H. G. MacNab, *The New Views of Mr Owen . . . of the Rev. Dr Bell and that of the New British and Foreign System of Mutual Instruction* (London, 1819), p. 212; cited in J. Lawson and H. Silver, *A Social History of Education in England* (1973), p. 241.

29 T. Bernard, *The Education of the Poor* (1809), p. 35; cited in M. G. Jones, *The Charity School Movement* (1930; repr. 1964), p. 337.

30 P. Chevallier *et al.*, *L'Enseignement français de la Révolution à nos jours* (1968), p. 64.

31 Statistics from Antoine Prost, *Histoire de l'enseignement en France 1800–1967* (1968), document 17: *Statistique de l'instruction primaire 1817–1887.*

32 R. D. Anderson, *Education in France 1848-1870* (1975), p. 155.

33 Monroe, op. cit.: s.v. 'Monitorial System', Vol. 4, p. 297.

34 On the monitorial method in Russia, and references to the foregoing passage, see generally B. Hollingworth, 'Lancasterian Schools in Russia', *Durham Research Review*, V, 17 (September 1966), pp. 59–71.

35 Ibid. p. 70.

36 Ibid.

37 *The Raleigh Register*, 1 April 1814; K & H, p. 135.

38 Oscar Browning, *Memories of Sixty Years at Eton, Cambridge and Elsewhere* (1860), pp. 62–70; cited in P. J. Gosden, *How They Were Taught: An Anthology of Contemporary Accounts of Learning and Teaching in England* (1969), pp. 82–3.

39 Ibid. p. 87.

40 Royal Commission to Inquire into the State, Discipline, Studies and Revenues of our University (Oxford and Cambridge) and of all and Singular Colleges in our said University (ies), 1852; cited from J. S. Maclure (ed.), *Educational Documents: England and Wales 1816–1963* (1965), pp. 63–9.

41 Royal Commission to Inquire into the Revenues and Management of certain Colleges and Schools, and the studies pursued and instruction given therein (1864); Maclure, op. cit. p. 85. The nine schools examined were Eton, Winchester, Westminster, Charterhouse, St Paul's, Merchant Taylors', Harrow, Rugby and Shrewsbury.

42 Royal Commission (Taunton Report) (1868); Maclure, op. cit. p. 95.

43 Herbert Spencer, *Education* (1861; 1929), p. 2.

44 Ibid. p. 49.

45 Devonshire Report (1875); Maclure, op. cit. p. 107.

46 Royal Commission to consider what are the best methods of establishing a well-organized system of secondary education in England . . . (Bryce Report) (1895); Maclure, op. cit. p. 147.

47 Ibid. p. 142.

48 V. H. H. Green, *British Institutions: The Universities* (1969), p. 105.

49 Cross Report, I, p. 138; cited in Lawson and Silver, op. cit. p. 340.

50 S. G. Checkland, op. cit. pp. 27, 215.

51 R. Mols, *Introduction à la démographie historique des villes d'Europe* (1954–6); in R. R. Palmer, *Atlas of World History* (1962), p. 194.

52 *Letter*, Lord John Russell to Lord Lansdowne, 4 February 1839; Maclure, op. cit. p. 43.

53 *Minutes*, Committee of the Council on Education, 25 August 1846 and 21 December 1846; Maclure, op. cit. pp. 52–3.

54 Royal Commission to Inquire into the State of Popular Education in England (Newcastle Report) (1861), I, p. 107; Lawson and Silver, op. cit. p. 287.

55 Newcastle Report, VI, p. 300; Maclure, op. cit. p. 74.
56 Quoted in Maclure, op. cit. p. 79.
57 Lawson and Silver, op. cit. p. 285.
58 Speech by W. E. Forster, House of Commons, 17 February 1870; Maclure, op. cit. p. 99.
59 See Maclure, op. cit. pp. 128 ff.
60 Report from the Poor Law Commissioners on the Training of Pauper Children (1841), appendix IX, pp. 391–3, Report by Edward Sims, 16 March 1840; in Gosden, op. cit. p. 12.
61 See J. W. Padberg, *Colleges in Controversy: The Jesuit Schools in France from Revival to Suppression 1815–1880* (1969).
62 Anderson, op. cit. p. 199.
63 Thiers, *La Commission extraparlementaire de 1849* (c. 1850), p. 31; quoted in Anderson, op. cit. p. 48.
64 Anderson, op. cit. p. 199.
65 Statistics collected in *Report of the United States Commissioner for Education* (1900), I, p. 781.
66 Eda Sagarra, *A Social History of Germany 1648–1914* (1977), p. 279. See also chapter 15, pp. 273–84 *passim*.
67 Friedrich Paulsen, *German Education: Past and Present* (1908), pp. 250 ff.
68 Cited in H. B. Dunkel, *Herbart and Herbartianism* (1970), p. 215.
69 Sagarra, op. cit. p. 419.

Chapter 10

1 Herder, *Ideen zur Philosophie der Geschichte der Menschheit* (1784); trans. T. Churchill, *Outlines of a Philosophy of the History of Man* (c. 1800), p. 91.
2 Humboldt, *Ansichten der Natur mit wissenschaftlichen Erläuterungen*, 3rd ed. (1849), Preface.
3 Humboldt, *Kosmos* (1862), Vol. 5, p. 5.
4 Much of the material on Humboldt and the *Naturphilosophie* movement comes from Margarita Bowen, *Empiricism and Geographical Thought* (1981).
5 Quoted in P. J. Gosden, *How They Were Taught* (1969), p. 7.
6 Elizabeth Mayo, *Lessons on Objects*, 6th ed. (1837), pp. 17–27; quoted in W. H. C. Stewart and W. P. McCann, *The Educational Innovators*, Vol. 1: 1750–1850 (1967), p. 151.
7 Froebel, *Letter to the Duke of Meiningen* (1827), in *Friedrich Fröbels gesammelte pädagogische Schriften*, ed. Wichard Lange (Berlin, 1862–3), I. 1. 89; trans. I. Lilley, *Friedrich Froebel: A Selection from his Writings* (1967), p. 33.
8 Froebel, *The Education of Man* (1826); Lilley, op. cit. p. 141. All translations from Froebel's *Collected Pedagogical Works* are from Lilley's collection.
9 Froebel, *Letter to the Duke of Meiningen*; Lilley, op. cit. p. 35.

10 Ibid. p. 36.

11 Ibid. p. 37.

12 Froebel, *The Education of Man*; Lilley, op. cit. p. 128.

13 In Lilley, op. cit. pp. 41, 156.

14 Froebel, *Pedagogics of the Kindergarten*; Lilley, op. cit. p. 93.

15 Froebel, *The Education of Man*; Lilley, op. cit. p. 52.

16 Ibid. p. 67.

17 Ibid. p. 136.

18 Ibid.

19 Ibid. p. 138.

20 Ibid. p. 141.

21 Ibid. pp. 48–9.

22 Froebel, *Letter to Karl Kristoph Friedrich Krause* (1828); Lilley, op. cit. p. 41.

23 Ibid. p. 42.

24 *Friedrich Fröbels gesammelte pädagogische Schriften*, ed. Lange, Vol. 2, p. 22; Lilley, op. cit. p. 102.

25 Quoted in Asa Briggs, *Victorian People* (1954; 1965), p. 250.

26 Following Dunkel, *Herbart and Herbartianism* (1970), pp. 209 ff.; which see for a fuller exposition.

27 Ibid. pp. 216–17.

28 Ibid. p. 232.

29 Ibid. p. 230.

30 Cecil Reddie, *Abbotsholme* (1900), p. 115.

31 'Trustees of Dartmouth College *v.* Woodward', *Reports of Cases Argued and Decided in the Supreme Court of the United States*, 4 Wheaton 555–654 (1819); in R. Hofstadter and W. Smith, *American Higher Education: A Documentary History* (1961), Vol. 1, pp. 207, 213–19 *passim*. (H & S.)

32 Researches of D. G. Tewkesbury, cited in Richard Hofstadter, 'The Great Retrogression: Presbyterians and Puritans', in *The Development of Academic Freedom in the United States* (1957), pp. 209–21, 238–51.

33 Quoted in E. W. Knight and C. L. Hall, *Readings in American Educational History* (1951), p. 270. (K & H.)

34 H. P. Tappan, *University Education* (1851), p. 43; H & S, Vol. 2, p. 488.

35 J. M. Hart, *German Universities* (1874); H & S, Vol. 2, pp. 571–2.

36 Noah Porter, *Inaugural Address* (1871), H & S, Vol. 2, pp. 699–700.

37 See C. W. Eliot, *Educational Reform: Essays and Addresses* (1898), pp. 125–48; H & S, Vol. 2, pp. 701–14.

38 Porter's *Letter* to Sumner and the latter's *Reply*; in H & S, Vol. 2, pp. 849–57.

39 Reported in L. R. Veysey, *The Emergence of the American University* (1965), p. 173.

40 R. M. Wenley, 'Can We Stem the Tide?', *Educational Review*, XXXIV (1907), pp. 242–3.

41 Text of the Convention Document 'On the Rights of Women' (1848) in K & H, pp. 713–16.

42 C. W. Eliot, *Inaugural Address* (1869); K & H, p. 718.

43 NEA, *Addresses and Journal of Proceedings* (1879), p. 98; K & H, p. 721.

44 Both quotations in K & H, p. 722.

45 *American Journal of Education*, I (1855), p. 368.

46 *New York Free Enquirer*, 7 October 1829; K & H, pp. 147–57.

47 *Boston Courier*, 28 August 1830; K & H, p. 147.

48 Quoted in K & H, p. 151n.

49 Ibid. p. 148.

50 Ibid. p. 149.

51 *Resolves of the General Court of the Commonwealth of Massachusetts* (1837), pp. 465–6; K & H, pp. 359–60.

52 Mann, *Twelfth Annual Report* to the Massachusetts State Board of Education (1848); K & H, pp. 165–6.

53 *Acts and Resolves of the General Court of Massachusetts in the Year 1852*, pp. 170–171; K & H, p. 365.

54 In addition to the play *The Melting Pot*, see also S. Feldstein and L. Costello, *The Ordeal of Assimilation: A Documentary History of the White Working Class* (1974); Part II. B, pp. 168–85, and Part IV, pp. 356–60.

55 Jane Addams, 'Foreign-Born Children in the Primary Grades', *Journal of Proceedings*, 36th Annual Meeting, National Education Association (1897), pp. 106–10; quoted in Feldstein and Costello, op. cit. p. 253.

56 Ibid.

57 Florence Kelley, 'Protection for American Children', *Child Labor Bulletin* (May 1914), pp. 14–19; in Feldstein and Costello, op. cit. pp. 294–9.

58 *Laws of Massachusetts* (January 1827), cp. XCLIII; K & H, p. 247.

59 See *Common School Journal*, 1 February 1839, and *Tenth Annual Report* of the Massachusetts State Board of Education (1846); in K & H, pp. 415–16.

60 E. W. Knight, 'A Century of Teacher-Education', *The Educational Forum*, IX (1945), pp. 149–61.

61 See Dunkel, op. cit. pp. 241–83.

62 Sales figures are in ibid. pp. 271, 278.

63 Rein, *Outlines of Pedagogics*, trans. C. C. and I. J. van Liew (1893).

64 Ibid. p. 104.

65 Ibid. p. 99.

66 Ibid. p. 75.

67 Ibid. p. 87.

68 Ibid. pp. 109–10.

69 De Garmo, *First Yearbook of the National Herbart Society* (1902), p. 7.

70 Charles McMurry, *The Elements of General Method, Based on the Principles of Herbart*, 2nd ed. (1903), p. 56.

71 Ibid. p. 51.
72 See ibid. *passim* and, respectively, pp. 54–5, 249, 310.
73 Ibid. p. 6.
74 Ibid. p. 236.
75 Ibid. p. 237.
76 Ibid. p. 235.
77 Ibid. p. 249.
78 C. and F. McMurry, *The Method of the Recitation* (1897; rev. ed. 1903), p. 3.
79 Ibid.
80 Ibid. p. 10.
81 Ibid. pp. 91, 107–8.
82 Ibid. p. 118.
83 Ibid. p. 198.
84 Ibid. p. 219.
85 Ibid. pp. 168–9.
86 Ibid. pp. 288–94.
87 Ibid. p. 289.
88 Ibid. p. 290.

Chapter 11

1 The best account of the life and work of Owen is J. F. C. Harrison, *Quest for the New Moral World: Robert Owen and the Owenites in Britain and America* (1969). There is a fine short biography of his life and ideas by G. D. H. Cole in the introduction to the Everyman edition of *A New View of Society and Other Writings* (1927).
2 Preface to Third Essay. All ensuing quotations from Owen's writings are from the edition by Cole, op. cit. This quotation, p. 10.
3 Owen, *To the British Master Manufacturers*, p. 140.
4 Owen, *On the Employment of Children in Manufactories*, p. 130.
5 Ibid. p. 137.
6 Owen, *A New View of Society*, Dedication to Fourth Essay, p. 11.
7 See F. E. and F. P. Manuel, *French Utopias: An Anthology of Ideal Societies* (1966; repr. 1971).
8 See W. H. G. Armytage, *Heavens Below: Utopian Experiments in England 1560–1960* (1961).
9 Owen, *A New View of Society*, p. 17.
10 Ibid. Fourth Essay, p. 63.
11 Owen, *Report to the County of Lanark*, p. 246.
12 Ibid. p. 268.
13 Ibid. p. 284.
14 Ibid. p. 288.

15 Ibid. p. 294.
16 Ibid. p. 292.
17 Ibid. p. 283.
18 Owen, *A New View of Society*, p. 75.
19 Owen, *Report*, pp. 282–3.
20 Quoted in W. A. C. Stewart and W. P. McCann, *The Educational Innovators* (1967), Vol. 1, p. 73, n. 94.
21 The story is in Harrison, op. cit.
22 Stewart and McCann, op. cit. pp. 74–82.
23 Ibid. p. 85.
24 English translation by G. C. Iggers, *The Doctrine of Saint-Simon: An Exposition*, First Year, 1828–9 (1958; repr. 1972).
25 Ibid. First Session, 'On the Necessity of a New Social Doctrine', p. 1.
26 Ibid. Ninth Session, 'Education', p. 141.
27 Ibid. p. 153.
28 Ibid. pp. 162–3.
29 Following the translation of Frank Manuel, *Design for Utopia: Selected Writings of Charles Fourier* (1901; repr. 1971).
30 Fourier, *Théorie de l'unité universelle*, Vol. 4, 2nd ed. (1838), p. 1; coll. in Manuel, op. cit. p. 67.
31 Ibid. Vol. 4, p. 188; Manuel, op. cit. pp. 73–4.
32 Owen, *A New View of Society*, p. 48.
33 *The Doctrine of Saint-Simon: An Exposition*, Ninth Session, p. 140.
34 Marx and Engels, *Manifesto of the Communist Party* (1848); coll and trans. in R. C. Tucker (ed.), *The Marx–Engels Reader* (1972), p. 335.
35 Ibid. p. 345.
36 Ibid. p. 361.
37 Engels, *Socialism: Utopian and Scientific*; Tucker, op. cit. p. 622.
38 Ibid. p. 621.
39 Marx, *Critique of the Gotha Programme*; Tucker, op. cit. p. 382.
40 For Plato, the references are *Republic*, IV. 476a ff.; for Aristotle, *Posterior Analytics*, II. xix (99b) ff.
41 The standard recent exposition, which considers 'the ghost in the machine' as a linguistic fallacy, namely, a 'category mistake', is Gilbert Ryle, *The Concept of Mind* (1949; repr. 1963).
42 There is a growing literature on the perception and study of childhood, for which see J. Cleverley and D. C. Phillips, *From Locke to Spock: Influential Models of the Child in Modern Western Thought* (1976) and its bibliography, pp. 115–17.
43 Montessori, *The Montessori Method: Scientific Pedagogy*, trans. A. E. George (1912), reprinted and revised as *The Discovery of the Child*, trans. M. A. Johnstone (1948), p. 20.

44 Ibid. p. 5.
45 E. M. Standing, *The Montessori Revolution in Education* (1962; repr. 1966), p. 88.
46 Scott Nearing, *Education in Soviet Russia* (1926), p. 100.
47 A recent monograph is Rita Kramer, *Maria Montessori: A Biography* (1976).
48 A detailed history of English progressive education is Stewart and McCann, op. cit. See especially Vol. 2, by W. A. Stewart, *Progressive Schools 1881–1967*. For Reddie, see pp. 9 ff. and pp. 243–67.
49 Ibid. Vol. 2, pp. 66 ff.
50 Ibid. pp. 154 ff.
51 Ibid. p. 86.
52 Ibid. p. 220.
53 Ibid. p. 226.

Chapter 12

1 Peirce, *Collected Papers of Charles Sanders Peirce* (1931–5), Vol. 5, para. 2. For an expanded commentary on the significance of this dictum, see W. B. Gallie, *Peirce and Pragmatism* (1952), chapter 1.
2 Following Gallie, op. cit. pp. 26 ff.
3 This correspondence has been collected in R. B. Perry, *The Thought and Character of William James*, 2 vols (Boston: Little, Brown, 1935).
4 James, *Talks to Teachers* (1899; repr. 1958), pp. 23–4.
5 Ibid. p. 129.
6 Ibid. p. 36.
7 Ibid. p. 125.
8 Ibid.
9 Ibid. p. 87.
10 Ibid. p. 96.
11 L. Cremin, *The Transformation of the School* (1962), pp. 4, 5.
12 Ibid. pp. 131 ff. for a fuller account of Parker at Chicago.
13 Dewey, *The School and Society* (1900; repr. 1956), pp. 173–4.
14 Ibid.
15 John Adams, *The Herbartian Psychology Applied to Education* (1897), pp. 46, 49.
16 Dewey, *How We Think* (1933), p. 99.
17 Dewey, 'International Law and the War System', *The Christian Century*, 18 October 1923; repr. in *Characters and Events* (1929), Vol. 2, pp. 650–65.
18 Dewey, *Art as Experience* (1935), p. 23.
19 Dewey, *Democracy and Education* (1916), p. 149.
20 Dewey, *The Quest for Certainty* (1929), p. 17.
21 *Oxford Dictionary of the Christian Church*, ed. F. L. Cross (1957), s.v. 'Gifford Lectures', p. 557.
22 Dewey, *The Quest for Certainty*, pp. 287–8.

23 Ibid. p. 291.
24 Ibid. p. 151.
25 Ibid. p. 154.
26 Ibid. p. 156.
27 Ibid. p. 155.
28 Cremin, op. cit. pp. 24 ff. Acknowledgement is made to the invaluable assistance afforded by this monograph.
29 Ibid. pp. 154–60.
30 Ibid. pp. 215–20.
31 C. A. Bowers, *The Progressive Educator and the Depression: The Radical Years* (1969), p. 10. Essential reading for an understanding of the 1930s.
32 Ibid. p. 111.
33 Quoted in ibid. p. 13.
34 Pius XI, *Divini illius magistri (Rappresentanti in terra)* (1929); in *Five Great Encyclicals* (New York: Paulist Press, 1939), p. 63.
35 Ibid. p. 55.
36 Cremin, op. cit. p. 229.
37 *Progressive Education*, I, 1 (April 1924), p. 3.
38 Cremin, op. cit.

Chapter 13

1 These literacy statistics are reported by the respective countries concerned, collected in *The World in Figures*, edited by The Economist Newspaper (1976), p. 18.
2 Ibid.
3 W. S. Deffenbaugh, 'Compulsory Attendance Laws in the United States', *Bulletin*, United States Bureau of Education, No. 2 (1914), p. 10.
4 The figures come from the statistical analyses of the United States Office of Education, Washington, DC.
5 *Acts of the General Assembly of the Commonwealth of Kentucky* (1904), pp. 181–2; coll. in E. W. Knight and C. L. Hall, *Readings in American Educational History* (1951), cited hereafter as K & H.
6 'Cardinal Principles of Secondary Education', *Bulletin*, Department of the Interior, Bureau of Education, No. 35 (Washington: Government Printing Office, 1918).
7 Act quoted in J. S. Maclure, *Educational Documents: England and Wales 1816– 1963* (1965), p. 154.
8 Ibid.
9 *Education Act 1918*, Statement by H. A. L. Fisher, 10 August 1917; Maclure, op. cit. pp. 174–5.

10 D. H. Akenson, *The Irish Education Experiment: The National System in the Nineteenth Century* (1970), p. 140.

11 Ibid. p. 377.

12 Nathaniel Burwash, *Egerton Ryerson* (1903), pp. 189–91.

13 *Mirari vos*, 15 August 1932; coll. and trans. in Anne Fremantle, *The Papal Encyclicals in their Historical Context* (1956), p. 127.

14 *Quanta cura* and *Syllabus errorum* in Fremantle, op. cit. pp. 135 ff.

15 Georges Dupeux, *French Society 1789–1970* (1976), p. 158.

16 *Lettres d'institutrices rurales d'autrefois*; quoted and trans. in Dupeux, op. cit. pp. 185–6.

17 Quoted in David Thomson, *Europe Since Napoleon* (1966), p. 367.

18 Albert Thibaudet, *La République des professeurs* (1927); Dupeux, op. cit. pp. 184–5.

19 Quoted, with a fuller documentation, in W. D. Halls, *Society, Schools and Progress in France* (1965), p. 27.

20 Pierre Bourdieu, 'L'École conservatrice', *Revue française de sociologie*, VII (1966), pp. 225 ff.; trans. also in J. Eggleston (ed.), *Contemporary Research in the Sociology of Education* (1974), pp. 32–46.

21 Pierre Bourdieu, 'Cultural Reproduction and Social Reproduction', in R. Brown, *Knowledge, Education and Cultural Change* (1973), p. 80.

22 Quoted in N. Ascherson, *The King Incorporated: Leopold II in the Age of Trusts* (1963), p. 139.

23 There is little English material on either Sanz or Giner; an account will be found in J. B. Trend, *The Origins of Modern Spain* (1934; repr. 1965).

24 A. Ramos Oliviera, *Politics, Economics and Men of Modern Spain 1808–1946* (1946), p. 452.

25 A. H. de Oliviera Marques, *History of Portugal*, 2nd ed. (1976), Vol. 2, p. 30. The educational statistics that follow are from that work.

26 Ibid. p. 31.

27 Ibid. pp. 203 ff. Also, Economist Newspaper, op. cit. p. 18.

28 L. Minio-Paluello, *Education in Fascist Italy* (1946), p. 15. This monograph has been followed in the ensuing section.

29 Ibid.

30 H. S. Harris, *The Social Philosophy of Giovanni Gentile* (1960), pp. 55 ff. Acknowledgement is made to that monograph and many personal discussions with Harris on the issues discussed here.

31 Gentile, *Per la scuola primaria di stato* (1907); quoted and trans. in Harris, op. cit. p. 62, n. 71.

32 *Opera omnia di Benito Mussolini*, ed. E. and D. Susmel (Florence: La Fenice, 1951–62), Vol. 24, pp. 75–6, 89; quoted in S. W. Halperin, *Mussolini and Italian Fascism* (1964), p. 70.

33 For greater detail, see Minio-Paluello, op. cit. Part IV, chapters 4, 5, 6, pp. 195–218.
34 See H. P. Bleuel, *Strength Through Joy: Sex and Society in Nazi Germany* (*Das saubere Reich*, 1972); trans. J. M. Brownjohn (1973), p. 164; also, R. Gruneberger, *A Social History of the Third Reich* (1971; repr. 1974), p. 363.
35 Hermann Rauschning, *Hitler Speaks* (1939), p. 51; quoted in Bleuel, op. cit. p. 140.
36 Gruneberger, op. cit. pp. 367 ff.
37 Bleuel, op. cit. p. 182.
38 Ibid. p. 156.
39 W. L. Shirer, *The Rise and Fall of the Third Reich* (1960), p. 252.

Chapter 14

1 *Russia at the Close of the Sixteenth Century*, [including] *Of the Russe Common Wealth* (London, 1591; repr. Hakluyt Society, 1856), Vol. 20, p. 63.
2 Ibid. p. 112.
3 Quoted in W. H. E. Johnson, *Russia's Educational Heritage* (1950), p. 21.
4 *Ukase*; coll. and trans. in L. J. Oliva, *Peter the Great* (1970), p. 48.
5 *Ukase*; ibid. pp. 53–4.
6 Vasili Klyuchevsky, *Peter the Great* (1910; repr. and trans. 1958), p. 263.
7 J. H. Billington, *The Icon and the Axe* (1970), p. 290.
8 For statistics and foregoing ideas, see R. D. Charques, *A Short History of Russia* (1956), p. 183.
9 P. Ignatiev, D. M. Odinetz, P. J. Novgorotsev, *Russian Schools and Universities in the World War* (1929), p. 31.
10 Cited in D. B. Leary, *Education and Autocracy in Russia* (1919), p. 49.
11 Ignatiev *et al*., op. cit. pp. 5 ff.
12 Ibid. p. 10.
13 Ibid. p. 20.
14 Ibid. p. 39.
15 Ibid.
16 Ibid. p. 36.
17 Ibid. p. 100.
18 Sheila Fitzpatrick, *The Commissariat of Enlightenment* (1970).
19 *Circular of the People's Commissaire of Education to All Regional Commissioners of Education*, 24 December 1917; coll. and trans. M. Eastman, *Education and Art in Soviet Russia* (n.d., *c*. 1920).
20 US Commissioner of Education, *Report*, 30 June 1918, p. 88.
21 Cited in N. Hans and S. Hessen, *Educational Policy in Soviet Russia* (1930), p. 17.
22 See Fitzpatrick, op. cit. p. 1n.

23 *Provision for the Organization of Popular Education in the USSR*, Decree of the Workers' and Peasants' Government; Eastman, op. cit. p. 10.

24 US Commissioner of Education, op. cit. p. 89.

25 A. Lunacharsky, *First Report of the People's Commissar of Education* (1918).

26 People's Commissar Lepeshinsky, paper read at the First All-Russian Congress of Teacher-Internationalists, 2 June 1918; Eastman, op. cit. p. 15.

27 Lunacharsky, *Self-Education of the Workers: The Cultural Task of the Struggling Proletariat* (n.d., *c.* 1918).

28 Ibid.

29 Cited in Hans and Hessen, op. cit. p. 21.

30 Lunacharsky, *Self-Education.*

31 *Collection of Laws and Decrees of the Workers' and Peasants' Government* (1918), nos 76–7, art. 153; trans. Helen Rapp, in R. Schlesinger, *The Family in the USSR* (1949).

32 Schlesinger, op. cit. p. 33.

33 N. Semashko (People's Commissar of Health), *Health Protection in the USSR* (1934), pp. 82–4; in Schlesinger, op. cit. p. 44.

34 Marx, *Early Texts*, ed. and trans. D. McLellan (1971), p. 148.

35 István Mészáros, *Marx's Theory of Alienation*, 3rd ed. (London: Merlin Press, 1972), pp. 93 ff. and chapter 3 *passim.*

36 Lepeshinsky; in Eastman, op. cit. pp. 19–20.

37 Lunacharsky, 'Declaration of the Principles of the Socialist School', in *Narodnoe Prosveshcheniye*, No. 10, 6 June 1918.

38 *The Institute for Child Study*; in Eastman, op. cit. p. 36.

39 Education Act of 16 October 1918; Hans and Hessen, op. cit. p. 18.

40 B. Pares, *Russia* (1949), pp. 66–7.

41 M. Epshtein, 'Besprizorniki v SSSR', *Bolshaya Sovetskaya Entsiklopediya*, Vol. 5 (1927), p. 786.

42 Marx, *Capital*, I. iv. 9; Everyman ed. (1951), Vol. 1, p. 522.

43 Marx, *Der Vorbote* (Geneva, 1866), No. 10, p. 151.

44 Coll. in *Lenin on Youth* (1967), p. 58.

45 Quoted in T. Woody, *New Minds: New Men?* (1932), p. 49.

46 Quoted by I. Merzon, *Na Putiakh k Novoy Shkole* (1924); quoted in S. M. Teitelbaum, 'The Dalton Plan in the Soviet Schools', *Harvard Educational Review*, XVII, 2 (Spring 1947), pp. 91 ff.

47 Shatsky, quoted in T. Woody, op. cit. p. 48.

48 S. Nearing, *Education in Soviet Russia* (1926), p. 35.

49 L. Wilson, *The New Schools in New Russia* (1928), p. 65.

50 Nearing, op. cit. p. 99.

51 A. Pinkevitch, *The New Education in the Soviet Republic* (1929), p. 7.

52 Wilson, op. cit. pp. 27–8.

53 N. K. Krupskaya, 'International Children's Week', *Pravda*, 24–30 July 1923; in *On Education* (1957), pp. 107–8.

54 N. K. Krupskaya, 'The Young Pioneer Movement as a Pedagogical Problem', *Uchitelskaya Gazeta*, No. 15, 8 April 1927; *On Education*, p. 118.

55 Nearing, op. cit. p. 98.

56 Pinkevitch, op. cit. p. vi.

57 Sidney and Beatrice Webb, *Soviet Communism – A New Civilization?* (1936), Vol. 2, p. 897.

58 Krupskaya, *On Education*, pp. 118–22.

59 Nearing, op. cit. p. 42.

60 Ibid. p. 46.

61 So described by George Counts.

62 *Decree* of the CEC of the RSFSR, April 1929.

63 *Urok* is the Russian word for lesson, on a traditional Pestalozzian object-lesson or Herbartian five-step model.

64 V. Samarin, 'The Soviet School, 1936–42'; in G. L. Kline (ed.), *Soviet Education* (1957), p. 32.

65 Ibid.

66 'On the Pedological Distortion of the System of the Narkomprosov', Decree of the Central Committee of the Communist Party, 4 July 1936, reported in *Izvestia*.

67 B. King, *Changing Man: The Education System of the USSR* (1937), p. 108.

68 G. Counts, 'Education in the USSR', *New Republic*, 13 February 1935, pp. 8–11.

69 B. King, 'The New Decrees on Soviet Education', *British-Russian Gazette and Trade Outlook* (January 1933), pp. 105–7.

70 Stalin, *Voprosi Leninizma*, 11th ed. (Moscow: Gosudarstvennoe Izdatel'stvo Nauk RSFSR, 1947), p. 490; also in Stalin, *Problems of Leninism* (Moscow: Foreign Languages Publishing House, 1947), p. 523.

71 A. M. Pankratova (ed.), *Istoriya SSSR* (1955), Iz. 14, pp. 338, 339.

72 Makarenko's writings in Russian have been published in numerous editions. The standard edition of his collected works is *Sochineniya v Semi Tomakh* (Moscow, 1857).

73 For a general study of Makarenko's life and work see James Bowen, *Soviet Education: Anton Makarenko and the Years of Experiment* (1962); also, *Anton S. Makarenko e lo sperimentalismo sovietico*, trans. B. Bellerate (Florence: La Nuova Italia Editrice, 1973). For an account of Makarenko's methods as interpreted and practised in the USSR recently, see U. Bronfennbrenner, 'Soviet Methods of Character Education: Some Implications for Research', *American Psychologist*, XVII (1962), pp. 550–65.

74 Much of the translation from Russian sources has been done by the present author and merged, generally, into the text. Throughout I have tried to

avoid the translation of *chelovek* as 'man' and have used, wherever possible, its alternative meaning of 'person'.

75 In this respect compare the subsequent work of Jean Piaget and Lawrence Kohlberg, especially the latter's 'Moral Education in the Schools: A Developmental View', *School Review*, LXXIV (1966), pp. 1–30.

76 Ibid.

77 A translation of this decree, made and edited by G. S. Counts, has been issued under the title *Krushchev and the Central Committee Speak on Education* (1959).

Chapter 15

1 *Thought and Language* was issued in English translation in 1962 by MIT Press, Cambridge, Massachusetts, and had undergone twelve printings by 1975. It contains a critical bibliography and useful introductions by Jerome Bruner, and the translators, E. Hanfmann and G. Vakar.

2 Ibid. p. 5.

3 The full story is told in Z. A. Medvedev, *The Rise and Fall of T. D. Lysenko* (1969).

4 A. A. Smirnov, 'The Development of Soviet Psychology', in R. B. Winn (ed. and trans.), *Soviet Psychology* (1961), pp. 16–18 and *passim*.

5 Report of the Harvard Committee, *General Education in a Free Society* (1945), p. xiii.

6 Ibid. p. 10.

7 Ralph H. Turner, 'Sponsored and Contest Mobility and the School System', coll. in Earl Hopper (ed.), *Readings in the Theory of Educational Systems* (London: Hutchinson, 1971).

8 For a fuller discussion, see Raymond Lyon, 'Developments in the Economics of Education over the Past Twenty Five Years', *International Review of Education*, XXV, 2 (1979).

9 Mark Blaug (ed.), *Economics of Education*, 2 vols (1968), Vol. 1, pp. 7–8.

10 See William D. Walls, 'The Psychology of Education', *Int. Rev. of Education*, XXV, 2 (1979).

11 Ibid.

12 See Erik Sven Nordenbo, 'Philosophy of Education in the Western World: Developmental Trends During the Last Twenty Five Years', *Int. Rev. of Education*, XXV, 2 (1979).

13 L. Kohlberg, 'Moral Education in the Schools: A Developmental View', *School Review*, LXXIV (1966), pp. 1–30.

14 See Bogdan Suchodolski, 'Philosophy and Education', and Torsten Husén, 'General Theories in Education: A Twenty Five Year Perspective', both collected in *Int. Rev. of Education*, XXV, 2 (1979).

15 John Wilson *et al.*, *Introduction to Moral Education* (1967), p. 18.

16 Jean Piaget, *The New Methods: Their Psychological Foundations* (1935); repr. in *Science of Education and the Psychology of the Child*, trans. D. Coltman (1971), p. 180.

17 *Psychologie et pédagogie* (1969); coll. in *Science of Education and the Psychology of the Child*, p. 27.

18 See Kohlberg, op. cit.

19 P. Bourdieu, 'L'École conservatrice', *Revue française de sociologie*, VII (1966), pp. 225 ff.; see also 'Cultural Reproduction and Social Reproduction', in R. Brown, *Knowledge, Education and Cultural Change* (1974).

20 P. L. Berger and T. Luckman, *The Social Construction of Reality* (1967).

21 See C. F. Kaestle (ed.), 'Education and American Society: New Historical Interpretations', *History of Education*, VII, 3 October 1978.

22 R. Gombin, *Les Origines du gauchisme* (1971).

23 The transliterated Chinese title is *wu-ch'an chieh-chi wen-hua ta ko-ming*; given in Neale Hunter, *Shanghai Journal: An Eyewitness Account of the Cultural Revolution* (1969), p. 5.

24 In *Selected Works of Mao Tse-tung*, 4 vols (1967), Vol. 1, pp. 295–309.

25 Ibid. p. 295.

26 R. Gombin, *The Origins of Modern Leftism*, trans. M. K. Perl (1975), pp. 9, 13.

27 For a highly readable, succinct account of the response, see W. K. Richmond, *Education and Schooling* (1975).

28 This movement is well illustrated in two collections of readings: R. Brown (ed.), *Knowledge, Education and Cultural Change* (1973), and J. Eggleston (ed.), *Contemporary Research in the Sociology of Education* (1974).

29 J. S. Coleman *et al.*, *Equality of Educational Opportunity* (Washington, DC: US Government Printing Office, 1966).

30 J. W. Douglas *et al.*, *All Our Future* (London: Davies, 1968); quoted by Tyrell Burgess, Foreword, in C. Jencks *et al.*, *Inequality* (New York: Basic Books, 1972; repr. Harmondsworth: Penguin, 1975), p. 1.

31 Jencks *et al.*, op. cit. p. 265.

32 There is now a growing literature on the politicization of education: one of the most forceful is Sam Bowles and Herbert Gintis, *Schooling in Capitalist America* (New York: Basic Books, 1976). See also Maurice Kogan, *The Politics of Educational Change* (London: Fontana, 1978), and Peter Raggatt and Merrill Evans (eds), *Urban Education 3: The Political Context* (London: Ward Lock, 1977).

33 W. L. Guttsman, *The British Political Elite* (London: MacGibbon and Kee, 1968).

34 Thorstein Veblen, *The Theory of the Leisure Class* (New York: Macmillan, 1899); C. Wright Mills, *The Power Elite* (New York: Oxford University Press, 1956); R. J. Lampman, *The Share of Top Wealth-Holders in National Wealth 1922–1956* (Princeton, NJ: Princeton University Press, 1962).

35 A. Jones (ed.), *Economics and Equality* (London: Philip Adam, 1976).
36 Michael Crozier (ed.), *Crisis of Democracy* (The Trilateral Commission) (New York: New York University Press, 1974). This quotation from Sam Bowles, 'Can the Trilateral Commission Make Democracy Safe for Capitalism?', in Greg Crough *et al.*, *Australia and World Capitalism* (Ringwood, Victoria: Penguin, 1980), p. 202.
37 Bowles, op. cit.
38 Ibid. p. 203.
39 Attending the Kyoto conference were, among others: James Carter, Zbigniew Brzezinski, Walter Mondale, Michael Blumenthal, Harold Brown, Richard Holbrooke, Warren Christoper, Warren Cooper, Andrew Young, Fred Bergsten, Cyrus Vance.
40 Kogan, op. cit.
41 A literature is growing rapidly, a good example in English being Richard Bernstein, *The Restructuring of Social and Political Theory* (Oxford: Blackwell, 1976; London: Methuen, 1979).
42 The concept was developed by Margarita Bowen, and is presented in *Empiricism and Geographical Thought* (1981).
43 Toffler, *Future Shock* (London: Pan, 1971), p. 360.
44 In 1977 the UNESCO Institute for Education, Hamburg, commissioned the present author to edit the Jubilee Issue of the *International Review of Education* under the title *Contemporary Educational Theory: A Critical Assessment*. See James Bowen (ed.), *International Review of Education*, Jubilee Issue, XXV, 2 (1979), for a fuller discussion of these matters.
45 This conceptual change is discussed in Peter Hall (ed.), *Europe 2000* (1977), *passim*.
46 Kuhn, *The Structure of Scientific Revolutions* (1962).

Bibliography

This is not an exhaustive list of works consulted; it mainly contains specific items referred to in the Notes.

ADAMS, J. *The Herbartian Psychology Applied to Education*. London: Isbister, 1897.

ADAMSON, J. W. *Pioneers of Modern Education in the Seventeenth Century*. New York: Teachers College, Columbia University, 1905; repr. 1971.

AKENSON, D. H. *The Irish Education Experiment: The National System of Education in the Nineteenth Century*. London: Routledge and Kegan Paul, 1970.

ALTICK, R. *The English Common Reader*. Chicago: Chicago University Press, 1957.

ANDERSON, R. D. *Education in France 1848–1870*. Oxford: Clarendon Press, 1975.

ARMYTAGE, W. H. G. *Heavens Below: Utopian Experiments in England 1560–1960*. London: Routledge and Kegan Paul, 1961.

ARTZ, F. B. *The Development of Technical Education in France 1500–1850*. Cambridge, Mass.: MIT Press, 1966.

ASCHERSON, N. *The King Incorporated: Leopold II in the Age of Trusts*. London: Allen and Unwin, 1963.

ASHLEY, M. *A History of Europe 1648–1815*. Englewood Cliffs, NJ: Prentice-Hall, 1973.

BACON, F. *The Advancement of Learning*. 1623. Ed. G. W. Kitchin. 1915. Repr. London: Dent, 1954.

—— *Novum Organum*. 1623. [Trans. R. J. Ellis and J. Spedding.] London: Routledge, n.d. [*c.* 1858].

—— *New Atlantis*. 1627. Ed. A. B. Gough. Oxford: Clarendon Press, 1924.

—— *Selections*. Ed. M. T. McClure. London: Scribner's, 1928.

BARNARD, H. C. *The Port-Royalists on Education: Extracts from the writing of the Port-Royalists*. Cambridge: Cambridge University Press, 1918.

—— *The French Tradition in Education: Ramus to Mme Necker de Saussure*. Cambridge: Cambridge University Press, 1922.

—— *Madame de Maintenon and St Cyr*. London: Black, 1934.

—— *Education and the French Revolution*. Cambridge: Cambridge University Press, 1969.

BASEDOW, J. B. *Elementarwerk mit den Kupfertafeln Chodowieckis*. 1770–2. Leipzig: Ernst Wiegandt, 1909. Facsimile ed. Hildesheim: Georg Olms, 1972.

BATTERSBY, W. J. *St John Baptist de la Salle*. London: Burns and Oates, 1957.

BEALES, A. C. F. *Education under Penalty*. London: University of London, The Athlone Press, 1963.

BEAUMONT, G. de. 'On Prison Reform'. In S. Drescher (ed. and trans.), *Tocqueville and Beaumont on Social Reform*. New York: Harper, 1968.

BELL, A. *An Analysis of the Experiment in Education Made at Egmore near Madras*. London: T. Bensley, 1807.

BERGER, P. L., and LUCKMAN, T. *The Social Construction of Reality*. Harmondsworth: Penguin, 1967.

BERLIN, I. *The Age of Enlightenment*. New York: Mentor, 1956.

BERNAL, J. D. *Science in History*. 4 vols. Harmondsworth: Penguin, 1969.

BETTENSON, H. *Documents of the Christian Church*. 2nd ed. London: Oxford University Press, 1963.

BILLINGTON, J. H. *The Icon and the Axe*. New York: Random House, 1970.

BLAUG, M. *Economics of Education*. 2 vols. Harmondsworth: Penguin, 1968.

BLEUEL, H. P. *Strength Through Joy: Sex and Society in Nazi Germany*. (*Das saubere Reich*. 1972.) Trans. J. M. Brownjohn. London: Secker and Warburg, 1973. Repr. London: Pan, 1976.

BOWEN, J. *Soviet Education: Anton Makarenko and the Years of Experiment*. Madison: University of Wisconsin Press, 1962.

—— *A History of Western Education*. Volume 1: *The Ancient World: Orient and Mediterranean*. London and New York: Methuen and St Martin's Press, 1972. Barcelona: Herder, 1976. Milan: Mondadori, 1979. Volume 2: *Civilization of Europe: Sixth to Sixteenth Century*. London and New York: Methuen and St Martin's Press, 1975. Barcelona: Herder, 1979. Milan: Mondadori, 1980.

—— (ed.) *Contemporary Educational Theory: A Critical Assessment*. 25th Jubilee Issue, *International Review of Education*, XXV, 2. UNESCO Institute of Education. The Hague: Martinus Nijhoff, 1979.

BOWEN, M. J. *Empiricism and Geographical Thought: From Francis Bacon to Alexander von Humboldt*. Cambridge: Cambridge University Press, 1981.

BOWERS, C. A. *The Progressive Educator and the Depression: The Radical Years*. New York: Random House, 1969.

BOYLE, R. *The Works*. Facsimile repr. of 1772 London ed. Ed. D. McKie. Hildesheim: Georg Olms, 1965.

BRIGGS, A. *Victorian People*. London: Odhams, 1954. Harmondsworth: Penguin, 1965.

BRINSLEY, J. *Ludus literarius, or The Grammar Schoole*. London: Felix Kingston for John Bellamie, 1627. Ed. E. T. Campagnac. Repr. Liverpool and London: Liverpool University Press and Constable, 1917.

BRONOWSKI, J., and MAZLISH, B. *The Western Intellectual Tradition*. Harmondsworth: Penguin, 1963.

BROWN, H. *Scientific Organizations in Seventeenth Century France*. Baltimore: Williams and Wilkins, 1934. Repr. New York: Russell and Russell, 1967.

BROWN, R. *Knowledge, Education and Cultural Change*. London: Tavistock, 1973.

BRUNSCHWIG, H. *Enlightenment and Romanticism in Eighteenth-Century Prussia*. Chicago: Chicago University Press, 1949.

BUCHNER, E. F. *The Educational Theory of Immanuel Kant*. Philadelphia: Lippincott, 1904. Repr. New York: AMS Press, 1971.

BURTT, E. A. (ed.) *The English Philosophers from Bacon to Mill*. New York: Modern Library, 1939.

BURWASH, N. *Egerton Ryerson*. Toronto: Geo. N. Morang, 1903.

CHADWICK, H. 'The Scots College at Douai', *English Historical Review*, LVI (1941).

CHARQUES, R. D. *A Short History of Russia*. New York: E. P. Dutton, 1956.

CHECKLAND, S. G. *The Rise of Industrial Society in England 1815–1885*. London: Longmans, Green, 1964.

CHEVALLIER, P., et al. *L'Enseignement français de la Révolution à nos jours*. Paris: Mouton, 1968.

CIPOLLA, C. *The Fontana Economic History of Europe: The Sixteenth and Seventeenth Centuries*. London: Collins, 1974.

—— *Literacy and Development in the West*. Harmondsworth: Penguin, 1969.

CLEVERLEY, J., and PHILLIPS, D. C. *From Locke to Spock: Influential Models of the Child in Modern Western Thought*. Melbourne: Melbourne University Press, 1976.

COE, R. N. 'The Idea of "Natural Order" in French Education', *British Journal of Educational Studies*, II, 2 (May 1957).

COHN, N. *The Pursuit of the Millennium: Revolutionary Millennarians and Mystical Anarchists of the Middle Ages*. London: Secker and Warburg, 1957. 3rd rev. ed. London: Paladin, 1970.

COMENIUS, J. A. *Opera didactica omnia*. 1657. 2 vols. Prague: Academia Scientiarum Bohemslovenica, 1957.

—— *Labyrinth of the Heart, and Paradise of the World*. Trans. Count Lützow. London: Dent, 1901.

—— *The Way of Light*. Trans. E. T. Campagnac. Liverpool: Liverpool University Press, 1938.

—— *Analytical Didactic*. Ed. V. Jelinek. Chicago: Chicago University Press, 1953.

—— *The School of Infancy*. Ed. E. Eller. Chapel Hill: University of North Carolina Press, 1956.

—— *Comenius in England: Documents Relating to the Visit and Relations to the Royal Society*. Ed. and trans. R. F. Young. London: Humphrey Milford, 1932.

—— *John Amos Comenius on Education*. Ed. Jean Piaget. New York: Teachers College, Columbia University, 1957.

COOK, T. G. (ed.) *The History of Education in Europe*. London: Methuen, for History of Education Society, 1974.

COULTON, G. G. *Medieval Panorama*. 2 vols. Cambridge: Cambridge University Press, 1938. Repr. London: Fontana, 1961.

CRANFIELD, G. A. *The Development of the Provincial Newspaper 1700–1760*. Oxford: Clarendon Press, 1962.

CREMIN, L. *The Transformation of the School*. New York: Alfred Knopf, 1962.

CRESSY, D. *Education in Tudor and Stuart England*. New York: St Martin's Press, 1976.

CROCKER, L. G. *The Age of Enlightenment*. London: Macmillan, 1969.

DEANE, P. *The First Industrial Revolution*. Cambridge: Cambridge University Press, 1969.

DE GARMO, C. *First Yearbook of the National Herbart Society*. Bloomington, Ill.: Public School Publishing Co., 1902.

DE MAUSE, L. *The History of Childhood*. New York: Psychohistory Press, 1974.

DESCARTES, R. *Œuvres de Descartes*. Paris: Leopold Cerf, 1909.

—— *The Philosophical Works of Descartes*. Trans. E. S. Haldane and G. R. T. Ross. 2 vols. 1911. Cambridge: Cambridge University Press, 1967.

—— *Philosophical Writings*. Trans. and ed. E. Anscombe and P. T. Geach. London: Nelson, 1966.

—— *Philosophical Letters*. Trans. A. Kenny. Oxford: Clarendon Press, 1970.

DEWEY, J. *The School and Society*. Chicago: Chicago University Press, 1900.

—— *How We Think*. London: D. C. Heath, 1910; rev. ed. 1933.

—— *Democracy and Education*. New York: Macmillan, 1916.

—— *The Quest for Certainty*. New York: Minton, Balch, 1929.

—— *Characters and Events*. New York: Henry Holt, 1929.

—— *Art as Experience*. New York: Minton, Balch, 1935.

DIDEROT, D., D'ALEMBERT *et al*. *Encyclopedia*. Selections ed. and trans. N. S. Hoyt and T. Cassirer. Indianapolis: Bobbs-Merrill, 1965.

DOMUS GALILAEANA. *Celebrazione della Accademia del Cimento nel Tricentario della Fondazione*. Pisa: Presso la Domus Galilaeana, 1957.

DOWLING, P. J. *The Hedge Schools of Ireland*. Dublin: Talbot Press, 1935.

DUNKEL, H. B. *Herbart and Education.* New York: Random House, 1969.

—— *Herbart and Herbartianism: An Educational Ghost Story.* Chicago: Chicago University Press, 1970.

DUPEUX, G. *French Society 1789–1970.* Trans. P. Wait. London: Methuen, 1976.

DURKAN, J. 'Education in the Century of the Reformation'. In D. McRoberts (ed.), *Essays on the Scottish Reformation 1513–1625.* Glasgow: Burns, 1962.

DURY, J. *The Reformed School, and The Reformed Library Keeper.* London: William Du Gard, 1650. Facsimile repr. Menston: The Scolar Press, 1972.

—— *The Reformed School.* Ed. H. M. Knox. Liverpool: Liverpool University Press, 1958.

EASTMAN, M. *Education and Art in Soviet Russia in the Light of Official Decrees and Documents.* New York: Socialist Publication Society, n.d. [*c.* 1920].

ECONOMIST NEWSPAPER. *The World in Figures.* London: The Economist, 1976.

EDWARDS, R. D. *An Atlas of Irish History.* London: Methuen, 1973.

EGGLESTON, J. (ed.) *Contemporary Research in the Sociology of Education.* London: Methuen, 1974.

EHLER, S. Z., and MORRALL, J. B. (trans. and eds) *Church and State through the Centuries: Historic Documents with Commentaries.* London: Burns and Oates, 1954.

ELWELL, C. E. *The Influence of the Enlightenment on the Catholic Theory of Religious Education in France 1750–1850.* Cambridge, Mass.: Harvard University Press, 1944.

Enciclopedia Mondadori delle Scienze. Milan: Mondadori, 1968.

FARRELL, A. P. *The Jesuit Code of Liberal Education: Development and Scope of the Ratio Studiorum.* Milwaukee: Bruce Publishing Co., 1938.

FELDSTEIN, S., and COSTELLO, L. *The Ordeal of Assimilation: A Documentary History of the White Working Class.* New York: Doubleday, Anchor, 1974.

FÉNELON. *Fénelon on Education.* A translation of the *Traité de l'éducation des filles* and other documents illustrating Fénelon's educational theories and practice. Trans. and introd. H. C. Barnard. Cambridge: Cambridge University Press, 1966.

FICHTE, J. G. *Addresses to the German Nation.* Trans. R. F. Jones and G. H. Turnbull. Chicago and London: Open Court, 1922; repr. 1956.

—— *The Vocation of Man.* Ed. and trans. R. M. Chisholm. New York: Liberal Arts Press, 1956.

FITZPATRICK, S. *The Commissariat of Enlightenment.* Cambridge: Cambridge University Press, 1970.

FORD, P. L. (ed.) *The New England Primer.* Facsimile of the 1727 ed. New York: Teachers College, Columbia University, 1962.

FOURIER, C. *Design for Utopia: Selected Writings of Charles Fourier.* Trans. F. Manuel. 1901. Repr. New York: Schocken, 1971.

FREMANTLE, A. *The Papal Encyclicals in their Historical Context*. New York: Mentor, 1956.

FROEBEL, F. *Friedrich Froebel: A Selection from His Writings*. Trans. E. M. Lilley. Cambridge: Cambridge University Press, 1967.

GAETANO, A. L. 'G. B. Gelli and the Rebellion against Latin', *Studies in the Renaissance* (1966), XIII.

GALILEI, G. *Dialogue Concerning the Two Chief World Systems: Ptolemaic and Copernican*. 1632. Trans. W. Drake. Berkeley: University of California Press, 1953.

GALLIE, W. B. *Peirce and Pragmatism*. Harmondsworth: Penguin, 1952.

GEYL, P. *Napoleon: For and Against*. Trans. O. Renier. London: Cape, 1949. Repr. Harmondsworth: Penguin, 1965.

GIBSON, R. W. *Francis Bacon: A Bibliography of His Works and of Baconiana to the Year 1750*. Oxford: Scrivener Press, 1950.

GILBERT, H. *Queene Elizabethes Achademy*. Ed. F. J. Furnivall. London: Early English Text Society, 1869.

GOMBIN, R. *Les Origines du gauchisme*. Paris: Éditions du Seuil, 1971. Trans. M. K. Perl. *The Origins of Modern Leftism*. Harmondsworth: Penguin, 1975.

GOODY, J. *Literacy in Traditional Societies*. Cambridge: Cambridge University Press, 1968.

GOSDEN, P. J. *How They Were Taught: An Anthology of Contemporary Accounts of Learning and Teaching in England*. Oxford: Blackwell, 1969.

GREEN, V. H. H. *British Institutions: The Universities*. Harmondsworth: Penguin, 1969.

GRENDLER, P. F. *Critics of the Italian World 1530–1560*. Madison: University of Wisconsin Press, 1969.

—— 'The Rejection of Learning in Mid-Cinquecento Italy', *Studies in the Renaissance* (1966), XIII.

GRUNEBERGER, R. *A Social History of the Third Reich*. 1971. Repr. Harmondsworth: Penguin, 1974.

GUIMPS, R. de. *Pestalozzi: His Life and Work*. London: Swann Sonnenschein, 1890.

GUTEK, G. L. *Pestalozzi and Education*. New York: Random House, 1968.

HALL, P. (ed.) *Europe 2000*. London: Duckworth, 1977.

HALLS, W. D. *Society, Schools and Progress in France*. Oxford: Pergamon Press, 1965.

HALPERIN, S. W. *Mussolini and Italian Fascism*. Princeton, NJ: Van Nostrand Anchor, 1964.

HANS, N. *New Trends in Education in the Eighteenth Century*. London: Routledge and Kegan Paul, 1951.

—— and HESSEN, S. *Educational Policy in Soviet Russia*. London: King and Son, 1930.

HARING, C. H. *The Spanish Empire in America*. New York: Harcourt, Brace, World, 1947; repr. with corrections, 1952.

HARRIS, H. S. *The Social Philosophy of Giovanni Gentile*. Urbana: University of Illinois Press, 1960.

HARRISON, J. F. C. *Quest for the New Moral World: Robert Owen and the Owenites in Britain and America*. New York: Scribner's, 1969.

HARTWELL, R. W. *The Causes of the Industrial Revolution*. London: Methuen, 1967.

HARVARD UNIVERSITY COMMITTEE. *General Education in a Free Society*. Cambridge, Mass.: Harvard University Press, 1945.

HEAFFORD, M. R. *Pestalozzi: His Thought and its Relevance Today*. London: Methuen, 1967.

HEGEL, G. F. W. *Reason in History*. Ed. and trans. R. S. Hartman. New York: Liberal Arts Press, 1953.

HELM, P. J. *History of Europe 1450–1660*. London: Bell, 1961.

HERBART, J. F. *The Aesthetic Presentation of the World*. 1804. Trans. H. M. and E. Felkin. London: Swann Sonnenschein, 1892.

—— *The Science of Education*. 1806. Trans. H. M. and E. Felkin. London: Swann Sonnenschein, 1892. Boston: D. C. Heath, 1896.

—— *A Text-Book in Psychology*. 1816. Trans. M. K. Smith. New York: D. Appleton, 1897.

—— *Outlines of Educational Doctrine*. 1835. Trans. A. F. Lange. New York: Macmillan, 1901.

—— *The ABC of Sense Perception and Minor Pedagogical Works*. New York: D. Appleton, 1896.

HERDER, J. G. von. *Outlines of a Philosophy of the History of Man*. Trans. T. Churchill, *c.* 1800. Facsimile ed. New York: Bergman, n.d.

HERR, R. *The Eighteenth-Century Revolution in Spain*. Princeton, NJ: Princeton University Press, 1958; repr. 1969.

HILL, C. *Reformation to Industrial Revolution*. Harmondsworth: Penguin, 1967.

HOBBES, T. *Leviathan*. 1651. Ed. M. Oakeshott. Oxford: Blackwell, 1946; 2nd ed. 1955.

HOFSTADTER, R. *The Development of Academic Freedom in the United States*. New York: Columbia University Press, 1957.

—— and SMITH, W. *American Higher Education: A Documentary History*. 2 vols. Chicago: Chicago University Press, 1961.

HOLLINGWORTH, B. 'Lancasterian Schools in Russia', *Durham Research Review*, V, 17 (September 1966).

HOOLE, C. *A New Discovery of the Art of Teaching Schoole, in Four Small Treatises*. Ed. E. T. Campagnac. Liverpool and London: Liverpool University Press and Constable, 1913.

HUMBOLDT, A. von. *Kosmos*. 5 vols. Stuttgart: Cotta, 1845–62.

—— *Ansichten der Natur mit wissenschaftlichen Erläuterungen.* 3rd ed. Stuttgart and Tübingen: Cotta, 1849.

HUNTER, N. *Shanghai Journal: An Eyewitness Account of the Cultural Revolution.* Boston: Beacon Press, 1969.

IGNATIEV, P., ODINETZ, D. M., and NOVGOROTSEV, P. J. *Russian Schools and Universities in the World War.* New Haven, Conn.: Yale University Press, 1929.

INGLIS, B. *Poverty and the Industrial Revolution.* London: Hodder and Stoughton, 1971. Repr. London: Panther, 1972.

JAMES, W. *Talks to Teachers.* 1899. Repr. New York: W. W. Norton, 1958.

JOHNSON, C. *Old-Time Schools and School-Books.* 1904. Repr. New York: Dover, 1963.

JOHNSON, F. R. 'Gresham College: Precursor of the Royal Society', *Journal of the History of Ideas,* I, 4 (1945).

JOHNSON, W. H. E. *Russia's Educational Heritage.* Pittsburgh: Carnegie Institute of Technology Press, 1950.

JONES, M. G. *The Charity School Movement: A Study of Eighteenth-Century Puritanism in Action.* Cambridge: Cambridge University Press, 1938. Repr. London: Frank Cass, 1964.

JORDAN, W. K. *Philanthropy in England 1480–1660: A Study of the Changing Pattern of English Social Aspirations.* London: Allen and Unwin, 1959.

KANT, I. *Sämmtliche Werke.* Ed. Rosenkranz and Schubert. Leipzig: Voss, 1839.

—— *Kant's Critique of Practical Reason and Other Works on the Theory of Ethics.* Trans. T. K. Abbott. 1873; 6th ed. 1909. Repr. London: Longmans, 1963.

—— *Critique of Pure Reason.* 1st ed. (A) 1781; 2nd ed. (B) 1787. Trans. Norman Kemp Smith. London: Macmillan, 1952.

—— *Prolegomena to any Future Metaphysics that will be able to Present itself as a Science.* 1783. Trans. P. G. Lucas. Manchester: Manchester University Press, 1953.

—— *Philosophical Correspondence 1759–1799.* Ed. and trans. Arnulf Zweig. Chicago: Chicago University Press, 1967.

—— *Education (Über Pädagogik).* 1803. Trans. A. Churton. Ann Arbor: University of Michigan Press, 1960.

—— *On History.* Ed. L. W. Beck. Indianapolis: Bobbs-Merrill, 1963.

KHRUSHCHEV, N. *Krushchev and the Central Committee Speak on Education.* Trans. G. Counts. Pittsburgh: Pittsburgh University Press, 1959.

KING, B. *Changing Man: The Education System of the USSR.* New York: Viking Press, 1937.

KLINE, G. L. (ed.) *Soviet Education.* New York: Columbia University Press, 1957.

KLYUCHEVSKY, V. *Peter the Great.* Trans. L. Archibald. 1910. Repr. New York: Random House, 1958.

KNIGHT, E. W., and HALL, C. L. *Readings in American Educational History.* New York: Appleton-Century-Crofts, 1951.

KNOWLES, D. *The Religious Orders in England*. Vol. 2: *The End of the Middle Ages*. Cambridge: Cambridge University Press, 1955.

KNOX, J. *John Knox's History of the Reformation in Scotland*. Ed. W. C. Dickinson. 2 vols. London: Thomas Nelson, 1949.

KRAMER, R. *Maria Montessori: A Biography*. New York: Putnam's, 1976.

KRUPSKAYA, N. K. *On Education: Selected Speeches and Articles*. Trans. G. P. Ivanov-Mumjiev. Moscow: Foreign Languages Publishing House, 1957.

KUHN, T. *The Structure of Scientific Revolutions*. Chicago: Chicago University Press, 1962.

LA FONTAINERIE, F. de. *French Liberalism and Education in the Eighteenth Century: Writings of La Chalotais, Turgot, Diderot and Condorcet on National Education*. New York: Burtt Franklin, 1971.

LANCASTER, J. *Improvements in Education*. 1802. 3rd. ed. London: Darton and Harvey, 1805.

—— *An Account of a Remarkable Establishment of Education at Paris*. London: J. Lancaster, 1809.

—— *The British System of Education*. London: Longman, 1810.

LANDO, O. 'The *Paradossi* of Ortensio Lando'. In W. G. Rice (ed.), *Essays and Studies in English and Comparative Literature*, VIII. Ann Arbor: University of Michigan Press, 1932.

LAWSON, J., and SILVER, H. *A Social History of Education in England*. London: Methuen, 1973.

LEARY, D. B. *Education and Autocracy in Russia: From the Origins to the Bolsheviki*. Buffalo, NY: University of Buffalo Press, 1919.

LEIBNIZ, G. W. von. *New Essays Concerning Human Understanding*. 1765. Trans. A. G. Langley. 1896. Repr. La Salle, Ill.: Open Court, 1949.

—— *Selections*. Ed. P. P. Weiner. New York: Scribner's, 1951.

LENIN, V. I. *Lenin on Youth*. Moscow: Progress Publishers, 1967.

LOCKE, J. *The Works*. London: Tegg, Sharp, 1823.

—— *Essays on the Law of Nature*. Trans. W. von Leyden. Oxford: Clarendon Press, 1954.

—— *The Educational Writings of John Locke*. Ed. J. L. Axtell. Cambridge: Cambridge University Press, 1968.

—— *John Locke: Prophet of Common Sense*. Ed. M. V. C. Jeffreys. London: Methuen, 1967.

LUNACHARSKY, A. *Self-Education of the Workers: The Cultural Task of the Struggling Proletariat*. London: Workers' Socialist Federation, n.d. [c. 1918].

LUTHER, M. D. *Martin Luthers Werke*. Weimar: Herman Böhlaus Nachfolger, 1883.

MCGRATH, P. *Papists and Puritans under Elizabeth I*. London: Blandford Press, 1967.

MCLACHLAN. *English Education under the Test Acts: Being the History of the Non-*

Conformist Academies 1662–1820. Manchester: Manchester University Press, 1931.

MACLURE, J. S. *Educational Documents: England and Wales 1816–1963*. London: Chapman and Hall, 1965.

MCMANNERS, J. *French Ecclesiastical Society under the Ancien Régime: A Study of Angers in the Eighteenth Century*. Manchester: Manchester University Press, 1960.

MACMURRAY, J. *The Self as Agent*. Gifford Lectures 1953. London: Faber, 1957.

MCMURRY, C. *The Elements of General Method Based on the Principles of Herbart*. 1889. Rev. ed. Bloomington, Ill.: Public School Publishing Co., 1903.

—— and MCMURRY, F. *The Method of the Recitation*. 1897. New York: Macmillan, 1903.

MCROBERTS, D. *Essays on the Scottish Reformation 1513–1625*. Glasgow: Burns, 1962.

MANUEL, F. E. and F. P. *French Utopias: An Anthology of Ideal Societies*. 1966. Repr. New York: Schocken, 1971.

MAO TSE-TUNG. *Selected Works*. 4 vols. Peking: Foreign Languages Press, 1967.

MARX, K. *Early Texts*. Ed. and trans. D. McLellan. Oxford: Clarendon Press, 1971.

—— *Capital*. Trans. E. and C. Paul. Everyman Library. London: Dent, 1930; repr. 1951.

—— *The Marx–Engels Reader*. Ed. R. C. Tucker. New York: W. W. Norton, 1972.

MEDVEDEV, A. A. *The Rise and Fall of T. D. Lysenko*. New York: Doubleday, Anchor, 1969.

MILL, J. *James Mill on Education*. Ed. W. H. Burston. Cambridge: Cambridge University Press, 1969.

MILTON, J. *Tractate of Education*. 1644. Ed. D. Browning. Cambridge: Cambridge University Press, 1897.

MINIO-PALUELLO, L. *Education in Fascist Italy*. London: Oxford University Press, 1946.

MOLS, R. *Introduction à la démographie historique des villes d'Europe du 14e au 18e siècle*. 3 vols. Gembloux, Belgium: Duculot, 1954–6.

MONROE, P. *Thomas Platter and the Educational Renaissance of the Sixteenth Century*. New York: Appleton, 1904.

—— (ed.) *A Cyclopedia of Education*. 5 vols. New York: Macmillan, 1911–13.

MONTAIGNE, M. de. *The Essays of Michel Seigneur de Montaigne*. Trans. J. C. Cotton. 3rd ed. London: Ward, Lock, Tyler, 1700.

—— *Essays of Montaigne*. Ed. P. Chubb. Trans. J. Florio. London: Walter Scott Publishing Co., n.d.

—— *Œuvres complètes*. Ed. A. Thibaudet and M. Rat. Bibliothèque de la Pléiade. Bruges: Gallimard, 1962.

MONTESSORI, M. *The Montessori Method: Scientific Pedagogy as Applied to Child Education in the 'Children's Houses'*. Trans. Anne E. George. New York: F. A. Stokes, 1912.

—— *The Discovery of the Child*. Trans. Mary A. Johnstone. Adyar, Madras: Kalakshetra Publications, 1948.

MONTGOMERY, J. W. *Cross and Crucible: Johann Valentin Andreae (1586–1654), Phoenix of the Theologians*. 2 vols. The Hague: Martinus Nijhoff, 1973.

MOORE, P. *Watchers of the Stars: The Scientific Revolution*. London: Michael Joseph, 1973.

NEARING, S. *Education in Soviet Russia*. New York: International Publishers, 1926.

NEUBERG, V. *Popular Education in Eighteenth-Century England*. London: Woburn Press, 1971.

NOONE, J. B. 'Rousseau's Theory of Natural Law as Conditional', *Journal of the History of Ideas*, XXXIII, 1 (January–March 1972).

OLIVA, L. J. *Peter the Great*. Englewood Cliffs, NJ: Prentice-Hall, 1970.

OLIVIERA MARQUES, A. H. de. *History of Portugal*. 2nd ed. 2 vols. New York: Columbia University Press, 1976.

ORNSTEIN, M. *The Role of the Scientific Societies in the Seventeenth Century*. Chicago: Chicago University Press, 1938.

OWEN, R. *A New View of Society and Other Writings*. Everyman Library. London: Dent, 1927.

PADBERG, J. W. *Colleges in Controversy: The Jesuit Schools in France from Revival to Suppression 1815–1880*. Cambridge, Mass.: Harvard University Press, 1969.

PALMER, R. R. *Atlas of World History*. Chicago: Rand McNally, 1962.

—— *The School of the French Revolution*. Princeton, NJ: Princeton University Press, 1975.

PANKRATOVA, A. M. (ed.) *Istoriya SSSR*. 3 vols. Moscow: Institut Istorii Academii Nauk SSR, 1955.

PARES, B. *Russia*. Rev. ed. New York: Mentor, 1949.

PARKER, I. *The Dissenting Academies*. Cambridge: Cambridge University Press, 1914.

PASSMORE, J. *The Perfectibility of Man*. New York: Scribner's, 1970.

PAULSEN, F. *German Education: Past and Present*. 1906. Trans. T. Lorenz. London: T. Fisher Unwin, 1908.

PEIRCE, C. S. *Collected Papers*. Cambridge, Mass.: Harvard University Press, 1931–5.

PESTALOZZI, J. H. *Leonard and Gertrude*. 1781. Trans. E. Channing. Boston: D. C. Heath, 1910.

—— *How Gertrude Teaches Her Children*. 1802. Trans. L. E. Holland and F. C. Turner. London: Swann Sonnenschein, 1894.

—— *Letters on Early Education (Addressed to J. P. Greaves)*. 1827. Syracuse, NY: C. W. Bardeen, 1898.

PETTY, W. *The Advice of W.P. to Mr Samuel Hartlib, for the Advancement of Some Particular Parts of Learning.* London: 1648.

PIAGET, J. *Science of Education and the Psychology of the Child.* Trans. D. Coltman. New York: Viking Press, 1971.

PINKEVITCH, A. P. *The New Education in the Soviet Republic.* Trans. N. Perlmutter. New York: John Day, 1929.

PROST, A. *Histoire de l'enseignement en France 1800–1967.* Paris: Armand Colin, 1968.

PURVER, M. *The Royal Society: Concept and Creation.* London: Routledge and Kegan Paul, 1967.

RABELAIS, F. *Œuvres complètes.* 1552–67. Ed. J. Boulenger. Bibliothèque de la Pléiade. Bruges: Gallimard, 1955.

—— *The Five Books of Gargantua and Pantagruel.* 1567. Trans. J. Le Clerq. New York: Modern Library, 1944.

RAMOS OLIVIERA, A. *Politics, Economics and Men of Modern Spain 1808–1946.* London: Victor Gollancz, 1946.

RANDALL, J. H. *The School of Padua and the Emergence of Modern Science.* Padua: Antenore, 1961.

REDDIE, C. *Abbotsholme.* London: G. Allen, 1900.

REIN, W. *Outlines of Pedagogics.* Trans. C. C. and I. J. van Liew. London: Swann Sonnenschein, 1893.

RICHMOND, K. *Education and Schooling.* London: Methuen, 1975.

RODERICK, A. J. (ed.) *Wales Through the Ages.* 2 vols. Swansea: Christopher Davies, 1959–60.

ROUSSEAU, J.-J. *Œuvres complètes.* Ed. B. Gagnebin and M. Raymond. Paris: Garnier, 1960–4.

—— *Minor Educational Writings.* Ed. and trans. W. Boyd, 1910. Repr. New York: Teachers College, Columbia University, 1962.

ROWSE, A. L. *The England of Elizabeth: The Structure of Society.* London: Macmillan, 1950.

RUDÉ, G. *Paris and London in the Eighteenth Century: Studies in Popular Protest.* London: Collins, 1952.

—— *Europe in the Eighteenth Century: Aristocracy and the Bourgeois Challenge.* London: Weidenfeld and Nicholson, 1972. Repr. London: Sphere, 1972.

RUSH, B. *Selected Writings of Benjamin Rush.* Ed. D. D. Runes. New York: Philosophical Library, 1947.

RYLE, G. *The Concept of Mind.* London: Hutchinson, 1949. Repr. Harmondsworth: Penguin, 1963.

SAGARRA, E. *A Social History of Germany 1648–1914.* London: Methuen, 1977.

SAINT-SIMON. *The Doctrine of Saint-Simon: An Exposition.* 1828–9. Ed. and trans. G. G. Iggers, 1958. Repr. New York: Schocken, 1972.

SALMON, D. (ed.) *The Practical Parts of Lancaster's Improvements and Bell's Experiments*. Cambridge: Cambridge University Press, 1932.

SARGENT, W. L. 'On the Progress of Elementary Education', *Journal of the Royal Statistical Society*, XXX (1867).

SCHLESINGER, R. *The Family in the USSR: Documents and Readings*. Trans. H. Rapp. London: Routledge and Kegan Paul, 1949.

SCOTT, D. F. S. *Wilhelm von Humboldt and the Idea of a University*. Durham: University of Durham, 1960.

SHIRER, W. L. *The Rise and Fall of the Third Reich*. New York: Simon and Schuster, 1960.

SILVER, H. (ed.) *Equal Opportunity in Education*. London: Methuen, 1973.

SIZER, T. R. (ed.) *Tne Age of the Academies*. New York: Teachers College, Columbia University, 1964.

SMITH, N. K. *New Studies in the Philosophy of Descartes*. London: Macmillan, 1952.

SPELL, J. R. *Rousseau in the Spanish World Before 1833: A Study in Franco-Spanish Literary Relations*. Austin: University of Texas Press, 1938. Repr. New York: Octagon Books, 1969.

SPENCER, H. *Education: Intellectual, Moral and Physical*. London: Rationalist Press, 1861. Repr. London: Watts, 1929.

SPINKA, M. *John Amos Comenius: That Incomparable Moravian*. Chicago: Chicago University Press, 1943.

SPRAT, T. *The History of the Royal Society of London for the Improving of Natural Knowledge*. 1667. Facsimile reprint. Ed. J. I. Cope and H. W. Hones. London: Routledge and Kegan Paul, 1959.

STANDING, E. M. *Maria Montessori: Her Life and Work*. Hollis and Carter, 1957. Repr. New York: Mentor-Omega, 1962.

—— *The Montessori Revolution in Education*. Fresno, California: The Academy Guild Press, 1962. Repr. New York: Schocken, 1966.

STEWART, W. H. C. *The Educational Innovators*. Vol. 2. London: Macmillan, 1968.

—— and MCCANN, W. P. *The Educational Innovators*. Vol. 1: 1750–1850. London: Macmillan, 1967.

STONE, L. *The Crisis of the Aristocracy 1558–1641*. Oxford: Clarendon Press, 1965.

—— 'The Educational Revolution in England 1560–1640', *Past and Present*, XXVIII (1964).

STOWE, A. M. *English Grammar Schools in the Reign of Queen Elizabeth*. New York: Teachers College, Columbia University, 1908.

SYLVESTER, D. W. *Educational Documents 800–1816*. London: Methuen, 1970.

TAYLOR, A. J. P. *The Course of German History*. Repr. London: Methuen, 1961.

THOMSON, D. *Europe Since Napoleon*. Harmondsworth: Penguin, 1966.

TOBIAS, J. J. *Crime and Industrial Society in the Nineteenth Century*. Harmondsworth: Penguin, 1972.

TREADGOLD, D. *The West in Russia and China: Religious and Secular Thought in Modern Times.* Vol. 1: *Russia 1472–1917.* Cambridge: Cambridge University Press, 1973.

TREND, J. B. *The Origins of Modern Spain.* Cambridge: Cambridge University Press, 1934. Repr. New York: Russell and Russell, 1965.

TREVOR-ROPER, H. 'The Scottish Enlightenment', *Studies on Voltaire and the Eighteenth Century*, LVIII. Geneva: Institut et Musée Voltaire, 1967.

TROUTON, R. *Peasant Renaissance in Yugoslavia 1900–1950: A Study of the Development of Peasant Society as Affected by Education.* London: Routledge and Kegan Paul, 1952.

TURNBULL, G. H. *Hartlib, Dury and Comenius: Gleanings from Hartlib's Papers.* Liverpool and London: Liverpool University Press and Hodder and Stoughton, 1947.

TURNER, B. *Equality for Some: The Story of Girls' Education.* London: Ward Lock, 1974.

ULICH, R. *Three Thousand Years of Educational Wisdom.* Cambridge: Cambridge University Press, 1954.

VENTURI, F. *Utopia and Reform in the Enlightenment.* Cambridge: Cambridge University Press, 1971.

VEYSEY, L. R. *The Emergence of the American University.* Chicago: Chicago University Press, 1965.

VYGOTSKY, L. S. *Thought and Language.* Trans. E. Hanfmann and G. Vakar. Cambridge, Mass.: MIT Press, 1962.

WARD, A. *Collected Papers.* Vol. 1. Cambridge: Cambridge University Press, 1921.

WEBB, S. and B. *Soviet Communism – A New Civilization?* 2 vols. New York: Scribner's, 1936.

WEBSTER, C. (ed.) *Samuel Hartlib and the Advancement of Learning.* Cambridge: Cambridge University Press, 1970.

WESLEY, J. *The Works of John Wesley.* London: Wesleyan Conference Office, 1872. Facsimile repr. Grand Rapids, Mich.: Zondervan Publishing House, n.d.

WHITE, F. R. *Famous Utopias of the Renaissance.* New York: Packard, 1946. Repr. New York: Hendricks House, 1955.

WILLIAMS, M. (ed.) *Revolutions 1775–1830.* Harmondsworth: Penguin, 1971.

WILSON, J., *et al. Introduction to Moral Education.* Harmondsworth: Penguin, 1967.

WILSON, L. *The New Schools in New Russia.* Vanguard Studies of Soviet Russia. [No printer or place], 1928.

WINN, R. B. (ed. and trans.) *Soviet Psychology.* New York: Philosophical Library, 1961.

WOODY, T. *New Minds: New Men?* New York: Macmillan, 1932.

YATES, F. A. *The French Academies of the Sixteenth Century.* London: Warburg Institute, University of London, 1947.

Index

Seguin, Édouard, early psychologist, 393
sense perception: advanced by Bacon, 42;
accepted by Descartes, 60; Locke's arguments as the basis of all knowledge, 173,
175; opposed by Pestalozzi in the doctrine
of *Anschauung*, 228; but accepted as basis of
learning, 229; as *aisthesis* in Herbart's
theory, 233; *see also* empiricism; faculty
theory of the mind
sex: and adult roles in Rousseau, 191; advice
on, 191–2
Shatsky, Stanislav, and polytechnization,
507–8
Smith, Adam, new economic theory in
Wealth of Nations, 143
social Darwinism: advanced by Spencer, 346;
position of 1930 conservatives, 438
'social empiricism', and responsible action,
554
social theory: Hobbes and Locke on the
social contract, 173; Rousseau's desire for
social reconstruction, 186, ideas on the
social contract, 186ff.; and relation to
justice, 194–5; de Tracy supports élitism,
251; Hegel's theory of the corporate state,
263–6, and of history as objectification of
Geist, 264; Dewey's interest in, 417, in his
Democracy and Education, 423ff.; Counts'
criticisms of American Society, 436–7
socialism: *Loi Falloux* designed to counter, in
France, 317; Froebel's kindergarten accused of, 341; in France: Saint-Simon,
382–3, Fourier, 383–5; in Germany:
Marx's concept of scientific socialism, 386;
Fabian socialism, 388; in depression
America, 437, accepted by American
teachers, 437; taught in Soviet schools,
509–10; and revisionist educational historiography, 536; and Modern Leftism, 540–1
Société pour l'Instruction Élémentaire, 1815, in-
troduces monitorial system, 256, 298–9, 315
Society for Promoting Christian Knowledge
(SPCK): founded 1699, 143; provide basic
literacy for the poor, 144; educational
activities, 144; extends to Scotland, 149, to
Wales, 154–5, to Ireland, 158–9; influenced
by Francke, 165; decline in the nineteenth
century, 291
Society for the Propagation of the Gospel in
Foreign Parts (SPG): founded 1701, 143;
missionaries in American colonies, 269
Society of Jesus, *see* Jesuits
Solomon's House, Bacon's institute of learn-
ing, 43–5, 82; influence on Petty, 98
Soviet Union: rejects Montessori method,
400; admired by American socialists, 437;

educational history of, 498–515 *passim*;
officially founded, 508; Stalinist period,
512–21 *passim*; dominates post-war Eastern
Europe, 523
Spain: in the sixteenth century, bulwark of
Catholicism, 3ff.; education in the seventeenth century, 125–6; Rousseau's ideas in,
201; modern era, 465–8; Catholic supremacy under Alfonso XII, 465–6; period of
extreme bourgeois reaction in education,
467; attempted educational reforms in 1931
of Second Republic, 467–8; reactionary
educational policies of Franco, 468
Spencer, Herbert, advocate of scientific empiricism, 305–6
Spener, Jakob, and Pietism, 164
Stakhanovism, in the Soviet system, 515
state, for Hegel, the agency of progress, 265
Steiner, Rudolf, founds Anthroposophy,
builds the Goetheanum, 391; the Freie
Waldorfschule, 405
Stoglav, 486
Stoy, Karl Volkmar, promotes scientific
teacher preparation, 349
Studia humanitatis, strongly rejected in
sixteenth-century Italy by the *poligrafi*,
76–7
Sturm, Johann, school in Strasbourg, 9, 12;
a model for the Huguenots, 34
Sunday School movement, and Raikes, 291

tabula rasa: in Bacon's theory, 45–6; in Locke,
174, 176–7, 178; central to Helvétius'
theory, 180; challenged by Pestalozzi, 226;
accepted by Herbart, 234, by James Mill,
289; rejected by Froebel, 337
Tappan, Henry T.: and American universities, 354; recommended the Prussian model,
355
Taunton Commission, 1864 inquiry into
English grammar schools, 304–5
teacher certification: in Napoleonic France,
254; in early twentieth-century USA, 432;
in Belgium, 461
teacher training: first college in Europe
founded by La Salle, 119; Austrian reference to in 1774, 127; pedagogical seminar
of Heyne at Göttingen, 163; Francke's
seminar, 166; Kant's involvement, 212,
217; Swiss concern for, 223; Herbart's
Pedagogical Seminar, 234; concept of the
normal school, 250; in Napoleonic France,
254–5; nineteenth-century English pressures for improvement, 305; James Kay
and the normal school movement, 309–10;
French laws of 1889, 456; Cross Commis-